CLASSICS OF WESTERN THOUGHT

Volume
II

Middle Ages, Renaissance, and Reformation

FOURTH EDITION

Kevin J. Ray

CLASSICS OF WESTERN THOUGHT

Under the General Editorship of
Thomas H. Greer
Michigan State University

Volume **I**
The Ancient World
FOURTH EDITION
Edited by Donald S. Gochberg
Michigan State University

Volume **II**
Middle Ages, Renaissance, and Reformation
FOURTH EDITION
Edited by Karl F. Thompson
Michigan State University

Volume **III**
The Modern World
FOURTH EDITION
Edited by Edgar E. Knoebel
Michigan State University

Volume **IV**
The Twentieth Century
Edited by Donald S. Gochberg
Michigan State University

CLASSICS OF WESTERN THOUGHT

Volume
II

Middle Ages, Renaissance, and Reformation

FOURTH EDITION

Edited by
Karl F. Thompson
Michigan State University

HARCOURT BRACE JOVANOVICH, PUBLISHERS

San Diego   New York   Chicago   Austin   Washington, D.C.

London   Sydney   Tokyo   Toronto

Introduction to the *Classics* Series

Writings by the great minds of the Western tradition offer modern Westerners the best possible introduction to their humanistic heritage. To provide such an introduction, the editors of this series have brought together works that we consider classics of the Western tradition—of Western *thought*, in the broad sense. For the most part, these volumes of primary documents are intended for use in college-level courses in humanities or the history of civilization, normally in the company of a brief narrative text. One such text, designed especially for use with this series, is my *Brief History of the Western World*, Fifth Edition (Harcourt Brace Jovanovich, 1987).

The number and range of documents in Western civilization are, of course, enormous, and good reasons can always be advanced for choosing one work over another. We have sought works that are truly *classic*, that is to say, valuable both for their intrinsic merit and for having exerted a paramount influence on their own and later times—works that display judgment applied to observation as well as creative thought and literary skill. In deciding upon the length and quantity of selections, we have aimed to keep in balance two considerations: having each selection long enough to give a clear view of the author's ideas and, at the same time, offering selections from a substantial number of the foremost writers.

The documents appear for the most part in chronological order, in four manageable volumes: *The Ancient World* (Volume I); *Middle Ages, Renaissance, and Reformation* (Volume II); *The Modern World* (Volume III); and *The Twentieth Century* (Volume IV). Each document is introduced by a brief account of the author's life, his or her role in the shaping of the Western tradition, and the significance of the particular work. As in the selection of the writings themselves, we have kept student and instructor constantly in mind.

In this Fourth Edition of the first three volumes of the *Classics*, we have added a number of documents especially suited to the interests of today's readers. (These are noted specifically in the editor's preface to each of the revised volumes.) Most of the selections in the preceding edition have been kept; in several instances they now appear in attractive new translations. Clear and concise footnotes have been extended throughout these volumes in order to explain parts of documents that might otherwise be obscure. As a result of all these improvements, we believe that readers will find these *Classics*, more than ever, an enjoyable aid to understanding the Western intellectual heritage.

Thomas H. Greer
General Editor

Preface to
the Fourth Edition

This second volume of the *Classics of Western Thought* series presents some of the more significant achievements of Western culture during the period following the decline of classical civilization and extending into the beginning of the modern era, that is, the period from A.D. 500 to 1600. The readings are arranged in chronological order, save for occasional deviations that respect the traditional divisions of Western history into Middle Ages, Renaissance, and Reformation.

During the early Middle Ages, Europe struggled to develop its own distinctive civilization, and by the year 1000 a culture with certain marked characteristics had evolved. The people of the Middle Ages saw their world as a marvelously intricate but orderly arrangement by which everyone was assigned a place and function in society in accordance with God's will. We remember this era as the Age of Faith, envy its spiritual stability, and admire the subtlety of its philosophy, which, using Aristotle's methods, deduced from the revealed truths of Christianity the harmonious interplay of cause and effect everywhere in God's creation. The noble aspirations of chivalry we can still admire, and we honor the medieval conception, inspired by the dual heritage of Rome and Christianity, of a universal state. The harsh actualities of medieval life contrasted with the ideals of the age, and these, too, were graphically depicted by contemporary writers. Sure that the world was a place of trial and testing, medieval people were equally certain that, to use the words of Dante, greatest of medieval poets, "In His will is our peace."

By the fifteenth century, the form and content of Western culture were again being reshaped, and the medieval world and its ideals began to give place to the modern. This period of transition, known as the

Renaissance, was an age of discovery, in which, paradoxically, changes often resulted from a diligent, scholarly examination of the literature and philosophy of the ancient world. Writers, scholars, and artists, with an increased sense of individualism, rejected medieval habits of mind and strove to emulate the cultural achievements of Greece and Rome. Notable changes also occurred to accommodate growing trade and commerce. The age of exploration saw European culture spread throughout the world, and nationalism and expediency, as noted by Machiavelli, displaced medieval political beliefs and practices.

The sixteenth century brought the Reformation and, with it, the dissolution of the Christian unity of the Middle Ages. During this period the foundations of modern Protestantism were laid, and the Roman Church enforced clerical discipline, reaffirmed its traditional teachings, and strengthened its organization. Many of the key points of the religious controversy are set forth in the selections from Calvin, Luther, and St. Ignatius of Loyola.

By the end of the period covered by this volume, the changes wrought by the Renaissance and Reformation had been fairly well assimilated into Western art, thought, and life.

This Fourth Edition of *Middle Ages, Renaissance, and Reformation* contains several important additions that further reveal the spirit and thought of the period.

Two new selections illustrate the breadth and complexity of religious experience during the Middle Ages. One is from St. Catherine of Siena's *Dialogue*, a basic work of long-lasting influence in the history of religious mysticism. The other is a popular story, by an unknown author, of one of the miracles of Our Lady; it is a typical expression of the veneration and reverence accorded the Virgin Mary.

Two stirring orations by Queen Elizabeth I of England are also added. They show the mastery of politics and power of this early modern ruler.

A penetrating insight into the special world of Renaissance art is found in Giorgio Vasari's biographies of Leonardo da Vinci and Michelangelo; the excerpts included in this new edition are especially valuable as first-hand accounts by a fellow artist.

A different selection from Cervantes' *Don Quixote* than the one previously used gives us a better idea of the narrative scope of the story and of the complex character of its hero.

Introductions and footnotes have been revised throughout the volume.

These changes provide broader understanding of an era of Western cultural development that strongly influenced following periods—and that continues to offer spiritual, artistic, and intellectual resources to present-day societies and individuals.

Karl F. Thompson

Contents

CLASSICS OF WESTERN THOUGHT

Volume
II

Middle Ages, Renaissance, and Reformation

FOURTH EDITION

PRINCIPAL RELIGIOUS AND INTELLECTUAL CENTERS
OF EUROPE (c.1300–1600)

Cathedral   Shrine (Relics)

University   Monastery

MILES
0   300

NORTH SEA
BALTIC SEA
ATLANTIC OCEAN
MEDITERRANEAN SEA

Edinburgh
Glasgow
Durham
Dublin
York
Lincoln
Cambridge
Oxford
Bury St. Edmunds
Bath
London
Salisbury
Canterbury
Amsterdam
Rotterdam
Antwerp
Brussels
Cologne
Mont St. Michel
Paris
Amiens
Aachen
Fulda
Chartres
Reims
Mainz
Worms
Orleans
Clairvaux
Vezelay
Citeaux
Poitiers
St. Gall
Cluny
Bordeaux
Basel
Roncesvalle
Geneva
Compostella
Milan
Padua
Venice
Burgos
Albi
Toulouse
Avignon
Bologna
Pisa
Rimini
Salamanca
Montepellier
Florence
Urbino
Coimbra
Assisi
Lisbon
Toledo
Barcelona
Siena
Rome
Monte Cassino
Cordoba
Naples
Salerno
Palermo

Copenhagen
Lund
Wittenberg
Prague
Vienna

1

St. Benedict of Nursia

The Rule of St. Benedict

*T*HE *leading figure in the origin and growth of the monastic movement was St. Benedict of Nursia (ca. 480–ca. 543). As a young man, St. Benedict fled from the immorality of Rome and for three years led a life of solitary contemplation, prayer, and strict austerity in a lonely hillside cave. Impressed by his devoutness and sincerity, the members of an ascetic religious community persuaded him to become their governor. They proved undependable and ungovernable, however; and St. Benedict, with a few chosen disciples, left that community to establish a monastery on Monte Cassino, midway between Rome and Naples. This foundation has been associated ever since with his name and has become one of the chief centers of religious life in western Europe. The monastery (in the Western sense of a community of work and prayer) found a model here, and* The Rule of St. Benedict, *reflecting his mature spiritual wisdom, became a guide in the development of monasticism as a major institution of medieval Europe.*

Judged by the standards of its day, The Rule *did not prescribe a life of excessive austerity. This wise discretion, recognizing both the strength of men's idealism and the limits of their physical capacities, distinguishes* The Rule *and accounts in no small measure for its success. St. Benedict believed in a communal discipline that would help the individual monk live according to his vows of poverty, chastity, and obedience; and that would also permit him time to work in the fields and shops of the monastery, and to read and study. St. Benedict's precepts were binding on the abbot as well as on the monks. The monastery thus became, under the influence of St. Benedict, a self-sufficient community whose primary aim was service to God through work and prayer.*

The qualities necessary for an abbot.—The abbot who is worthy to rule over a monastery ought always to bear in mind by what name he is called and to justify by his life his title of superior. For he represents Christ in the monastery, receiving his name from the saying of the apostle:[1] "Ye have received the Spirit of adoption, whereby we cry, Abba, Father" [Rom. 8:15]. Therefore the abbot should not teach or command anything contrary to the precepts of the Lord, but his commands and his teaching should be in accord with divine justice. He should always bear in mind that both his teaching and the obedience of his disciples will be inquired into on the dread day of judgment. For the abbot should know that the shepherd will have to bear the blame if the Master finds anything wrong with the flock. Only in case the shepherd has displayed all diligence and care in correcting the fault of a restive and disobedient flock will he be freed from blame at the judgment of God, and be able to say to the Lord in the words of the prophet: "I have not hid thy righteousness within my heart; I have declared thy faithfulness and thy salvation" [Ps. 40:10]; but "they despising have scorned me" [Ezek. 20:27]. Then shall the punishment fall upon the flock who scorned his care and it shall be the punishment of death. The abbot ought to follow two methods in governing his disciples: teaching the commandments of the Lord to the apt disciples by his words, and to the obdurate and the simple by his deeds. And when he teaches his disciples that certain things are wrong, he should demonstrate in his own life by not doing those things, lest when he has preached to others he himself should be a castaway [1 Cor. 9:27], and lest God should sometime say to him, a sinner: "What hast thou to do to declare my statutes, or that thou shouldest take my covenant in thy mouth? Seeing that thou hatest instruction, and castest my words behind thee" [Ps. 50:16, 17], or "Why beholdest thou the mote that is in thy brother's eye, but considerest not the beam that is in thine own eye?" [Matt. 7:3]. Let there be no respect of persons in the monastery. Let the abbot not love one more than another, unless it be one who excels in good works and in obedience. The freeman is not to be preferred to the one who comes into the monastery out of servitude, unless there be some other good reason. But if it seems right and fitting to the abbot, let him show preference to anyone of any rank whatsoever; otherwise let them keep their own

---

[1]St. Paul. Medieval writers often refer to him simply as the Apostle.

THE RULE OF ST. BENEDICT   St. Benedict of Nursia, *The Rule of St. Benedict*, in *A Source Book for Medieval History*, Oliver J. Thatcher and Edgar Holmes McNeal (New York: Charles Scribner's Sons, 1905), 435–37, 440–46, 450–51, 459, 464, 467–76.

places. For whether slave or free, we are all one in Christ [Gal. 3:28] and bear the same yoke of servitude to the one Lord, for there is no respect of persons with God [Rom. 2:11]. For we have special favor in His sight only in so far as we excel others in all good works and in humility. Therefore, the abbot should have the same love toward all and should subject all to the same discipline according to their respective merits. In his discipline the abbot should follow the rule of the apostle who says: "Reprove, rebuke, exhort" [2 Tim. 4:2]. That is, he should suit his methods to the occasion, using either threats or compliments, showing himself either a hard master or a loving father, according to the needs of the case. Thus he should reprove harshly the obdurate and disobedient, but the obedient, the meek, and the gentle he should exhort to grow in grace. We advise also that he rebuke and punish those who neglect and scorn his teaching. He should not disregard the transgressions of sinners, but should strive to root them out as soon as they appear, remembering the peril of Eli, the priest of Siloam [1 Sam. chaps. 1–4]. Let him correct the more worthy and intelligent with words for the first or second time, but the wicked and hardened and scornful and disobedient he should punish with blows in the very beginning of their fault, as it is written: "A fool is not bettered by words" [cf. Prov. 17:10]; and again "Thou shalt beat him with the rod, and shalt deliver his soul from hell" [Prov. 23:14].

The abbot should always remember his office and his title, and should realize that as much is intrusted to him, so also much will be required from him. Let him realize how difficult and arduous a task he has undertaken, to rule the hearts and care for the morals of many persons, who require, one encouragements, another threats, and another persuasion. Let him so adapt his methods to the disposition and intelligence of each one that he may not only preserve the flock committed to him entire and free from harm, but may even rejoice in its increase . . .

• • •

Obedience.—The first grade of humility is obedience without delay, which is becoming to those who hold nothing dearer than Christ. So, when one of the monks receives a command from a superior, he should obey it immediately, as if it came from God himself, being impelled thereto by the holy service he has professed and by the fear of hell and the desire of eternal life. Of such the Lord says: "As soon as he heard of me, he obeyed me" [Ps. 17:44]; and again to the apostles, "He that heareth you, heareth me" [Luke 10:16]. Such disciples, when they are commanded, immediately abandon their own business and their own plans, leaving undone what they were at work upon. With ready hands and willing feet they hasten to obey the commands of their superior, their act following on the heels of his command, and both the order and the fulfilment occurring, as it were, in the same moment of time—such promptness does the fear of the Lord inspire.

Good disciples who are inspired by the desire for eternal life gladly take up that narrow way of which the Lord said: "Narrow is the way which leadeth unto life" [Matt. 7:14]. They have no wish to control their own lives or to obey their own will and desires, but prefer to be ruled by an abbot, and to live in a monastery, accepting the guidance and control of another. Surely such disciples follow the example of the Lord who said: "I came not to do mine own will, but the will of him that sent me" [John 6:38]. But this obedience will be acceptable to God and pleasing to men only if it be not given fearfully, or halfheartedly, or slowly, or with grumbling and protests. For the obedience which is given to a superior is given to God, as he himself has said: "Who heareth you, heareth me" [Luke 10:16]. Disciples ought to obey with glad hearts, "for the Lord loveth a cheerful giver" [2 Cor. 9:7]. If the disciple obeys grudgingly and complains even within his own heart, his obedience will not be accepted by God, who sees his unwilling heart; he will gain no favor for works done in that spirit, but, unless he does penance and mends his ways, he will rather receive the punishment of those that murmur against the Lord's commands.

• • •

Humility.—Now the first step of humility is this, to escape destruction by keeping ever before one's eyes the fear of the Lord, to remember always the commands of the Lord, for they who scorn him are in danger of hell-fire, and to think of the eternal life that is prepared for them that fear him. So a man should keep himself in every hour from the sins of the heart, of the tongue, of the eyes, of the hands, and of the feet. He should cast aside his own will and the desires of the flesh; he should think that God is looking down on him from heaven all the time, and that his acts are seen by God and reported to him hourly by his angels. For the prophet shows that the Lord is ever present in the midst of our thoughts, when he says: "God trieth the hearts and the reins" [Ps. 7:9], and again, "The Lord knoweth the thoughts of men" [Ps. 94:11], and again he says: "Thou hast known my thoughts from afar" [Ps. 139:2], and "The thoughts of a man are known to thee" [Ps. 76:11]. So a zealous brother will strive to keep himself from perverse thoughts by saying to himself: "Then only shall I be guiltless in his sight, if I have kept me from mine iniquity" [Ps. 18:23]. And the holy Scriptures teach us in divers places that we should not do our own will; as where it says: "Turn from thine own will" [Ecclesiasticus 18:30]; and where we ask in the Lord's Prayer that his will be done in us; and where it warns us: "There is a way that seemeth right unto a man, but the end thereof are the ways of death" [Prov. 14:12]; and again, concerning the disobedient: "They are corrupt and abominable in their desires" [Ps. 14:1]. And we should always remember that God is aware of our fleshly desires; as the prophet says, speaking to the Lord: "All my desire is before thee" [Ps. 38:9]. Therefore, we should shun evil desires, for death lieth in the way of the lusts; as the Scripture shows, saying: "Go not after thy lusts" [Ecclesiasticus 18:30]. Therefore since the eyes of the Lord are upon the good and the wicked, and since "the Lord looked down from heaven upon the children of men to see if there were any that did understand and seek God" [Ps. 14:2], and since our deeds are daily reported to him by the angels whom he assigns to each one of us; then, surely, brethren, we should be on our guard every hour, lest at any time, as the prophet says in the Psalms, the Lord should look down upon us as we are falling into sin, and should spare us for a space, because he is merciful and desires our conversion, but should say at the last: "These things hast thou done and I kept silence" [Ps. 50:21].

The second step of humility is this, that a man should not delight in doing his own will and desires, but should imitate the Lord who said: "I came not to do mine own will, but the will of him that sent me" [John 6:38]. And again the Scripture saith: "Lust hath its punishment, but hardship winneth a crown."

The third step of humility is this, that a man be subject to his superior in all obedience for the love of God, imitating the Lord, of whom the apostle says: "He became obedient unto death" [Phil. 2:8].

The fourth step of humility is this, that a man endure all the hard and unpleasant things and even undeserved injuries that come in the course of his service, without wearying or withdrawing his neck from the yoke, for the Scripture saith: "He that endureth to the end shall be saved" [Matt. 10:22], and again: "Comfort thy heart and endure the Lord" [Ps. 27:14]. And yet again the Scripture, showing that the faithful should endure all unpleasant things for the Lord, saith, speaking in the person of those that suffer: "Yea, for thy sake are we killed all the day long; we are counted as sheep for the slaughter" [Ps. 44:22]; and again, rejoicing in the sure hope of divine reward: "In all things, we are more than conquerors through him that loved us" [Rom. 8:37]; and again in another place: "For thou, O God, hast proved us; thou hast tried us as silver is tried; thou broughtest us into the net, thou laidst affliction upon our loins" [Ps. 66:10 f]; and again to show that we should be subject to a superior: "Thou hast placed men over our heads" [Ps. 66:12]. Moreover, the Lord bids us suffer injuries patiently, saying: "Whosoever shall smite thee on the right cheek, turn to him the other also. And if any man will sue thee at the law, and take away thy coat, let him have thy cloak also. And whosoever shall compel thee to go a mile, go with him twain" [Matt. 5:39–41]. And with the apostle Paul we should suffer with false brethren, and endure persecution, and bless them that curse us.

The fifth step of humility is this, that a man should not hide the evil thoughts that arise in his heart or the sins which he has committed in secret, but should humbly confess them to his abbot; as the Scripture exhorteth us, saying: "Commit thy way unto the Lord, trust also in him" [Ps. 37:5]; and again: "O, give thanks unto the Lord, for he is good; for his mercy endureth forever" [Ps. 106:1]; and yet again the prophet saith: "I have acknowledged my sin unto thee, and mine iniquity have I not hid. I said, I will confess my transgressions unto the Lord; and thou forgavest the iniquity of my sin" [Ps. 32:5].

The sixth step of humility is this, that the monk should be contented with any lowly or hard condition in which he may be placed, and should always look upon himself as an unworthy laborer, not fitted to do what is intrusted to him; saying to himself in the words of the prophet: "I was reduced to nothing and was ignorant; I was as a beast before thee and I am always with thee" [Ps. 73:22 f].

The seventh step of humility is this, that he should not only say, but should really believe in his heart that he is the lowest and most worthless of all men, humbling himself and saying with the prophet: "I am a worm and no man; a reproach of men, and despised of all people" [Ps. 22:6]; and "I that was exalted am humbled and confounded" [Ps. 88:15]; and again: "It is good for me that I have been afflicted, that I might learn thy statutes" [Ps. 119:71].

• • •

The order of divine worship during the day.—The prophet says: "Seven times a day do I praise thee" [Ps. 119:164]; and we observe this sacred number in the seven services of the day; that is, matins, prime, terce, sext, nones, vespers, and completorium; for the hours of the daytime are plainly intended here, since the same prophet provides for the nocturnal vigils, when he says in another place: "At midnight I will rise to give thanks unto thee" [Ps. 119:62]. We should therefore praise the Creator for his righteous judgments at the aforesaid times: matins, prime, terce, sext, nones, vespers, and completorium; and at night we should rise to give thanks unto Him.[2]

• • •

The daily labor of the monks.—Idleness is the great enemy of the soul, therefore the monks should always be occupied, either in manual labor or in holy reading. The hours for these occupations should be arranged according to the seasons, as follows: From Easter to the first of October, the monks shall go to work at the first hour and labor until the fourth hour, and the time from the fourth to the sixth hour shall be spent in reading. After dinner, which comes at the sixth hour, they shall lie down and rest in silence; but anyone who wishes may read, if he does it so as not to disturb anyone else. Nones shall be observed a little earlier, about the middle of the eighth hour, and the monks shall go back to work, laboring until vespers. But if the conditions of the locality or the needs of the monastery, such as may occur at harvest time, should make it necessary to labor longer hours, they shall not feel themselves ill-used, for true monks should live by the labor of their own hands, as did the apostles and the holy fathers. But the weakness of human nature must be taken into account in making these arrangements. From the first of October to the beginning of Lent, the monks shall have until the full second hour for reading, at which hour the service of terce shall be held. After terce, they shall work at their respective tasks until the ninth hour. When the ninth hour sounds they shall cease from labor and be ready for the service at the second bell. After dinner they shall spend the time in reading the lessons and the psalms. During Lent the time from daybreak to the third hour shall be devoted to reading, and then they shall work at their appointed tasks

---

[2]Medieval custom divided the day into twelve equal periods, beginning with sunrise and ending with sunset. The night was similarly divided. Seven services were held daily: matins, about daybreak; prime, the first part of the day; terce, the third part of the day; sext, the sixth part of the day; nones, the ninth part of the day; vespers in the evening; completorium, or compline, was the last service. Vigils were services held during the night.

until the tenth hour. At the beginning of Lent each of the monks shall be given a book from the library of the monastery which he shall read entirely through. One or two of the older monks shall be appointed to go about through the monastery during the hours set apart for reading, to see that none of the monks are idling away the time, instead of reading, and so not only wasting their own time but perhaps disturbing others as well. Anyone found doing this shall be rebuked for the first or second offence, and after that he shall be severely punished, that he may serve as a warning and an example to others. Moreover, the brothers are not to meet together at unseasonable hours. Sunday is to be spent by all the brothers in holy reading, except by such as have regular duties assigned to them for that day. And if any brother is negligent or lazy, refusing or being unable profitably to read or meditate at the time assigned for that, let him be made to work, so that he shall at any rate not be idle. The abbot shall have consideration for the weak and the sick, giving them tasks suited to their strength, so that they may neither be idle nor yet be distressed by too heavy labor.

Monks should not have personal property.—The sin of owning private property should be entirely eradicated from the monastery. No one shall presume to give or receive anything except by the order of the abbot; no one shall possess anything of his own, books, paper, pens, or anything else; for monks are not to own even their own bodies and wills to be used at their own desire, but are to look to the father [abbot] of the monastery for everything. So they shall have nothing that has not been given or allowed to them by the abbot; all things are to be had in common according to the command of the Scriptures, and no one shall consider anything as his own property. If anyone has been found guilty of this most grievous sin, he shall be admonished for the first and second offence, and then if he does not mend his ways he shall be punished.

All the brothers are to be treated equally.—It is written: "Distribution was made unto every man as he had need" [Acts 4:35]. This does not mean that there should be respect of persons, but rather consideration for infirmities. The one who has less need should give thanks to God and not be envious; the one who has greater need should be humbled because of his infirmity, and not puffed up by the greater consideration shown him. Thus all members of the congregation shall dwell together in peace. Above all let there be no complaint about anything, either in word or manner, and if anyone is guilty of this let him be strictly disciplined.

•   •   •

Silence is to be kept after completorium.—The monks should observe the rule of silence at all times, but especially during the hours of the night. This rule shall be observed both on fast-days and on other days, as follows: on other than fast-days, as soon as the brothers rise from the table they shall sit down together, while one of them reads from the Collations[3] or the lives of the fathers or other holy works. But the reading at this time shall not be from the Heptateuch[4] or from the books of the Kings, which are not suitable for weak intellects to hear at this hour and may be read at other times. On fast-days the brethren shall assemble a little while after vespers, and listen to readings from the Collations. All shall be present at this reading except those who have been given other duties to be done at this time, and after the reading of four or five pages, or as much as shall occupy an hour's time, the whole congregation shall meet for completorium. After completorium no one shall be allowed to speak to another, unless some unforeseen occasion arises, as that of caring for guests, or unless the abbot has to give a command to some one; and in these cases such speaking as is necessary shall be done quietly and gravely. If anyone breaks this rule of silence he shall be severely disciplined.

•   •   •

Monks are not to receive letters or anything.—No monk shall receive letters or gifts or anything from his family or from any persons on the outside, nor shall he send anything, except by the command of the abbot. And if anything has been sent to the monastery for him he shall not receive it unless he has first shown it to the abbot and received his permission. And if the abbot orders such a thing to be received, he may yet bestow it upon anyone whom he chooses, and the brother to whom it was sent shall acquiesce without ill-will, lest he give occasion to the evil one by his discontent. If anyone breaks this rule, he shall be severely disciplined.

The vestiarius [one who has charge of the clothing] and the calciarius [one who has charge of the footwear].—The brothers are to be provided with

[3]Collections of religious writings.
[4]The first seven books of the Old Testament.

clothes suited to the locality and the temperature, for those in colder regions require warmer clothing than those in warmer climates. The abbot shall decide such matters. The following garments should be enough for those who live in moderate climates: A cowl and a robe apiece (the cowl to be of wool in winter and in summer light or old); a rough garment for work; and shoes and boots for the feet. The monks shall not be fastidious about the color and texture of these clothes, which are to be made of the stuff commonly used in the region where they dwell, or of the cheapest material. The abbot shall also see that the garments are of suitable length and not too short. When new garments are given out the old ones should be returned, to be kept in the wardrobe for the poor. Each monk may have two cowls and two robes to allow for change at night and for washing; anything more than this is superfluous and should be dispensed with as being a form of luxury. The old boots and shoes are also to be returned when new ones are given out. Those who are sent out on the road shall be provided with trousers, which shall be washed and restored to the vestiary when they return. There shall also be cowls and robes of slightly better material for the use of those who are sent on journeys, which also shall be given back when they return. A mattress, a blanket, a sheet, and a pillow shall be sufficient bedding. The beds are to be inspected by the abbot frequently, to see that no monk has hidden away anything of his own in them, and if anything is found there which has not been granted to that monk by the abbot, he shall be punished very severely. To avoid giving occasion to this vice, the abbot shall see that the monks are provided with everything that is necessary: cowl, robe, shoes, boots, girdle, knife, pen, needle, handkerchief, tablets, etc. For he should remember how the fathers did in this matter, as it is related in the Acts of the Apostles: "There was given unto each man according to his need" [Acts 2:45]. He should be guided in this by the requirements of the needy, rather than by the complaints of the discontented, remembering always that he shall have to give an account of all his decisions to God on the day of judgment.

The table of the abbot.—The table of the abbot shall always be for the use of guests and pilgrims, and when there are no guests the abbot may invite some of the brothers to eat with him. But in that case, he should see that one or two of the older brothers are always left at the common table to preserve the discipline of the meal.

Artisans of the monastery.—If there are any skilled artisans in the monastery, the abbot may permit them to work at their chosen trade, if they will do so humbly. But if any one of them is made proud by his skill in his particular trade or by his value to the monastery, he shall be made to give up that work and shall not go back to it until he has convinced the abbot of his humility. And if the products of any of these trades are sold, those who conduct the sales shall see that no fraud is perpetrated upon the monastery. For those who have any part in defrauding the monastery are in danger of spiritual destruction, just as Ananias and Sapphira[5] for this sin suffered physical death. Above all, avarice is to be avoided in these transactions; rather the prices asked should be a little lower than those current in the neighborhood, that God may be glorified in all things.

The way in which new members are to be received.—Entrance into the monastery should not be made too easy, for the apostle says: "Try the spirits, whether they are of God" [1 John 4:1]. So when anyone applies at the monastery, asking to be accepted as a monk, he should first be proved by every test. He shall be made to wait outside four or five days, continually knocking at the door and begging to be admitted; and then he shall be taken in as a guest and allowed to stay in the guest chamber a few days. If he satisfies these preliminary tests, he shall be made to serve a novitiate of at least one year, during which he shall be placed under the charge of one of the older and wiser brothers, who shall examine him and prove, by every possible means, his sincerity, his zeal, his obedience, and his ability to endure shame. And he shall be told in the plainest manner all the hardships and difficulties of the life which he has chosen. If he promises never to leave the monastery [*stabilitas loci*] the rule shall be read to him after the first two months of his novitiate, and again at the end of six more months, and finally, four months later, at the end of his year. Each time he shall be told that this is the guide which he must follow as a monk, the reader saying to him at the end of the reading: "This is the law under which you have expressed a desire to live; if you are able to obey it, enter; if not, depart in peace." Thus he shall have been given every chance for mature deliberation and every opportunity to refuse the yoke of service. But if he still persists in asserting his eagerness to enter and his willingness to obey the rule and the commands of his superiors, he shall then be received into the congregation,

[5]A husband and wife who perished because of their attempt to cheat the Apostles (Acts 5: 1–11)

with the understanding that from that day forth he shall never be permitted to draw back from the service or to leave the monastery. The ceremony of receiving a new brother into the monastery shall be as follows: first he shall give a solemn pledge, in the name of God and his holy saints, of constancy, conversion of life, and obedience (*stabilitas loci, conversio morum, obedientia*);[6] this promise shall be in writing drawn up by his own hand (or, if he cannot write, it may be drawn up by another at his request, and signed with his own mark), and shall be placed by him upon the altar in the presence of the abbot, in the name of the saints whose relics are in the monastery. Then he shall say: "Receive me, O Lord, according to thy word, and I shall live; let me not be cast down from mine expectation" [Ps. 119:116]; which shall be repeated by the whole congregation three times, ending with the "Gloria Patri." Then he shall prostrate himself at the feet of all the brothers in turn, begging them to pray for him, and therewith he becomes a member of the congregation. If he has any property he shall either sell it all and give to the poor before he enters the monastery, or else he shall turn it over to the monastery in due form, reserving nothing at all for himself; for from that day forth he owns nothing, not even his own body and will. Then he shall take off his own garments there in the oratory, and put on the garments provided by the monastery. And those garments which he put off shall be stored away in the vestiary, so that if he should ever yield to the promptings of the devil and leave the monastery, he shall be made to put off the garments of a monk, and to put on his own worldly clothes, in which he shall be cast forth. But the written promise which the abbot took from the altar where he placed it shall not be given back to him, but shall be preserved in the monastery.

The presentation of children.—If persons of noble rank wish to dedicate their son to the service of God in the monastery, they shall make the promise for him, according to the following form: they shall bind his hand and the written promise along with the consecrated host[7] in the altarcloth and thus offer him to God. And in that document they shall promise under oath that their son shall never receive any of the family

---

[6]The vows that a monk had to take may be summed up as follows: (1) *stabilitas loci,* stability of place, steadfastness; that is, he took a vow never to leave the monastery and give up the monastic life; (2) *conversio morum,* conversion of life; that is, to give up all secular and worldly practices and to conform to the ideals and standards of the monastic life; (3) observance of the rule; (4) obedience, that is, to the abbot and to all his superiors; (5) chastity; and (6) poverty. The last three are generally meant when "monastic vows" are spoken of.

[7]The consecrated wafer or bread of the Eucharist.

property, from them or any other person in any way whatsoever. If they are unwilling to do this, and desire to make some offering to the monastery for charity and the salvation of their souls, they may make a donation from that property, reserving to themselves the usufruct[8] during their lives, if they wish. This shall all be done so clearly that the boy shall never have any expectations that might lead him astray, as we know to have happened. Poor people shall do the same when they offer their sons; and if they have no property at all they shall simply make the promise for their son and present him to the monastery with the host before witnesses.

---

[8]Right to use a piece of property.

2

The Song of Roland

THE Song of Roland *is probably the best example of the* chansons de geste, *or poetic tales of adventure, popular in the Middle Ages. Put in writing some three hundred years after the events it purports to describe,* The Song of Roland *was probably composed and recited by professional entertainers, or jongleurs, operating along the pilgrim route to the shrine of St. James at Compostella in northwestern Spain. Though the hero of the poem is vassal to the French king Charlemagne, the connection with history is tenuous. Charlemagne did campaign in northern Spain in 778, however; and, on his return to France, suffered the loss of the rear guard of his army, ambushed at Roncesvalles in the Pyrenees mountains. The hero, Roland, commands the rear guard on this campaign, having been put in command at the suggestion of Ganelon, a jealous traitor in league with the Saracen (Muslim) king Marsilla, whose forces carry out the ambush. Oliver, Roland's companion, thrice urges Roland to sound the horn Oliphant for aid, but Roland's pride keeps him from doing so until it is too late. Summoned at last by Roland's horn, Charlemagne returns and destroys the Saracen army (after God, in response to Charlemagne's prayer, has ordered the sun to stand still to allow the French forces sufficient daylight). Ganelon afterward offers the specious defense that he wanted revenge on Roland but did not intend treachery against Charlemagne. However, his guilt proved in trial by combat, he is duly executed. The poem closes with Charlemagne's dream, in which God commands the king to prepare for further battles against the forces of Islam.*

The excerpt presented here is the climax of the poem—the death of Roland. Inevitably, the epic evokes comparisons with Homer's Iliad: *like Achilles, Roland embodies the ideals of his age, and his stubborn rashness and pride cause the death of his friend and disaster for many others. Unlike the* Iliad, The Song of Roland *is oversimple in characterization; but its color and symbolism and its*

14

vigorous language convey the qualities that gave feudalism its vitality: a sense of religious mission in the war against evil, high regard for personal honor, and mutual loyalty of vassal and overlord.

91

Roland has gone into the Spanish pass
On Veillantif, his good swift horse.
He bears his arms, they are very becoming to him.
As for his spear, the knight brandishes it,
He twirls the tip against the sky,
A pure white ensign is lashed to its point,
The fringes flap against his hands.
He has a well-proportioned body, his face is open and smiling.
His companion follows right behind him,
And the men of France call him their protector.
He looks fiercely toward the Saracens
And amicably and gently toward the French,
And he spoke to them in comradely fashion:
"My lord barons, move forward at a slow trot!
These pagans are heading for a great massacre.
Today we shall have a fine and noble battle,
No king of France ever had such a worthy challenge."
As he speaks, the armies close in.   AOI.[1]

• • •

128

Count Roland sees the great slaughter of his men.
He calls his companion Oliver:
"Dear sir, dear comrade, in God's name, what do you make of this?

---

[1]The letters AOI appear after many stanzas. Their meaning is not clear, but they may be notices to the reciter to utter some exclamation to indicate heightened significance and to arouse the listeners' attention.

THE SONG OF ROLAND   From *The Song of Roland*, translated by Gerard J. Brault (University Park: The Pennsylvania State University Press, 1978). © The Pennsylvania State University Press, 1978. Reprinted by permission of The Pennsylvania State University Press. [Pp. 73–74, 105–119, 120–53.]

You see so many good knights lying on the ground!
Sweet France, the fair, is to be pitied,
How impoverished she is now of such knights!
O dear King, what a shame you're not here!
Dear Oliver, how shall we do it,
How shall we break the news to him?"
Oliver said: "I don't know how to reach him.
I'd rather die than have something to blame ourselves for."   AOI.

129

Roland said: "I shall sound the oliphant.[2]
Charles, who is going through the pass, will hear it.
I give you my word that the Franks will return now."
Oliver said: "That would be dishonorable
And a reproach to all your relatives,
The shame of it would last the rest of their lives!
When I told you to, you did nothing at all,
Don't expect my consent to do it now.
If you sound the horn, it will not be a brave act.
See how bloody both your arms are!"
The Count replies: "I have struck mighty fine blows!"   AOI.

130

Roland says: "Our battle is hard,
I shall sound the horn and Charles will hear it."
Oliver said: "That would not be a heroic deed!
When I told you to, comrade, you did not deign to.
If the King had been here, we would have suffered no harm.
Those who are with him over there are not to be blamed."
Oliver said: "By this beard of mine,
If I manage to see my fair sister Alda again,
You shall never lie in her arms!"   AOI.

131

Roland said: "Why are you angry with me?"
The other replies: "Comrade, you brought it on yourself,

---

[2]Roland's horn, so called because it was made from the tusk of an elephant (*oliphant* being an old form of the word).

For heroism tempered with common sense is a far cry from
    madness;
Reasonableness is to be preferred to recklessness.
Frenchmen have died because of your senselessness.
We shall never again be of service to Charles.
If you had believed me, my lord would have come,
We would have fought [and won] this battle,
King Marsile would be captured or slain.
I have come to rue your prowess, Roland!
Charlemagne will not have any help from us.
There shall never be such a man again until Judgment Day.
You will die here and France will be dishonored.
Today our loyal companionage comes to an end,
Before nightfall, our parting will be very sad."   AOI.

132

The Archbishop hears them quarreling.
He urges on his horse with his pure gold spurs,
He comes up to them, he began to reprove them:
"Sir Roland and you, Sir Oliver,
In God's name I beg you, don't argue!
Sounding the horn would be of no use to us now,
Nevertheless it is best:
The King will come, he will be able to avenge us,
The men of Spain must not return home joyful.
Our Frenchmen will dismount,
They will find us dead and cut to pieces.
They will raise us in coffins on sumpters,[3]
They will shed tears of sorrow and pity for us.
They will bury us in hallowed ground within church walls,
Neither wolves, nor pigs, nor dogs will devour us."
Roland replies: "Well said, sir."   AOI.

133

Roland has brought the oliphant up to his mouth,
He grasps it firmly, he sounds it with all his might.
The mountains are high and the sound travels a great distance,

[3]Pack mules.

They heard it echo a full thirty leagues away.
Charles heard it, all his men too.
The King said: "Our men are giving battle!"
But Ganelon contradicted him:
"If anyone else said this, it would seem a great lie!"   AOI.

134

Count Roland, with pain and suffering,
With great agony sounds his oliphant.
Bright blood comes gushing from his mouth,
The temple of his brain has burst.
The sound of the horn he is holding carries very far,
Charles, who is going through the pass, hears it.
Duke Naimes heard it, the Franks[4] listen for it.
The King says: "I hear Roland's horn!
He'd never sound it if he weren't fighting."
Ganelon replies: "There's no battle!
You're old now, you're grizzled and white-haired,
Yet such words make you seem a child.
You know Roland's great folly perfectly well,
It's a wonder God suffers him so. . . .
He sounds his horn all day long for a mere hare.
He's showing off now before his peers,
No force on earth would dare challenge him in the field.
Ride on! Why are you stopping?
The Fatherland is very far ahead of us."   AOI.

135

Count Roland's mouth is bleeding,
The temple of his brain has burst.
He sounds the oliphant in agony and in pain,
Charles heard it, and his Frenchmen too.
The King said: "That horn has been blowing a long time!"
Duke Naimes replies: "A worthy knight is pouring out his suffering!
There is a battle, so help me.

[4]The French.

The one who begs you to pretend you have heard nothing has
    betrayed him.
To arms, shout your battle cry,
Save your noble household:
You hear as plain as can be Roland signaling his distress!"

136

The Emperor has ordered his trumpets to be sounded.
The French dismount, they arm themselves
With hauberks,[5] helmets, and gilded swords.
They have fine shields and long and sturdy spears,
And white, red, and blue ensigns.
All the knights of the army mount their war-horses,
They spur furiously until they are out of the pass.
They say to one another:
"If only we could see Roland before he's killed,
We would strike mighty blows with him!"
But what is the use? They have tarried too long.

137

The afternoon has brightened up, as has the day.
The equipment shines in the sun,
Hauberks and helmets blaze forth great flashes,
The shields, too, which are beautifully painted with flowers,
The spears, and the golden ensigns.
The Emperor rides furiously,
And the French are vexed and angry.
They are all crying bitterly,
And they have great fear for Roland.
The King has Count Ganelon seized,
He turns him over to the kitchen help in his employ.
He calls Besgon, their master:
"Guard him well, as befits the felon that he is!
He has betrayed my household."
The head cook takes charge of him, he assigns this duty to a hundred
    of his fellows
From the kitchen, the most reliable and the toughest.

---

[5]Coats of chain mail.

They pluck out his beard and his moustache,
Each strikes him four blows with his fist;
They thrash him soundly with rods and sticks,
They put an iron collar around his neck,
And they chain him like a bear.
They placed him shamefully on a sumpter.
They guard him until they deliver him back to Charles.

138

The mountains are high, shadowy, and massive,   AOI.
The valleys deep and the waters swift.
The trumpets sound in the rear and in front,
And all respond to the oliphant's call.
The Emperor rides furiously,
And the French are angry and vexed.
They are all weeping and showing distress,
And they pray God to protect Roland
Until they arrive together on the battlefield:
With him they will strike properly.
But what is the use? It is of no avail,
They tarry too long, they cannot be there in time.   AOI.

139

King Charles rides like fury,
His white beard is spread over his hauberk.
The knights from France all spur furiously,
They are all in a state of blind anger
For not being with Roland, the captain,
Who is fighting the Saracens of Spain.
He is so badly hurt I do not think his soul can remain in him.
God! what men, the sixty who are in his company!
No king or captain ever had finer.   AOI.

140

Roland gazes at the mountains and hills.
He sees so many men from France lying dead,
He weeps over them like a noble knight:

"My lord barons, God have mercy on you!
May He grant Paradise to all your souls,
May He cause them to lie among the holy flowers!
I have never seen worthier knights than you,
You have served me constantly and for so long!
You have conquered such great nations for Charles!
The Emperor raised you, but how unfortunate the outcome!
Land of France, you are a very sweet realm,
Today made desolate by such a cruel disaster!
French knights, I see you dying for my sake:
I cannot protect or save you.
May God, who never did lie, help you!
Oliver, my friend, I must not fail you,
I shall die of sorrow if nothing else kills me.
Comrade, sir, let's go strike again!"

141

Count Roland has returned to the battlefield,
He holds Durendal, he strikes like a worthy knight.
He cuts Faldron of Pui in two
And twenty-four of the most esteemed Saracens.
There shall never be a man more bent on revenge.
As the stag runs before the hounds,
So the pagans flee before Roland.
The Archbishop said: "You are doing very well!
That's the sort of valor any knight must have
Who bears arms and sits astride a good horse!
He must be strong and fierce in battle,
Otherwise he is not worth four pennies,
Instead he should be in one of those monasteries
Praying all the time for our sins."
Roland replies: "Strike, do not spare them!"
When they heard this, the Franks attacked again.
There were very heavy losses among the Christians.

• • •

145

The pagans, seeing that there were few Frenchmen left,
Become overconfident and are much relieved.

One said to the other: "The Emperor is in the wrong."
Marganice sat astride a sorrel horse,
He urges him on with his golden spurs,
He strikes Oliver from behind full in the back.
He broke the white hauberk away from his body,
He pushed his spear through his chest, until it came out in front.
Afterward he said: "You've taken quite a blow!
Charlemagne left you in the pass, that's his misfortune!
He did us wrong, it's not right that he should boast about it,
For on you alone I have taken ample revenge for all our losses."

146

Oliver feels that he has received a mortal blow.
He holds Halteclere, whose steel was shiny,
He strikes Marganice on his pointed golden helmet,
He knocks its flower and crystal ornaments to the ground,
He cuts his head down to the front teeth,
He delivered his blow and threw him down dead.
Afterward he said: "Damn you, pagan!
I don't say that Charles hasn't suffered any losses;
But before any woman or lady you may have seen
You shall not boast, in the realm you came from,
That you have taken anything worth a penny from me,
Nor inflicted any harm on me or anyone else."
Then he cries out to Roland for help.   AOI.

147

Oliver feels that he has received a mortal wound,
He will never slake his thirst for revenge.
He strikes now like a true knight in the thick of the press,
He hacks through spears and shields,
Feet, fists, saddles, and sides.
Anyone having seen him dismembering Saracens,
Piling one corpse on top of another,
Would remember a true knight.
He does not want to forget Charles's battle cry,
He shouts "Monjoie!"[6] loud and clear.

[6]The poet says later that Charlemagne's battle cry comes from Joyeuse, the name of
  Charlemagne's sword.

He calls Roland, his friend and his peer:
"Comrade, sir, do come next to me!
We shall part with great sadness today."   AOI.

148

Roland looks Oliver in the face,
It is wan, livid, colorless, and pale.
Bright blood streaks the length of his body,
It falls to the ground in spurts.
"God!" says the Count, "I don't know what to do now.
Comrade, sir, your valor, what a shame!
There will never be anyone who will measure up to you.
Alas, fair France, how bereft you shall remain
Of worthy knights, how ruined and fallen!
The Emperor will suffer a heavy loss because of this."
Having said this, he faints upon his horse.   AOI.

149

See now Roland, who has fainted upon his horse,
And Oliver, who has suffered a mortal wound.
He has lost so much blood that his eyes are clouded,
He cannot see clearly enough far and near
To be able to recognize any mortal.
Encountering his companion,
He strikes him on his helmet of gold wrought with gems,
He hacks through it completely down to the nasal,
But he did not touch his head.
After this blow, Roland looked at him,
He asked him softly and gently:
"Comrade, sir, are you doing this on purpose?
Look, it's Roland who loves you so!
You haven't challenged me in any way!"
Oliver said: "I hear you speaking now.
I do not see you, may the Lord God see you!
I struck you, please forgive me for this!"
Roland replies: "I have suffered no injury,
I forgive you this here and before God."
After he said this, they bowed to each other,
See them now parting with such affection!

150

Oliver feels that death is gripping him hard,
Both eyes are rolling in his head,
He loses hearing and vision completely.
He dismounts, he lies down on the ground,
He confesses his sins in a loud voice.
With both hands joined and raised toward heaven,
He prays God to grant him Paradise,
He blessed Charles and fair France,
And his companion Roland above all others.
His heart fails him, his helmet drops forward,
His whole body falls to the ground,
The Count is dead, he lingers no more.
Noble Roland weeps over him and laments over him,
You shall never hear a sadder man on earth!

• • •

157

The pagans say: "The Emperor is returning,   AOI.
Listen to the bugle calls of the men from France!
If Charles comes, it will mean losses for us.
If Roland lives, our war begins anew,
We have lost Spain, our land."
Four hundred of them assemble, wearing helmets,
Those who consider themselves to be the best on the battlefield,
They make a heavy and savage attack upon Roland.
For his part, the Count now has much to do.   AOI.

158

When Count Roland sees them coming,
He makes himself so strong, so fierce, so sharp!
He will not give in to them as long as he is alive.
He sits astride the horse called Veillantif,
He urges him on with his pure gold spurs,
He attacks them all in the thick of the press,
Archbishop Turpin is with him.
One pagan said to the other: "Come on, my friend!

We have heard the bugles of the men from France.
Charles, the mighty king, is returning!"

159

Count Roland never cared for any coward,
Villain, or evil man with a bad character,
Or any knight if he were not a good fighter.
He called Archbishop Turpin:
"My lord, you are on foot and I am on horseback,
For love of you, I shall make a stand here.
We shall endure together the good and the bad,
I shall not abandon you for any man alive.
In a moment we shall pay the pagans back for this attack,
The best blows are those of Durendal."
The Archbishop said: "Damn anyone who will not strike hard!
Charles, who will avenge us well, is returning."

160

The pagans say: "We were born for such misfortune!
What a cruel day has dawned for us this day!
We have lost our lords and our peers,
Brave Charles is returning with his great army.
We hear the clear bugles of the men from France,
The noise from those shouting 'Monjoie!' is great.
Count Roland is so fierce,
He shall never be vanquished by any man alive.
Let's throw our spears at him, then let him be."
So they did this with a rain of darts and wigars,
Spears, lances, and feathered mizraks.[7]
They pierced and punctured Roland's shield,
And shattered and broke the metal links of his hauberk,
But not a spear entered his body.
However, they wounded Veillantif in thirty places
Under the Count, and they left him dead.
The pagans flee, thus letting him be.
Count Roland now remains on foot.   AOI.

---

[7]Wigars and mizraks were also weapons for throwing.

161

The pagans flee, angry and vexed,
They strive with all their might to reach Spain.
Count Roland does not have any way to pursue them,
He has lost his war-horse Veillantif,
Willy-nilly, he now remains on foot.
He went to help Archbishop Turpin,
He unlaced his golden helmet from his head,
He took off the light white hauberk.
And he cut his under-tunic all in pieces,
He puts the strips in his great wounds.
Then he embraced him against his breast,
Afterward he laid him softly on the green grass.
Roland begged him very gently:
"Oh, noble man, pray give me leave!
Our companions, whom we held so dear,
Are dead now and we must not abandon them.
I want to go look for them and identify them,
To lay them out and line them up before you."
The Archbishop said: "Go and then return!
This battlefield is yours, thank God, yours and mine."

162

Roland turns and goes away, he wanders through the field all alone,
He searches the valleys and he searches the mountains.
There he found Gerin and his companion Gerier,
And he found Berengier and Atton;
There he found Anseïs and Samson,
He found old Gerard of Roussillon.
The knight took them one by one,
He came back with them to the Archbishop,
He lined them up before his knees.
The Archbishop cannot help crying,
He raises his hand, he gives his blessing.
Afterward he said: "You are to be pitied, my lords!
May God in His Glory have all your souls!
May He place them among the holy flowers!
My own death is causing me such anguish,
I shall never see the mighty Emperor!"

163

Roland turns and goes away, he sets out to search the field,
He found his companion Oliver.
He embraced him tight against his breast,
He comes to the Archbishop as best he can,
He laid him with the others on a shield,
And the Archbishop absolved them and crossed them.
Then the sorrow and the pity intensify.
Roland says: "Good comrade Oliver,
You were the son of Duke Renier,
Who held the march of the Valley of Runers.
When it comes to smashing lances and piercing shields,
Vanquishing and dismaying villains,
Aiding and counseling worthy men,
Vanquishing and dismaying evildoers,
There is no finer knight in any land!"

164

Count Roland sees his peers dead
And Oliver, whom he loved so well,
He was moved with pity, he begins to weep.
His face lost all its color.
He suffered such pain that he could no longer stand,
Willy-nilly, he falls to the ground.
The Archbishop said: "You are to be pitied, worthy knight!"

165

When the Archbishop saw Roland faint,
He suffered greater anguish than ever before.
He stretched out his hand and took the oliphant.
At Roncevaux there is a running stream,
He wants to go there, he will give some water to Roland.
He turns and goes away with short, faltering steps.
He is so weak that he cannot go any farther,
He has not the strength to, he has lost too much blood.
In less time than it would take a man to cover a single acre,
His heart fails him and he falls forward.
His death is gripping him hard.

166

Count Roland recovers from his swoon,
He rises to his feet, but he is suffering great pain.
He gazes uphill and he gazes downhill:
On the green grass, beyond his companions,
He sees the noble warrior lying,
It is the Archbishop, whom God sent in his name.
The Archbishop says his confession, he gazes upward,
He has joined and raised both hands toward heaven,
And he prays God to grant him Paradise.
Charles's warrior Turpin is dead.
By fighting great battles and preaching many fine sermons,
He was always a relentless fighter against the pagans.
May God grant him his holy blessing!   AOI.

• • •

168

Roland feels that death is near,
His brain is coming out through his ears.
He prays God to call his Peers,
And then, for his own sake, he prays the angel Gabriel.
He took the oliphant so as not to incur any blame,
And his sword Durendal with his other hand.
Where no crossbow can shoot a bolt,
He goes in the direction of Spain to a fallow field.
He climbs a hill and halts beneath two beautiful trees.
There are four objects made of marble there.
He fell backward on the green grass,
He fainted there, for death is near.

169

The mountains are high and the trees are very high,
There are four shiny marble objects there.
Count Roland faints on the green grass.
A Saracen is watching him all the while,
He feigns death and lies amid the others.
He smeared his body and his face with blood,

He rises to his feet and makes a dash forward.
He was well proportioned, strong, and very brave,
Through pride he embarks upon an act of fatal folly.
He seized Roland's body and his weapons,
And he said these words: "Charles's nephew is vanquished!
I shall carry this sword to Arabia."
But as the Saracen was pulling, the Count came round a bit.

170

Roland feels the Saracen stealing his sword from him,
He opened his eyes and said these words to him:
"I don't believe you're one of our men!"
He holds on to the oliphant, he does not want to part with it
    for a single moment,
And he strikes him on the helmet, whose gold is
    wrought with gems.
He smashes the steel, the head, the bones,
He knocked both his eyes out of his head,
He tumbled him over dead at his feet.
Afterward he says: "Dirty pagan, whatever possessed you
To seize me rightly or wrongly?
No one will hear of this without thinking you were mad.
My oliphant is split at the wide end now,
The crystal and the gold ornaments have fallen off."

171

Roland notices that his sight is failing him,
He rises to his feet and exerts himself to the utmost,
All color has faded from his face.
There is a dark stone in front of him,
He strikes it ten blows in bitterness and frustration.
The steel grates, but it is not smashed or nicked.
"Oh," said the Count, "Holy Mary, help me!
Oh, Durendal, noble one, you are to be pitied!
Since I am finished, I no longer have you in my care.
I have won so many battles in the field with you
And conquered so many vast lands
Over which white-bearded Charles rules!

May no turn–tail ever possess you!
A very good knight has owned you for a long time,
Never again shall there be such a sword in blessed France."

172

Roland struck the sardonyx stone,
The steel grates, but it does not break or nick.
Seeing that he cannot smash it,
He begins to lament over it to himself:
"Oh, Durendal, how beautiful you are, how clear, how bright!
How you shine and flash against the sun!
Charles was in the valleys of Maurienne
When God instructed him from heaven on high by His angel
To give you to a captain count:
So the great, noble king girded me with it.
With it I conquered Anjou and Brittany,
With it I conquered Poitou and Maine,
With it I conquered Normandy the free,
With it I conquered Provence and Aquitaine,
Lombardy and all Romagna;
With it I conquered Bavaria and all Flanders,
Burgundy, all Poland,
And Constantinople, which rendered homage to him,
And he does as he wishes in Saxony;
With it I conquered Scotland, Iceland,
And England, which he held under his jurisdiction;
With it I conquered so many countries and lands
Over which white-bearded Charles rules.[8]
I feel sad and heavy-hearted for this sword,
I would rather die than have it remain with the pagans.
God, our Father, do not let France be dishonored in this way!"

173

Roland struck a dark stone,
He whacks off more than I can say.
The sword grates, but neither shatters nor breaks,

---

[8]Roland's list of conquests has little basis in fact, but it suits the exaggerated tone of the epic.

It rebounds upward toward heaven.
The Count, seeing that he cannot smash it,
Laments over it softly to himself:
"Oh, Durendal, how beautiful you are and how very holy!
There are many relics in the golden hilt:
Saint Peter's tooth, some of Saint Basil's blood,
Some of my lord Saint Denis's hair,
Some of Saint Mary's clothing.
It is not right for the pagans to own you,
You must be served by Christians.
May no coward ever possess you!
With you I conquered many vast lands
Over which white-bearded Charles rules,
And the Emperor is powerful and mighty as a consequence."

174

Roland feels that death is overcoming him,
It descends from his head to his heart.
He ran beneath a pine tree,
He lay down prone on the green grass.
He places his sword and his oliphant beneath him.
He turned his head toward the pagan army:
He did this because he earnestly desires
That Charles and all his men say
That the noble Count died as a conqueror.
He beats his breast in rapid succession over and over again.
He proffered his gauntlet to God for his sins.   AOI.

175

Roland feels that his time is up,
He is on a steep hill, his face turned toward Spain.
He beat his breast with one hand:
"Mea culpa,[9] Almighty God,
For my sins, great and small,
Which I committed from the time I was born
To this day when I am overtaken here!"
He offered his right gauntlet to God,
Angels from heaven descend toward him.   AOI.

[9]"My fault; I am to blame."

176

Count Roland lay beneath a pine tree,
He has turned his face toward Spain.
He began to remember many things:
The many lands he conquered as a brave knight,
Fair France, the men from whom he is descended,
Charlemagne, his lord, who raised him.
He cannot help weeping and sighing.
But he does not wish to forget prayers for his own soul,
He says his confession in a loud voice and prays for God's mercy:
"True Father, who never lied,
Who resurrected Saint Lazarus from the dead
And saved Daniel from the lions,
Protect my soul from all perils
Due to the sins I committed during my life!"
He proffered his right gauntlet to God,
Saint Gabriel took it from his hand.
He laid his head down over his arm,
He met his end, his hands joined together.
God sent His angel Cherubin
And Saint Michael of the Peril,
Saint Gabriel came with them.
They bear the Count's soul to Paradise.

• • •

179

The Emperor orders his bugles to be sounded,
Then the brave man rides off with his great army.
They have made the men of Spain turn tail,
They are in hot pursuit and all join in.
When the King sees the afternoon light waning,
He dismounts on the green grass in a meadow,
He prostrates himself on the ground and prays the Lord God
That He stop the sun for him,
That He postpone nightfall and prolong daylight.
Now there appears to him an angel who regularly speaks with him,
He promptly commands the King:
"Ride, Charles, for you do not lack daylight!

God knows that you have lost the flower of France.
You can now avenge yourself on this crime-ridden people."
When he heard this, the Emperor mounted up   AOI.

180

God performed a very great miracle for Charlemagne,
For the sun stood still.
The pagans flee, the Franks pursue them relentlessly.
They overtake them in the Val Tenebros,
Spurring on, they pursue them toward Saragossa,
Slaying them with mighty blows.
They cut off their getaway and main escape routes.
The Ebro River is before them now:
It is very deep, fearsome, and rapid,
There is no barge, galley, or lighter.
The pagans cry out to Tervagant, one of their gods,
Then jump in, but they receive no protection.
The men in full armor weigh the heaviest,
Some go swirling down to the bottom;
The others go floating downstream.
The survivors, however, swallowed so much water
That they all drowned in fearful pain.
The French cry out: "You are to be pitied, Roland!"   AOI.

181

Charles sees that all the pagans are dead,
Some killed, but most of them drowned—
His knights win a huge mass of booty in the process—
Then the noble King dismounted,
He lies on the ground, he thanked God.
When he rises, the sun has set.
The Emperor said: "It is time to bivouac,
It is too late to return to Roncevaux.
Our horses are tired and exhausted:
Remove their saddles and the bridles from their heads,
And let them refresh themselves in these meadows.
The Franks reply: "Well said, sire."   AOI.

182

The Emperor has pitched camp.
The French dismount in the deserted land,
They have taken the saddles away from their horses,
They remove the golden bridles from their heads,
They turn them loose in the meadows, there is abundant
    fresh grass there;
They have no other provisions for them.
Anyone who is very tired sleeps on the bare ground.
That night they do not mount guard at all.

183

The Emperor lies down in a meadow,
The brave man sets his great spear down next to his head.
That night he does not wish to take off his armor,
He has put on his shiny saffron hauberk,
Laced on his helmet of gold wrought with gems,
Girded Joyeuse—it has always been without peer—
Which changes color thirty times a day.
We can say a good deal about the Lance
With which Our Lord was wounded on the Cross:
Charles has its tip, thanks be to God,
He had it mounted in the golden pommel of his sword.
Because of this honor and because of this grace,
The name Joyeuse was given to the sword.
French knights must not forget it:
They derive their battle cry "Monjoie!" from it,
That is why no people on earth can withstand them.

3

Chrétien de Troyes

Lancelot

*T*HE *trumpets that sounded in* The
Song of Roland *summoned men to battle for God and feudal lord. In the
centuries following Roland's exploits at Roncesvalles, medieval society became
increasingly sophisticated and self-conscious. Men were concerned not only
about their prowess on the field of battle but about proper deportment at court
and castle. Reflecting and inspiring this changed attitude, poetry and fiction
became preoccupied with social conduct. In addition to valor in knightly
combats, the heroes of narratives were required to exhibit courtly behavior,
refined manners, and deference to upper-class women. The result was a code of
conduct that made love an ennobling ideal—a conception that has been one of the
distinguishing marks of European culture. According to some scholars, the
influence of this code on society equaled that of the changes wrought by the
Renaissance.*

*"Romances," as the medieval world knew them, were narratives, usually in
verse, of knightly adventures and supernatural occurrences in long-ago times
and faraway places. Chrétien de Troyes, of whose life we know nothing save
that he resided at the court of Champagne in France in the latter part of the
twelfth century, was the first to put the legends of King Arthur and the knights
of the Round Table into the framework of a romance. The following selection is
a prose translation of Chrétien's romance,* Lancelot. *It illustrates the code of
courtly love in the hero's complete submission to his lady's whims, in his
devotion alike to religion and to love, and in the tension that arose from his
pledging his honor to the service of both his lady and his feudal lord. The full
title of this romance,* Lancelot, or The Knight of the Cart, *is a hint to the
reader that the mysterious knight of the first section who incurs the shame of
riding in a peasant cart is really Lancelot, worthiest of Arthur's knights and for a
long time in love with the queen.*

Upon a certain Ascension Day[1] King Arthur had come from Caerleon, and had held a very magnificent court at Camelot[2] as was fitting on such a day. After the feast the King did not quit his noble companions, of whom there were many in the hall. The Queen was present, too, and with her many a courteous lady able to converse in French. And Kay, who had furnished the meal, was eating with the others who had served the food. While Kay was sitting there at meat, behold there came to court a knight, well equipped and fully armed, and thus the knight appeared before the King as he sat among his lords. He gave him no greeting, but spoke out thus: "King Arthur, I hold in captivity knights, ladies, and damsels who belong to thy dominion and household; but it is not because of any intention to restore them to thee that I make reference to them here; rather do I wish to proclaim and serve thee notice that thou hast not the strength or the resources to enable thee to secure them again. And be assured that thou shalt die before thou canst ever succour them."

The King replies that he must needs endure what he has not the power to change; nevertheless, he is filled with grief. Then the knight makes as if to go away, and turns about, without tarrying longer before the King; but after reaching the door of the hall, he does not go down the stairs, but stops and speaks from there these words: "King, if in thy court there is a single knight in whom thou hast such confidence that thou wouldst dare to entrust to him the Queen that he might escort her after me out into the woods whither I am going, I will promise to await him there, and will surrender to thee all the prisoners whom I hold in exile in my country if he is able to defend the Queen and if he succeeds in bringing her back again." Many who were in the palace heard this challenge, and the whole court was in an uproar.

Kay, too, heard the news as he sat at meat with those who served. Leaving the table, he came straight to the King, and as if greatly enraged, he began to say: "O King, I have served thee long, faithfully, and loyally; now I take my leave, and shall go away, having no desire to serve thee more." The King was grieved at what he heard, and as soon as he could, he thus replied to him: "Is this serious, or a joke?" And Kay replied: "O King, fair sire, I have no desire to jest, and I take my leave

---

[1]The fortieth day after Easter on which Christ's ascension into heaven is celebrated.

[2]Caerleon . . . Camelot, cities in Arthur's legendary kingdom.

LANCELOT   From the book *Arthurian Romances* by Chrétien de Troyes. Translated by W. W. Comfort. Everyman's Library Edition. [New York, 1955.] Reprinted by permission of J. M. Dent & Sons Ltd. [Pp. 270–75, 308–10, 326–33, 358–59.]

quite seriously. No other reward or wages do I wish in return for this service I have given you. My mind is quite made up to go away immediately." "Is it in anger or in spite that you wish to go?" the King inquired; "seneschal,[3] remain at court, as you have done hitherto, and be assured that I have nothing in the world which I would not give you at once in return for your consent to stay." "Sire," says Kay, "No need of that. I would not accept for each day's pay a measure of fine pure gold."

Thereupon, the King in great dismay went off to seek the Queen. "My lady," he says, "you do not know the demand that the seneschal makes of me. He asks me for leave to go away, and says he will no longer stay at court; the reason of this I do not know. But he will do at your request what he will not do for me. Go to him now, my lady dear. Since he will not consent to stay for my sake, pray him to remain on your account, and if need be, fall at his feet, for I should never again be happy if I should lose his company." The King sends the Queen to the seneschal, and she goes to him. Finding him with the rest, she went up to him, and said: "Kay, you may be very sure that I am greatly troubled by the news I have heard of you. I am grieved to say that I have been told it is your intention to leave the King. How does this come about? What motive have you in your mind? I cannot think that you are so sensible or courteous as usual. I want to ask you to remain: stay with us here, and grant my prayer." "Lady," he says, "I give you thanks; nevertheless, I shall not remain." The Queen again makes her request, and is joined by all the other knights. And Kay informs her that he is growing tired of a service which is unprofitable. Then the Queen prostrates herself at full length before his feet. Kay beseeches her to rise, but she says that she will never do so until he grants her request. Then Kay promises her to remain, provided the King and she will grant in advance a favour he is about to ask. "Kay," she says, "both I and he will grant it, whatever it may be. Come now, and we shall tell him that upon this condition you will remain." So Kay goes away with the Queen to the King's presence. The Queen says: "I have had hard work to detain Kay; but I have brought him here to you with the understanding that you will do what he is going to ask." The King sighed with satisfaction, and said that he would perform whatever request he might make.

"Sire," says Kay, "hear now what I desire, and what is the gift you have promised me. I esteem myself very fortunate to gain such a boon

---

[3] A seneschal was the manager of a noble or royal household.

with your consent. Sire, you have pledged your word that you would entrust to me my lady here, and that we should go after the knight who awaits us in the forest." Though the King is grieved, he trusts him with the charge, for he never went back upon his word. But it made him so ill-humoured and displeased that it plainly showed in his countenance. The Queen, for her part, was sorry too, and all those of the household say that Kay had made a proud, outrageous, and mad request. Then the King took the Queen by the hand, and said: "My lady, you must accompany Kay without making objection." And Kay said: "Hand her over to me now, and have no fear, for I shall bring her back perfectly happy and safe." The King gives her into his charge, and he takes her off. After them all the rest go out, and there is not one who is not sad. You must know that the seneschal was fully armed, and his horse was led into the middle of the courtyard, together with a palfrey, as is fitting, for the Queen. The Queen walked up to the palfrey, which was neither restive nor hard-mouthed. Grieving and sad, with a sigh the Queen mounts, saying to herself in a low voice, so that no one could hear: "Alas, alas, if you only knew it, I am sure you would never allow me without interference to be led away a step." She thought she had spoken in a very low tone; but Count Guinable heard her, who was standing by when she mounted.

When they started away, as great a lament was made by all the men and women present as if she already lay dead upon a bier. They do not believe that she will ever in her life come back. The seneschal in his impudence takes her where that other knight is awaiting her. But no one was so much concerned as to undertake to follow him; until at last my lord Gawain thus addressed the King his uncle: "Sire," he says, "you have done a very foolish thing, which causes me great surprise; but if you will take my advice, while they are still near by, I and you will ride after them, and all those who wish to accompany us. For my part, I cannot restrain myself from going in pursuit of them at once. It would not be proper for us not to go after them, at least far enough to learn what is to become of the Queen, and how Kay is going to comport himself." "Ah, fair nephew," the King replied, "you have spoken courteously. And since you have undertaken the affair, order our horses to be led out bridled and saddled that there may be no delay in setting out."

The horses are at once brought out, all ready and with the saddles on. First the King mounts, then my lord Gawain, and all the others rapidly. Each one, wishing to be of the party, follows his own will and starts away. Some were armed, but there were not a few without their arms. My lord Gawain was armed, and he bade two squires lead by the bridle two extra steeds. And as they thus approached the forest, they saw Kay's horse running out; and they recognized him, and saw that both reins of the bridle were broken. The horse was running wild, the stirrup-straps all stained with blood, and the saddle-bow was broken and damaged. Every one was chagrined at this, and they nudged each other and shook their heads. My lord Gawain was riding far in advance of the rest of the party, and it was not long before he saw coming slowly a knight on a horse that was sore, painfully tired, and covered with sweat. The knight first saluted my lord Gawain, and his greeting my lord Gawain returned. Then the knight, recognising my lord Gawain, stopped and thus spoke to him: "You see, sir, my horse is in a sweat and in such case as to be no longer serviceable. I suppose that those two horses belong to you; now, with the understanding that I shall return the service and the favour, I beg you to let me have one or the other of them, either as a loan or outright as a gift." And he answers him: "Choose whichever you prefer." Then he who was in dire distress did not try to select the better or the fairer or the larger of the horses, but leaped quickly upon the one which was nearer to him, and rode him off. Then the one he had just left fell dead, for he had ridden him hard that day, so that he was used up and overworked.

The knight without delay goes pricking through the forest, and my lord Gawain follows in pursuit of him with all speed, until he reaches the bottom of a hill. And when he had gone some distance, he found the horse dead which he had given to the knight, and noticed that the ground had been trampled by horses, and that broken shields and lances lay strewn about, so that it seemed that there had been a great combat between several knights, and he was very sorry and grieved not to have been there. However, he did not stay there long, but rapidly passed on until he saw again by chance the knight all alone on foot, completely armed, with helmet laced, shield hanging from his neck, and with his sword girt on. He had overtaken a cart. In those days such a cart served the same purpose as does a pillory now; and in each good town where there are more than three thousand such carts nowadays, in those times there was only one, and this, like our pillories, had to do service for all those who commit murder or treason, and those who are guilty of any delinquency, and for thieves who have stolen others' property or have forcibly seized it on the roads. Whoever was convicted of any crime was placed upon a cart and dragged through all the streets, and he lost henceforth all his legal rights, and was never afterward heard, honoured, or welcomed in any court. The carts were so dreadful in those days that the saying was then first used: "When thou dost see and meet a cart, cross thyself and call upon God, that no evil may befall thee."

The knight on foot, and without a lance, walked behind the cart, and saw a dwarf sitting on the shafts, who held, as a driver does, a long goad in his hand. Then he cries out: "Dwarf, for God's sake, tell me now if thou hast seen my lady, the Queen, pass by here." The miserable, low-born dwarf would not give him any news of her, but replied: "If thou wilt get up into the cart I am driving thou shalt hear to-morrow what has happened to the Queen." Then he kept on his way without giving further heed. The knight hesitated only for a couple of steps before getting in. Yet, it was unlucky for him that he shrank from the disgrace, and did not jump in at once; for he will later rue his delay. But common sense, which is inconsistent with love's dictates, bids him refrain from getting in, warning him and counselling him to do and undertake nothing for which he may reap shame and disgrace. Reason, which dares thus speak to him, reaches only his lips, but not his heart; but love is enclosed within his heart, bidding him and urging him to mount at once upon the cart. So he jumps in, since love will have it so, feeling no concern about the shame, since he is prompted by love's commands. And my lord Gawain presses on in haste after the cart, and when he finds the knight sitting in it, his surprise is great. "Tell me," he shouted to the dwarf, "if thou knowest anything of the Queen." And he replied: "If thou art so much thy own enemy as is this knight who is sitting here, get in with him, if it be thy pleasure, and I will drive thee along with him." When my lord Gawain heard that, he considered it great foolishness, and said that he would not get in, for it would be dishonourable to exchange a horse for a cart: "Go on, and wherever thy journey lies, I will follow after thee."

[Jeered at because of his shameful ride in the peasant cart, Lancelot nevertheless perseveres in his quest. He learns that the Queen and Sir Kay are held captive in the mysterious Land of Gorre, where many of Arthur's subjects are imprisoned. After many combats, adventures, and temptations, he wins his way to the perilous entrance to Gorre. *Ed.*]

At the end of this very difficult bridge they[4] dismount from their steeds and gaze at the wicked-looking stream, which is as swift and

---

[4]Lancelot and two knights who have accompanied him thus far.

raging, as black and turgid, as fierce and terrible as if it were the devil's stream; and it is so dangerous and bottomless that anything falling into it would be as completely lost as if it fell into the salt sea. And the bridge, which spans it, is different from any other bridge; for there never was such a one as this. If any one asks of me the truth, there never was such a bad bridge, nor one whose flooring was so bad. The bridge across the cold stream consisted of a polished, gleaming sword; but the sword was stout and stiff, and was as long as two lances. At each end there was a tree-trunk in which the sword was firmly fixed. No one need fear to fall because of its breaking or bending, for its excellence was such that it could support a great weight. But the two knights who were with the third were much discouraged; for they surmised that two lions or two leopards would be found tied to a great rock at the other end of the bridge. The water and the bridge and the lions combine so to terrify them that they both tremble with fear, and say: "Fair sire, consider well what confronts you; for it is necessary and needful to do so. This bridge is badly made and built, and the construction of it is bad. If you do not change your mind in time, it will be too late to repent. You must consider which of several alternatives you will choose. Suppose that you once get across (but that cannot possibly come to pass, any more than one could hold in the winds and forbid them to blow, or keep the birds from singing, or re-enter one's mother's womb and be born again—all of which is as impossible as to empty the sea of its water); but even supposing that you got across, can you think and suppose that those two fierce lions that are chained on the other side will not kill you, and suck the blood from your veins, and eat your flesh and then gnaw your bones? For my part, I am bold enough, when I even dare to look and gaze at them. If you do not take care, they will certainly devour you. Your body will soon be torn and rent apart, for they will show you no mercy. So take pity on us now, and stay here in our company! It would be wrong for you to expose yourself intentionally to such mortal peril." And he, laughing, replies to them: "Gentlemen, receive my thanks and gratitude for the concern you feel for me: it comes from your love and kind hearts. I know full well that you would not like to see any mishap come to me; but I have faith and confidence in God, that He will protect me to the end. I fear the bridge and stream no more than I fear this dry land; so I intend to prepare and make the dangerous attempt to cross. I would rather die than turn back now."

The others have nothing more to say; but each weeps with pity and heaves a sigh. Meanwhile he prepares, as best he may, to cross the stream, and he does a very marvellous thing in removing the armour from his feet and hands. He will be in a sorry state when he reaches the other side. He is going to support himself with his bare hands and feet upon the sword, which was sharper than a scythe, for he had not kept on his feet either sole or upper or hose. But he felt no fear of wounds upon his hands or feet; he preferred to maim himself rather than to fall from the bridge and be plunged in the water from which he could never escape. In accordance with this determination, he passes over with great pain and agony, being wounded in the hands, knees, and feet. But even this suffering is sweet to him: for Love, who conducts and leads him on, assuages and relieves the pain. Creeping on his hands, feet, and knees, he proceeds until he reaches the other side. Then he recalls and recollects the two lions which he thought he had seen from the other side; but, on looking about, he does not see so much as a lizard or anything else to do him harm. He raises his hand before his face and looks at his ring, and by this test he proves that neither of the lions is there which he thought he had seen, and that he had been enchanted and deceived; for there was not a living creature there. When those who had remained behind upon the bank saw that he had safely crossed, their joy was natural; but they do not know of his injuries. He, however, considers himself fortunate not to have suffered anything worse. The blood from his wounds drips on his shirt on all sides. Then he sees before him a tower, which was so strong that never had he seen such a strong one before: indeed, it could not have been a better tower.

At the window there sat King Bademagu, who was very scrupulous and precise about matters of honour and what was right, and who was careful to observe and practise loyalty above all else; and beside him stood his son, who always did precisely the opposite so far as possible, for he found his pleasure in disloyalty, and never wearied of villainy, treason, and felony. From their point of vantage they had seen the knight cross the bridge with trouble and pain. Meleagant's colour changed with the rage and displeasure he felt; for he knows now that he will be challenged for the Queen; but his character was such that he feared no man, however strong or formidable. If he were not base and disloyal, there could no better knight be found; but he had a heart of wood, without gentleness and pity. What enraged his son and roused his ire, made the king happy and glad. The king knew of a truth that he who had crossed the bridge was much better than any one else. For no one would dare to pass over it in whom there dwelt any of that evil nature which brings more shame upon those who possess it than prowess brings of honour to the virtuous. For prowess cannot accomplish so much as wickedness and sloth can do: it is true beyond a doubt that it is possible to do more evil than good.

[Lancelot, almost beaten by Meleagant, the evil son of the King of Gorre, is so inspired by the sight of Guinevere that he triumphs and gains the promise of the Queen's release. Through a misunderstanding, Guinevere believes that Lancelot has been killed and grieves to the point of death. He meanwhile believes a false report of her death and attempts to kill himself. They are each saved, however, at the very last minute by hearing that the other is alive. *Ed.*]

. . . The Queen yearns ardently for the arrival of her lover and her joy. She has no desire this time to bear him any grudge. But rumour, which never rests but runs always unceasingly, again reaches the Queen to the effect that Lancelot would have killed himself for her sake, if he had had the chance. She is happy at the thought that this is true, but she would not have had it happen so for anything, for her sorrow would have been too great. Thereupon Lancelot arrived in haste. . . .

This time the Queen did not lower her eyes to the ground, but she went to meet him cheerfully, honouring him all she could, and making him sit down by her side. Then they talked together at length of all that was upon their hearts, and love furnished them with so much to say that topics did not lack. And when Lancelot sees how well he stands, and that all he says finds favour with the Queen, he says to her in confidence: "Lady, I marvel greatly why you received me with such a countenance when you saw me the day before yesterday, and why you would not speak a word to me: I almost died of the blow you gave me, and I had not the courage to dare to question you about it, as I now venture to do. I am ready now, lady, to make amends, when you have told me what has been the crime which has caused me such distress." Then the Queen replies: "What? Did you not hesitate for shame to mount the cart? You showed you were loath to get in, when you hesitated for two whole steps. That is the reason why I would neither address nor look at you." "May God save me from such a crime again," Lancelot replies, "and may God show me no mercy, if you were not quite right! For God's sake, lady, receive my amends at once, and tell me, for God's sake, if you can ever pardon me." "Friend, you are quite forgiven," the Queen replies; "I pardon you willingly." "Thank you for that, lady," he then says; "but I cannot tell you here all that I should like to say; I should like to talk with you more at leisure, if possible." Then the Queen indicates a window by her glance rather than with her finger, and says: "Come through the garden to-night and speak with me at yonder window, when every one inside has gone to sleep. You will not be able to get in: I shall be inside and you outside; to gain entrance will be impossible. I shall be able to touch you only with my lips or hand, but, if you please, I will stay there until morning for love of you. Our bodies cannot be joined, for close beside me in my room lies Kay the seneschal, who is still suffering from his wounds. And the door is not open, but is tightly closed and guarded well. When you come, take care to let no spy catch sight of you." "Lady," says he, "if I can help it, no spy shall see me who might think or speak evil of us." Then, having agreed upon this plan, they separate very joyfully.

Lancelot leaves the room in such a happy frame that all his past troubles are forgotten. But he was so impatient for the night to come that his restlessness made the day seem longer than a hundred ordinary days or than an entire year. If night had only come, he would gladly have gone to the trysting place. Dark and sombre night at last won its struggle with the day, and wrapped it up in its covering, and laid it away beneath its cloak. When he saw the light of day obscured, he pretended to be tired and worn, and said that, in view of his protracted vigils, he needed rest. You, who have ever done the same, may well understand and guess that he pretends to be tired and goes to bed in order to deceive the people of the house; but he cared nothing about his bed, nor would he have sought rest there for anything, for he could not have done so and would not have dared, and furthermore he would not have cared to possess the courage or the power to do so. Soon he softly rose, and was pleased to find that no moon or star was shining, and that in the house there was no candle, lamp, or lantern burning. Thus he went out and looked about, but there was no one on the watch for him, for all thought that he would sleep in his bed all night. Without escort or company he quickly went out into the garden, meeting no one on the way, and he was so fortunate as to find that a part of the garden-wall had recently fallen down. Through this break he passes quickly and proceeds to the window, where he stands, taking good care not to cough or sneeze, until the Queen arrives clad in a very white chemise. She wore no cloak or coat, but had thrown over her a short cape of scarlet cloth and shrew-mouse fur.

As soon as Lancelot saw the Queen leaning on the window-sill behind the great iron bars, he honoured her with a gentle salute. She promptly returned his greeting, for he was desirous of her, and she of him. Their talk and conversation are not of vulgar, tiresome affairs. They draw close to one another, until each holds the other's hand. But they are so distressed at not being able to come together more completely, that they curse the iron bars. Then Lancelot asserts that, with the Queen's consent, he will come inside to be with her, and that the bars cannot keep him out. And the Queen replies: "Do you not see how the bars are stiff to bend and hard to break? You could never so twist, pull or drag at them as to dislodge one of them." "Lady," says he, "have no fear of that. It would take more than these bars to keep me out. Nothing but your command could thwart my power to come to you. If you will but grant me your permission, the way will open before me. But if it is not your pleasure, then the way is so obstructed that I could not possibly pass through." "Certainly," she says, "I consent. My will need not stand in your way; but you must wait until I retire to my bed again, so that no harm may come to you, for it would be no joke or jest if the seneschal, who is sleeping here, should wake up on hearing you. So it is best for me to withdraw, for no good could come of it, if he should see me standing here." "Go then, lady," he replies; "but have no fear that I shall make any noise. I think I can draw out the bars so softly and with so little effort that no one shall be aroused."

Then the Queen retires, and he prepares to loosen the window. Seizing the bars, he pulls and wrenches them until he makes them bend and drags them from their places. But the iron was so sharp the end of his little finger was cut to the nerve, and the first joint of the next finger was torn; but he who is intent upon something else paid no heed to any of his wounds or to the blood which trickled down. Though the window is not low, Lancelot gets through it quickly and easily. First he finds Kay asleep in his bed, then he comes to the bed of the Queen, whom he adores and before whom he kneels, holding her more dear than the relic of any saint. And the Queen extends her arms to him and, embracing him, presses him tightly against her bosom, drawing him into the bed beside her and showing him every possible satisfaction: her love and her heart go out to him. It is love that prompts her to treat him so; and if she feels great love for him, he feels a hundred thousand times as much for her. For there is no love at all in other hearts compared with what there is in his; in his heart love was so completely embodied that it was niggardly toward all other hearts. Now Lancelot possesses all he wants, when the Queen voluntarily seeks his company and love, and when he holds her in his arms, and she holds him in hers. Their sport is so agreeable and sweet, as they kiss and fondle each other, that in truth such a marvellous joy comes over them as was never heard or known. But their joy will not be revealed by me, for in a story it has no place. Yet, the most choice and delightful satisfaction was precisely that of which our story must not speak.

That night Lancelot's joy and pleasure were very great. But, to his sorrow, day comes when he must leave his mistress' side. It cost him such pain to leave her that he suffered a real martyr's agony. His heart now stays where the Queen remains; he has not the power to lead it away, for it finds such pleasure in the Queen that it has no desire to leave her: so his body goes, and his heart remains. But enough of his body stays behind to spot and stain the sheets with the blood which has fallen from his fingers. Full of sighs and tears, Lancelot leaves in great distress. He grieves that no time is fixed for another meeting, but it cannot be. Regretfully he leaves by the window through which he had entered so happily. He was so badly wounded in the fingers that they were in a sorry state; yet he straightened the bars and set them in their place again, so that from neither side, either before or behind, was it evident that any one had drawn out or bent any of the bars. When he leaves the room, he bows and acts precisely as if he were before a shrine; then he goes with a heavy heart, and reaches his lodgings without being recognised by any one. He throws himself naked upon his bed without awaking any one, and then for the first time he is surprised to notice the cuts in his fingers; but he is not at all concerned, for he is very sure that the wound was caused by dragging the window bars from the wall. Therefore he was not at all worried, for he would rather have had both arms dragged from his body than not enter through the window. But he would have been very angry and distressed, if he had thus injured and wounded himself under any other circumstances.

In the morning, within her curtained room, the Queen had fallen into a gentle sleep; she had not noticed that her sheets were spotted with blood, but she supposed them to be perfectly white and clean and presentable. Now Meleagant, as soon as he was dressed and ready, went to the room where the Queen lay. He finds her awake, and he sees the sheets spotted with fresh drops of blood, whereupon he nudges his companions and, suspicious of some mischief, looks at the bed of Kay the seneschal, and sees that his sheets are blood-stained too, for you must know that in the night his wounds had begun to bleed afresh. Then he said: "Lady, now I have found the evidence that I desired. It is very true that any man is a fool to try to confine a woman: he wastes his efforts and his pains. He who tries to keep her under guard loses her sooner than the man who takes no thought of her. A fine watch, indeed, has been kept by my father, who is guarding you on my behalf! He has succeeded in keeping you from me, but, in spite of him, Kay the seneschal has looked upon you last night, and has done what he pleased with you, as can readily be proved." "What is that?" she asks. "Since I must speak, I find blood on your sheets, which proves the fact. I know it and can prove it, because I find on both your sheets and his the blood which issued from his wounds: the evidence is very strong."

Then the Queen saw on both beds the bloody sheets, and marvelling, she blushed with shame and said: "So help me God, this blood which I see upon my sheets was never brought here by Kay, but my nose bled during the night, and I suppose it must be from my nose." In saying so, she thinks she tells the truth. "By my head," says Meleagant, "there is nothing in what you say. Swearing is of no avail, for you are taken in your guilt, and the truth will soon be proved." Then he said to the guards who were present: "Gentlemen, do not move, and see to it that the sheets are not taken from the bed until I return. I wish the king to do me justice, as soon as he has seen the truth." Then he searched until he found him, and falling at his feet, he said: "Sire, come to see what you have failed to guard. Come to see the Queen, and you shall see the certain marvels which I have already seen and tested. But, before you go, I beg you not to fail to be just and upright toward me. You know well to what danger I have exposed myself for the Queen; yet, you are no friend of mine and keep her from me under guard. This morning I went to see her in her bed, and I remarked that Kay lies with her every night. Sire, for God's sake, be not angry if I am disgruntled and if I complain. For it is very humiliating for me to be hated and despised by one with whom Kay is allowed to lie." "Silence!" says the king; "I don't believe it." "Then come, my lord, and see the sheets and the state in which Kay has left them. Since you will not believe my words, and since you think I am lying, I will show you the sheets and the quilt covered with blood from Kay's wounds." "Come now," says the king; "I wish to see for myself, and my eyes will judge of the truth."

Then the king goes directly to the room, where the Queen got up at his approach. He sees that the sheets are blood-stained on her bed and on Kay's alike, and he says: "Lady, it is going badly now, if what my son has said is true." Then she replies: "So help me God, never even in a dream was uttered such a monstrous lie. I think Kay the seneschal is courteous and loyal enough not to commit such a deed, and besides, I do not expose my body in the market-place, nor offer it of my own free will. Surely, Kay is not the man to make an insulting proposal to me, and I have never desired and shall never desire to do such a thing myself." "Sire, I shall be much obliged to you," says Meleagant to his father, "if Kay shall be made to atone for this outrage, and the Queen's shame thus be exposed. It devolves upon you to see that justice is done, and this justice I now request and claim. Kay has betrayed King Arthur his lord, who had such confidence in him that he entrusted to him what he loved most in the world." "Let me answer, sire," says Kay, "and I shall exonerate myself. May God have no mercy upon my soul when I leave this world, if I ever lay with my lady! Indeed, I should rather be dead than ever do my lord such an ugly wrong, and may God never grant me better health than I have now but rather kill me on the spot, if such a thought ever entered my mind! But I know that my wounds bled profusely last night, and that is the reason why my sheets are stained with blood. That is why your son suspects me, but surely he has no right to do so."

And Meleagant answers him: "So help me God, the devils and demons have betrayed you. You grew too heated last night and, as a result of your exertions, your wounds have doubtless bled afresh. There is no use in your denying it; we can see it, and it is perfectly evident. It is right that he should atone for his crime, who is so plainly taken in his guilt. Never did a knight with so fair a name commit such iniquity as this, and yours is the shame for it." "Sire, sire," says Kay to the king, "I will defend the Queen and myself against the accusation of your son. He harasses and distresses me, though he has no ground to treat me so." "You cannot fight," the king replies; "you are too ill." "Sire, if you will allow it, I will fight with him, ill as I am, and will show him that I am not guilty of the crime which he imputes to me." But the Queen, having secretly sent word to Lancelot, tells the king that she will present a knight who will defend the seneschal, if Meleagant dares to urge this charge. Then Meleagant said at once: "There is no knight without exception, even were he a giant, whom I will not fight until one of us is defeated."

Then Lancelot came in, and with him such a rout of knights that the whole hall was filled with them. As soon as he had entered, in the hearing of all, both young and old, the Queen told what had happened, and said: "Lancelot, this insult has been done me by Meleagant. In the presence of all who hear his words he says I have lied, if you do not make him take it back. Last night, he asserted, Kay lay with me, because he found my sheets, like his, all stained with blood; and he says that he [Kay] stands convicted, unless he will undertake his own defence, or unless some one else will fight the battle on his behalf." Lancelot says: "You need never use arguments with me. May it not please God that either you or he should be thus discredited! I am ready to fight and to prove to the extent of my power that he never was guilty of such a thought. I am ready to employ my strength in his behalf, and to defend him against this charge." Then Meleagant jumped up and said: "So help me God, I am pleased and well satisfied with that; no one need think that I object." And Lancelot said: "My lord king, I am well acquainted with suits and laws, with trials and verdicts: in a question of veracity an oath should be taken before the fight." Meleagant at once replies: "I agree to take an oath; so let the relics be brought at once, for I know well that I am right." And Lancelot answers him: "So help me God, no one who ever knew Kay the seneschal would doubt his word on such a point." Then they call for their horses, and ask that their arms be brought. This is promptly done, and when the valets had armed them, they were ready for the fight. Then the holy relics are brought forth: Meleagant steps forward, with Lancelot by his side, and both fall on their knees. Then Meleagant, laying his hands upon the relics, swears unreservedly: "So help me God and this holy relic, Kay the seneschal lay with the Queen in her bed last night and had his pleasure with her." "And I swear that thou liest," says Lancelot, "and furthermore I swear that he neither lay with her nor touched her. And may it please God to take vengeance upon him who has lied, and may He bring the truth to light! Moreover, I will take another oath and swear, whoever may dislike it or be displeased, that if I am permitted to vanquish Meleagant to-day, I will show him no mercy, so help me God and these relics here!" The king felt no joy when he heard this oath.

[The Queen allows the fight between Lancelot and Meleagant to be stopped before either is victor. She returns to Arthur's court, but Lancelot is treacherously imprisoned by Meleagant. He gains freedom long enough to participate, disguised, in the tournament presided over by the Queen, in which he willingly incurs shame by obeying her command to do his worst. But when she commands him to do his best, he triumphs over all contestants. Lancelot is imprisoned once more by Meleagant and, at last, escapes; then he challenges Meleagant to fight before King Arthur and the court. *Ed.*]

In the field there stood a sycamore as fair as any tree could be; it was wide-spread and covered a large area, and around it grew a fine border of thick fresh grass which was green at all seasons of the year. Under this fair and stately sycamore, which was planted back in Abel's time, there rises a clear spring of water which flows away hurriedly. The bed of the spring is beautiful and as bright as silver, and the channel through which the water flows is formed, I think, of refined and tested gold, and it stretches away across the field down into a valley between the woods. There it pleases the King to take his seat where nothing unpleasant is in sight. After the crowd has drawn back at the King's command, Lancelot rushes furiously at Meleagant as at one whom he hates cordially, but before striking him, he shouted with a loud and commanding voice: "Take your stand, I defy you! And take my word, this time you shall not be spared." Then he spurs his steed and draws back the distance of a bow-shot. Then they drive their horses toward each other at top speed, and strike each other so fiercely upon their resisting shields that they pierced and punctured them. But neither one is wounded, nor is the flesh touched in this first assault. They pass each other without delay, and come back at the top of their horses' speed to renew their blows on the strong, stout shields. Both of the knights are strong and brave, and both of the horses are stout and fast. So mighty are the blows they deal on the shields about their necks that the lances passed clean through, without breaking or splintering, until the cold steel reached their flesh. Each strikes the other with such force that both are borne to earth, and no breast-strap, girth, or stirrup could save them from falling backward over their saddle-bow, leaving the saddle without an occupant. The horses run riderless over hill and dale, but they kick and bite each other, thus showing their mortal hatred.

As for the knights who fell to earth, they leaped up as quickly as possible and drew their swords, which were engraved with chiselled lettering. Holding their shields before the face, they strive to wound each other with their swords of steel. Lancelot stands in no fear of him, for he knew half as much again about fencing as did his antagonist, having learned it in his youth. Both dealt such blows on the shield slung from their necks, and upon their helmets barred with gold, that they crushed and damaged them. But Lancelot presses him hard and gives him a mighty blow upon his right arm which, though encased in mail, was unprotected by the shield, severing it with one clean stroke. And when he felt the loss of his right arm, he said that it should be dearly sold. If it is at all possible, he will not fail to exact the price; he is in such pain and wrath and rage that he is well-nigh beside himself, and he has a poor opinion of himself, if he cannot score on his rival now. He rushes at him with the intent to seize him, but Lancelot forestalls his plan, for with his trenchant sword he deals his body such a cut as he will not recover from until April and May be passed. He smashes his nose-guard against his teeth, breaking three of them in his mouth. And Meleagant's rage is such that he cannot speak or say a word; nor does he deign to cry for mercy, for his foolish heart holds tight in such constraint that even now it deludes him still. Lancelot approaches and, unlacing his helmet, cuts off his head. Never more will this man trouble him: it is all over with him as he falls dead. Not a soul who was present there felt any pity at the sight. The King and all the others there are jubilant and express their joy. Happier than they ever were before, they relieve Lancelot of his arms, and lead him away exultingly.

4

Medieval Lyric Poetry

W_E *have seen an example of the medieval epic in* The Song of Roland *and of the medieval romance in* Chrétien de Troyes' Lancelot. *Too often overlooked, however, is the gift of the Middle Ages for lyric verse, a talent that appears both in religious poems, such as the following selection's* Canticle of the Sun *by St. Francis of Assisi (1182–1226), and in more secular forms and subjects. In the songs of wandering scholars, or in the margins of manuscripts in monastic libraries (where a scribe might jot down some poem he had composed or remembered having heard), or in chance collections, we find some of the choicest medieval Latin lyrics. All of the other poems except the last in the following selection are from a collection of songs, poems, and plays compiled in the thirteenth century at a Benedictine monastery in southern Germany. After the dissolution of the monastery, the manuscript remained undiscovered until early in the nineteenth century. These lyrics are especially attractive for their use of rhyme and accent (admirably preserved in the following translations), which sound so natural to the modern ear but were seldom used in Greek or Latin verse. They show yet another aspect of the Middle Ages in their intense awareness and enjoyment of the beauty of this world. The translator has termed "When Diana lighteth late her crystal lamp" the high point of medieval secular verse.*

ST. FRANCIS OF ASSISI

The Canticle of the Sun

Most high, omnipotent, good Lord
Praise, glory, and honour and benediction, all are Thine.
To Thee alone do they belong, most High,
And there is no man fit to mention Thee.

Praise be to Thee, my Lord, with all Thy creatures,
Especially to my worshipful brother sun,
The which lights up the day, and through him dost
   Thou brightness give;
And beautiful is he and radiant with splendour great;
Of Thee, most High, signification gives.

Praised be my Lord, for sister moon and for the stars,
In heaven Thou hast formed them clear and precious and fair.

Praised be my Lord for brother wind
And for the air and clouds and fair and every kind of weather,
By the which Thou givest to Thy creatures nourishment.

Praised be my Lord for sister water,
The which is greatly helpful and humble and precious and pure.

Praised be my Lord for brother fire,
By the which Thou lightest up the dark.
And fair is he and gay and mighty and strong.

Praised be my Lord for our sister, mother earth,
The which sustains and keeps us
And brings forth diverse fruits with grass and flowers bright.

Praised be my Lord for those who for Thy love forgive
And weakness bear and tribulation.
Blessed those who shall in peace endure,
And by Thee, most High, shall they be crowned.

Praised be my Lord for our sister, the bodily death,
From the which no living can flee.
Woe to them who die in mortal sin;

MEDIEVAL LYRIC POETRY   St. Francis of Assisi, "The Canticle of the Sun," in *The Writings of Saint Francis of Assisi*, trans. P. Robinson (Philadelphia: Dolphin, 1906), 86.

Blessed those who shall find themselves in Thy most holy will,
For the second death shall do them no ill.

Praise ye and bless ye my Lord, and give Him thanks,
And be subject unto Him with great humility.

MS. OF BENEDICTBEUERN

Let's Away with Study

Let's away with study,
  Folly's sweet.
Treasure all the pleasure
  Of our youth:
Time enough for age
  To think on Truth.
So short a day,
And life so quickly hasting,
And in study wasting
  Youth that would be gay!

'Tis our spring that's slipping,
  Winter draweth near,
  Life itself we're losing,
  And this sorry cheer
Dries the blood and chills the heart,
  Shrivels all delight.
Age and all its crowd of ills
  Terrifies our sight.
So short a day,
And life so quickly hasting,
And in study wasting
  Youth that would be gay!

Let us as the gods do,
  'Tis the wiser part:

MEDIEVAL LYRIC POETRY   (ca. 1000–ca. 1400) Selections are reprinted from *Medieval Latin Lyrics*, translated by Helen Waddell, with the permission of W. W. Norton & Company, Inc. All Rights Reserved, 1977. Reprinted by permission of Constable Publishers. [Pp. 185–87, 189–91, 203–205, 265–67, 269–71, 275–77.]

Leisure and love's pleasure
   Seek the young in heart
Follow the old fashion,
   Down into the street!
Down among the maidens,
   And the dancing feet!
So short a day,
And life so quickly hasting,
And in study wasting
   Youth that would be gay!

There for the seeing
   Is all loveliness,
White limbs moving
   Light in wantonness.
Gay go the dancers,
   I stand and see,
Gaze, till their glances
   Steal myself from me.
So short a day,
And life so quickly hasting,
And in study wasting
   Youth that would he gay!

When Diana[1] Lighteth Late Her Crystal Lamp

When Diana lighteth
Late her crystal lamp,
Her pale glory kindleth
From her brother's fire,
Little straying west winds
Wander over heaven,
Moonlight falleth,
And recalleth
With a sound of lute-strings shaken,
Hearts that have denied his reign
To love again.

[1]Roman goddess of the moon.

Hesperus, the evening star,
To all things that mortal are,
Grants the dew of sleep.

Thrice happy Sleep!
The antidote to care,
Thou dost allay the storm
Of grief and sore despair;
Through the fast-closed gates
Thou stealest light;
Thy coming gracious is
As Love's delight.

Sleep through the wearied brain
Breathes a soft wind
From fields of ripening grain,
The sound
Of running water over clearest sand,
A millwheel turning, turning slowly round,
These steal the light
From eyes weary of sight.

Love's sweet exchange and barter, then the brain
Sinks to repose;
Swimming in strangeness of a new delight
The eyelids close;
Oh sweet the passing o'er from love to sleep.
But sweeter the awakening to love.

Under the kind branching trees
Where Philomel[2] complains and sings
Most sweet to lie at ease,
Sweeter to take delight
Of beauty and the night
On the fresh springing grass,
With smell of mint and thyme,
And for Love's bed, the rose.
Sleep's dew doth ever bless,
But most distilled on lovers' weariness.

[2]The nightingale.

To You, Consummate Drinkers

To you, consummate drinkers,
    Though little be your drought,
Good speed be to your tankards,
    And send the wine about.
Let not the full decanter
    Sleep on its round,
And may unheard of banter
    In wit abound.

If any cannot carry
    His liquor as he should,
Let him no longer tarry,
    No place here for the prude.
No room among the happy
    For modesty.
A fashion only fit for clowns,
    Sobriety.

If such by chance are lurking
    Let them be shown the door;
He who good wine is shirking,
    Is one of us no more.
A death's head is his face to us,
    If he abide.
Who cannot keep the pace with us,
    As well he died.

Should any take upon him
    To drink without a peer,
Although his legs go from him,
    His speech no longer clear,
Still for his reputation
    Let him drink on,
And swig for his salvation
    The bumper down.

But between god and goddess,
    Let there no marriage be,
For he whose name is Liber
    Exults in liberty.

Let none his single virtue
    Adulterate,
Wine that is wed with water is
    Emasculate.

Queen of the sea we grant her,
    Goddess without demur,
But to be bride to Bacchus[3]
    Is not for such as her.
For Bacchus drinking water
    Hath no man seen;
Nor ever hath his godship
    Baptized been.

The Grace of Giving

Right and wrong they go about
    Cheek by jowl together.
Lavishness can't keep in step
    Avarice his brother.
Virtue, even in the most
    Unusual moderation,
Seeking for the middle course,
    Vice on either side it, must
Look about her with the most
    Cautious contemplation.

You'll remember to have read
    In the works of Cato,[4]
Where it plainly is set forth
    "Walk but with the worthy."
If then you have set your mind
    On the grace of giving,
This of first importance is,
    He who now your debtor is,

---

[3]Roman god of wine.
[4]Roman statesman, called "the Censor," 234–149 B.C.

Can he be regarded as
　　Worthily receiving?

Giving otherwise is but
　　Virtue by repute,
Naught but secondary good,
　　Not the absolute.
But would you be generous
　　With security,
Have your glory on account,
　　Value full with each amount,
Hesitate no more, but give
　　What you have to me.

So by My Singing Am I Comforted

So by my singing am I comforted
　Even as the swan that singing makes death sweet,
For from my face is gone the wholesome red,
And soft grief in my heart is sunken deep.
　　For sorrow still increasing,
　　And travail unreleasing,
　　And strength from me fast flying,
　　And I for sorrow dying,
Dying, dying, dying,
Since she I love cares nothing for my sighing.

If she whom I desire would stoop to love me,
　I should look down on Jove;[5]
If for one night my lady would lie by me,
　And I kiss the mouth I love,
　　Then come Death unrelenting,
　　With quiet breath consenting,
　　I go forth unrepenting,
Content, content, content,
That such delight were ever to me lent.

[5]Chief god of Roman religion.

Innocent breasts, when I have looked upon them,
   Would that my hands were there,
How have I craved, and dreaming thus upon them,
   Love wakened from despair.
      Beauty on her lips flaming,
      Rose red with her shaming,
      And I with passion burning
      And with my whole heart yearning
For her mouth, her mouth, her mouth,
That on her beauty I might slake my drouth.

ANONYMOUS THIRTEENTH-CENTURY MS.

Down from the Branches Fall the Leaves

Down from the branches fall the leaves,
A wanness comes on all the trees,
   The summer's done;
And into his last house in heaven
   Now goes the sun.

Sharp frost destroys the tender sprays,
Birds are a–cold in these short days.
   The nightingale
Is grieving that the fire of heaven
   Is now grown pale.

The swollen river rushes on
Past meadows whence the green has gone,
   The golden sun
Has fled our world. Snow falls by day,
   The nights are numb.

About me all the world is stark,
And I am burning; in my heart
   There is a fire,
A living flame in me, the maid
   Of my desire.

Her kisses, fuel of my fire,
Her tender touches, flaming higher.
   The light of light

Dwells in her eyes: divinity
  Is in her sight.

Greek fire[6] can be extinguished
By bitter wine; my fire is fed
  On other meat.
Yea, even the bitterness of love
  Is bitter-sweet.

[6]An incendiary material used in ancient and medieval warfare, said to have kept on burning even in water.

5

Maimonides

The Guide for the Perplexed

MAIMONIDES, *or Moses ben Maimon (1135–1204), philosopher, physician, and master of rabbinical literature, was born to a prominent Jewish family in Cordoba, Spain. He was educated there by his learned father and with his family later emigrated to Egypt where, in Cairo, he attained a position of leadership in the Jewish community. With his appointment as court physician to the sultan Saladin, his medical skill became known and valued by many Muslims and Christians. Maimonides is said to have been invited to England by King Richard the Lion Hearted, but to have declined.*

Maimonides and such Muslim philosophers as al-Farabi, Avicenna, and Averroës strengthened influence of Aristotle on Western civilization through their commentaries on his philosophy, which were translated and circulated widely in Europe. Indeed, Aristotle's thought spread throughout the medieval world, culminating in the Scholastic philosophers, especially St. Thomas Aquinas. In Maimonides' Guide for the Perplexed, *Aristotle is regarded as having the highest human intellect, excepting persons who have received divine inspiration.*

The "perplexed" for whom Maimonides writes are those who cannot decide between following the lead of their own speculations or following authority. Maimonides has in mind devout Jews who know science and who are perplexed by the literal meanings of religious Law, but a similar dilemma faces believers of all faiths.

In the following excerpts from The Guide, *Maimonides deals with basic questions confronting philosophy and religion such as whether the universe will last forever or come to an end; the relationship of form and matter in inanimate objects and in human beings; whether the universe has a purpose or not; and the relationship between God's will and natural causation in controlling events in this world.*

Written originally in Arabic, The Guide was soon translated into Hebrew and then into Latin at the court of Frederick II, Holy Roman emperor and king of Sicily. Thus its influence extended into Europe, and the fame of Maimonides grew. The well-known expression "From Moses to Moses there was none like Moses," suggests that in some people's judgment Moses Maimonides surpassed every religious thinker and teacher since the biblical Moses.

PART II: CHAPTER 27

The Theory of a Future Destruction of the Universe is not Part of the Religious Belief taught in the Bible

We have already stated that the belief in the Creation is a fundamental principle of our religion; but we do not consider it a principle of our faith that the Universe will again be reduced to nothing. It is not contrary to the tenets of our religion to assume that the Universe will continue to exist for ever. It might be objected that everything produced is subject to destruction, as has been shown; consequently the Universe, having had a beginning, must come to an end. This axiom cannot be applied according to our views. We do not hold that the Universe came into existence, like all things in Nature, as the result of the laws of Nature. For whatever owes its existence to the action of physical laws is, according to the same laws, subject to destruction: the same law which caused the existence of a thing after a period of non-existence, is also the cause that the thing is not permanent; since the previous non-existence proves that the nature of that thing does not necessitate its permanent existence. According to our theory, taught in Scripture, the existence or non-existence of things depends solely on the will of God and not on fixed laws, and, therefore, it does not follow that God must destroy the Universe after having created it from noth-

THE GUIDE FOR THE PERPLEXED   From Moses ben Maimon, *The Guide for the Perplexed*, translated by M. Friedlander, 2d. ed., 1904, repr. 1956 (New York: Dover Publications), 201–202, 261–62, 272–73, 285–87.

ing. It depends on His will. He may, according to His desire, or according to the decree of His wisdom, either destroy it, or allow it to exist, and it is therefore possible that He will preserve the Universe for ever, and let it exist permanently as He Himself exists. It is well known that our Sages[1] never said that the throne of glory will perish, although they assumed that it has been created. No prophet or sage ever maintained that the throne of glory will be destroyed or annihilated; but, on the contrary, the Scriptural passages speak of its permanent existence. We are of opinion that the souls of the pious have been created, and at the same time we believe that they are immortal. Some hold, in accordance with the literal meaning of the Midrashim,[2] that the bodies of the pious will also enjoy everlasting happiness. Their notion is like the well-known belief of certain people, that there are bodily enjoyments in Paradise. In short, reasoning leads to the conclusion that the destruction of the Universe is not a certain fact. There remains only the question as to what the prophets[3] and our Sages say on this point; whether they affirm that the world will certainly come to an end, or not. Most people amongst us believe that such statements have been made, and that the world will at one time be destroyed. I will show you that this is not the case; and that, on the contrary, many passages in the Bible speak of the permanent existence of the Universe. Those passages which, in the literal sense, would indicate the destruction of the Universe, are undoubtedly to be understood in a figurative sense, as will be shown. If, however, those who follow the literal sense of the Scriptural texts reject our view, and assume that the ultimate certain destruction of the Universe is part of their faith, they are at liberty to do so. But we must tell them that the belief in the destruction is not necessarily implied in the belief in the Creation; they believe it because they trust the writer, who used a figurative expression, which they take literally. Their faith, however, does not suffer by it.

. . .

[1] Jewish commentators on Scripture. By Scripture and Bible Maimonides means Hebrew Scripture, that is, the Old Testament.

[2] Detailed expositions and interpretations of passages of Scripture.

[3] Persons (for instance the Old Testament prophets) who speak for God or as though under divine guidance.

PART III: CHAPTER 13

The Universe has No other Purpose than its own Existence

Intelligent persons are much perplexed when they inquire into the purpose of the Creation. I will now show how absurd this question is. . . . An agent that acts with intention must have a certain ulterior object in that which he performs. This is evident, and no philosophical proof is required. It is likewise evident that that which is produced with intention has passed over from non-existence to existence. It is further evident, and generally agreed upon, that the being which has absolute existence, which has never been and will never be without existence, is not in need of an agent. We have explained this before. The question, "What is the purpose thereof?" cannot be asked about anything which is not the product of an agent; therefore we cannot ask what is the purpose of the existence of God. He has not been created. According to these propositions it is clear that the purpose is sought for everything produced intentionally by an intelligent cause; that is to say, a final cause must exist for everything that owes its existence to an intelligent being: but for that which is without a beginning, a final cause need not be sought, as has been stated by us. After this explanation you will understand that there is no occasion to seek the final cause of the whole Universe, neither according to our theory of the Creation, nor according to the theory of Aristotle, who assumes the Eternity of the Universe. For according to Aristotle, who holds that the Universe has not had a beginning, an ultimate final cause cannot be sought even for the various parts of the Universe. Thus it cannot be asked, according to his opinion, What is the final cause of the existence of the heavens? Why are they limited by this measure or by that number? Why is matter of this description? What is the purpose of the existence of this species of animals or plants? Aristotle considers all this as the result of a permanent order of things. Natural Philosophy investigates into the object of everything in Nature, but it does not treat of the ultimate final cause, of which we speak in this chapter. . . .

We remain firm in our belief that the whole Universe was created in accordance with the will of God, and we do not inquire for any other cause or object. Just as we do not ask what is the purpose of God's existence, so we do not ask what was the object of His will, which is the cause of the existence of all things with their present properties, both those that have been created and those that will be created. . . .

• • •

PART III: CHAPTER 17

Five Theories concerning Providence

There are different theories concerning Divine Providence; they are all ancient, known since the time of the Prophets, when the true Law was revealed to enlighten these dark regions. . . .

This is our theory, or that of our Law. I will show you [first] the view expressed on this subject in our prophetical books, and generally accepted by our Sages. I will then give the opinion of some later authors among us, and lastly, I will explain my own belief. The theory of man's perfectly free will is one of the fundamental principles of the Law of our Teacher Moses, and of those who follow the Law. According to this principle man does what is in his power to do, by his nature, his choice, and his will; and his action is not due to any faculty created for the purpose. All species of irrational animals likewise move by their own free will. This is the Will of God; that is to say, it is due to the eternal divine will that all living beings should move freely, and that man should have power to act according to his will or choice within the limits of his capacity. Against this principle we hear, thank God, no opposition on the part of our nation. Another fundamental principle taught by the Law of Moses is this: Wrong cannot be ascribed to God in any way whatever; all evils and afflictions as well as all kinds of happiness of man, whether they concern one individual person or a community, are distributed according to justice; they are the result of strict judgment that admits no wrong whatever. Even when a person suffers pain in consequence of a thorn having entered into his hand, although it is at once drawn out, it is a punishment that has been inflicted on him [for sin], and the least pleasure he enjoys is a reward [for some good action]; all this is meted out by strict justice; as is said in Scripture, "all his ways are judgment" (Deut. xxxii. 4); we are only ignorant of the working of that judgment. . . .

My opinion on this principle of Divine Providence I will now explain to you. In the principle which I now proceed to expound I do not rely on demonstrative proof, but on my conception of the spirit of the Divine Law, and the writings of the Prophets. The principle which I accept is far less open to objections, and is more reasonable than the opinions mentioned before. It is this: In the lower or sublunary portion of the Universe Divine Providence does not extend to the individual members of species except in the case of mankind. It is only in this species that the incidents in the existence of the individual beings, their good and evil fortunes, are the result of justice, in accordance with the words, "For all His ways are judgment." But I agree with Aristotle as regards all other living beings, and à fortiori[4] as regards plants and all the rest of earthly creatures. For I do not believe that it is through the interference of Divine Providence that a certain leaf drops [from a tree], nor do I hold that when a certain spider catches a certain fly, that this is the direct result of a special decree and will of God in that moment; it is not by a particular Divine decree that the spittle of a certain person moved, fell on a certain gnat in a certain place, and killed it; nor is it by the direct will of God that a certain fish catches and swallows a certain worm on the surface of the water. In all these cases the action is, according to my opinion, entirely due to chance, as taught by Aristotle. Divine Providence is connected with Divine intellectual influence, and the same beings which are benefited by the latter so as to become intellectual, and to comprehend things comprehensible to rational beings, are also under the control of Divine Providence, which examines all their deeds in order to reward or punish them. It may be by mere chance that a ship goes down with all her contents, as in the above-mentioned instance, or the roof of a house falls upon those within; but it is not due to chance, according to our view, that in the one instance the men went into the ship, or remained in the house in the other instance; it is due to the will of God, and is in accordance with the justice of His judgments, the method of which our mind is incapable of understanding. . . .

All that is mentioned of the history of Abraham, Isaac, and Jacob is a perfect proof that Divine Providence extends to every man individually. But the condition of the individual beings of other living creatures is undoubtedly the same as has been stated by Aristotle. On that account it is allowed, even commanded, to kill animals; we are permitted to use them according to our pleasure. The view that other living beings are only governed by Divine Providence in the way described by Aristotle, is supported by the words of the Prophet Habakkuk. When he perceived the victories of Nebuchadnezzar, and saw the multitude of those slain by him, he said, "O God, it is as if men were abandoned, neglected, and unprotected like fish and like worms of the earth." He thus

[4] All the more.

shows that these classes are abandoned. This is expressed in the following passage: "And makest men as the fishes of the sea, as the creeping things, that have no ruler over them. They take up all of them with the angle," etc. (Hab. i. 14, 15). The prophet then declares that such is not the case; for the events referred to are not the result of abandonment, forsaking, and absence of Providence, but are intended as a punishment for the people, who well deserved all that befell them. He therefore says: "O Lord, Thou hast ordained them for judgment, and O mighty God, Thou hast established them for correction" (*ibid.* ver. 12). Our opinion is not contradicted by Scriptural passages like the following: "He giveth to the beast his food" (Ps. cxlvii. 9); "The young lions roar after their prey, and seek their meat from God" (*ibid.* civ. 21); "Thou openest thine hand, and satisfiest the desire of every living thing" (*ibid.* cxlv. 16); or by the saying of our Sages: "He sitteth and feedeth all, from the horns of the unicorns even unto the eggs of insects." There are many similar sayings extant in the writings of our Sages, but they imply nothing that is contrary to my view. All these passages refer to Providence in relation to species, and not to Providence in relation to individual animals. The acts of God are as it were enumerated; how He provides for every species the necessary food and the means of subsistence. This is clear and plain. Aristotle likewise holds that this kind of Providence is necessary, and is in actual existence. Alexander also notices this fact in the name of Aristotle, viz., that every species has its nourishment prepared for its individual members; otherwise the species would undoubtedly have perished. It does not require much consideration to understand this. There is a rule laid down by our Sages that it is directly prohibited in the Law to cause pain to an animal, and is based on the words: "Wherefore hast thou smitten thine ass?" etc. (Num. xxii. 32). But the object of this rule is to make us perfect; that we should not assume cruel habits; and that we should not uselessly cause pain to others; that, on the contrary, we should be prepared to show pity and mercy to all living creatures, except when necessity demands the contrary: "When thy soul longeth to eat flesh," etc. (Deut. xii. 20). We should not kill animals for the purpose of practicing cruelty, or for the purpose of play. It cannot be objected to this theory, Why should God select mankind as the object of His special Providence, and not other living beings? For he who asks this question must also inquire, Why has man alone, of all species of animals, been endowed with intellect? The answer to this second question must be, according to the three afore-mentioned theories: It was the Will of God, it is the decree of His Wisdom, or it is in accordance with the laws of Nature. The same answers apply to the first question. Understand thoroughly my theory, that I do not ascribe to God ignorance of anything or any kind of weakness; I hold that Divine Providence is related and closely connected with the intellect, because Providence can only proceed from an intelligent being, from a being that is itself the most perfect Intellect. Those creatures, therefore, which receive part of that intellectual influence, will become subject to the action of Providence in the same proportion as they are acted upon by the Intellect. This theory is in accordance with reason and with the teaching of Scripture, whilst the other theories previously mentioned either exaggerate Divine Providence or detract from it. In the former case they lead to confusion and entire nonsense, and cause us to deny reason and to contradict that which is perceived with the senses. The latter case, viz., the theory that Divine Providence does not extend to man, and that there is no difference between man and other animals, implies very bad notions about God; it disturbs all social order, removes and destroys all the moral and intellectual virtues of man.

6

St. Thomas Aquinas

Summation of the Catholic Faith

ST. *Thomas Aquinas (ca. 1225–*
1274) received his early education at the monastery of Monte Cassino and, over
the objections of his family, entered the Dominican order at age eighteen. How
little the formative years sometimes tell about an individual's potentialities is
exemplified by the fact that Aquinas, known to his fellow students as the
"Dumb Ox," became a Doctor of Theology, the "Angelic Doctor" of the
medieval Church and universities throughout Europe. He lectured at Paris,
Rome, and Bologna, engaged in the affairs of the Church, and wrote
monumental treatises on theology. Preferring the life of scholarship to the
dignity and power of office, Aquinas refused the archbishopric of Naples and the
abbacy of Monte Cassino. He died while journeying to a council where
reconciliation of the Greek and Latin Churches was to have been discussed.
Aquinas was officially declared a saint some half-century after his death, and no
theologian save Augustine has had a greater influence on the theology and
philosophy of the Western world. By a directive of 1879, Pope Leo XIII
advised members of the Catholic clergy to take the teachings of Aquinas as the
basis of their own theological position.

The supreme figure in "scholasticism," the medieval philosophical effort to
harmonize faith and reason, Aquinas distinguishes in his Summation of the
Catholic Faith *(Summa Contra Gentiles) between truth discerned by hu-*
man reason and that imparted by revelation—both of which are necessary.
Revelation is contained in the Scriptures, but also comes through the teachings of
the Church Fathers and the decisions of Church councils. Reason is not, for
Aquinas, merely a function of the individual mind, but rather the "natural
truth" (or "natural law") which reaches our understanding through philosophy.
These two kinds of truth—reason and revelation—are complementary, for they
spring from the same source, that is, from God, the Prime Mover. The

following selection, with its many quotations from the Scriptures and from Aristotle, illustrates the characteristic method of thought and proof in scholastic philosophy.

ON THE WAY IN WHICH DIVINE TRUTH IS TO BE MADE KNOWN

The way of making truth known is not always the same, and, as the Philosopher[1] has very well said, "it belongs to an educated man to seek such certitude in each thing as the nature of that thing allows." The remark is also introduced by Boethius.[2] But, since such is the case, we must first show what way is open to us in order that we may make known the truth which is our object.

There is a twofold mode of truth in what we profess about God. Some truths about God exceed all the ability of the human reason. Such is the truth that God is triune. But there are some truths which the natural reason also is able to reach. Such are that God exists, that He is one, and the like. In fact, such truths about God have been proved demonstratively by the philosophers, guided by the light of the natural reason.

That there are certain truths about God that totally surpass man's ability appears with the greatest evidence. Since, indeed, the principle of all knowledge that the reason perceives about some thing is the understanding of the very substance of that being (for according to Aristotle "what a thing is" is the principle of demonstration), it is necessary that the way in which we understand the substance of a thing determines the way in which we know what belongs to it. Hence, if the human intellect comprehends the substance of some thing, for example, that of a stone or of a triangle, no intelligible characteristic belonging to that thing surpasses the grasp of the human reason. But this does not happen to us in the case of God. For the human intellect is not able to reach a comprehension of the divine substance through its natural

---

[1] Medieval writers customarily refer to Aristotle as the Philosopher.

[2] Roman statesman and philosopher (480–524).

SUMMATION OF THE CATHOLIC FAITH   From *On the Truth of the Catholic Faith* by St. Thomas Aquinas, translated by Anthony Pegis, copyright © 1955 by Doubleday & Company, Inc. Reprinted by permission of the publisher. [Pp. 63–66, 71–75.]

power. For, according to its manner of knowing in the present life, the intellect depends on the senses for the origin of knowledge; and so those things that do not fall under the senses cannot be grasped by the human intellect except in so far as the knowledge of them is gathered from sensible things. Now, sensible things cannot lead the human intellect to the point of seeing in them the nature of the divine substance; for sensible things are effects that fall short of the power of their cause. Yet, beginning with sensible things, our intellect is led to the point of knowing about God that He exists, and other such characteristics that must be attributed to the First Principle. There are, consequently, some intelligible truths about God that are open to the human reason; but there are others that absolutely surpass its power.

We may easily see the same point from the gradation of intellects. Consider the case of two persons of whom one has a more penetrating grasp of a thing by his intellect than does the other. He who has the superior intellect understands many things that the other cannot grasp at all. Such is the case with a very simple person who cannot at all grasp the subtle speculations of philosophy. But the intellect of an angel surpasses the human intellect much more than the intellect of the greatest philosopher surpasses the intellect of the most uncultivated simple person; for the distance between the best philosopher and a simple person is contained within the limits of the human species, which the angelic intellect surpasses. For the angel knows God on the basis of a more noble effect than does man; and this by as much as the substance of an angel, through which the angel in his natural knowledge is led to the knowledge of God, is nobler than sensible things and even than the soul itself, through which the human intellect mounts to the knowledge of God. The divine intellect surpasses the angelic intellect much more than the angelic surpasses the human. For the divine intellect is in its capacity equal to its substance, and therefore it understands fully what it is, including all its intelligible attributes. But by his natural knowledge the angel does not know what God is, since the substance itself of the angel, through which he is led to the knowledge of God, is an effect that is not equal to the power of its cause. Hence, the angel is not able, by means of his natural knowledge, to grasp all the things that God understands in Himself; nor is the human reason sufficient to grasp all the things that the angel understands through his own natural power. Just as, therefore, it would be the height of folly for a simple person to assert that what a philosopher proposes is false on the ground that he himself cannot understand it, so (and even more so) it is the acme of stupidity for a man to suspect as false what is divinely revealed through the ministry of the angels simply because it cannot be investigated by reason.

The same thing, moreover, appears quite clearly from the defect that we experience every day in our knowledge of things. We do not know a great many of the properties of sensible things, and in most cases we are not able to discover fully the natures of those properties that we apprehend by the senses. Much more is it the case, therefore, that the human reason is not equal to the task of investigating all the intelligible characteristics of that most excellent substance.

The remark of Aristotle likewise agrees with this conclusion. He says that "our intellect is related to the prime beings, which are most evident in their nature, as the eye of an owl is related to the sun."

Sacred Scripture also gives testimony to this truth. We read in Job: "Peradventure thou wilt comprehend the steps of God, and wilt find out the Almighty perfectly?" (11:7). And again: "Behold, God is great, exceeding our knowledge" (Job 36:26). And St. Paul: "We know in part" (I Cor. 13:9).

We should not, therefore, immediately reject as false, following the opinion of the Manicheans[3] and many unbelievers, everything that is said about God even though it cannot be investigated by reason.

• • •

THE TRUTHS THE HUMAN REASON IS NOT ABLE TO INVESTIGATE ARE FITTINGLY PROPOSED TO MEN FOR BELIEF

Now, perhaps some will think that men should not be asked to believe that the reason is not adequate to investigate, since the divine Wisdom provides in the case of each thing according to the mode of its nature. We must therefore prove that it is necessary for man to receive from God as objects of belief even those truths that are above the human reason.

No one tends with desire and zeal towards something that is not already known to him. But, as we shall examine later on in this work, men are ordained by the Divine Providence toward a higher good than human fragility can experience in the present life. That is why it was

---

[3]A sect that believed in two contending principles of good (light, soul) and evil (darkness, body).

necessary for the human mind to be called to something higher than the human reason here and now can reach, so that it would thus learn to desire something and with zeal tend towards something that surpasses the whole state of the present life. This belongs especially to the Christian religion, which in a unique way promises spiritual and eternal goods. And so there are many things proposed to men in it that transcend human sense. The Old Law, on the other hand, whose promises were of a temporal character, contained very few proposals that transcended the inquiry of the human reason. Following this same direction, the philosophers themselves, in order that they might lead men from the pleasure of sensible things to virtue, were concerned to show that there were in existence other goods of a higher nature than these things of sense, and that those who gave themselves to the active or contemplative virtues would find much sweeter enjoyment in the taste of these higher goods.

It is also necessary that such truth be proposed to men for belief so that they may have a truer knowledge of God. For then only do we know God truly when we believe Him to be above everything that it is possible for man to think about Him; for, as we have shown, the divine substance surpasses the natural knowledge of which man is capable. Hence, by the fact that some things about God are proposed to man that surpass his reason, there is strengthened in man the view that God is something above what he can think.

Another benefit that comes from the revelation to men of truths that exceed the reason is the curbing of presumption, which is the mother of error. For there are some who have such a presumptuous opinion of their own ability that they deem themselves able to measure the nature of everything; I mean to say that, in their estimation, everything is true that seems to them so, and everything is false that does not. So that the human mind, therefore, might be freed from this presumption and come to a humble inquiry after truth, it was necessary that some things should be proposed to man by God that would completely surpass his intellect.

A still further benefit may also be seen in what Aristotle says in the *Ethics*. There was a certain Simonides who exhorted people to put aside the knowledge of divine things and to apply their talents to human occupations. He said that "he who is a man should know human things, and he who is mortal, things that are mortal." Against Simonides Aristotle says that "man should draw himself towards what is immortal and divine as much as he can." And so he says in the *De animalibus* that, although what we know of the higher substances is very little, yet that little is loved and desired more than all the knowledge that we have about less noble substances. He also says in the *De caelo et mundo*[4] that when questions about the heavenly bodies can be given even a modest and merely plausible solution, he who hears this experiences intense joy. From all these considerations it is clear that even the most imperfect knowledge about the most noble realities brings the greatest perfection to the soul. Therefore, although the human reason cannot grasp fully the truths that are above it, yet, if it somehow holds these truths at least by faith, it acquires great perfection for itself.

Therefore it is written: "For many things are shown to thee above the understanding of men" (Ecclus. 3:25). Again: "So the things that are of God no man knoweth but the Spirit of God. But to us God hath revealed them by His Spirit" (I Cor. 2:11, 10).

TO GIVE ASSENT TO THE TRUTHS OF FAITH IS NOT FOOLISHNESS EVEN THOUGH THEY ARE ABOVE REASON

Those who place their faith in this truth, however, "for which the human reason offers no experimental evidence," do not believe foolishly, as though "following artificial fables" (II Peter 1:16). For these "secrets of divine Wisdom" (Job 11:6) the divine Wisdom itself, which knows all things to the full, has deigned to reveal to men. It reveals its own presence, as well as the truth of its teaching and inspiration, by fitting arguments; and in order to confirm those truths that exceed natural knowledge, it gives visible manifestation to works that surpass the ability of all nature. Thus, there are the wonderful cures of illnesses, there is the raising of the dead, and the wonderful immutation[5] in the heavenly bodies; and what is more wonderful, there is the inspiration given to human minds, so that simple and untutored persons, filled with the gift of the Holy Spirit, come to possess instantaneously the highest wisdom and the readiest eloquence. When these arguments were examined, through the efficacy of the abovementioned proof, and not the violent assault of arms or the promise of pleasures, and (what is most wonderful of all) in the midst of the tyranny of the persecutors, an innumerable throng of people, both simple and most learned, flocked

---

[4] Concerning heaven and earth.
[5] Change, transformation.

to the Christian faith. In this faith there are truths preached that surpass every human intellect; the pleasures of the flesh are curbed; it is taught that the things of the world should be spurned. Now, for the minds of mortal men to assent to these things is the greatest of miracles, just as it is a manifest work of divine inspiration that, spurning visible things, men should seek only what is invisible. Now, that this has happened neither without preparation nor by chance, but as a result of the disposition of God, is clear from the fact that through many pronouncements of the ancient prophets God had foretold that He would do this. The books of these prophets are held in veneration among us Christians, since they give witness to our faith.

The manner of this confirmation is touched on by St. Paul: "Which," that is, human salvation, "having begun to be declared by the Lord, was confirmed unto us by them that hear Him: God also bearing them witness of signs, and wonders, and divers miracles, and distributions of the Holy Ghost" (Heb. 2:3–4).

This wonderful conversion of the world to the Christian faith is the clearest witness of the signs given in the past; so that it is not necessary that they should be further repeated, since they appear most clearly in their effect. For it would be truly more wonderful than all signs if the world had been led by simple and humble men to believe such lofty truths, to accomplish such difficult actions, and to have such high hopes. Yet it is also a fact that, even in our own time, God does not cease to work miracles through His saints for the confirmation of the faith.

• • •

THE TRUTH OF REASON IS NOT OPPOSED TO THE TRUTH OF THE CHRISTIAN FAITH

Now, although the truth of the Christian faith which we have discussed surpasses the capacity of the reason, nevertheless that truth that the human reason is naturally endowed to know cannot be opposed to the truth of the Christian faith. For that with which the human reason is naturally endowed is clearly most true; so much so, that it is impossible for us to think of such truths as false. Nor is it permissible to believe as false that which we hold by faith, since this is confirmed in a way that is so clearly divine. Since, therefore, only the false is opposed to the truth, as is clearly evident from an examination of their definitions, it is impossible that the truth of faith should be opposed to those principles that the human reason knows naturally.

Furthermore, that which is introduced into the soul of the student by the teacher is contained in the knowledge of the teacher—unless his teaching is fictitious, which it is improper to say of God. Now, the knowledge of the principles that are known to us naturally has been implanted in us by God; for God is the Author of our nature. These principles, therefore, are also contained by the divine Wisdom. Hence, whatever is opposed to them is opposed to the divine Wisdom, and, therefore, cannot come from God. That which we hold by faith as divinely revealed, therefore, cannot be contrary to our natural knowledge.

Again. In the presence of contrary arguments our intellect is chained, so that it cannot proceed to the knowledge of the truth. If, therefore, contrary knowledges were implanted in us by God, our intellect would be hindered from knowing truth by this very fact. Now, such an effect cannot come from God.

And again. What is natural cannot change as long as nature does not. Now, it is impossible that contrary opinions should exist in the same knowing subject at the same time. No opinion or belief, therefore, is implanted in man by God which is contrary to man's natural knowledge.

Therefore, the Apostle[6] says: "The word is nigh thee, even in thy mouth and in thy heart. This is the word of faith, which we preach" (Rom. 10:8). But because it overcomes reason, there are some who think that it is opposed to it: which is impossible.

The authority of St. Augustine[7] also agrees with this. He writes as follows: "That which truth will reveal cannot in any way be opposed to the sacred books of the Old and the New Testament."

From this we evidently gather the following conclusion: whatever arguments are brought forward against the doctrines of faith are conclusions incorrectly derived from the first and self-evident principles imbedded in nature. Such conclusions do not have the force of demonstration; they are arguments that are either probable or sophistical. And so, there exists the possibility to answer them.

---

[6] St. Paul. Medieval writers often refer to him simply as the Apostle.
[7] A bishop, writer, and leading theologian of the early Church (354–430).

7

St. Thomas Aquinas

Summation of Knowledge

ST. *Thomas Aquinas intended his second great work,* Summation of Knowledge *(traditionally entitled, in Latin,* Summa Theologica*), to be the harmonization of all knowledge. The 631 questions dealt with and the 10,000 objections raised (which are answered by the use of Aristotelian logic and quotation from authority) range from the nature and attributes of God to the relationship between Christian morality and the everyday concerns of trade and commerce. "Of Cheating, Which Is Committed in Buying and Selling" and "Of the Sin of Usury" from the* Summation of Knowledge *reveal not only the method of Aquinas and the comprehensiveness of his philosophy, but how the Church attempted to deal during the Middle Ages with a question that was becoming difficult to cope with: How to reconcile the practices of budding capitalism with traditional economic theory and orthodox religious beliefs.*

OF CHEATING, WHICH IS COMMITTED IN BUYING AND SELLING

We must now consider those sins which relate to voluntary commutations.[1] First, we shall consider cheating, which is committed in buying and selling; secondly, we shall consider usury, which occurs in loans.

[1]Exchanges in trade, substitutions of one kind of payment for another.

SUMMATION OF KNOWLEDGE From St. Thomas Aquinas, *Summa Theologica*, trans. Fathers of the English Dominican Province (New York: Benziger, 1947), 1513–14, 1516–19. Reprinted by permission of the publisher.

*Whether It is Lawful to Sell a Thing
for More Than Its Worth?*

We proceed thus to the First Article:—

Objection 1. It would seem that it is lawful to sell a thing for more than its worth. In the commutations of human life, civil laws determine that which is just. Now according to these laws it is just for buyer and seller to deceive one another . . . and this occurs by the seller selling a thing for more than its worth, and the buyer buying a thing for less than its worth. Therefore it is lawful to sell a thing for more than its worth.

Obj. 2. Further, that which is common to all would seem to be natural and not sinful. Now Augustine relates that the saying of a certain jester was accepted by all, *You wish to buy for a song and to sell at a premium*, which agrees with the saying of Prov. xx. 14, *It is naught, it is naught, saith every buyer: and when he is gone away, then he will boast*. Therefore it is lawful to sell a thing for more than its worth.

Obj. 3. Further, it does not seem unlawful if that which honesty demands be done by mutual agreement. Now, according to the Philosopher . . . in the friendship which is based on utility, the amount of the recompense for a favor received should depend on the utility accruing to the receiver: and this utility sometimes is worth more than the thing given, for instance if the receiver be in great need of that thing, whether for the purpose of avoiding a danger, or of deriving some particular benefit. Therefore, in contracts of buying and selling, it is lawful to give a thing in return for more than its worth.

On the contrary, It is written (Matth. vii. 12): *All things . . . whatsoever you would that men should do to you, do you also to them*. But no man wishes to buy a thing for more than its worth. Therefore no man should sell a thing to another man for more than its worth.

I answer that, It is altogether sinful to have recourse to deceit in order to sell a thing for more than its just price, because this is to deceive one's neighbor so as to injure him. Hence Tully[2] says . . . *Contracts should be entirely free from double-dealing: the seller must not impose upon the bidder, nor the buyer upon one that bids against him*.

But apart from fraud, we may speak of buying and selling in two ways. First, as considered in themselves, and from this point of view, buying and selling seem to be established for the common advantage of both parties, one of whom requires that which belongs to the other, and vice versa, as the Philosopher states. . . . Now whatever is established

---

[2]Marcus Tullius Cicero (106–43 B.C.), Roman orator, statesman, and Stoic philosopher.

for the common advantage, should not be more of a burden to one party than to another, and consequently all contracts between them should observe equality of thing and thing. Again, the quality of a thing that comes into human use is measured by the price given for it, for which purpose money was invented. . . . Therefore if either the price exceed the quantity of the thing's worth, or, conversely, the thing exceed the price, there is no longer the equality of justice: and consequently, to sell a thing for more than its worth, or to buy it for less than its worth, is in itself unjust and unlawful.

Secondly we may speak of buying and selling, considered as accidentally tending to the advantage of one party, and to the disadvantage of the other: for instance, when a man has great need of a certain thing, while another man will suffer if he be without it. In such a case the just price will depend not only on the thing sold, but on the loss which the sale brings on the seller. And thus it will be lawful to sell a thing for more than it is worth in itself, though the price paid be not more than it is worth to the owner. Yet if the one man derive a great advantage by becoming possessed of the other man's property, and the seller be not at a loss through being without that thing, the latter ought not to raise the price, because the advantage accruing to the buyer, is not due to the seller, but to a circumstance affecting the buyer. Now no man should sell what is not his, though he may charge for the loss he suffers.

On the other hand if a man find that he derives great advantage from something he has bought, he may, of his own accord, pay the seller something over and above: and this pertains to his honesty.

Reply Obj. 1. As stated above . . . human law is given to the people among whom there are many lacking virtue, and it is not given to the virtuous alone. Hence human law was unable to forbid all that is contrary to virtue; and it suffices for it to prohibit whatever is destructive of human intercourse, while it treats other matters as though they were lawful, not by approving of them, but by not punishing them. Accordingly, if without employing deceit the seller disposes of his goods for more than their worth, or the buyer obtain them for less than their worth, the law looks upon this as licit, and provides no punishment for so doing, unless the excess be too great, because then even human law demands restitution to be made, for instance if a man be deceived in regard to more than half the amount of the just price of a thing.

On the other hand the Divine law leaves nothing unpunished that is contrary to virtue. Hence, according to the Divine law, it is reckoned unlawful if the equality of justice be not observed in buying and selling: and he who has received more than he ought must make compensation to him that has suffered loss, if the loss be considerable. I add this condition, because the just price of things is not fixed with mathematical precision, but depends on a kind of estimate, so that a slight addition or subtraction would not seem to destroy the equality of justice.

Reply Obj. 2. As Augustine says . . . *this jester, either by looking into himself or by his experience of others, thought that all men are inclined to wish to buy for a song and sell at a premium. But since in reality this is wicked, it is in every man's power to acquire that justice whereby he may resist and overcome this inclination.* And then he gives the example of a man who gave the just price for a book to a man who through ignorance asked a low price for it. Hence it is evident that this common desire is not from nature but from vice, wherefore it is common to many who walk along the broad road of sin.

Reply Obj. 3. In commutative justice we consider chiefly real equality. On the other hand, in friendship based on utility we consider equality of usefulness, so that the recompense should depend on the usefulness accruing, whereas in buying it should be equal to the thing bought.

. . .

OF THE SIN OF USURY

We must now consider the sin of usury, which is committed in loans. . . .

Whether It Is a Sin to Take Usury for Money Lent?

We proceed thus to the First Article:—

Objection 1. It would seem that it is not a sin to take usury[3] for money lent. For no man sins through following the example of Christ. But Our Lord said of Himself (Luke xix. 23): *At My coming I might have exacted it*, i.e. the money lent, *with usury*. Therefore it is not a sin to take usury for lending money.

Obj. 2. Further, according to Ps. xviii. 8, *The law of the Lord is unspotted*, because, to wit, it forbids sin. Now usury of a kind is allowed in the Divine law, according to Deut. xxiii. 19, 20. *Thou shalt not*

[3]Interest payment.

fenerate[4] *to thy brother money, nor corn, nor any other thing, but to the stranger:* nay more, it is even promised as a reward for the observance of the Law, according to Deut. xxviii. 12: *Thou shalt fenerate to many nations, and shalt not borrow of any one.* Therefore it is not a sin to take usury.

Obj. 3. Further, in human affairs justice is determined by civil laws. Now civil law allows usury to be taken. Therefore it seems to be lawful.

Obj. 4. Further, the counsels are not binding under sin. But, among other counsels we find (Luke vi. 35): *Lend, hoping for nothing thereby.* Therefore it is not a sin to take usury.

Obj. 5. Further, it does not seem to be in itself sinful to accept a price for doing what one is not bound to do. But one who has money is not bound in every case to lend it to his neighbor. Therefore it is lawful for him sometimes to accept a price for lending it.

Obj. 6. Further, silver made into coins does not differ specifically from silver made into a vessel. But it is lawful to accept a price for the loan of a silver vessel. Therefore it is also lawful to accept a price for the loan of a silver coin. Therefore usury is not in itself a sin.

Obj. 7. Further, anyone may lawfully accept a thing which its owner freely gives him. Now he who accepts the loan, freely gives the usury. Therefore he who lends may lawfully take the usury.

On the contrary, It is written (Exod. xxii. 25): *If thou lend money to any of thy people that is poor, that dwelleth with thee, thou shalt not be hard upon them as an extortioner, nor oppress them with usuries.*

I answer that, To take usury for money lent is unjust in itself, because this is to sell what does not exist, and this evidently leads to inequality which is contrary to justice.

In order to make this evident, we must observe that there are certain things the use of which consists in their consumption: thus we consume wine when we use it for drink, and we consume wheat when we use it for food. Wherefore in such like things the use of the thing must not be reckoned apart from the thing itself, and whoever is granted the use of the thing, is granted the thing itself; and for this reason, to lend things of this kind is to transfer the ownership. Accordingly if a man wanted to sell wine separately from the use of the wine, he would be selling the same thing twice, or he would be selling what does not exist, wherefore he would evidently commit a sin of injustice. In like manner he commits an injustice who lends wine or wheat, and asks for double pay-

[4]Lend money for interest.

ment, viz. one, the return of the thing in equal measure, the other, the price of the use, which is called usury.

On the other hand, there are things the use of which does not consist in their consumption. thus to use a house is to dwell in it, not to destroy it. Wherefore in such things both may be granted: for instance, one may hand over to another the ownership of his house while reserving to himself the use of it for a time, or vice versa, he may grant the use of the house, while retaining the ownership. For this reason a man may lawfully make a charge for the use of his house, and, besides this, revendicate[5] the house from the person to whom he has granted its use, as happens in renting and letting a house.

Now money, according to the Philosopher . . . was invented chiefly for the purpose of exchange: and consequently the proper and principal use of money is its consumption or alienation whereby it is sunk in exchange. Hence it is by its very nature unlawful to take payment for the use of money lent, which payment is known as usury: and just as a man is bound to restore other ill-gotten goods, so is he bound to restore the money which he has taken in usury.

Reply Obj. 1. In this passage usury must be taken figuratively for the increase of spiritual goods which God exacts from us, for He wishes us ever to advance in the goods which we receive from Him: and this is for our own profit not for His.

Reply Obj. 2. The Jews were forbidden to take usury from their brethren, i.e. from other Jews. By this we are given to understand that to take usury from any man is evil simply, because we ought to treat every man as our neighbor and brother, especially in the state of the Gospel, whereto all are called. Hence it is said without any distinction in Ps. xiv. 5: *He that hath not put out his money to usury*, and (Ezech. xviii. 8): *Who hath not taken usury*. They were permitted, however, to take usury from foreigners, not as though it were lawful, but in order to avoid a greater evil, lest, to wit, through avarice to which they are prone according to Is. lvi. 11, they should take usury from the Jews who were worshippers of God.

Where we find it promised to them as a reward, *Thou shalt fenerate to many nations*, etc., fenerating is to be taken in a broad sense for lending, as in Ecclus. xxix. 10, where we read: *Many have refused to fenerate, not out of wickedness*, i.e. they would not lend. Accordingly the Jews are promised in reward an abundance of wealth, so that they would be able to lend to others.

---

[5]Reclaim.

Reply Obj. 3. Human laws leave certain things unpunished, on account of the condition of those who are imperfect, and who would be deprived of many advantages, if all sins were strictly forbidden and punishments appointed for them. Wherefore human law has permitted usury, not that it looks upon usury as harmonizing with justice, but lest the advantage of many should be hindered. Hence it is that in civil law it is stated that *those things according to natural reason and civil law which are consumed by being used, do not admit of usufruct,* and that *the senate did not (nor could it) appoint a usufruct to such things, but established a quasi-usufruct,* namely by permitting usury. Moreover the Philosopher, led by natural reason, says . . . that *to make money by usury is exceedingly unnatural.*

Reply Obj. 4. A man is not always bound to lend, and for this reason it is placed among the counsels. Yet it is a matter of precept not to seek profit by lending: although it may be called a matter of counsel in comparison with the maxims of the Pharisees, who deemed some kinds of usury to be lawful, just as love of one's enemies is a matter of counsel. Or again, He speaks here not of the hope of usurious gain, but of the hope which is put in man. For we ought not to lend or do any good deed through hope in man, but only through hope in God.

Reply Obj. 5. He that is not bound to lend, may accept repayment for what he has done, but he must not exact more. Now he is repaid according to equality of justice if he is repaid as much as he lent. Wherefore if he exacts more for the usufruct of a thing which has no other use but the consumption of its substance, he exacts a price of something non-existent: and so his exaction is unjust.

Reply Obj. 6. The principal use of a silver vessel is not its consumption, and so one may lawfully sell its use while retaining one's ownership of it. On the other hand the principal use of silver money is sinking it in exchange, so that it is not lawful to sell its use and at the same time expect the restitution of the amount lent. It must be observed, however, that the secondary use of silver vessels may be an exchange, and such use may not be lawfully sold. In like manner there may be some secondary use of silver money; for instance, a man might lend coins for show, or to be used as security.

Reply Obj. 7. He who gives usury does not give it voluntarily simply, but under a certain necessity, in so far as he needs to borrow money which the owner is unwilling to lend with usury.

8

Papal Documents

THE controversy that lasted through much of the medieval period between the pope and such temporal (secular) rulers as the king of France and the Holy Roman emperor generated many treatises that in turn influenced medieval political thought and action. Indeed political doctrines and arguments in the Middle Ages always raised religious questions; for, according to medieval belief, whatever people did in their daily lives directly influenced their prospects for salvation. Therefore, whoever had the responsibility for governing the day-to-day activities of the people should also be involved in providing for their spiritual welfare. The basic issue in the controversy was this: should the ruler of the state share in the responsibility for his subjects' spiritual welfare, or should the Church have sole responsibility for the spiritual welfare of all Christians and thus be independent of and superior to secular authority?

The three documents that follow state the medieval case for the independence of the Church and for its superiority to secular authority. The first of these is Dictatus Papae, written about 1090. (Important papal documents are usually entitled with the first two words, in Latin, of their text.) Ascribed formerly to Pope Gregory VII, it is now thought to be a compilation of opinions gathered from several sources. But whether or not written by Gregory himself, it undoubtedly represents the principles that guided him in his long struggle with the Holy Roman emperor.

The second document is Clericis Laicos, a papal "bull" (decree), of Boniface VIII. Although written in 1296, two centuries later than the Dictatus Papae, it is based on the same doctrines as the earlier work. This bull is of additional interest because it addresses a very practical issue: the rejection of claims by the kings of France and England that they could tax the Church and clergy to support the state in times of crisis. Feeling that such claims threaten the

85

independence of the Church, Pope Boniface asserts the right of the pope to allow such taxation or to forbid it as he sees fit.

The third document, also by Pope Boniface VIII, is the bull Unam Sanctam. *Written in 1302 and directed against the king of France, it deals with the question of the authority of any king over the Church within his realm. Strongly opposed to such authority, it is considered the classic expression of papal claims to universal supremacy.*

These three documents embody the basic case made in medieval times for the authority of the Church. Dante has them in mind when he argues against the pope and in behalf of the authority of the Holy Roman emperor (see pp. 92–98).

DICTATUS PAPAE

1. That the Roman church was established by God alone.
2. That the Roman pontiff alone is rightly called universal.
3. That he alone has the power to depose and reinstate bishops.
4. That his legate,[1] even if he be of lower ecclesiastical rank, presides over bishops in council, and has the power to give sentence of deposition against them.
5. That the pope has the power to depose those who are absent [*i.e.,* without giving them a hearing].
6. That, among other things, we ought not to remain in the same house with those whom he has excommunicated.[2]
7. That he alone has the right, according to the necessity of the occasion, to make new laws, to create new bishoprics, to make a monastery of a chapter of canons, and *vice versa*, and either to divide a rich bishopric or to unite several poor ones.
8. That he alone may use the imperial insignia.
9. That all princes shall kiss the foot of the pope alone.
10. That his name alone is to be recited in the churches.
11. That the name applied to him belongs to him alone.
12. That he has the power to depose emperors.

---

[1] A papal ambassador.

[2] Cut off from the rites and fellowship of the Church.

PAPAL DOCUMENTS   Taken from *A Source Book for Medieval History,* Oliver J. Thatcher and Edgar Holmes McNeal (New York: Charles Scribner's Sons, 1905), pp. 136–38, 311–17.

13. That he has the right to transfer bishops from one see to another when it becomes necessary.
14. That he has the right to ordain as a cleric anyone from any part of the church whatsoever.
15. That anyone ordained by him may rule [as bishop] over another church, but cannot serve [as priest] in it, and that such a cleric may not receive a higher rank from any other bishop.
16. That no general synod[3] may be called without his order.
17. That no action of a synod and no book shall be regarded as canonical without his authority.
18. That his decree can be annulled by no one, and that he can annul the decrees of anyone.
19. That he can be judged by no one.
20. That no one shall dare to condemn a person who has appealed to the apostolic seat.[4]
21. That the important cases of any church whatsoever shall be referred to the Roman church [that is, to the pope].
22. That the Roman church has never erred and will never err to all eternity, according to the testimony of the holy scriptures.
23. That the Roman pontiff who has been canonically ordained is made holy by the merits of St. Peter, according to the testimony of St. Ennodius, bishop of Pavia, which is confirmed by many of the holy fathers, as is shown by the decrees of the blessed pope Symmachus.
24. That by his command or permission subjects may accuse their rulers.
25. That he can depose and reinstate bishops without the calling of a synod.
26. That no one can be regarded as catholic who does not agree with the Roman church.
27. That he has the power to absolve subjects from their oath of fidelity to wicked rulers.

CLERICIS LAICOS

It is said that in times past laymen practiced great violence against the clergy, and our experience clearly shows that they are doing so at present, since they are not content to keep within the limits prescribed

---

[3]An assembly of high officials of the Church.
[4]Rome.

for them, but strive to do that which is prohibited and illegal. And they pay no attention to the fact that they are forbidden to exercise authority over the clergy and ecclesiastical persons and their possessions. But they are laying heavy burdens on bishops, churches, and clergy, both regular[5] and secular,[6] by taxing them, levying contributions on them, and extorting the half, or the tenth, or the twentieth, or some other part of their income and possessions. They are striving in many ways to reduce the clergy to servitude and to subject them to their own sway. And we grieve to say it, but some bishops and clergy, fearing where they should not, and seeking a temporary peace, and fearing more to offend man than God, submit, improvidently rather than rashly, to these abuses [and pay the sums demanded], without receiving the papal permission. Wishing to prevent these evils, with the counsel of our brethren, and by our apostolic authority, we decree that if any bishops or clergy, regular or secular, of any grade, condition, or rank, shall pay, or promise, or consent to pay to laymen any contributions, or taxes, or the tenth, or the twentieth, or the hundredth, or any other part of their income or of their possessions, or of their value, real or estimated, under the name of aid, or loan, or subvention, or subsidy, or gift, or under any other name or pretext, without the permission of the pope, they shall, by the very act, incur the sentence of excommunication. And we also decree that emperors, kings, princes, dukes, counts, barons, *podestà*, *capitanei*, and governors of cities, fortresses, and of all other places everywhere, by whatever names such governors may be called, and all other persons of whatever power, condition, or rank, who shall impose, demand, or receive such taxes, or shall seize, or cause to be seized, the property of churches or of the clergy, which has been deposited in sacred buildings, or shall receive such property after it has been seized, or shall give aid, counsel, or support in such things either openly or secretly, shall by that very act incur the sentence of excommunication. We also put under the interdict[7] all communities which shall be culpable in such matters. And under the threat of deposition we strictly command all bishops and clergy, in accordance with their oath of obedience, not to submit to such taxes without the express permission of the pope. They shall not pay anything under the pretext that they had already promised or agreed to do so before the prohibition

[5]In religious orders: under a regula (rule).
[6]Serving in the world, like parish priests.
[7]Mass excommunication of all persons living in a specified area.

came to their knowledge. They shall not pay, nor shall the above-named laymen receive anything in any way. And if the ones shall pay, or the others receive anything, they shall by that very act fall under the sentence of excommunication. From this sentence of excommunication and interdict no one can be absolved except in the moment of death, without the authority and special permission of the pope. . . .

UNAM SANCTAM

The true faith compels us to believe that there is one holy catholic apostolic church, and this we firmly believe and plainly confess. And outside of her there is no salvation or remission of sins, as the Bridegroom says in the Song of Solomon: "My dove, my undefiled is but one; she is the only one of her mother, she is the choice one of her that bare her" [Song of Sol. 6:9]; which represents the one mystical body, whose head is Christ, but the head of Christ is God [1 Cor. 11.3]. In this church there is "one Lord, one faith, one baptism" [Eph. 4:5]. For in the time of the flood there was only one ark, that of Noah, prefiguring the one church, and it was "finished above in one cubit" [Gen. 6:16], and had but one helmsman and master, namely, Noah. And we read that all things on the earth outside of this ark were destroyed. This church we venerate as the only one, since the Lord said by the prophet: "Deliver my soul from the sword; my darling from the power of the dog" [Ps. 22:20]. He prayed for his soul, that is, for himself, the head; and at the same time for the body; and he named his body, that is, the one church, because there is but one Bridegroom [cf. John 3:29], and because of the unity of the faith, of the sacraments, and of his love for the church. This is the seamless robe of the Lord which was not rent but parted by lot [John 19:23]. Therefore there is one body of the one and only church, and one head, not two heads, as if the church were a monster. And this head is Christ and his vicar, Peter and his successors; for the Lord himself said to Peter: "Feed my sheep" [John 21:16]. And he said "my sheep," in general, not these or those sheep in particular; from which it is clear that all were committed to him. If therefore Greeks or anyone else say that they are not subject to Peter and his successors, they thereby necessarily confess that they are not of the sheep of Christ. For the Lord says in the Gospel of John, that there is one fold and only one shepherd [John 10:16]. By the words of the gospel we are taught that the two swords, namely, the spiritual authority and the temporal are in the power of the church. For when the apostles said "Here are two swords" [Luke 22:38]—that is, in the church, since it was the apostles who were speaking—the Lord did not answer, "It is too much," but "It is enough." Whoever denies that the temporal sword is in the power of Peter does not properly understand the word of the Lord when he said: "Put up thy sword into the sheath" [John 18:11]. Both swords, therefore, the spiritual and the temporal, are in the power of the church. The former is to be used by the church, the latter for the church; the one by the hand of the priest, the other by the hand of kings and knights, but at the command and permission of the priest. Moreover, it is necessary for one sword to be under the other, and the temporal authority to be subjected to the spiritual; for the apostle says, "For there is no power but of God: and the powers that are ordained of God" [Rom. 13:1]; but they would not be ordained [*i.e.,* arranged or set in order; note the play on the words] unless one were subjected to the other, and, as it were, the lower made the higher by the other. For, according to St. Dionysius, [8] it is a law of divinity that the lowest is made the highest through the intermediate. According to the law of the universe all things are not equally and directly reduced to order, but the lowest are fitted into their order through the intermediate, and the lower through the higher. And we must necessarily admit that the spiritual power surpasses any earthly power in dignity and honor, because spiritual things surpass temporal things. We clearly see that this is true from the paying of tithes, from the benediction, from the sanctification, from the receiving of the power, and from the governing of these things. For the truth itself declares that the spiritual power must establish the temporal power and pass judgment on it if it is not good. Thus the prophecy of Jeremiah concerning the church and the ecclesiastical power is fulfilled: "See, I have this day set thee over the nations and over the kingdoms, to root out, and to pull down, and to destroy, and to throw down, to build, and to plant" [Jer. 1:10]. Therefore if the temporal power errs, it will be judged by the spiritual power, and if the lower spiritual power errs, it will be judged by its superior. But if the highest spiritual power errs, it can not be judged by men, but by God alone. For the apostle says: "But he that is spiritual judgeth all things, yet he himself is judged of no man" [1 Cor. 2:15]. Now this authority, although it is given to man and exercised through man, is not human, but divine. For it was given by the word of the Lord to Peter, and the rock was made firm to him and his successors, in Christ

[8]Bishop of Rome, 259–68.

himself, whom he had confessed. For the Lord said to Peter: "Whatsoever thou shalt bind on earth shall be bound in heaven: and whatsoever thou shalt loose on earth shall be loosed in heaven" [Matt. 16:19]. Therefore whosoever resisteth this power thus ordained of God, resisteth the ordinance of God [Rom. 13.2], unless there are two principles (beginnings), as Manichæus pretends there are. But this we judge to be false and heretical. For Moses says that, not in the beginnings, but in the beginning [note the play on words], God created the heaven and the earth [Gen. 1:1]. We therefore declare, say, and affirm that submission on the part of every man to the bishop of Rome is altogether necessary for his salvation.

9
Dante Alighieri
On Monarchy

*D*ANTE *Alighieri (1265–1321),*
greatest of the Italian poets, was born in Florence to a family that, originally of
the feudal class, had belonged to the urban commercial class for several genera-
tions. As a youth he was caught up in intellectual interests and, under the
influence of the scholar Brunetto Latini, mastered the literature and philosophy
of the ancient world. A friend of the poets and artists of his time, Dante knew the
famous painter Giotto well and was a member of the culturally aggressive
society of Florence.

His life was repeatedly (and usually adversely) affected by the civil turmoil
of his native city, which reflected the larger struggle between the papacy and the
Holy Roman Empire. Holding public office for a while, Dante became involved
in this civic strife and later was banished on pain of being burned alive if he
returned to Florence. Dante wandered thereafter from city to city, taking service
with successive patrons until he retired to Ravenna, where he died.

The Latin treatise De Monarchia *(On Monarchy), written between*
1310 and 1316, contains Dante's mature political ideas and summarizes the
arguments for one side of the chief political controversy of the Middle Ages: Was
the pope or the emperor the supreme temporal ruler? Put another way, the
question was whether the state was to be independent or under the control of the
Church. The popes had claimed authority over secular rulers by virtue of their
appointment by God as His vicars on earth. The popes also claimed that, since
they were responsible for the fate of human souls in the hereafter, they ought to
have control over what people do in this world to enhance their chances of
salvation. Dante—employing the scholastic method, in which specific points
are deduced from generally accepted principles—rejects these arguments. In
the following selection he argues for the necessity of a temporal monarchy
and attempts to prove logically that the emperor receives his power directly
from God.

The question pending investigation . . . concerns two great luminaries, the Roman Pontiff[1] and the Roman Prince,[2] and the point at issue is whether the authority of the Roman Monarch . . . derives from God directly, or from some vicar or minister of God, by whom I mean the successor of Peter, veritable keeper of the keys of the kingdom of heaven.

• • •

Those men to whom the entire subsequent discussion is directed assert that the authority of the Empire depends on the authority of the Church, just as the inferior artisan depends on the architect. They are drawn to this by divers opposing arguments, some of which they take from Holy Scripture, and some from certain acts performed by the Chief Pontiff, and by the Emperor himself; and they endeavor to make their conviction reasonable.

From the same gospel they quote the saying of Christ to Peter, "Whatsoever thou shalt loose on earth shall be loosed in heaven," and understand this saying to refer alike to all the Apostles, according to the text of Matthew and John. They reason from this that the successor of Peter has been granted of God power to bind and loose all things, and then infer that he has power to loose the laws and decrees of the Empire, and to bind the laws and decrees of the temporal kingdom. Were this true, their inference would be correct.

But we must reply to it by making a distinction against the major premise of the syllogism which they employ. Their syllogism is this: Peter had power to bind and loose all things; the successor of Peter has like power with him; therefore the successor of Peter has power to loose and bind all things. From this they infer that he has power to loose and bind the laws and decrees of the Empire.

I concede the minor premise, but the major only with distinction. Wherefore I say that "all," the symbol of the universal, which is implied in "whatsoever" is never distributed beyond the scope of the distributed term. When I say, "All animals run," the distribution of "all" comprehends whatever comes under the genus "animal." But when I say, "All men run," the symbol of the universal only refers to whatever

[1]The pope. Dante also uses Chief Pontiff, Vicar of God, and Head Shepherd as titles for the pope.

[2]The Holy Roman emperor.

ON MONARCHY   *The De Monarchia of Dante Alighieri,* trans. Aurelia Henry (Boston: Houghton Mifflin, 1904), 137, 164, 166–68, 170–74, 196–206.

comes under the term "man." And when I say, "All grammarians run," the distribution is narrowed still further.

Therefore we must always determine what it is over which the symbol of the universal is distributed; then, from the recognized nature and scope of the distributed term, will be easily apparent the extent of the distribution. Now, were "whatsoever" to be understood absolutely when it is said, "Whatsoever thou shalt bind," he would certainly have the power they claim; nay, he would have even greater power, he would be able to loose a wife from her husband, and, while the man still lived, bind her to another—a thing he can in no wise do. He would be able to absolve me, while impenitent—a thing which God himself cannot do.

So it is evident that the distribution of the term under discussion is to be taken, not absolutely, but relatively to something else. A consideration of the concession to which the distribution is subjoined will make manifest this related something. Christ said to Peter, "I will give unto thee the keys of the kingdom of heaven"; that is, I will make thee doorkeeper of the kingdom of heaven. Then he adds, "and whatsoever," that is, "everything which," and He means thereby, "Everything which pertains to that office thou shalt have power to bind and loose." And thus the symbol of the universal which is implied in "whatsoever" is limited in its distribution to the prerogative of the keys of the kingdom of heaven. Understood thus, the proposition is true, but understood absolutely, it is obviously not. Therefore I conclude that although the successor of Peter has authority to bind and loose in accordance with the requirements of the prerogative granted to Peter, it does not follow, as they claim, that he has authority to bind and loose the decrees or statutes of Empire, unless they prove that this also belongs to the office of the keys. But we shall demonstrate further on that the contrary is true.

They quote also the words in Luke which Peter addressed to Christ, saying, "Behold, here are two swords," and they assert that the two ruling powers were predicted by those two swords, and because Peter declared they were "where he was," that is, "with him," they conclude that according to authority these two ruling powers abide with Peter's successor.

To refute this we must show the falsity of the interpretation on which the argument is based. Their assertion that the two swords which Peter designated signify the two ruling powers before spoken of, we deny outright, because such an answer would have been at variance with Christ's meaning, and because Peter replied in haste, as usual, with regard to the mere external significance of things.

A consideration of the words preceding it and of the cause of the words will show that such an answer would have been inconsistent with Christ's meaning. Let it be called to mind that this response was made on the day of the feast, which Luke mentions earlier, saying, "Then came the day of unleavened bread, when the passover must be killed."[3] At this feast Christ had already foretold His impending passion, in which He must be parted from His disciples. Let it be remembered also that when these words were uttered, all the twelve disciples were together; wherefore a little after the words just quoted Luke says, "And when the hour was come, He sat down, and the twelve Apostles with him." Continuing the discourse from this place he reaches the words, "When I sent you without purse, and scrip, and shoes, lacked ye anything?" And they answered, "Nothing." Then said He unto them, "But now, he that hath a purse, let him take it, and likewise his scrip: and he that hath no sword, let him sell his garment, and buy one." The meaning of Christ is clear enough here. He did not say, "Buy or procure two swords," but "twelve"; for it was in order that each of the twelve disciples might have one that He said to them, "He that hath no sword, let him buy one." And He spake thus to forewarn them of the persecution and contempt the future should bring, as though he would say, "While I was with you ye were welcomed, now shall ye be turned away. It behooves you, therefore, to prepare for yourselves those things which before I denied to you, but for which there is present need." If Peter's reply to these words had carried the meaning ascribed to it, the meaning would have been at variance with that of Christ, and Christ would have censured Him, as he did oftentimes, for his witless answers. However, He did not do so, but assented, saying to him, "It is enough," meaning, "I speak because of necessity; but if each cannot have a sword, two will suffice."

And that Peter usually spoke of the external significance of things is shown in his quick and unthinking presumption, impelled, I believe, not only by the sincerity of his faith, but by the purity and simplicity of his nature. To this characteristic presumption all those who write of Christ bear witness.

• • •

---

[3]A lamb was customarily sacrificed at the feast of Passover.

Although by the method of reduction to absurdity it has been shown ... that the authority of Empire has not its source in the Chief Pontiff, yet it has not been fully proved, save by an inference, that its immediate source is God, seeing that if the authority does not depend on the Vicar of God, we conclude that it depends on God Himself. For a perfect demonstration of the proposition we must prove directly that the Emperor, or Monarch, of the world has immediate relationship to the Prince of the universe, who is God.

In order to realize this, it must be understood that man alone of all beings holds the middle place between corruptibility and incorruptibility, and is therefore rightly compared by philosophers to the horizon which lies between the two hemispheres. Man may be considered with regard to either of his essential parts, body or soul. If considered in regard to the body alone, he is perishable; if in regard to the soul alone, he is imperishable. So the Philosopher spoke well of its incorruptibility when he said in the second book *On the Soul*, "And this only can be separated as a thing eternal from that which perishes."

If man holds a middle place between the perishable and imperishable, then, inasmuch as every mean shares the nature of the extremes, man must share both natures. And inasmuch as every nature is ordained for a certain ultimate end, it follows that there exists for man a twofold end, in order that as he alone of all beings partakes of the perishable and the imperishable, so he alone of all beings should be ordained for two ultimate ends. One end is for that in him which is perishable, the other for that which is imperishable.

Ineffable Providence has thus designed two ends to be contemplated of man: first, the happiness of this life, which consists in the activity of his natural powers, and is prefigured by the terrestrial Paradise; and then the blessedness of life everlasting, which consists in the enjoyment of the countenance of God, to which man's natural powers may not attain unless aided by divine light, and which may be symbolized by the celestial Paradise.

To these states of blessedness, just as to diverse conclusions, man must come by diverse means. To the former we come by the teachings of philosophy, obeying them by acting in conformity with the moral and intellectual virtues; to the latter through spiritual teachings which transcend human reason, and which we obey by acting in conformity with the theological virtues, Faith, Hope, and Charity. Now the former end and means are made known to us by human reason, which the philosophers have wholly explained to us; and the latter by the Holy

Spirit, which has revealed to us supernatural but essential truth through the Prophets and Sacred Writers, through Jesus Christ, the coeternal Son of God, and through His disciples. Nevertheless, human passion would cast all these behind, were not men, like horses astray in their brutishness, held to the road by bit and rein.

Wherefore a twofold directive agent was necessary to man, in accordance with the twofold end; the Supreme Pontiff to lead the human race to life eternal by means of revelation, and the Emperor to guide it to temporal felicity by means of philosophic instruction. And since none or few—and these with exceeding difficulty—could attain this port, were not the waves of seductive desire calmed, and mankind made free to rest in the tranquillity of peace, therefore this is the goal which he whom we call the guardian of the earth and Roman Prince should most urgently seek; then would it be possible for life on this mortal threshing-floor to pass in freedom and peace. The order of the world follows the order inherent in the revolution of the heavens. To attain this order it is necessary that instruction productive of liberality and peace should be applied by the guardian of the realm, in due place and time, as dispensed by Him who is the ever present Watcher of the whole order of the heavens. And He alone foreordained this order, that by it in His Providence He might link together all things, each in its own place.

If this is so, and there is none higher than He, only God elects and only God confirms. Whence we may further conclude that neither those who are now, nor those who in any way whatsoever have been, called Electors[4] have the right to be so called; rather should they be entitled heralds of divine providence. Whence it is that those in whom is vested the dignity of proclamation suffer dissension among themselves at times, when, all or part of them being shadowed by the clouds of passion, they discern not the face of God's dispensation.

It is established, then, that the authority of temporal Monarchy descends without mediation from the fountain of universal authority. And this fountain, one in its purity of source, flows into multifarious channels out of the abundance of its excellence.

Methinks I have now approached close enough to the goal I had set myself, for I have taken the kernels of truth from the husks of false-hood, in that question which asked whether the office of Monarchy was

---

[4] The Holy Roman emperor was selected by vote of the leading princes of the Empire, who were known as Electors.

essential to the welfare of the world, and in the next which made inquiry whether the Roman people rightfully appropriated the Empire, and in the last which sought whether the authority of the Monarch derived from God immediately, or from some other. But the truth of this final question must not be restricted to mean that the Roman Prince shall not be subject in some degree to the Roman Pontiff, for felicity that is mortal is ordered in a measure after felicity that is immortal. Wherefore let Caesar[5] honor Peter as a first-born son should honor his father, so that, refulgent with the light of paternal grace, he may illumine with greater radiance the earthly sphere over which he has been set by Him who alone is Ruler of all things spiritual and temporal.

[5]Caesar here means the Holy Roman emperor, and Peter refers to the pope.

10

Dante Alighieri

The Divine Comedy:
The Inferno

T HE Divine Comedy, *begun by Dante about 1300, is the poet's greatest work and has traditionally caused him to be ranked among the most celebrated poets of all time. Dante called his poem the* Commedia; *the epithet "Divina" was added some two centuries later. A comedy only in the medieval sense of having a fortunate ending, the poem describes the experiences of the human soul after death. Dante recounts his own imaginary pilgrimage—under the guidance of the Roman poet Vergil— through Hell and up the mount of Purgatory, until at last he arrives in Paradise, where he is welcomed by the soul of his idealized Beatrice.*

Thoroughly learned in the medieval scholasticism of St. Thomas Aquinas, skilled in Latin poetry (although he wrote his Comedy *in Italian), and familiar with the symbolism of medieval art and legend (the leopard, lion, and wolf of the first canto, for instance, probably represent lust, violence, and fraud), Dante combines these elements of his knowledge in the poem. The following selection is taken from* The Inferno, *the first part of the* Comedy, *as translated by John Ciardi, one of America's most distinguished modern poets. In it Dante narrates his encounters with great figures of the classic past who, according to medieval belief, could not receive salvation because they had lived before Christ's redemption of mankind. They are not punished but remain in "limbo." In the lower circles of Hell, he views the torments of sinners, among whom he sees the famous lovers Paolo and Francesca, and the unfortunate Ugolino of Pisa. In the final canto of* The Inferno, *Dante emerges at last from the pit of Hell on Easter morn and sees again the stars of Heaven. Freed from despair, he will go on toward the ascent to Paradise, which he narrates in* The Purgatorio *and* The Paradiso *(the concluding parts of* The Comedy*).*

CANTO I

Midway in our life's journey, I went astray
   from the straight road and woke to find myself
   alone in a dark wood. How shall I say

what wood that was! I never saw so drear,
   so rank, so arduous a wilderness!
   Its very memory gives a shape to fear.

Death could scarce be more bitter than that place!
   But since it came to good, I will recount
   all that I found revealed there by God's grace.

How I came to it I cannot rightly say,
   so drugged and loose with sleep had I become
   when I first wandered there from the True Way

But at the far end of that valley of evil
   whose maze had sapped my very heart with fear!
   I found myself before a little hill

and lifted up my eyes. Its shoulders glowed
   already with the sweet rays of that planet
   whose virtue leads men straight on every road,

and the shining strengthened me against the fright
   whose agony had wracked the lake of my heart
   through all the terrors of that piteous night.

Just as a swimmer, who with his last breath
   flounders ashore from perilous seas, might turn
   to memorize the wide water of his death—

so did I turn, my soul still fugitive
   from death's surviving image, to stare down
   that pass that none had ever left alive.

And there I lay to rest from my heart's race
   till calm and breath returned to me. Then rose
   and pushed up that dead slope at such a pace

THE DIVINE COMEDY: THE INFERNO   From *The Inferno* by Dante Alighieri, translated by John Ciardi. Copyright © 1954, 1982 by John Ciardi. Reprinted by arrangement with New American Library, New York, New York. [Pp. 28–32, 34–39, 42–46, 49–54, 58–62, 271, 275–77, 283–87.]

each footfall rose above the last. And lo!
    almost at the beginning of the rise
    I faced a spotted Leopard, all tremor and flow

and gaudy pelt. And it would not pass, but stood
    so blocking my every turn that time and again
    I was on the verge of turning back to the wood.

This fell at the first widening of the dawn
    as the sun was climbing Aries[1] with those stars
    that rode with him to light the new creation.

Thus the holy hour and the sweet season
    of commemoration did much to arm my fear
    of that bright murderous beast with their good omen.

Yet not so much but what I shook with dread
    at sight of a great Lion that broke upon me
    raging with hunger, its enormous head

held high as if to strike a mortal terror
    into the very air. And down his track,
    a She-Wolf drove upon me, a starved horror

ravening and wasted beyond all belief.
    She seemed a rack for avarice, gaunt and craving.
    Oh many the souls she has brought to endless grief!

She brought such heaviness upon my spirit
    at sight of her savagery and desperation,
    I died from every hope of that high summit.

And like a miser—eager in acquisition
    but desperate in self-reproach when Fortune's wheel
    turns to the hour of his loss—all tears and attrition

I wavered back; and still the beast pursued,
    forcing herself against me bit by bit
    till I slid back into the sunless wood.

[1]The Ram, a sign of the zodiac. The time indicated is the dawn of Good Friday in the year 1300.

And as I fell to my soul's ruin, a presence
gathered before me on the discolored air,
the figure of one who seemed hoarse from long silence.[2]

At sight of him in that friendless waste I cried:
"Have pity on me, whatever thing you are,
whether shade or living man." And it replied:

"Not man, though man I once was, and my blood
was Lombard, both my parents Mantuan.
I was born, though late, *sub Julio*,[3] and bred

in Rome under Augustus in the noon
of the false and lying gods. I was a poet
and sang of old Anchises' noble son[4]

who came to Rome after the burning of Troy.
But you—why do *you* return to these distresses
instead of climbing that shining Mount of Joy

which is the seat and first cause of man's bliss?"
"And are you then that Virgil and that fountain
of purest speech?" My voice grew tremulous:

"Glory and light of poets! now may that zeal
and love's apprenticeship that I poured out
on your heroic verses serve me well!

For you are my true master and first author,
the sole maker from whom I drew the breath
of that sweet style whose measures have brought me honor.

See there, immortal sage, the beast I flee.
For my soul's salvation, I beg you, guard me from her,
for she has struck a mortal tremor through me."

And he replied, seeing my soul in tears:
"He must go by another way who would escape
this wilderness, for that mad beast that fleers

---

[2]This figure is Vergil (70–19 B.C.), author of the *Aeneid*.
[3]In the time of Julius Caesar.
[4]Aeneas, whose adventures in coming to Italy are told in the *Aeneid*.

before you there, suffers no man to pass.
  She tracks down all, kills all, and knows no glut,
  but, feeding, she grows hungrier than she was.

She mates with any beast, and will mate with more
  before the Greyhound[5] comes to hunt her down.
  He will not feed on lands nor loot, but honor

and love and wisdom will make straight his way.
  He will rise between Feltro and Feltro,[6] and in him
  shall be the resurrection and new day

of that sad Italy for which Nisus died,
  and Turnus, and Euryalus, and the maid Camilla.[7]
  He shall hunt her through every nation of sick pride

till she is driven back forever to Hell
  whence Envy first released her on the world.
  Therefore, for your own good, I think it well

you follow me and I will be your guide
  and lead you forth through an eternal place.
  There you shall see the ancient spirits tried

in endless pain, and hear their lamentation
  as each bemoans the second death of souls.
  Next you shall see upon a burning mountain[8]

souls in fire and yet content in fire,
  knowing that whensoever it may be
  they yet will mount into the blessed choir.

To which, if it is still your wish to climb,
  a worthier spirit shall be sent to guide you.
  With her shall I leave you, for the King of Time,[9]

---

[5]Perhaps a reference to one of the Scala family, rulers of Verona.

[6]Verona is between the towns of Feltro and Montefeltro.

[7]Persons in Vergil's *Aeneid*. They died in the battles fought between the Trojan followers of Aeneas and the inhabitants of the district around Rome.

[8]Purgatory, where the sins of the penitent are burned away.

[9]God.

who reigns on high, forbids me to come there
    since, living, I rebelled against his law.[10]
    He rules the waters and the land and air

and there holds court, his city and his throne.
    Oh blessed are they he chooses!" And I to him:
    "Poet, by that God to you unknown,

lead me this way. Beyond this present ill
    and worse to dread, lead me to Peter's gate
    and be my guide through the sad halls of Hell."

And he then: "Follow." And he moved ahead
in silence, and I followed where he led.

CANTO II

The light was departing. The brown air drew down
    all the earth's creatures, calling them to rest
    from their day-roving, as I, one man alone,

prepared myself to face the double war
    of the journey and the pity, which memory
    shall here set down, nor hesitate, nor err.

O Muses![11] O High Genius! Be my aid!
    O Memory, recorder of the vision,
    here shall your true nobility be displayed!

Thus I began: "Poet, you who must guide me,
    before you trust me to that arduous passage,
    look to me and look through me—can I be worthy?

You sang how the father of Sylvius,[12] while still
    in corruptible flesh won to that other world,
    crossing with mortal sense the immortal sill.

But if the Adversary of all Evil
    weighing his consequence and who and what
    should issue from him, treated him so well—

[10]Because he lived before the time of Christ and had not accepted God's law, his soul could not enter Paradise.

[11]In Greek mythology, goddesses associated with literature, the arts, and sciences.

[12]Aeneas. His journey to the underworld is narrated in the *Aeneid*.

that cannot seem unfitting to thinking men,
  since he was chosen father of Mother Rome
  and of her Empire by God's will and token.

Both, to speak strictly, were founded and foreknown
  as the established Seat of Holiness
  for the successors of Great Peter's throne.

In that quest, which your verses celebrate,
  he learned those mysteries from which arose
  his victory and Rome's apostolate.

There later came the chosen vessel, Paul,
  bearing the confirmation of that Faith
  which is the one true door to life eternal.

But I—how should I dare? By whose permission?
  I am not Aeneas. *I* am not Paul.
  Who could believe me worthy of the vision?

How, then, may I presume to this high quest
  and not fear my own brashness? You are wise
  and will grasp what my poor words can but suggest."

As one who unwills what he wills, will stay
  strong purposes with feeble second thoughts
  until he spells all his first zeal away—

so I hung back and balked on that dim coast
  till thinking had worn out my enterprise,
  so stout at starting and so early lost.

"I understand from your words and the look in your eyes,"
  that shadow of magnificence answered me,
  "your soul is sunken in that cowardice

that bears down many men, turning their course
  and resolution by imagined perils,
  as his own shadow turns the frightened horse.

To free you of this dread I will tell you all
  of why I came to you and what I heard
  when first I pitied you. I was a soul

among the souls of Limbo,[13] when a Lady[14]
  so blessed and so beautiful, I prayed her
  to order and command my will, called to me.

Her eyes were kindled from the lamps of Heaven.
  Her voice reached through me, tender, sweet, and low.
  An angel's voice, a music of its own:

'O gracious Mantuan whose melodies
  live in earth's memory and shall live on
  till the last motion ceases in the skies,

my dearest friend, and fortune's foe, has strayed
  onto a friendless shore and stands beset
  by such distresses that he turns afraid

from the True Way, and news of him in Heaven
  rumors my dread he is already lost.
  I come, afraid that I am too-late risen.

Fly to him and with your high counsel, pity,
  and with whatever need be for his good
  and soul's salvation, help him, and solace me.

It is I, Beatrice, who send you to him.
  I come from the blessed height for which I yearn.
  Love called me here. When amid Seraphim[15]

I stand again before my Lord, your praises
  shall sound in Heaven.' She paused, and I began:
  'O Lady of that only grace that raises

feeble mankind within its mortal cycle
  above all other works God's will has placed
  within the heaven of the smallest circle;

so welcome is your command that to my sense,
  were it already fulfilled, it would yet seem tardy.
  I understand, and am all obedience.

---

[13]The region bordering hell where the souls of the righteous unbaptized, born befo
Christ, or beyond the boundaries of Christendom, must remain.

[14]Beatrice, the young woman whom Dante had loved in his youth. His idealized love f
her remained a life-long inspiration.

[15]The highest order of angelic beings.

But tell me how you dare to venture thus
   so far from the wide heaven of your joy
   to which your thoughts yearn back from this abyss.'

'Since what you ask,' she answered me, 'probes near
   the root of all, I will say briefly only
   how I have come through Hell's pit without fear.

Know then, O waiting and compassionate soul,
   that is to fear which has the power to harm,
   and nothing else is fearful even in Hell.

I am so made by God's all-seeing mercy
   your anguish does not touch me, and the flame
   of this great burning has no power upon me.

There is a Lady in Heaven[16] so concerned
   for him I send you to, that for her sake
   the strict decree is broken. She has turned

and called Lucia[17] to her wish and mercy
   saying: 'Thy faithful one is sorely pressed;
   in his distresses I commend him to thee.'

Lucia, that soul of light and foe of all
   cruelty, rose and came to me at once
   where I was sitting with the ancient Rachel,[18]

saying to me: 'Beatrice, true praise of God,
   why dost thou not help him who loved thee so
   that for thy sake he left the vulgar crowd?

Dost thou not hear his cries? Canst thou not see
   the death he wrestles with beside that river
   no ocean can surpass for rage and fury?

No soul of earth was ever as rapt to seek
   its good or flee its injury as I was—
   when I had heard my sweet Lucia speak—

[16]The Virgin Mary.
[17]The patron saint of sight, who here symbolizes Divine Light.
[19]In the Bible, wife of Jacob and mother of Joseph and Benjamin.

to descend from Heaven and my blessed seat
  to you, laying my trust in that high speech
  that honors you and all who honor it.'

She spoke and turned away to hide a tear
  that, shining, urged me faster. So I came
  and freed you from the beast that drove you there,

blocking the near way to the Heavenly Height.
  And now what ails you? Why do you lag? Why
  this heartsick hesitation and pale fright

when three such blessed Ladies lean from Heaven
  in their concern for you and my own pledge
  of the great good that waits you has been given?"

As flowerlets drooped and puckered in the night
  turn up to the returning sun and spread
  their petals wide on his new warmth and light—

just so my wilted spirits rose again
  and such a heat of zeal surged through my veins
  that I was born anew. Thus I began:

"Blesséd be that Lady of infinite pity,
  and blesséd be thy taxed and courteous spirit
  that came so promptly on the word she gave thee.

Thy words have moved my heart to its first purpose.
  My Guide! My Lord! My Master! Now lead on:
  one will shall serve the two of us in this."

He turned when I had spoken, and at his back
I entered on that hard and perilous track.

CANTO III

I AM THE WAY INTO THE CITY OF WOE.
I AM THE WAY TO A FORSAKEN PEOPLE.
I AM THE WAY INTO ETERNAL SORROW.

SACRED JUSTICE MOVED MY ARCHITECT.
I WAS RAISED HERE BY DIVINE OMNIPOTENCE,
PRIMORDIAL LOVE AND ULTIMATE INTELLECT.

ONLY THOSE ELEMENTS TIME CANNOT WEAR
WERE MADE BEFORE ME, AND BEYOND TIME I STAND.
ABANDON ALL HOPE YE WHO ENTER HERE.

These mysteries I read cut into stone
    above a gate. And turning I said: "Master,
    what is the meaning of this harsh inscription?"

And he then as initiate to novice:
    "Here must you put by all division of spirit
    and gather your soul against all cowardice.

This is the place I told you to expect.
    Here you shall pass among the fallen people,
    souls who have lost the good of intellect."

So saying, he put forth his hand to me,
    and with a gentle and encouraging smile
    he led me through the gate of mystery.

Here sighs and cries and wails coiled and recoiled
    on the starless air, spilling my soul to tears.
    A confusion of tongues and monstrous accents toiled

in pain and anger. Voices hoarse and shrill
    and sounds of blows, all intermingled, raised
    tumult and pandemonium that still

whirls on the air forever dirty with it
    as if a whirlwind sucked at sand. And I,
    holding my head in horror, cried: "Sweet Spirit,

what souls are these who run through this black haze?"
    And he to me: "These are the nearly soulless
    whose lives concluded neither blame nor praise.

They are mixed here with that despicable corps
    of angels who were neither for God nor Satan,
    but only for themselves. The High Creator

scourged them from Heaven for its perfect beauty,
    and Hell will not receive them since the wicked
    might feel some glory over them." And I:

"Master, what gnaws at them so hideously
    their lamentation stuns the very air?"
    "They have no hope of death," he answered me,

"and in their blind and unattaining state
    their miserable lives have sunk so low
    that they must envy every other fate.

No word of them survives their living season.
    Mercy and Justice deny them even a name.
    Let us not speak of them: look, and pass on."

I saw a banner there upon the mist.
    Circling and circling, it seemed to scorn all pause.
    So it ran on, and still behind it pressed

a never-ending rout of souls in pain.
    I had not thought death had undone so many
    as passed before me in that mournful train.

And some I knew among them; last of all
    I recognized the shadow of that soul
    who, in his cowardice, made the Great Denial.[19]

At once I understood for certain: these
    were of that retrograde and faithless crew
    hateful to God and to His enemies.

These wretches never born and never dead
    ran naked in a swarm of wasps and hornets
    that goaded them the more the more they fled.

and made their faces stream with bloody gouts
    of pus and tears that dribbled to their feet
    to be swallowed there by loathsome worms and maggots.

Then looking onward I made out a throng
    assembled on the beach of a wide river,
    whereupon I turned to him: "Master, I long

to know what souls these are, and what strange usage
    makes them as eager to cross as they seem to be
    in this infected light." At which the Sage:

---

[19]Pope Celestine V, who renounced the papacy in 1294. Dante evidently thought that Celestine put selfish regard for his own salvation above his duty to the Church.

"All this shall be made known to you when we stand
   on the joyless beach of Acheron."[20] And I
   cast down my eyes, sensing a reprimand

in what he said, and so walked at his side
   in silence and ashamed until we came
   through the dead cavern to that sunless tide.

There, steering toward us in an ancient ferry
   came an old man with a white bush of hair,
   bellowing: "Woe to you depraved souls! Bury

here and forever all hope of Paradise:
   I come to lead you to the other shore,
   into eternal dark, into fire and ice.

And you who are living yet, I say begone
   from these who are dead." But when he saw me stand
   against his violence he began again:

"By other windings and by other steerage
   shall you cross to that other shore. Not here! Not here!
   A lighter craft than mine must give you passage."

And my Guide to him: "Charon,[21] bite back your spleen:
   this has been willed where what is willed must be,
   and is not yours to ask what it may mean."

The steersman of that marsh of ruined souls,
   who wore a wheel of flame around each eye,
   stifled the rage that shook his woolly jowls.

But those unmannered and naked spirits there
   turned pale with fear and their teeth began to chatter
   at sound of his crude bellow. In despair

they blasphemed God, their parents, their time on earth,
   the race of Adam, and the day and the hour
   and the place and the seed and the womb that gave them birth.

---

[20]In Greek and Roman mythology, the river in the underworld across which souls of the
dead are ferried.

[21]The ferryman who takes souls of the dead across Acheron.

But all together they drew to that grim shore
   where all must come who lose the fear of God.
   Weeping and cursing they come for evermore,

and demon Charon with eyes like burning coals
   herds them in, and with a whistling oar
   flails on the stragglers to his wake of souls.

As leaves in autumn loosen and stream down
   until the branch stands bare above its tatters
   spread on the rustling ground, so one by one

the evil seed of Adam in its Fall
   cast themselves, at his signal, from the shore
   and streamed away like birds who hear their call.

So they are gone over that shadowy water,
   and always before they reach the other shore
   a new noise stirs on this, and new throngs gather.

"My son," the courteous Master said to me,
   "all who die in the shadow of God's wrath
   converge to this from every clime and country.

And all pass over eagerly, for here
   Divine Justice transforms and spurs them so
   their dread turns wish: they yearn for what they fear.

No soul in Grace comes ever to this crossing;
   therefore if Charon rages at your presence
   you will understand the reason for his cursing."

When he had spoken, all the twilight country
   shook so violently, the terror of it
   bathes me with sweat even in memory:

the tear-soaked ground gave out a sigh of wind
   that spewed itself in flame on a red sky,
   and all my shattered senses left me. Blind,

like one whom sleep comes over in a swoon,
I stumbled into darkness and went down.

CANTO IV

A monstrous clap of thunder broke apart
   the swoon that stuffed my head; like one awakened
   by violent hands, I leaped up with a start.

And having risen; rested and renewed,
   I studied out the landmarks of the gloom
   to find my bearings there as best I could.

And I found I stood on the very brink of the valley
   called the Dolorous Abyss, the desolate chasm
   where rolls the thunder of Hell's eternal cry,

so depthless-deep and nebulous and dim
   that stare as I might into its frightful pit
   it gave me back no feature and no bottom.

Death-pale, the Poet spoke: "Now let us go
   into the blind world waiting here below us.
   I will lead the way and you shall follow."

And I, sick with alarm at his new pallor,
   cried out, "How can I go this way when you
   who are my strength in doubt turn pale with terror?"

And he: "The pain of these below us here,
   drains the color from my face for pity,
   and leaves this pallor you mistake for fear.

Now let us go, for a long road awaits us."
   So he entered and so he led me in
   to the first circle and ledge of the abyss.

No tortured wailing rose to greet us here
   but sounds of sighing rose from every side,
   sending a tremor through the timeless air,

a grief breathed out of untormented sadness,
   the passive state of those who dwelled apart,
   men, women, children—a dim and endless congress.

And the Master said to me: "You do not question
   what souls these are that suffer here before you?
   I wish you to know before you travel on

that these were sinless. And still their merits fail,
    for they lacked Baptism's grace, which is the door
    of the true faith *you* were born to. Their birth fell

before the age of the Christian mysteries,
    and so they did not worship God's Trinity
    in fullest duty. I am one of these.

For such defects are we lost, though spared the fire
    and suffering Hell in one affliction only:
    that without hope we live on in desire."

I thought how many worthy souls there were
    suspended in that Limbo, and a weight
    closed on my heart for what the noblest suffer.

"Instruct me, Master, and most noble Sir,"
    I prayed him then, "better to understand
    the perfect creed that conquers every error:

has any, by his own or another's merit,
    gone ever from this place to blessedness?"
    He sensed my inner question and answered it:

"I was still new to this estate of tears
    when a Mighty One descended here among us,[22]
    crowned with the sign of victorious years.

He took from us the shade of our first parent,
    of Abel, his pure son, of ancient Noah,
    of Moses, the bringer of law, the obedient.

Father Abraham, David the King,
    Israel with his father and his children,
    Rachel, the holy vessel of His blessing,

and many more He chose for elevation
    among the elect. And before these, you must know,
    no human soul had ever won salvation."

---

[22]A reference to the medieval belief that Christ descended into the afterworld between
Good Friday and Easter and released the souls of worthy Old Testament personages and
led them to Heaven.

We had not paused as he spoke, but held our road
and passed meanwhile beyond a press of souls
crowded about like trees in a thick wood.

And we had not traveled far from where I woke
when I made out a radiance before us
that struck away a hemisphere of dark.

We were still some distance back in the long night,
yet near enough that I half-saw, half-sensed,
what quality of souls lived in that light.

"O ornament of wisdom and of art,
what souls are these whose merit lights their way
even in Hell. What joy sets them apart?"

And he to me: "The signature of honor
they left on earth is recognized in Heaven
and wins them ease in Hell out of God's favor."

And as he spoke a voice rang on the air:
"Honor the Prince of Poets; the soul and glory
that went from us returns. He is here! He is here!"

The cry ceased and the echo passed from hearing;
I saw four mighty presences come toward us
with neither joy nor sorrow in their bearing.

"Note well," my Master said as they came on,
"that soul that leads the rest with sword in hand
as if he were their captain and champion.

It is Homer, singing master of the earth.
Next after him is Horace, the satirist,
Ovid is third, and Lucan is the fourth.[23]

Since all of these have part in the high name
the voice proclaimed, calling me Prince of Poets,
the honor that they do me honors them."

[23]Four leading poets of the Greco-Roman world.

So I saw gathered at the edge of light
    the masters of that highest school whose song
    outsoars all others like an eagle's flight.

And after they had talked together a while,
    they turned and welcomed me most graciously,
    at which I saw my approving Master smile.

And they honored me far beyond courtesy,
    for they included me in their own number,
    making me sixth in that high company.

So we moved toward the light, and as we passed
    we spoke of things as well omitted here
    as it was sweet to touch on there. At last

we reached the base of a great Citadel
    circled by seven towering battlements
    and by a sweet brook flowing round them all.

This we passed over as if it were firm ground.
    Through seven gates I entered with those sages
    and came to a green meadow blooming round.[24]

There with a solemn and majestic poise
    stood many people gathered in the light,
    speaking infrequently and with muted voice.

Past that enameled green we six withdrew
    into a luminous and open height
    from which each soul among them stood in view.

And there directly before me on the green
    the master souls of time were shown to me.
    I glory in the glory I have seen!

Electra stood in a great company
    among whom I saw Hector and Aeneas
    and Caesar in armor with his falcon's eye.

I saw Camilla, and the Queen Amazon
    across the field. I saw the Latian King
    seated there with his daughter by his throne.

---

[24]A description of Elysium, where, according to Greek mythology, the souls of the virtuous dwelt.

And the good Brutus who overthrew the Tarquin:
    Lucrezia, Julia, Marcia, and Cornelia;[25]
    and, by himself apart, the Saladin.[26]

And raising my eyes a little I saw on high
    Aristotle, the master of those who know,
    ringed by the great souls of philosophy.

All wait upon him for their honor and his.
    I saw Socrates and Plato at his side
    before all others there. Democritus

who ascribes the world to chance, Diogenes,
    and with him there Thales, Anaxagoras,
    Zeno, Heraclitus, Empedocles.[27]

And I saw the wise collector and analyst—
    Dioscorides[28] I mean. I saw Orpheus[29] there,
    Tully, Linus, Seneca the moralist,[30]

Euclid the geometer, and Ptolemy,[31]
    Hippocrates, Galen, Avicenna,
    and Averrhoës of the Great Commentary.[32]

I cannot count so much nobility;
    my longer theme pursues me so that often
    the word falls short of the reality.

The company of six is reduced by four.
    My Master leads me by another road
    out of that serenity to the roar

and trembling air of Hell. I pass from light
    into the kingdom of eternal night.

[25]Electra . . . Cornelia: figures in history and legend.

[26]A twelfth-century sultan of Egypt.

[27]Democritus . . . Empedocles: Greek philosophers.

[28]A first-century Greek physician and writer on medicine.

[29]In Greek mythology, a musician whose playing enchanted all nature.

[30]Tully (Cicero), Linus (Livy), Seneca: Roman writers and philosophers.

[31]A second-century Egyptian astronomer; devised the earth-centered astronomical system that was widely accepted in the Middle Ages.

[32]Hippocrates and Galen were ancient writers on medicine. Avicenna and Averrhoës were Muslim philosophers, physicians, and commentators of the eleventh and twelfth centuries.

from CANTO V

I came to a place stripped bare of every light
  and roaring on the naked dark like seas
  wracked by a war of winds. Their hellish flight

of storm and counterstorm through time foregone,
  sweeps the souls of the damned before its charge.
  Whirling and battering it drives them on,

and when they pass the ruined gap of Hell
  through which we had come, their shrieks begin anew.
  There they blaspheme the power of God eternal.

And this, I learned, was the never ending flight
  of those who sinned in the flesh, the carnal and lusty
  who betrayed reason to their appetite.

• • •

At last I spoke: "Poet, I should be glad
  to speak a word with those two swept together[33]
  so lightly on the wind and still so sad."

And he to me: "Watch them. When next they pass,
  call to them in the name of love that drives
  and damns them here. In that name they will pause."

Thus, as soon as the wind in its wild course
  brought them around, I called: "O wearied souls!
  if none forbid it, pause and speak to us."

As mating doves that love calls to their nest
  glide through the air with motionless raised wings,
  borne by the sweet desire that fills each breast—

Just so those spirits turned on the torn sky
  from the band where Dido[34] whirls across the air;
  such was the power of pity in my cry.

---

[33]Paolo and Francesca da Rimini, who lived in the thirteenth century. The story of their
tragic love was well known in Dante's time.
[34]The queen of Carthage who killed herself when Aeneas abandoned her.

"O living creature, gracious, kind, and good,
  going this pilgrimage through the sick night,
  visiting us who stained the earth with blood,

were the King of Time our friend, we would pray His peace
  on you who have pitied us. As long as the wind
  will let us pause, ask of us what you please.

The town where I was born lies by the shore
  where the Po descends into its ocean rest
  with its attendant streams in one long murmur.

Love, which in gentlest hearts will soonest bloom
  seized my lover with passion for that sweet body
  from which I was torn unshriven to my doom.

Love, which permits no loved one not to love,
  took me so strongly with delight in him
  that we are one in Hell, as we were above.

Love led us to one death. In the depths of Hell
  Caïna[35] waits for him who took our lives."
  This was the piteous tale they stopped to tell.

And when I had heard those world-offended lovers
  I bowed my head. At last the Poet spoke:
  "What painful thoughts are these your lowered brow covers?"

When at length I answered, I began: "Alas!
  What sweetest thoughts, what green and young desire
  led these two lovers to this sorry pass."

Then turning to those spirits once again,
  I said: "Francesca, what you suffer here
  melts me to tears of pity and of pain.

But tell me: in the time of your sweet sighs
  by what appearances found love the way
  to lure you to his perilous paradise?"

---

[35] A variant of the name Cain. In this region are confined those who, like Cain in the Bible, killed blood relatives. Francesca was married to Gianciotto Malatesta but fell in love with his brother Paolo. The lovers were slain by Gianciotto, whose soul was condemned to a lower circle than were the lovers' souls.

And she: "The double grief of a lost bliss
   is to recall its happy hour in pain.
   Your Guide and Teacher knows the truth of this.

But if there is indeed a soul in Hell
   to ask of the beginning of our love
   out of his pity, I will weep and tell:

On a day for dalliance we read the rhyme
   of Lancelot, how love had mastered him.[36]
   We were alone with innocence and dim time.

Pause after pause that high old story drew
   our eyes together while we blushed and paled;
   but it was one soft passage overthrew

our caution and our hearts. For when we read
   how her fond smile was kissed by such a lover,
   he who is one with me alive and dead

breathed on my lips the tremor of his kiss.
   That book, and he who wrote it, was a pander.
   That day we read no further." As she said this,

the other spirit, who stood by her, wept
   so piteously, I felt my senses reel
   and faint away with anguish. I was swept

by such a swoon as death is, and I fell,
   as a corpse might fall, to the dead floor of Hell.

from CANTOS XXXII *and* XXXIII

. . . I saw two souls together
   in a single hole, and so pinched in by the ice
   that one head made a helmet for the other.

As a famished man chews crusts—so the one sinner
   sank his teeth into the other's nape
   at the base of the skull, gnawing his loathsome dinner.

---

[36]The story was that of Lancelot's love for Queen Guinevere.

Tydeus in his final raging hour
  gnawed Menalippus' head with no more fury
  than this one gnawed at skull and dripping gore.[37]

"You there," I said, "who show so odiously
  your hatred for that other, tell me why
  on this condition: that if in what you tell me

you seem to have a reasonable complaint
  against him you devour with such foul relish,
  I, knowing who you are, and his soul's taint,

may speak your cause to living memory,
God willing the power of speech be left to me."

The sinner raised his mouth from his grim repast
  and wiped it on the hair of the bloody head
  whose nape he had all but eaten away. At last

he began to speak: "You ask me to renew
  a grief so desperate that the very thought
  of speaking of it tears my heart in two.

I was Count Ugolino, I must explain;
  this reverend grace is the Archbishop Ruggieri:[38]
  now I will tell you why I gnaw his brain.

That I, who trusted him, had to undergo
  imprisonment and death through his treachery,
  you will know already. What you cannot know—

that is, the lingering inhumanity
  of the death I suffered—you shall hear in full:
  then judge for yourself if he has injured me.

• • •

[37]A Greek legend relates that both Tydeus and Menalippus were mortally wounded fighting each other. In his dying rage, Tydeus gnawed his enemy's head.

[38]Ruggieri betrayed Ugolini after they had conspired to gain control of a faction in the civil strife in Pisa in 1288. Ugolini was imprisoned with his sons and left to die of starvation.

You are cruelty itself if you can keep
   your tears back at the thought of what foreboding
   stirred in my heart; and if you do not weep,

at what are you used to weeping?—The hour when food
   used to be brought, drew near. They were now awake,
   and each was anxious from his dream's dark mood.

And from the base of that horrible tower I heard
   the sound of hammers nailing up the gates:
   I stared at my sons' faces without a word.

I did not weep: I had turned stone inside.
   They wept. 'What ails you, Father, you look so strange,'
   my little Anselm, youngest of them, cried.

But I did not speak a word nor shed a tear:
   not all that day nor all that endless night,
   until I saw another sun appear.

When a tiny ray leaked into that dark prison
   and I saw staring back from their four faces
   the terror and the wasting of my own,

I bit my hands in helpless grief. And they,
   thinking I chewed myself for hunger, rose
   suddenly together. I heard them say:

'Father, it would give us much less pain
   if you ate us: It was you who put upon us
   this sorry flesh; now strip it off again.'

I calmed myself to spare them. Ah! hard earth,
   why did you not yawn open? All that day
   and the next we sat in silence. On the fourth,

Gaddo, the eldest, fell before me and cried,
   stretched at my feet upon that prison floor:
   'Father, why don't you help me?' There he died.

And just as you see me, I saw them fall
   one by one on the fifth day and the sixth.
   Then, already blind, I began to crawl

from body to body shaking them frantically.
    Two days I called their names, and they were dead.
    Then fasting overcame my grief and me."

His eyes narrowed to slits when he was done,
    and he seized the skull again between his teeth
    grinding it as a mastiff grinds a bone.

• • •

CANTO XXXIV

"On march the banners of the King of Hell,"
    my Master said. "Toward us. Look straight ahead:
    can you make him out at the core of the frozen shell?"

Like a whirling windmill seen afar at twilight,
    or when a mist has risen from the ground—
    just such an engine rose upon my sight

stirring up such a wild and bitter wind
    I cowered for shelter at my Master's back,
    there being no other windbreak I could find.

I stood now where the souls of the last class
    (with fear my verses tell it) were covered wholly;
    they shone below the ice like straws in glass.

Some lie stretched out; others are fixed in place
    upright, some on their heads, some on their soles;
    another, like a bow, bends foot to face.

When we had gone so far across the ice
    that it pleased my Guide to show me the foul creature
    which once had worn the grace of Paradise,

he made me stop, and, stepping aside, he said:
    "Now see the face of Dis![39] This is the place
    where you must arm your soul against all dread."

Do not ask, Reader, how my blood ran cold
    and my voice choked up with fear. I cannot write it:
    this is a terror that cannot be told.

---

[39]Another name for Satan.

I did not die, and yet I lost life's breath:
   imagine for yourself what I became,
   deprived at once of both my life and death.

The Emperor of the Universe of Pain
   jutted his upper chest above the ice;
   and I am closer in size to the great mountain

 the Titans[40] make around the central pit,
   than they to his arms. Now, starting from this part,
   imagine the whole that corresponds to it!

If he was once as beautiful as now
   he is hideous, and still turned on his Maker,
   well may he be the source of every woe!

With what a sense of awe I saw his head
   towering above me! for it had three faces:
   one was in front, and it was fiery red;

the other two, as weirdly wonderful,
   merged with it from the middle of each shoulder
   to the point where all converged at the top of the skull;

the right was something between white and bile;
   the left was about the color that one finds
   on those who live along the banks of the Nile.

Under each head two wings rose terribly,
   their span proportioned to so gross a bird:
   I never saw such sails upon the sea.

They were not feathers—their texture and their form
   were like a bat's wings—and he beat them so
   that three winds blew from him in one great storm:

it is these winds that freeze all Cocytus.[41]
   He wept from his six eyes, and down three chins
   the tears ran mixed with bloody froth and pus.

---

[40]In Greek mythology, gigantic gods whom Zeus overcame and cast down into tl underworld.

[41]A lake of ice in the lowest section of Hell.

In every mouth he worked a broken sinner
　　between his rake-like teeth. Thus he kept three
　　in eternal pain at his eternal dinner.

For the one in front the biting seemed to play
　　no part at all compared to the ripping: at times
　　the whole skin of his back was flayed away.

"That soul that suffers most," explained my Guide,
　　"is Judas Iscariot, he who kicks his legs
　　on the fiery chin and has his head inside.

Of the other two, who have their heads thrust forward,
　　the one who dangles down from the black face
　　is Brutus: note how he writhes without a word.

And there, with the huge and sinewy arms, is the soul
　　of Cassius.[42]—But the night is coming on
　　and we must go, for we have seen the whole."

Then, as he bade, I clasped his neck, and he,
　　watching for a moment when the wings
　　were opened wide, reached over dexterously

and seized the shaggy coat of the king demon;
　　then grappling matted hair and frozen crusts
　　from one tuft to another, clambered down.

When we had reached the joint where the great thigh
　　merges into the swelling of the haunch,
　　my Guide and Master, straining terribly,

turned his head to where his feet had been
　　and began to grip the hair as if he were climbing;
　　so that I thought we moved toward Hell again.

"Hold fast!" my Guide said, and his breath came shrill
　　with labor and exhaustion. "There is no way
　　but by such stairs to rise above such evil."

---

[42]In medieval legend, Judas, who betrayed Christ, and Brutus and Cassius, who slew
　Julius Caesar, were the leading examples of treachery.

At last he climbed out through an opening
  in the central rock, and seated me on the rim;
  then joined me with a nimble backward spring.

I looked up, thinking to see Lucifer
  as I had left him, and I saw instead
  his legs projecting high into the air.

Now let all those whose dull minds are still vexed
  by failure to understand what point it was
  I had passed through, judge if I was perplexed.

"Get up. Up on your feet," my Master said.
  "The sun already mounts to middle tierce,[43]
  and a long road and hard climbing lie ahead."

It was no hall of state we had found there,
  but a natural animal pit hollowed from rock
  with a broken floor and a close and sunless air.

"Before I tear myself from the Abyss,"
  I said when I had risen, "O my Master,
  explain to me my error in all this:

where is the ice? and Lucifer—how has he
  been turned from top to bottom: and how can the sun
  have gone from night to day so suddenly?"

And he to me: "You imagine you are still
  on the other side of the center where I grasped
  the shaggy flank of the Great Worm of Evil

which bores through the world—you *were* while I climbed down,
  but when I turned myself about, you passed
  the point to which all gravities are drawn.

You are under the other hemisphere where you stand;
  the sky above us is the half opposed
  to what which canopies the great dry land.

Under the mid-point of that other sky
  the Man who was born sinless and who lived
  beyond all blemish, came to suffer and die.

[43]According to medieval reckoning, tierce was the third part of the day. Middle tierce
  would be about 7:30 A.M.

You have your feet upon a little sphere
    which forms the other face of the Judecca.[44]
    There it is evening when it is morning here.

And this gross Fiend and Image of all Evil
    who made a stairway for us with his hide
    is pinched and prisoned in the ice-pack still.

On this side he plunged down from heaven's height,
    and the land that spread here once hid in the sea
    and fled North to our hemisphere for fright;

and it may be that moved by the same fear,
    the one peak that still rises on this side
    fled upward leaving this great cavern here."

Down there, beginning at the further bound
    of Beelzebub's[45] dim tomb, there is a space
    not known by sight, but only by the sound

of a little stream descending through the hollow
    it has eroded from the massive stone
    in its endlessly entwining lazy flow.

My Guide and I crossed over and began
    to mount that little known and lightless road
    to ascend into the shining world again.

He first, I second, without thought of rest
    we climbed the dark until we reached the point
    where a round opening brought in sight the blest

and beauteous shining of the Heavenly cars.
And we walked out once more beneath the Stars.

[44]The section of the floor of Hell immediately surrounding the pit in which Satan is embedded. The name is derived from Judas.

[45]Another name for Satan.

11

St. Catherine of Siena

The Dialogue

ST. *Catherine of Siena (1347–1380)*
*lived in a time of extraordinary troubles and turmoil. The black plague
devastated Italy, civil wars among the city states raged unceasingly, and the
Church was on the brink of disintegration.*

*In her native city of Siena she was known for her piety and for her zealous
care for the victims of the plague. Although she became a member of the
Dominican religious order, she continued to live and work outside of the
convent. Her influence spread beyond Siena. She took an active part in Church
affairs and in politics not only through personal encounters but also through
numerous letters addressed to popes, kings, governors, and military leaders,
upbraiding them for their failures and offering advice and counsel.*

*She became involved with Church policy at the highest level. She re-
proached Pope Gregory XI so strenuously for not ending the so-called "exile" of
the papacy (when for almost seventy years the popes resided in Avignon in
France) that he at last gave in to her scolding and moved to Rome in 1377. With
equally vigorous indignation she wrote to kings and military leaders, pointing
out that it was their responsibility to stop warfare among Christians and to unite
in resuming the crusades against the Muslims.*

*St. Catherine's role in politics and in the Church was an important one. But
perhaps of even more importance and enduring influence was her role as a
leading figure in the history of religious mysticism. Her Dialogue, from which
the following selection is taken, describes her mystical experience as if she (or her
soul, as she prefers to say) were actually conversing with God. She writes of her
experience as a withdrawal into the "inner cell" of her being where she
communes with God in an intensely personal relationship that transcends the
rituals of formal religious practice.*

The Dialogue *gives an insight into the inner life of the religious mystic and an understanding of the strength of the motivations of those who, like St. Catherine, lead lives of unceasing and inflexible dedication to their religious beliefs. Canonized by the Church in 1461 and declared a patron saint of Italy in 1939 by Pope Pius XII, her memory and influence continue to the present day.*

As the soul[1] comes to know herself she also knows God better, for she sees how good he has been to her. In the gentle mirror of God she sees her own dignity: that through no merit of hers but by his creation she is the image of God. And in the mirror of God's goodness she sees as well her own unworthiness, the work of her own sin. For just as you can better see the blemish on your face when you look at yourself in a mirror, so the soul who in true self-knowledge rises up with desire to look at herself in the gentle mirror of God with the eye of understanding sees all the more clearly her own defects because of the purity she sees in him.

Now as light and knowledge grew more intense in this soul, a sweet bitterness was both heightened and mellowed. The hope that first Truth had given her mellowed it. But as a flame burns higher the more fuel is fed it, the fire in this soul grew so great that her body could not have contained it. She could not, in fact, have survived had she not been encircled by the strength of him who is strength itself.

Thus cleansed by the fire of divine charity, which she had found in coming to know herself and God, and more hungry than ever in her hope for the salvation of the whole world and the reform of holy Church, she stood up with confidence in the presence of the supreme Father. She showed him the leprosy of holy Church and the wretchedness of the world, speaking to him as with the words of Moses:

"My Lord, turn the eye of your mercy on your people and on your mystic body, holy Church. How much greater would be your glory if

---

[1]St. Catherine uses "her soul," "she," "that soul," as well as "I" to refer to herself.

THE DIALOGUE   Reprinted from *Catherine of Siena: The Dialogue*, Suzanne Noffke, O.P., trans. From *The Classics of Western Spirituality*. Copyright © 1980 by the Missionary Society of St. Paul the Apostle in the State of New York. Used by permission of Paulist Press. [Pp. 48–50, 53–57, 60–63.]

you would pardon so many and give them the light of knowledge! For then they would surely all praise you, when they see that your infinite goodness has saved them from deadly sin and eternal damnation. How much greater this than to have praise only from my wretched self, who have sinned so much and am the cause and instrument of every evil! So I beg you, divine eternal Love, to take your revenge on me, and be merciful to your people. I will not leave your presence till I see that you have been merciful to them.

"For what would it mean to me to have eternal life if death were the lot of your people, or if my faults especially and those of your other creatures should bring darkness upon your bride, who is light itself? It is my will, then, and I beg it as a favor, that you have mercy on your people with the same eternal love that led you to create us in your image and likeness. You said, 'Let us make humankind in our image and likeness.' And this you did, eternal Trinity, willing that we should share all that you are, high eternal Trinity! You, eternal Father, gave us memory to hold your gifts and share your power. You gave us understanding so that, seeing your goodness, we might share the wisdom of your only-begotten Son. And you gave us free will to love what our understanding sees and knows of your truth, and so share the mercy of your Holy Spirit.

"Why did you so dignify us? With unimaginable love you looked upon your creatures within your very self, and you fell in love with us. So it was love that made you create us and give us being just so that we might taste your supreme eternal good.

"Then I see how by our sin we lost the dignity you had given us. Rebels that we were, we declared war on your mercy and became your enemies. But stirred by the same fire that made you create us, you decided to give this warring human race a way to reconciliation, bringing great peace out of our war. So you gave us your only-begotten Son, your Word, to be mediator between us and you. He became our justice taking on himself the punishment for our injustices. He offered you the obedience you required of him in clothing him with our humanity, eternal Father, taking on our likeness and our human nature!

"O depth of love! What heart could keep from breaking at the sight of your greatness descending to the lowliness of our humanity? We are your image, and now by making yourself one with us you have become our image, veiling your eternal divinity in the wretched cloud and dung heap of Adam. And why? For love! You, God, became human and we have been made divine! In the name of this unspeakable love, then, I beg you—I would force you even!—to have mercy on your creatures."

God let himself be forced by her tears and chained by her holy desire. And turning to her with a glance at once full of mercy and of sadness he said:

"I want you to understand this, my daughter: I created humankind anew in the blood of my only-begotten Son and reestablished them in grace, but they have so scorned the graces I gave them and still give them! They go from bad to worse, from sin to sin, constantly repaying me with insults. And they not only fail to recognize my graces for what they are, but sometimes even think I am abusing them—I who want nothing but their sanctification! I tell you it will go harder for them in view of the grace they have received, and they will be deserving of greater punishment. They will be more severely punished now that they have been redeemed by my Son's blood than they would have been before that redemption, before the scar of Adam's sin was removed.

"It is only reasonable that those who receive more should give more in return, and the greater the gift, the greater the bond of indebtedness. How greatly were they indebted to me, then, since I had given them their very existence, creating them in my image and likeness! They owed me glory, but they stole it from me and took it to themselves instead. They violated the obedience I had laid on them and so became my enemies. But with humility I destroyed their pride: I stooped to take on their humanity, rescued them from their slavery to the devil, and made them free. And more than this—can you see?—through this union of the divine nature with the human, God was made human and humanity was made God."

Then that soul stood before the divine majesty deeply joyful and strengthened in her new knowledge. What hope she had found in the divine mercy! What unspeakable love she had experienced! For she had seen how God, in his love and his desire to be merciful to humankind in spite of their enmity toward him, had given his servants a way to force his goodness and calm his wrath. So she was glad and fearless in the face of the world's persecution, knowing that God was on her side. And the fire of her holy longing grew so strong that she would not rest there, but with holy confidence made her plea for the whole world. . . .

"Have mercy, eternal God, on your little sheep, good shepherd that you are! Do not delay with your mercy for the world, for already it almost seems they can no longer survive! Everyone seems bereft of any oneness in charity with you, eternal Truth, or even with each other: I mean, whatever love they have for each other has no grounding in you."

Then God, like one drunk with love for our good, found a way to fire up an even greater love and sorrow in that soul. He showed her with what love he had created us (as we have already begun to tell) and he said:

"See how they all lash out at me! And I created them with such burning love and gave them grace and gifts without number—all freely, though I owed them nothing! But see, daughter, how they strike back at me with every sort of sin, but most of all with their wretched and hateful selfishness, that breeding ground of every evil, and with this selfish love they have poisoned the whole world. I have shown you how love of me bears every good that is brought to birth for others. By the same principle this sensual selfishness (which is born of pride just as my love is born of charity) is the bearer of every evil.

"This evil they do by means of other people. For love of me and love of others are inseparable. And those who have not loved me have cut themselves off as well from any love of their neighbors. This is why I said—and I explained it to you—that every good and every evil is done by means of your neighbors.

"How many charges I could bring against humankind! For they have received nothing but good from me, and they repay me with every sort of hateful evil. But I have told you that my wrath would be softened by the tears of my servants, and I say it again: You, my servants, come into my presence laden with your prayers, your eager longing, your sorrow over their offense against me as well as their own damnation, and so you will soften my divinely just wrath.

"Know that no one can escape my hands, for I am who I am, whereas you have no being at all of yourselves. What being you have is my doing; I am the Creator of everything that has any share in being. But sin is not of my making, for sin is nonbeing. Sin is unworthy of any love, then, because it has no part in me. Therefore, my creatures offend me when they love sin, which they should not love, and hate me, to whom they owe love because I am supremely good and gave them being with such burning love. But they cannot escape me: Either I will have them in justice because of their sin, or I will have them in mercy.

"Open the eye of your understanding, then, and look at my hand, and you will see that what I have told you is true."

So in obedience to the most high Father, she raised her eyes, and she saw within his closed fist the entire world. And God said:

"My daughter, see now and know that no one can be taken away from me. Everyone is here as I said, either in justice or in mercy. They are mine; I created them, and I love them ineffably. And so, in spite of their wickedness, I will be merciful to them because of my servants, and I will grant what you have asked of me with such love and sorrow."

The fire within that soul blazed higher and she was beside herself as if drunk, at once gloriously happy and grief-stricken. She was happy in her union with God, wholly submerged in his mercy and savoring his vast goodness; but to see such goodness offended brought her grief. She knew, though, that God had shown her his creatures' sinfulness to rouse her to intensify her concern and longing. And so she offered thanks to the divine majesty.

As she felt her emotions so renewed in the eternal Godhead, the force of her spirit made her body break into a sweat. (For her union with God was more intimate than was the union between her soul and her body.) The holy fire of love grew so fierce within her that its heat made her sweat water, but it was not enough. She longed to see her body sweat blood, so she said to herself:

"Alas, my soul! You have frittered your whole life away, and for this have all these great and small evils come upon the world and holy Church! So I want you to heal them now with a sweat of blood."

Indeed, this soul remembered well what Truth had taught her: that she should always know herself and God's goodness at work in her, and that the medicine by which he willed to heal the whole world and to soothe his wrath and divine justice was humble, constant, holy prayer. So, spurred on by holy desire, she roused herself even more to open the eye of her understanding. She gazed into divine charity and there she saw and tasted how bound we are to love and seek the glory and praise of God's name through the salvation of souls. . . .

[And God said:] "You are the workers I have hired for the vineyard of holy Church. When I gave you the light of holy baptism I sent you by my grace to work in the universal body of Christianity. You received your baptism within the mystic body of holy Church by the hands of my ministers, and these ministers I have sent to work with you. You are to work in the universal body. They, however, have been placed within the mystic body to shepherd your souls by administering the blood to you through the sacraments you receive from them, and by rooting out from you the thorns of deadly sin and planting grace within you. They are my workers in the vineyard of your souls, ambassadors for the vineyard of holy Church.

"Do you know what course I follow, once my servants have completely given themselves to the teaching of the gentle loving Word? I prune them, so that they will bear much fruit—cultivated fruit, not wild. Just as the gardener prunes the branch that is joined to the vine so that it will yield more and better wine, but cuts off and throws into the fire the branch that is barren, so do I the true gardener act. When my servants remain united to me I prune them with great suffering so that they will bear more and better fruit, and virtue will be proved in them. But those who bear no fruit are cut off and thrown into the fire. . . .

"Keep in mind that each of you has your own vineyard. But every one is joined to your neighbors' vineyards without any dividing lines. They are so joined together, in fact, that you cannot do good or evil for yourself without doing the same for your neighbors.

"All of you together make up one common vineyard, the whole Christian assembly, and you are all united in the vineyard of the mystic body of holy Church from which you draw your life. In this vineyard is planted the vine, which is my only-begotten Son, into whom you must be engrafted. Unless you are engrafted into him you are rebels against holy Church, like members that are cut off from the body and rot.

"It is true that while you have time you can get yourselves out of the stench of sin through true repentance and recourse to my ministers. They are the workers who have the keys to the wine cellar, that is, the blood poured forth from this vine. (And this blood is so perfect in itself that you cannot be deprived of its benefits through any fault in the minister.)

"It is charity that binds you to true humility—the humility that is found in knowing yourself and me. See, then, that it is as workers that I have sent you all. And now I am calling you again, because the world is failing fast. The thorns have so multiplied and have choked the seed so badly that it will produce no fruit of grace at all.

"I want you, therefore, to be true workers. With deep concern help to till the souls in the mystic body of holy Church. I am calling you to this because I want to be merciful to the world as you have so earnestly begged me."

And the soul, restless in her great love, answered:

"O immeasurably tender love! Who would not be set afire with such love? What heart could keep from breaking? You, deep well of charity, it seems you are so madly in love with your creatures that you could not live without us! Yet you are our God, and have no need of us. Your greatness is no greater for our well-being, nor are you harmed by any harm that comes to us, for you are supreme eternal Goodness. What could move you to such mercy? Neither duty nor any need you have of us (we are sinful and wicked debtors!)—but only love!

"If I see clearly at all, supreme eternal Truth, it is I who am the thief, and you have been executed in my place. For I see the Word, your Son, nailed to a cross. And you have made him a bridge for me, as you have shown me, wretched servant that I am! My heart is breaking and yet cannot break for the hungry longing it has conceived for you! . . . "

12

The Tumbler of Our Lady

IN addition to formal worship in the
churches and cathedrals of medieval Europe, there evolved religious traditions
embodied in popular tales and legends as well as in special religious observances.
The most popular and widespread were those concerning the Virgin Mary.
Why this should be so is variously explained as the appeal Mary had to the
popular imagination and to the desire for a less demanding and rigorous aspect
of religion than the formal sacramental system and prescribed rituals of
the Church.

The intensity of this attitude is seen in the many cathedrals dedicated to her
(Notre Dame de Paris, "Our Lady of Paris," for example) and in the Lady
Chapels dedicated to the Virgin Mary that are part of virtually every church of
any size throughout Europe. Members of the clergy, merchants, nobles, and
peasants all found in her a consoling figure, quick to pity and quick to forgive, an
intercessor who would plead in their behalf to a stern and awesome God, whose
judgments could otherwise be severe and unyielding.

A host of stories circulated, telling how Mary obtained mercy and forgiveness
for her devotees, however sinful, who prayed sincerely to her. These stories
appeared in an extraordinary variety, ranging from pleasantly charming (like
the story included here) to the robust and morally dubious. In some, the Virgin
shows her loving acceptance of the veneration of simple, artless folk; in others,
she saves the lives of thieves and murderers; in still others, she protects wayward
nuns and young women who repent and pray for forgiveness only after they
have enjoyed a life of sin. All of these stories have in common, however, the
image of the Virgin Mary smiling sadly, forgivingly, and sympathetically at all
who devoutly kneel before her.

This story is about a *tumbler*—an acrobat, or gymnast, who performed at fairs and in the streets of towns. Tiring of his strenuous life, he entered the monastery at Clairvaux (in France), which had been founded by St. Bernard and which was known for its dedication to the veneration of the Virgin Mary. The tumbler gave the monastery all he owned: horses, clothes, and money.

He was a good man but unable to take part in the religious services because he had never learned to do anything but dance and perform acrobatics. He could not memorize prayers, not even "Our Father," or the Creed, or "Hail Mary," or anything to help save his soul. Moreover, the other monks never spoke to him, for they had taken the vow of silence. Every one of them served God in whatever way he could: the priests at the altar, the deacons reading their gospels, the subdeacons reading their epistles. At night they were singing, and even the acolytes were busy, one singing verses, another saying the lesson. Even the most ignorant could say "Our Father."

The tumbler was afraid that when they saw he was doing nothing in return for his meals and lodging they would send him away. He wept and cried out to Mary, asking her to pray to God the Father to save him and show him how to serve God and the Virgin so that he would deserve what he was given in the monastery.

As he wandered around the monastery one day, he came to a crypt where there was an altar and above it a statue of Our Lady. The bells of the monastery began to ring, calling everyone to mass. But the tumbler suddenly decided to stay in the little chapel. "Now," he cried, "I'll do all my tricks and stunts right here. I'll do what I know how to do. I won't go on getting my food and doing nothing in return for it. Others serve the Mother of God by singing; I will serve her in her chapel and in my own way by leaping and tumbling and doing all the tricks I've learned."

He took off his heavy gown and placed it by the altar, but lest his naked body show, he kept his long jacket on. He then turned humbly to the statue and prayed: "Lady, into your care I give my body and soul. Dear Queen, sweet Lady, do not scorn what I am going to do, for I only wish to please you and serve you in good faith, with God's help. I do not know how to chant or read. But I will show you what I can do best

THE TUMBLER OF OUR LADY   Anonymous verse narrative of the thirteenth century. Abridged version translated by the editor from the text established by L. Clédat, *Chrestomathie du Moyen Age*, Paris, 1884, pp. 231–38.

to please you. For, Lady, you are never unkind to those who serve you well. Such as I am, I offer myself to you."

Then he began to leap and dance with both long and short steps, now low, now high. At last he knelt before the image, bowed, and said, "Dear and sweet Queen, pity me from your tender heart and do not reject my offering." He continued then with all the somersaults and leaps and turns of all the places he had been in France, and in Spain, Brittany, and Lorraine.

He held his hand to his forehead and looked most humbly at the image of the Mother of God. "Lady," he said, "I do this all for you. I dare to say and boast that it is not for my pleasure. For I serve you for your pleasure and joy. And, Lady, you are my joy." He went on leaping and dancing in honor of Our Lady as long as the mass lasted. Then, overcome with weariness, his body covered with sweat, he sank down unconscious before the altar.

The little tumbler continued with these devotions every day and sometimes several times a day. Another monk, curious about his frequent disappearances from the regular services, followed him and saw all that he did. He ran off to tell the abbot.

The abbot and the monk came to watch, hiding behind a pillar in the crypt. They saw all of the tumbler's dancing and leaping. When at last he sank down exhausted and drenched with sweat, it was Our Lady herself, whom he had served so well, that came to his aid.

The abbot, looking hard to see well, beheld Our Lady descending through an opening in the vaulting of the crypt. She was glorious beyond anything ever seen, with gold and precious gems adorning her rich robes. With her came angels and archangels, who stood beside her and gathered around the little tumbler to help and comfort him. As he somehow sensed their presence, his heart began to regain its strength.

The gentle and radiant Queen held a white cloth with which she fanned the little tumbler lying before the altar. The lovely lady cooled his neck and body and face, but the poor man did not see or know that around him was gathered such a splendid company.

Some time after this, the abbot summoned the tumbler to come before him. The tumbler was afraid that he would be expelled from the monastery and he wept. The abbot prolonged his uncertainty by demanding to be told everything about his life in the monastery. But when he had finished doing so, the abbot comforted the poor man, telling him that his conduct was approved of and that he should keep on with his devotions. Happiness and joy overwhelmed the poor tumbler. He fell ill and had to remain in his bed. He was distraught at not being able to perform his devotions ever again.

Everyone in the monastery gathered around his deathbed. Then Our Lady appeared with her angels, who, singing, carried the little tumbler to heaven.

13
Geoffrey Chaucer

Canterbury Tales: The Prologue, The Prologue of the Pardoner's Tale, The Pardoner's Tale, and The Reeve's Tale

G EOFFREY Chaucer (ca. 1340–
1400), the first of the great English poets, affords an example of the cosmopolitan, sophisticated quality of medieval literature at its best. At ease in the literary conventions of French, Italian, and Latin poetry, Chaucer was also successful in the world of practical affairs. In his youth he had seen military service in France and had been a member of diplomatic missions to France and Italy. Although his many government posts and benefits may not have been bestowed on him for his literary achievements, there can be no doubt that, even during his lifetime, Chaucer enjoyed wide acclaim as a writer.

Canterbury Tales, Chaucer's masterpiece, was composed during the latter years of the fourteenth century. It is, on the one hand, a tribute to the medieval ideal society composed of clergy, nobility, and commoners; on the other hand, it is a shrewd depiction of individual follies and vices, which suggest a decline in medieval society and its institutions.

The setting of the Tales is a pilgrimage of some thirty persons, drawn from the various ranks of society, to visit the shrine of St. Thomas à Becket, a twelfth-century martyr and defender of the Church. Each pilgrim is to tell two stories on the road to Canterbury and two on the return journey. Chaucer identifies the pilgrims in medieval fashion, noting their dress and emblems of rank. Thus, his characters represent a cross section of the society of the time. Furthermore, his skill in characterization creates a gallery of distinct, vivid individuals. These sketches make up The Prologue, some of which is given in the following selection.

The stories usually suit the character of the narrator and range from the elegant stylizations of courtly romance in The Knight's Tale to the crude anecdotes of the miller and the reeve. Although Chaucer never completed his *collection of stories (only twenty-three pilgrims get their turn), he succeeds in presenting a vivid picture of medieval society and, in a broader sense, the whole range of human behavior*

THE PROLOGUE

When April with his showers sweet with fruit
The drought of March has pierced unto the root
And bathed each vein with liquor that has power
To generate therein and sire the flower;
When Zephyr[1] also has, with his sweet breath,
Quickened again, in every holt and heath,
The tender shoots and buds, and the young sun
Into the Ram[2] one half his course has run,
And many little birds make melody
That sleep through all the night with open eye
(So Nature pricks them on to ramp and rage)—
Then do folk long to go on pilgrimage,
And palmers to go seeking out strange strands,
To distant shrines well known in sundry lands.
And specially from every shire's end
Of England they to Canterbury wend,
The holy blessed martyr[3] there to seek
Who helped them when they lay so ill and weak.
  Befell that, in that season, on a day
In Southwark, at the Tabard, as I lay
Ready to start upon my pilgrimage
To Canterbury, full of devout homage,
There came at nightfall to that hostelry
Some nine and twenty in a company

[1]The west wind.

[2]Aries, the first sign of the zodiac. The sun passes through Aries in the spring.

[3]St. Thomas à Becket, twelfth-century martyr whose shrine was in Canterbury cathedral.

CANTERBURY TALES   Reprinted from *The Canterbury Tales* translated by J. U. Nicholson. Copyright © 1934 by Covici Friede, Inc. Used by permission of Crown Publishers, Inc. [Pp. 1–10, 13–18, 19–22, 109–119, 293–97, 302–310.]

Of sundry persons who had chanced to fall
In fellowship, and pilgrims were they all
That toward Canterbury town would ride.
The rooms and stables spacious were and wide,
And well we there were eased, and of the best.
And briefly, when the sun had gone to rest,
So had I spoken with them, every one,
That I was of their fellowship anon,
And made agreement that we'd early rise
To take the road, as you I will apprise.
   But none the less, whilst I have time and space,
Before yet farther in this tale I pace,
It seems to me accordant with reason
To inform you of the state of every one
Of all of these, as it appeared to me,
And who they were, and what was their degree,
And even how arrayed there at the inn;
And with a knight thus will I first begin.

The Knight

A knight there was, and he a worthy man,
Who, from the moment that he first began
To ride about the world, loved chivalry,
Truth, honour, freedom and all courtesy.
Full worthy was he in his liege-lord's war,
And therein had he ridden (none more far)
As well in Christendom as heathenesse,
And honoured everywhere for worthiness.
   At Alexandria, he, when it was won;
Full oft the table's roster he'd begun
Above all nations' knights in Prussia.
In Latvia raided he, and Russia,
No christened man so oft of his degree.
In far Granada[4] at the siege was he
Of Algeciras, and in Belmarie.
At Ayas was he and at Satalye
When they were won; and on the Middle Sea

---

[4]This name and the names in the following lines are those of cities and places in Spain,
North Africa, or elsewhere around the Mediterranean (the Middle Sea).

At many a noble meeting chanced to be.
Of mortal battles he had fought fifteen,
And he'd fought for our faith at Tramissene
Three times in lists, and each time slain his foe.
This self-same worthy knight had been also
At one time with the lord of Palatye
Against another heathen in Turkey:
And always won he sovereign fame for prize.
Though so illustrious, he was very wise
And bore himself as meekly as a maid.
He never yet had any vileness said,
In all his life, to whatsoever wight.
He was a truly perfect, gentle knight.
But now, to tell you all of his array,
His steeds were good, but yet he was not gay.
Of simple fustian wore he a jupon.[5]
Sadly discoloured by his habergeon;[6]
For he had lately come from his voyage
And now was going on this pilgrimage.

The Squire

With him there was his son, a youthful squire,
A lover and a lusty bachelor,
With locks well curled, as if they'd laid in press.
Some twenty years of age he was, I guess.
In stature he was of an average length,
Wondrously active, aye, and great of strength.
He'd ridden sometime with the cavalry
In Flanders, in Artois, and Picardy,
And borne him well within that little space
In hope to win thereby his lady's grace.
Prinked out he was, as if he were a mead,
All full of fresh-cut flowers white and red.
Singing he was, or fluting, all the day;
He was as fresh as is the month of May.
Short was his gown, with sleeves both long and wide.

[5]A tunic.
[6]Coat of mail.

Well could he sit on horse, and fairly ride.
He could make songs and words thereto indite,
Joust, and dance too, as well as sketch and write.
So hot he loved that, while night told her tale,
He slept no more than does a nightingale.
Courteous he, and humble, willing and able,
And carved before his father at the table.

•   •   •

The Prioress

There was also a nun, a prioress,
Who, in her smiling, modest was and coy;
Her greatest oath was but "By Saint Eloy!"[7]
And she was known as Madam Eglantine.
Full well she sang the services divine,
Intoning through her nose, becomingly;
And fair she spoke her French, and fluently,
After the school of Stratford-at-the-Bow,[8]
For French of Paris was not hers to know.
At table she had been well taught withal,
And never from her lips let morsels fall,
Nor dipped her fingers deep in sauce, but ate
With so much care the food upon her plate
That never driblet fell upon her breast.
In courtesy she had delight and zest.
Her upper lip was always wiped so clean
That in her cup was no iota seen
Of grease, when she had drunk her draught of wine.
Becomingly she reached for meat to dine.
And certainly delighting in good sport,
She was right pleasant, amiable—in short.
She was at pains to counterfeit the look
Of courtliness, and stately manners took.
And would be held worthy of reverence.
    But, to say something of her moral sense,
She was so charitable and piteous

[7]Patron saint of goldsmiths and renowned for his courtesy and refined manners.
[8]A place near London. The prioress comes from the convent located there.

That she would weep if she but saw a mouse
Caught in a trap, though it were dead or bled.
She had some little dogs, too, that she fed
On roasted flesh, or milk and fine white bread.
But sore she'd weep if one of them were dead,
Or if men smote it with a rod to smart:
For pity ruled her, and her tender heart.
Right decorous her pleated wimple was;
Her nose was fine; her eyes were blue as glass;
Her mouth was small and therewith soft and red;
But certainly she had a fair forehead;
It was almost a full span broad, I own,
For, truth to tell, she was not undergrown.
Neat was her cloak, as I was well aware.
Of coral small about her arm she'd bear
A string of beads and gauded all with green;
And therefrom hung a brooch of golden sheen
Whereon there was first written a crowned "A,"
And under, *Amor vincit omnia.*[9]
Another little NUN with her had she,
Who was her chaplain; and of PRIESTS she'd three.

• • •

The Monk

A monk there was, one made for mastery,
An outrider,[10] who loved his venery;[11]
A manly man, to be an abbot able.
Full many a blooded horse had he in stable:
And when he rode men might his bridle hear
A-jingling in the whistling wind as clear,
Aye, and as loud as does the chapel bell
Where this brave monk was master of the cell.
The rule of Maurus or Saint Benedict,[12]
By reason it was old and somewhat strict,

[9]Love conquers all.
[10]A monk who supervised the monastery farms and estates.
[11]Hunting.
[12]St. Benedict was the founder of Western monasticism; St. Maurus was his disciple.

This said monk let such old things slowly pace
And followed new-world manners in their place.
He cared not for that text a clean-plucked hen
Which holds that hunters are not holy men;
Nor that a monk, when he is cloisterless,
Is like unto a fish that's waterless;
That is to say, a monk out of his cloister.
But this same text he held not worth an oyster;
And I said his opinion was right good.
What? Should he study as a madman would
Upon a book in cloister cell? Or yet
Go labour with his hands and swink and sweat,
As Austin[13] bids? How shall the world be served?
Let Austin have his toil to him reserved.
Therefore he was a rider day and night;
Greyhounds he had, as swift as bird in flight.
Since riding and the hunting of the hare
Were all his love, for no cost would he spare.
I saw his sleeves were purfled at the hand
With fur of grey, the finest in the land;
Also, to fasten hood beneath his chin,
He had of good wrought gold a curious pin:
A love-knot in the larger end there was.
His head was bald and shone like any glass,
And smooth as one anointed was his face.
Fat was this lord, he stood in goodly case.
His bulging eyes he rolled about, and hot
They gleamed and red, like fire beneath a pot;
His boots were soft; his horse of great estate.
Now certainly he was a fine prelate:
He was not pale as some poor wasted ghost.
A fat swan loved he best of any roast.
His palfrey was as brown as is a berry.

The Friar

A friar there was, a wanton and a merry,
A limiter,[14] a very festive man.

---

[13]St. Augustine, bishop and leader of the early Church, directed his followers to engage in manual labor.

[14]A friar licensed to beg for his order in a certain, limited area.

In all the Orders Four[15] is none that can
Equal his gossip and his fair language.
He had arranged full many a marriage
Of women young, and this at his own cost.
Unto his order he was a noble post.
Well liked by all and intimate was he
With franklins[16] everywhere in his country,
And with the worthy women of the town:
For at confessing he'd more power in gown
(As he himself said) than a good curate,
For of his order he was licentiate.[17]
He heard confession gently, it was said,
Gently absolved too, leaving naught of dread.
He was an easy man to give penance
When knowing he should gain a good pittance;
For to a begging friar, money given
Is sign that any man has been well shriven.
For if one gave (he dared to boast of this),
He took the man's repentance not amiss.
For many a man there is so hard of heart
He cannot weep however pains may smart.
Therefore, instead of weeping and of prayer,
Men should give silver to poor friars all bare.
His tippet was stuck always full of knives
And pins, to give to young and pleasing wives.
And certainly he kept a merry note:
Well could he sing and play upon the rote.
At balladry he bore the prize away.
His throat was white as lily of the May;
Yet strong he was as ever champion.
In towns he knew the taverns, every one,
And every good host and each barmaid too—
Better than begging lepers, these he knew.
For unto no such solid man as he
Accorded it, as far as he could see,
To have sick lepers for acquaintances.
There is no honest advantageousness

---

[15]The four orders of friars: Augustinians, Carmelites, Dominicans, Franciscans.
[16]Well-to-do independent farmers.
[17]Licensed to hear confessions.

In dealing with such poverty-stricken curs;
It's with the rich and with big victuallers.
And so, wherever profit might arise,
Courteous he was and humble in men's eyes.
There was no other man so virtuous.
He was the finest beggar of his house;
A certain district being farmed to him,
None of his brethren dared approach its rim;
For though a widow had no shoes to show,
So pleasant was his *In principio*,[18]
He always got a farthing ere he went.
He lived by pickings, it is evident.
And he could romp as well as any whelp.
On love days could he be of mickle help.
For there he was not like a cloisterer,
With threadbare cope as is the poor scholar,
But he was like a lord or like a pope.
Of double worsted was his semi-cope,
That rounded like a bell, as you may guess.
He lisped a little, out of wantonness,
To make his English soft upon his tongue;
And in his harping, after he had sung,
His two eyes twinkled in his head as bright
As do the stars within the frosty night.
This worthy limiter was named Hubert.

The Merchant

There was a merchant with forked beard, and girt
In motley gown, and high on horse he sat,
Upon his head a Flemish beaver hat;
His boots were fastened rather elegantly.
He spoke his notions out right pompously,
Stressing the times when he had won, not lost.
He would the sea were held at any cost
Across from Middleburgh to Orwell town.[19]

---

[18]In the beginning—which are the opening words of the Gospel according to St. John.

[19]Middleburgh in Holland and Orwell in England were important ports for the wool trade.

At money-changing he could make a crown.
This worthy man kept all his wits well set;
There was no one could say he was in debt,
So well he governed all his trade affairs
With bargains and with borrowings and with shares.
Indeed, he was a worthy man withal,
But, sooth to say, his name I can't recall.

The Clerk

A clerk[20] from Oxford was with us also,
Who'd turned to getting knowledge, long ago.
As meagre was his horse as is a rake,
Nor he himself to fat, I'll undertake,
But he looked hollow and went soberly.
Right threadbare was his overcoat; for he
Had got him yet no churchly benefice,
Nor was so worldly as to gain office.
For he would rather have at his bed's head
Some twenty books, all bound in black and red,
Of Aristotle and his philosophy
Than rich robes, fiddle, or gay psaltery.
Yet, and for all he was philosopher,
He had but little gold within his coffer;
But all that he might borrow from a friend
On books and learning he would swiftly spend,
And then he'd pray right busily for the souls
Of those who gave him wherewithal for schools.
Of study took he utmost care and heed.
Not one word spoke he more than was his need;
And that was said in fullest reverence
And short and quick and full of high good sense.
Pregnant of moral virtue was his speech;
And gladly would he learn and gladly teach.

• • •

[20]The term *clerk* was applied to any ecclesiastical student as well as to the person who had taken holy orders.

The Franklin

There was a franklin[21] in his company;
White was his beard as is the white daisy.
Of sanguine temperament by every sign,
He loved right well his morning sop in wine.
Delightful living was the goal he'd won,
For he was Epicurus'[22] very son,
That held opinion that a full delight
Was true felicity, perfect and right.
A householder, and that a great, was he;
Saint Julian[23] he was in his own country.
His bread and ale were always right well done;
A man with better cellars there was none.
Baked meat was never wanting in his house,
Of fish and flesh, and that so plenteous
It seemed to snow therein both food and drink
Of every dainty that a man could think.
According to the season of the year
He changed his diet and his means of cheer.
Full many a fattened partridge did he mew,
And many a bream and pike in fish-pond too.
Woe to his cook, except the sauces were
Poignant and sharp, and ready all his gear.
His table, waiting in his hall alway,
Stood ready covered through the livelong day.
At county sessions[24] was he lord and sire,
And often acted as a knight of shire.[25]
A dagger and a trinket-bag of silk
Hung from his girdle, white as morning milk.
He had been sheriff and been auditor;
And nowhere was a worthier vavasor.[26]

[21]An independent owner of considerable property.

[22]Greek philosopher reputed to have taught that pleasure is the highest good.

[23]Patron saint of hospitality.

[24]Meetings of the county's justices of the peace.

[25]Member of parliament for his county.

[26]A substantial landholder.

The Haberdasher, the Carpenter, the Weaver, the Dyer, and the Arras-Maker

A haberdasher and a carpenter,
An arras-maker,[27] dyer, and weaver
Were with us, clothed in similar livery,
All of one sober, great fraternity.
Their gear was new and well adorned it was;
Their weapons were not cheaply trimmed with brass,
But all with silver; chastely made and well
Their girdles and their pouches too, I tell.
Each man of them appeared a proper burgess
To sit in guildhall on a high dais.[28]
And each of them, for wisdom he could span,
Was fitted to have been an alderman;[29]
For chattels they'd enough, and, too, of rent;
To which their goodwives gave a free assent,
Or else for certain they had been to blame.
It's good to hear "Madam" before one's name,
And go to church when all the world may see,
Having one's mantle borne right royally.

• • •

The Physician

With us there was a doctor of physic;
In all this world was none like him to pick
For talk of medicine and surgery;
For he was grounded in astronomy.[30]
He often kept a patient from the pall
By horoscopes and magic natural.
Well could he tell the fortune ascendent
Within the houses for his sick patient.
He knew the cause of every malady,

[27]Tapestry weaver.
[28]A citizen worthy of sitting on the platform at town council meetings.
[29]A senior member of a town council.
[30]Actually, the physician relies on astrology.

Were it of hot or cold, of moist or dry,
And where engendered, and of what humour;
He was a very good practitioner.
The cause being known, down to the deepest root,
Anon he gave to the sick man his boot.
Ready he was, with his apothecaries,
To send him drugs and all electuaries;
By mutual aid much gold they'd always won—
Their friendship was a thing not new begun.
Well read was he in Esculapius,[31]
And Deiscorides, and in Rufus,
Hippocrates, and Hali, and Galen,
Serapion, Rhazes, and Avicen,
Averrhoës, Gilbert, and Constantine,
Bernard, and Gatisden, and John Damascene.
In diet he was measured as could be,
Including naught of superfluity,
But nourishing and easy. It's no libel
To say he read but little in the Bible.
In blue and scarlet he went clad, withal,
Lined with a taffeta and with sendal;
And yet he was right chary of expense;
He kept the gold he gained from pestilence.
For gold in physic is a fine cordial,
And therefore loved he gold exceeding all.

The Wife of Bath

There was a housewife come from Bath, or near,
Who—sad to say—was deaf in either ear.
At making cloth she had so great a bent
She bettered those of Ypres and even of Ghent.[32]
In all the parish there was no goodwife
Should offering make before her, on my life;
And if one did, indeed, so wroth was she
It put her out of all her charity.

---

[31]Here the physician begins to rattle off a list of ancient and medieval doctors and writers on medicine.

[32]Cities in Belgium famous for clothmaking.

Her kerchiefs were of finest weave and ground;
I dare swear that they weighed a full ten pound
Which, of a Sunday, she wore on her head.
Her hose were of the choicest scarlet red,
Close gartered, and her shoes were soft and new.
Bold was her face, and fair, and red of hue.
She'd been respectable throughout her life,
With five churched husbands bringing joy and strife,
Not counting other company in youth;
But thereof there's no need to speak, in truth.
Three times she'd journeyed to Jerusalem;
And many a foreign stream she'd had to stem;
At Rome she'd been, and she'd been in Boulogne,
In Spain at Santiago, and at Cologne.
She could tell much of wandering by the way:
Gap-toothed was she, it is no lie to say.
Upon an ambler easily she sat,
Well wimpled, aye, and over all a hat
As broad as is a buckler or a targe;
A rug was tucked around her buttocks large,
And on her feet a pair of sharpened spurs.
In company well could she laugh her slurs.
The remedies of love she knew, perchance,
For of that art she'd learned the old, old dance.

The Parson

There was a good man of religion, too,
A country parson, poor, I warrant you;
But rich he was in holy thought and work.
He was a learned man also, a clerk,
Who Christ's own gospel truly sought to preach;
Devoutly his parishioners would he teach.
Benign he was and wondrous diligent.
Patient in adverse times and well content,
As he was oft times proven; always blithe,
He was right loath to curse to get a tithe,
But rather would he give, in case of doubt,
Unto those poor parishioners about,
Part of his income, even of his goods.

Enough with little, coloured all his moods.
Wide was his parish, houses far asunder,
But never did he fail, for rain or thunder,
In sickness, or in sin, or any state,
To visit to the farthest, small and great,
Going afoot, and in his hand a stave.
This fine example to his flock he gave,
That first he wrought and afterwards he taught;
Out of the gospel then that text he caught,
And this figure he added thereunto—
That, if gold rust, what shall poor iron do?
For if the priest be foul, in whom we trust,
What wonder if a layman yield to lust?
And shame it is, if priest take thought for keep,
A shitty shepherd, shepherding clean sheep.
Well ought a priest example good to give,
By his own cleanness, how his flock should live.
He never let his benefice for hire,
Leaving his flock to flounder in the mire,
And ran to London, up to old Saint Paul's
To get himself a chantry[33] there for souls,
Nor in some brotherhood did he withhold;
But dwelt at home and kept so well the fold
That never wolf could make his plans miscarry;
He was a shepherd and not mercenary.
And holy though he was, and virtuous,
To sinners he was not impiteous,
Nor haughty in his speech, nor too divine,
But in all teaching prudent and benign.
To lead folk into Heaven but by stress
Of good example was his busyness.
But if some sinful one proved obstinate,
Be who it might, of high or low estate,
Him he reproved, and sharply, as I know.
There is nowhere a better priest, I trow.
He had no thirst for pomp or reverence,
Nor made himself a special, spiced conscience,
But Christ's own lore, and His apostles' twelve
He taught, but first he followed it himselve.

[33]A fund to pay for daily masses for the repose of souls.

The Plowman

With him there was a plowman, was his brother,
That many a load of dung, and many another
Had scattered, for a good true toiler, he,
Living in peace and perfect charity.
He loved God most, and that with his whole heart
At all times, though he played or plied his art,
And next, his neighbour, even as himself.
He'd thresh and dig, with never thought of pelf,
For Christ's own sake, for every poor wight,
All without pay, if it lay in his might.
He paid his taxes, fully, fairly, well,
Both by his own toil and by stuff he'd sell.
In a tabard he rode upon a mare.

• • •

The Miller

The miller was a stout churl, be it known,
Hardy and big of brawn and big of bone;
Which was well proved, for when he went on lam
At wrestling, never failed he of the ram.
He was a chunky fellow, broad of build;
He'd heave a door from hinges if he willed,
Or break it through, by running, with his head.
His beard, as any sow or fox, was red,
And broad it was as if it were a spade.
Upon the coping of his nose he had
A wart, and thereon stood a tuft of hairs,
Red as the bristles in an old sow's ears;
His nostrils they were black and very wide.
A sword and buckler bore he by his side.
His mouth was like a furnace door for size.
He was a jester and could poetize,
But mostly all of sin and ribaldries.
He could steal corn and full thrice charge his fees;
And yet he had a thumb of gold, begad.
A white coat and blue hood he wore, this lad.
A bagpipe he could blow well, be it known,
And with that same he brought us out of town.

• • •

The Reeve

The reeve[34] he was a slender, choleric man,
Who shaved his beard as close as razor can.
His hair was cut round even with his ears;
His top was tonsured like a pulpiteer's.
Long were his legs, and they were very lean,
And like a staff, with no calf to be seen.
Well could he manage granary and bin;
No auditor could ever on him win.
He could foretell, by drought and by the rain,
The yielding of his seed and of his grain.
His lord's sheep and his oxen and his dairy,
His swine and horses, all his stores, his poultry,
Were wholly in this steward's managing;
And, by agreement, he'd made reckoning
Since his young lord of age was twenty years;
Yet no man ever found him in arrears.
There was no agent, hind, or herd who'd cheat
But he knew well his cunning and deceit;
They were afraid of him as of the death.
His cottage was a good one, on a heath;
By green trees shaded with this dwelling-place.
Much better than his lord could he purchase.
Right rich he was in his own private right,
Seeing he'd pleased his lord, by day or night,
By giving him, or lending, of his goods,
And so got thanked—but yet got coats and hoods.
In youth he'd learned a good trade, and had been
A carpenter, as fine as could be seen.
This steward sat a horse that well could trot,
And was all dapple-grey, and was named Scot.
A long surcoat of blue did he parade,
And at his side he bore a rusty blade.
Of Norfolk was this reeve of whom I tell,
From near a town that men call Badeswell.
Bundled he was like friar from chin to croup,
And ever he rode hindmost of our troop.

[34]Probably the manager of an estate.

The Summoner

A summoner[35] was with us in that place,
Who had a fiery-red, cherubic face,
For eczema he had; his eyes were narrow
As hot he was, and lecherous, as a sparrow;
With black and scabby brows and scanty beard;
He had a face that little children feared.
There was no mercury, sulphur, or litharge,
No borax, ceruse, tartar, could discharge,
Nor ointment that could cleanse enough, or bite,
To free him of his boils and pimples white,
Nor of the bosses resting on his cheeks.
Well loved he garlic, onions, aye and leeks,
And drinking of strong wine as red as blood.
Then would he talk and shout as madman would.
And when a deal of wine he'd poured within,
Then would he utter no word save Latin.
Some phrases had he learned, say two or three,
Which he had garnered out of some decree;
No wonder, for he'd heard it all the day;
And all you know right well that even a jay
Can call out "Wat" as well as can the pope.
But when, for aught else, into him you'd grope,
'Twas found he'd spent his whole philosophy;
Just *"Questio quid juris"*[36] would he cry.
He was a noble rascal, and a kind;
A better comrade 'twould be hard to find.
Why, he would suffer, for a quart of wine,
Some good fellow to have his concubine
A twelve-month, and excuse him to the full
(Between ourselves, though, he could pluck a gull).
And if he chanced upon a good fellow,
He would instruct him never to have awe,
In such a case, of the archdeacon's curse,
Except a man's soul lie within his purse;
For in his purse the man should punished be.
"The purse is the archdeacon's Hell," said he.

[35]A summoner was an official who called delinquents before church courts.
[36]"The question is what aspect of law [applies]."

But well I know he lied in what he said,
A curse ought every guilty man to dread
(For curse can kill, as absolution save),
And 'ware *significavit*[37] to the grave.
In his own power had he, and at ease,
The boys and girls of all the diocese,
And knew their secrets, and by counsel led.
A garland had he set upon his head,
Large as a tavern's wine-bush on a stake;
A buckler had he made of bread they bake.

The Pardoner

With him there rode a gentle pardoner[38]
Of Rouncival,[39] his friend and his compeer;
Straight from the court of Rome had journeyed he.
Loudly he sang "Come hither, love, to me,"
The summoner joining with a burden round;
Was never horn of half so great a sound.
This pardoner had hair as yellow as wax,
But lank it hung as does a strike of flax;
In wisps hung down such locks as he'd on head,
And with them he his shoulders overspread;
But thin they dropped, and stringy, one by one.
But as to hood, for sport of it, he'd none,
Though it was packed in wallet all the while.
It seemed to him he went in latest style,
Dishevelled, save for cap, his head all bare.
As shiny eyes he had as has a hare.
He had a fine veronica[40] sewed to cap.
His wallet lay before him in his lap,
Stuffed full of pardons brought from Rome all hot.
A voice he had that bleated like a goat.
No beard had he, nor ever should he have,
For smooth his face as he'd just had a shave;

---

[37]A writ or order sending an excommunicated person to imprisonment.

[38]A pardoner was a distributor of papal indulgences (pardons) which granted remission of punishment in purgatory.

[39]A religious hospital in London.

[40]A representation of the face of Jesus on a cloth.

I think he was a gelding or a mare.
But in his craft, from Berwick unto Ware,
Was no such pardoner in any place.
For in his bag he had a pillowcase
The which, he said, was Our True Lady's veil:
He said he had a piece of the very sail
That good Saint Peter had, what time he went
Upon the sea, till Jesus changed his bent.
He had a latten[41] cross set full of stones,
And in a bottle had he some pig's bones.
But with these relics, when he came upon
Some simple parson, then this paragon
In that one day more money stood to gain
Than the poor dupe in two months could attain.
And thus, with flattery and suchlike japes,
He made the parson and the rest his apes.
But yet, to tell the whole truth at the last,
He was, in church, a fine ecclesiast.
Well could he read a lesson or a story,
But best of all he sang an offertory;
For well he knew that when that song was sung,
Then might he preach, and all with polished tongue,
To win some silver, as he right well could;
Therefore he sang so merrily and so loud.
    Now have I told you briefly, in a clause,
The state, the array, the number, and the cause
Of the assembling of this company
In Southwark, at this noble hostelry
Known as the Tabard Inn, hard by the Bell.

[The Pardoner is one of the most vividly drawn portraits in literature. His prologue and narrative are outstanding examples of Chaucer's proficiency in combining crucial social issues with dramatically presented, psychologically accurate characterizations. *Ed.*]

THE PROLOGUE OF THE PARDONER'S TALE

"Masters," quoth he, "in churches, when I preach,
I am at pains that all shall hear my speech,
And ring it out as roundly as a bell,

---

[41]Made of copper and zinc alloy.

For I know all by heart the thing I tell.
My theme is always one, and ever was:
'Radix malorum est cupiditas.'[42]
  "First I announce the place whence I have come.
And then I show my pardons, all and some.
Our liege-lord's seal on my patent perfect,
I show that first, my safety to protect,
And then no man's so bold, no priest nor clerk,
As to disturb me in Christ's holy work;
And after that my tales I marshall all.
Indulgences of pope and cardinal,
Of patriarch and bishop, these I do
Show, and in Latin speak some words, a few,
To spice therewith a bit my sermoning
And stir men to devotion, marvelling.
Then show I forth my hollow crystal-stones,
Which are crammed full of rags, aye, and of bones;
Relics are these, as they think, every one.
Then I've in latten box a shoulder bone
Which came out of a holy Hebrew's sheep.
'Good men,' say I, 'my words in memory keep;
If this bone shall be washed in any well,
Then if a cow, calf, sheep, or ox should swell
That's eaten snake, or been by serpent stung,
Take water of that well and wash its tongue,
And 'twill be well anon; and furthermore,
Of pox and scab and every other sore
Shall every sheep be healed that of this well
Drinks but one draught; take heed of what I tell.
And if the man that owns the beasts, I trow,
Shall every week, and that before cock-crow,
And before breakfast, drink thereof a draught,
As that Jew taught of yore in his priestcraft,
His beasts and all his store shall multiply.
And, good sirs, it's a cure for jealousy;
For though a man be fallen in jealous rage,
Let one make of this water his pottage
And nevermore shall he his wife mistrust,

---

[42]"The root of evil is greed."

Though he may know the truth of all her lust,
Even though she'd taken two priests, aye, or three.
   "'Here is a mitten, too, that you may see.
Who puts his hand therein, I say again,
He shall have increased harvest of his grain,
After he's sown, be it of wheat or oats,
Just so he offers pence or offers groats.
   "'Good men and women, one thing I warn you,
If any man be here in church right now
That's done a sin so horrible that he
Dare not, for shame, of that sin shriven be,
Or any woman, be she young or old,
That's made her husband into a cuckold,
Such folk shall have no power and no grace
To offer to my relics in this place.
But whoso finds himself without such blame,
He will come up and offer, in God's name,
And I'll absolve him by authority
That has, by bull, been granted unto me.'
  "By this fraud have I won me, year by year,
A hundred marks, since I've been pardoner.
I stand up like a scholar in pulpit,
And when the ignorant people all do sit,
I preach, as you have heard me say before,
And tell a hundred false japes, less or more.
I am at pains, then, to stretch forth my neck,
And east and west upon the folk I beck,
As does a dove that's sitting on a barn.
With hands and swift tongue, then, do I so yarn
That it's a joy to see my busyness.
Of avarice and of all such wickedness
Is all my preaching, thus to make them free
With offered pence, the which pence come to me.
For my intent is only pence to win,
And not at all for punishment of sin.
When they are dead, for all I think thereon
Their souls may well black-berrying have gone!
For, certainly, there's many a sermon grows
Ofttimes from evil purpose, as one knows;
Some for folks' pleasure and for flattery,

To be advanced by all hypocrisy,
And some for vainglory, and some for hate.
For, when I dare not otherwise debate,
Then do I sharpen well my tongue and sting
The man in sermons, and upon him fling
My lying defamations, if but he
Has wronged my brethren or—much worse—wronged me.
For though I mention not his proper name,
Men know whom I refer to, all the same,
By signs I make and other circumstances.
Thus I pay those who do us displeasances.
Thus spit I out my venom under hue
Of holiness, to seem both good and true.
    "But briefly my intention I'll express;
I preach no sermon, save for covetousness.
For that my theme is yet, and ever was,
'*Radix malorum est cupiditas.*'
Thus can I preach against that self-same vice
Which I indulge, and that is avarice.
But though myself be guilty of that sin,
Yet can I cause those other folk to win
From avarice and really to repent.
But that is not my principal intent.
I preach no sermon, save for covetousness;
This should suffice of that, though, as I guess.
    "Then do I cite examples, many a one,
Out of old stories and of time long gone,
For vulgar people all love stories old;
Such things they can re-tell well and can hold.
What? Think you that because I'm good at preaching
And win me gold and silver by my teaching
I'll live of my free will in poverty?
No, no, that's never been my policy!
For I will preach and beg in sundry lands;
I will not work and labour with my hands,
Nor baskets weave and try to live thereby,
Because I will not beg in vain, say I.
I will none of the apostles counterfeit;
I will have money, wool, and cheese, and wheat,
Though it be given by the poorest page,
Or by the poorest widow in village,

And though her children perish of famine.
Nay! I will drink good liquor of the vine
And have a pretty wench in every town.
But harken, masters, to conclusion shown:
Your wish is that I tell you all a tale.
Now that I've drunk a draught of musty ale,
By God, I hope that I can tell something
That shall, in reason, be to your liking.
For though I am myself a vicious man,
Yet I would tell a moral tale, and can,
The which I'm wont to preach more gold to win.
Now hold your peace! my tale I will begin."

THE PARDONER'S TALE

In Flanders, once, there was a company
Of young companions given to folly,
Riot and gambling, brothels and taverns;
And, to the music of harps, lutes, gitterns,
They danced and played at dice both day and night,
And ate also and drank beyond their might,
Whereby they made the devil's sacrifice
Within that devil's temple, wicked wise,
By superfluity both vile and vain.
So damnable their oaths and so profane
That it was terrible to hear them swear;
Our Blessed Saviour's Body they did tear;[43]
They thought the Jews had rent Him not enough;
And each of them at others' sins would laugh.
Then entered dancing-girls of ill repute,
Graceful and slim, and girls who peddled fruit,
Harpers and bawds and women selling cake,
Who do their office for the Devil's sake,
To kindle and blow the fire of lechery,
Which is so closely joined with gluttony;
I call on holy writ, now, to witness
That lust is in all wine and drunkenness.

• • •

[43]It was believed that swearing inflicted pain on the body of Christ.

Now these three roisterers, whereof I tell,
Long before prime was rung by any bell,
Were sitting in a tavern for to drink;
And as they sat they heard a small bell clink
Before a corpse being carried to his grave;
Whereat one of them called unto his knave:
"Go run," said he, "and ask them civilly
What corpse it is that's just now passing by,
And see that you report the man's name well."
   "Sir," said the boy, "it needs not that they tell.
I learned it, ere you came here, full two hours;
He was, by gad, an old comrade of yours;
And he was slain, all suddenly, last night,
When drunk, as he sat on his bench upright;
An unseen thief, called Death, came stalking by,
Who hereabouts makes all the people die,
And with his spear he clove his heart in two
And went his way and made no more ado.
He's slain a thousand with this pestilence;
And, master, ere you come in his presence,
It seems to me to be right necessary
To be forewarned of such an adversary:
Be ready to meet him for evermore.
My mother taught me this, I say no more."
   "By holy Mary," said the innkeeper,
"The boy speaks truth, for Death has slain, this year,
A mile or more hence, in a large village,
Both man and woman, child and hind and page.
I think his habitation must be there;
To be advised of him great wisdom 'twere,
Before he did a man some dishonour."
   "Yea, by God's arms!" exclaimed this roisterer,
"Is it such peril, then, this Death to meet?
I'll seek him in the road and in the street,
As I now vow to God's own noble bones!
Hear, comrades, we're of one mind, as each owns;
Let each of us hold up his hand to other
And each of us become the other's brother,
And we three will go slay this traitor Death;
He shall be slain who's stopped so many a breath,

By God's great dignity, ere it be night."
    Together did these three their pledges plight
To live and die, each of them for the other,
As if he were his very own blood brother.
And up they started, drunken, in this rage,
And forth they went, and towards that village
Whereof the innkeeper had told before.
And so, with many a grisly oath, they swore
And Jesus' blessed body once more rent—
"Death shall be dead if we find where he went."
    When they had gone not fully half a mile,
Just as they would have trodden over a stile,
An old man, and a poor, with them did meet,
This ancient man full meekly them did greet,
And said thus: "Now, lords, God keep you and see!"
    The one that was most insolent of these three
Replied to him: "What? Churl of evil grace,
Why are you all wrapped up, except your face?
Why do you live so long in so great age?"
    This ancient man looked upon his visage
And thus replied: "Because I cannot find
A man, nay, though I walked from here to Ind
Either in town or country who'll engage
To give his youth in barter for my age;
And therefore must I keep my old age still,
As long a time as it shall be God's will.
Not even Death, alas! my life will take;
Thus restless I my wretched way must make,
And on the ground, which is my mother's gate,
I knock with my staff early, aye, and late,
And cry: 'O my dear mother, let me in!
Lo, how I'm wasted, flesh and blood and skin!
Alas! When shall my bones come to their rest?
Mother, with you fain would I change my chest,
That in my chamber so long time has been,
Aye! For a haircloth rag to wrap me in!'
But yet to me she will not show that grace,
And thus all pale and withered is my face.
    "But, sirs, in you it is no courtesy
To speak to an old man despitefully,

Unless in word he trespass or in deed.
In holy writ you may, yourselves, well read
'Before an old man, hoar upon the head,
You should arise.' Which I advise you read,
Nor to an old man any injury do
More than you would that men should do to you
In age, if you so long time shall abide;
And God be with you, whether you walk or ride.
I must pass on now where I have to go."

   "Nay, ancient churl, by God it sha'n't be so,"
Cried out this other hazarder, anon;
"You sha'n't depart so easily, by Saint John!
You spoke just now of that same traitor Death,
Who in this country stops our good friends' breath.
Hear my true word, since you are his own spy,
Tell where he is or you shall rue it, aye
By God and by the holy Sacrament!
Indeed you must be, with this Death, intent
To slay all us young people, you false thief."

   "Now, sirs," said he, "if you're so keen, in brief,
To find out Death, turn up this crooked way,
For in that grove I left him, by my fay,
Under a tree, and there he will abide;
Nor for your boasts will he a moment hide.
See you that oak? Right there you shall him find.
God save you, Who redeemed all humankind,
And mend your ways!"—thus said this ancient man.

   And every one of these three roisterers ran
Till he came to that tree; and there they found,
Of florins of fine gold, new-minted, round,
Well-nigh eight bushels full, or so they thought.
No longer, then, after this Death they sought,
But each of them so glad was of that sight,
Because the florins were so fair and bright,
That down they all sat by this precious hoard.
The worst of them was first to speak a word.

   "Brothers," said he, "take heed to what I say;
My wits are keen, although I mock and play.
This treasure here Fortune to us has given
That mirth and jollity our lives may liven,

And easily as it's come, so will we spend.
Eh! By God's precious dignity! Who'd pretend,
Today, that we should have so fair a grace?
But might this gold be carried from this place
Home to my house, or if you will, to yours—
For well we know that all this gold is ours—
Then were we all in high felicity.
But certainly by day this may not be;
For men would say that we were robbers strong,
And we'd, for our own treasure, hang ere long.
This treasure must be carried home by night
All prudently and slyly, out of sight.
So I propose that cuts among us all
Be drawn, and let's see where the cut will fall;
And he that gets the short cut, blithe of heart
Shall run to town at once, and to the mart,
And fetch us bread and wine here, privately.
And two of us shall guard, right cunningly,
This treasure well; and if he does not tarry,
When it is night we'll all the treasure carry
Where, by agreement, we may think it best."
   That one of them the cuts brought in his fist
And bade them draw to see where it might fall;
And it fell on the youngest of them all;
And so, forth toward the town he went anon.
And just as soon as he had turned and gone,
That one of them spoke thus unto the other:
   "You know well that you are my own sworn brother,
So to your profit I will speak anon.
You know well how our comrade is just gone;
And here is gold, and that in great plenty,
That's to be parted here among us three.
Nevertheless, if I can shape it so
That it be parted only by us two,
Shall I not do a turn that is friendly?"
   The other said: "Well, now, how can that be?
He knows well that the gold is with us two.
What shall we say to him? What shall we do?"
   "Shall it be secret?" asked the first rogue, then,
"And I will tell you in eight words, or ten,

What we must do, and how bring it about."
"Agreed," replied the other, "Never doubt,
That, on my word, I nothing will betray."
"Now," said the first, "we're two, and I dare say
The two of us are stronger than is one.
Watch when he sits, and soon as that is done
Arise and make as if with him to play;
And I will thrust him through the two sides, yea.
The while you romp with him as in a game,
And with your dagger see you do the same;
And then shall all this gold divided be,
My right dear friend, just between you and me;
Then may we both our every wish fulfill
And play at dice all at our own sweet will."
And thus agreed were these two rogues, that day
To slay the third, as you have heard me say.

This youngest rogue who'd gone into the town,
Often in fancy rolled he up and down
The beauty of those florins new and bright.
"O Lord," thought he, "if so be that I might
Have all this treasure to myself alone,
There is no man who lives beneath the throne
Of God that should be then so merry as I."
And at the last the Fiend, our enemy,
Put in his thought that he should poison buy
With which he might kill both his fellows; aye,
The Devil found him in such wicked state,
He had full leave his grief to consummate;
For it was utterly the man's intent
To kill them both and never to repent.
And on he strode, no longer would he tarry,
Into the town, to an apothecary,
And prayed of him that he'd prepare and sell
Some poison for his rats, and some as well
For a polecat that in his yard had lain,
The which, he said, his capons there had slain,
And fain he was to rid him, if he might,
Of vermin that thus damaged him by night.

The apothecary said: "And you shall have
A thing of which, so God my spirit save,

In all this world there is no live creature
That's eaten or has drunk of this mixture
As much as equals but a grain of wheat,
That shall not sudden death thereafter meet;
Yea, die he shall, and in a shorter while
Than you require to walk but one short mile;
This poison is so violent and strong."

This wicked man the poison took along
With him boxed up, and then he straightway ran
Into the street adjoining, to a man,
And of him borrowed generous bottles three;
And into two his poison then poured he;
The third one he kept clean for his own drink.
For all that night he was resolved to swink
In carrying the florins from that place.
And when this roisterer, with evil grace,
Had filled with wine his mighty bottles three,
Then to his comrades forth again went he.

What is the need to tell about it more?
For just as they had planned his death before,
Just so they murdered him, and that anon.
And when the thing was done, then spoke the one:
"Now let us sit and drink and so be merry,
And afterward we will his body bury."
And as he spoke, one bottle of the three
He took wherein the poison chanced to be
And drank and gave his comrade drink also,
For which, and that anon, lay dead these two.
I feel quite sure that Doctor Avicenna[44]
Within the sections of his *Canon* never
Set down more certain signs of poisoning
Than showed these wretches two at their ending.
Thus ended these two homicides in woe;
Died thus the treacherous poisoner also.

O cursed sin, full of abominableness!
O treacherous homicide! O wickedness!
O gluttony, lechery, and hazardry!

---

[44]Muslim writer on medicine and commentator on Aristotle. His book *Canon of Medicine* was known in the Western medieval world.

O blasphemer of Christ with villainy,
And with great oaths, habitual for pride!
Alas! Mankind, how may this thing betide
That to thy dear Creator, Who thee wrought,
And with His precious blood salvation bought,
Thou art so false and so unkind, alas!
   Now, good men, God forgive you each trespass,
And keep you from the sin of avarice.
My holy pardon cures and will suffice,
So that it brings me gold, or silver brings,
Or else, I care not—brooches, spoons or rings.
Bow down your heads before this holy bull!
Come up, you wives, and offer of your wool!
Your names I'll enter on my roll, anon,
And into Heaven's bliss you'll go, each one.
For I'll absolve you, by my special power,
You that make offering, as clean this hour
As you were born.
               And lo, sirs, thus I preach.
And Jesus Christ, who is our souls' great leech,
So grant you each his pardon to receive;
For that is best; I will not you deceive.
   But, sirs, one word forgot I in my tale;
I've relics in my pouch that cannot fail,
As good as England ever saw, I hope,
The which I got by kindness of the pope.
If gifts your change of heart and mind reveal,
You'll get my absolution while you kneel.
Come forth, and kneel down here before, anon,
And humbly you'll receive my full pardon;
Or else receive a pardon as you wend,
All new and fresh as every mile shall end,
So that you offer me each time, anew,
More gold and silver, all good coins and true.
It is an honour to each one that's here
That you may have a competent pardoner
To give you absolution as you ride,
For all adventures that may still betide.
Perchance from horse may fall down one or two,
Breaking his neck, and it might well be you.

See what insurance, then, it is for all
That I within your fellowship did fall,
Who may absolve you, both the great and less,
When soul from body passes, as I guess.
I think our host might just as well begin,
For he is most enveloped in all sin.
Come forth, sir host, and offer first anon,
And you shall kiss the relics, every one,
Aye, for a groat! Unbuckle now your purse."

   "Nay, nay," said he, "then may I have Christ's curse!
It sha'n't be," said he, "as I've hope for riches,
Why, you would have me kissing your old breeches,
And swear they were the relics of a saint,
Though with your excrement 'twere dabbed like paint.
By cross Saint Helen[45] found in Holy Land,
I would I had your ballocks in my hand
Instead of relics in a reliquary;
Let's cut them off, and them I'll help you carry;
They shall be shrined within a hog's fat turd."

   This pardoner, he answered not a word;
So wrathy was he no word would he say.

   "Now," said our host, "I will no longer play
With you, nor any other angry man."

   But at this point the worthy knight began,
When that he saw how all the folk did laugh:
"No more of this, for it's gone far enough;
Sir pardoner, be glad and merry here;
And you, sir host, who are to me so dear,
I pray you that you kiss the pardoner.
And, pardoner, I pray you to draw near,
And as we did before, let's laugh and play."
And then they kissed and rode forth on their way.

[In keeping with Chaucer's plans to present in *Canterbury Tales* the full range of taste among the different social classes, the popular taste for comic, bawdy stories is represented by the story told about a miller by the Reeve (who, a carpenter, is attempting to get back at the Miller for his comical story about an unfortunate carpenter). The popular tale on which the story is based is

---

[45]Mother of the Emperor Constantine; she was reputed to have found the cross on which Christ was crucified.

enlivened through local color and narrative adroitness; and the Canterbury pilgrims, despite their different social classes, all seem to listen with amusement. *Ed.*]

THE REEVE'S TALE

At Trumpington, not far from Cambridge town,
There is a bridge wherethrough a brook runs down,
Upon the side of which brook stands a mill;
And this is very truth that now I tell.
A miller dwelt there, many and many a day;
As any peacock he was proud and gay.
He could mend nets, and he could fish, and flute,
Drink and turn cups, and wrestle well, and shoot;
And in his leathern belt he did parade
A cutlass with a long and trenchant blade.
A pretty dagger had he in his pouch;
There was no man who durst this man to touch.
A Sheffield whittler[46] bore he in his hose;
Round was his face and turned-up was his nose.
As bald as any ape's head was his skull;
He was a market-swaggerer to the full.
There durst no man a hand on him to lay,
Because he swore he'd make the beggar pay.
A thief he was, forsooth, of corn and meal,
And sly at that, accustomed well to steal.
His name was known as arrogant Simpkin.
A wife he had who came of gentle kin;
The parson of the town her father was.
With her he gave full many a pan of brass,
To insure that Simpkin with his blood ally.
She had been bred up in a nunnery;
For Simpkin would not have a wife, he said,
Save she were educated and a maid
To keep up his estate of yeomanry.
And she was proud and bold as is a pie.[47]
A handsome sight it was to see those two;
On holy days before her he would go

---

[46] An especially keen knife. Sheffield was famous for the manufacture of cutlery.
[47] A magpie, a noisy, chattering bird.

With a broad tippet bound about his head;
And she came after in a skirt of red,
While Simpkin's hose were dyed to match that same.
There durst no man to call her aught but dame;
Nor was there one so hardy, in the way,
As durst flirt with her or attempt to play,
Unless he would be slain by this Simpkin
With cutlass or with knife or with bodkin.[48]
For jealous folk are dangerous, you know,
At least they'd have their wives to think them so.
Besides, because she was a dirty bitch,
She was as high as water in a ditch;
And full of scorn and full of back-biting.
She thought a lady should be quite willing
To greet her for her kin and culture, she
Having been brought up in that nunnery.

A daughter had they got between the two,
Of twenty years, and no more children, no,
Save a boy baby that was six months old;
It lay in cradle and was strong and bold.
This girl right stout and well developed was,
With nose tip-tilted and eyes blue as glass,
With buttocks broad, and round breasts full and high,
But golden was her hair, I will not lie.

The parson of the town, since she was fair,
Was purposeful to make of her his heir,
Both of his chattels and of his estate,
But all this hinged upon a proper mate.
He was resolved that he'd bestow her high
Into some blood of worthy ancestry;
For Holy Church's goods must be expended
On Holy Church's blood, as it's descended.
Therefore he'd honour thus his holy blood,
Though Holy Church itself became his food.

Large tolls this miller took, beyond a doubt,[49]
With wheat and malt from all the lands about;
Of which I'd specify among them all

---

[48]Small dagger.
[49]In folklore, millers were notorious for stealing from customers.

A Cambridge college known as Soler Hall;
He ground their wheat and all their malt he ground.
    And on a day it happened, as they found,
The manciple[50] got such a malady
That all men surely thought that he should die.
Whereon this miller stole both flour and wheat
A hundredfold more than he used to cheat;
For theretofore he stole but cautiously,
But now he was a thief outrageously,
At which the warden scolded and raised hell;
The miller snapped his fingers, truth to tell,
And cracked his brags and swore it wasn't so.
    There were two poor young clerks, whose names I know,
That dwelt within this Hall whereof I say.
Willful they were and lusty, full of play,
And (all for mirth and to make revelry)
After the warden eagerly did they cry
To give them leave, at least for this one round,
To go to mill and see their produce ground;
And stoutly they proclaimed they'd bet their neck
The miller should not steal one half a peck
Of grain, by trick, nor yet by force should thieve;
And at the last the warden gave them leave.
John was the one and Alain was that other;
In one town were they born, and that called Strother,
Far in the north, I cannot tell you where.
    This Alain, he made ready all his gear,
And on a horse loaded the sack anon.
Forth went Alain the clerk, and also John,
With good sword and with buckler at their side.
John knew the way and didn't need a guide,
And at the mill he dropped the sack of grain.
"Ah, Simon, hail, good morn," first spoke Alain.
"How fares it with your fair daughter and wife?"
    "Alain! Welcome," said Simpkin, "by my life,
And John also. How now? What do you here?"
    "Simon," said John, "by God, need makes no peer;[51]

---

[50]Steward or purchasing agent.
[51]"Necessity knows no law."

He must himself serve who's no servant, eh?
Or else he's but a fool, as all clerks say.
Our manciple—I hope he'll soon be dead,
So aching are the grinders in his head—
And therefore am I come here with Alain
To grind our corn and carry it home again;
I pray you speed us thither, as you may."
    "It shall be done," said Simpkin, "by my fay.
What will you do the while it is in hand?"
    "By God, right by the hopper will I stand,"
Said John, "and see just how the corn goes in;
I never have seen, by my father's kin,
Just how the hopper waggles to and fro."
    Alain replied: "Well, John, and will you so?
Then will I get beneath it, by my crown,
To see there how the meal comes sifting down
Into the trough; and that shall be my sport.
For, John, in faith, I must be of your sort;
I am as bad a miller as you be."
    The miller smiled at this, their delicacy,
And thought: "All this is done but for a wile;
They think there is no man may them beguile;
But, by my thrift, I will yet blear their eyes,
For all the tricks in their philosophies.
The more odd tricks and stratagems they make,
The more I'll steal when I begin to take.
In place of flour I'll give them only bran.
'The greatest clerk is not the wisest man,'
As once unto the grey wolf said the mare.[52]
But all their arts—I rate them not a tare."
    Out of the door he went, then, secretly,
When he had seen his chance, and quietly;
He looked up and looked down, until he found
The clerks' horse where it stood, securely bound,
Behind the mill, under an arbour green;
And to the horse he went, then, all unseen;
He took the bridle off him and anon,

---

[52]A folk story told of a wolf who wanted to buy a mare's foal. The mare said that the price was written on her hind hoof. When the wolf tried to read it, he was kicked senseless.

When the said horse was free, why he was gone
Toward the fen, for wild mares ran therein,
And with a neigh he went, through thick and thin.
    This miller straight went back and no word said,
But did his business and with these clerks played,
Until their corn was fairly, fully ground.
But when the flour was sacked and the ears bound,
This John went out, to find his horse away,
And so he cried: "Hello!" and "Weladay!
Our horse is lost! Alain, for Jesus' bones
Get to your feet, come out, man, now, at once!
Alas, our warden's palfrey's lost and lorn!"
    This Alain forgot all, both flour and corn,
Clean out of mind was all his husbandry,
"What? Which way did he go?" began to cry.
    The wife came bounding from the house, and then
She said: "Alas! Your horse went to the fen,
With the wild mares, as fast as he could go.
A curse light on the hand that tied him so,
And him that better should have knotted rein!"
    "Alas!" quoth John, "Alain, for Jesus' pain,
Lay off your sword, and I will mine also;
I am as fleet, God knows, as is a roe;
By God's heart, he shall not escape us both!
Why didn't you put him in the barn? My oath!
Bad luck, by God, Alain, you are a fool!"
    These foolish clerks began to run and roll
Toward the marshes, both Alain and John.
    And when the miller saw that they were gone,
He half a bushel of their flour did take
And bade his wife go knead it and bread make.
He said: "I think those clerks some trickery feared;
Yet can a miller match a clerkling's beard,
For all his learning; let them go their way.
Look where they go, yea, let the children play,
They'll catch him not so readily, by my crown!"
    Those simple clerks went running up and down
With "Look out! Halt! Halt! Down here! 'Ware the rear!
Go whistle, you, and I will watch him here!"
But briefly, till it came to utter night,

They could not, though they put forth all their might,
That stallion catch, he always ran so fast,
Till in a ditch they trapped him at the last.

    Weary and wet, as beast is in the rain,
Came foolish John and with him came Alain.
"Alas," said John, "the day that I was born!
Now are we bound toward mockery and scorn.
Our corn is stolen, folk will call us fools,
The warden and the fellows at the schools,
And specially this miller. Weladay!"

    Thus John complained as he went on his way
Toward the mill, with Bayard[53] once more bound.
The miller sitting by the fire he found,
For it was night, and farther could they not;
But, for the love of God, they him besought
For shelter and for supper, for their penny.

    The miller said to them: "If there be any,
Such as it is, why you shall have your part.
My house is small, but you have learned your art;
You can, by metaphysics, make a place
A full mile wide in twenty feet of space.
Let us see now if this place will suffice,
Or make more room with speech, by some device."

    "Now, Simon," said John, "by Saint Cuthbert's beard,
You're always merry and have well answered.
As I've heard, man shall take one of two things:
Such as he finds, or take such as he brings.
But specially, I pray you, mine host dear,
Give us some meat and drink and some good cheer,
And we will pay you, truly, to the full.
With empty hand no man takes hawk or gull;
Well, here's our silver, ready to be spent."

    This miller to the town his daughter sent
For ale and bread, and roasted them a goose,
And tied their horse, that it might not go loose;
And then in his own chamber made a bed,
With sheets and with good blankets fairly spread,
Not from his bed more than twelve feet, or ten.

---

[53]A common name for a horse.

The daughter made her lone bed near the men,
In the same chamber with them, by and by;
It could not well be bettered, and for why?
There was no larger room in all the place.
They supped and talked, and gained some small solace,
And drank strong ale, that evening, of the best.
Then about midnight all they went to rest.

Well had this miller varnished his bald head,
For pale he was with drinking, and not red.
He hiccoughed and he mumbled through his nose,
As he were chilled, with humours lachrymose.
To bed he went, and with him went his wife.
As any jay she was with laughter rife,
So copiously was her gay whistle wet.
The cradle near her bed's foot-board was set,
Handy for rocking and for giving suck.
And when they'd drunk up all there was in crock,
To bed went miller's daughter, and anon
To bed went Alain and to bed went John.
There was no more; they did not need a dwale.[54]
This miller had so roundly bibbed his ale
That, like a horse, he snorted in his sleep,
While of his tail behind he kept no keep.
His wife joined in his chorus, and so strong,
Men might have heard her snores a full furlong;
And the girl snored, as well, for company.

Alain the clerk, who heard this melody,
He poked at John and said: "Asleep? But how?
Did you hear ever such a song ere now?
Lo, what a compline is among them all!
Now may the wild-fire on their bodies fall!
Who ever heard so outlandish a thing?
But they shall have the flour of ill ending.
Through this long night there'll be for me no rest;
But never mind, 'twill all be for the best.
For, John," said he, "so may I ever thrive,
As, if I can, that very wench I'll swive.
Some recompense the law allows to us;

---

[54]A drink to put them to sleep.

For, John, there is a statute which says thus,
That if a man in one point be aggrieved,
Yet in another shall he be relieved.
Our corn is stolen, to that there's no nay,
And we have had an evil time this day.
But since I may not have amending, now,
Against my loss I'll set some fun—and how!
By God's great soul it shan't be otherwise!"
    ˙ This John replied: "Alain, let me advise.
The miller is a dangerous man," he said,
"And if he be awakened, I'm afraid
He may well do us both an injury."
    But Alain said: "I count him not a fly."
And up he rose and to the girl he crept.
This wench lay on her back and soundly slept,
Until he'd come so near, ere she might spy,
It was too late to struggle, then, or cry;
And, to be brief, these two were soon as one.
Now play, Alain! For I will speak of John.
    This John lay still a quarter-hour, or so,
Pitied himself and wept for all his woe.
"Alas," said he, "this is a wicked jape!
Now may I say that I am but an ape.
Yet has my friend, there, something for his harm;
He has the miller's daughter on his arm.
He ventured, and his pains are now all fled,
While I lie like a sack of chaff in bed;
And when this jape is told, another day,
I shall be held an ass, a milksop yea!
I will arise and chance it, by my fay!
'Unhardy is unhappy,' as they say."
    And up he rose, and softly then he went
To find the cradle for expedient,
And bore it over to his own foot-board.
    Soon after this the wife no longer snored,
But woke and rose and went outside to piss,
And came again and did the cradle miss,
And groped round, here and there, but found it not.
"Alas!" thought she, "my way I have forgot.
I nearly found myself in the clerks' bed.

Eh, *ben'cite*, [55] but that were wrong!" she said.
And on, until by cradle she did stand.
And, groping a bit farther with her hand,
She found the bed, and thought of naught but good,
Because her baby's cradle by it stood,
And knew not where she was, for it was dark;
But calmly then she crept in by the clerk,
And lay right still, and would have gone to sleep.
But presently this John the clerk did leap,
And over on this goodwife did he lie.
No such gay time she'd known in years gone by.
He pricked her hard and deep, like one gone mad.
And so a jolly life these two clerks had
Till the third cock began to crow and sing.
      Alain grew weary in the grey dawning,
For he had laboured hard through all the night;
And said: "Farewell, now, Maudy, sweet delight!
The day is come, I may no longer bide;
But evermore, whether I walk or ride,
I am your own clerk, so may I have weal."
      "Now, sweetheart," said she, "go and fare you well!
But ere you go, there's one thing I must tell.
When you go walking homeward past the mill,
Right at the entrance, just the door behind,
You shall a loaf of half a bushel find
That was baked up of your own flour, a deal
Of which I helped my father for to steal.
And, darling, may God save you now and keep!"
And with that word she almost had to weep.
      Alain arose and thought: "Ere it be dawn,
I will go creep in softly by friend John."
And found the cradle with his hand, anon.
"By God!" thought he, "all wrong I must have gone;
My head is dizzy from my work tonight,
And that's why I have failed to go aright.
I know well, by this cradle, I am wrong,
For here the miller and his wife belong."
And on he went, and on the devil's way,

[55]"God bless [me]."

Unto the bed wherein the miller lay.
He thought to have crept in by comrade John,
So, to the miller, in he got anon,
And caught him round the neck, and softly spake,
Saying: "You, John, you old swine's head, awake,
For Christ's own soul, and hear a noble work,
For by Saint James, and as I am a clerk,
I have, three times in this short night, no lack,
Swived that old miller's daughter on her back,
While you, like any coward, were aghast."
  "You scoundrel," cried the miller, "you trespassed?
Ah, traitor false and treacherous clerk!" cried he,
"You shall be killed, by God's own dignity!
Who dares be bold enough to bring to shame
My daughter, who is born of such a name?"
  And by the gullet, then, he caught Alain.
And pitilessly he handled him amain,
And on the nose he smote him with his fist.
Down ran the bloody stream upon his breast;
And on the floor, with nose and mouth a-soak,
They wallowed as two pigs do in a poke.
And up they came, and down they both went, prone,
Until the miller stumbled on a stone,
And reeled and fell down backwards on his wife,
Who nothing knew of all this silly strife;
For she had fallen into slumber tight
With John the clerk, who'd been awake all night.
But at the fall, from sleep she started out.
"Help, holy Cross of Bromholm!"[56] did she shout,
"In *manus tuas*,[57] Lord, to Thee I call!
Simon, awake, the Fiend is on us all!
My heart is broken, help, I am but dead!
There lies one on my womb, one on my head!
Help, Simpkin, for these treacherous clerks do fight!"
  John started up, as fast as well he might,
And searched along the wall, and to and fro,

---

[56]A relic believed to be a piece of the cross on which Christ was crucified. It was kept at Bromholm, in the east of England.
[57]"Into thy hands."

To find a staff; and she arose also,
And knowing the room better than did John,
She found a staff against the wall, anon;
And then she saw a little ray of light,
For through a hole the moon was shining bright;
And by that light she saw the struggling two,
But certainly she knew not who was who,
Except she saw a white thing with her eye.
And when she did this same white thing espy,
She thought the clerk had worn a nightcap here.
And with the staff she nearer drew, and near,
And, thinking to hit Alain on his poll,
She fetched the miller on his bald white skull,
And down he went, crying out, "Help, help, I die!"
The two clerks beat him well and let him lie;
And clothed themselves, and took their horse anon.
And got their flour, and on their way were gone.
And at the mill they found the well-made cake
Which of their meal the miller's wife did bake.

 Thus is the haughty miller soundly beat,
And thus he's lost his pay for grinding wheat,
And paid for the two suppers, let me tell,
Of Alain and of John, who've tricked him well,
His wife is taken, also his daughter sweet;
Thus it befalls a miller who's a cheat.
And therefore is this proverb said with truth,
"An evil end to evil man, forsooth."
The cheater shall himself well cheated be.
And God, Who sits on high in majesty,
Save all this company, both strong and frail!
Thus have I paid this miller with my tale.

14

Everyman

*M*EDIEVAL *drama was originally an addition to the Church's liturgy for some special day's observance, such as the Easter service when the clergy might reenact the scene at the tomb; gradually, however, it became an independent form. Although separate from the rituals of the Church, drama continued throughout the Middle Ages to be exclusively religious. In many towns, especially in England, plays were entrusted to the care of guilds. Presented on wagon stages rolled from place to place in the streets during the celebrations of the great Church festivals, the plays often took the form of a sequence of scenes illustrating biblical narratives: the Creation, the Flood (given, naturally, by the carpenters guild; after all, who would be better skilled at building the ark?), the Nativity, and so on. They came to include some secular matter, as, for instance, the comic interludes of the* Shepherds Play, *in which the rustic clowning of the shepherds and a thieving cottager accompany the story of the Nativity.*

The fifteenth century witnessed the full flowering of medieval drama. Audiences in streets and innyards could enjoy not only dramatizations of biblical stories, but plays telling of other miraculous incidents in the lives of the saints. Strolling companies of professionals also put on "morality plays," in which such personified abstractions as Faith, Hope, and Charity contested with World, Flesh, and Devil for the human soul. This view of the world as a testing place, where one learns through suffering how to follow the path of salvation, was congenial to the medieval mind. In the play Everyman, *originally Dutch but translated and produced in several English versions before the close of the fifteenth century, we find in simple but moving terms the universal experience of mankind encountering death and divine judgment. The following translation preserves, for the most part, the word order and erratic rhyme pattern of the original. The spelling, however, has been modernized.*

Dramatis Personae

GOD	GOODS	STRENGTH
DEATH	GOOD-DEEDS	DISCRETION
EVERYMAN	KNOWLEDGE	FIVE WITS
FELLOWSHIP	CONFESSION	ANGEL
KINDRED	BEAUTY	DOCTOR

GOD SPEAKS

GOD.   I perceive here in my majesty,
        How that all creatures be to me unkind,
        Living without dread in worldly prosperity:
        Of spiritual sight the people be so blind,
        Drowned in sin, they know me not for their God;
        In worldly riches is all their mind,
        They fear not my righteousness, the sharp rod;
        My love that I showed when I for them died
        They forget clean, and shedding of my blood red;
        I hanged between two it cannot be denied;
        To give them life I suffered to be dead;
        I healed their feet, with thorns hurt was my head;
        I could do no more than I did truly,
        And now I see the people do clean forsake me:
        They use the seven deadly sins damnable,
        As pride, covetousness, wrath and lechery,
        Now in the world be made commendable:
        And thus they leave of angels the heavenly company,
        Every man liveth so after his own pleasure,
        And yet of their life they be nothing sure:
        I see the more than I them forbear
        The worse they be from year to year;
        All that liveth decayeth fast,
        Therefore I will in all the haste
        Have a reckoning of every man's person;
        For, if I leave the people thus alone
        In their life and wicked tempests,
        Verily they will become much worse than beasts:

EVERYMAN *Everyman*, in *Dodsley's Old Plays*, ed. W. C. Hazlitt (London: Reeves & Turner, 1874), I, 100–42. (This is an adaptation.)

For now one would by envy another up eat;
Charity they do all clean forget:
I hoped well that every man
In my glory should make his mansion,
And thereto I had them all elect;
But now I see, like traitors deject,
They thank me not for the pleasure that I to them meant,
Nor yet for their being that I them have lent:
I proffered the people great multitude of mercy,
And few there be that asketh it heartily;
They be so encumbered with worldly riches,
That needs on them I must do justice,
On every man living without fear.—
Where art thou, Death, thou mighty messenger?

DEATH.   Almighty God, I am here at your will,
Your commandment to fulfill.

GOD.   Go thou to Everyman,
And show him in my name,
A pilgrimage he must on him take,
Which he in nowise may escape;
And that he bring with him a sure reckoning,
Without delay or any tarrying.

DEATH.   Lord, I will in the world go run over all,
And cruelly out search both great and small;
Every man will I beset that liveth beastly,
Out of God's laws, and dreadeth not folly:
He that loveth riches I will strike with my dart
His sight to blind, and from heaven to depart,
Except that alms be his good friend,
In hell for to dwell world without end.
Lo, yonder I see Everyman walking:
Full little he thinketh on my coming;
His mind is on fleshly lusts, and his treasure;
And great pain it shall cause him to endure
Before the Lord heaven king.—
Everyman, stand still: whither art thou going
Thus gayly? hast thou thy maker forgot?

EVERYMAN.   Why asketh thou?
Wouldst thou know?

DEATH.   Yes, sir, I will show you;

In great haste I am sent to thee
From God out of his majesty.
EVERYMAN.   What, sent to me!
DEATH.   Yes, certainly:
   Though thou hast forgot him here,
   He thinketh on thee in the heavenly sphere;
   As, ere we depart, thou shalt know.
EVERYMAN.   What desireth God of me?
DEATH.   That shall I show thee;
   A reckoning he will needs have
   Without any longer respite.

             • • •

EVERYMAN.   Full unready I am such reckoning to give:
   I know thee not; what messenger art thou?
DEATH.   I am Death, that no man dreadeth;
   For every man I rest, and no man spareth,
   For it is God's commandment
   That all to me should be obedient.
EVERYMAN.   O Death, thou comest when I had thee least in mind:
   In thy power it lieth me to save;
   Yet of my good will I give thee, if thou will be kind,
   Yea, a thousand pounds shalt thou have.
   And defer this matter till another day.
DEATH.   Everyman, it may not be by no way;
   I set not by gold, silver nor riches,
   Nor by pope, emperor, king, duke nor princes;
   For, if I would receive gifts great,
   All the world I might get;
   But my custom is clean contrary:
   I give thee no respite, come hence, and not tarry.
EVERYMAN.   Alas, shall I have no longer respite?
   I may say, Death giveth no warning:
   To think on thee it maketh my heart sick;
   For all unready is my book of reckoning:
   But twelve years if I might have abiding,
   My accounting book I would make so clear
   That my reckoning I should not need to fear.
   Wherefore, Death, I pray thee for God's mercy,
   Spare me till I be provided of remedy.

DEATH.   Thee availeth not to cry, weep and pray:
　　　　But haste thee lightly that thou were going this journey:
　　　　And prove thy friends if thou can;
　　　　For, know thou well, the tide abideth no man,
　　　　And in the world each living creature
　　　　For Adam's sin must die of nature.
EVERYMAN.   Death, if I should this pilgrimage take,
　　　　And my reckoning surely make,
　　　　Show me, for Saint Charity,[1]
　　　　Should I not come again shortly?
DEATH.   No, Everyman, if thou be once there,
　　　　Thou mayst never more come here,
　　　　Trust me verily.
EVERYMAN.   O gracious God, in the high seat celestial,
　　　　Have mercy on me in this most need.—
　　　　Shall I have no company from this vale terrestrial
　　　　Of mine acquaintance that way me to lead?
DEATH.   Yea, if any be so hardy,
　　　　That would go with thee, and bear thee company:
　　　　Hie thee that thou were gone to God's magnificence,
　　　　Thy reckoning to give before his presence.
　　　　What, thinkest thou thy life is given thee,
　　　　And thy worldly goods also?
EVERYMAN.   I had thought so, verily.
DEATH.   Nay, nay; it was but lent thee,
　　　　For as soon as thou art gone,
　　　　Another awhile shall have it, and then go therefrom,
　　　　Even as thou hast done.
　　　　Everyman, thou art mad! Thou hast thy wits five;
　　　　And here on earth will not amend thy life;
　　　　For suddenly I do come.
EVERYMAN.   O wretched caitiff, whither shall I flee,
　　　　That I might escape this endless sorrow!—
　　　　Now, gentle Death, spare me till to-morrow,
　　　　That I may amend me
　　　　With good advisement.
DEATH.   Nay, thereto I will not consent,
　　　　Nor no man will I respite;

---

[1]A way of saying "Blessed Charity."

But to the heart suddenly I shall smite
Without any advisement.
And now out of thy sight I will me hie;
See thou make thee ready shortly,
For thou mayst say, this is the day
That no man living may escape away.

EVERYMAN.   Alas! I may well weep with sighs deep:
Nor have I no manner of company
To help me in my journey, and me to keep;
And also my writing is full unready.
How shall I do now for to excuse me!

. . .

To whom were I best my complaint to make?
What, if I to Fellowship thereof spake,
And showed him of this sudden chance!
For in him is all my reliance;
We have in the world so many a day
Been good friends in sport and play.
I see him yonder, certainly;
I trust that he will bear me company,
Therefore to him will I speak to ease my sorrow.
Well met, good Fellowship; and good-morrow.

FELLOWSHIP.   Everyman, good-morrow by this day:
Sir, why lookest thou so piteously?
If anything be amiss, I pray thee, me say,
That I may help to remedy.

. . .

EVERYMAN.   Then be you a good friend at need;
I have found you true here before.

FELLOWSHIP.   And so ye shall evermore;
For, in faith, if thou go to hell,
I will not forsake thee by the way.

EVERYMAN.   Ye speak like a good friend, I believe you well;
I shall deserve it if I may.

FELLOWSHIP.   I speak of no deserving, by this day;
For he that will say and nothing do,
Is not worthy with good company to go:

Therefore show me the grief of your mind,
As to your friend most lovingly and kind.
EVERYMAN.   I shall show you how it is
  Commanded, I am to go a journey,
  A long way, hard and dangerous;
  And give a straight account without delay
  Before the high judge Adonai:[2]
  Wherefore I pray you, bear me company,
  As ye have promised, in this journey.
FELLOWSHIP.   That is matter, indeed; promise is duty,
  But if I should take such a voyage on me,
  I know it well it should be to my pain:
  Also it makes me afraid certain.
  But let us take counsel here as well as we can,
  For your words would fear a strong man.
EVERYMAN.   Why, ye said—if I had need,
  Ye would me never forsake quick indeed,
  Though it were to hell truly.
FELLOWSHIP.   So I said, certainly;
  But such pleasures be set aside, the sooth to say,
  And also if we took such a journey,
  When should we come again?
EVERYMAN.   Nay, never again till the day of doom.
FELLOWSHIP.   In faith, then will not I come there:
  Who hath you these tidings brought?
EVERYMAN.   Indeed, Death was with me here.
FELLOWSHIP.   Now, by God that all hath bought,
  If Death were the messenger,
  For no man that is living to-day
  I will not go that loath journey,
  Not for the father that begat me.
EVERYMAN.   Ye promised otherwise, pardy.[3]
FELLOWSHIP.   I know well I said so truly,
  And yet if thou wilt eat and drink, and make good cheer,
  Or haunt to women the lusty company,
  I would not forsake you while the day is clear,
  Trust me verily.

---

[2] A name for God often used in the Old Testament.
[3] Indeed, in truth.

EVERYMAN.   Yea, thereto ye would be ready:
    To go to mirth, solace and play.
    Your mind will sooner apply
    Than to bear me company in my long journey.
FELLOWSHIP.   Now, in good faith, I will not that way;
    But if thou will murder, or any man kill,
    In that I will help thee with a good-will.

• • •

EVERYMAN.   Whither away, Fellowship? will you forsake me?
FELLOWSHIP.   Yes, by my say; to God I betake thee.
EVERYMAN.   Farewell, good Fellowship; for this my heart is sore:
    Adieu forever, I shall see thee no more.
FELLOWSHIP.   In faith, Everyman, farewell now at the end;
    For you I will remember that parting is mourning.
EVERYMAN.   Alack! shall we thus depart, indeed?
    Aye! Lady, help, without any more comfort,
    Lo, Fellowship forsaketh me in my most need:
    For help in this world whither shall I resort?
    Fellowship here before with me would merry make;
    And now little sorrow for me doth he take.
    It is said, in prosperity men friends may find,
    Which in adversity be full unkind.
    Now, whither for succor shall I flee,
    Since that Fellowship hath forsaken me?
    To my kinsmen I will truly,
    Praying them to help me in my necessity;
    I believe that they will do so;
    For kind will creep where it may not go.
    I will go say; for yonder I see them go:—
    Where be ye now, my friends and kinsmen?
KINDRED.   Here be we now at your commandment:
    Cousin, I pray you, show us your intent
    In any wise, and not spare.

• • •

EVERYMAN.   Gramercy,[4] my friends and kinsmen kind;
    Now shall I show you the grief of my mind.

[4]Equivalent to "many thanks."

I was commanded by a messenger,
That is a high king's chief officer;
He bade me go a pilgrimage to my pain,
And, I know well, I shall never come again:
Also I must give a reckoning straight;
For I have a great enemy that hath me in wait,
Which intendeth me for to hinder.

KINDRED.   What account is that which we must render?
That would I know.

EVERYMAN.   Of all my works I must show,
How I have lived, and my days spent;
Also of ill deeds that I have used
In my time this life was me lent,
And of all virtues that I have refused:
Therefore I pray you, go thither with me
To help to make my account, for Saint Charity.

KINDRED.   What, to go thither? Is that the matter?
Nay, Everyman, I had rather fast on bread and water,
All this five year and more.

EVERYMAN.   Alas, that ever I was born!
For now shall I never be merry,
If that you forsake me.

KINDRED.   Aye, sir; what, ye be a merry man:
Take good heart to you, and make no moan.
But one thing I warn you, by Saint Ann,
As for me ye shall go alone.

EVERYMAN.   My Kindred, will you not with me go?

KINDRED.   No, by our Lady, I have the cramp in my toe:
Trust not to me; for, so God me speed,
I will deceive you in your most need.

• • •

EVERYMAN.   Aye, Jesus, is all come here to?
Lo, fair words maketh fools vain;
They promise, and nothing will do certain.
My kinsmen promised me faithfully
For to abide with me steadfastly;
And now fast away do they flee:
Even so Fellowship promised me.
What friend were best for me to provide?

I lose my time here longer to abide;
Yet in my mind a thing there is,—
All my life I have loved riches;
If that my good now help me might,
He would make my heart full light:
I will speak to him in this distress.—
Where art thou, my Goods and Riches?
GOODS.   Who calleth me? Everyman? what, hast thou haste?
I lie here in corners trussed and piled so high,
And in chests I am locked so fast,
Also sacked in bags, thou mayst see with thine eye,
I cannot stir; in packs low I lie:
What would ye have, lightly me say?
EVERYMAN.   Come hither, Good, in all the haste thou may;
For of counsel I must desire thee.
GOODS.   Sir, if ye in the world have sorrow or adversity,
That can I help you to remedy shortly.
EVERYMAN.   It is another disease that grieveth me;
In this world it is not, I tell thee so,
I am sent for another way to go,
To give a straight account general
Before the highest Jupiter[5] of all:
And all my life I have had joy and pleasure in thee,
Therefore I pray thee go with me;
For, peradventure, thou mayst before God Almighty
My reckoning help to clean and purify,
For it is said ever among
That money maketh all right that is wrong.
GOODS.   Nay, Everyman, I sing another song;
I follow no man on such voyages,
For, if I went with thee,
Thou should fare much the worse for me:
For because on me thou did set thy mind,
Thy reckoning I have made blotted and blind,
That thine account thou cannot make truly;
And that hast thou for the love of me.
EVERYMAN.   That would grieve me full sore,
When I should come to that fearful answer:
Up, let us go thither together.

[5]Not the Roman god but God, the one god and judge of all.

GOODS.   Nay, not so; I am too brittle, I may not endure:
   I will follow no man one foot be ye sure.
EVERYMAN.   Alas, I have thee loved, and had great pleasure
   All my life days on good and treasure.
GOODS.   That is to thy damnation without lessening,
   For my love is contrary to the love everlasting;
   But if thou had me loved moderately during,
   As, to the poor give part of me,
   Then shouldst thou not in this dolor be,
   Nor in this great sorrow and care.
EVERYMAN.   Lo, now was I deceived ere I was aware,
   And all I suppose was misspending of time.
GOODS.   What, thinkest thou that I am thine?
EVERYMAN.   I had thought so.
GOODS.   Nay, Everyman, I say no:
   As for a while I was lent thee;
   A season thou hast had me in prosperity;
   My condition is man's soul to kill,
   If I save one, a thousand I do spill:
   Believest thou that I will follow thee?
   Nay, from this world not verily.
EVERYMAN.   I had believed otherwise.
GOODS.   Therefore to thy soul Good is a thief,
   For when thou art dead, this is my guise,
   Another to deceive in this same wise,
   As I have done thee, and all to his soul's reprieve.
EVERYMAN.   O false Good, cursed thou be,
   Thou traitor to God that has deceived me,
   And caught me in thy snare.
GOODS.   Mary, thou brought thyself in care,
   Whereof I am glad,
   I must needs laugh, I cannot be sad.
EVERYMAN.   Aye, Good, thou hast had long my hearty love;
   I gave thee that which should be the Lord's above:
   But wilt thou not go with me, indeed?
   I pray thee truth to say.
GOODS.   No, so God me speed;
   Therefore farewell, and have good-day.
EVERYMAN.   O, to whom shall I make my moan!

• • •

Of whom shall I now counsel take?
I think that I shall never speed
Till that I go to my Good-deed;
But, alas! she is so weak
That she can neither go nor speak:
Yet will I venture on her now.—
My Good-deeds, where be you?

GOOD-DEEDS.   Here I lie, cold in the ground;
Thy sins hath me so bound,
That I cannot stir.

EVERYMAN.   O Good-deeds, I stand in fear;
I must you pray of counsel,
For help now should come right well.

GOOD-DEEDS.   Everyman, I have understanding,
That ye be summoned an account to make
Before Messias[6] of Jerusalem king,
And you do wish that journey with you will I take.

EVERYMAN.   Therefore I come to you my moan to make:
I pray you, that ye will go with me.

GOOD-DEEDS.   I would full fain, but I can not stand verily.

EVERYMAN.   Why, has there anything on you fall?

GOOD-DEEDS.   Yes, sir, I may thank you of all;
If ye had perfectly cheered me,
Your book of count full ready had been.
Look, the books of your works and deeds eke;
Aye, see how they lie under the feet,
To your soul's heaviness.

EVERYMAN.   Our Lord Jesus help me,
For one letter here I cannot see.

GOOD-DEEDS.   There is a blind reckoning in time of distress.

EVERYMAN.   Good-deeds, I pray you, help me in this need,
Or else I am forever damned, indeed;
Therefore help me to make reckoning
Before the Redeemer of all things,
That king is, and was, and ever shall.

GOOD-DEEDS.   Everyman, I am sorry for your fall,
And fain would I help you if I were able.

EVERYMAN.   Good-deeds, your counsel I pray you give me.

GOOD-DEEDS.   That shall I do verily:

[6]Christ.

Though that on my feet I may not go,
I have a sister that shall with you also,
Called Knowledge, which shall with you abide,
To help you make that dreadful reckoning.

KNOWLEDGE.   Everyman, I will go with thee, and be thy guide,
In thy most need to go by thy side.

EVERYMAN.   In good condition I am now in everything,
And am whole content with this good thing,
Thanked be God my creator.

GOOD-DEEDS.   And when he hath brought you there,
Where thou shalt heal thee of thy smart,
Then go you with your reckoning and your good deeds
together,
For to make you joyful at heart
Before the blessed Trinity.

EVERYMAN.   My Good-deeds, gramercy;
I am well content certainly
With your words sweet.

KNOWLEDGE.   Now go we together lovingly
To Confession, that cleansing river.

EVERYMAN.   For joy I weep: I would we were there;
But, I pray you, give me perception,
Where dwelleth that holy man Confession?

KNOWLEDGE.   In the house of salvation;
We shall find him in that place,
That shall us comfort by God's grace.—
Lo, this is Confession: kneel down, and ask mercy;
For he is in good conceit[7] with God Almighty.

EVERYMAN.   O glorious fountain that all uncleanliness doth clarify,
Wash from me the spots of vice unclean,
That on me no sin may be seen;
I come with Knowledge for my redemption,
Redempt with heart and full contrition,
For I am commanded a pilgrimage to take,
And great accounts before God to make.
Now I pray you, Shrift,[8] mother of salvation,
Help my good deeds for my piteous exclamation.

---

[7]Favor.
[8]Absolution, forgiveness of sin.

CONFESSION.   I know your sorrows well, Everyman:
    Because with Knowledge ye come to me,
    I will you comfort as well as I can;
    And a precious jewel I will give thee,
    Called penance, voider of adversity:
    Therewith shall your body chastised be
    With abstinence and perseverance in God's service;
    Here shall you receive that scourge of me,
    Which is penance strong that ye must endure,
    To remember thy Saviour was scourged for thee
    With sharp scourges, and suffered it patiently:
    So must thou, ere thou escape that painful pilgrimage.—
    Knowledge, keep him in this voyage,
    And by that time Good-deeds will be with thee;
    But in any wise be seeker of mercy,
    For your time draweth fast; if ye will saved be,
    Ask God mercy and he will grant truly:
    When with the scourge of penance man doth him bind,
    The oil of forgiveness then shall he find.
EVERYMAN.   Thanked be God for his gracious work;
    For now I will my penance begin:
    This hath rejoiced and lighted my heart,
    Though the knots be painful and hard within.
KNOWLEDGE.   Everyman, look your penance that ye fulfill,
    What pain that ever it to you be;
    And Knowledge shall give you counsel at will,
    How your account ye shall make clearly.
EVERYMAN.   O eternal God, O heavenly figure,
    O way of righteousness, O goodly vision,
    Which descended down in a virgin pure
    Because he would Everyman redeem,
    Which Adam forfeited by his disobedience,
    O blessed Godhead elect and high divine,
    Forgive my grievous offence;
    Here I cry thee mercy in this presence:
    O ghostly treasure, O ransomer and redeemer
    Of all the world, hope and conductor,
    Mirror of joy, foundator of mercy,
    Which illumineth heaven and earth thereby,
    Hear my clamorous complaint, though it late be,

Receive my prayers; unworthy in this heavy life
Though I be, a sinner most abominable,
Yet let my name be written in Moses' table.—[9]
O Mary, pray to the maker of all things
Me for to help at my ending.
And save me from the power of my enemy;
For Death assaileth me strongly:
And, Lady, that I may by means of thy prayer
Of your son's glory be a partner,
By the means of his passion, I it crave;
I beseech you, help my soul to save.—
Knowledge, give me the scourge of penance,
My flesh therewith shall give acquaintance;
I will now begin, if God give me grace.

KNOWLEDGE.   Everyman, God give you time and space:
Thus I bequeath you in the hands of our Saviour;
Now may you make your reckoning sure.

EVERYMAN.   In the name of the holy Trinity,
My body sore punished shall be,
Take this body for the sin of the flesh;
Also thou delightest to go gay and fresh;
And in the way of damnation thou did me bring,
Therefore suffer now strokes of punishing:
Now of penance I will wade the water clear,
To save me from purgatory that sharp fire.

GOOD-DEEDS.   I thank God, now I can walk and go,
And am delivered of my sickness and woe;
Therefore with Everyman I will go, and not spare,
His good works I will help him to declare.

KNOWLEDGE.   Now, Everyman, be merry and glad;
Your Good-deeds cometh now, ye may not be sad:
Now is your Good-deeds whole and sound,
Going upright upon the ground.

EVERYMAN.   My heart is light, and shall be evermore;
Now will I smite faster than I did before.

GOOD-DEEDS.   Everyman, pilgrim, my special friend,
Blessed be thou without end;
For thee is prepared the eternal glory:

[9]The list of the saved or redeemed.

Ye have me made whole and sound,
Therefore I will abide by thee in every stound.[10]

EVERYMAN.   Welcome, my Good-deeds, now I hear thy voice
I weep for very sweetness of love.

KNOWLEDGE.   Be no more sad, but ever rejoice,
God seeth thy living in his throne above;
Put on this garment to thy behove,
Which is wet with your tears,
Or else before God you may it miss,
When ye to your journey's end come shall.

EVERYMAN.   Gentle Knowledge, what do ye it call?

KNOWLEDGE.   It is a garment of sorrow,
From pain it will you borrow;
Contrition it is,
That getteth forgiveness,
It pleaseth God passing well.

GOOD-DEEDS.   Everyman, will you wear it for your heal?

EVERYMAN.   Now blessed be Jesus, Mary's son;
For now have I on true contrition:
And let us go now without tarrying.—
Good-deeds, have we clear our reckoning?

GOOD-DEEDS.   Yea, indeed, I have it here.

[Everyman confesses his sins to the priest and receives extreme unction.
Accompanied by Knowledge, Discretion, Strength, Beauty, and Five-Wits, he
comes to his grave, where all save Good-deeds bid him farewell. *Ed.*]

EVERYMAN.   Methinks, alas! that I must be gone
To make my reckoning, and my debts pay;
For, I see, my time is nigh spent away.—
Take example, all ye that this do hear or see,
How they that I love best do forsake me;
Except my Good-deeds, that abideth truly.

GOOD-DEEDS.   All earthly things is but vanity,
Beauty, Strength and Discretion do man forsake,
Foolish friends, and kinsmen, that fair spake;
All fleeth save Good-deeds, and that am I.

EVERYMAN.   Have mercy on me, God most mighty,—
And stand by me thou mother and maid, holy Mary.

_____

[10]Moment.

GOOD-DEEDS.   Fear not, I will speak for thee.

EVERYMAN.   Here I cry God mercy.

GOOD-DEEDS.   Shorten our end and diminish our pain:
Let us go, and never come again.

EVERYMAN.   Into thy hands, Lord, my soul I commend,
Receive it, Lord, that it be not lost;
As thou me boughtest, so me defend,
And save me from the fiend's boast,
That I may appear with that blessed host
That shall be saved at the day of doom.

• • •

KNOWLEDGE.   Now hath he suffered that we all shall endure,
The Good-deeds shall make all sure;
Now hath he made ending:
Me thinketh that I hear angels sing,
And make great joy and melody,
Where every man's soul received shall be.

THE ANGEL.   Come, excellent elect spouse to Jesus,
Here above thou shalt go,
Because of thy singular virtue:
Now the soul is taken the body from,
Thy reckoning is crystal clear;
Now shalt thou into the heavenly sphere,
Unto which all ye shall come
That liveth well before the day of doom.

DOCTOR.[11]   This moral men may have in mind;
Ye hearers, take it of worth, old and young,
And forsake pride, for he deceiveth you in the end,
And remember Beauty, Five-wits, Strength and Discretion,
They all at the last do Everyman forsake,
Save his Good-deeds, there doth he take:
But beware, and if they be small,
Before God he hath no help at all;
None excuse may be there for Everyman:
Alas! how shall he do then,
For after death amends may no man make;
For then mercy and pity doth him forsake;

---

[11]A scholar or learned man.

If his reckoning be not clean when he doth come,
God will say—*Ite, maledicti, in ignem aeternum:*[12]
And he that hath his account whole and sound,
High in heaven he shall be crowned;
Unto which place God bring us all thither,
That we may live body and soul together;
Thereto help the Trinity:
Amen, say ye, for Saint Charity.

[12]Go, accursed, into everlasting fire.

15

Christine de Pisan

The Book of the Duke of True Lovers

*T*HE *medieval period, for all its rigidly defined class and sex roles, saw some remarkable exceptions to the general relegation of women to inferior status. Women were important in the Church, as heads of female religious orders; in politics, as rulers of principalities; in literature, as patrons of writers and as writers themselves. Christine de Pisan (1363–ca. 1430) has the distinction of being probably the first woman to support herself by means of her writings. She wrote sometimes as a woman defending her sex against the customary slights and condemnations of contemporary male authors, and sometimes as a writer in tune with the "reading public" of the time.*

Christine de Pisan's father came to France from the small Italian town of Pazzano (hence the name Pisan in its French form), and his "advice" or counsel based on astrology apparently won him the favor of many important persons, including King Charles V. Christine then spent a studious childhood in and about the French court, and throughout her life enjoyed the acquaintance of great and noble personages. She was married at age fifteen to the secretary of the royal household. Her husband died in 1389, leaving her a widow at age twenty-six. She chose to support herself and her three small children by using her talent for writing and from the beginning enjoyed success.

Her Book of the Duke of True Lovers *(ca. 1400) is included here because its plot is on the one hand thoroughly typical of its time and on the other quite unusual. It is typical in having the youth woo his lady through displays of bravery that alternate with symptoms of lovesickness; the lady in turn encourages and discourages him. She, moreover, is married to someone else, which makes her relationship with the hero more interesting, perilous, and perforce secret. As usual, love ennobles their attitudes, purifies their motivations, and so on. The difference between this story and more typical ones, however, is that it is apparently based on an actual happening. An acquaintance had told Christine of his early romance with an older woman, of how he wooed and won her using the expected gamesmanship of love even though he was at the time subject to certain inconvenient requirements of the real world: the youthful lover must worry about getting home late, and he has to ask his parents for money to carry on his courtship.*

Such day-to-day concerns did not trouble the characters of Chrétien de Troyes' Lancelot, *for they lived entirely in a make-believe world. Christine de Pisan's story, written two centuries later than* Lancelot, *shows us both how the later medieval writers continued to use the conventions of the old romances and how people in the real world imitated them. An especially interesting aspect of the story is the insight it gives into the behavior expected of women in the later Middle Ages.*

———

[The narrator (the youthful duke), distantly related to the lady of the story, tells how he met her on a day in summer.]

[One day while hunting] we went along a path which I had often followed . . . and nearby was a strong and impressive castle, but I will not tell you its name.

At the time there was visiting in the castle a princess known to many as so good and beautiful and virtuous that all esteemed her highly. Since we just happened to be passing by, we did not know she was there, but as soon as we came near the castle we saw a fine company of ladies coming to meet us. They welcomed us in a polite and gracious manner.

The lady of whom everyone spoke so well came out of her chamber and stood there gracefully, neither proudly nor haughtily, but, as all agreed, in such a way as became her noble rank and high station. When we saw her, we bowed to her, as was proper, whereupon she came towards us. She gave me her ungloved hand and kissed me and said, "I did not know you were coming. You are indeed welcome, but what brings you here now?"

My cousin (who was with me) replied, "Well, my lady, we were just out enjoying ourselves, and we did not know you were here. Chance brings us here, but God be praised for so favoring us that we find so warm a welcome."

THE BOOK OF THE DUKE OF TRUE LOVERS   An abridgement and translation made by the editor from the original French.

The good and lovely lady laughed at this, and answered, "Well, then, let us go and amuse ourselves."

So we went down into a green meadow, and she went with us to a very pretty spot and drew me to her side to sit down beside her. Large cushions of golden silk were brought for her to sit on under the shade of a willow where, beneath the trees, the waters of a spring ran fair and clear through a channel skillfully cut through the tender green foliage. She sat down with me beside her, and the others went off and sat here and there beside the spring. Then she felt obliged to ask me questions, for I confess that I did not know at that time how to talk with ladies, for I was still somewhat young.

She began by asking me about the journey from which I had just returned, especially about what was happening at the court of the king and queen and about the behavior and appearance of the court ladies. I told her what I could recall, and I remember that we talked of many things.

It is now time to tell how that malady of lovesickness began from which I suffered so much. It is curious that I now fell deeply in love with her whom I had often seen but of whom I had never thought much. It was as if someone should cross the sea and explore many lands searching for what he might find close at hand, but which he does not see until another points it out to him. Thus it happened to me, for I did not perceive the graciousness of my dear lady until love taught me. Before then I had only hoped to see such a woman so that I could give my heart to her. And now I had beside me what I had gone elsewhere to seek. When she spoke to me, her speech and gentle and gracious demeanor delighted me so much that I was speechless. I watched her closely and contemplated her beauty, since she seemed to me more elegant, more graceful, and sweeter than I had ever before noticed.

Then her gentle, laughing eyes, filled with the force of love, stirred up my heart so that I did not know how to speak to her. She must truly have thought my look and manner foolish, since I did not move either hand or foot but changed color so often when she looked at me that it might have seemed that I trembled with fear. How shall I put it briefly? If I wanted to be made love's prisoner, I certainly did not fail.

When I had stayed in this place for almost a third of the summer's day, my cousin spoke to me. "Take you leave now, for I really believe that you have detained my lady too long here, and it is time for supper."

Then the noble and courteous lady, both fair and good, invited me to sup with her, but I excused myself. I lingered only a short while longer, and then I rose to leave, but first it was fitting that we drink some wine. When we had drunk and eaten a little, I asked her if I could escort her to the castle, but the fair one said no. So, without more delay, I took my leave of her and of the others.

When we reached my home, night had already closed in. My father was looking into the courtyard, and he sternly asked where I had been all day. I had hurried back because I feared and dreaded his anger, and when I saw him at the window I wished greatly that he had been somewhere else. However, I dismounted and knelt to greet him. I did not say anything, and he left.

I went to my room where I had supper. I was thoughtful and sad, and my friends tried to cheer me up with many stories, but my thoughts were elsewhere. It seemed to me that I still saw her face to face, she who had captured my heart. When bedtime came, I lay down in a comfortable bed, but I don't believe that I slept more than an hour and a half. I was afraid that she for whom I felt such sweet longing might not think about things as I did.

I did not yet, however, feel the fierce and ardent desire which makes lovers burn with fever and then grow pale and pine away with worry. That was yet to come. At the time I thought only of how I could be happy and merry and have expensive things and fancy clothes and be so generous and behave so honorably that everyone would praise me so highly that my lady would be pleased with my good behavior. I wanted to improve my manners and put aside the boyish habits and behavior which up until then made me awkward. I therefore begged my parents so hard that I got what I wanted, which was to have gold and silver to spend freely and to dress fashionably. I then chose an emblem and a motto in which my lady's name was hidden in such a way that no one could recognize it. I ordered horses for jousting and arranged for a festival and planned many other things.

The festival was quickly arranged. Jousts were announced at which whoever fought well could win valuable jewels. Twenty knights would come to this tournament who would joust with all comers.

On the appointed day the festival was held in a pleasant meadow where, placed at the end of a glade, was a castle with six high towers. In the meadow large and spacious tents were set up, as well as platforms for seats and many pavilions.

On the day that had been set, my sweet lady arrived before nightfall. A fine company of noble people met her, together with minstrels, whose drums and trumpets made the hills and valleys resound. I was filled with joy when I saw my lady coming toward me, and nothing could have made me happier. I met her with a noble retinue, approaching her and greeting her, as she did me.

She said, "You put yourself to great trouble, fair cousin, for it must be inconvenient to come to meet me at such a time."

Talking thus with a happy countenance to my sweet and dear lady, I rode beside her as we approached the castle. It surely seemed to me that I had sufficient reward for my trouble, for my happiness was doubled because it seemed to me that she looked at me more tenderly than she had ever done before. We arrived at the castle where we found waiting many fair ladies who politely knelt before her.

In the courtyard she was received with much joy. I then escorted her through the rooms to her chamber. Then servants brought wine and sweetmeats, and the fair lady asked me to share some with her. After this we withdrew and left her to rest awhile, and I went to get dressed.

In order to have a dance in the German fashion and so that nothing should be lacking to make the festival perfect, I had had a hundred rich costumes made with my emblem on them. I remember that twenty of them which the knights wore were of green velvet and embroidered cloth of gold.

When we were dressed, we appeared before my lady. There we found a good number of ladies and young women of the countryside who had already arrived for the festival. Without delaying, I greeted my lady and all of them, and I really believe that I was blushing. Nevertheless, I said, "My lady, it is time for supper." I then took her by the hand and led her to the hall. The knights led the ladies, and the minstrels blew their trumpets so that the whole place echoed with sound, and the feast was good to look upon.

When we had supped and had dessert, we drank. Then the minstrels came forward and played their horns with pleasant harmonies. In a little while dancing began, joyous and gay, and because of the happy festival, everyone joined in happily.

I waited no longer, but went directly to ask my lady to dance. For a little while she declined, but at last said yes. So I took her hand and led her to dance. Then I escorted her back to her seat. Make no mistake, I was so carried away by love for her that I felt overcome by delight to be near her. I thought that this was heaven and desired nothing better.

So we danced happily the greater part of the night. Then the revel ended, for it was time to retire. I led her who was as fair as amber to her chamber, where we spoke many courteous words. When she had looked at me in a way to stir my passion, we ate some sweetmeats, and I bade her good night and took my leave of all.

Like one who is carried away by love, I was impatient for morning when I could see my lady. I arose from bed as soon as I decently could. Already the house was full of brave and valiant knights and squires, who were even then practicing with foils.

When I was ready and the mass was said, I went out, but not seeing my lady, I was sad. I went to look for her and found her, for she was at mass.

When she came from the chapel I courteously greeted her. She said tenderly, "Welcome, fair cousin. Take good care, for everyone who wants to win a fair lady must appear at the tournament."

I smiled and was courageous enough to say, "I want to make a request of you, my lady, and if you grant it, I shall be very happy. My request is that you give me, if it pleases you, a sleeve from one of your dresses and a garland of myrtle to wear on my helmet. I think that if you gave me a kingdom, it would not please me more!"

My lady was thoughtful for awhile and at last said, "Surely, fair cousin, it would gain you more to have these from some other lady for whom you could perform knightly and courageous deeds. There are many worthy ladies here, if you want to have a token for your helmet as you go to perform feats of chivalry. This you should receive from your lady love and not from me. But I do not say that I want to refuse or that I am unwilling to grant your request, for I would do even more for you. But I would not want anyone to know of it."

Then she took a knife and cut off a sleeve with ermine from one of her dresses of cloth of gold and gave it to me. I gave her many thanks for this, and I also had from her the green garland and I was happy and glad. I said that I would wear it on my helmet, and I would joust for love of her, but she must understand that I still had to learn how to do such things.

Dinner was ready soon on that day of summer. We all dined quickly in our chambers. Then we went to the meadow where the tournament was to be held, and we dismounted before the beautiful pavilions. The armor was already there, and the lances were made ready and the warhorses tried out. You could see their high saddles with stirrups, white and red and green and covered with emblems, shields of many colors and painted lances. Already there was a great crowd of common folk and much noise and uproar.

Then the general tournament began. The trumpets made joyous sounds, and the heralds made their proclamations, and the knights on their noble battle horses, according to their several ranks, fought eagerly. My lady, and many other ladies, each of them beautiful to see, twenty ladies with fair long blonde hair adorned with garlands, were seated in one place. Loveliest and foremost of them all was the lady who was first in my thoughts. They were all dressed in gowns of white silk embroidered with gold of special pattern.

You can be very sure that many jousts were run that day, and it must have been pleasing to those who watched, since those who fought tried hard to merit attention and to beat each other so as to win the ladies' favors. You could see many a thrust parried quickly, and one overthrowing another in the thick of the fight, and another blow aimed at the opening of the visor or at shield or helmet. One had his helmet struck off, and someone came to carry him off. Lances were broken and blows sounded, and the trumpets were blown so loud that God's thunder could not have been heard. Hard blows were given on either side.

At last I rode out from my pavilion swifter than a hawk. I was well supported by my stirrups. My armor was all white, and my horse's caparison was white also. Neither red or green or any other color was to be seen except fine gold. My companions came out with me. All were armed in white, and our company carried white lances. I had had the sleeve my lady gave me fastened firmly to my helmet so that it could not be torn off. I put the green garland on my helmet also and set out with my fine company with great desire to see my sweet goddess.

Full of happiness I arrived at the jousting place and looked at the place where she was. I saw her tender glance, and therefore did not fear any misfortune. I rode before her and quickly closed my helmet and went to my place. In her presence, a noble count brought me my lance and said to me that it would be a shame if I did not joust well, since I wore so noble a crest.

Then, with lance lowered and wanting to keep it well placed, I did not hesitate but spurred my charger against another's who was coming toward me. We did not falter, but since it is not right to tell of one's own exploits, I will not tell anything about them except that the fair lady thought that I had done so well that she graciously praised me highly, and at the end awarded me the prize for those who were with me. I gladly took it, with the kind agreement of the ladies, and thus you may know for sure that for my age I did well that day, as well as I could. If I did anything brave, I deserve no praise for it, for it was surely love and not my ability that was the cause. Without doubt there could be found in the company many experienced knights better than myself. But I believe that the ladies gave it to me because they saw how eager I was.

The pleasant festival lasted for three whole days. All were welcome and put at their ease. Then the festivities came to an end, but my lady did not leave for a whole month, for I had asked her husband to allow her to stay, and he agreed.

You can imagine what joy I had in this pleasant visit. Every hour I wondered how to plan things to amuse and entertain her. One day I had baths made ready and stoves heated and tubs placed in white pavilions in a suitable location. It happened that I went there when my lady was in the bath. She was not glad to see me, but I felt happy when I looked upon her fair flesh as white as lily. This delighted me greatly, as you who hear tell of it can well imagine. On another day we went hunting, and on another we went to the river to fish. In such ways we passed a whole month in many enjoyable pastimes.

But in the midst of my happiness love bound my heart more fast than ever and held it so violently that a great desire to be loved was aroused in me, and before the festival ended no other being could have been more miserable. I could not be happy if I did not see her and gaze constantly upon her, which I never tired of doing, and it seemed to me that I could never spend enough time with her. You can believe that I lacked the skill to hide the sorrow I felt. Although I would not reveal my thought to anyone, I was nevertheless so troubled in my mind and in such turmoil that in spite of myself my face revealed my state of mind. I was now sad, now merry. Like someone who has been forsaken, I often wept so bitterly that it seemed to me likely that I would die of grief and sorrow. I grew pale, I trembled, I blushed, and often changed color and broke into a sweat for fear. I became upset to the point where my strength failed me. I neither drank nor ate with any appetite, nor could I get much sleep, so that I got into a state where I grew worse and worse. No one knew what ailed me, for by no means would I speak to anyone about my state of mind, nor would I, even to save my life, confess it to her whom I loved. Nevertheless, she often asked what ailed me and said that I should tell her how I was and not hide anything from her. She said that I should speak to her without fear, for I must believe that she would do all in her power to help me.

For a long time my lady comforted me thus, but nevertheless I dared not for all the gold in the world let her know the weight which oppressed my heart. Thus, in deep melancholy I wept and sighed. I became so filled with love that I do not know what more to say concerning it except that I had a troublesome and painful acquaintance with it and lacked from that time on the quiet and pleasurable peace of mind which I had enjoyed before. My heart was plunged into another peril, for I came to reject all comfort and to make of sorrow a pitiless guest. For a long time I remained in this state, not daring to ask her for her love for fear of her refusal.

[At last, after some encouraging hints from the lady, the young duke speaks to her about his love. On her return home, they exchange messages, and she devises a way for him to visit her secretly with the aid of the young duke's cousin, who is also related to the lady, and of the lady's maid servant. The story resumes with the arrival of the two youths at the lady's castle. *Ed.*]

We dismounted outside the gate, and I put on different clothes. My cousin went on, and I waited with the horses and was careful not to be recognized. He invented an excuse for being there at that hour. He had come on a pressing matter which had suddenly come up, and he had to talk with the lord of the castle about it at once. He was told that the lord was not there, nor would he return for some months. He replied that in that case great loss would result.

Then my very dear lady hurried to a window which looked down into the courtyard and said, "What chance brings my cousin here? Go and let down the drawbridge right away. If I don't know what he asks, I cannot tell if he brings urgent news from someone."

My cousin was then led to her by two young women. When he reached her and greeted her, she asked him, "Has someone died or why have you come so late? I haven't seen you for a week. Tell me what it is."

He replied that it was no use for him to stay, since he could not see the lord and master, which he regretted. It was best for him to leave.

She answered that he should not do that but let her know everything without delay.

Then he said, "It would be best that my attendant, who is holding the horses at the gate, bring me the letter I gave him to carry. Some one should tell him to come here right away."

Then with a bold air my lady ordered her secretary to do so. My cousin, being very careful, came to the chamber door and said to me,

"Give me the letter at once." And then he said to the secretary, "Send him away quickly, for there is nothing more for him to do here, and it is not right for an attendant to remain in the room now."

My cousin said this because a light was shining in the chamber by which I might be recognized and discovered. He took the big letter which I carried in my jacket and led my lady aside and, reading it, indicated how serious was the matter described. Meanwhile, as my lady had ordered, the secretary had me go into the unlighted chamber of a wise, cautious, and respected lady, who was acquainted with everything and whose chamber was connected with the lady's.

As soon as the letter had been read before everyone, my cousin prepared to leave with a show of great regret. But my lady forbade him to go and said that he must certainly remain there or she would complain to her lord and husband about him. In this way she made him stay.

She talked for a long time with him and at last, so that people would not wonder about it, she said that it was time to retire and that there was no reason for anyone to keep guard in her chamber. So that there would be no suspicion or doubt about his staying until that late hour, a bed was prepared for him in a room at a distance where he was escorted to rest, accompanied by the most trustworthy of the castle retinue.

She then undressed and went to bed in her room where her maids were still present. She did not stay in bed long, but got up and dressed again and, complaining that she did not feel well, ordered a fire lit in the chamber where I was. I hid until the servant had made a fire. Then my lady came wrapped in a long robe. She did not bring with her any of her waiting-women except one, the one mentioned before whom she had chosen to trust.

Then the lady who was her companion came to get me and led me to my lady. I could hardly greet her for I was nervous and hardly knew where I was. Nevertheless, I said, "Sweet lady, may God save you, body and soul."

"Friend, you are very welcome," she said, and she made me sit beside her. As soon as I looked at her, I was almost beside myself. My lady saw this very well, and she gave me a kiss, for which I thanked her humbly many times.

My lady, whom my troubled and uncertain heart reveres, then began to speak: "Have I done what you wanted, fair sir, in bringing you here so secretly? Is this what a friend should do? Do not deceive me in any way now, but tell me if you can and while you have the chance what you want."

Trembling with joy and sighing, I then said, "Sweet lady, on my oath I do not know how to say what I would like to say. Therefore, very dear lady, please understand and recognize that I am altogether yours, body and soul. I cannot say more than that."

She came close and put her arm around my neck and, laughing, said, "It is up to me then to speak for us both, since you cannot remember anything to say. Yet I really believe that love favors me so much that I do not think I could say a single word about what I believe you want to speak that would not be proper for me to say."

The other lady who was there began to smile and said, "Since I see you are already in agreement in this matter, I really can recognize that love makes fools of the wisest."

My lady said to me, "My friend, since love has made us agree, we don't have to ask if we love one another. I really believe that love can claim us both as his servants, which does not make me sad. Nevertheless, dear friend, even though I trust you in this affair and I will not conceal anything, I do not know what you intend. I tell you that no matter how much love you see in me, and however I may seem in word or look to be pleased or happy, and although I may kiss and embrace you, never for a moment imagine that I want to do anything shameful or for which I could be blamed. Dear friend, I warn you, since I don't want you to say that I gave myself to you, I swear that I will never do anything to ruin my honor. And so, once and for all, I swear to you truthfully that as soon as I see, either from your behavior or expression, that you wish otherwise, you will never see me again. I do not know if I am wrong in this, but I do not seek to refuse you any other pleasure by which a lady can enslave her lover. And if it were not wrong, I would give my heart wholly to you and would give up everything for you to use as you want. But I promise you loyalty and true friendship, and I am willing to prefer you to all others if that will satisfy you. So tell me what you want while you have time and opportunity, for I want to know."

When she whom I adore stopped talking, I answered, "My lady, it almost kills me to hear you speak this way. The love, goodness, and favor you show me would satisfy me very well, and I hope that you will never imagine that I am unwilling to agree to everything you command. Nothing that you wish can make me grieve, so I cannot be unhappy about this, for are you not my loved one? Should I not behave according to the way you want me to? When I want to do otherwise, may I perish, body and soul. Good God! how happy I ought to be because I see that you love me and call me your dear friend. I possess what I want, and I don't wish for anything more. I think that I am well rewarded.

"I must not speak ill of love that enables me to gain such great joy. Therefore, fair and gentle one, I thank you humbly, for from now on I shall wear the crown of a lover; I shall put aside bad habits and behave virtuously, as I must do in order to be like a valiant man. And finally, sweet lady, I could not be happier, no matter how much I talk about it."

Then my lady, in whom there is every grace, embraced me very tenderly and kissed me more than a hundred times. I remained happy this way all night, and believe this, you lovers who are listening, I was very much at my ease. Many sweet words filled with joy were spoken that night. And she, in whom there is every goodness, taught me how, in spite of all who might be displeased, I could find the way and place to see her quite often.

Thus we passed the time, but the night seemed brief to me. When day came, which made me sad, embracing and kissing me a hundred times and giving me sweet, loving looks, she said, "Farewell, dear love." And she locked me in the chamber all alone and went to her own room.

Later, dressed as a page, I was led out by the discreet secretary who knew what was going on.

[What really happened that night must be left to the reader's imagination, for the elaborate language and eloquent sentiments somewhat color and conceal actuality. In any event, the youthful duke and his lady meet often. This happy state of affairs ends, however, when the lady's trusted companion has to leave the lady's castle to return to her own home. The lady then writes to a former friend and companion, the Lady La Tour, asking if she would come to stay at the lady's castle and help her continue the affair. The friend replies in an unexpected manner with a lengthy condemnation of the lady's behavior and a lecture on the deportment expected of a proper lady of the time. *Ed.*]

The Lady La Tour writes:

My lady, I have heard certain rumors about your conduct which grieve me from the bottom of my heart because I fear that you will ruin your good name. I fear that your actions tend that way, for it is fitting for every princess and high-born lady, since she is placed above others in honor and social position to exceed others in virtue, goodness, wisdom, manners and disposition so that she can give an example to other women. It is proper that she be devout toward God, have a tranquil, gentle, and calm demeanor, and in her amusements be restrained and without excess, that she laugh in moderation and not without cause, and have a dignified walk, a modest look, and gracious gestures, with a kindly response and a courteous word for everyone. Her dress and attire should be rich but not affected. She should be polite when she welcomes strangers, restrained in her speech and not too familiar, not hasty or changeable in giving opinions, never appearing harsh, capricious, or ill-tempered. She should never be difficult to wait upon but sympathetic and kind to her servants, not proud but generous within reason; and she should be able to recognize goodness and discretion in those who are her best servants and to keep them close to her and reward them according to what they deserve. She should not trust flatterers but recognize them and send them away. She should not believe gossip readily nor be in the habit of whispering either to strangers or to intimate friends in secret or solitary places and in particular not to any of her personal servants or waiting women, so that no one will be able to think that she knows more than another of her private business. She should never make jests with anyone in the presence of others unless the jest is understood by all, so that those listening will not imagine that there is some idle secret between them. She should not stay in her room by herself too long or too often but should sometimes retire and at other times be with others.

Although the behavior I have described and all other actions befitting a noble princess used to be followed by you, you now act quite differently, so they say. For you amuse yourself much more and have become more talkative and mirthful than you used to be. When the outer signs change it is a sign that the disposition has altered. Now you want to be away from others except one or two of your waiting-women with whom you talk privately even when others are present. You titter and gossip secretly, as if you understood each other, and no other company pleases you but these. Others cannot serve you to your liking. These things make your servants envious and make them think that you are in love with someone. . . .

My lady, for God's sake be careful not to be deceived by such foolish thoughts. For as far as happiness is concerned, be assured that in love affairs there are a hundred thousand more griefs, cares, and risks, especially for ladies, than there are times of happiness.

Love itself brings with it many troubles, and the fear that it will be found out makes such pleasure costly. As to the saying that "There cannot be any harm in this, since it will not lead to sin," my lady, no one can be so sure of herself as to be certain that she will never lose control of herself however good her resolutions may be. Truly, it is hardly possible for nothing to happen or for it not to be found out. For where there is fire there is always smoke, but sometimes there is smoke without fire. And to say "I shall make a man valiant because of love" is, I declare, very foolish, for you ruin yourself to benefit another. And as to saying "I shall have gained a true friend and servant," good God! what could such a friend or servant do for a lady? If she were in any trouble, he would not dare do anything for her, for fear of dishonoring her.

Again, my lady, if you or any other should excuse yourselves by saying "My situation is a sad one, for I have little freedom and happiness. Because of this I can have pleasure without doing wrong in order to cure my melancholy and to pass the time," you may be quite sure that such excuses do not help, for he who sets fire to his own house in order to burn his neighbor's is very foolish. She who bears with a husband patiently and without shaming herself increases her reputation and her honor. And as to pleasure, surely a noble lady, indeed any woman, can find pleasure if she wants to without such love. There are enough lawful and suitable pleasures to enjoy and with which to pass time without melancholy.

I do not know what more I can write to you except that to the utmost of my power I humbly beg you not to take what I have written amiss. Please be assured of my good intentions which compel me to say what I have said. I would very much rather do my duty by faithfully admonishing you and making you angry than either advise you harmfully or keep silent in order to keep your good will.

[The lady is dismayed on reading this letter. She sends it to the young duke, who is likewise distressed. They see each other less frequently thereafter, and he sets out on adventures, one of which takes him abroad for ten years. He and the lady are still in love, but neither of them thinks of doing anything decisive, and their romance ebbs away. *Ed.*]

16

Giovanni Boccaccio

The Decameron

G IOVANNI Boccaccio (1313–
1375), a great admirer and biographer of Dante, was the first to lecture on The
Divine Comedy under the auspices of the city of Florence, which had banished
Dante and then, some years after his death, had endowed a lectureship in his
honor. Dante's masterpiece is for the most part a medieval poem; Boccaccio's
own works are usually thought of as belonging to the Renaissance period. The
best-known work, The Decameron, written between 1348 and 1358, exem-
plifies narrative realism, has racy wit and humor, and is to be enjoyed for itself
and not primarily for high moral or religious truth. Whereas Dante's universe
was based upon the Ptolemaic system of spheres with earth at its center, and had
St. Thomas Aquinas's Summa Theologica as its philosophical guide,
Boccaccio's Decameron frees itself from all obligations save that of telling a
series of cleverly concocted stories. Although he knew the classics and was a
serious humanist scholar and writer of Latin treatises, Boccaccio wrote the
stories (and all the works for which he is now remembered) in Italian.

Most of the one hundred stories of The Decameron were well known
among his contemporaries, but the superior ease with which Boccaccio tells them
made his versions distinctive. In Boccaccio's time, a writer was supposed to show
skill in handling conventional material rather than originality or novelty in
inventing plots. The stories of The Decameron are supposedly narrated by a
group of gay, witty, and worldly young people who enjoy telling tales; some of
the stories are mocking, some are sad, and some are outrageously bawdy. The
following selection begins with the opening pages of The Decameron, a
description of the plague-stricken city from which the group of young men and
women flee to take refuge in a villa overlooking Florence. The narratives that
follow were favorites in Boccaccio's time, when stories involving honor, pride,
and love were especially popular.

In the year of our blessed Savior's Incarnation, 1348, that memorable plague ravaged the excellent city, far beyond all the rest in Italy; which plague, by operation of the heavenly bodies, or rather for our enormous iniquities, by the just anger of God was sent upon us mortals. Some few years before, it began in the East, sweeping thence an innumerable quantity of living souls, extending itself afterward from place to place westward, until it seized on the said city, where neither human skill nor Providence could find any prevention, even though the city was cleansed of many impurities by the diligent officers ordered to that task. Besides the prevention of all sick persons' entrance, all possible precautions were daily used for the preservation of health. There were also incessant prayers and the supplications of devout people for the abatement of so dangerous a sickness.

About the beginning of the year it also began in a very strange manner, yet not as it had done in the eastern countries where anyone afflicted with the ailment would show signs of inevitable death by bleeding at the nose. But here it began either under the armpits or in the groin with certain swellings, in some to the bigness of an apple, in others like an egg, which in the vulgar speech was termed a botch or a boil. In very short time after, the deadly boils would spread to all parts of the body; whereupon the disease showed itself by black or blue spots, which would appear on the arms of many, or on their thighs, and every part of the body—in some, great and few; in others, small and thick.

Now, as the boil at the beginning was an assured sign of near approaching death, so the spots proved likewise. It seemed that the physician's advice, medicines, or any other remedy, were all useless. It plainly appeared that because of the nature of the illness and the ignorance of the physicians no cure was to be found. Moreover, besides the number of those who were skilled in medicine, there were a great many, both men and women, who without any knowledge of medicine at all became physicians; so that not only few were healed, but wellnear all died within three days after the aforementioned signs were seen, some sooner, and others later—commonly without fever or any other complications.

This pestilence was of great power and violence. For not only healthful persons speaking to the sick, or coming to see them, or airing clothes to comfort them were taken ill; but even those who touched

THE DECAMERON *The Decameron of Giovanni Boccaccio*, ed. Henry Morley (London: Routledge, 1895), 10–13, 102–10. (This is an adaptation.)

their garments or any food upon which a sick person had fed, or anything else he had used contracted the disease in what seemed a miraculous way. Among which marvels let me tell you one thing, which if others had not seen it as well as I, I could hardly be persuaded to write down: the quality of this contagion was of such virulence that the clothes or anything else touched by a dying person proved deadly to any beast or animal, dog or cat, that lay upon or even touched them.

My own eyes saw, among many others, proof of this one day. Some rags of linen and wool torn from a wretched person dead of that disease lay in the open street, and two swine searching for food tossed and tumbled the clothes with their snouts. Whereupon they turned about twice or thrice and fell down dead. This occurrence and other similar ones caused fears and imaginings in those who looked on, often causing them to fly away from the sick and from touching anything that had been near an ill person, for they thought that thus their health could be preserved.

There were some who thought that living soberly and in abstinence would be sufficient protection; so, joining together, they lived apart from all other company, shut up in houses where none had been sick. And there, for their greater security, they used delicate foods and excellent wines, avoiding luxury and refusing to speak to one another, not looking out of the windows or heeding the cries of the dying or watching the corpses being carried to burial. But with their music and pleasure, they lived in hope. Others were of a contrary opinion. They said that there was no medicine for such a dangerous ailment better than to drink hard and be merry. So they sang continually, went everywhere, satisfied their every appetite, laughing at and mocking every sad spectacle. They vowed to spend day and night thus, and they went from tavern to tavern, living without any restraint and abandoning all of their possessions. Most of the houses of the city became common, and strangers entered and did what they pleased without any let or hindrance.

Yet in all of this mean behavior they were wise enough to shun as much as possible the weak and sickly. In the misery and affliction of our city, the authority of the laws, both human and divine, was destroyed through the death of the lawful ministers and officers. For they all died, or lay so sick or in want of servants and attendants, that they could not carry out any duty. Hence everyone did as he pleased.

Between these two extremities of behavior there were others of more moderate temperament, not being so careful as the first, nor drinking so heedlessly as the second, but using all things sufficient for their appetites, and not shutting themselves up. They walked in the streets, some carrying nosegays of flowers, others odiferous herbs and spiceries, holding them to their noses in the belief that they could protect the brain against the noisome stench of dead carcases. Some others there were of even more inhuman mind (though perhaps they had the surest remedy) who said that the best medicine for the pestilence was to be away from it. Caring for nobody but themselves, many men and women forsook the city, their own houses, their parents, kindred, and friends, and fled. They seemed to believe that the wrath of God, punishing men with his plague, would fall on none save those inside the city. Or else they believed that the ending of all things had come.

Now these people, with their diversity of opinions, did not all die, nor did they all escape. Many among them, falling sick and having set an example by their own flight, died altogether forsaken. So it was that one citizen fled after another, and one neighbor had no care of another. The terror of the time so afflicted the hearts of men that brother forsook brother, uncle abandoned nephew, and wife left husband. Incredible as it seems, fathers and mothers fled away from their own children. As a result a countless number of men and women fell sick and, finding no charity among their friends, became dependent upon untrustworthy servants, who served them only for extravagant wages. Yet even that kind of help was hard to find and consisted mostly of men and women unskilled and ignorant, unfit for anything except to bring the sick person what he called for, or to sit by and await the hour of his death. Even so, the desire for gain which led many to undertake this service often caused their own death.

In this calamity, when the sick were forsaken by neighbors, kindred, and friends, there arose a custom never heard of before. A woman, young, fair, or noble, falling sick, often had to depend upon a man's help. Without any shame she would show any part of her body, just as she would to another woman. If the woman recovered, it sometimes happened that this occasioned further dishonest behavior. Many, being more modest, refused such disgraceful help, choosing rather to die than by such help to be cured.

Because of the lack of effective remedies and the violence of the contagion the multitude of them that died night and day was so great that it was a dreadful sight to behold or even to hear about. Necessity caused behavior quite different from that of former times when it was the custom (as it is now again) for women, relatives, neighbors, and friends to meet at the deceased's house and there express their sorrow for their loss. Or they would assemble before the door and with the priests conduct the dead body with funeral pomp of torchlight and singing to the church chosen by the deceased. But these decent customs, after the fury of the pestilence began to increase, were ignored, and other new customs came in their place. People died without having any women about them, but multitudes also perished without any witness as to how, when, or in what manner they departed. There were few women mourners, or none, to exhibit the outward shows of grief; but there were many who lived only in idleness, like immodest women heedless of their own welfare.

Very few would accompany the body to the grave, not even the neighbors, even though the deceased had been an honorable citizen. Only the meanest kind of people, grave-diggers, coffin-bearers, and the like, who served only for money, made up the procession. The coffin being mounted on their shoulders, they would run with it hastily to the nearest church with four or six poor priests following, sometimes without lights, and, a short service being said, the body would be irreverently thrown into the first open grave they found.

[Toward the end of the third day of the young people's stay in the villa outside Florence, it becomes the turn of one of the young ladies to tell a story. She chooses the tale of Giletta of Narbonne. *Ed.*]

There lived some time ago in the kingdom of France a gentleman named Isnarde, Count of Roussillon. Because he was continually ill, he kept a physician in his house, a Master Gerard of Narbonne. Count Isnarde had only one son, very young and fair, named Bertram, with whom the children of the retainers had their education. Among them was Giletta, daughter of the physician. Her affection for young Bertram was most unusual in so young a maiden. Old Count Isnarde dying, young Bertram became a ward of the King and was sent to Paris to remain under the royal protection. Young Giletta grieved long and hard at the loss of her dear Bertram.

A few years after, her father also died, and then her desire became set on visiting Paris herself to see the young Count. She awaited only time and opportunity to start her journey. But her friends to whose care she had been committed, because of her rich dowry, watched closely her walks and behavior, so she could not by any means escape. She was old enough for marriage, which increased her love for the Count and at the same time led her to refuse without any explanation the matches proposed by her friends. By this time the Count had become a gallant young gentleman, able to choose his own wife. Hence her affections were all the more aroused by fear that he would choose someone else.

It was widely known that the King of France was in a very dangerous condition because of a strange tumor on his stomach, which, being ill-tended, became a fistula. It afflicted him daily with extraordinary pain. No physician being found that could offer any hope of a cure, but instead only increased his suffering, the King despaired of all help and listened to no further advice. Giletta was very joyful at this, for she hoped that this could be a reason for her journey. If the disease were no more than she believed it to be, she could easily cure it, and then she could win Bertram as her husband. Therefore, recalling the rules of medicine which by long practice and experience she had learned of her father, she compounded certain herbs together into a powder and set off for Paris.

Having arrived there, she first sought for a glimpse of Bertram, the saint that had caused her pilgrimage. Next, she gained access to the King, humbly asking his majesty to grant her sight of his fistula. When the King saw her modest looks he knew her for a discreet young gentlewoman. He therefore laid the fistula open to her inspection. When she had seen and felt it, she assured the King that she knew herself able to cure it. "Sire," she said, "if your Highness will trust me, I hope, without any peril to your life or even the least pain, to make you whole and sound within eight days' time."

The King began to smile at this, saying, "How is it possible for you, being a young maiden, to do that which the best physicians in Europe are not able to do? I praise your kindness and will not be unthankful for your willingness, but I am fully determined to use no more counsel or to try any more medicines."

Giletta replied, "Great King, let not my skill and experience be despised because I am young and a maiden, for I do not depend on my own knowledge, but upon the gracious assistance of Heaven and some rules of skilled observation which I learned of the reverend Gerard of Narbonne, who was my father and a physician of great fame during the whole of his life."

Hearing these words, the King began to admire her gracious de- meanor and said to himself, "How do I know whether this young woman is sent to me by the direction of Heaven or not? Why should I not make proof of her skill? Her promise is to cure me in a short time and without any pain or affliction. She shall not have come so far just to return again with only the loss of her labor. I am resolved to try her skill." He then spoke to her: "Fair maiden, if you cause me to break my determination and then fail to cure me, what can you expect to follow?"

"Whatsoever, great King," said she, "shall please you. Let me be strongly guarded, yet not hindered when I am carrying on the cure. And then if I do not perfectly heal you within eight days, let a good fire be made and consume my body to ashes. But if I accomplish the cure and set your Highness free from all further trouble, what recompense shall come to me?"

The King praised the confidence she had in her own skill, and replied, "Fair maiden, because you are a maid and unmarried, if you succeed and I find myself fully cured, I will match you with some gentleman in marriage who shall be honorable and of good reputation. And I shall furnish you with a good dowry as well."

"My gracious sovereign," she said, "I am most heartily thankful that your Highness will procure a marriage for me, but I desire to have the husband I shall choose, by your gracious favor. But I shall not choose any of your sons or any member of the royal house."

This the King gladly granted, and young Giletta began to minister the cure. Within fewer days than her limited time, the King was sound and perfectly cured. When he perceived this, he said to her, "Believe me, gracious maid, most worthily have you won yourself a husband. Name him, and you shall have him."

She replied, "Then I have won Count Bertram of Roussillon, whom I have loved from my infancy, and cannot love any other."

The King was not eager to grant the young Count's hand to her, but his solemn promise and his royal word, which he would not by any means break, had been given. He therefore commanded that the Count be sent for and spoke to him thus: "Noble Count, it is not unknown to us that you are a gentleman of great honor, and it is our royal pleasure to free you from your wardship so that you may return home and arrange matters for the reception of the wife whom we have decided to give you."

The Count answered the King with most humble thanks, but wanted to know who his wife was to be.

"She is the young gentlewoman," replied the King, "who by the grace of Heaven has saved my life."

The Count knew her, of course, and thought that although she was fair, her humble birth made her unworthy of him. He disdainfully answered the King thus: "Would your Highness give me a quack doctor for my wife, one that deals in powders and pills? I hope I am able to do much better for myself."

"Would you have us break our oath which we have given to this virtuous maid for the recovery of our health? She will have no other reward but Count Bertram for her husband."

"Sir," replied the Count, "you may dispossess me of all that is mine, because I am your ward and subject. And you may choose whom you will for my wife. But allow me to tell you that this marriage will be over my objection and I will never agree willingly to it."

"Sir," said the King, "it is our will that it should be so. She is virtuous, fair and wise. She loves you most affectionately. With her you will lead a more happy life than with the greatest lady in our kingdom."

The Count stood silent and discontented, but the King commanded preparations for the wedding, and when the appointed time had arrived, the Count, against his will, received his wife from the King.

When all of this was done, the Count requested permission of the King to leave for his own home for the consummation of the marriage there. But instead of riding home, the Count went to Tuscany, where he heard of a war between the Florentines and Siennese. The Florentines welcomed him and made him captain of a company.

The poor, forsaken, newly-married Countess was hardly pleased with such dishonorable treatment, yet, discreetly hiding her disappointment and hoping by her virtuous demeanor to induce him to return, she rode to Roussillon where all of the people received her very lovingly. Now because of the Count's long absence, all things were disordered: mutinies, quarrels, civil dissensions, had even caused much bloodshed. But she, like the wise and provident lady she was, brought order again. The Count's vassals came to admire her so much that they greatly condemned the Count's unkindness toward her.

When the whole county of Roussillon, by her policy and wisdom, was fully pacified, she chose two knights, whom she sent to the Count, her husband, to let him know that if it was because of her that he stayed away from his home, she would gladly leave and no longer trouble him. He replied harshly, "Let her do as she wants. I'll not live with her or anywhere near her. Tell her from me that when she gets this ring from my finger to wear on hers, and when she holds in her arms a child that I have begotten on her, then I'll come to live with her." The ring that he meant was the dearest thing he possessed, and he was never known to take it from his finger because he believed it had special powers.

The two knights knew that these conditions were impossible, but they got nothing more from the Count and sorrowfully took his reply back to their lady. She was, of course, dismayed at the severity of his rejection, but nevertheless began to scheme how she could satisfy these conditions and have her husband and his love. Having decided what to do, she called together all of the Count's vassals and told them how she had attempted to persuade the Count to return and how he had spurned her. She then revealed that rather than force the Count to live in exile, she herself would leave and spend the rest of her life on pilgrimages and in deeds of charity, praying always for the Count's soul and her own. She urged them then to undertake the government of the Count's domain and to let him know of her leaving and her decision never to return to Roussillon. Everyone wept on hearing her and tried, in vain, to dissuade her.

Having bade farewell to everyone, but not telling where she was going, she left, accompanied by only her maid and one kinsman. She wore a pilgrim's habit, yet she provided herself with plenty of money and jewels.

She went directly to Florence, where she took lodging with a poor widow and pretended to live contentedly as a pilgrim (though she was impatiently longing for news of the Count). The very next day she saw him ride past the house at the head of his company. She recognized him, of course, but asked the widow who he was.

"A stranger who calls himself Count of Roussillon," replied the widow. "He is well thought of in the city and is in love with a neighbor of mine, a young gentlewoman who lives with her mother, a worthy and honest woman. She is unmarried only because of her poverty."

The Countess listened carefully and debated with herself what to do. Having learned the name of the lady and her daughter and where they lived, she, still wearing her pilgrim's clothes, visited them. She found mother and daughter living in poverty, and asked the mother for a few words in private. When they were alone, the Countess said, "We have both suffered from bad fortune. But you can, if you will, help us both and bring comfort to us both."

"Believe me," answered the lady, "I would do anything within the limits of honesty."

The Countess then said, "I must rely on your trust and fidelity, for if I do not have them, both of us may be ruined."

"Tell me anything you want," replied the old lady, "and be assured that I shall never deceive you."

The Countess then told the whole story of her love from the beginning to the present moment, revealing her true identity and the purpose of her coming to Florence. So well did she speak that the old lady believed her altogether, especially since she had heard from others some of the Countess's story of misfortune. All of this made her more compassionate for the Countess's plight.

When the Countess had told all of her past history, she went on: "Among my miseries and misfortunes, which have almost broken my heart to retell, there are two things that I must overcome if I am ever to have my husband and his love. Yet these two things I can accomplish with your help, if what I have heard is true. You can tell if this is so. Since my arrival in this city, it has been told me that my husband, the Count, is deeply in love with your daughter."

"If the Count," replied the lady, "loves my daughter and already has a wife, he will find that his greatness will not help him to dishonor her just because she is poor. It is true that there may be some love on the part of the Count, but I shall do whatever I can for you, for I prize my daughter's honesty as highly as he does his proud honor."

"Madam," said the Countess, "I thank you for your offer. But before I ask you to do anything more, let me tell you what I intend to do for you. Your daughter is beautiful and ready for marriage, but, I hear, is prevented from doing so for want of a dowry. In recompense of the favor I am going to ask of you, I shall give you as much as you think necessary for her dowry."

Poverty made the poor lady's agreement quick. Moreover, she had a noble heart, and said, "Countess, how can I serve you so as to deserve such a generous offer? If the act is honest and I can preserve my reputation, I would gladly help you. You may then do as you see fit about a reward."

"Then, Madam," replied the Countess, "tell the Count, by some trustworthy messenger, that your daughter is ready to give herself to him if she receives, as his pledge of honor, the ring he wears on his little finger, which, as she has no doubt heard, he treasures very much. If he sends the ring, you shall give it to me and then send word to him that your daughter is ready to receive him. Then let him come secretly at night to your house where I, instead of your daughter, shall go to bed with him. Thus, unknown to him, I may with luck conceive his child. At the proper time, with his child in my arms and his ring on my finger, I may gain his love and live thereafter with him as a good wife should with her husband. And you will have been the cause of this good fortune."

The old lady thought that all of this would be difficult to achieve and might cause scandal about her daughter. Nevertheless, considering that she could be the means to a good end by enabling the virtuous Countess to reform an erring husband, she promised to help. Within a few days, she very cleverly saw to it that the ring was obtained, despite the Count's reluctance to part with it; and she succeeded in putting the Countess in her daughter's bed, where the Count, by God's grace, ardently begat two fine sons whom the Countess bore in due time.

Thus the old lady gave the Countess full possession of her husband many times, but always secretly and in the dark, so that the Count never suspected that he lay with his own wife and was being cheated of the woman whom he thought he possessed. Moreover, when he left in the mornings, always before daybreak so as to avoid suspicion, he often gave her jewels and other gifts which the Countess carefully treasured.

Perceiving definitely that she was with child, she at last told the old lady that she would no longer trouble her. "Madam," she said, "I thank Heaven and you because my desire has been so well satisfied. It is time for me to reward you and take my leave. You may make any demand of me you please, but not as a wage, because that would seem base and mercenary. What you receive of me is an honorable recompense for honorable and virtuous assistance, such as any honest lady in similar distress should be able to expect."

Although poverty might well have urged the lady to demand an extravagant sum, she asked for only a hundred pounds as friendly assistance toward her daughter's wedding. And she asked for that with a becoming hesitancy. But the Countess gave her five hundred pounds and many costly jewels besides.

Then the Countess returned to her lodgings at the widow's house. The old lady and her daughter left Florence. The Count was distressed, but never heard any further word of her or her daughter, who was married happily and honorably.

Not long after, Count Bertram was recalled to Roussillon, where he willingly went, having heard that his wife was no longer there. The Countess remained in Florence until the birth of her twin sons, who greatly resembled their father. She was most careful of their nursing, and when they were old enough to travel, went to Montpellier where she rested for a time. Learning that the Count was to hold his court on All Saints Day, she joined there the throng of lords and knights and ladies. Clad in her pilgrim's habit, she entered the great hall where all the tables were spread for the feast. Pushing through the crowd, with her two children in her arms, she kneeled at last before the Count and, weeping copiously, spoke to him: "Worthy lord, I am your poor, despised, and unfortunate wife who, in order to allow you to return to your own home, have gone begging through the world. And now I hope that you will honorably live up to your own strict conditions, stated to the two knights whom I sent to you. These conditions I was commanded to obey. Behold, here in my arms, not one son begotten by you, but two, and your ring on my finger besides. If you are a man of honor, now is the time, after my long and tedious journey, for you to welcome me as your own true wife."

The Count was astonished, for he knew his ring quite well, and both children were so perfectly like him that everyone agreed that he must be their father. Upon his asking how all this could have happened, the Countess told the whole assembly the entire story. Moreover, she repeated their talk abed and showed the jewels that he had given her. All of these proofs of his shame and her devotion to her husband compelled him to acknowledge that she told the whole truth.

Therefore, commending her constancy, wit, and courage, he kissed the two sweet little boys and, to keep his promise, as he was urged to do by all, especially the ladies, he accepted the Countess as his lawful wife. Folding her in his arms and tenderly kissing her, he bade her welcome as his virtuous, loyal, and loving wife, as she would be for him forever. He knew that she had more becoming dresses in the house, and he requested several ladies of the court to accompany her to her chamber and help her rid herself of the pilgrim's garb and put on her most becoming dress, her wedding dress. He termed her his wife indeed and gave thanks to the King for having forced him to wed. Now was Count Bertram of Roussillon truly married to the fair Giletta of Narbonne.

[On the fifth day, one of the youths tells the following story* of Federigo's Falcon. *Ed.*]

A young man named Federigo, son of Messer Filippo Alberighi, was praised above all youths in Tuscany for his deeds in arms and for his gallantry. As so often happens with worthy men, he fell in love with a lady. She was called Giovanna and was judged to be one of the most beautiful and most gracious women in Florence. To gain her love he took part in tournaments, gave parties, sent presents, and spent his money recklessly. But she, being as modest as she was beautiful, paid no attention to these things nor to the man who did them.

*A modernization, by the editor, of the version presented by Edward Hutton in his 1620 translation of the *Decameron*.

Spending constantly all that he could and acquiring nothing, he found his wealth vanishing, as was to be expected. He became poor, without anything left except a little farm where he lived as cheaply as possible, and one other thing—a falcon, one of the best in the world. Nevertheless, his love continued as strong as ever. But since he could not keep on living in the city as he wanted to, he moved to Campi where his little estate was. There he flew his falcon whenever he could; he was in debt to no one; and he patiently put up with being poor.

Now it happened that while Federigo was continuing in his unhappiness, the husband of Giovanna became ill and, coming close to death, made his will. He was a very wealthy man and named his son, already fairly well grown, as his heir. Always having loved Giovanna dearly, he named her to have his fortune if his son should die without lawful children of his own. He then died, and Giovanna was a widow.

That summer, as is customary for our ladies, she went to the country with her son to stay at her estate, which happened to be very near Federigo's. The boy became friends with Federigo and acquainted with Federigo's farm and delighted with the birds and dogs. Often seeing Federigo's falcon flying, he badly wanted to have it. But he couldn't bring himself to ask, seeing how dear it was to Federigo.

Matters were continuing like that when the boy became ill. His mother was very much grieved, for he was her only child, and she loved him as dearly as possible, taking care of him all day long and never ceasing to comfort him. She kept on asking if there was anything he wanted, begging him to tell her and promising that she would certainly get it if it were at all possible.

The boy, hearing her promise so often, said, "Dear mother, if you could get Federigo's falcon for me, I would get well soon."

Hearing this, the lady paused a while and began thinking what she ought to do. She knew that Federigo had loved her for a long time and had never received a single glance from her. She wondered, "How can I send or go to ask for this falcon which, from what I hear, is the best that has ever flown and is, moreover, the only thing he lives for? How can I be so selfish that I want to take it away from a kind man who has no other pleasure at all?"

Troubled by what she had thought, as well as by feeling sure that she would get the falcon if she asked for it, she did not know what to say. She kept quiet, not answering her son. Finally, though, so great was her love for her son, she made up her mind to please him no matter what she had to do. She decided not to send for the falcon but to go and ask for it herself.

"My son," she said, "try to feel better and get well and strong because I promise that the first thing I shall do tomorrow morning is to go for the falcon and bring it to you." The boy was happy with that and showed some improvement right away.

On the following morning, Giovanna took another lady with her for company and went to Federigo's little cottage and asked for him. Since it was not the season for hawking, he had not been out for several days. He was in his garden busy with putting things in order. Hearing that Lady Giovanna was at the door asking for him, he was greatly surprised and happily ran to greet her. She, seeing him coming, came to meet him with ladylike graciousness. Federigo welcomed her with a respectful bow.

She said, "Good day, Federigo." And then she continued, "I have come to make up for all the hurt you have had in loving me more than you should. I shall make it up to you this way: I intend to dine with you in your home today, together with my friend."

Federigo humbly replied to this, "My lady, I do not remember any harm I ever received from you, but so much good that if I was ever worth anything it was because of your virtue and the love I had for you. Indeed, this kindness of yours in coming here is more dear than it would be if I had as much of my fortune as I once had, since you have come to so poor a host."

Having spoken thus, he escorted her into the house, but with great embarrassment, and from there into the garden. Not having anyone else who could entertain her, he said, "My lady, since there is no one else, this good woman, wife of that laborer there, will keep you company while I go to have the table set."

With all the hardships caused by his poverty, he had not been aware until then of the want he had been reduced to by the way in which he had wasted his riches. But that morning, not finding anything with which to entertain the lady for whose love he had honored many guests, he was remorseful. Not knowing what to do and cursing his misfortune, he was beside himself, running here and there, finding neither money nor anything to pawn.

It was growing late and he wanted very much to honor the lady with something. But he did not want to borrow from the gardener or anyone else. His eye chanced to fall on his fine falcon sitting on its perch in the tiny living room. Having nothing else to use, he took it and found it plump. He thought it would make a good dish for so fine a lady. And so, without another thought, he wrung its neck and had his little servant girl pluck and dress it right away and put it on the spit to roast quickly.

He had the table set with the whitest cloths, of which he still had a few, and with a happy countenance returned to the lady in the garden. He told her that dinner, such as he could provide, was ready. The lady and her friend got up and went to the table. Without knowing what there was to eat, together with Federigo who served them eagerly, they ate the pretty falcon.

Then getting up from the table they spent a while conversing pleasantly. It then seemed time to the lady to say why she had come, so she began speaking courteously to Federigo.

"Federigo, remembering your past life and my modesty, which perhaps you have thought of as cruelty and harshness, I have no doubt that you will be surprised at my boldness when you hear the chief reason for my coming here. But if you had children you would know how strong love for them can be, and it seems to me certain that you would excuse me. But since you have none, and I, though I have only one and cannot escape the common law of motherhood whose force compels me, I must, despite all that is right and proper, ask of you a gift, something which I know is extremely dear to you. The reason for this is that there is no other pleasure or sport or consolation left you by your misfortune. That gift is—your falcon, which my little boy wants so much that if I don't bring it to him I'm afraid that his sickness will become worse and something will happen so that I will lose him. Because of this, I pray you not by the love you have for me, for that does not bring obligation, but because of your nobility which you have shown by your behavior to be greater than anyone else's. Please give me the falcon so I can say that with this gift I have saved my son's life and for which he will be indebted to you always."

Hearing what the lady requested and knowing that he could not give her what she asked for because he had given her the falcon to eat, Federigo began to weep so hard that he could not say a word. She thought at first that he wept because of grief at giving the falcon away rather than for any other reason. She was going to say that she didn't want it. However, she kept quiet and waited for him to reply.

He answered, "My lady, since it pleased God that I should fall in love with you, I have often thought that luck was against me. But all that is nothing to what has happened now. I can never be at peace now, considering that you came to my poor house, where you never visited when I was rich, and asked me for a little gift. Fortune has made it so that I cannot grant it. And why that is I will tell you quickly. When I heard that you in your kindness wanted to dine with me, I thought of your rank and worth, and it seemed proper to serve something better than is usually served to others. Therefore, remembering the falcon which you ask me for, and its excellence, I thought it food worthy of you. Today you had it roasted on a platter. I thought it very well done. But now I see you preferred it otherwise, and I am so struck with grief at not being able to help you that I believe I shall never have any peace."

Having said this, he showed the feathers, beak, and claws to prove the truth of what he had said.

When she heard and saw this, the lady at first blamed him for having killed so fine a falcon just to give a woman something to eat. But then she began to think approvingly of his greatness of spirit which poverty had not subdued and never could subdue. Giving up hope of having the falcon and being therefore even more concerned about her son's health, she thanked Federigo for his honoring her and for his good will. She left sadly and returned to her son. He, either because he was sad at not being able to have the falcon or because his illness was destined to become fatal, did not live many days but died, to his mother's extreme grief.

She grieved tearfully for a long time. But she was still young and very rich, and her brothers kept on urging her to marry again. She did not want to do so, but they insisted. She remembered Federigo's courage and his recent brave generosity in killing so wonderful a falcon to honor her. She said to her brothers, "I would prefer, if you would let me, to stay as I am without remarrying. You insist on my marrying, but I will take no one for a husband but Federigo degli Alberighi."

They laughed at her mockingly. "Silly woman, what do you mean! Why choose him when he doesn't have a cent to his name?"

But she replied, "Brothers, I know very well how it is—as you say. But I would rather have a man who lacks wealth than wealth which lacks a man."

The brothers listened to her and, knowing Federigo to be a good man though poor, gave her to him together with all her money.

Married to the woman he dearly loved and, moreover, having lots of money, Federigo had no more troubles and lived happily with her to the end of his days.

17

Petrarch

My Secret

PETRARCH (1304–1374) or, to use
the Italian form of his name, Francesco Petrarca, is often considered the founder
of humanism. Through his inexhaustible industry in scholarship he brought the
mind of western Europe into sympathetic contact with classical antiquity. He
was also the first to collect a private library of any size and to advocate the
preservation of Greek and Latin manuscripts. In his life and work humanism is
well illustrated. The orator, the poet, and the scholar (Petrarch was skilled in all
these roles) of that time were, in effect, obliged to pursue and disseminate
learning, secure individual integrity, and harmonize classical genius with
divine revelation. Classical learning, requiring the study and preparation of
accurate texts of the works of Greek and Roman writers, was thought necessary
to the perfection of the intellect and the civilization of habits. Although Petrarch
himself failed to master Greek, the following generation of scholars made
knowledge of Greek a necessary attainment for the learned. In the ensuing
centuries humanism came to mean the cultivation of the human personality so
that the individual, with liberated intelligence and talent, could lead a life of
dignity, self-reliance, and creativeness.

Of Florentine parentage, Petrarch lived by choice at Avignon, the seat of the
papacy during the greater part of the fourteenth century, and was often a guest in
the palaces of despots and princes in Italy. For the most part, however, he
followed a life of solitary study. Petrarch is best known today for his Italian
sonnets to Laura, which combine the conventional chivalrous love poetry of
southern France and concepts of Platonic idealism. His contemporaries knew
him more for his Latin epic, Africa, modeled on Vergil's Aeneid, and for his
patriotic odes honoring Italy. In a spectacular ceremony in Rome in 1341,
Petrarch was crowned with a laurel wreath as the foremost poet and scholar
of his time.

My Secret (Secretum Meum), *from which the following excerpt is* *taken, is Petrarch's imaginary dialogue with St. Augustine, the fourth-century* *bishop, scholar, and leading theologian of the early Church. In responding to* *Augustine's questions, Petrarch (or, as he calls himself, Franciscus) tries to* *justify his own life and to examine his own beliefs. In doing so, he calls into* *question many of the everyday values of his society as well as its abstract* *generalizations about life and religious beliefs.*

BOOK I

AUGUSTINUS.   What are you doing, poor little man? What are you dreaming? What do you look forward to? Have you then forgotten all your miseries? Don't you remember that you are mortal?

FRANCISCUS.   Certainly I remember it. In fact, that thought never comes to me without bringing a twinge of terror.

AUGUSTINUS.   I wish you did remember it, as you say. You would save me a lot of trouble. The best way to despise properly the temptations of this life is to remember one's own misery and meditate assiduously on death. The thought of death should penetrate to the very marrow of your bones.

FRANCISCUS.   It does indeed. But the thought of death doesn't seem to banish my distress of mind.

AUGUSTINUS.   Anyone who seriously longs to cast off his distresses cannot be disappointed of his desire.

FRANCISCUS.   What's this? Everybody wants to get rid of his woes, and very few have been able to. Most people are unhappy against their will.

AUGUSTINUS.   I thought you were more intelligent. If you had properly absorbed the true and helpful words of the philosophers you have read, if in fact you had studied for yourself and not for others, if you had drawn from the reading of so many books a rule for your own life instead of seeking vaingloriously the windy applause of the vulgar, you wouldn't say such stupid things.

MY SECRET   From *Petrarch and His World* by Morris Bishop, copyright © 1963 by Indiana University Press. Reprinted by permission of the publisher. Further use is prohibited by law. [Pp. 194–207, 210–13.]

FRANCISCUS. You make me blush like a schoolboy. But still I don't know what for.

AUGUSTINUS. For many things; but first of all for your idea that a man can be unhappy against his will.

FRANCISCUS. Ah, I'll stop blushing! Everybody knows that poverty, pain, ignominy, diseases, death, come against our will and without our agency. Hence it's easy to recognize our distresses and easy to hate them, but it's not easy to get rid of them. The first two points are in our power, the third is in the power of fortune.

AUGUSTINUS. Your impudence makes me angrier than your mistakes. Idiot, have you forgotten the words of the philosophers and saints, that no one can be made miserable by such miseries? If virtue alone renders man happy, the contrary of virtue must render him unhappy.

FRANCISCUS. That's Stoic doctrine,[1] more theoretical than practical.

AUGUSTINUS. Are we agreed on this, that a man becomes unhappy only through vice?

FRANCISCUS. Well, I've noticed that many, including me, are chiefly tormented by our inability to shake off the yoke of vices, although we have struggled all our lives to that end with all our powers. So one may admit that many are very miserable against their will, while grieving and hoping for deliverance.

AUGUSTINUS. I'll tell you the method of deliverance. The first step is to meditate on death and human infelicity; the second is to struggle with intense desire to rise.

FRANCISCUS. It hasn't worked with me.

AUGUSTINUS. In men's minds there is a perverse and pestilent longing to deceive oneself. You men should fear the frauds you perpetrate on yourselves. Everyone esteems himself at more than his worth and loves himself more than is due. The deceived is never separate from the deceiver.

FRANCISCUS. You've said that before. But as far as I can remember I have never deceived myself. I can only wish I hadn't been deceived by others.

AUGUSTINUS. Right now you are deceiving yourself, in boasting that you have never deceived yourself. Do you think that anyone can sin perforce? Sin is a voluntary action; if the will is lacking, the act ceases to be sinful.

---

[1] Stoic philosophers of Greece and Rome taught that the acceptance of one's fate brought peace of mind and happiness.

FRANCISCUS.   I'll have to grant that. I feel it in myself and I conjecture it in others. I suspect that I am being punished, that since I didn't stand upright when I could, now that I want to rise from my abjection I no longer can.

AUGUSTINUS.   Instead of "I no longer can," you should say: "I no longer wish to."

FRANCISCUS.   I'll never confess that. Heaven knows—no man does—how I have suffered and how I have longed to rise.

AUGUSTINUS.   Conscience may well have made you weep, but it has not made you change your intentions. Certainly you could have reformed, if you had really wished to. Look at my own story, in my Confessions.[2]

FRANCISCUS.   I know all about that. Every time I read your Confessions I am moved by two contrary feelings, hope and fear. Sometimes it seems to me, in tears, that I am reading not another's story but the record of my own pilgrimage.

AUGUSTINUS.   You must learn from it to desire your amelioration passionately. Consult your own conscience. It is the best interpreter of virtue; it is the infallible, truthful judge of your thoughts and acts. It will tell you that you have never properly aspired to salvation.

FRANCISCUS.   My conscience tells me that is true. But how can this great desire work?

AUGUSTINUS.   In opening a way through difficulties. The desire for virtue is a large part of virtue. And this desire can arise only through the extinction of other desires. One must dare to say: "I have nothing further in common with the body; I am revolted by all the visible world; I aspire to greater felicities."

FRANCISCUS.   How can one attain this state?

AUGUSTINUS.   First, as I have already recommended, by the constant remembrance of your mortality.

FRANCISCUS.   So I don't meditate on death?

AUGUSTINUS.   Very rarely, in fact, and so limply that your meditation does not penetrate to the depths of your calamities.

FRANCISCUS.   I thought the opposite.

AUGUSTINUS.   I am not talking about what you thought, but about what you ought to think. You ought to think constantly about the

[2]In his autobiographical *Confessions*, Augustine told of his own spiritual turmoil, struggle, and final success.

fragility of your state and bear constantly before your eyes the image of your mortality. Few think profoundly that they must necessarily die. You must ever aspire to that life wherein you will cease to be mortal. So you must look continually on the picture of a dying man, on the chilling limbs, the burning, sweating breast, the gasping breath, the receding, filming, tear-filled eyes, the livid face, the sunken cheeks, the yellowed teeth, the sharp nose, the foam at the lips, the thick, dry tongue, the strangle in the throat, the revolting smell, and above all the horror of a face without intelligence.

FRANCISCUS. I see that I must tell myself the whole truth.

AUGUSTINUS. Think also of the final judgment, when you must give an account of all your deeds and words, when you can put no trust in wit and eloquence, riches and power, bodily beauty or worldly fame. You must think of heaven and hell not as possible but as necessary and inevitable. Then you may be sure that you have not meditated in vain.

FRANCISCUS. You terrify me. And yet such meditations are familiar to me, especially at night, when the spirit, released from its day-time cares, collects itself within itself. Then I compose myself in the attitude of a dying man, and I picture vividly to myself the hour of death and all its horrible accompaniments, so that sometimes I seem to look into hell; and I am so shattered by this vision that I rise up all trembling, and I frighten anyone who is present by crying: "Alas, what is happening to me? And what will happen? Mercy, O dear Jesus, aid me!" I fall in a sort of fit; and when I tell my friends of it I move them to tears. Such being my case, what holds me back? What obstacle lies in my way, so that my nightmare medita-tions bring me only terror, but I remain what I was before, like those who have never known such experiences? I am worse off than they, for they enjoy their pleasures, whereas for me every pleasure is blended with bitterness.

AUGUSTINUS. You should rather be happy because you are aware of your state. There is hope for you. You must reflect forever on the imminence of death, thanking God for his warnings. As for these midnight phantasms, they are not divinely sent, but are the pro-ducts of a tortured spirit. Your salutary purpose for reform is weakened by the excessive mobility of your mind. Hence your inward discord, the anxiety of a mind that tortures itself and cannot bring itself to wash away its own stains. While it recognizes its own tortuous ways it does not desert them; while it fears the imminent danger it does not conjure it away.

FRANCISCUS.   Alas, wretched man that I am!

AUGUSTINUS.   Good! You are shaken out of your torpor. Now let us repose a little in silence, and leave the rest to tomorrow.

FRANCISCUS.   That is what I need: repose and silence.

BOOK II

AUGUSTINUS.   Did you sleep well?

FRANCISCUS.   Well enough.

AUGUSTINUS.   Let's return to our subject. Many evils assail you, but you don't realize how many and how mighty are your enemies. Let's take the capital sins in their order. First, the most grievous sin of pride. How petty are the superiorities you look on with complacency! You are proud of your intellect, of your reading of many books; you glory in your own high talk and in the shape of your mortal body. And yet you recognize how often that fine intellect fails you, and in how many ways you can't equal the competence of the simplest of men. I'm putting it mildly; there are mean, common animals whose powers you could never imitate by any application. And you would glory in your intelligence! All your reading, what good has it done you? Of all the books you have read, how much has clung in your spirit and taken root there, to produce fruit in its time? Examine yourself, and you will find that all you know, in comparison with what you don't know, is only a tiny trickle compared with the ocean. And what is the use of knowing many things if, when you have learned the dimensions of heaven and earth, the measure of the seas, the courses of the stars, the virtues of plants and stones, the secrets of nature, you still don't know yourself? What difference does it make that others applaud your words, if these are not approved by your own inward judgment? What can be more puerile, nay, insane, than, in your heedlessness and sloth, to spend your time in the study of words, to find your pleasure in talk, not even to perceive your own shame with your bleary eyes? You are like those birds that, according to the story, so delight in their own sweet song that they die of it. How often have I heard you complain that neither tongue nor pen could express the ideas that were clear enough in your thought!

What then is this rhetoric, so limited and frail that it can't embrace its own subjects or possess what it has embraced! So much for pride of mind! And as for your pride of body, what pleases you therein? Perhaps its vigor and health? Nothing could be more idiotic. A weakness arising from the slightest causes, the attacks of illness, the bite of a worm, a poisonous exhalation, may make an end of body. Or perhaps you think you're handsome, and you look admiringly on your features and complexion? Have you forgotten the fable of Narcissus?[3] And the revolting ugliness beneath the skin? And the approach of age's decay?

FRANCISCUS.   Hold on a minute! You say I boast of my intelligence. Well, the only intelligence I claim is that I have never trusted it. Why should I be proud of reading many books, from which I have derived little learning but much distress of mind? You accuse me of seeking glory in fine language when, as you admit, my chief torment is that it can't suffice to express my ideas. And when you talked seriously about my beautiful body you almost made me laugh. So I have put my hope in this wretched mortal frame, which daily warns me of its frailty? Heaven forbid! I admit that when I was a boy I took pleasure in showing off my fine face and licking down my hair, but such vanity disappeared with my youth.

AUGUSTINUS.   There is much I could say in reply, but I prefer to let your conscience shame you. You try to hide your pride, but you reveal it in your depreciation of others. That revelation of self-esteem is more unpleasant than undue exaltation of oneself. I would much rather see you exalt others, even though preserving your own primacy, than watch you trample them down and then haughtily display a shield of humility, made of the scorn of others.

FRANCISCUS.   As you like. I have no very high opinion either of myself or of others. I don't like to say outright what I have learned to think of most men.

AUGUSTINUS.   Well, let's pass on to the other points. Of envy I absolve you. But what about greed for temporal goods?

FRANCISCUS.   Come, come! I never heard anything more absurd. There's nothing I'm freer from than avarice.

AUGUSTINUS.   Not so free as you think. And not so free either from ambition. What are these incessant cares and worries of yours? You

---

[3]A Greek myth about a young man who fell in love with his own reflection (in a pool of water).

may say that you want to be in a position to help your friends. But that would be just a noble excuse.

FRANCISCUS.   I'm not inhuman enough to be unmoved by concern for my friends, especially those who are endeared to me by their virtue and merit. Some I admire, some I venerate, some I love, some I pity. On the other hand I'm not so high-minded as to ruin myself for my friends. I have to think of my own future, provide a competence for old age, and hence combine some material concern with my cultivation of the Muses.

AUGUSTINUS.   A useless labor, and a senseless one. You can get along with very little. You were never so well off as when you were wandering alone and carefree in the hills. Then you thought yourself the richest and happiest of mortals; but now you have abandoned that frugal country peace. You began to despise the berries of your bushes, the rough clothing, and life among peasants, and you have come to learn cupidity amid the city's tumults. You are still hesitant, perhaps because you are caught in the snares of sin, or perhaps because God wills that where you passed your youth under the discipline of others you should, though your own master, drag out a sad old age.

FRANCISCUS.   Well, if I try to provide against poverty in that sad old age, what is wrong with that?

AUGUSTINUS.   The wrong is that you are forever concerned with the ephemeral, and you forget the eternal. Nothing is more senseless than to suffer poverty forever, out of fear of suffering it for a day.

FRANCISCUS.   True; but my desires are modest and limited. I don't want abundance; but I don't want to live in need.

AUGUSTINUS.   Only the gods don't live in need. Don't you know that man is the most needy of all the animals? Cease to hope for the impossible; content yourself with man's lot, and learn to have both too much and too little, to surpass and to be surpassed. You can't shake off the yoke of fortune that rests on the necks of kings. You can be freed from it only when, conquering human passions, you submit yourself totally to the rule of virtue. Then you will be free, needing nothing, subject to no man, finally a king, powerful and absolutely happy.

FRANCISCUS.   I wish that I could wish for nothing. But I am dragged on by perverse habit. I feel forever something unsatisfied in my heart.

AUGUSTINUS.   Let us speak of ambition. Examine your heart and you
will find that it has no little place there.

FRANCISCUS.   You think it was nothing that I have fled the cities
whenever I could, disdaining assemblies and public ceremonies,
seeking the woods and country peace, forswearing vain honors?
And I hear myself accused of ambition!

AUGUSTINUS.   You mortals renounce many things not because you
despise them but because you despair of attaining them. You
·haven't proved to me that you haven't desired honors, but only
that you hate the trouble of seeking them. Don't hope to hide
behind a finger, as the saying goes. This flight from the cities, this
longing for the woods of which you are so proud, doesn't excuse
you; it's just a shift of blame. All kinds of roads lead to the same
goal; and believe me, though you have left the trodden highway,
you are trying to reach on a byway those ambitious ends you claim
to despise. Your insistence on free time, your solitude, your in-
curiosity about normal human occupations, your studies, whose
purpose is glory, all prove your ambition. But let's get on. I won't
mention gluttony; you're free of that. And wrath is no serious fault
of yours. But there are more dangerous passions for you.

FRANCISCUS.   Good God, what more dangerous can remain?

AUGUSTINUS.   How great are the flames of lust?

FRANCISCUS.   Sometimes they are so great that I grieve that I wasn't
born insensible. I would rather be a motionless stone than feel the
upheavals of my body. Sometimes I think I have risen above them;
and then I fall again, with bitterness of spirit, into the old miseries.

AUGUSTINUS.   I am not surprised, for I was a witness of your struggles, and I saw you rise and fall; and now, in pity for your prostrate
state, I have proposed to bring you aid.

FRANCISCUS.   I thank you. But what human power remains to help
me?

AUGUSTINUS.   None; only divine power. A man cannot be chaste
without God's gift. You must beg for this gift, humbly and often
with tears. He does not deny what is properly asked.

FRANCISCUS.   I have done that so often that I almost fear to bore him.

AUGUSTINUS.   Not humbly enough, not soberly enough. You have
always reserved a little place for future desires; you have always set
the term of your prayers too far ahead. I speak out of experience;
the same thing happened to me. I used to pray: "Lord, grant me to

live chaste; but not right away; pretty soon." But a man who prays for tomorrow loses today.

FRANCISCUS.   I shall then pray assiduously, without weariness, shame, or despair.

AUGUSTINUS.   Good. And keep in mind the words of Plato, that nothing hinders knowledge of the divine more than the carnal appetites and the flame of lust. But since we are to return to this subject, I shall deal now with other grievous wounds of your spirit. You are afflicted by a calamitous ailment, which the moderns call *accidia* and the ancients *aegritudo*, or depression, or acute melancholy.

FRANCISCUS.   The very name makes me shudder.

AUGUSTINUS.   I am not surprised, since you have suffered from it long and grievously.

FRANCISCUS.   I admit it. The assaults of the other passions are brief and they contain their modicum of pleasure, but this plague holds me so close that sometimes it tortures me day and night, robbing me of light and life, plunging me into hell. But strangely enough I feed so upon tears and pain with a kind of atrocious black satisfaction that I am unwilling to be torn from them.

AUGUSTINUS.   What is the cause of your depression? Illness, misfortune?

FRANCISCUS.   All kinds of causes. Specific reasons; and in general my abhorrence and contempt for the human condition.

AUGUSTINUS.   What especially afflicts you?

FRANCISCUS.   Everything I see, hear, and feel.

AUGUSTINUS.   Gad! There is nothing you like?

FRANCISCUS.   Nothing—or not very much.

AUGUSTINUS.   All this is what I have called accidia. You loathe all your own concerns.

FRANCISCUS.   Other people's too.

AUGUSTINUS.   Even your advantages, which others envy?

FRANCISCUS.   Only the most wretched of creatures could envy a wretched man.

AUGUSTINUS.   You think that fortune has been unkind to you?

FRANCISCUS.   Very unkind, very evil, very arrogant, very cruel.

AUGUSTINUS.   Well, everybody can't be first.

FRANCISCUS.   I don't want to be first. No one has had more modest ambitions than I, but no one has gained them with more difficulty.

I call Truth to witness that I have never desired to stand first. I abhor an existence filled with care and trouble; I much prefer a middle state, Horace's golden mean, *aurea mediocritas*. But even that I haven't been able to attain. Forever doubtful of the future, with my mind in suspense, I have gained no pleasure from fortune's favors. As you know, I have always been dependent on others, and that's the unhappiest of states.

AUGUSTINUS.   You would have it that you alone of all men might live free from care? Very few indeed have been able to live for themselves alone, and the happiest are those who have lived for others. There must be other reasons for your melancholy.

FRANCISCUS.   Don't you know that cruel stroke of fate, which in a single day struck me down, and all my hopes, and my property, and my family and home?[4]

AUGUSTINUS.   I see your eyes flash. Let's go on, for this is no time to deal with that matter.

FRANCISCUS.   Then there's my life in this most horrible of cities.[5] Sometimes it seems to me that I have descended into hell. How can I do here anything really good, think honest thoughts, write proper poetry?

AUGUSTINUS.   Plenty of others, and great men, too, have suffered in the same way. You came of your own free will to this city and to this state of mind, and by your own free will you can escape. You can train your ears to listen to the city's din with pleasure, as to a waterfall. By such devices you can banish your melancholy.

FRANCISCUS.   I must yield to you, although I am not entirely convinced. At least, my condition no longer seems so wretched as it did. Let us now postpone further talk till tomorrow.

BOOK III

AUGUSTINUS.   I haven't yet touched your deepest and most persistent troubles. You are fastened by two mighty chains. You are like a miser in prison shackled by golden fetters; you would like to get free, but you don't want to lose them. But there's a law in this

---

[4]The death of his father and the loss of his inheritance occurred on the same day.

[5]Avignon, the city in southern France in which Petrarch lived for many years.

prison: if you don't throw off the chains you can't go free. And you love them; you even boast of them.

FRANCISCUS.   What are these chains you're talking about?

AUGUSTINUS.   Love and glory.

FRANCISCUS.   Gods above, what's this I hear? So you call love and glory chains, and if I permit it you'll take them from me? You want to rob me of the loveliest things in life, and condemn to darkness the fairest part of my being?

AUGUSTINUS.   I'm going to try to, though I doubt if I succeed. Tell me, don't you think love is the utmost madness?

FRANCISCUS.   The fact is, love depends on its object. It can be called either the ugliest passion of the spirit or its noblest activity. If I adore a wicked, contemptible woman, that is madness; but if a rare exemplar of virtue attracts me and I devote myself to loving and venerating her, what of that?

AUGUSTINUS.   There's no difference. In both cases you bid farewell to reason and to awareness of truth.

FRANCISCUS.   You're wasting your time. I've never loved anything foul, anything that was not very beautiful.

AUGUSTINUS.   Even beautiful things can be loved foully.

FRANCISCUS.   Do you know who it is you're talking about?

AUGUSTINUS.   I have thoroughly considered my subject. We are going to talk about a mortal woman, whom you have been admiring and celebrating during a large part of your life.[6] I am amazed at your long insanity.

FRANCISCUS.   Don't be offensive. Do you realize that you are referring to a woman whose mind, ignoring earthly cares, burns with celestial desires? In whose aspect, as truth is truth, shines heavenly beauty? Whose behavior is an example of perfect virtue? Whose voice, whose eyes, are more than mortal, whose very walk seems no human action? Think of that, please, and you will realize what sort of language you must use.

AUGUSTINUS.   Poor fool! So for sixteen years you have fed your flame with false cajolements! How you have suffered! But in the end, when those eyes close in death, you will be ashamed that you tied your immortal soul to a mortal body and you will blush to recall what you have so exalted.

---

[6]Petrarch wrote his love sonnets to a woman named Laura, the wife of a citizen of Avignon.

FRANCISCUS.   God forbid! I shall not live to see her death.

AUGUSTINUS.   How do you know? She is getting older; that splendid body, worn out with illness and with frequent childbirths, has already lost much of its old vigor. It is folly to submit your soul to any such mortal thing.

FRANCISCUS.   I have not done so. I have never loved her body so much as her soul. My delight was in her character, transcending mortality, resembling that of the angels. So if—the mere utterance makes me shudder—if she should die first, I would appease my grief by saying, with Laelius,[7] wisest of the Romans: "I loved her virtue, which has not been spent."

AUGUSTINUS.   Well, pour all the praise you like on your little woman. I won't contradict you. She's a queen, a saint, if you like, or as Virgil said, a goddess, a sister of Phoebus,[8] a nymph. But her great virtue won't help to excuse your errors.

FRANCISCUS.   I call Truth[9] here by our side to witness that in my love there has never been anything base, lewd, or in any way culpable, except perhaps in its excess. Nothing more wholly beautiful than my love can be conceived.

AUGUSTINUS.   I'm sorry to hear such nonsense from one who ought to think more clearly.

FRANCISCUS.   Whatever I am is due to her. I should never have gained my present reputation, however one may judge it, if she hadn't tended with her noble sympathy that tiny little seed of virtue that nature sowed in my breast. She recalled my youthful spirit from all turpitude, pulled me back, as they say, with a hook, and forced me to look upward. How could I fail to be transformed by her character? Never has any slanderer, however scurrilous, attacked her good name or dared to find anything reprehensible in her actions, words, or even gestures. Even those who leave nothing unsoiled spared her, in admiration and reverence. It is not strange that her good fame inspired in me the desire for fame, and eased my labors to that end. From my young manhood I longed for nothing else than to please her, who alone had pleased me. You know how, to

[7]A Roman nobleman, man of letters, and close friend of Petrarch.

[8]In Roman mythology Phoebus Apollo, god of the sun, was the twin brother of Diana, goddess of the moon and of chastity.

[9]The figure, or spirit, of Truth is imagined as sitting in silent judgment throughout the dialogue.

gain that end, I spurned the temptations of a myriad pleasures and subjected myself prematurely to laborious cares. And you order me to forget her or to love her more temperately!

AUGUSTINUS.   You make me sick at my stomach.

FRANCISCUS.   Why, pray?

AUGUSTINUS.   Because to think falsely is a sign of ignorance; but to proclaim the false impudently is a sign both of ignorance and of vainglory.

FRANCISCUS.   How can you prove that I have either thought or said anything false?

AUGUSTINUS.   By everything you have said! First of all when you say that she has made you what you are. The fact is that she has prevented you from developing. What a man you might have been, if she hadn't captured you with her beauty! It is kind nature that made you what you were; she prevented you from becoming what you might have been, or rather you threw it away for her, for she is innocent. Her beauty seemed to you so sweet and attractive that you destroyed your native possibilities in your longings and wailings. And you boast that she preserved you from all turpitudes! Perhaps she did save you from many, but she forced you into greater calamities. For one who drives us to our downfall while keeping us out of various filthy courses, or who inflicts a mortal wound while healing some minor scratches, can hardly be called our liberator, but rather our murderer. So she whom you call your guide has saved you from foul actions only to lay you out on a splendid bier. And as for her teaching you to look upward, to disdain the mass of men, what else is that than making you slave to her alone, forgetful and scornful of all else on earth? There is nothing worse for a man among men. When you recall that she involved you in innumerable labors you are certainly telling the truth. But you got a good deal out of them! And as for your boast that she made you seek for fame, well, that is the worst burden on your soul. In short, this woman you exalt so highly is ruining you.

FRANCISCUS.   What do you mean?

AUGUSTINUS.   She has distracted your mind from the love of the Creator and has turned it to the love of the creature. You have loved the Creator only as the artificer who made that beautiful body.

FRANCISCUS.   I protest to Truth here present and to my conscience that I never loved her body more than her soul! As she has grown older and her bodily beauty has dwindled I have been the more constant. Although the flower of youth visibly fades with the passage of time, the beauty of her spirit kept increasing, and this has kept me faithful.

AUGUSTINUS.   Are you trying to fool me? If that spirit had inhabited a squalid body, would you have loved it as much?

FRANCISCUS.   I don't dare to assert that, for the spirit is invisible. But if the spirit should make itself manifest, no doubt I would love a beautiful spirit even in an ugly habitation.

AUGUSTINUS.   You are playing on words. For if you can love only what is evident to the eyes, you love the body. However, I won't deny that her spirit and her character have added fuel to your flames, just as her very name greatly increased your passion. You loved body and soul together, and both of them immoderately. And you have fallen into great disasters because of this love.

FRANCISCUS.   That I will never admit, even if you put me to torture.

AUGUSTINUS.   Do you remember your boyhood, your love of God, your meditations on death, your religious feeling, your love of virtue?

FRANCISCUS.   I remember very well, and I grieve that as I have grown older my merits have decreased.

AUGUSTINUS.   When did you lose these good habits?

FRANCISCUS.   I came to a parting of the ways, and I took the downward path. And I have never been able to find the right way again.

AUGUSTINUS.   How old were you when this happened?

FRANCISCUS.   It was in the midst of youth's fevers. If you wait a moment, I can recollect the exact year.

AUGUSTINUS.   And when did this woman's beauty first appear to you?

FRANCISCUS.   Oh, that I'll never forget!

AUGUSTINUS.   How do those two times match?

FRANCISCUS.   Well, in fact her appearance in my life and my steps astray happened at about the same time.

AUGUSTINUS.   That's what I was after. And this glorious woman, this guide to heaven, why didn't she hold you by the hand and show you the right road?

FRANCISCUS.   She did all she could. Unmoved by my prayers and blandishments, in spite of her youth and mine and in spite of certain circumstances that might have moved a heart of stone, she kept her feminine purity and remained firm, impregnable. Isn't that something? She showed me my duty; and when I went my headstrong way she preferred to abandon me rather than to follow me.

AUGUSTINUS.   Ah, then you did sometimes have base desires! You denied that before. Well, that's the familiar madness of lovers, always saying: "Will I, nill I, nill I, will I." You don't know what you want or what you don't want.

FRANCISCUS.   You've tricked me. If perhaps I had such desires at the time, youthful ardor caused them. Now I know better. But she never wavered in her womanly virtue. If at the time I protested against it, now I am glad of it, and I thank her.

AUGUSTINUS.   It's hard to trust someone who has fallen once. That flame of yours may be less intense, it hasn't been extinguished. And in ascribing so much merit to your beloved, in absolving her, you are condemning yourself. Love has made you wretched; that's what I began by saying. Earthly love leads to the forgetfulness of God; it has brought you to the miserable state you have described. In your folly, you were not even content with gazing on her living face, the source of your woes, and you obtained from an illustrious artist a painted image and carried it around with you, to have something to cry over forever. You sought out everything that would provoke and irritate your emotion. And—the final proof of an unhinged mind—you were as much allured by her beautiful name as by her body, and with incredible folly you cultivated every punning significance of it! You loved the laurel, whether of emperors or poets, because it chimed with her name. You could hardly write a poem without dragging in the laurel. And since you couldn't hope for the imperial wreath, you longed for the laurel crown of poetry as immoderately as you had loved the lady. You will be shocked some day when you reflect how much effort you spent in obtaining it, though I grant that you were often borne on the wings of inspiration. Don't speak; I know what is in your mind. I know that you were a poet before you fell in love. But the difficulties and dangers in the way of success would have delayed your effort, if the memory of that sweetest of names hadn't spurred you on over land and sea to Rome and Naples, where finally you gained what you had lusted for so ardently.[10] Anyone

---

[10]Petrarch had been honored in public ceremonies in Rome and Naples. In Rome he was crowned with a wreath of laurel, symbolic of his high achievement in poetry and scholarship.

who doesn't take this as an indication of notable madness must be mad himself.

FRANCISCUS.   What do you want me to do? Despair?

AUGUSTINUS.   First we'll look for remedies. Cicero says that many think of driving out an old love with a new one, as a nail drives out a nail. That's good advice. A mind dispersed on many objects has the more difficulty in concentrating on one. But the danger is that if you cast off this passion, which I admit is one of the nobler sort, you may get entangled in many, and become, instead of a lover, a libertine. I won't disapprove of your passing from one subjection to another, for perhaps in such excursions you may find your liberty, or a lighter servitude; but I would much reprobate your bowing your neck to a series of sordid involvements.

FRANCISCUS.   May the patient interrupt the doctor for a moment? Let me tell you this—I can never love anyone else. My eyes are so used to gazing upon her, my mind is so used to admiring her, that all that is not she seems dark and ugly. So if you command me to love another in order to free myself from love, you are asking the impossible. It's all over; I am done for.

AUGUSTINUS.   Then you must find some external remedy. Can you persuade yourself to run away?

FRANCISCUS.   Painful though it would be, I could do so.

AUGUSTINUS.   If you can, you're saved. How can you be secure in this place, where remain so many vestiges of your old wounds, where you are oppressed by the present and the past? . . . You are too old to play the passionate lover. Most men don't reach your present age.[11] Renounce the follies of youth; extinguish the ardors of adolescence. Don't be forever thinking of what you have been; look around you to realize what you are now.

FRANCISCUS.   Do you know what brings me a little comfort? She is getting old along with me.

AUGUSTINUS.   Perhaps you think it's more decent for you to love her when you're both old than to fall in love with a girl? As a matter of fact love is all the uglier as there is less basis for love. You should therefore be ashamed that your mind never changes, while the body is continually changing. That is a subject for reflection, which, as I said, is Cicero's third cure of love. Meditate on your manhood, on the nobility of the human spirit, on the fragility and

---

[11]Petrarch was thirty-eight years old when he wrote *My Secret*.

filth of the body, on the brevity of life, on the flight of time, on the
certainty of death. Think how revolting it is to be the world's
laughingstock, how improper your behavior is for your clerical
profession. Recall all your sufferings for her sake, all your lamentations and tears. Think, at the same time, of her ungrateful and
supercilious bearing, how, if she was occasionally kind, it was
more briefly than the blowing of a summer breeze. Think how you
have added to her fame, and how much she has subtracted from
your own life, and how you have protected her own fair name,
while she has always been perfectly unconcerned about your state.
Think how she has distracted you from the love of God, how she
has interfered with the completion of the works you have in hand.
And finally think of what she actually is! Few consider with a
realizing sense the filthiness of the feminine body. Repel every
recollection of your past preoccupations and all thought of the
past. And besiege heaven with your prayers; tire the ears of the
heavenly king. Let no night or day pass without tears and supplications. But we've talked enough about this. Now I come to your
final fault, which I must undertake to cure. You are unduly desirous of worldly glory and of immortality for your name.

FRANCISCUS.   I must confess it. I cannot restrain this appetite.

AUGUSTINUS.   But it is to be feared that the longing for vain immortality may block the road to true immortality. Worldly fame is
nothing but the diffuse gabble of many tongues. It is a gust of air,
the breath of many men. You despise the vulgar mob; but you
delight in the silly little words of the very men whose actions you
condemn. Worse, you find the summit of your felicity therein!
What is the purpose of your perpetual labors, your night vigils, the
fervency of your studies? You may answer: "To learn something
useful for my life;" but you already know all that is needful for life
and death. It would be better for you to apply what you know to
your conduct. And I notice that you have tried in most of your
works to tickle the public taste, to please the very people you
particularly dislike, plucking posies, in your poems, histories, and
speeches, to enrapture your hearers. And not content with their
ephemeral applause, you have lusted for fame among posterity.
Thus you started a big history of Romans, from Romulus to Titus;
and without finishing that, you dispatched a poetic craft to Africa.
And so, writing of others, you forget yourself. And death may
strike you down before you finish either task.

FRANCISCUS.   I have been afraid of that. I once fell seriously ill, and I thought I was going to die. And what tortured me most was the thought that I was leaving my *Africa* half finished. As I didn't want anyone else to edit it, I had determined to burn it with my own hands. That is a bitter memory.

AUGUSTINUS.   You confirm me in my judgment. But suppose you had plenty of time, leisure, tranquillity, without dull periods or physical weakness, that you were spared all those interruptions that have interfered with your writing, that every condition was favorable. What great thing to you think you would accomplish?

FRANCISCUS.   No doubt some brilliant, rare, excellent book.

AUGUSTINUS.   The more excellent it might be, the more it would detract from the care of your soul. And how vain and transitory is earthly fame!

FRANCISCUS.   Oh, I know all that old stuff of the philosophers about the vanity of human wishes and so forth. But I don't expect to become a god and embrace eternity. Human fame is enough for me. That's what I long for. Being mortal, I desire only mortal rewards.

AUGUSTINUS.   What a calamity, if you are telling the truth! If you don't want immortal rewards, if you don't look to eternity, you are condemned to earth. Your fate is sealed; there is no hope for you.

FRANCISCUS.   All I meant was this: I treat mortal things as mortal, and I don't affront the nature of things by vast, unreasonable desires. I don't abandon eternal concerns; I just defer them.

AUGUSTINUS.   Take care! Death may strike at any moment. Time is short; it is dangerous to make any postponement.

FRANCISCUS.   Still, there is some reason in my stand. That glory which it is permissible to hope for must be sought while we are here below. The greater glory will be enjoyed in heaven by those who will be admitted there; they won't even think of earthly glory. So this is the order: the care for mortal things must come first in mortal minds; eternal concerns will succeed in their turn to the transitory.

AUGUSTINUS.   What a foolish little man you are! You think that all the joys of earth and heaven will shower upon you at your summons! What is earth in comparison with heaven? I hate to hear you sneer at the "old stuff" of the philosophers. Is the geometrical proof that our earth is tiny, just a long island of land, old stuff? Is it old stuff that of the world's five so-called zones the middle one is uninhabit-able by men because of the sun's heat, the extreme one to north and south burdened by intolerable cold and perpetual ice, so that only the two temperate zones are habitable? It is doubtful whether the antipodes are inhabited; I don't think so myself. That leaves only the north temperate zone, which, according to some, is divided into two parts, one reserved for our uses, the other cut off by the northern Ocean, which forbids our access to it. In this tiny world glory is of small account.

FRANCISCUS.   Do you then order me to give up my studies and live ingloriously?

AUGUSTINUS.   I will never advise you to live without glory, but I admonish you not to prefer the quest of glory to that of virtue. I will lay down this rule: take no heed for glory; the less you long for it the more of it you will gain. A man would be mad who would bustle about under the midday sun to show others his shadow, and no less mad is he who, in the ardors of life, tries to promote his own fame. Go to your goal, and your shadow will follow you. You wear yourself out writing books; you're making a great mistake, for you forget your own advantage in trying to bring advantage to others, and thus in the vain hope of glory you waste unwitting this brief span of life.

FRANCISCUS.   What shall I do then? Shall I leave my books unfinished? Wouldn't it be more sensible to hurry them to a conclusion, if God grants it, and then, being freed of these tasks, to give myself wholly to higher things? I can't calmly leave half done works that have cost me so much.

AUGUSTINUS.   I know where the shoe pinches. You would rather abandon yourself than your little books. Lay down the burden of your histories; the deeds of the Romans have been sufficiently celebrated by themselves and by others. Abandon Africa[12] and leave it to its inhabitants. You won't increase either Scipio's[13] glory or your own. He can't be any further exalted; you are just creeping along behind him. So surrender all these works, and at last give yourself back to yourself! And, to return to the point from which we started, begin to think deeply about death, which little by little

---

[12]Petrarch was writing an epic poem about the Romans in Africa.

[13]Scipio the Elder (237–183 B.C.) was a hero of Rome's war against Carthage (in Africa).

and all unconscious you are approaching. You are part of the great procession; exulting in the prime of your life, you are treading on the heels of others; but others are treading on yours. Remember Cicero: "All the life of a philosopher is meditation on death." You can find the right path by listening to your own spirit, which tells you: "This is the way home." I pray God that he may accompany you and bring your wandering steps to safety.

FRANCISCUS.   Oh, may your prayer be granted, and by God's favor may I come safe out of the maze, free of my own self-deceptions and delusions! And may the storms of my spirit subside, and the world be silent, and fortune molest me no more!

18

Giovanni Pico della Mirandola

Oration on the Dignity of Man

GIOVANNI Pico, Count of Mirandola (1463–494), provides a perfect example of the brilliant, young, restless intellectual of the Renaissance. Repelled by the traditional curriculum of the University of Bologna, Pico spent several years wandering through Italy and France, collecting a library, acquiring a remarkable miscellaneous knowledge of the Greek and Latin classics, and studying Hebrew, Chaldee, and Arabic. He was especially interested in the occult and in Neoplatonism. These studies seemed to him to promise an understanding of the divine mystery that underlies all religions.

As a youth of twenty-four, Pico confidently offered to defend in public disputation nine hundred propositions, which represented his own conclusions in philosophy and theology. Despite the interest generated by his audacity, the disputation was never held, for some of the theses suggested by Pico aroused suspicions of heresy.

Pico took all knowledge as his province and attempted to show the truth of Christianity as both a religion and a philosophy by bringing into intellectual harmony the traditional classics and the philosophies of Hebraism and Islam. With his handsome appearance, keen intelligence, and restless and quick perceptions, Pico made a vivid impression upon his contemporaries—a living proof of the Platonic "Ideal Youth," as one of his philosophically minded admirers termed him. Pico's Oration on the Dignity of Man, originally intended as an introductory speech for the disputation proposed in 1487, is an excellent reflection of the aspirations of Renaissance humanism.

I have read in the records of the Arabians, reverend Fathers, that Abdala the Saracen,[1] when questioned as to what on this stage of the world, as it were, could be seen most worthy of wonder, replied: "There is nothing to be seen more wonderful than man." In agreement with this opinion is the saying of Hermes Trismegistus: "A great miracle, Asclepius, is man."[2] But when I weighed the reason for these maxims, the many grounds for the excellence of human nature reported by many men failed to satisfy me—that man is the intermediary between creatures, the intimate of the gods, the king of the lower beings, by the acuteness of his senses, by the discernment of his reason, and by the light of his intelligence the interpreter of nature, the interval between fixed eternity and fleeting time, and (as the Persians say) the bond, nay, rather, the marriage song of the world, on David's testimony[3] but little lower than the angels. Admittedly great though these reasons be, they are not the principal grounds, that is, those which may rightfully claim for themselves the privilege of the highest admiration. For why should we not admire more the angels themselves and the blessed choirs of heaven? At last it seems to me I have come to understand why man is the most fortunate of creatures and consequently worthy of all admiration and what precisely is that rank which is his lot in the universal chain of Being—a rank to be envied not only by brutes but even by the stars and by minds beyond this world. It is a matter past faith and a wondrous one. Why should it not be? For it is on this very account that man is rightly called and judged a great miracle and a wonderful creature indeed.

But hear, Fathers, exactly what this rank is and, as friendly auditors, conformably to your kindness, do me this favor. God the Father, the supreme Architect, had already built this cosmic home we behold, the most sacred temple of His godhead, by the laws of His mysterious wisdom. The region above the heavens He had adorned with Intelli-

---

[1] Abd Allah (late sixth and early seventh century), probably a cousin of Muhammed.

[2] Hermes Trismegistus was the name used for an otherwise unknown writer on astrology and magic. Medieval writers attributed to him many treatises from late antiquity. Asclepius is a speaker in one of Hermes' dialogues.

[3] Psalm 8:5.

ORATION ON THE DIGNITY OF MAN   Giovanni Pico della Mirandola, *Oration on the Dignity of Man*, trans. Elizabeth L. Forbes. Reprinted from *The Renaissance Philosophy of Man*, edited by Ernst Cassirer, Paul O. Kristeller, and John H. Randall, Jr., by permission of The University of Chicago Press. Copyright 1948 by The University of Chicago. All rights reserved. [Pp. 223–27, 229–35.]

gences, the heavenly spheres He had quickened with eternal souls, and the excrementary and filthy parts of the lower world He had filled with a multitude of animals of every kind. But, when the work was finished, the Craftsman kept wishing that there were someone to ponder the plan of so great a work, to love its beauty, and to wonder at its vastness. Therefore, when everything was done (as Moses and Timaeus[4] bear witness), He finally took thought concerning the creation of man. But there was not among His archetypes that from which He could fashion a new offspring, nor was there in His treasure-houses anything which He might bestow on His new son as an inheritance, nor was there in the seats of all the world a place where the latter might sit to contemplate the universe. All was now complete; all things had been assigned to the highest, the middle, and the lowest orders. But in its final creation it was not the part of the Father's power to fail as though exhausted. It was not the part of His wisdom to waver in a needful matter through poverty of counsel. It was not the part of His kindly love that he who was to praise God's divine generosity in regard to others should be compelled to condemn it in regard to himself.

At last the best of artisans ordained that that creature to whom He had been able to give nothing proper to himself should have joint possession of whatever had been peculiar to each of the different kinds of being. He therefore took man as a creature of indeterminate nature and, assigning him a place in the middle of the world, addressed him thus: "Neither a fixed abode nor a form that is thine alone nor any function peculiar to thyself have we given thee, Adam, to the end that according to thy longing and according to thy judgment thou mayest have and possess what abode, what form, and what functions thou thyself shalt desire. The nature of all other beings is limited and constrained within the bounds of laws prescribed by Us. Thou, constrained by no limits, in accordance with thine own free will, in whose hand We have placed thee, shalt ordain for thyself the limits of thy nature. We have set thee at the world's center that thou mayest from thence more easily observe whatever is in the world. We have made thee neither of heaven nor of earth, neither mortal nor immortal, so that with freedom of choice and with honor, as though the maker and molder of thyself, thou mayest fashion thyself in whatever shape thou shalt prefer. Thou shalt have the power to degenerate into the lower

---

[4]The person for whom Plato's dialogue embodying a theory of creation is named.

forms of life, which are brutish. Thou shalt have the power, out of thy soul's judgment, to be reborn into the higher forms, which are divine."

O supreme generosity of God the Father, O highest and most marvelous felicity of man! To him it is granted to have whatever he chooses, to be whatever he wills. Beasts as soon as they are born (so says Lucilius)[5] bring with them from their mother's womb all they will ever possess. Spiritual beings, either from the beginning or soon thereafter, become what they are to be for ever and ever. On man when he came into life the Father conferred the seeds of all kinds and the germs of every way of life. Whatever seeds each man cultivates will grow to maturity and bear in him their own fruit. If they be vegetative, he will be like a plant. If sensitive, he will become brutish. If rational, he will grow into a heavenly being. If intellectual, he will be an angel and the son of God. And if, happy in the lot of no created thing, he withdraws into the center of his own unity, his spirit, made one with God, in the solitary darkness of God, who is set above all things, shall surpass them all. Who would not admire this our chameleon? Or who could more greatly admire aught else whatever? It is man who Asclepius of Athens, arguing from his mutability of character and from his self-transforming nature, on just grounds says was symbolized by Proteus[6] in the mysteries. Hence those metamorphoses renowned among the Hebrews and the Pythagoreans.[7]

For the occult theology of the Hebrews sometimes transforms the holy Enoch[8] into an angel of divinity whom they call "Mal'akh Adonay Shebaoth," and sometimes transforms others into other divinities. The Pythagoreans degrade impious men into brutes and, if one is to believe Empedocles,[9] even into plants. Mohammed, in imitation, often had this saying on his tongue: "They who have deviated from divine law become beasts," and surely he spoke justly. For it is not the bark that makes the plant but its senseless and insentient nature; neither is it the hide that makes the beast of burden but its irrational, sensitive soul; neither is it the orbed form that makes the heavens but their undeviating order; nor is it the sundering from body but his spiritual intelligence

---

[5] Roman poet (second century B.C.).

[6] In Greek mythology, a powerful sea god, who could assume the shape of animals and monsters.

[7] Followers of the Greek philosopher Pythagoras (sixth century B.C.).

[8] Old Testament prophet.

[9] Greek philosopher (fifth century B.C.).

that makes the angel. For if you see one abandoned to his appetites crawling on the ground, it is a plant and not a man you see; if you see one blinded by the vain illusions of imagery, as it were of Calypso,[10] and, softened by their gnawing allurement, delivered over to his senses, it is a beast and not a man you see. If you see a philosopher determining all things by means of right reason, him you shall reverence: he is a heavenly being and not of this earth. If you see a pure contemplator, one unaware of the body and confined to the inner reaches of the mind, he is neither an earthly nor a heavenly being; he is a more reverend divinity vested with human flesh.

Are there any who would not admire man, who is, in the sacred writings of Moses and the Christians, not without reason described sometimes by the name of "all flesh," sometimes by that of "every creature," inasmuch as he himself molds, fashions, and changes himself into the form of all flesh and into the character of every creature? For this reason the Persian Euanthes, in describing the Chaldaean[11] theology, writes that man has no semblance that is inborn and his very own but many that are external and foreign to him; whence this saying of the Chaldaeans: "Hanorish tharah sharinas," that is, "Man is a being of varied, manifold, and inconstant nature." But why do we emphasize this? To the end that after we have been born to this condition—that we can become what we will—we should understand that we ought to have especial care to this, that it should never be said against us that, although born to a privileged position, we failed to recognize it and became like unto wild animals and senseless beasts of burden, but that rather the saying of Asaph the prophet should apply: "Ye are all angels and sons of the Most High,"[12] and that we may not, by abusing the most indulgent generosity of the Father, make for ourselves that freedom of choice He has given into something harmful instead of salutary. Let a certain holy ambition invade our souls, so that, not content with the mediocre, we shall pant after the highest and (since we may if we wish) toil with all our strength to obtain it.

Let us disdain earthly things, despise heavenly things, and, finally, esteeming less whatever is of the world, hasten to that court which is beyond the world and nearest to the Godhead. There, as the sacred

---

[10]A sea nymph in Homer's *Odyssey*. Pico evidently means Circe, an enchantress, who changed men into beasts.

[11]The Chaldeans were an ancient Semitic people who ruled in Mesopotamia in the seventh and sixth centuries B.C.

[12]Psalm 82:6.

mysteries relate, Seraphim, Cherubim, and Thrones[13] hold the first places; let us, incapable of yielding to them, and intolerant of a lower place, emulate their dignity and their glory. If we have willed it, we shall be second to them in nothing.

• • •

Then let us fill our well-prepared and purified soul with the light of natural philosophy, so that we may at last perfect her in the knowledge of things divine. And lest we be satisfied with those of our faith, let us consult the patriarch Jacob,[14] whose form gleams carved on the throne of glory. Sleeping in the lower world but keeping watch in the upper, the wisest of fathers will advise us. But he will advise us through a figure (in this way everything was wont to come to those men) that there is a ladder extending from the lowest earth to the highest heaven, divided in a series of many steps, with the Lord seated at the top, and angels in contemplation ascending and descending over them alternately by turns.

If this is what we must practice in our aspiration to the angelic way of life, I ask: "Who will touch the ladder of the Lord either with fouled foot or with unclean hands?" As the sacred mysteries have it, it is impious for the impure to touch the pure. But what are these feet? What these hands? Surely the foot of the soul is that most contemptible part by which the soul rests on matter as on the soil of earth, I mean the nourishing and feeding power, the tinder of lust, and the teacher of pleasurable weakness. Why should we not call the hands of the soul its irascible power, which struggles on its behalf as the champion of desire and as plunderer seizes in the dust and sun what desire will devour slumbering in the shade? These hands, these feet, that is, all the sentient part whereon resides the attraction of the body which, as they say, by wrenching the neck holds the soul in check, lest we be hurled down from the ladder as impious and unclean, let us bathe in moral philosophy as if in a living river. Yet this will not be enough if we wish to be companions of the angels going up and down on Jacob's ladder, unless we have first been well fitted and instructed to be promoted duly from step to step, to stray nowhere from the stairway, and to engage in the alternate comings and goings. Once we have achieved this by the art of

---

[13]In early Christian belief, seraphim, cherubim, and thrones were the three highest orders of angels.

[14]Jacob dreamed that he saw angels ascending and descending a ladder that extended from earth to heaven (Genesis 28:12–13).

discourse or reasoning, then, inspired by the Cherubic spirit,[15] using philosophy through the steps of the ladder, that is, of nature, and penetrating all things from center to center, we shall sometimes descend, with titanic force rending the unity like Osiris[16] into many parts, and we shall sometimes ascend, with the force of Phoebus[17] collecting the parts like the limbs of Osiris into a unity, until, resting at last in the bosom of the Father who is above the ladder, we shall be made perfect with the felicity of theology.

Let us also inquire of the just Job,[18] who entered into a life-covenant with God before he himself was brought forth into life, what the most high God requires above all in those tens of hundreds of thousands who attend him. He will answer that it is peace, in accord with what we read in him: "He maketh peace in his high places." And since the middle order expounds to the lower orders the counsel of the highest order, let Empedocles the philosopher expound to us the words of Job the theologian. He indicates to us a twofold nature present in our souls, by one side of which we are raised on high to the heavenly regions, and by the other side plunged downward into the lower, through strife and friendship or through war and peace, as he witnesses in the verses in which he makes complaint that he is being driven into the sea, himself goaded by strife and discord into the semblance of a madman and a fugitive from the gods.

Surely, Fathers, there is in us a discord many times as great; we have at hand wars grievous and more than civil, wars of the spirit which, if we dislike them, if we aspire to that peace which may so raise us to the sublime that we shall be established among the exalted of the Lord, only philosophy will entirely allay and subdue in us. In the first place, if our man but ask a truce of his enemies, moral philosophy will check the unbridled inroads of the many-sided beast and the leonine passions of wrath and violence. If we then take wiser counsel with ourselves and learn to desire the security of everlasting peace, it will be at hand and will generously fulfil our prayers. After both beasts are felled like a sacrificed sow, it will confirm an inviolable compact of holiest peace between flesh and spirit. Dialectic will appease the tumults of reason

[15]The contemplative spirit.

[16]Egyptian god who was slain and dismembered. The fragments of his body were pieced together by his wife, the goddess Isis, and he was restored to life.

[17]Apollo, the Greco-Roman sun god.

[18]Old Testament figure who, despite his sufferings, proclaimed his enduring faith in God.

made confused and anxious by inconsistencies of statement and soph-
isms of syllogisms. Natural philosophy will allay the strife and differences of opinion which vex, distract, and wound the spirit from all
sides. But she will so assuage them as to compel us to remember that,
according to Heraclitus,[19] nature was begotten from war, that it was on
this account repeatedly called "strife" by Homer, and that it is not,
therefore, in the power of natural philosophy to give us in nature a true
quiet and unshaken peace but that this is the function and privilege of
her mistress, that is, of holiest theology. She will show us the way and
as comrade lead us to her who, seeing us hastening from afar, will
exclaim "Come to me, ye who have labored. Come and I will restore
you. Come to me, and I will give you peace, which the world and
nature cannot give you."

When we have been so soothingly called, so kindly urged, we shall
fly up with winged feet, like earthly Mercuries,[20] to the embraces of our
blessed mother and enjoy that wished-for peace, most holy peace,
indivisible bond, of one accord in the friendship through which all
rational souls not only shall come into harmony in the one mind which
is above all minds but shall in some ineffable way become altogether
one. This is that friendship which the Pythagoreans say is the end of all
philosophy. This is that peace which God creates in his heavens, which
the angels descending to earth proclaimed to men of good will, that
through it men might ascend to heaven and become angels. Let us wish
this peace for our friends, for our century. Let us wish it for every home
into which we go; let us wish it for our own soul, that through it she
shall herself be made the house of God, and to the end that as soon as
she has cast out her uncleanness through moral philosophy and dialectic, adorned herself with manifold philosophy as with the splendor of a
courtier, and crowned the pediments of her doors with the garlands of
theology, the King of Glory may descend and, coming with his Father,
make his stay with her. If she show herself worthy of so great a guest,
she shall, by the boundless mercy which is his, in golden raiment like a
wedding gown, and surrounded by a varied throng of sciences, receive
her beautiful guest not merely as a guest but as a spouse from whom she
will never be parted. She will desire rather to be parted from her own
people and, forgetting her father's house and herself, will desire to die in
herself in order to live in her spouse, in whose sight surely the death of

---

[19]Greek philosopher (fifth century B.C.).
[20]In Roman mythology Mercury was the speedy messenger of Jupiter.

his saints is precious—death, I say, if we must call death that fulness of life, the consideration of which wise men have asserted to be the aim of philosophy.

Let us also cite Moses himself, but little removed from the springing abundance of the holy and unspeakable wisdom by whose nectar the angels are made drunk. Let us hearken to the venerable judge in these words proclaiming laws to us who are dwellers in the desert loneliness of this body: "Let those who, as yet unclean, still need moral philosophy, live with the people outside the tabernacle under the sky, meanwhile purify themselves like the priests of Thessaly. Let those who have already ordered their conduct be received into the sanctuary but not quite yet touch the holy vessels; let them first like zealous Levites[21] in the service of dialectic minister to the holy things of philosophy. Then when they have been admitted even to these, let them now behold the many-colored robe of the higher palace of the Lord, that is to say, the stars; let them now behold the heavenly candlestick divided into seven lights; let them now behold the fur tent, that is, the elements, in the priesthood of philosophy, so that when they are in the end, through the favor of theological sublimity, granted entrance into the inner part of the temple, they may rejoice in the glory of the Godhead with no veil before his image." This of a surety Moses commands us and, in commanding, summons, urges, and encourages us by means of philosophy to prepare ourselves a way, while we can, to the heavenly glory to come.

But indeed not only the Mosaic and Christian mysteries but also the theology of the ancients show us the benefits and value of the liberal arts, the discussion of which I am about to undertake. For what else did the degrees of the initiates observed in the mysteries of the Greeks mean? For they arrived at a perception of the mysteries when they had first been purified through those expiatory sciences, as it were, moral philosophy and dialectic. What else can that perception possibly be than an interpretation of occult nature by means of philosophy? Then at length to those who were so disposed came that ΕΠΟΠΤΕΙΑ [Initiation in the Eleusinian[22] mysteries], that is to say, the observation of things divine by the light of theology. Who would not long to be initiated into such sacred rites? Who would not desire, by neglecting all human concerns, by despising the goods of fortune, and by disregarding those

---

[21]In the Bible, members of the tribe of Levi were chosen to assist the priests.

[22]One of the most important of the ancient Greek secret religious rituals.

of the body, to become the guest of the gods while yet living on earth, and, made drunk by the nectar of eternity, to be endowed with the gifts of immortality though still a mortal being? Who would not wish to be so inflamed with those Socratic frenzies sung by Plato in the *Phaedrus*,[23] that, by the oarage of feet and wings escaping speedily from hence, that is, from a world set on evil, he might be borne on the fastest of courses to the heavenly Jerusalem? Let us be driven, Fathers, let us be driven by the frenzies of Socrates, that they may so throw us into ecstasy as to put our mind and ourselves in God. Let us be driven by them, if we have first done what is in our power. For if through moral philosophy the forces of our passions have by a fitting agreement become so intent on harmony that they can sing together in undisturbed concord, and if through dialectic our reason has moved progressively in a rhythmical measure, then we shall be stirred by the frenzy of the Muses and drink the heavenly harmony with our inmost hearing. Thereupon Bacchus, the leader of the Muses,[24] by showing in his mysteries, that is, in the visible signs of nature, the invisible things of God to us who study philosophy, will intoxicate us with the fulness of God's house, in which, if we prove faithful, like Moses, hallowed theology shall come and inspire us with a doubled frenzy. For, exalted to her lofty height, we shall measure therefrom all things that are and shall be and have been in indivisible eternity; and, admiring their original beauty, like the seers of Phoebus, we shall become her own winged lovers. And at last, roused by ineffable love as by a sting, like burning Seraphim rapt from ourselves, full of divine power we shall no longer be ourselves but shall become He Himself Who made us.

If anyone investigates the holy names of Apollo, their meanings and hidden mysteries, these amply show that that god is no less a philosopher than a seer; but, since Ammonius[25] has sufficiently examined this subject, there is no reason why I should now treat it otherwise. But, Fathers, three Delphic[26] precepts may suggest themselves to your minds, which are very necessary to those who are to go into the most sacred and revered temple, not of the false but of the true Apollo, who lights every soul as it enters this world. You will see that they give us no other advice than that we should with all our strength embrace this

---

[23]Platonic dialogue in which Socrates discusses the nature of inspiration and love.

[24]Bacchus was the Greek god of wine and of musical and poetic inspiration.

[25]A third-century Christian philosopher.

[26]Oracular or solemn—an allusion to Apollo's oracle at Delphi.

threefold philosophy which is the concern of our present debate. For the saying μηδὲν ἄγαν, that is, "Nothing too much," prescribes a standard and rule for all the virtues through the doctrine of the Mean, with which moral philosophy duly deals. Then the saying γνῶϑι σεαυτόν, that is, "Know thyself," urges and encourages us to the investigation of all nature, of which the nature of man is both the connecting link and, so to speak, the "mixed bowl." For he who knows himself in himself knows all things, as Zoroaster[27] first wrote, and then Plato in his *Alcibiades*. When we are finally lighted in this knowledge by natural philosophy, and nearest to God are uttering the theological greeting, εἶ, that is, "Thou art," we shall likewise in bliss be addressing the true Apollo on intimate terms.

---

[27]Founder of an ancient Persian religion (*ca.* 626–*ca.* 551 B.C.).

19

Desiderius Erasmus

The Praise of Folly

DESIDERIUS Erasmus of Rotter-
dam (ca. 1466–1536) dominated the European world of letters in the early
sixteenth century. Under pressure from his guardians, he became an Augustinian monk and was ordained a priest; he was, however, permitted to leave the
monastery and to travel extensively. Although he remained a devout Christian
all his life, he lived more as a scholar than as a priest. Wherever people were
interested in learning, there Erasmus went. He journeyed to England, for
instance, to lecture on Greek at Cambridge and became fast friends with English
scholars, especially Sir Thomas More, at whose suggestion Erasmus wrote
The Praise of Folly (1509). In recognition of his life of constant scholarly endeavor, he has been called the "Prince of Humanists" and "Schoolmaster to
the Renaissance."

Erasmus, keenly aware of the corrupt practices of the Church, was a strong
proponent of reform. His edition of the Greek New Testament gave a scholarly
impetus to reform, while his forthright criticism of abuses encouraged critical
examination of traditional practices and beliefs. Religion for Erasmus was both
a personal matter and a question of scholarship and doctrine. Revolt against
religious authority, however, seemed to him to lead only to religious anarchy;
instead, he advocated gradual reform from within. Erasmus therefore appealed
to people's reason and sense of humor, refusing to take up the defense of the rebel
Luther at the Diet of Worms, but, on the other hand, refusing to be merely a
spokesman for the orthodox views of the Church. Neither a servant of reform
nor a slave of reaction, he was disliked by both parties.

Erasmus's Praise of Folly is an ironical survey of sixteenth-century European society. Folly—presented in the guise of a goddess of ancient mythology—
is the speaker; she describes the vanities and nonsense of those who, in their
ignorance, greed, and envy, are—in effect—her worshipers. Some of her

followers are easily recognized: the vain and proud merchant, the angry and jealous husband, the silly rich woman. But Folly (as is shown in the following excerpt) also finds her devotees among people in universities, in the institutions of the Church, and in the courts of princes and kings. Erasmus's wit, masked as Folly, delights in searching them out and exposing their shortcomings; these characterizations would, Erasmus hoped, persuade his readers to bring about reforms of their own lives and beliefs as well as of society and the Church.

[Folly speaks.]

First of all, who does not know that the earliest period of a man's life is by far the happiest for him and by far the most pleasant for all about him? What is it in children, that we should kiss them the way we do, and cuddle them, and fondle them—so that even an enemy would give aid to one of that age—except this enchantment of folly, which prudent nature carefully bestows on the newly born; so that by this pleasure, as a sort of prepayment, they win the favor of their nurses and parents and make these forget the pains of bringing them up. After this comes adolescence. How welcome it is in every home! How well everyone wishes it! How studiously does everyone promote it, how officiously they lend it the helping hand! But, I ask, whence comes this grace of youth? Whence but from me, by whose favor the young know so little—and how lightly worn is that little! And presently when lads grown larger begin, through experience and discipline, to have some smack of manhood, I am a liar if by the same token the brightness of their beauty does not fade, their quickness diminish, their wit lose its edge, their vigor slacken. The farther one gets from me, then, the less and less he lives, until *molesta senectus* (that is, irksome old age) arrives, hateful to others, to be sure, but also and more so to itself.

Old age would not be tolerable to any mortal at all, were it not that I, out of pity for its troubles, stand once more at its right hand; and just as the gods of the poets customarily save, by some metamorphosis or other, those who are dying, in like manner I bring those who have one

THE PRAISE OF FOLLY   Desiderius Erasmus, *The Praise of Folly*, trans. by Hoyt Hopewell Hudson. Copyright 1941 © 1969 by Princeton University Press; Princeton Paperback 1970. Excerpts, pp. 16–17, 56–59, 76–81, 85–88, 93–100, 125. Reprinted by permission of Princeton University Press.

foot in the grave back to their infancy again, for as long as possible; so
that the folk are not far off in speaking of them as "in their second
childhood." If anyone would like to know the method of bringing
about this alteration, I shall not conceal it. I lead them to my spring of
Lethe[1]—for that stream rises in the Fortunate Isles, and only a little
rivulet of it flows in the underworld—so that then and there they may
drink draughts of forgetfulness. With their cares of mind purged away,
by gentle stages they become young again. But now, you say, they
merely dote, and play the fool. Yes, quite so. But precisely this it is to
renew one's infancy. Is to be childish anything other than to dote and
play the fool? As if in that age the greatest joy were not this, that one
knows nothing! For who does not dread and shun as a prodigy the boy
who has a man's wisdom? As the proverb current among the folk has it,
"I hate a boy of premature wisdom." Who could bear to converse or
transact business with an old man who should join to his long experience of things, an equal vigor of mind and sharpness of judgment?
Hence it is that an old man dotes, thanks to me.

•   •   •

Then what shall I say of the people who so happily fool themselves
with forged pardons for sins, measuring out time to be spent in purgatory as if with an hour-glass, and figuring its centuries, years, months,
days, and hours as if from a mathematical table, beyond possibility of
error? Or I might speak of those who will promise themselves any and
every thing, relying upon certain charms or prayers devised by some
pious impostor either for his soul's sake or for money, to bring them
wealth, reputation, pleasure, plenty, good health, long life, and a green
old age, and at last a seat next to Christ's in heaven—but they do not
wish to get it too soon. That is to say, when the pleasures of this life
have finally failed them, willy-nilly, though they struggled tooth and
nail to hold on to them, then it is time for the bliss of heaven to arrive.

I fancy that I see some merchant or soldier or judge laying down one
small coin from his extensive booty and expecting that the whole
cesspool of his life will be at once purified. He conceives that just so
many perjuries, so many lustful acts, so many debauches, so many
fights, murders, frauds, lies, and so many breaches of faith, are bought
off as by contract; and so bought off that with a clean slate he may start

[1] In Greek mythology the souls of those who drank the water of Lethe forgot their
previous existence.

from scratch upon a new round of sins. And who are more foolish, yet who more happy, than those who promise themselves something more than the highest felicity if they daily recite those seven verses of the *Psalms*? The seven, I mean, which some devil, a playful one, but blabbing rather than crafty, is believed to have pointed out to St. Bernard after he had been duped by the saint's trick.[2] Things like that are so foolish, you know, that I am almost ashamed of them myself; yet they stand approved not only by the common people but even by teachers of religion. And is it not almost as bad when the several countries each lay claim to a particular saint of their own, and then assign particular powers respectively to the various saints and observe for each one his own peculiar rites of worship? One saint assists in time of toothache, another is propitious to women in travail, another recovers stolen goods, a fourth stands by with help in a shipwreck, and still another keeps the sheep in good repair; and so of the rest, though it would take too long to specify all of them. Some of them are good for a number of purposes, particularly the Virgin Mother, to whom the common people tend to attribute more than to the Son.

Yet what do men ask of these saints except things that pertain to folly? Think a bit: among all those consecrated gifts which you see covering the walls of some churches, and even hung on the ceiling, do you ever find one given in gratitude for an escape from folly, or because the giver has been made any whit wiser? One person has come safe to land. A second survived being run through in a duel. One no less fortunately than bravely got away from a battlefield, leaving the rest to fight. Another was brought near to the gallows, but by favor of some saint who is friendly to thieves he has decided that he should go on relieving those who are burdened with too much wealth. Another escaped in a jailbreak. Another came through a fever, in spite of his doctor. The poisoned drink of another, by loosening his bowels, served to cure him instead of kill him, not at all to the joy of his wife, who lost both her labor and her expenses. Another's cart was turned over, but he drove both horses home safely. Another was dug out of the debris of a fallen house. Another, caught in the act by a husband, made good his escape. No one gives thanks for a recovery from being a fool. So sweet it is not to be wise that mortal men will pray to be delivered from anything sooner than from Folly.

---

[2]According to legend, the devil revealed which seven verses insured salvation when St. Bernard said that he intended to recite all of the Psalms daily in order to be sure of saying the correct ones.

But why should I launch out upon this ocean of superstition? "For if I had a hundred tongues, a hundred mouths, a voice of brass, I could not set forth all the shapes of fools or run over all the names of folly." Yet the whole life of Christian folk everywhere is full of fanaticisms of this kind. Our priests allow them, without regret, and even foster them, being aware of how much money is wont to accrue from this source. In this posture of affairs, suppose that some odious wise man were to step up and sing out this, which is true: "You will not die badly if you live well. You get quit of your sins if you add to the money payment a hatred of evil-doing, add tears, watchings, prayers, fastings; and if you alter the whole basis of your life. This or that saint will be gracious to you if you emulate his goodness." If the wise man, I say, were to start howling out things like that, just see from what contentment, and into what a turmoil, he would all of a sudden drive the souls of men!

• • •

Among men of learned professions, the lawyers may claim first place for themselves, nor is there any other class quite so self-satisfied; for while they industriously roll up the stone of Sisyphus by dint of weaving together six hundred laws in the same breath, no matter how little to the purpose, and by dint of piling glosses upon glosses and opinions upon opinions, they contrive to make their profession seem the most difficult of all. What is really tedious commends itself to them as brilliant. Let us put in with them the logicians and sophists, a breed of men more loquacious than the famed brass kettles at Dodona;[3] any one of them can out-chat twenty picked women. They would be happier, however, if they were merely talkative, and not quarrelsome as well, to such a degree that they will stubbornly cut and thrust over a lock of goat's wool, quite losing track of the truth in question while they go on disputing. Their self-love makes them happy, and equipped with three syllogisms they will unhesitatingly dare to join battle upon any subject with any man. Mere forwardness brings them back unbeaten, though you match Stentor[4] against them.

Near these march the scientists, reverenced for their beards and the fur on their gowns, who teach that they alone are wise while the rest of mortal men flit about as shadows. How pleasantly they dote, indeed, while they construct their numberless worlds, and measure the sun,

[3]The voice of the oracle of Zeus at Dodona, a place in northern Greece, was supposed to be heard in a wind whose sound was magnified by brass gongs.
[4]A Greek warrior in the Trojan war who was famous for his loud voice.

moon, stars, and spheres as with thumb and line. They assign causes for lightning, winds, eclipses, and other inexplicable things, never hesitating a whit, as if they were privy to the secrets of nature, artificer of things, or as if they visited us fresh from the council of the gods. Yet all the while nature is laughing grandly at them and their conjectures. For to prove that they have good intelligence of nothing, this is a sufficient argument: they can never explain why they disagree with each other on every subject. Thus knowing nothing in general, they profess to know all things in particular; though they are ignorant even of themselves, and on occasion do not see the ditch or the stone lying across their path, because many of them are blear-eyed or absent-minded; yet they proclaim that they perceive ideas, universals, forms without matter, primary substances, quiddities, and ecceities—things so tenuous, I fear, that Lynceus[5] himself could not see them. When they especially disdain the vulgar crowd is when they bring out their triangles, quadrangles, circles, and mathematical pictures of the sort, lay one upon the other, intertwine them into a maze, then deploy some letters as if in line of battle, and presently do it over in reverse order—and all to involve the uninitiated in darkness. Their fraternity does not lack those who predict future events by consulting the stars, and promise wonders even more magical; and these lucky scientists find people to believe them.

Perhaps it were better to pass over the theologians in silence, and not to move such a Lake Camarina,[6] or to handle such an herb *Anagyris foetida*,[7] as that marvellously supercilious and irascible race. For they may attack me with six hundred arguments, in squadrons, and drive me to make a recantation; which if I refuse, they will straightway proclaim me an heretic. By this thunderbolt they are wont to terrify any toward whom they are ill-disposed. No other people are so loth to acknowledge my favors to them; yet the divines are bound to me by no ordinary obligations. They are happy in their self-love, and as if they already inhabited the third heaven they look down from a height on all other mortal men as on creatures that crawl on the ground, and they come near to pitying them. They are protected by a wall of scholastic definitions, arguments, corollaries, implicit and explicit propositions; they have so many hideaways that they could not be caught even by the

---

[5]A figure in Greek legend who could see over one hundred miles and through tree trunks.
[6]A lake in Sicily known for its evil odor.
[7]A plant noted for its bad smell.

net of Vulcan;[8] for they slip out on their distinctions, by which also they cut through all knots as easily as with a double-bitted axe from Tenedos,[9] and they abound with newly-invented terms and prodigious vocables. Furthermore, they explain as pleases them the most arcane matters, such as by what method the world was founded and set in order, through what conduits original sin has been passed down along the generations, by what means, in what measure, and how long the perfect Christ was in the Virgin's womb, and how accidents subsist in the Eucharist without their subject.

• • •

Paul could exhibit faith; but when he said, "Faith is the substance of things hoped for, the evidence of things not seen," he did not define it doctorally. The same apostle, though he exemplified charity supremely well, divided and defined it with very little logical skill in his first epistle to the Corinthians, Chapter 13. And no doubt the apostles consecrated the Eucharist devoutly enough; but suppose you had questioned them about the *terminus a quo* and the *terminus ad quem*,[10] or about transubstantiation—how the body is in many places at once, the difference between the body of Christ when in heaven, when on the Cross, when in the sacrament of the Eucharist, about the point when transubstantiation occurs (seeing that the prayer effecting it is a discrete quantity having extension in time)—they would not have answered with the same acuteness, I suggest, with which the sons of Scotus[11] distinguish and define these matters. The apostles knew the mother of Jesus, but who among them has demonstrated philosophically just how she was kept clear from the sin of Adam, as our theologians have done? Peter received the keys, received them from One who did not commit them to an unworthy person, and yet I doubt that he ever understood—for Peter never did attain to subtlety—that a person who did not have knowledge could have the key to knowledge. They went about baptizing everywhere, and yet they never taught what is the formal, the material, the efficient, and the final cause of baptism, nor is mention made by them that it has both a delible character and an indelible one.

---

[8]The Greek god Vulcan (or Hephaestus) fashioned a net to catch Mars and Venus making love.

[9]A proverbial symbol of quick and severe justice.

[10]Starting point and conclusion.

[11]Scotists, or followers of Duns Scotus, a scholastic theologian (*ca.* 1265–1308).

They worshipped, to be sure, but in spirit, following no other teaching than that of the Gospel, "God is a spirit, and they that worship Him must worship Him in spirit and in truth." It seems never to have been revealed to them that a picture drawn with charcoal on a wall ought to be worshipped with the same worship as Christ himself—at least if it is drawn with two fingers outstretched and the hair unshorn, and has three sets of rays in the nimbus fastened to the back of the head. For who would comprehend these things if he had not consumed all of thirty-six years upon the physics and metaphysics of Aristotle and the Scotists?

In similar wise, the apostles preach grace, and yet they never determined what the difference is between grace freely given and grace that makes one deserving. They urge us to good works, but do not separate work, work working, and work that has been worked. At all times they inculcate charity, but do not distinguish charity which is infused from that which is acquired, or explain whether charity is an accident or a substance, created or uncreated. They abhor sin, but may I be shot if they could define scientifically what it is we call sin, unless they had the luck to be instructed by the spirit of the Scotists.

• • •

Coming nearest to these in felicity are the men who generally call themselves "the religious" and "monks"—utterly false names both, since most of them keep as far away as they can from religion and no people are more in evidence in every sort of place. But I do not see how anything could be more dismal than these monks if I did not succor them in many ways. For though people as a whole so detest this race of men that meeting one by accident is supposed to be bad luck, yet they flatter themselves to the queen's taste. For one thing, they reckon it the highest degree of piety to have no contact with literature, and hence they see to it that they do not know how to read. For another, when with asinine voices they bray out in church those psalms they have learned, by rote rather than by heart, they are convinced that they are anointing God's ears with the blandest of oil. Some of them make a good profit from their dirtiness and mendicancy, collecting their food from door to door with importunate bellowing; nay, there is not an inn, public conveyance, or ship where they do not intrude, to the great disadvantage of the other common beggars. Yet according to their account, by their very dirtiness, ignorance, want of manners, and insolence, these delightful fellows are representing to us the lives of the apostles.

What is funnier than to find that they do everything by rule, employing, as it were, the methods of mathematics; and to slip up is a great crime. There must be just so many knots for each shoe and the shoe-string must be of a certain color; the habit must be decked with just so much trimming; the girdle must be of a certain material and the width of so many straws; the cowl of a certain shape and a certain number of bushels in capacity; the hair so many fingers long; and one must sleep just so many hours. Who does not see that all this equality is really very unequal, in view of the great diversity of bodies and temperaments? Yet on the basis of such details they hold other people as mere nutshells. What is more, the members of one order, amid all their professions of apostolic charity, will turn and condemn the members of some other, making an admirable hubbub over the way their habit is belted or the slightly darker color of it. Among the monks you will see some so rigorously pious that they will wear no outer garment unless it be of Cilician goat's hair, while their inner garment is of Milesian wool; some others, on the contrary, are linen on the outside, but still wool underneath. Members of certain orders start back from the mere touch of a piece of money as if it were aconite. They do not, however, withdraw from the touch of a glass of wine, or of a woman. In short, all orders take remarkable care that nothing in their way of life shall be consistent; nor is it so much their concern to be like Christ as to be unlike each other. Thus a great part of their felicity derives from their various names. Those of one order delight to call themselves Cordeliers, but among them some are Coletes, some Minors, some Minims, some Crutched. Again, there are the Benedictines and the Bernardines; the Bridgetines and the Augustinians; the Williamists and the Jacobines;[12] as if it were not enough to be called Christians.

The greater number of them work so hard at their ceremonies and at maintaining the minutiae of tradition that they deem one heaven hardly a suitable reward for their labors; never recalling that the time will come when, with all these things held of no account, Christ will demand a reckoning of that which He has prescribed, namely, charity. One friar will then show a paunch which has been padded out with every kind of

---

[12]Cordeliers . . . Jacobines: orders of monks and friars.

fish; another will spill out a hundred bushels of hymns. Another will count off so many myriads of fasts, and will lay the blame for his almost bursting belly upon his having always broken his fasts by a single dinner. Another will point to a pile of ceremonies so big that seven ships could scarcely carry it. Another will boast that for sixty years he never touched money, except when his fingers were protected by two pairs of gloves. Another will wear a cowl so dirty and greasy that no sailor would deign to put it on. Another will celebrate the fact that for more than fifty-five years he lived the life of a sponge, always fastened to one spot. Another will show a voice grown hoarse with assiduous chanting; another, a lethargy contracted by living alone; another, a tongue grown dumb under his vow of silence. But Christ, interrupting their boasts, which otherwise would go on endlessly, will say: ". . . I recognize one commandment which is truly mine, and of that I hear nothing. . . . I promised the inheritance of my Father, not to cowls, orisons, or fasts, but to works of charity." . . .

• • •

. . . And at this point it pleases me to touch upon kings and nobles of the court, by whom I am worshipped sincerely and, as becomes gentlemen, frankly. And indeed, if they had so much as half an ounce of sound wisdom, what life were more dismal than theirs or more to be avoided? For let a person weigh in his mind how heavy a burden rests on the shoulders of anyone wishing to act the true prince, and he will not conclude that sovereignty is a thing worth using perjury and parricide to gain. He will consider that one who grasps the helm of great affairs must further the public, not his private, interest and give his mind to nothing except as it concerns the general good; he must not deviate a finger's breadth from the laws of which he is author and executor; he must himself be warrant for the integrity of all officials and magistrates; he is one person who is exposed to all eyes, and like a favorable star he has power, by the good influence of his conduct, to bring salvation in human affairs; or like a fatal comet he may bring destruction in his train. The vices of other men are not so deeply felt or so widely communicated. A prince is in such a position that if he lapses ever so slightly from honesty, straightway a dangerous and vital infection spreads to many people. Then the lot of princes brings with it a host of things which tend to lead them from righteousness, such as pleasure, liberty, adulation, and excess; so that he must endeavor more earnestly and watch more vigilantly lest, beguiled by these, he fail of his duty. Finally, to say nothing of treasons, hatreds, and other perils or dreads, there stands above his own crown that true King who will call him to account for even the least of his trespasses; and the accounting will be the more severe as the empire he ruled was the more mighty. I say that if the prince weighed these things, and many more like them, within himself—and he would do so, were he wise—I am afraid he could neither sleep nor eat in any joy.

But as it is, with my assistance, kings leave all these concerns to the gods, take care of themselves nicely, and grant no hearing to anyone unless he knows how to speak pleasant things, because solicitude must not get a foothold in their minds. They believe they have played the part of a sovereign to the hilt if they diligently go hunting, feed some fine horses, sell dignities and offices at a profit to themselves, and daily devise new measures by which to drain away the wealth of citizens and sweep it into their own exchequer. All this, of course, is done in due form, under new-found names, so that even when most unjust it shall carry some appearance of equity; and they take care to add a little sweetening so that in any event they may secure for themselves the hearts of the people. Fashion me now a man such as princes commonly are, a man ignorant of the laws, almost an enemy of the public welfare, intent upon private gain, addicted to pleasure, a hater of learning, a hater, too, of liberty and truth, thinking about anything except the safety of the state, and measuring all things by his own desire and profit. Then put on him a golden chain, symbolizing the union of all virtues linked together; set on him a crown adorned with gems, which is to remind him that he ought to surpass others in every heroic quality. In addition, give him a scepter, emblem of justice and of a heart in no way corrupted, and finally a scarlet robe, badge of a certain eminent love for the realm. If a prince really laid his own life alongside these symbols, I believe he would have the grace to be ashamed of his finery. He would be afraid some nosy satirist might turn the whole spectacle, suited as it is for high tragedy, into laughter and derision.

Now what shall I say about the noble courtiers? Though nothing is more venal, more servile, more witless, or more contemptible than most of them, yet they desire to seem the foremost of created things. Here is one point, however, in which they are as modest as one could wish: they are satisfied to carry about on their bodies gold, gems, scarlet, and the other insignia of wisdom and the virtues, but the reality of these they leave for the use of others. They find themselves abundantly happy in being allowed to speak of the king as "our master," in having learned how to turn a compliment in three words, and in knowing how to repeat on occasion those courteous titles of Your Grace, Your Lordship, and Your Majesty; in having cast off shame beyond other men, and in flattering handsomely. For these are the arts which truly become the nobleman and courtier. For the rest, if you look more closely at their whole way of life, you are sure to find them "mere Phaeacians, suitors of Penelope, and"—you know the rest of the verse,[13] which Echo can give you better than I. They sleep until noon, when a hired chaplain comes to their bedside and swiftly runs through matins before they are half up. Then to breakfast, which is barely got through when dinner-time comes along. After dinner come dice, checkers, cards, jesters, fools, whores, dalliance, and horse-play. Meanwhile there must be a round or two of drinks. Then back to supper, with toasts after it—not just a toast, by Jove! And in this fashion do their hours, days, months, years, and lives glide away with no boredom. For myself it is as good as a hearty meal to watch these high-flyers, observing how every one of the ladies will think herself nearer to gods the longer train she trails; while one of the noblemen will shove past another by using his elbow, in order that he may seem to stand a little closer to Jove; and each is the more pleased with himself the heavier chain he can carry about on his neck, as if he were showing off his strength rather than his wealth.

Our popes, cardinals, and bishops for some time now have earnestly copied the state and practice of princes, and come near to beating them at their own game. Let a bishop but consider what his alb, the white emblem of sincerity, should teach him, namely, a life in every way blameless; and what is signified on his part by the two-horned miter, the two peaks bound by the same knot—I suppose it is a perfect knowledge of the Old and New Testaments; what is meant by covering his hands with gloves, a clean administration of the sacrament and one unsullied by any taint of human concerns; what the crozier symbolizes, most watchful care of the flock put under his charge; what is indicated by the cross that is carried before him, to wit, a victory over all carnal affections. If he would contemplate these and other lessons of the sort, I say, would he not lead a sad and troubled life? But as it is, they do well enough by way of feeding themselves; as for the other, the care of the

---

[13]The quotation is from Homer's *Odyssey* and is part of its rather unflattering description of the suitors who sought the hand of Penelope, Odysseus' queen, while Odysseus was away for many years.

sheep, they delegate that to Christ himself, or else refer it to their suffragans, as they call them, or other deputies. Nor do they keep in mind the name they bear, or what the word "bishop" means—labor, vigilance, solicitude. Yet in raking in moneys they truly play the bishop, overseeing everything—and overlooking nothing.

In a similar way the cardinals, if they considered the fact that they have succeeded to the places of the apostles, would see that the same works are required of them as were performed by their predecessors; that they are not lords, but stewards, of spiritual things, and that shortly they are to render an exact account of what they hold in trust. Yes, let them too philosophize a bit concerning their vestments, and question themselves in this fashion: "What does the whiteness of this upper garment mean? Is it not a notable and singular purity of heart? What the crimson lower garment? Is it not a burning love of God? What, again, that outer robe flowing down in broad folds and spreading over the mule of his Exalted Reverence, though it would suffice to cover a camel? Is it not charity ample enough to embrace all men in its helpfulness, by way of teaching, exhorting, chastising, admonishing, ending wars, resisting wicked princes, and freely spending blood—not money alone—for the flock of Christ? And wherefore all this money, anyway, for those who hold the places of the needy apostles?" If they would weigh these things, I repeat, they would not be so ambitious for the post, and would willingly give it up, or at least they would lead a toilsome and watchful life of the sort lived by those ancient apostles.

As to these Supreme Pontiffs who take the place of Christ, if they tried to emulate His life, I mean His poverty, labors, teaching, cross, and contempt for safety, if even they thought upon the title of Pope—that is, Father—or the addition "Most Holy," who on earth would be more afflicted? Who would purchase that seat at the price of every resource and effort? Or who defend it, when purchased, by the sword, by poison, or by anything else? Were wisdom to descend upon them, how it would inconvenience them! Wisdom, did I say? Nay, even a grain of salt would do it—a grain of that salt which is spoken of by Christ. It would lose them all that wealth and honor, all those possessions, triumphal progresses, offices, dispensations, tributes, and indulgences; it would lose them so many horses, mules, and retainers; so many pleasures. (See how I have comprehended in a few words many marketsful, a great harvest, a wide ocean, of goods!) In place of these it would bring vigils, fasts, tears, prayers, sermons, studies, sighs, and a thousand troublesome tasks of the sort. Nor should we pass over the circumstance that all those copyists and notaries would be in want, as would all those advocates, promoters, secretaries, muleteers, grooms, bankers, and pimps—I was about to add something more tender, though rougher, I am afraid, on the ears. In short, that great host of men which burdens—I beg your pardon, I mean adorns—the Roman See would beg for their bread. This would be inhuman and downright abominable, and, what is more accursed, those very princes of the church and true lights of the world would themselves be reduced to a staff and a wallet.

As it is now, what labor turns up to be done they hand over to Peter and Paul, who have leisure for it. But the splendor and the pleasure they take care of personally. And so it comes about—by my doing, remember—that scarcely any kind of men live more softly or less oppressed with care; believing that they are amply acceptable to Christ if with a mystical and almost theatrical finery, with ceremonies, and with those titles of Beatitude and Reverence and Holiness, along with blessing and cursing, they perform the office of bishops. To work miracles is primitive and old-fashioned, hardly suited to our times; to instruct the people is irksome; to interpret the Holy Scriptures is pedantry; to pray is otiose; to shed tears is distressing and womanish; to live in poverty is sordid; to be beaten in war is dishonorable and less than worthy of one who will hardly admit kings, however great, to kiss his sacred foot; and finally, to die is unpleasant, to die on the cross a disgrace.

There remain only those weapons and sweet benedictions of which Paul speaks, and the popes are generous enough with these: interdictions, excommunications, reexcommunications, anathematizations, pictured damnations, and the terrific lightning-bolt of the bull, which by its mere flicker sinks the souls of men below the floor of hell. And these most holy fathers in Christ, and vicars of Christ, launch it against no one with more spirit than against those who, at the instigation of the devil, try to impair or to subtract from the patrimony of Peter. Although this saying of Peter's stands in the Gospel, "We have left all and followed Thee," yet they give the name of his patrimony to lands, towns, tribute, imposts, and moneys. On behalf of these things, inflamed by zeal for Christ, they fight with fire and sword, not without shedding of Christian blood; and then they believe they have defended the bride of Christ in apostolic fashion, having scattered what they are pleased to designate as "her enemies." As if the church had any enemies more pestilential than impious pontiffs who by their silence allow

Christ to be forgotten, who enchain Him by mercenary rules, adulterate His teachings by forced interpretations, and crucify Him afresh by their scandalous life!

• • •

But indeed I have long since forgotten myself and run out of bounds. If anything I have said shall seem too saucy or too glib, stop and think: 'tis Folly, and a woman, that has spoken. But of course you will also remember that Greek proverb, "Even a foolish man will often speak a word in season," unless, perhaps, you assume that this does not extend to women. I see that you are expecting a peroration, but you are just too foolish if you suppose that after I have poured out a hodgepodge of words like this I can recall anything that I have said. There is an old saying, "I hate a pot-companion with a memory." Here is a new one: "I hate a hearer that remembers anything."

And so farewell. . . . Applaud . . . live . . . drink . . . O most distinguished initiates of Folly!

20

Niccolò Machiavelli

The Prince

N$ICCOLÒ$ Machiavelli (1469–
1527), *for a time an ambassador and secretary of the Republic of Florence, was
exiled when the Medici family returned to power in 1512. During his exile he
wrote* The Prince *(1513), which was circulated in manuscript form but not
published until 1532, five years after his death. In his later years, Machiavelli
was permitted to return to Florence and was commissioned by the Medicis to
write* The History of Florence. *He was not, however, entrusted by them with
any other important official post.*

*The influence of Machiavelli was profound in his own day and has continued
so into our own. He departed from conventional medieval political theory, with
its endless comparisons of the body politic to the human body—the king or
prince representing the head and the people representing the body and limbs, and
so on. Nor did Machiavelli agree with the many who regarded the prince as the
divinely appointed ruler; in his treatise,* The Prince, *the state is considered
entirely secular, and nothing happens to a state save by the application of power.
The ruler's whole duty is to maintain order and to keep the state strong. In order
to do this, the prince must gain and retain power by whatever means are
available. The Romans, Machiavelli felt, were the best practitioners of this
policy, and his writings are full of admiration for them—notably, his perceptive
and analytical* Discourses on Livy.

*Unfortunately for his reputation, the name of Machiavelli became associated
chiefly with* The Prince, *which is, in the opinion of many, a lesser work than
his* Discourses on Livy. *He was attacked bitterly by those who regarded him
as an embodiment of evil ("Old Nick himself"—the name coined for him by
English mockers) and by more astute practitioners of tyranny who, according to
Voltaire, disliked him because he gave away their trade secrets. In literature and
legend Machiavelli's name became synonymous with the villain who, excusing*

his actions with the doctrine that the end justifies the means, uses any method to gain power and enjoys crime for its own sake. In defense of Machiavelli one can cite his hope of uniting Italy so that the ceaseless local wars and invasions would end. He can also be viewed as simply an objective reporter of the actual state of affairs in the Italy of his time.

NICCOLÒ MACHIAVELLI TO LORENZO THE MAGNIFICENT, SON OF PIERO DE' MEDICI

Those who want to gain a prince's favor usually offer him those things they value most or that they think he likes best. So we often see people giving him horses, armor, cloth of gold, gems, and similar ornaments suitable to their position. Wishing to offer Your Magnificence something on my behalf as evidence of my devotion, I find nothing in my possessions I value higher than the knowledge of the actions of great men, which I have gained from long experience of the affairs of today and from constant study of the past. I have carefully examined and thought about these matters for a long time, and now I have written it all down in a small volume, which I send to Your Magnificence.

Although I judge this book unworthy for you to receive, I am confident that you will generously accept it, especially when you recall that I can give no greater gift than to help you understand in a very short time what it has taken me many years and many dangers and much discomfort to learn.

• • •

A prince, first of all, should have no other object or thought in mind than war and how to wage it. He must not take up anything else to be skillful in, for war is the only art essential to those who govern. It is, moreover, of such great value that it not only keeps in power those who have been born rulers, but often helps men of humble origin to rise to high rank. On the other hand, when princes turn their attention more to luxuries than to war, they lose their power. The chief cause of losing

THE PRINCE   From the introduction and chapters 14–19, 26. Translation by the editor, based on the texts in *Opere*, Firenze, 1843; *Opere*, Milano, 1873–77; and *Il Principe di Niccolò Machiavelli*, Oxford, 1891.

power is neglect of the art of war; the chief means of acquiring power is skill in the art of war.

Francesco Sforza,[1] because he had his own army, rose from private citizen to duke of Milan. His descendants, wanting to avoid the hardships of war, became private citizens instead of dukes. Among other misfortunes that being unskilled in arms brings you is that it makes others despise you, and that is a disgrace against which a prince must guard, as I will explain later. There is no possible equality between an armed man and one who is unarmed. It is unreasonable to suppose that the armed man will willingly obey the unarmed one or that the unarmed one will be safe among armed servants. For when one feels superior and the other suspicious, it is impossible for them to work well together. A prince who does not understand military affairs will, in addition to the other misfortunes I have described, lose the esteem of his soldiers and will be unable to trust them.

He should, therefore, never think of anything else than military training. In peacetime he ought to pay more attention to it than even in time of war. He can do this in two ways: first, with action; the second, with study. As to action, besides keeping his forces well trained and disciplined, he ought to go hunting often and thus keep his body used to hardship. He will also in this way learn the nature of the land, how the mountains rise up, how the valleys open, how the plains extend, and will discover the nature of the rivers and swamps. He ought to pay greatest attention to all of this, for this knowledge is useful in two ways: first, he comes to know his own country and can better plan its defense; then, by knowledge and experience of these places, he can easily understand any other location it becomes necessary to know about. Since the hills, valleys, plains, rivers, and swamps of Tuscany, for example, have a certain similarity to those of other provinces, knowledge of the appearance of one province can easily lead to an understanding of others. The prince who lacks this lacks the first qualification which a military leader ought to have, for this teaches him how to find the enemy, to select his campgrounds, to lead his forces, to plan battles, and to besiege territories to his advantage.

Philopoemen,[2] prince of the Achaeans, among other things for which writers praised him, never thought of anything but methods of

---

[1] A military leader who overthrew the weak government of Milan in 1450 and became its duke. His son Lodovico Il Moro was driven from power in 1499 by Louis XII of France.

[2] Greek soldier, patriot, and statesman (253–184 B.C.).

waging war, even in peacetime. When he was in the country with his friends, he often stopped and questioned them: "If the enemy were on that hill, and we were here with our army, which of us would have the advantage? How could we advance toward him and still maintain good order? If we wanted to retreat, how should we do so? If they retreated, how should we follow?" As he went along, he put before them all the things which might happen to an army. He listened to their opinions and gave his own with supporting arguments, so that because of this constant discussion nothing could happen when he was leading his army for which he did not have an answer.

As to the exercise of the mind, however, the prince ought to read history and study the actions of distinguished men to see how they conducted themselves in war and to examine the reasons for their victories and their defeats so that he can imitate the former and avoid the latter. Above all, he ought to do as some great men have done in the past who took as a model someone praised and glorified and kept his deeds and actions before them. It is said that Alexander the Great imitated Achilles; Caesar, Alexander; and Scipio, Cyrus.[3] . . . A wise prince ought to do likewise and never remain idle in peacetime. He ought to put these examples to use so that if fortune turns against him he will be ready to resist her. . . .

We must now see what methods and rules a prince should use in dealing with his subjects and his friends. Because I know that many have written about this, I fear that my writing about it will be judged presumptuous, since I disagree in this matter completely with the opinions of others. But since I intend to write something useful to those who understand, it seems to me more practical to go directly to the actual truth of the matter than to speculate about it. Many have imagined republics and principalities that have never been seen or known really to exist. But there is such a difference between how we live and how we ought to live that he who turns away from what actually does occur for the sake of what ought to occur, does something that will ruin him rather than save him. For he who wants to be a good man all the time will be ruined among so many who are not good. It is therefore necessary for a prince who wants to survive to learn how *not* to be good and to use goodness, or not use it, according to what needs to be done.

[3] Achilles: legendary Greek hero of the Trojan war. Caesar: Roman general and statesman (first century B.C.). Alexander: conqueror of the eastern Mediterranean world (fourth century B.C.). Scipio: Roman general, victor over Carthage (236–184 B.C.). Cyrus: founder of Persian empire (sixth century B.C.).

Leaving aside, then, those matters which concern only an imaginary prince and talking about those things that are real, I say that all men, and especially princes because they are situated higher, exhibit certain qualities which bring them either blame or praise. Thus, one is termed liberal or generous, another miserly or stingy . . . one is thought unselfish, another greedy; one cruel, another compassionate; one unreliable, another trustworthy; one effeminate and cowardly, another fierce and courageous; one humane, another proud; one lascivious, another chaste; one frank, the other crafty; one harsh, the other easygoing; one serious, the other lightminded; one religious, the other an unbeliever; and so on.

I know that everyone will admit that it would be very fine for a prince to have all of the qualities mentioned above that are judged good. But because human nature will not allow it, they cannot all be possessed or maintained. It is necessary, therefore, that the prince be clever enough to know how to avoid a bad reputation for having those vices which might endanger his position, and if he can do so, he should also avoid those vices that are not dangerous to his position. But if he cannot do so, he can let them persist with less worry. He must not care if he gets a bad reputation on account of those vices without which he could not protect the state; because, all things considered, we find that some things which seem to be virtues would, if followed, lead to ruin, whereas something else which seems vicious will bring about security and well-being.

• • •

Beginning now with the first of the qualities mentioned above, I say that it would be well to be thought liberal or generous. Nevertheless, liberality used to such a degree that you are known for it, is harmful to you. If you practice it moderately, as one ought to, no one will know about it, and you will be blamed for the opposite vice. If, on the other hand, you want to gain a reputation for being liberal or generous, you must not omit any extravagance, to such an extent that a prince who does so will use up his resources. It will then become necessary at last, if he wants to keep on being known for his liberality, for him to tax his people heavily, to extort money from them, and do everything possible just to get money.

This will begin to make his subjects hate him, and when he becomes poor no one will think much of him. Thus, having harmed many and benefited few by his generosity, he will be subject to all kinds of hardships and all kinds of dangers. If he realizes this and wants to change his ways, he is immediately blamed for becoming stingy

A prince, therefore, being unable to use this virtue of liberality or generosity to the point where it is recognized without harming himself, ought not, if he is wise, object to being termed stingy. For as time passes he will be termed more liberal when people see that because of his thriftiness his income is enough both to defend himself against those who make war against him and to begin his own enterprises without burdening the people. Such a prince is actually liberal to those from whom he takes nothing, who are numerous, and stingy to those to whom he does not give, who are few.

In our times we have not seen any great achievements except the ones performed by those considered stingy. The others have failed. Pope Julius II,[4] though he used his reputation for generosity to win the papacy, did not try to maintain it afterwards because he wanted to be able to wage war. The present king of France[5] has made many wars without imposing heavy taxes on his people because the extra expenditures were paid for by his long-term economies. The present king of Spain,[6] if he had continued being liberal, would not have begun or completed so many undertakings.

For these reasons a prince ought to care little about being thought stingy if he thereby avoids robbing his subjects and can still defend himself, and if he does not become poor and contemptible or is not forced to become greedy. For this vice of stinginess is one of those that will enable him to rule. If someone says that Caesar came to power by using liberality and many others attained high rank by being generous or being thought so, I reply that you are already a prince or you are on the way to becoming one. In the first case, this liberality is dangerous; in the second it is quite necessary to be considered generous. Caesar was one of those who wished to come to power in Rome. But if, after attaining power, he had lived and had not decreased his expenditures, he would have destroyed his authority. And if someone should reply that there have been many princes considered to be very generous and who have done great deeds with their armies, I say that either the prince

[4]As pope, from 1503 to 1513, he was an energetic military leader in behalf of the temporal and political power of the papacy.
[5]Louis XII (reigned 1498–1515).
[6]Ferdinand II (reigned 1474–1516), called "the Catholic."

spends his own money and his subjects' or someone else's. In the first case, he ought be careful; in the other case, he should not neglect in any way being very generous.

Generosity is necessary for the prince who marches with his army and lives on plunder, loot, and ransoms, and uses other people's wealth. Otherwise his soldiers would not follow him. You can be very generous with what does not belong to you or to your subjects, as were Cyrus, Caesar, and Alexander. To spend others' money does not harm your reputation but helps it. It is only spending your own money that hurts you. There is nothing that uses itself up like generosity. For while you use it, you lose the power to use it, and you become either poor and despised or, in order to escape poverty, you become greedy and hated. Above all, a prince must guard against being despised and hated, and generosity or liberality brings you to one or the other condition. However, it is wiser to be known as stingy, which brings you disgrace without hatred, than trying to be known as liberal, which necessarily makes you known as rapacious; having a reputation for that brings disgrace and hatred. . . .

Proceeding to the other qualities mentioned before, I say that every prince ought to wish to be thought merciful and not cruel, but he ought to be careful not to misuse that mercy. Cesare Borgia[7] was considered cruel; nevertheless, his cruelty pacified the Romagna, united it, and restored it to peace and loyalty. If this is well thought through, it will be seen to have been more merciful than the people of Florence who, in order to avoid being called cruel, allowed Pistoia to be destroyed.[8] Hence, a prince ought not to worry about a reputation for being cruel in order to keep his subjects unified and loyal, for with a very few examples of cruelty he will prove more merciful than those who, because of too much leniency, allow disorder to erupt, whence arise murders and lootings. For these harm a whole community, whereas the executions ordered by the prince harm only individuals. And of all princes, it is impossible for a new one to avoid the reputation of being cruel because new states are full of dangers. Vergil says in Dido's words: "Harsh times and the newness of the state force me to do such things and to guard all my lands."[9] Nevertheless, the prince should be cautious

---

[7]Son of Pope Alexander VI, and known for his skillful but ruthless tactics. The Romagna is a district in north-central Italy.

[8]Florence did not intervene to subdue civil strife in the nearby city of Pistoia when it was under Florentine control. As a result, the city was ruined.

[9]In his *Aeneid* the Roman poet Vergil describes the successful rule of Dido, legendary queen of Carthage.

in judging and acting, but not timid. He should proceed in a temperate manner, with prudence and humanity, so that overconfidence does not make him careless, or excessive suspicions make him intolerable.

From this rises a question: is it better to be loved than feared, or the reverse? The answer is that the prince should be both feared and loved, if possible. But since it is difficult for the two to go together, it is much safer to be feared than loved, if one of the two has to be given up. For it can be said of men in general that they are ungrateful, talkative, tricky, and deceitful, eager to avoid dangers, anxious for gain. While you are doing them favors, they are all yours, offering you blood, possessions, life, and children, as I said before, when need for these is remote; but when you need them, they turn on you. And the prince who has trusted their words without making other preparations is ruined, for friendships gained by favors, and not by greatness and nobility, cannot be counted upon when needed. Men care less about offending someone who makes himself loved than one who makes himself feared, because love is supported by a chain of obligation, which because of man's debased nature, is broken at every occasion for selfish profit; but fear, maintained by dread of punishment, never fails.

Nevertheless, the prince should make himself feared in such a way that if he does not gain love, he at least avoids hatred. For to be feared and not to be hated go very well together. This can always be done if the prince refrains from taking the property and women of his subjects. And when indeed it is necessary to take someone's life, it should be when there is sufficient justification and obvious cause. But above all he should refrain from taking the property of others, for men forget the death of their father sooner than the loss of their property. Moreover, reasons for taking property are never lacking, and he who begins to live by extortion always finds reasons to take the goods of others, whereas reasons for taking life are fewer and less lasting.

But when the prince is with the army and commands a great number of soldiers it is altogether necessary that he pay no attention to being called cruel, because if he is not cruel he cannot keep his army together or ready for service. Among the marvelous actions of Hannibal[10] there is cited this: he had a large army made up of many kinds of men, but he led them through a foreign land without any disagreement arising either among them or with their commander, either in misfortune or in good times. This cannot have come from anything other than his

---

[10]Carthaginian general (247–183 B.C.) whose army crossed the Alps into Italy and defeated the Romans in several major battles.

inhuman cruelty, which, together with his many other qualities, always made his soldiers respect him and think him terrible. Without this, his other virtues would not have been enough to produce such an effect. Writers have thought too little about this when on the one hand they admire his achievements, and on the other blame the principal cause of those achievements.

The fact that his other qualities would not have been enough can be seen in the example of Scipio, a man very famous in his own time and in all times that we know anything about. His armies mutinied when he was in Spain. This resulted from nothing other than too much kindness, which allowed the soldiers more freedom than goes with military discipline. This fault was condemned in the Senate by Fabius Maximus[11] who called him the corruptor of the Roman militia. And when the Locrians[12] were destroyed by one of his officers, Scipio did not avenge them nor did he punish the officer's disobedience, owing to his easy-going nature. Thus, when someone in the Senate wanted to make excuses for him, he said that there were many men who knew better how not to make mistakes than to punish the mistakes of others. This characteristic would in time have ruined Scipio's fame and glory if he had kept on with it as a commander, but living under the Senate's command this bad quality was not merely hidden but was part of his fame.

I conclude, therefore, that as far as being feared or loved are concerned, men love as they please but fear as the prince wills. A wise prince ought to rely on what is in his power and not in the power of others, only being careful to avoid being hated, as I have pointed out. . . .

Everyone knows how praiseworthy it is for a prince to keep his word and to live honestly and not be deceitful. Nevertheless, experience shows that princes in our times who have done great things have cared little for honesty; they have known how to confuse men's minds with their cleverness and have finally defeated those who put their faith in honesty.

You ought to realize, therefore, that there are two ways of fighting: one according to laws, the other with force. The first is appropriate to men, the second to animals. But often the first is not enough, and it is necessary to turn to the second. Therefore, it is necessary for a prince to

[11]Roman statesman (third century B.C.).
[12]Citizens of Locri, a town in Sicily.

know very well the methods of both animal and man. This lesson was secretly taught by writers of antiquity, who tell how Achilles and many other princes of ancient times were given to the centaur Chiron,[13] so that he could raise and teach them. Their having as tutor a creature half-animal and half-man indicates the need of a prince's knowing how to use the nature of both and that one cannot bring success without the other.

Therefore, since it is necessary for a prince to know well how to act like an animal, he should choose the natures of the fox and the lion; for the lion cannot defend himself from traps, and the fox cannot defend himself from wolves. A prince needs to be a fox to know about traps, and a lion to terrify the wolves. Those who behave only like the lion do not understand this. Therefore, a prudent ruler ought not to keep faith when to do so would be disadvantageous and when the reasons for making promises no longer exist. If all men were good, this precept would not be good. But since they are bad and would not keep their promises to you, it is not necessary for you to keep yours to them. A prince never lacks good reason to excuse his breaking his word. One could give innumerable modern examples of this and show how many peace treaties and promises have been broken and made ineffective by the untrustworthiness of princes. He who has best known how to act like a fox has succeeded best. But he who has this talent has to know how to keep it hidden and to pretend and deceive. Men are so simple and yield to the needs of the present so readily that he who deceives will always find those who let themselves be deceived.

I do not wish to remain silent about one recent example. Alexander VI[14] did nothing else but deceive men and thought of nothing else, yet he always found the opportunity to do so. There never was a man who had greater success in affirming something; and the more oaths he used in affirming it, the sooner he broke his promise. Nevertheless, his deceptions always succeeded in the way he wanted, for he knew the way of the world.

It is not necessary, then, for a prince to have the good qualities mentioned above, but it is necessary to seem to have them. I would even say this: to have them and use them all the time is dangerous, but seeming to have them is useful. He should seem to be pious, faithful,

---

[13] A mythical creature, half horse and half man, that was reputed to have been the educator of several legendary Greek heroes.

[14] As Pope, from 1492 to 1503, he was known for his astute but devious political maneuvering.

humane, honest, religious, and to be so. But he should have his mind so prepared that when occasion requires, he is able to change to the opposite. And it must be understood that a prince, especially a new prince, cannot observe all those things for which men are considered good; it is often necessary to act contrary to faith, charity, humanity, and religion in order to maintain the state. It is therefore necessary for him to have the ability to change his mind according to the way the winds of fortune and conditions require. If possible, he ought not, as I have said before, turn away from what is good, but he should be able to do evil if necessary.

A prince should be very careful that nothing ever comes from his mouth that is not full of the aforementioned [good] qualities. Those who see and hear him should think him all compassion, all faith, all integrity, all humaneness, all religion. And nothing is more necessary to seem to have than the last quality. For people in general judge more with their eyes than with their minds. Everyone can see; few have understanding. Everyone sees what you seem to be; few know what you really are. And those few do not dare oppose the opinion of the many, who have the power of the state to support them. In the actions of individuals, especially princes, when there is no judge to appeal to, people look at the results.[15] A prince only has to conquer and maintain the state. His means will always be considered honorable, and everyone will praise them because the common crowd is always deceived by appearances and by the way things turn out. In the world the crowd is everything. The few are isolated when the crowd is in control. A certain prince of the present time, whom it would be well not to mention by name,[16] always preaches peace and fidelity but is actually a great enemy of both. Either of these qualities, had he followed them, would often have taken from him his reputation or his state. . . .

Since I have spoken of the most important of the qualities mentioned above, I want to discuss the others briefly, with this generalization: the prince should pay attention, as has been said before, to avoiding those things which make him hated and despised. As long as he succeeds in this, he will have done his part and will not find danger in other vices. Hatred, as I have said, comes from being greedy and seizing his subjects' property and women. He must refrain from doing these things.

---

[15]"In the actions . . . results." Some translations condense Machiavelli's sentence to "The end justifies the means."

[16]Probably Ferdinand II of Spain, who was on good terms with the Medici rulers of Florence.

For most men live contentedly as long as they are not deprived of their property or honor. Then he has to contend only with the ambition of a few, which he can easily control in many ways. He is judged contemptible if he is thought changeable, frivolous, effeminate, cowardly, and irresolute. A prince ought to guard against these as from a dangerous reef. He must try to show by his actions his greatness, spirit, seriousness, and bravery. In governing the affairs of his subjects, he must make his decisions irrevocable. He ought to maintain such a reputation that no one would think of deceiving or cheating him.

The prince who earns such an opinion for himself has a great reputation. If a prince has a great reputation, it is difficult to plot against him or to attack him so long as he is thought to have great ability and the respect of his subjects. Therefore, a prince must fear two things: one from inside his state because of his subjects, the other from outside because of foreign enemies. He can defend himself from the latter with good weapons and good friends, and he will always have good friends if he has good arms. Conditions inside the state will remain quiet when conditions outside are quiet, unless they are already stirred up by a conspiracy. When attacked from outside, if he has ruled and lived as I have said, and if he stands firm, he will repel all attacks as the Spartan Nabis[17] did. But concerning his subjects when external matters are stable, he still has to be wary of their plots. The prince can be quite safe from these if he avoids being hated and if he keeps the people satisfied, which will of course happen as I have already explained.

One of the most effective safeguards a prince can have against conspiracies is not being hated by the people, for every conspirator believes that he will please the people by killing the prince. But if he thinks he will offend them by doing so, he does not dare to carry out the action because the difficulties encountered by conspirators are very many. Experience shows that there have been many conspiracies, and few have turned out well because a conspirator cannot act alone. He can get companions only from among those who, he thinks, are discontented. And just as soon as you have revealed your plot to a malcontent, you give him the means to be contented. . . . He sees on the one hand certain gain and on the other an uncertain prospect full of danger. He would have to be a rare friend to you or a fierce enemy of the prince to keep his word to you.

[17]Spartan military leader (third century B.C.) who executed eighty of his own soldiers in order to make the others fight more bravely.

To put the matter briefly, I say that a conspirator can know nothing but anxiety, jealousy, and fear of punishment, which terrifies him. But on the prince's side there are the prestige of his office, the laws, and the power of his friends and the state that defend him. When the good will of the people is added to all of these, it is impossible that anyone would be so foolhardy as to conspire. Whereas a conspirator usually has to be afraid before committing the act, in this case he also has to be afraid afterwards, for he will have the people for his enemy too, and he will have no hope of any escape.

•   •   •

Having considered everything in the foregoing discussion, I ask myself if the time has not come in Italy for a new prince to succeed and whether conditions are not favorable for a prudent and capable person to introduce methods which would benefit him and do good for the mass of people. It seems to me that so many things come together to benefit a new prince that I do not know of any time more favorable for doing so. And if, as I have said, the Israelites had to be slaves in Egypt so that the power of Moses could become evident; and the Persians had to be oppressed by the Medes so that the greatness of Cyrus[18] could be recognized; and the Athenians had to be scattered so that the excellence of Theseus[19] could be revealed; then in order to reveal the greatness of the Italian spirit, it was necessary for Italy to be reduced to her present situation and that she be more enslaved than the Hebrews, more oppressed than the Persians, more scattered than the Athenians, without a leader, without order, beaten, plundered, impoverished, overrun, and suffering every kind of disaster.

And although before now some persons have shown signs that could be judged indications of their having been chosen by God for Italy's redemption, it happened that later on they were rejected by fortune.

So Italy remains, as if lifeless, and waits for the one, whoever he may be, who can heal her wounds, put an end to the plundering of Lombardy, Tuscany, and Naples, and cure her of those sores that have been festering for so long a time. She can be seen praying to God to send

---

[18]In the course of founding the Persian Empire, Cyrus defeated the Medes, who had been a major power in southwest Asia.

[19]Theseus, legendary hero, was said to have united the villages of the region around Athens into a single city-state.

someone who can save her from this barbarous cruelty and outrage. See how ready she is and willing to follow a banner if only someone would raise it.

There is no one to be seen in whom we can put our hope except in your own illustrious family,[20] because your good fortune and strength, favored by God and the Church which your family now rules, enable it to become the leader of this redemption. This will not be very difficult if you recall the deeds and lives of the persons I have named before. And although these were unusual and extraordinary, they were men and each one had less opportunity than exists at present. For their enterprise was not more just than this, nor easier, nor was God more their friend than yours.

Here is a great, just cause: a war is just when it is necessary, and arms are holy for him whose only hope is in arms. Everything is perfectly ready. Nor can it be very difficult where there is great willingness, if only the methods I have mentioned are followed. Moreover, we have seen extraordinary wonders performed by God: the sea has parted; a cloud has shown the way; the rock has poured out water; manna has rained down.[21] Everything has contributed to your greatness. The rest is for you to do. God does not want to do everything, lest he take away our free will and the share in glory which belongs to us.

It is not remarkable that none of the Italians mentioned before has been able to do what we hope your illustrious House will do, nor that in so many revolutions and military operations in Italy it seems that military ability has disappeared. This happens because the old tactics were not good and there has not been anyone who has been able to find new ones. Nothing brings so much honor to a man who rises to power as the new laws and methods devised by him.

These things, when they are well done and contain greatness in them, make him revered and wondered at. And in Italy there is no lack of opportunity for introducing all kinds of reforms. Here there is a great power in the limbs if only it were not lacking in the head. You can see in duels and small scale combats how the Italians are superior in strength, dexterity, and cleverness. But when it comes to armies there is no comparison. It is all caused by the inferiority of the leaders, for those

---

[20]That is, the Medici family.

[21]References to the miraculous circumstances of Moses' leading the Israelites out of bondage.

who know are not obeyed, and everyone thinks he knows. No one has yet been able to raise himself so high by his ability and fortune that others obey. Because of this it has happened in the wars of the past twenty years that whenever there has been an entirely Italian army, it has always failed. Proof of this was first Taro, then Alessandria, Capua, Genoa, Vaila, Bologna, and Mestri.[22]

If your illustrious House, then, wishes to emulate those famous men who redeemed their countries, it is necessary first of all to have as the real beginning of all undertakings your own army. For you cannot have more faithful or more loyal or better soldiers. And although individually they may be good, they become even better when united and when they see that they are commanded by their prince and are respected and trusted by him. It is necessary, therefore, that you get such forces ready in order to be able to defend yourself with Italian strength against foreigners.

Although the Swiss and Spanish infantry may be looked upon as terrifying, nevertheless each has its faults, so that a third kind could not only resist them but be confident of defeating them. For the Spanish cannot withstand cavalry attacks, and the Swiss fear infantry that attacks as resolutely as they. Hence it is seen and is evident from experience that the Spanish cannot withstand French cavalry, and the Swiss are destroyed by Spanish infantry. Although a complete example of the latter has not actually been seen, yet it was almost observed in the battle of Ravenna, when the Spanish infantry attacked German battalions which deploy in the same way as the Swiss. The Spanish, because of their agility and use of their shields, got underneath the Germans' pikes and attacked them safely, whereas the Germans had no way of resisting. If the cavalry had not charged, they would have been annihilated.

It is possible, then, to know the drawbacks of these kinds of infantry and to organize a new kind which could resist cavalry and would not fear opposing infantry. To do this, one must create new weapons and a different kind of organization. These are things which, when used for the first time, give fame and glory to a new prince.

This opportunity must not be allowed to pass. Italy after so long a time sees her redeemer. I cannot express the love with which he would be greeted in all the provinces which have suffered from being overrun

---

[22]Battles that took place in Italy at the end of the fifteenth century and the beginning of the sixteenth.

by foreigners, with what thirst for vengeance, with what firm faith, what piety, what tears! What gates would be shut against him? What people would deny him obedience? What envy would oppose him? What Italian would fail to revere him?

This barbarian rule stinks in the nostrils of everyone. May your illustrious House undertake this task with that spirit and hope with which just causes are undertaken, so that under your banner our fatherland will become noble, and under its protection Petrarch's saying will become true:

> Against the furious foe
> Virtue herself will take up arms. The fight
> Will then be brief. Not slow
> Are Italian hearts to keep our honor bright.[23]

---

[23]Lines from Petrarch's patriotic verses, *My Italy* (*Italia Mia*), which have remained familiar and loved to the present day.

21

Baldassare Castiglione

The Courtier

*B*ALDASSARE *Castiglione (1478–
1529) is himself one of the best examples of the ideal Renaissance gentleman
described in his prose dialogue,* The Courtier. *A man of many careers—
including man of letters, adviser to princes, and official of the Church—
Castiglione was always faithful to his code of gentlemanly honor. For several
years he resided at the court of Guidobaldo da Montefeltro, Duke of Urbino,
representing the duke on several diplomatic missions, including one trip to
England and the court of Henry VII. Later, Castiglione was involved in one of
the major quarrels of the century—between Pope Clement VII and the Holy
Roman Emperor, Charles V. Castiglione lived his last years in Spain, where he
entered the Church and became Bishop of Avila.*

Castiglione's The Courtier, *written in 1514 and published in 1528, is an
expression of the Renaissance at its best. Translated into English in 1561 by Sir
Thomas Hoby, the work exerted a great influence upon Shakespeare's contemporaries and stands even now as the classic expression of the aristocratic credo. It
purports to be the record of conversations of a group of witty and learned men and
women (whose thinking was influenced by the new learning of the Renaissance)
who gathered in the evenings in the hall of the ducal palace of Urbino—the most
princely residence in Italy, according to contemporary opinion. The discussions
deal with the ethical, intellectual, military, sporting, and social gifts and
abilities of the ideal gentleman. As the following selection opens, Count
Ludovico da Canossa is setting forth what he considers to be the qualities of the
ideal gentleman-courtier. The others then join in with their contributions to this
description of the well-born, well-bred ideal gentleman whose attributes summa-
rize not only the aristocratic tradition in Western culture, but many shaping
ideals of Western culture as a whole.*

[Count Ludovico speaks.]

"I wish, then, that this Courtier[1] of ours should be nobly born and of gentle race; because it is far less unseemly for one of ignoble birth to fail in worthy deeds, than for one of noble birth, who, if he strays from the path of his predecessors, stains his family name, and not only fails to achieve but loses what has been achieved already; for noble birth is like a bright lamp that manifests and makes visible good and evil deeds, and kindles and stimulates to virtue both by fear of shame and by hope of praise. And since this splendour of nobility does not illumine the deeds of the humbly born, they lack that stimulus and fear of shame, nor do they feel any obligation to advance beyond what their predecessors have done; while to the nobly born it seems a reproach not to reach at least the goal set them by their ancestors. And thus it nearly always happens that both in the profession of arms and in other worthy pursuits the most famous men have been of noble birth, because nature has implanted in everything that hidden seed which gives a certain force and quality of its own essence to all things that are derived from it, and makes them like itself: as we see not only in the breeds of horses and of other animals, but also in trees, the shoots of which nearly always resemble the trunk; and if they sometimes degenerate, it arises from poor cultivation. And so it is with men, who if rightly trained are nearly always like those from whom they spring, and often better; but if there be no one to give them proper care, they become like savages and never reach perfection.

"It is true that, by favour of the stars or of nature, some men are endowed at birth with such graces that they seem not to have been born, but rather as if some god had formed them with his very hands and adorned them with every excellence of mind and body. So too there are many men so foolish and rude that one cannot but think that nature brought them into the world out of contempt or mockery. Just as these can usually accomplish little even with constant diligence and good training, so with slight pains those others reach the highest summit of excellence. And to give you an instance: you see my lord Don Ippolito

---

[1]The meaning here is probably simply a gentleman who can live easily and comfortably in cultivated society.

THE COURTIER   Baldassare Castiglione, *The Book of the Courtier*, trans. Leonard E. Opdycke (New York: Scribner, 1901), 22–26, 59–66, 86–88, 175–79, 297–99, 308–09.

d'Este, Cardinal of Ferrara,[2] who has enjoyed such fortune from his birth, that his person, his aspect, his words and all his movements are so disposed and imbued with this grace, that—although he is young—he exhibits among the most aged prelates such weight of character that he seems fitter to teach than to be taught; likewise in conversation with men and women of every rank, in games, in pleasantry and in banter, he has a certain sweetness and manners so gracious, that whoso speaks with him or even sees him, must needs remain attached to him forever.

"But to return to our subject: I say that there is a middle state between perfect grace on the one hand and senseless folly on the other; and those who are not thus perfectly endowed by nature, with study and toil can in great part polish and amend their natural defects. Besides his noble birth, then, I would have the Courtier favoured in this regard also, and endowed by nature not only with talent and beauty of person and feature, but with a certain grace and (as we say) air that shall make him at first sight pleasing and agreeable to all who see him; and I would have this an ornament that should dispose and unite all his actions, and in his outward aspect give promise of whatever is worthy the society and favour of every great lord."

Here, without waiting longer, my lord Gaspar Pallavicino[3] said:

"In order that our game may have the form prescribed, and that we may not seem to slight the privilege given us to contradict, I say that this nobility of birth does not appear to me so essential in the Courtier; and if I thought I were saying what was new to any of us, I should cite instances of many men born of the noblest blood who have been full of vices; and on the other hand, of many men among the humbly born who by their virtue have made their posterity illustrious. And if what you just said to be true, namely that there is in everything this occult influence of the original seed, then we should all be in the same case, because we had the same origin, nor would any man be more noble than another. But as to our differences and grades of eminence and obscurity, I believe there are many other causes: among which I rate fortune to be chief; for we see her holding sway in all mundane affairs, often amusing herself by lifting to heaven whom she pleases (although wholly without merit), and burying in the depths those most worthy to be exalted.

---

[2]The cardinal, a friend of Leonardo da Vinci, had become an archbishop by age twenty-four.

[3]One of the younger members of the court and a close friend of Castiglione.

"I quite agree with what you say as to the good fortune of those endowed from birth with advantages of mind and body: but this is seen as well among the humbly born as among the nobly born, since nature has no such subtle distinctions as these; and often, as I said, the highest gifts of nature are found among the most obscure. Therefore, since this nobility of birth is won neither by talent nor by strength nor by craft, and is rather the merit of our predecessors than our own, it seems to me too extravagant to maintain that if our Courtier's parents be humbly born, all his good qualities are spoiled, and that all those other qualifications that you mentioned do not avail to raise him to the summit of perfection; I mean talent, beauty of feature, comeliness of person, and that grace which makes him always charming to everyone at first sight."

Then Count Ludovico[4] replied:

"I do not deny that the same virtues may rule the low-born and the noble: but (not to repeat what we have said already or the many other arguments that could be adduced in praise of noble birth, which is honoured always and by everyone, it being reasonable that good should beget good), since we have to form a Courtier without flaw and endowed with every praiseworthy quality, it seems to me necessary to make him nobly born, as well for many other reasons as for universal opinion, which is at once disposed in favour of noble birth. For if there be two Courtiers who have as yet given no impression of themselves by good or evil acts, as soon as the one is known to have been born a gentleman and the other not, he who is low-born will be far less esteemed by everyone than he who is high-born, and will need much effort and time to make upon men's minds that good impression which the other will have achieved in a moment and merely by being a gentleman.

· · ·

"But to come to some details, I am of opinion that the principal and true profession of the Courtier ought to be that of arms; which I would have him follow actively above all else, and be known among others as bold and strong, and loyal to whomsoever he serves. And he will win a reputation for these good qualities by exercising them at all times and in all places, since one may never fail in this without severest censure. And

---

[4] Ludovico da Canossa, friend and relation of Castiglione, later entered the service of the king of France. He was also a friend of Erasmus and Raphael.

just as among women, their fair fame once sullied never recovers its first lustre, so the reputation of a gentleman who bears arms, if once it be in the least tarnished with cowardice or other disgrace, remains forever infamous before the world and full of ignominy. Therefore the more our Courtier excels in this art, the more he will be worthy of praise; and yet I do not deem essential in him that perfect knowledge of things and those other qualities that befit a commander; since this would be too wide a sea, let us be content, as we have said, with perfect loyalty and unconquered courage, and that he be always seen to possess them. For the courageous are often recognized even more in small things than in great; and frequently in perils of importance and where there are many spectators, some men are to be found, who, although their hearts be dead within them, yet, moved by shame or by the presence of others, press forward almost with their eyes shut, and do their duty God knows how. While on occasions of little moment, when they think they can avoid putting themselves in danger without being detected, they are glad to keep safe. But those who, even when they do not expect to be observed or seen or recognized by anyone, show their ardour and neglect nothing, however paltry, that may be laid to their charge,—they have that strength of mind which we seek in our Courtier.

"Not that we would have him look so fierce, or go about blustering, or say that he has taken his cuirass to wife, or threaten with those grim scowls that we have often seen in Berto;[5] because to such men as this, one might justly say that which a brave lady jestingly said in gentle company to one whom I will not name at present; who, being invited by her out of compliment to dance, refused not only that, but to listen to the music, and many other entertainments proposed to him,— saying always that such silly trifles were not his business; so that at last the lady said, 'What is your business, then?' He replied with a sour look, 'To fight.' Then the lady at once said, 'Now that you are in no war and out of fighting trim, I should think it were a good thing to have yourself well oiled, and to stow yourself with all your battle harness in a closet until you be needed, lest you grow more rusty than you are'; and so, amid much laughter from the bystanders, she left the discomfited fellow to his silly presumption.

"Therefore let the man we are seeking, be very bold, stern, and always among the first, where the enemy are to be seen; and in every

---

[5]A clown or buffoon attached to the papal court as an entertainer on social occasions.

other place, gentle, modest, reserved, above all things avoiding ostentation and that impudent self-praise by which men ever excite hatred
and disgust in all who hear them.

• • •

"I would have him more than passably accomplished in letters, at
least in those studies that are called the humanities, and conversant not
only with the Latin language but with the Greek, for the sake of the
many different things that have been admirably written therein. Let
him be well versed in the poets, and not less in the orators and historians, and also proficient in writing verse and prose, especially in this
vulgar tongue of ours; for besides the enjoyment he will find in it, he
will by this means never lack agreeable entertainment with ladies, who
are usually fond of such things. And if other occupations or want of
study prevent his reaching such perfection as to render his writings
worthy of great praise, let him be careful to suppress them so that
others may not laugh at him, and let him show them only to a friend
whom he can trust: because they will at least be of this service to him,
that the exercise will enable him to judge the work of others. For it very
rarely happens that a man who is not accustomed to write, however
learned he may be, can ever quite appreciate the toil and industry of
writers, or taste the sweetness and excellence of style, and those latent
niceties that are often found in the ancients.

"Moreover these studies will also make him fluent and, as
Aristippus[6] said to the tyrant, confident and assured in speaking with
everyone. Hence I would have our Courtier keep one precept fixed in
mind; which is that in this and everything else he should be always on
his guard, and diffident rather than forward, and that he should keep
from falsely persuading himself that he knows that which he does not
know. For by nature we all are fonder of praise than we ought to be, and
our ears love the melody of words that praise us more than any other
sweet song or sound; and thus, like sirens' voices, they are often the
cause of shipwreck to him who does not close his ears to such deceptive
harmony. Among the ancient sages this danger was recognized, and
books were written showing in what way the true friend may be
distinguished from the flatterer. But what does this avail, if there be
many, nay a host, of those who clearly perceive that they are flattered,

---

[6]Greek philosopher (fourth century B.C.) who lived for a time at the court of Dionysius,
the tyrant (ruler) of Syracuse in Sicily.

yet love him who flatters them, and hold him in hatred who tells them the truth? And often when they find him who praises them too sparing in his words, they even help him and say such things of themselves, that the flatterer is put to shame, most impudent though he be.

"Let us leave these blind ones to their errour, and have our Courtier of such good judgment that he will not take black for white, or have more self-confidence than he clearly knows to be well founded; and especially in those peculiarities which (if you remember) messer Cesare[7] in his game said we had often used as an instrument to bring men's folly to light. On the contrary, even if he well knows the praises bestowed upon him to be true, let him not err by accepting them too openly or confirming them without some protest; but rather let him as it were disclaim them modestly, always showing and really esteeming arms as his chief profession, and all other good accomplishments as an ornament thereto. And particularly among soldiers let him not act like those who insist on seeming soldiers in learning, and learned men among soldiers. In this way, for the reasons we have alleged, he will avoid affectation, and even the middling things that he does, shall seem very great."

Messer Pietro Bembo[8] here replied:

"Count, I do not see why you insist that this Courtier, being lettered and endowed with so many other admirable accomplishments, should hold everything as an ornament of arms, and not arms and the rest as an ornament of letters; which without other accompaniment are as superiour in dignity to arms, as the mind is to the body, for the practice of them properly pertains to the mind, as that of arms does to the body."

Then the Count replied:

"Nay, the practice of arms pertains to both mind and body. But I would not have you judge in such a cause, messer Pietro, for you would be too much suspected of bias by one of the two sides: and as the controversy has already been long waged by very wise men, there is no need to renew it; but I regard it as settled in favour of arms, and would have our Courtier so regard it too, since I may form him as I wish. And if you are of contrary mind, wait till you hear of a contest wherein he who defends the cause of arms is allowed to use arms, just as those who defend letters make use of letters in their defence; for if everyone avails himself of his proper weapons, you shall see that men of letters will be worsted."

[7]Messer (lord) Cesare Gonzaga, cousin of Castiglione.

[8]Poet, courtier, and papal secretary to Leo X, Bembo became a cardinal in 1539 and spent his remaining years in Rome.

"Ah," said messer Pietro, "a while ago you blamed the French for prizing letters little, and told what glorious lustre is shed on man by letters and how they make him immortal, and now it seems you have changed your mind. Do you not remember that

> Before the famous tomb of brave Achilles
> Thus spake the mighty Alexander, sighing:
> 'O happy youth, who found so clear a trumpet,
> And lofty bard to make thy deeds undying!'[9]

And if Alexander envied Achilles not for his deeds, but for the fortune that had granted him the happiness of having his exploits celebrated by Homer, we may conclude that Alexander esteemed Homer's poems above Achilles's arms. For what other judge do you wait then, or for what other sentence upon the dignity of arms and letters, than that pronounced by one of the greatest commanders that have ever been?"

Then the Count replied:

"I blame the French for thinking that letters are a hindrance to the profession of arms, and I hold that learning is more proper to no one than to a warrior; and in our Courtier I would have these two accomplishments joined and each aided by the other, as is most proper: nor do I think I have changed my mind in this. But as I said, I do not wish to discuss which of the two is more worthy of praise. It is enough that men of letters almost never select for praise any but great men and glorious deeds, which in themselves merit praise for the mere essential quality from which they spring; besides this they are very noble material for writers: which is a great ornament, and in part the cause of perpetuating writings, which perhaps would not be so much read and appreciated if they lacked their noble theme, but vain and of little moment.

"And if Alexander was envious that Achilles should be praised by Homer, it does not therefore follow that he esteemed letters above arms; wherein if he had felt himself as far behind Achilles as he deemed all those who wrote of him were behind Homer, I am sure he would far rather have desired fine acts on his part than fine speeches on the part of others. Hence I believe that saying of his to have been a tacit eulogy of himself, and that he was expressing a desire for what he thought he did not possess (that is, the supreme excellence of a writer), and not for what he believed he already had attained (that is, prowess in arms, wherein he did not deem Achilles at all his superior). Thus he called

---

[9]These lines about Alexander and Achilles are the opening of a sonn

Achilles happy, as if hinting that although his own fame had hitherto not been so celebrated in the world as Achilles's, which was made bright and illustrious by that poem so divine,—it was not because his valour and merits were less or deserving of less praise, but because fortune bestowed upon Achilles that miracle of nature as a glorious trumpet for his achievements. Perhaps also he wished to incite some noble genius to write about him, by showing that this must be as pleasing to him as were his love and veneration for the sacred monuments of letters: whereof we have spoken long enough for the present."

"Nay, too long," replied my lord Ludovico Pio;[10] "for I believe that in the whole world it would be impossible to find a receptacle large enough to hold all the things you would have in our Courtier."

Then the Count said:

"Wait a little, for there are many more that he must have."

"In that case," replied Pietro da Napoli,[11] "Grasso de' Medici[12] would have a great advantage over messer Pietro Bembo."

Here everyone laughed, and the Count began anew and said:

"My lords, you must know that I am not content with the Courtier unless he be also a musician and unless, besides understanding and being able to read notes, he can play upon divers instruments. For if we consider rightly, there is to be found no rest from toil or medicine for the troubled spirit more becoming and praiseworthy in time of leisure, than this; and especially in courts, where besides the relief from tedium that music affords us all, many things are done to please the ladies, whose tender and gentle spirit is easily penetrated by harmony and filled with sweetness. Thus it is no marvel that in both ancient and modern times they have always been inclined to favour musicians, and have found refreshing spiritual food in music."

Then my lord Gaspar said:

"I admit that music as well as many other vanities may be proper to women and perhaps to some that have the semblance of men, but not to those who really are men; for these ought not to enervate their mind with delights and thus induce therein a fear of death."

"Say not so," replied the Count; "for I shall enter upon a vast sea in praise of music. And I shall call to mind how it was always celebrated and held sacred among the ancients, and how very sage philosophers

[10]Military leader, distant cousin of Emilia Pia, the companion of the Duchess of Urbino.

[11]Member of the entourage of Pope Julius II.

[12]Nickname of a fat servant of the Medici. Bembo in contrast was slender.

were of opinion that the world is composed of music, that the heavens make harmony in their moving, and that the soul, being ordered in like fashion, awakes and as it were revives its powers through music.

"Thus it is written that Alexander was sometimes excited by it so passionately, that he was forced almost against his will to leave the banquet table and rush to arms; and when the musician changed the temper of the tune, he grew calm again, lay aside his arms, and returned to the banquet table. Moreover I will tell you that grave Socrates learned to play the cithern at a very advanced age. And I remember having once heard that Plato and Aristotle would have the man of culture a musician also; and they show by a host of arguments that the power of music over us is very great, and (for many reasons which would be too long to tell now) that it must needs be taught from childhood, not so much for the mere melody that we hear, but for the power it has to induce in us a fresh and good habit of mind and an habitual tendency to virtue, which renders the soul more capable of happiness, just as bodily exercise renders the body more robust; and that music is not only no hindrance in the pursuits of peace and war, but is very helpful therein.

"Again, Lycurgus[13] approved of music in his harsh laws. And we read that in their battles the very warlike Lacedemonians[14] and Cretans used the cithern and other dulcet instruments; that many very excellent commanders of antiquity, like Epaminondas,[15] practised music; and that those who were ignorant of it, like Themistocles,[16] were far less esteemed. Have you not read that music was among the first accomplishments which the worthy old Chiron[17] taught Achilles in tender youth, whom he reared from the age of nurse and cradle, and that the sage preceptor insisted that the hands which were to shed so much Trojan blood, should be often busied with the cithern? Where is the soldier who would be ashamed to imitate Achilles,—to say nothing of many other famous commanders whom I could cite?

"Therefore seek not to deprive our Courtier of music, which not only soothes men's minds, but often tames wild beasts; and he who

[13]Lawgiver of ancient Sparta.

[14]Spartans.

[15]Theban statesman and general (fourth century B.C.).

[16]Athenian general and statesman (fifth century B.C.).

[17]In Greek mythology, the centaur (half horse, half man) who was the teacher of the youthful Achilles and Hercules.

enjoys it not, may be sure that his spirit is ill attuned. See what power it has, to make (as once it did) a fish submit to be ridden by a man upon the boisterous sea. We find it used in holy temples to render praise and thanks to God; and we must believe that it is pleasing to Him and that He has given it to us as most sweet alleviation for our fatigues and troubles. Wherefore rough toilers of the field under a burning sun often cheat their weariness with crude and rustic song. With music the rude peasant lass, who is up before the day to spin or weave, wards off her drowsiness and makes her toil a pleasure; music is very cheering pastime for poor sailors after rain, wind and tempest: a solace to tired pilgrims on their long and weary journeys, and often to sorrowing captives in their chains and fetters. Thus, as stronger proof that melody even if rude is very great relief from every human toil and care, nature seems to have taught it to the nurse as chief remedy for the continual wailing of frail children, who by the sound of her voice are brought restful and placid sleep, forgetful of the tears so proper to them and given us in that age by nature as a presage of our after life."

As the Count now remained silent for a little, the Magnifico Giuliano[18] said:

"I do not at all agree with my lord Gaspar. Nay I think, for the reasons you give and for many others, that music is not only an ornament but a necessity to the Courtier. Yet I would have you declare in what way this and the other accomplishments that you prescribe for him, are to be practised, and at what time and in what manner. For many things that are praiseworthy in themselves often become very inappropriate when practised out of season, and on the other hand, some that seem of little moment are highly esteemed when made use of opportunely."

Then the Count said:

"Before we enter upon that subject, I wish to discuss another matter, which I deem of great importance and therefore think our Courtier ought by no means to omit: and this is to know how to draw and to have acquaintance with the very art of painting.

"And do not marvel that I desire this art, which to-day may seem to savour of the artisan and little to befit a gentleman; for I remember having read that the ancients, especially throughout Greece, had their boys of gentle birth study painting in school as an honourable and

---

[18]Youngest child of Lorenzo de' Medici, he later became governor of Florence and a general of the papal armies.

necessary thing, and it was admitted to the first rank of liberal arts; while by public edict they forbade that it be taught to slaves. Among the Romans too, it was held in highest honour, and the very noble family of the Fabii took their name from it; for the first Fabius was given the name *Pictor*,[19] because,—being indeed a most excellent painter, and so devoted to painting that when he painted the walls of the temple of Health,—he inscribed his own name thereon; for although he was born of a family thus renowned and honoured with so many consular titles, triumphs and other dignities, and although he was a man of letters and learned in the law, and numbered among the orators,—yet he thought to add splendour and ornament to his fame by leaving a memorial that he had been a painter. Nor is there lack of many other men of illustrious family, celebrated in this art; which besides being very noble and worthy in itself, is of great utility, and especially in war for drawing places, sites, rivers, bridges, rocks, fortresses, and the like; since however well we may keep them in memory (which is very difficult), we cannot show them to others.

"And truly he who does not esteem this art, seems to me very unreasonable; for this universal fabric that we see,—with the vast heaven so richly adorned with shining stars, and in the midst the earth girdled by the seas, varied with mountains, valleys and rivers, and bedecked with so many divers trees, beautiful flowers and grasses,— may be said to be a great and noble picture, composed by the hand of nature and of God; and whoever is able to imitate it, seems to me deserving of great praise: nor can it be imitated without knowledge of many things, as he knows well who tries. Hence the ancients greatly prized both the art and the artist, which thus attained the summit of highest excellence; very sure proof of which may be found in the antique marble and bronze statues that yet are seen."

[The conversation turns to the courtier's ability in sports. Lord Federico[20] speaks. *Ed.*]

"This dancing of yours in the sun pleases me not in any way, nor do I see what gain there is in it. But in my opinion whoever cares to wrestle or run or leap with peasants, ought to do so as a matter of practice and out of courtesy as we say, not in rivalry with them. And a man ought to be almost sure of winning; else let him not engage, because it is too

---

[19]Roman senator and historian (third century B.C.). *Pictor* means painter.

[20]Federico Fregoso, distinguished diplomat, student of philology and oriental languages, later became a cardinal.

unseemly and shameful a thing, and beneath his dignity, to see a gentleman vanquished by a peasant, and especially at wrestling. Hence I think it is well to abstain, at least in the presence of many, for the gain of beating is very small and the loss of being beaten is very great.

"The game of tennis also is nearly always played in public, and is one of those sports to which a crowd lends much distinction. Therefore I would have our Courtier practise this, and all the others except the handling of arms, as something that is not his profession, and let him show that he does not seek or expect praise for it, nor let him seem to devote much care or time to it, although he may do it admirably. Nor let him be like some men who delight in music, and in speaking with anyone always begin to sing under their breath whenever there is a pause in the conversation. Others always go dancing as they pass through streets and churches. Others, when they meet a friend in the piazza or anywhere else, at once put themselves in posture as if for fencing or wrestling, according to their favourite humour."

Here messer Cesare Gonzaga said:

"A young cardinal we have in Rome does better than that; for out of pride in his fine bodily frame, he conducts into his garden all who come to visit him (even although he has never seen them before), and urgently presses them to strip to the doublet and try a turn with him at leaping."

Messer Federico laughed; then he went on:

"There are certain other exercises that can be practised in public and in private, like dancing; and in this I think the Courtier ought to have a care, for when dancing in the presence of many and in a place full of people, it seems to me that he should preserve a certain dignity, albeit tempered with a lithe and airy grace of movement; and although he may feel himself to be very nimble and a master of time and measure, let him not attempt those agilities of foot and double steps which we find very becoming in our friend Barletta,[21] but which perhaps would be little suited to a gentleman. Yet in a room privately, as we are now, I think he may try both, and may dance morris–dances and brawls; but not in public unless he be masked, when it is not displeasing even though he be recognized by all.

"Indeed there is no better way of displaying oneself in such matters at public sports, either armed or unarmed; because disguise carries with it a certain freedom and licence, which among other things enable a

---

[21]Musician and dancer at the court of Urbino.

man to choose a part for which he feels himself qualified, and to use care and elaboration upon the chief point of the thing wherein he would display himself, and a certain nonchalance as to that which does not count,—which greatly enhances the charm: as for a youth to array himself like an old man, yet in easy dress so as to be able to show his vigour; a cavalier in the guise of a rustic shepherd or some other like costume, but with a perfect horse and gracefully bedecked in character;—because the mind of the spectators is quick to fill out the image of that which is presented to the eyes at first glance; and then seeing the thing turn out much better than the costume promised, they are amused and delighted.

"But in these sports and shows where masks are worn, it would not be seemly for a prince to try to enact the part of a prince, because that pleasure which the spectators find in novelty would be in great measure lacking, since it is news to no one that the prince is the prince; and he, conscious that besides the prince he is trying to play the prince, loses the freedom to do all those things that are beneath a prince's dignity. And if there were any contest in these sports, especially with arms, he might even make men think that he chose to impersonate a prince in order not to be beaten but spared by others; moreover were he to do in sport the same that it behooves him to do in earnest upon occasion, he would deprive his own proper action of dignity, and make it almost seem as if that too were sport. But at such times, if the prince lays aside his character of prince, and mingles equally with his inferiors yet in such fashion as to be recognizable, by renouncing his own rank he attains a higher one, in that he prefers to excel the rest not by authority but by merit, and to show that his worth is not enhanced by the fact that he is a prince.

"I say then that in these martial sports the Courtier ought to use the like discretion, according to his rank. In horseback vaulting too, in wrestling, running and leaping, I should be well pleased to have him shun the vulgar crowd, or at most let himself be very rarely seen; for there is not on earth a thing so excellent but the ignorant will tire of it and hold it of small account, if they see it often.

"As to music I hold the same opinion: hence I would not have our Courtier behave like many, who are no sooner come anywhere (even into the presence of gentlemen with whom they have no acquaintance), than without waiting to be urged they set about doing what they know and often what they do not know; so that it seems as if they had come only for the purpose of showing themselves, and had that for their chief profession. Therefore let the Courtier resort to music as a pastime and almost unwillingly, and not before vulgar people nor very many. And although he may know and understand that which he is doing, in this too I would have him hide the study and pains that are necessary in everything one would do well, and seem to value this accomplishment lightly in himself, but by practising it admirably make others value it highly."

[The ladies demand that the gentlemen tell what qualities they would attribute to a lady worthy of the attention of the ideal courtier. *Ed.*]

Then my lady Duchess[22] said:

"Do not wander from your subject, my lord Magnifico, but hold to the order given you and describe the Court Lady, to the end that so noble a Lady as this may have someone competent to serve her worthily."

The Magnifico continued:

"Then, my Lady, to show that your commands have power to induce me to essay even that which I know not how to do, I will speak of this excellent Lady as I would have her; and when I have fashioned her to my liking, not being able then to have another such, like Pygmalion[23] I will take her for my own.

"And although my lord Gaspar has said that the same rules which are set the Courtier, serve also for the Lady, I am of another mind; for while some qualities are common to both and as necessary to man as to woman, there are nevertheless some others that befit woman more than man, and some are befitting man to which she ought to be wholly a stranger. The same I say of bodily exercises; but above all, methinks that in her ways, manners, words, gestures and bearing, a woman ought to be very unlike a man; for just as it befits him to show a certain stout and sturdy manliness, so it is becoming in a woman to have a soft and dainty tenderness with an air of womanly sweetness in her every movement, which, in her going or staying or saying what you will, shall always make her seem the woman, without any likeness of a man.

"Now, if this precept be added to the rules that these gentlemen have taught the Courtier, I certainly think she ought to be able to profit by many of them, and to adorn herself with admirable accomplishments,

---

[22]Elisabetta Gonzaga, Duchess of Urbino; she was renowned for her wit and learning.

[23]Greek legendary sculptor. The goddess Venus brought his statue of a woman to life after he had fallen in love with it.

as my lord Gaspar says. For I believe that many faculties of the mind are as necessary to woman as to man; likewise gentle birth, to avoid affectation, to be naturally graceful in all her doings, to be mannerly, clever, prudent, not arrogant, not envious, not slanderous, not vain, not quarrelsome, not silly, to know how to win and keep the favour of her mistress and of all others, to practise well and gracefully the exercises that befit women. I am quite of the opinion, too, that beauty is more necessary to her than to the Courtier, for in truth that woman lacks much who lacks beauty. Then, too, she ought to be more circumspect and take greater care not to give occasion for evil being said of her, and so to act that she may not only escape a stain of guilt but even of suspicion, for a woman has not so many ways of defending herself against false imputations as has a man.

"But as Count Ludovico has explained very minutely the chief profession of the Courtier, and has insisted it be that of arms, methinks it is also fitting to tell what in my judgment is that of the Court Lady: and when I have done this, I shall think myself quit of the greater part of my duty.

"Laying aside, then, those faculties of the mind that she ought to have in common with the Courtier (such as prudence, magnanimity, continence, and many others), and likewise those qualities that befit all women (such as kindness, discretion, ability to manage her husband's property and her house and children if she be married, and all those capacities that are requisite in a good housewife), I say that in a lady who lives at court methinks above all else a certain pleasant affability is befitting, whereby she may be able to entertain politely every sort of man with agreeable and seemly converse, suited to the time and place, and to the rank of the person with whom she may speak, uniting with calm and modest manners, and with that seemliness which should ever dispose all her actions, a quick vivacity of spirit whereby she may show herself alien to all indelicacy; but with such a kindly manner as shall make us think her no less chaste, prudent and benign, than agreeable, witty and discreet: and so she must preserve a certain mean (difficult and composed almost of contraries), and must barely touch certain limits but not pass them.

"Thus, in her wish to be thought good and pure, the Lady ought not to be so coy and seem so to abhor company and talk that are a little free, as to take her leave as soon as she finds herself therein; for it might easily be thought that she was pretending to be thus austere in order to hide something about herself which she feared others might come to know;

and such prudish manners are always odious. Nor ought she, on the other hand, for the sake of showing herself free and agreeable, to utter unseemly words or practise a certain wild and unbridled familiarity and ways likely to make that believed of her which perhaps is not true; but when she is present at such talk, she ought to listen with a little blush and shame.

"Likewise she ought to avoid an errour into which I have seen many women fall, which is that of saying and of willingly listening to evil about other women. For those women who, on hearing the unseemly ways of other women described, grow angry thereat and seem to disbelieve it and to regard it almost monstrous that a woman should be immodest,—they, by accounting the offence so heinous, give reason to think that they do not commit it. But those who go about continually prying into other women's intrigues, and narrate them so minutely and with such zest, seem to be envious of them and to wish that everyone may know it, to the end that like matters may not be reckoned as a fault in their own case; and thus they fall into certain laughs and ways that show they then feel greatest pleasure. And hence it comes that men, while seeming to listen gladly, usually hold such women in small respect and have very little regard for them, and think these ways of theirs are an invitation to advance farther, and thus often go such lengths with them as bring them deserved reproach, and finally esteem them so lightly as to despise their company and even find them tedious."

• • •

Having so far spoken, the Magnifico was silent and sat quiet, as if he had ended his discourse. Then my lord Gaspar said:

"Verily, my lord Magnifico, you have adorned this Lady well and given her excellent qualities. Yet methinks you have kept much to generalities, and mentioned some things in her so great that I think you were ashamed to explain them, and have rather desired than taught them, after the manner of those who sometimes wish for things impossible and beyond nature. Therefore I would have you declare to us a little better what are the bodily exercises proper to a Court Lady, and in what way she ought to converse, and what those many things are whereof you say it befits her to have knowledge; and whether you mean that she should use the prudence, the magnanimity, the continence, and the many other virtues you have named, merely to aid her in the government of her house, children, and family (which however you would not have her chief profession), or indeed in her conversation and graceful practise of those bodily exercises; and, by your faith, guard against setting these poor virtues to such menial duty that they must needs be ashamed of it."

The Magnifico laughed, and said:

"My lord Gaspar, you cannot help showing your ill will towards women. But in truth I thought I had said enough, and especially before such hearers; for I am quite sure there is no one here who does not perceive that in the matter of bodily exercises it does not befit women to handle weapons, to ride, to play tennis, to wrestle, and to do many other things that befit men."

Then the Unico Aretino[24] said:

"Among the ancients it was the custom for women to wrestle unclothed with men; but we have lost this good custom, along with many others."

Messer Cesare Gonzaga added:

"And in my time I have seen women play tennis, handle weapons, ride, go hunting, and perform nearly all the exercises that a cavalier can."

The Magnifico replied:

"Since I may fashion this Lady as I wish, not only am I unwilling to have her practise such vigourous and rugged manly exercises, but I would have her practise even those that are becoming to women, circumspectly and with that gentle daintiness which we have said befits her; and thus in dancing I would not see her use too active and violent movements, nor in singing or playing those abrupt and oft-repeated diminutions which show more skill than sweetness; likewise the musical instruments that she uses ought, in my opinion, to be appropriate to this intent. Imagine how unlovely it would be to see a woman play drums, fifes or trumpets, or other like instruments; and this because their harshness hides and destroys that mild gentleness which so much adorns every act a woman does. Therefore when she starts to dance or make music of any kind, she ought to bring herself to it by letting herself be urged a little, and with a touch of shyness which shall show that noble shame which is the opposite of effrontery."

[Cardinal Bembo praises the Platonic notion of ideal beauty. *Ed.*]

Messer Pietro Bembo was silent, and those gentlemen still urged him to speak further of this love and of the mode of enjoying beauty truly; and he at last said:

---

[24]Bernardo Accolti, a writer of popular verse and a visitor at many Italian courts.

"Methinks I have shown clearly enough that old men can love more happily than young, which was my thesis: therefore it does not become me to go further."

Count Ludovico replied:

"You have better shown the unhappiness of youths than the happiness of old men, whom as yet you have not taught what road to follow in this love of theirs, but have only told them to be guided by reason; and by many it is thought impossible for love to abide with reason."

Bembo still sought to put an end to his discourse, but my lady Duchess begged him to speak; and he began anew thus:

"Too unhappy would human nature be, if our soul (wherein such ardent desire can spring up easily) were forced to feed it solely upon that which is common to her with the beasts, and could not direct it to that other nobler part which is peculiar to herself. Therefore, since so indeed it pleases you, I have no wish to avoid discoursing upon this noble subject. And as I feel myself unworthy to speak of Love's most sacred mysteries, I pray him so to inspire my thought and tongue that I may be able to show this excellent Courtier how to love beyond the manner of the vulgar crowd; and since from boyhood up I have dedicated my whole life to him, so now also may my words comport with this intent and with his praise.

"I say, then, that as in youth human nature is so greatly prone to sense, the Courtier may be allowed to love sensually while he is young. But if afterwards in maturer years he chances still to be kindled with this amorous desire, he must be very wary and take care not to deceive himself by allowing himself to be led into those calamities which in the young merit more compassion than blame, and, on the contrary, in the old more blame than compassion.

• • •

"Therefore let him shun the blind judgment of sense, and with his eyes enjoy the splendour of his lady, her grace, her amorous sparkle, the laughs, the ways and all the other pleasant ornaments of her beauty. Likewise with his hearing let him enjoy the sweetness of her voice, the concord of her words, the harmony of her music (if his beloved be a musician). Thus will he feed his soul on sweetest food by means of these two senses—which have little of the corporeal and are ministers of reason—without passing in his desire for the body to any appetite less than seemly.

"Next let him obey, please and honour his lady with all reverence, and hold her dearer than himself, and prefer her convenience and pleasures to his own, and love in her not less the beauty of mind than that of body. Therefore let him take care not to leave her to fall into any kind of errour, but by admonition and good advice let him always seek to lead her on to modesty, to temperance, to true chastity, and see to it that no thoughts find place in her except those that are pure and free from every stain of vice; and by thus sowing virtue in the garden of her fair mind, he will gather fruits of fairest behaviour too, and will taste them with wonderful delight. And this will be the true engendering and manifesting of beauty in beauty, which by some is said to be the end of love.

"In such fashion will our Courtier be most acceptable to his lady, and she will always show herself obedient, sweet and affable to him, and as desirous of pleasing him as of being loved by him: and the wishes of both will be most virtuous and harmonious, and they themselves will thus be very happy."

Here my lord Morello[25] said:

"To engender beauty in beauty, forsooth, would be to beget a beautiful child in a beautiful woman; and pleasing him in this would seem to me a much clearer token that she loved her lover than treating him with the affability of which you speak."

Bembo laughed, and said:

"You must not go beyond bounds, my lord Morello; nor does a woman give a small token of her love when she gives her lover her beauty, which is so precious a thing, and by the ways that are the avenues to her soul (that is, sight and hearing) sends the glances of her eyes, the image of her face, her voice, her words, which strike home to the lover's heart and give him proof of her love."

[Lady Emilia[26] jestingly reproves one of the gentlemen for his doubting that women are capable of Platonic love. *Ed.*]

My lady Emilia laughed, and said:

"My lord Gaspar, if you return to wronging us so often, I promise you that you will not be pardoned again."

My lord Gaspar replied:

"No wrong is done you by saying that women's souls are not so purged of passion as those of men, nor given to contemplation, as messer Pietro said those must be who would taste divine love. Thus we do not read that any woman has had this grace, but that many men have

[25]Soldier and retainer of the court of Urbino; the only old courtier portrayed.
[26]Companion of the Duchess of Urbino.

had it, like Plato, Socrates, and Plotinus,[27] and many others; and so many of our holy Fathers, like St. Francis, upon whom an ardent spirit of love impressed the most holy seal of the five wounds: nor could aught but the power of love lift St. Paul to the vision of those mysteries whereof man is not allowed to speak; nor show St. Stephen the opened heavens."

Here the Magnifico Giuliano replied:

"In this, women will by no means be outdone by men; for Socrates himself confesses that all the mysteries of love which he knew were revealed to him by a woman, who was the famous Diotima; and the angel who wounded St. Francis with the fire of love, has also made several women of our age worthy of the same seal. You must remember, too, that St. Mary Magdalen had many sins forgiven her because she loved much, and perhaps with no less grace than St. Paul was she many times lifted to the third heaven by angelic love; and so many others, who (as I narrated yesterday more at large) for the love of Christ's name took no heed of life, nor were afraid of torments or any manner of death however horrible and cruel it might be; and they were not old, as messer Pietro would have our Courtier, but tender and delicate girls, and of that age wherein he says that sensual love ought to be allowed in men."

My lord Gaspar began making ready to reply, but my lady Duchess said:

"Of this let messer Pietro Bembo be the judge, and let us abide by his decision whether or not women are as capable of divine love as men are. But as the controversy between you might be too long, it will be well to postpone it until tomorrow."

"Nay, until this evening," said messer Cesare Gonzaga.

"How until this evening?" said my lady Duchess.

Messer Cesare replied:

"Because it is already day"; and he showed her the light that was beginning to come in through the cracks at the windows.

Then everyone rose to his feet in great surprise, for the discussion did not seem to have lasted longer than usual; but by reason of having been begun much later, and by its pleasantness, it had so beguiled the company that they had not perceived the flight of hours; nor was there anyone who felt the heaviness of sleep upon his eyes, which nearly always happens when the accustomed hour of sleep is passed in watch-

---

[27]Third-century Greek philosopher.

ing. The windows having then been opened on that side of the palace which looks towards the lofty crest of Mount Catria, they saw that a beautiful dawn of rosy hue was already born in the east, and that all the stars had vanished save Venus, sweet mistress of the sky, who holds the bounds of night and day; from which there seemed to breathe a gentle wind that filled the air with crisp coolness and began to waken sweet choruses of joyous birds in the murmuring forests of the hills hard by.

So, having reverently taken leave of my lady Duchess, they all started towards their chambers without light of torches, that of day being enough for them; and as they were about to quit the room, my lord Prefect[28] turned to my lady Duchess, and said:

"My Lady, to finish the controversy between my lord Gaspar and my lord Magnifico, we will come with our judge this evening earlier than we did yesterday."

My lady Emilia replied:

"On condition that if my lord Gaspar wishes to accuse women and put some fresh imputation upon them, as is his wont, he shall also give bond to sustain his charge, for I account him a shifty disputant."

---

[28]Francesco della Rovere, nephew and adopted heir of the Duke of Urbino.

22

Sir Thomas More

Utopia

SIR Thomas More (1478–1535) was
the leading English humanist of his generation. Successful in the profession of
law, he was also known as a man of keen wit and learning. In 1529, having
entered the service of King Henry VIII, More became Lord Chancellor, the
most important of the royal officers. He resigned this position in 1532, however,
in an attempt to avoid having to take part in the political and religious quarrels
that accompanied Henry's dynastic ambitions and his break with the papacy. So
important a man, however, was not allowed to remain in obscurity: On his
refusal to take any oath of loyalty to the king that would involve rejection of the
pope's authority, More was tried, found guilty of high treason, and beheaded.

Like his friend Erasmus, More injected a religious tone into his humanism.
Scholarship, a sense of humor, and the intention of reforming society and the
Church were common to the work of both men.

More's Utopia (1516) is an imaginary discourse by a fictional traveler to the
New World. The narrator, Raphael Hythloday, tells of the land of Utopia, a
name coined by More from the Greek word meaning "nowhere." Hythloday
describes the Utopians' socialized economy, their system of compulsory and
universal education for both men and women, and their austere life under the
firm discipline of a wise and benevolent prince, who is completely tolerant of all
religious views save atheism. More thus presents a picture of a society completely different from his own—one that is free from corruption in politics and
law, and, more significantly, free from the poverty and crime resulting from
selfish misuse of private property by the rich and powerful. Like Plato's
Republic, More's Utopia has been taken as a model by social reformers who
like to envisage an ideal society founded on perfect order and justice.

Farming is a science common to all, both men and women, and they are all expert. They are instructed from their youth, partly in school with lessons and precepts, and partly in the country near the city, where they learn not only by seeing agriculture practised but engaging in it also as a kind of play. Besides farming, which is common to all, everyone learns another craft as his own. Most commonly this is clothworking in wool or flax, or masonry, or blacksmithing, or carpentry. There are no other trades followed there by any great number. Their garments are of one fashion throughout the island (except that men and women wear different garments, and there is a difference between the married and unmarried). The style stays the same always, is handsome in appearance, allows free movement of the body, and is fit for both winter and summer. Every family makes its own clothes. But of other crafts every man learns one, as do the women. But the women, being weaker, are put to the easier crafts like working wool or flax. The more laborious tasks are entrusted to the men. For the most part, every man is brought up in his father's craft. They are naturally inclined to it; but if a youth wants to learn another, he is adopted by a family engaged in the occupation he wants to learn. His own father and the magistrate take care that he is given to an honest and worthy householder. Yes, and if any person, after he has learned one craft, wants to learn still another, he is permitted to do so.

When he has learned both, he follows the one he prefers, unless the city needs one more than the other. The chief, and almost the only duty of the officers is to see that no man is idle but that everyone works diligently at his own craft, yet not all day from early morning to late at night like beasts of burden. For this would be worse than the fate of slaves, which is, nevertheless, the life of workmen almost everywhere except in Utopia. For they divide the day and night into twenty-four equal hours and devote only six hours to work, three before noon. Then they go straight to dinner, and after dinner, when they have rested two hours, they work three hours and then have supper. About eight in the evening (counting one o'clock as the first hour after noon) they go to bed. Eight hours they give to sleep. In the hours not devoted to work, sleep, or meals, every man spends his time as he wishes. This is not intended to permit waste of time, however, but that, being free

UTOPIA   Sir Thomas More, *Utopia*, trans. Ralph Robinson (1556), reprinted (Cambridge: Cambridge University Press, 1888), 78–99, 143–47. (This is an adaptation.)

from their own occupations, they can devote some time to some other branch of learning. For it is a custom there to have daily lectures early in the mornings. Although only those who are specifically designated as students are forced to be present, a great number of all kinds of people, both men and women, attend. However, if any man would rather spend this time on his own occupation (for there are many whose minds are unsuited to liberal studies), he is not blamed but praised and commended as helping the common welfare.

After supper they spend an hour in play: in summer in their gardens, in winter in their common halls, where they dine and sup. There they practice music or engage in pleasant conversation. Dice and other such foolish and pernicious games are unknown. But they have some games not much unlike chess. One is the battle of numbers, in which one number wins over another. In another, the vices fight against virtues, as if in battle array. In this game, there is clearly shown the strife and discord that vices have among themselves, but also their unity and concord against the virtues; what vices are opposed to what virtues; how they assail virtues openly with power and strength; how they operate secretly with wiles and subtlety; what the virtues need for help and aid in overcoming the power of the vices; how they too can use craft; and finally by what means victory can be achieved.

One thing you must consider more clearly here, lest you be mistaken: seeing that they spend only six hours in work, you may perhaps think that they lack many necessary things. But this is not so. For that small time is not only sufficient but even too much for the provision of an abundant supply of all things necessary to life. You will understand this if you consider how many people in other countries live idly: almost all women, who are half the population, or, if the women be employed, the men are idle. Besides this, there is a great and idle company of priests and religious men, as they call them. Add to them all rich men, especially landowners commonly called gentlemen, and noblemen. Take in this number also their servants. I mean all that gang of vain swaggerers. Join to them also sturdy and ingenious beggars, disguising the idleness of their lives with some pretended deformity or disease. Truly, you shall find the goods used in daily life are produced by the labor of fewer than you thought.

Now, consider with yourself how few of those who do labor are employed in necessary work. For where money is the most important reward, many superfluous and vain occupations will flourish to cater to idle wants and foolish pleasures. But if the same multitude that now is occupied in such work were divided into the few occupations necessary to supply basic wants, there would be such a quantity of necessary goods produced that undoubtedly prices would be too little to support the workmen and artificers. If, however, all those now busy in worthless occupations and the whole flock of those that live in idleness and sloth, consuming and wasting more of the things produced by other men's labor than the laborers themselves do—if all these, I say, were engaged in worthwhile occupations, you can easily see how little time would be sufficient to provide us with everything necessary, either to supply basic commodities or to provide a certain amount of modest and natural pleasures.

The truth of this is demonstrated in Utopia, for there in the whole city and the adjoining countryside, there are scarcely five hundred (in addition to the sick and aged) of the entire population who are excused from labor. Among these are the officers who, although they are by law exempt from labor, nevertheless set a good example by their voluntary work. The same freedom from labor is also granted those who, recommended by the priests and elected by the officers, are given a permanent excuse from labor so that they may engage in learning. But if any of these does not live up to expectations, he is sent back to the rank of artificers. On the other hand, it often happens that a laborer spends all of his free time in learning and makes such progress that he is taken from his trade and promoted to the company of the learned. From this class of learned people are chosen the ambassadors, the priests, magistrates and finally the prince himself, whom they call, in their old tongue, Barzanes, and also by a newer name, Adamus.

The rest of the people are neither idle nor occupied in worthless tasks. It is easily seen, therefore, that in only a few hours much productive work is accomplished. Moreover, they do not need to spend as much work in the necessary occupations as other nations. In other places, the building and repairing of houses takes up many men's continual labor because unthrifty persons allow their houses to fall into decay, so that what might have been repaired with little cost must be entirely rebuilt with great cost by their successors. It often happens, too, that a house that cost one man a great sum does not please another, who neglects it and lets it fall into ruin. Then he builds another just as costly somewhere else. Among the Utopians, however, where everything is well managed and the commonwealth well ordered, it very seldom happens that a new plot is chosen for building. Not only do they find quick remedies for present faults, but also repair houses that are ready to fall. In this way their houses last long, with so little labor and few repairs needed that men engaged in this occupation sometimes have almost nothing to do and are ordered to hew lumber at home and square and trim stone so that if any work becomes necessary it can be more speedily done.

Now, sir, notice, I pray, how few workmen they need for their clothing. First of all, while they are at work they wear simple garments of leather or skins that will last seven years. When they go outdoors, they put on a cloak which hides the coarser apparel. These cloaks, throughout the entire island, are all of one color, that is, the natural color of the wool. Hence, they use much less woolen cloth than other countries, and at much less cost. Linen cloth is made with less labor and is, therefore, used more. But in linen only whiteness is prized; in wool only cleanliness. As for the smallness or fineness of the thread, it is unimportant. This is the reason that in other places four or five cloth gowns of different colors, and as many silk coats are not enough for one man. If he is a particular man, he may think ten too few, whereas there one garment will serve a man four years. Why should he want more? If he had them, he would not be better off or more protected from cold, nor handsomer in apparel.

Since they are all occupied in worthwhile occupations and a few workmen are sufficient in any one trade (this is the reason there is a plentiful supply of everything), they sometimes turn out a numerous company of people to mend the highways, if need be. Often, when they have no such work, a proclamation is made decreeing fewer hours of work. For the magistrates do not compel the citizens to engage unwillingly in unnecessary labor. In that commonwealth the chief and only aim is to spend as much time as possible in the free exercise and training of the mind, for in this they believe the chief felicity of life to consist.

• • •

Now I will tell how the citizens behave toward each other, how the people entertain and amuse themselves, and how they distribute their goods. First, the city consists of families, the families being made up of kindred. For women, when they are married at the legal age, become part of their husband's family. But the male children and all the male offspring continue in their own family, being governed by the eldest man, unless he is senile, in which case he is replaced by the next oldest.

But in order to prevent the number of citizens from increasing or decreasing, it is ordained that no family (there are 6,000 families in each city and nearby countryside) shall have fewer than ten children between the ages of thirteen and sixteen. Of children under this age, no number is set. This number is easily maintained by putting the children of larger families into smaller families. If by chance a city has more than can be accommodated, the excess is used in other cities. If the population of the entire island exceeds the set number, they choose citizens from every city to build up a town under their own laws in a neighboring land where there is waste land, accepting also natives of that country if they want to join and dwell with them. Thus joining and dwelling together, they easily agree in one way of life, to the great wealth of both peoples. For they manage things so by their laws that ground which was before neither good nor profitable for anyone becomes fruitful enough for both. If the natives will not dwell with them and accept their laws, they drive them out of the land they have taken for themselves. If the natives resist or rebel, they make war upon them. For they consider it a just war that is fought to dispossess people from land which they do not use and keep others from using.

If by chance the number in any city is so diminished that it cannot be filled up without reducing the proper number in the other cities (which they say happened only twice, by the plague, since the beginning of the island), they replenish the number with citizens brought from their own foreign towns. They would rather see these foreign towns decay and perish than any city of the island diminish.

But to return to the behavior of the citizens toward each other: the eldest, as I have said, rules the family, the wives and their husbands; the children help their parents, and, in short, all younger people assist their elders.

Every city is divided into four equal parts or quarters. In the midst of each quarter there is a market place for all kinds of things. There the products of every family's labor are brought into certain houses, and all kinds of commodities are stored in several barns or storehouses. From thence the father of every family, or every householder, takes whatever he needs and carries it with him without money, exchange, pawn, or pledge. Why should anything be denied him—seeing that there is abundance of everything and that no one will ask for more than he needs? Why should it be thought that men who know they will never be in want would ask for more than is merely enough? Certainly, fear of want causes covetousness and greed, but only in man does it cause pride, because man thinks it a glorious thing to excel in ostentatious and vain display of possessions. This vice has no place among the Utopians.

Next to the market places that I spoke of stand meat markets where herbs, fruits, bread, fish, and all sorts of four-footed beasts and wild fowl that furnish meat for humans are stored and offered. First, the filth is washed away in the clear running river outside the city at properly appointed places. Then the beasts are killed and washed by the bondmen. For they do not permit free citizens to become accustomed to killing beasts. They consider it kindness to let animals grow old and die naturally. Nor do they allow any unclean or filthy thing to be brought into the city lest stench infect the air and cause pestilence.

Moreover, every street has great halls equidistant from each other and each has its own name. In these halls dwell the officers, and every hall has thirty families assigned to it, fifteen on each side. The stewards of these halls come at a certain time to the meat markets where they receive meat according to the number of families in their hall. The first care of all, however, is the sick in the hospitals. For around the city, a little outside the walls, they have four hospitals, so large that they seem like four little towns. They are made so spacious that the sick will not be crowded and uncomfortable or those with contagious diseases so close to others as to endanger them with infection. These hospitals are so well built and furnished with everything necessary to health, and the attendants and physicians so diligent and skillful that, although no man is sent there against his will, sick persons would rather go to them than remain home.

After the hospital steward has received the kinds of meat prescribed by the physician, the best is equally divided among the halls. . . . To these halls at the dinner hour come all the inhabitants of the ward, summoned by trumpet. No one, however, is forbidden to get his own meat and take it home, for they know that no one will do so without reason. No man is forbidden to dine at home, but no one does so willingly. It would be foolish to take the trouble to prepare a bad dinner at home when they are welcome to good fare at the nearby hall.

In the hall, all menial service and drudgery are performed by bondmen. But the women of every family have charge of the cooking and dressing the meat. They sit at three tables or more, according to their number. The men sit on the bench next the wall; the women opposite, so that if any sudden illness should affect them, as often happens to women with child, they may leave quickly and go to the nursery.

The nurses stay with the infants in a special room, which always has a fire lit and a supply of clean water. Cradles are provided so they may lay the children down or take them out of their swaddling clothes and warm them before the fire and refresh them with play. Every mother nurses her own child unless death or sickness prevents. If that happens, the officers' wives quickly provide a nurse, which is not difficult, for those who can perform this service are glad to volunteer. This kind act is much praised, and the child that is nursed always regards his nurse as his natural mother.

Children under five are cared for by the nurses. All other children, both boys and girls, up to the age of marriage either serve at the tables or, if still too young, stand quietly by. Whatever is given them they eat, and they have no separate dinner time. . . . Their dinners are very short, but their suppers longer because a working period follows dinner, but after supper come sleep and rest. No supper is passed without music . . . and they burn gums and spices, and sprinkle perfume about, leaving nothing undone that affords pleasure. For they incline to the opinion that no harmless pleasure should be forbidden.

• • •

If anyone wants to visit friends in another city or to see the place itself, he can easily get permission from the officers or magistrates unless there is some good reason for refusal. No one journeys alone, but a group is sent, carrying letters from the prince showing that they have permission for the journey and setting the day of their required return. They have a wagon given them, with a bondman to drive the oxen. Unless they have women along, they send the wagon home because it is an impediment. Though they carry nothing with them, they never lack for anything during the whole trip. For wherever they stop, they are at home. If they stop at a place for more than a day, everyone falls to his own occupation and is welcomed by the workmen and companies of the same craft.

If any man on his own and without permission leaves his precinct, and does not have the prince's letters, he is apprehended as a fugitive or runaway and is rebuked, shamed, and punished. If he is caught again in that fault, he is punished with bondage.

If anyone wants to walk in the fields and countryside belonging to his own city, he is not forbidden, provided that he has obtained the consent of his father and wife. But no matter in what part of the country he chances to be, he is given no food until he has worked his forenoon's stint or done as much as is required before supper. Observing this law and its conditions, he may go wherever he wants within the territory of his own city. He shall thus be no less profitable to his city than if he were always within the limits.

You can see how little time they have for loitering; how they have no way of disguising idleness. There are no taverns, alehouses, brothels, nor any occasion for vice or wickedness, no corners for lurking, no places for evil councils or unlawful assembly. For everyone is always in plain sight, so of necessity he must apply himself to his customary labors or else engage in honest and laudable pastimes.

This fashion of life and work being common to all, they must of necessity have plenty of everything. And since they are all equal partners, no one is poor or needy. The national council where, as I have said, every city sends three men every year, as soon as it knows in what places there is abundance and where there is scarcity, immediately allocates the abundance of one place to make up the lack of another place. This they do freely without any payment, taking nothing from them to whom things are given; but those cities that have given their supplies to cities in need do receive at another time what they need from the cities they aided. So, the whole island is, as it were, one family or household.

When they have made sufficient provision for themselves, which they think must consist of two years' supply because of the uncertainty of the next year's harvest, they send the superfluous goods and crops to other countries: grain, honey, wool, flax, wood, dyestuffs, skins, wax, tallow, leather, and livestock. A seventh of these things they give freely to the poor of the country to which they export, the rest they sell at a reasonable price. By this trade they bring into their own country not only a great deal of gold and silver, but also whatever they lack at home, which is chiefly iron. Because they have practised this trade for a long time, they have more of these things than anyone will readily believe. Therefore, they now do not care whether they sell for cash or for credit. If for credit, they never accept the word of private individuals but the warranty of the whole city set forth in contracts.

• • •

They keep most of the treasure at home to use for extreme danger, especially to hire at great wages foreign soldiers. For they prefer to endanger mercenaries rather than their own citizens. They know that their enemies can be bribed, and weakened by hired traitors set to fight among themselves. For this purpose they keep a great treasure on hand. This treasure is not for hoarding but for use. I am almost afraid to say this, lest I not be believed, for I would hardly believe another man's telling this, if I had not seen it myself.

It usually happens that if a thing is strange and not familiar in our experience, it is difficult to believe. However, a wise and judicious judge of matters will not be surprised, since all of their laws and customs are so different from ours, if their use of gold and silver is interpreted by their customs, not ours. I mean that they use these not as money, but keep them in case of emergency. In the meantime they are used in such a way that no one prizes them as money.

Anyone can plainly see that money is less important than iron, for men cannot live without iron any more than without fire and water. Nature has given no utility to gold and silver that we cannot do without. Only the folly of men sets them in higher esteem because of their scarcity. But nature, a most kind and loving nurse, has placed the most necessary things ready to our use, as air, water, and earth, and has hidden farthest from us all vain and unprofitable things. Therefore, if these metals should be locked up in some tower, it might be suspected that the prince and council (as the populace is always foolishly imagining) intended by some device to deceive the commons and profit themselves. Furthermore, if they should make plate of the gold and silver and other finely and cunningly wrought stuff, and if at any time they should have to melt it down again to pay their soldiers, they see that men would be loath to part from those things that they took delight in.

To remedy all of this, they have found a means which, since it conforms to all of their other laws and customs (and so different from ours, which set so much store on gold, that it is incredible except to those who are very wise) renders gold worthless. For they eat and drink of vessels of earthenware and glass, beautifully made but of small value. Of gold and silver they commonly make chamber pots and other vessels that serve for the vilest uses not only in the common halls but in every man's private house. Furthermore, of the same metals they make great chains and fetters and gyves in which they chain their bondmen. Finally, some condemned persons must wear earrings of gold, finger rings of gold, and collars of gold, and circlets of gold around their heads. Thus, by all possible means, they make gold and silver a badge of reproach and infamy. These metals, which in other nations are valued as life itself, would, if taken from the Utopians, not be missed any more than one penny.

They also gather pearls by the seashore, and diamonds and garnets from certain rocks; yet they do not seek them out, but find them by chance and cut and polish them. They give them to their children, for they make much of young children and like to dress and ornament them so that when they grow up and see that only little children wear jewels and ornaments, they put aside their own voluntarily, without being counselled to do so by their parents, even as our own children, when grown, throw away their dolls and nuts and toys.

• • •

There are several kinds of religion, not only in different parts of the island but also within the same city. Some worship the sun as their god; some, the moon; some, other planets. There are those who worship a man, once excellently virtuous and gloriously famous, not only as god but also as the chiefest and highest god. But the majority of wise people, rejecting all of these creeds, believes that there is a certain divine power, unknown, everlasting, inexplicable, far above the capacity and reach of man's knowledge, dispersed throughout the universe, not in size but in virtue. Him they call the father of all. To him alone they attribute the beginning, growth, processes, changes, and endings of all things. Nor do they worship any deity save him. All the other sects, though they differ, agree on this one point with the wisest—that there is one chief and principal god, maker and ruler of the whole world, whom they all, in their language, term Mythra.

There is some disagreement, however, for some identify this god in one way, some in another fashion. For everyone takes his own god to be the one to whose divine might and majesty the power over all things is commonly attributed. However, they are beginning little by little to forsake these various superstitions and to agree in the religion which seems reasonably to excel the others. There is no doubt that the others would have been abolished long since if it had not been for the habit of ascribing any mischance befalling one who has changed his religion to the enmity of the god whom he was forsaking, as if the god were seeking revenge.

After they heard us speak of Christ, of his doctrine, laws, miracles, and the wonderful constancy of martyrs whose blood was willingly shed to bring the nations of the world into the faith, you would hardly believe how glad they were to accept the Word, either by the secret inspiration of God or because it came closest to that opinion which they already thought of among themselves as the best. I do think, however, that it helped when they heard us say that Christ bade his followers to have all things in common, and that the same communalism still exists among the best Christian groups.

Whatever the cause, many of them accepted our religion and were washed with the holy waters of baptism. Because among us four (no more of us were left alive, two having died) there was no priest, which I heartily regret, they could be instructed in all the points of our religion but lacked those sacraments which only priests can administer. They nevertheless understand them and earnestly desire them, even disputing among themselves whether, without the sending of a Christian bishop, one of their own people might receive the order of priesthood. Truly, they were intending to choose one, but at my departure had not yet done so.

Those who do not agree with Christianity fear no one who has been converted, nor do they speak against any one who has received Christianity. There was one exception, however. One of our company was severely punished. As soon as he was baptised he began, against our will, and with more earnestness than wisdom, to talk about Christ's religion, and became so vehement that he not only preferred our religion before all others but utterly despised and condemned all others, calling them profane and their followers wicked, devilish, and children of everlasting damnation. When he had argued this way for a long time, they seized him, accused and condemned him to exile, not as a despiser of religion but as a stirrer up of sedition among the people. For it is one of the most ancient laws among them that no one shall be blamed for arguing in defense of his own religion. For King Utopus, at the very beginning, heard that the inhabitants of the land were, before his coming there, in continual strife and dissension among themselves because of their religion. He also perceived that this dissension (in which several sects fought only for their own part of the country) was the only reason he was able to conquer the land. Therefore, when he had gained victory, his first decree was that it should be lawful for every man to favor and follow whatever religion he wished, and to do the best he could to bring others to his opinion so long as he did it peaceably, gently, quietly and soberly, without hasty and contentious rebuking and inveighing against others. If he could not by fair and gentle words induce others to his opinion, he must nevertheless refrain from violence and unpleasant and seditious language. He who was guilty of vehemence and strife was banished or placed in bondage.

King Utopus made this law not only for the maintenance of peace, which he saw threatened by continual strife and mortal hatred, but also because he thought this decree would help religion. Of religion he did not define or determine anything, not knowing whether God, desiring many different kinds of respect and worship, might not inspire different men with different kinds of religious beliefs. He thought it an unwise and foolish thing, and arrogant presumption, to compel all others, by threats of violence, to agree to the same belief as yourself. Furthermore, though there may be only one true religion, and all others superstition, he foresaw that (if the matter were handled with reason and restraint) the truth of the right doctrine would at last come to light. If contention and debate were continually used, however, the worst and most stubborn and obstinate men, who uphold their evil opinions most constantly, would win. The holiest and best religion would thus be trodden down and destroyed by violent superstition, as good corn is overgrown and choked by weeds and thorns. Therefore, he left all this matter unprescribed and gave to every man liberty and free choice to believe as he wished.

23

François Rabelais

Gargantua and Pantagruel: The Abbey of Thélème

*L*IKE *Erasmus and Sir Thomas More, François Rabelais (ca. 1490–1553) believed that entrenched institutions are more vulnerable to laughter and mockery than to forthright denunciation. The attack is doubly effective when contained in a literary work embodying a sincerely held conviction about human beings and society and presenting as well an amusing story. Whereas Erasmus is clever and incisively witty, Rabelais is wildly, discursively, and grossly funny. Nevertheless, as Renaissance humanists, their underlying assumptions concerning society are much alike.*

Rabelais knew the institutions he attacked from personal experience. Educated in a Benedictine monastery, he served for a while as a secular priest. But, after earning a medical degree, he turned to the practice of medicine as well as to writing. His writing provoked the attempted retaliation of clerical authorities, but he was protected by his patron, Cardinal Du Bellay, whom he served as private physician.

Rabelais' best-known work, Gargantua and Pantagruel *(1533–1535), appeared first in installments. Adopting a medieval legend narrating the exploits of the giant Gargantua and his son Pantagruel, it embellishes the original tale with Renaissance themes and circumstances. Gargantua's education, for example, is in the best and noblest ideas of the Renaissance. Gargantua then fights wars (filled with wildly extravagant episodes) against foolish opponents who epitomize the superstitious customs, as Rabelais saw them, of feudal society. A devoted follower in these campaigns is Brother John, a most unclerical cleric, whom Gargantua asks to found an "Abbey." This Abbey of Thélème, described in the following excerpt, is the opposite of a traditional monastic foundation; it is a satire on certain evils that, Rabelais felt, were characteristic of monasticism and, by extension, characteristic of much of the society of his time: fear and repression, mistrust, ignorance, unreasoning blind faith. The true society, Rabelais suggests, should be founded on the noble and humane principle that those who are well-bred and well-educated naturally lead decent, joyful lives. The motto of the Abbey, "Do what you will," is a trustworthy guiding principle for free people and for the liberated human spirit. For the good take pleasure in doing good.*

HOW GARGANTUA HAD THE ABBEY OF THÉLÈME BUILT FOR THE MONK

There only remained the monk to be provided for, and Gargantua wanted to make him abbot of Seuilly,[1] but he refused the post. He next proposed to give him the abbey of Bourgueil or of Saint-Florant, whichever would suit him better, or both, if he fancied them. But the monk answered categorically that he wanted neither charge nor government of monks.

'For how should I be able to govern others,' he said, 'when I don't know how to govern myself? If it seems to you that I have done you, and may in the future do you welcome service, give me leave to found an abbey after my own devices.'

This request pleased Gargantua, and he offered him all his land of Thélème, beside the River Loire, to within six miles of the great forest of Port-Huault. The monk then requested Gargantua to institute his religious order in an exactly contrary way to all others.

'First of all, then,' said Gargantua, 'you mustn't build walls round it. For all other abbeys have lofty walls (murs).'

'Yes,' said the monk, 'and not without reason. Where there's a *mur* before and a *mur* behind, there are plenty of murmurs, envy, and mutual conspiracy.'

Moreover, seeing that in certain monasteries in this world it is the custom that if any woman enters—I speak of chaste and honest women—they wash the place where she trod, it was ordained that if any monk or nun happened to enter here, the spot where he or she had

---

[1]Rabelais often alludes to real places (like Seuilly) and real people but writes about them as if they were in a world of fantasy. His geography, architecture, and descriptions of people are all tinged with fantasy. Thélème, for example, is an imaginary place, but it bears some resemblance to actual Renaissance architecture.

GARGANTUA AND PANTAGRUEL: THE ABBEY OF THÉLÈME   From François Rabelais, *Gargantua and Pantagruel*, translated by J. M. Cohen (Penguin Classics, 1955), copyright © J. M. Cohen, 1955. Reprinted by permission of Penguin Books, Ltd. [Pp. 149–60.]

stood should be scrupulously washed likewise. And because in the religious foundations of this world everything is encompassed, limited, and regulated by hours, it was decreed that there should be no clock or dial at all, but that affairs should be conducted according to chance and opportunity. For Gargantua said that the greatest waste of time he knew was the counting of hours—what good does it do?—and the greatest nonsense in the world was to regulate one's life by the sound of a bell, instead of by the promptings of reason and good sense. Item, because at that time they put no women into religious houses unless they were one-eyed, lame, hunchbacked, ugly, malformed, lunatic, half-witted, bewitched, and blemished, or men that were not sickly, low-born, stupid, or a burden on their family. . . .

'By the way,' said the monk, 'if a woman is neither fair nor good, what can you do with her?'

'Make her a nun,' said Gargantua.

'Yes,' said the monk, 'and a sempstress of shirts.'

It was decreed that here no women should be admitted unless they were beautiful, well-built, and sweet-natured, nor any men who were not handsome, well-built, and of pleasant nature also.

Item, because men never entered nunneries except secretly and by stealth, it was decreed that here there should be no women when there were no men, and no men when there were no women.

Item, because both men and women, once accepted into a monastic order, after their novitiate year, were compelled and bound to remain for ever, so long as they lived, it was decreed that both men and women, once accepted, could depart from there whenever they pleased, without let or hindrance.

Item, because ordinarily monks and nuns made three vows, that is of chastity, poverty, and obedience, it was decreed that there anyone could be regularly married, could become rich, and could live at liberty.

With regard to the lawful age of entry, women were to be received at from ten to fifteen, and men at from twelve to eighteen.

HOW THE THÉLÈMITES' ABBEY WAS BUILT AND ENDOWED

For the building and furnishing of the abbey Gargantua had counted out in ready money two million seven hundred thousand, eight hundred and thirty-one fine gold Agnus Dei crowns;[2] and for every year

---

[2]These coins and the coinages mentioned later are pretty fancies and the sums highly imaginary.

until the work was completed he assigned out of his income from the River Dive, one million, six hundred and sixty-nine thousand Sun crowns, and an equal number stamped with the sign of Pleiades. While for its foundation and upkeep he granted in perpetuity two million three hundred and sixty-nine thousand rose nobles as a freehold endowment, exempt from all burdens and services, and payable every year at the abbey gate; and this he confirmed in due letters-patent.

The building was hexagonal in shape and so planned that at each angle was built a large circular tower, sixty yards in diameter; and all were alike in size and architecture. The River Loire ran along its north side, and on its bank was placed one of the towers, named Arctic, and facing to the east was another named Calaer; the next in order was Anatole, after that came Mesembrine, then Hesperie, and lastly Cryere. Between each tower was a space of three hundred and twelve yards. The whole was built in six storeys, including the underground cellars. The second was vaulted to the shape of a high arch, and the rest of the ceilings were of Flanders plaster in circular patterns. The roof was covered in fine slates with a lead coping, which bore figures of grotesques and small animals, gilded and in great variety, and with gutters projecting from the walls between the casements, painted in gold-and-blue diagonals to the ground, where they flowed into great pipes, which all led into the river below the house.

The said building was a hundred times more magnificent than Bonnivet or Chambord or Chantilly.[3] For it contained nine thousand, three hundred and thirty-two apartments, each one provided with an inner chamber, a closet, wardrobe, and chapel, and each one giving on a great hall. Between each tower, in the middle of the said main building, was an internal winding stair, the steps of which were, some of porphyry, some of Numidian marble, and some of serpentine, but all twenty-two feet broad, three inches thick, and twelve in number between each landing. On each landing, there was a fine old-fashioned double-arcade through which the light was admitted, and through it one entered a lattice-windowed closet of the breadth of the stairway. The steps went on to the roof and there ended in a pavilion. By this same stair there was an entrance on each side into a great hall, and from the halls into the apartments.

From the Arctic tower to the Cryere tower ran the fine great libraries of Greek, Latin, Hebrew, French, Italian, and Spanish books, divided storey by storey according to their languages.

---

[3]Bonnivet, Chambord, and Chantilly were actual royal chateaux built in the sixteenth century.

In the centre was a marvellous winding staircase, the entrance to which was on the outside of the building through an arch thirty-six feet wide; and this was built of such size and symmetry that six men-at-arms with lance in rest could ride abreast up to the top of the whole building.

Between the Anatole tower and the Mesembrine tower were fine wide galleries, all painted with ancient feats of arms, histories, and views of the world; and in the middle was a similar ascent and gate to the one described on the river side. Above this gate was written in large Gothic letters the following inscription:

THE INSCRIPTION SET ABOVE THE GREAT GATE OF THÉLÈME

Enter not here, vile hypocrites and bigots,
Pious old apes, and puffed-up snivellers,
Wry-necked creatures sawnier than the Goths,
Or Ostrogoths, precursors of Gog and Magog,[4]
Woe-begone scoundrels, mock-godly sandal-wearers,
Beggars in blankets, flagellating canters,
Hooted at, pot-bellied, stirrers up of troubles,
Get along elsewhere to sell your dirty swindles.
    Your hideous deceits
    Would fill my fields and streets
    With villainy
    And with their falsity
    Would untune my song's notes,
    Your hideous deceits.
Enter not here, lawyers insatiable,
Ushers, lawyers' clerks, devourers of the people,
Holders of office, scribes, and pharisees,
Ancient judges who tie up good citizens
Like stray dogs with cord on their necks,
Your reward is earned now, and it is the gibbet.
So go and bray there. Here is done no violence,
Such as in your courts sets men fighting lawsuits.
    Lawsuits and wrangling
    Set us not jangling;
    We come here for pleasure.
    But may your leisure

---

[4]Gigantic creatures representative of nations that war against God.

Be filled up with tangling
Lawsuits and wrangling.
Enter not here, miserly usurers,
Gluttons and lechers, everlasting gatherers,
Tricksters and swindlers, mean pettifoggers,
Hunchbacked and snub-nosed, who in your lockers
Never have enough of gold coin and silver.
However much you pocket you're never satisfied.
You pile up still more, you mean-featured dastards,
May cruel death for this spoil your faces.
Most hideous of faces,
Take them and their grimaces,
Shave them elsewhere, for here
They're out of place, I fear.
Shift them to other places,
Most hideous of faces.
Enter not here, you rambling mastiff curs,
Morning nor evening, jealous, old and spiteful,
Nor you either, seditious mutineers,
Spirits, goblins, and fond husbands' familiars,
Greeks or Latins, more to be feared than wolves,
Nor you with your sores, gnawed to the bone by pox,
Take your ulcers elsewhere and show them to others,
Scabby from head to toe and brimful of dishonour,
Grace, honour, praise, and light
Are here our sole delight;
Of them we make our song,
Our limbs are sound and strong.
This blessing fills us quite,
Grace, honour, praise, and light.
Enter in here, and you shall be most welcome,
And having come, stay noble gentlemen!
Here is the place where income comes in well,
And having come affords good entertainment
For great and small, though thousands of them come.
Be then my cronies, my especial favourites,
Merry and nimble, jolly, gay, and sprightly,
And, in a word, the best of good companions.
All worthy gentlemen,
Keen witted and serene,

From every coarseness free,
Here find civility,
Among your hosts will reign,
All worthy gentlemen.
Enter in here, you who preach with vigour
Christ's Holy Gospel, never mind who scoffs,
Here you will find a refuge and a tower
Against the foeman's error, the picked arguments,
Which falsely seek to spread about their poison.
Enter, here let us found a faith profound,
And then let us confound by speech and writing,
All that are the foemen of the Holy Writ.

Our Holy Writ and Word
For ever shall be heard
In this most holy spot.
Each wears it on his heart,
Each wears it as a sword,
Our Holy Writ and Word.

Enter in here, you ladies of high lineage,
Here be frank and fearless, enter gaily in,
Flowers of all beauty, with heaven in your faces,
Upright in bearing, modest in behaviour,
Here you will find the dwelling-place of honour.
That noble gentleman who of this place was donor,
And gives rewards, has destined it for you.
He has provided gold sufficient for its upkeep.

Gold freely given,
A man's freely shriven,
In exchange for awards.
For it brings rewards
To all mortal men,
Gold freely given.

CONCERNING THE ESTABLISHMENT OF THE THÉLÈMITES' HOUSE

In the middle of the first court was a magnificent fountain of fine alabaster, on the top of which were the three Graces with horns of abundance, spouting water from their breasts, mouths, ears, eyes, and other physical orifices. The rooms of the building above this first court stood upon stout pillars of chalcedony and porphyry, with magnificent old-fashioned arches between; and inside were fine, long, spacious galleries, decorated with paintings, with horns of stags, unicorns, rhinoceroses, and hippopotami, with elephants' tusks and with other remarkable objects. The ladies' lodging stretched from the Arctic tower to the Mesembrine gate, the men occupying the rest. In front of this ladies' lodging, to provide them with entertainment, there was outside, between the first two towers, the tilt-yard, the riding ring, the theatre, and the swimming-bath with excellent baths on three levels, well provided with all necessary accommodation and with a store of myrrh-water.

Beside the river were the handsome pleasure-gardens, in the middle of which was a neat maze. Between the two other towers were the tennis and balloon-courts. On the side of the Cryere tower was the orchard, well stocked with all fruit trees planted in the pattern of the quincunx; and at the end of it was the great park, which teemed with all kinds of wild game. Between the third pair of towers were the butts for arquebus, bow, and cross-bow; the offices were in a single-storey building outside the Hesperie tower; the stables were beyond the offices; and in front of them was the falconry, managed by falconers most expert in their art, and annually stocked by Candians, Venetians, and Sarmatians with all manner of birds, the finest of their breed: eagles, gerfalcons, goshawks, great falcons, lanners, falcons, sparrow-hawks, merlins, and others, so well trained and tamed that when they flew from the castle to disport themselves over the fields, they would capture all the game they met. The hunting stables were a little further off, in the direction of the park.

Every hall, room, and closet was hung with various tapestry, according to the season of the year. All the floors were covered with green cloth. The beds were embroidered. In each retiring room was a crystal mirror, set in a fine gold frame embellished all round with pearls, and it was large enough to give a true reflection of the whole figure.

At the outer doors of the halls in the ladies' lodgings were the perfumers and barbers, through whose hands the men passed on their visits to the ladies. These attendants also provided the ladies' rooms each morning with rose-water, orange-water, and myrtle-water, and brought for each lady a precious casket, which breathed of every aromatic scent.

The ladies, at the foundation of this order, dressed according to their own taste and pleasure. Afterwards, of their own free will, they reformed themselves in the following fashion: they wore scarlet or pink stockings, which they drew exactly three inches above the knee and which were bordered with fine embroidery or slashing. Their garters were of the colour of their bracelets, and were tied above and below the knee. Their shoes, sandals, and slippers were of crimson, red, or violet velvet, and jagged in points like lobsters' beards. Over their smocks they wore a corset of pure silk camblet; and over this a farthingale of white, red, brown, grey, or some other colour, on top of which was a silver taffeta skirt embroidered with gold thread and close-patterned needlework; or according to a lady's taste and the temperature of the season, this skirt might be of satin, damask, or velvet, and orange, brown, green, ash-grey, blue, bright yellow, crimson, or white cloth, gold-thread work, or embroidery, as suited each feast-day. Their gowns, according to the season, were of cloth of gold fringed with silver, of red satin embroidered with gold-thread work, of white, blue, black, brown, taffeta, silken serge, silk camblet, velvet, cloth of silver, cloth of gold, gold thread, velvet, or satin picked out with gold in various patterns.

On some summer days, instead of gowns they wore beautiful light capes of the materials mentioned, or sleeveless Moorish cloaks of violet velvet with gold fringe over silver thread, or corded with gold and studded at the seams with little Indian pearls: and always a fine plume of feathers, matching the colour of their cuffs and spangled with little embroidered motifs in gold. In winter, on the other hand, they wore taffeta gowns of the colours already named, trimmed with the fur of spotted lynxes, black weasels, Calabrian martens, sables, and other costly furs.

Their beads, rings, neck-chains, and collars were of precious stones: carbuncles, rubies, spider rubies, diamonds, sapphires, emeralds, turquoises, garnets, agates, beryls, pearls, and magnificent margarites. Their head-dresses conformed to the season; in winter they followed the French fashion, in spring the Spanish, and in summer the Italian, except on feast days and Sundays, when they wore the French head-dress, which is more dignified and more befitting to matronly modesty.

The men were dressed in their fashions, with stockings on their legs of light wool or serge-cloth, scarlet, pink, black, or white. Their trunkhose were of velvet of the same colour, or of one almost matching, and were embroidered or pointed to their taste. Their doublets were of cloth of gold or silver, velvet, satin, damask, or taffeta of the same colour, cut, embroidered, and trimmed to perfection. Their points were of silk of the same colour, with tags of well-burnished gold. Their mantles and cloaks were of cloth of gold, gold tissue, cloth of silver, or velvet picked out according to their fancy. Their gowns were as costly as those of the ladies. Their belts were of silk, of the same colour as their doublets. Each wore a fine sword at his side, with a hilt of gold and a velvet scabbard of the colour of his hose, tipped with chased gold; also a dagger was to match. Their caps were of black velvet decorated with many rings and gold buttons, and with white plumes above them, neatly divided by gold spangles, at the end of which fine rubies, emeralds, etc. hung on wires.

But such was the sympathy between the men and the women, that each day they were dressed in like apparel, and to ensure that this should be so, certain gentlemen were appointed to tell the men each morning what colours the ladies intended to wear that day. For everything followed the ladies' decision.

Do not suppose, however, that any time was wasted by either men or women over these handsome clothes and rich accoutrements. For the masters of the wardrobe had all the clothing so neatly laid out each morning, and the chambermaids were so skilful, that in a minute they were all ready and dressed from head to foot. And in order that they might have these accoutrements close at hand, around the Thélème wood was a great block of houses, a mile and a half long, very smart and well arranged, in which lived the goldsmiths, jewellers, embroiderers, tailors, wire-workers, velvet-weavers, tapestry makers, and upholsterers; and there each man worked at his trade, and all of them for the aforesaid monks and nuns.

They were provided with supplies and material by the lord Nausiclete,[5] who brought seven ships to them each year from the Perlas and Cannibal Islands,[6] loaded with gold ingots, raw silk, pearls, and precious stones. And if any pearls began to look old and lose their natural whiteness, they restored them by their art, which was to give them to certain fine cocks, as castings are given to falcons.

THE RULES ACCORDING TO WHICH THE THÉLÈMITES LIVED

All their life was regulated not by laws, statutes, or rules, but according to their free will and pleasure. They rose from bed when they pleased, and drank, ate, worked, and slept when the fancy seized them.

[5]An invented name meaning "one who owns many ships."
[6]Newly discovered islands in the Caribbean sea.

Nobody woke them; nobody compelled them either to eat or to drink, or to do anything else whatever. So it was that Gargantua had established it. In their rules there was only one clause.

Do what you will

because people who are free, well-born, well-bred, and easy in honest company have a natural spur and instinct which drives them to virtuous deeds and deflects them from vice; and this they called honour. When these same men are depressed and enslaved by vile constraint and subjection, they use this noble quality which once impelled them freely towards virtue, to throw off and break this yoke of slavery. For we always strive after things forbidden and covet what is denied us.

Making use of this liberty, they most laudably rivalled one another in all of them doing what they saw pleased one. If some man or woman said, 'Let us drink,' they all drank; if he or she said, 'Let us play,' they all played; if it was 'Let us go and amuse ourselves in the fields,' everyone went there. If it were for hawking or hunting, the ladies, mounted on fine mares, with their grand palfreys following, each carried on their daintily gloved wrists a sparrow-hawk, a lanneret, or a merlin, the men carrying the other birds.

So nobly were they instructed that there was not a man or woman among them who could not read, write, sing, play musical instruments, speak five or six languages, and compose in them both verse and prose. Never were seen such worthy knights, so valiant, so nimble both on foot and horse; knights more vigorous, more agile, handier with all weapons than they were. Never were seen ladies so good-looking, so dainty, less tiresome, more skilled with the fingers and the needle, and in every free and honest womanly pursuit than they were.

For that reason, when the time came that anyone in that abbey, either at his parents' request or for any other reason, wished to leave it, he took with him one of the ladies, the one who had accepted him as her admirer, and they were married to one another; and if at Thélème they had lived in devotion and friendship, they lived in still greater devotion and friendship when they were married. Indeed, they loved one another to the end of their days as much as they had done on their wedding day.

24

Giorgio Vasari

Lives of the Artists

*T*HE change in the status of the arts
accompanying the cultural Renaissance is illustrated by Vasari's Lives of the
Artists. *In the Middle Ages, artists were classified as merely craftsmen. It
would hardly have occurred to anyone to record their lives and achievements.
But Vasari's sixteenth-century compilation of biographies of artists, with de-
scriptive listings of their works, was widely applauded.*

Giorgio Vasari (1511–1574) was a painter and architect himself. His Lives
of the Most Eminent Italian Architects, Painters, and Sculptors *(first
published in 1550 and enlarged in 1568) is usually referred to as the* Lives of
the Artists. *He wrote, he said, "not to acquire praise as a writer" but to revive
and preserve the memory "of these artists . . . whose names and works should not
remain prey to death and oblivion."*

*Vasari's work is especially valuable as a source of materials concerning
Renaissance art, for he knew personally the leading artists of his time. Michelangelo was Vasari's teacher, and the two remained constant and loyal friends.*

A recurrent theme in Vasari's Lives *is that the works of his contemporaries
constituted a rebirth, referring to the way in which the classical forms and spirit
of Greek and Roman art were "reborn" in the works of Renaissance artists.
More than mere imitation was involved, however, for acquaintance with the art
and thought of the ancient world, it was believed, would bring with it the
impulse to create with the same spirit as did the artists, writers, and philosophers
of the ancient world.*

Two excerpts from Vasari's Lives *are included. The first is from Vasari's*
Life of Leonardo da Vinci *(1452–1519). Leonardo was famous in his time,
his work being competed for by many patrons, including popes and kings. One
of the most complex personalities of all ages, he remains an enigma today as
historians and analysts repeatedly seek explanations for his stupendous and*

often erratic genius. They note his peculiarities and his triumphs (he wrote lefthanded and backwards, he was of prodigious physical strength, he was a mathematical genius, he painted very little but his few paintings are among the best ever done, and so on). Like Vasari, they also mention his engineering and scientific projects. Today, however, we can see more clearly the remarkable way in which Leonardo's work anticipated and encouraged the development of modern science, which had its roots in the Renaissance spirit of universal inquiry.

Michelangelo (1475–1564) embodied many characteristic qualities of the Renaissance. An individualistic, highly competitive genius (sometimes to the point of eccentricity), he created, for example, embodiments of power (his gigantic statues David and Moses), of perfect harmony and grace (the Pietà), of daring color and form (the Sistine Chapel ceiling); and he was the chief participant in the creation of one of the world's greatest works of imaginative genius (St. Peter's in Rome). His poetry expressed Platonic idealism blended with Christian faith. In him and his works Vasari saw confirmation of the Renaissance belief that the arts, far from being merely crafts or techniques, were actually creative activities akin to the creative power of God that brought form and being out of chaos.

LEONARDO DA VINCI (1452–1519)

The most heavenly gifts seem to be showered on certain human beings. Sometimes supernaturally, marvelously, they all congregate in one individual. Beauty, grace, and talent are combined in such bounty that in whatever that man undertakes, he outdistances all other men and proves himself to be specially endowed by the hand of God. He owes his pre-eminence not to human teaching or human power. This was seen and acknowledged by all men in the case of Leonardo da Vinci, who had, besides the beauty of his person (which was such that it has never been sufficiently extolled), an indescribable grace in every effortless act and deed. His talent was so rare that he mastered any subject to which he turned his attention. Extraordinary strength and remarkable facility were here combined. He had a mind of regal boldness and

LIVES OF THE ARTISTS From Vasari's *Lives of the Artists*, edited by Betty Burroughs, New York: Simon and Schuster, 1966. Copyright © 1946, 1973 by Betty Burroughs. Reprinted by permission of Simon & Schuster, Inc. [Pp. 187, 191–92, 194–96, 258–70, 276–78, 283–84, 291, 296–97.]

magnanimous daring. His gifts were such that his celebrity was world-wide, not only in his own day, but even more after his death, and so will continue until the end of time.

Truly admirable, indeed, and divinely endowed was Leonardo da Vinci, the son of Ser Piero da Vinci. He might have been a scientist if he had not been so versatile. But the instability of his character caused him to take up and abandon many things. In arithmetic, for example, he made such rapid progress during the short time he studied it that he often confounded his teacher by his questions. He also began the study of music and resolved to learn to play the lute, and as he was by nature of exalted imagination, and full of the most graceful vivacity, he sang and accompanied himself most divinely, improvising at once both verses and music. . . .

When Ludovico Sforza became duke of Milan in 1493, he invited Leonardo most ceremoniously to come and play the lute before him. Leonardo took an instrument he had himself constructed of silver in the shape of a horse's head, a form calculated to render the tone louder and more sonorous. Leonardo was one of the best *improvisatori* [improvisers] in verse of his time. He surpassed all the musicians who had assembled to perform and so charmed the duke by his varied gifts that the nobleman delighted beyond measure in his society. The duke prevailed on him to paint a Nativity for an altarpiece to be sent as a present to the Emperor [Maximilian I]. For the Dominican monks of Santa Maria delle Grazie at Milan, Leonardo painted the *Last Supper*. This is a most beautiful and admirable work. The master gave so much beauty and majesty to the heads of the Apostles that he was constrained to leave the Christ unfinished, convinced as he was that he could not render the divinity of the Redeemer. Even so, this work has always been held in the highest estimation by the Milanese and by foreigners as well. Leonardo rendered to perfection the doubts and anxieties of the Apostles, their desire to know by whom their Master is to be betrayed. All their faces show their love, terror, anger, grief, or bewilderment, unable as they are to fathom the meaning of the Lord. The spectator is also struck by the determination, hatred, and treachery of Judas. The whole is executed with the most minute exactitude. The texture of the tablecloth seems actually made of linen.

The story goes that the prior was in a great hurry to see the picture done. He could not understand why Leonardo should sometimes remain before his work half a day together, absorbed in thought. He would have him work away, as he compelled the laborers to do who were digging in his garden, and never put the pencil down. Not content with seeking to hurry Leonardo, the prior even complained to the duke, and tormented him so much that at length, he sent for Leonardo and courteously entreated him to finish the work. Leonardo, knowing the duke to be an intelligent man, explained himself as he had never bothered to do to the prior. He made it clear that men of genius are sometimes producing most when they seem least to labor, for their minds are then occupied in the shaping of those conceptions to which they afterward give form. He told the duke that two heads were yet to be done: that of the Saviour, the likeness of which he could not hope to find on earth and had not yet been able to create in his imagination in perfection of celestial grace; and the other, of Judas. He said he wanted to find features fit to render the appearance of a man so depraved as to betray his benefactor, his Lord, and the Creator of the world. He said he would still search but as a last resort he could always use the head of that troublesome and impertinent prior. This made the duke laugh with all his heart. The prior was utterly confounded and went away to speed the digging in his garden. Leonardo was left in peace.

The head of Judas, as we see it finished, is indeed the image of treachery and wickedness. The nobility of this painting, in composition and in high finish, made the king of France [Francis I] wish to remove it to his own kingdom. He attempted to find architects to frame it in wood that it might be transported without injury. He was not deterred by any consideration of cost, but as the painting was on the wall, he had to forgo his desire, and the Milanese kept their picture. . . .

For Francesco del Giocondo, Leonardo undertook to paint the portrait of Mona Lisa, his wife [*La Gioconda*], but, after loitering over it for four years, he left it unfinished. It is now in the possession of Francis, king of France.[1] Whoever desires to see how far art can imitate nature, may do so by observing this head wherein every subtlety and every peculiarity have been faithfully reproduced. The eyes are bright and moist, and around them are those pale, red, and slightly livid circles seen in life, while the lashes and eyebrows are represented with the closest exactitude with the separate hairs drawn as they issue from the skin, every turn being followed and all the pores exhibited in the most natural manner. The nose with its beautiful and delicately red nostrils might easily be believed to be alive. The mouth, admirable in outline, is rose tinted in harmony with the carnation of the cheeks, which seems

[1] It is now in the Louvre museum in Paris.

not painted, but of flesh and blood. He who looks earnestly at the pit of the throat must fancy he sees the beating of the pulse. It is a marvel of art. Mona Lisa was very beautiful, and while he painted her, Leonardo had someone near at hand to sing or play to her, or to amuse her with jests, to keep from her that look of melancholy so common in portraits. This picture, on the contrary, has so pleasing an expression and a smile to sweet that one must think it rather divine than human. It has ever been esteemed a wonderful work. . . .

When Leo X became pope, Leonardo went to Rome with Duke Giuliano de' Medici.[2] The pontiff was interested in philosophical inquiry and especially in alchemy. Leonardo made some fanciful figures of animals out of a wax paste, hollow and very light, which floated in the air when they were inflated, but fell to the ground as the air escaped. A gardener of the Belvedere one day brought in a curious lizard for which Leonardo made wings from the skins of other lizards. In these wings he put quicksilver, so that, when the animal walked, the wings moved with a tremulous motion. He then made eyes, horns, and a beard for the creature, which he tamed and kept in a cage. He showed it to his visitors, and all who saw it ran away terrified. More than once, he had the intestines of a sheep cleaned and scraped until they were so fine that they could be held in the hollow of the hand. Then he fastened one end to a pair of bellows in another room and blew them up so that they filled the whole room, which was a very large one. Anyone who was there had to take refuge in a corner. He made numbers of these follies and occupied himself with mirrors and optical instruments. He also made experiments in oils and varnishes[3] for painting. Leonardo received a commission for a picture from Pope Leo and immediately began to distill oils and herbs for the varnish, whereupon the pontiff remarked, "Alas! this man will do nothing at all, since he is thinking of the end before he has made a beginning."

There was constant discord between Michelangelo Buonarroti and Leonardo. Michelangelo even left Florence because of it, and Duke Giuliano excused him by saying that the pope had summoned him to Rome. When Leonardo heard of this, he departed for France to the court of the king [Francis I] who already owned several of his works and wished him to paint the cartoon[4] of Saint Anne. Leonardo kept him

---

[2]Giovanni de' Medici (1475–1521) took the title Leo X when he became pope in 1513. Duke Giuliano was his brother.

[3]Varnishing is the last step in completing an oil painting.

[4]A cartoon is a full-size sketch on paper done in preparation for a painting.

waiting, according to his custom, a long time. Finally, being old, he lay sick for many months. When he found himself near death he made every effort to acquaint himself with the doctrine of the Catholic ritual. Then he confessed himself with great penitence and devoutly received the sacrament, sustained, because he could not stand, by his servants and friends. The King, who used to visit him often, came immediately afterward to his room. Leonardo was lamenting to him his fear that he had offended God and man, since he had not labored in art as he should have done, when he was seized with a violent paroxysm, the forerunner of death. The king rose and supported his head to assist him, in the hope of alleviating his pain, and Leonardo departed this life in the arms of the monarch.

The death of Leonardo caused great sorrow to all who had known him. Nor was there ever an artist who did more to honor the art of painting. The radiance of his countenance, which was splendidly beautiful, brought cheer to the most melancholy. He was most persuasive and could make a man say "yes" or "no" as he desired. He was physically so strong that he could bend a horseshoe as if it were lead. His generous liberality offered hospitality to rich or poor, provided only that his guest was distinguished by talent or excellence. The poorest or most insignificant abode was adorned by his presence, and as the city of Florence was blessed by his birth, it suffered grievously by his death. To the art of painting he contributed a mode of deepening the shadows which the moderns have used to give force and relief to their figures. . . .

• • •

MICHELANGELO BUONARROTI (1475–1564)

While the artists who came after Giotto[1] were doing their best to imitate and to understand nature, bending every faculty to increase that high comprehension sometimes called intelligence, the Almighty took pity on their often fruitless labor. He resolved to send to earth a spirit capable of supreme expression in all the arts, one able to give form to painting, perfection to sculpture, and grandeur to architecture. The Almighty Creator also graciously endowed this chosen one with an

---

[1] Giotto di Bondone (1276?–1337?), Florentine painter and sculptor, leading artist of the early Renaissance. Vasari names many artists. Only those of major significance will be identified in footnotes.

understanding of philosophy and with the grace of poetry. And because he had observed that in Tuscany men were more zealous in study and more diligent in labor than in the rest of Italy, He decreed that Florence should be the birthplace of this divinely endowed spirit.

In the Casetino, therefore, in 1475, a son was born to Signor Lodovico di Leonardo di Buonarroti Simoni, a descendant of the noble family of the counts of Canossa. The child's mother was also of a very good family. Lodovico was then mayor of Chiusi-e-Caprese, near the spot where Saint Francis of Assisi received the stigmata.[2] . . .

Because Lodovico had many children and was far from rich, he placed his boys as apprentices in the weaver's trade. At school, Michelangelo did more drawing than studying. A friend of his, Granacci, who, though just a boy, was working for Domenico Ghirlandaio, used to bring Michelangelo drawings made by his master, who was then one of the foremost painters of all Italy. The result was that Michelangelo became apprenticed to Ghirlandaio by the time he was fourteen years old.

Lorenzo the Magnificent[3] at about this time engaged the sculptor Bertoldo . . . to form a school for sculptors. It is true that Bertoldo was old and could no longer work, but he was an excellent craftsman, especially in bronze. Lorenzo was concerned because there were no sculptors comparable to the many able painters of the day. He asked Ghirlandaio to recommend and bring to the school any promising young sculptors. . . . Michelangelo and Granacci, among others, were sent to the Medici gardens.[4] Lorenzo sent for Lodovico, Michelangelo's father, and formally arranged to receive Michelangelo into his princely household. The lad was then fifteen or sixteen. He stayed there four years, until the death of Lorenzo, receiving for himself an allowance of money and a purple cloak to wear, while his father, Lodovico, was made an official of the customs. . . . Michelangelo made the most of the unusual opportunity for study which the Medici collection afforded. He also studied Masaccio's frescoes in the church of the Carmine. Here in a brawl, the jeering Torrigiano[5] gave him that blow on the nose which disfigured him for life.

• • •

[2]Marks resembling the crucifixion wounds of Christ.
[3]Ruler of Florence and patron of the arts (1449–1492).
[4]Site of Lorenzo's collection of classical sculptures.
[5]One of Michelangelo's fellow apprentices.

In Rome Michelangelo made such great progress in both conception and facility of execution that even the uncultivated were impressed and saw that his work was beyond comparison with any other. The cardinal of St. Denis, a Frenchman, wished to leave a memorial of himself in Rome and one done by the hand of this most famous artist. He arranged to have Michelangelo carve a Pietà.[6] No sculptor, no matter how distinguished an artist, could add a single grace or improve this marble masterpiece in any way either in elegance or strength. In the body of the dead Christ, to say nothing of the admirable draperies, is shown the absolute perfection of research in anatomy; every vein, every muscle, every nerve is perfectly rendered as it appears in death. Besides, there is the beauty of the face, the exquisite expression. It is a marvel that the hand of an artist, in so short a time, can transform shapeless stone into a perfection of beauty seldom achieved by nature in the flesh. The love and care which Michelangelo lavished upon this group were such that he carved his name upon it, on the ribbon that crosses the Virgin's bosom. This is the only work he ever signed. Michelangelo had happened to find a large group of strangers from Lombardy looking at the Pietà one day. They were admiring it and one said that the artist was "Our Hunchback of Milan."[7] Michelangelo came back that night with a lantern and carved Michelangelo Buonarroti where all could see. He gained great fame from this work. I have heard dull-witted folk object that the Virgin is too young. They have not been able to understand Michelangelo's ideal conception of the nature of the Madonna's virginity.

Michelangelo's fame, because of the Pietà [and many other works] was so great that in 1503, when he was twenty-nine years old, he was invited to Rome by Pope Julius II.[8] His Holiness commissioned him to make his tomb. Months passed before the design was finally approved. Indeed, it outdid any monument, even the imperial tombs, in magnificence of superb ornament and wealth of figures. When it was accepted, Julius determined to rebuild the choir of Saint Peter's to make it a fit setting. . . .

The Moses,[9] ten feet high, was also completed. No modern work will ever approach it in beauty, no, nor ancient either. Seated in imposing dignity, the lawgiver rests one arm upon the tablet. With his other

[6]A representation in painting or sculpture of the Virgin Mary mourning the dead Christ.

[7]Christofano Gobbo (Christofano Solari) who worked in Milan 1490–1522. "Gobbo" means "hunchback" in Italian.

[8]Pope 1503–1513. Patron of Raphael and Michelangelo.

[9]One of the statues designed to be part of the Pope's tomb.

hand he restrains his flowing beard that descends so softly, hair by separate hair, as though the chisel had become a pencil. The countenance, sacred and mighty, is of the most sublime beauty. Dazzling in splendor, the lawgiver radiates his divinity. The draperies are beautifully handled and turned at the edges. The anatomical development, the muscles, and the veins of the hands are exhibited to the utmost perfection. The same may be said of the legs and feet. This Moses seems indeed the friend of God. . . .

Michelangelo set up one portion of the tomb; that is the shorter sides of it. While he was doing this, more of his marble arrived from Carrara. Because Michelangelo found His Holiness engaged with important news just received from Bologna, he advanced the money out of his own pocket. A few days later he sought an audience with the Pope but was told to have patience by a groom of the chambers who added that he had orders not to admit him. A bishop who stood near observed that possibly the groom was unacquainted with the person whom he refused to admit. The groom replied that he knew him only too well. "I, however," he added, "am here to do as my superiors command, and to obey the orders of the Pope." Displeased with this reply, the master left, bidding the attendant tell His Holiness, when next he should inquire for Michelangelo that he had gone elsewhere. He went at once to his dwelling, where he left instructions that all his belongings should be sold. He took horses that very night and left Rome.

When he arrived in Bologna, scarcely was his foot out of the stirrup before attendants hurried him to the Pope's presence. . . . He knelt before the Pope, who merely glanced at him, saying angrily, "It seems that you would not come to us, but were waiting for us to come to you!" (He thus alluded to the fact that Bologna is nearer Florence than is Rome.) Michelangelo excused himself and admitted that he had acted in anger, but said that he could not bear to be ordered away. If he was wrong, he hoped the Pope would forgive him.

Now the bishop, in an effort to smooth things over, said that one should not expect artists to know anything outside their vocation, ignorant as they always were. This remark threw the Pope into a furious rage. He rushed at the bishop with a stick he happened to have in his hand, crying, "It is you who are the ignoramus, with your impertinences such as we would never think of uttering!" And he drove him out, the ushers hurrying the bishop along with blows. His rage thus spent upon the prelate, the Pope bestowed his benediction on Michelangelo.

• • •

The Pope returned to Rome; and while Michelangelo was still working on the statue [of Moses], Bramante,[10] who was the friend and kinsman of Raphael and hostile to Michelangelo, influenced the mind of the Pope to drop the work on the tomb and to employ Michelangelo instead on the painting of the chapel of Pope Sixtus [Sistine Chapel] in the Vatican. Bramante told the pontiff it was an invitation to death to build a tomb while one lived. Bramante and Michelangelo's other rivals hoped to thwart Michelangelo in his sculpture, in which he was perfect, and compel him to paint in fresco, in which they expected him to prove himself inferior to Raphael. Or, should he succeed at painting, it was almost certain that he would be so enraged as to secure the success of their main purpose, which was to be rid of him.

Michelangelo returned to Rome, therefore, and found the Pope no longer disposed to have the tomb finished. He was asked instead to paint the ceiling of the chapel, a great and difficult labor. Our artist, aware of his own inexperience, excused himself from the undertaking. He proposed that the work be given to Raphael. The more he refused, the more the impetuous Pope insisted. A quarrel threatened. Michelangelo saw that the Pope was determined, so he resolved to accept the task. His Holiness ordered Bramante to prepare the scaffolding. This he did by suspending the ropes through perforations in the ceiling. Michelangelo asked how the holes were going to be filled in when the painting was done. Bramante replied that they could think about it when the time came. Michelangelo saw that the architect was either incapable or unfriendly, and he went straight to the Pope to say that the scaffolding would not do and that Bramante did not know how to construct one. Julius, in the presence of Bramante, replied that Michelangelo might make it his own way. This he did by the use of a method that did not injure the walls, and which has since been pursued by Bramante and others. Michelangelo gave the ropes that were taken from Bramante's scaffolding to a poor carpenter, who sold them for a sum that made up his daughter's dowry.

Michelangelo made arrangements to do the whole thing himself. He avoided everyone for fear of being asked to show the work. A more and more earnest desire to see it grew day by day. Now, Pope Julius always enjoyed seeing the progress of the works he had undertaken, the more if he was thwarted. Thus it happened that he went to see the chapel one day. Michelangelo did not recognize him and rushed out upon him with a plank of the scaffolding and drove him out in a fury.

[10]Donato Bramante (1444–1514), architect under whose supervision St. Peter's was begun in 1506.

Michelangelo told me that he refused to show the painting because of spots that had appeared on the wet plaster. In fact, he was in despair and refused to continue the work until Giuliano da Sangallo told him how the spots might be removed.

When it was half done, Pope Julius, who had gone more than once to see the work, mounting ladders with Michelangelo's assistance, insisted on having a public showing. Hasty and impatient, he would not wait for the finishing touches. In fact, when all Rome came hurrying to see the chapel, the Pope was the first to enter. He hardly waited for the dust from the removal of the scaffolding to settle. Then it was that Raphael of Urbino, who was very prompt in imitation, instantly changed his style and painted the *Prophets* and the *Sibyls*[11] in the church of Santa Maria della Pace. Bramante tried to make the Pope give the second half of the chapel to Raphael. Hearing of this, Michelangelo complained of Bramante to the Pope. He spared no pains to point out faults in Bramante's life as well as errors in his work. Julius commanded that Michelangelo should continue the work. He completed it in twenty months, without even so much help as a man to grind his colors. It is true that Michelangelo sometimes complained that the Pope hurried him constantly by asking when it would be finished. Once Michelangelo answered, "It will be done when I believe I have satisfied art." "And we command," rejoined the pontiff, "that you satisfy our wish to have it done quickly," adding that, if it were not at once completed, he would have Michelangelo thrown from the scaffolding.

When he heard this, our artist, who feared the Pope's fury, and with good cause, instantly removed the scaffolding without retouching the painting *a secco* [on dry plaster], as the older masters had done. He had wanted very much to add some gold and ultramarine to the draperies to enrich the whole. The Pope, too, heard from all who praised the chapel highly that these things were still wanting and would fain have had Michelangelo do it. But Michelangelo knew it would have been too great a labor to put up the scaffolding, so the pictures remained as they were. The Pope, who saw Michelangelo often, would sometimes say, "Let the chapel be enriched with bright colors and gold, it looks poor." Then Michelangelo would answer, "Holy Father, these were poor folk and holy men, besides, who despised riches and ornament." . . .

Down the center of the ceiling is the *History of the World*, from the Creation to the Deluge. The *Prophets* and the *Sibyls*, five on each side

[11]Women regarded as prophetesses in ancient Greece and Rome.

and one at each end, are painted on the corbels. The lunettes portray the genealogy of Christ. Michelangelo used no perspective, nor any one fixed point of sight, but was satisfied to paint each division with perfection of design. Truly this chapel has been, and is, the very light of our art. Everyone capable of judging stands amazed at the excellence of this work, at the grace and flexibility, the beautiful truth of proportion of the exquisite nude forms. These are varied in every way in expression and form. Some of the figures are seated, some are in motion, while others hold up festoons of oak leaves and acorns, the device of Pope Julius.

All the world hastened to behold this marvel and was overwhelmed, speechless with astonishment. The Pope rewarded Michelangelo with rich gifts and planned still greater works. Michelangelo sometimes remarked that he was aware that the pontiff really esteemed his abilities. When the Pope was sometimes rude and rough, he always soothed the injury by gifts and favors. Once, for example, Michelangelo asked leave to go to Florence for the festival of San Giovanni and begged also for some money for the journey. Pope Julius said, "Well! but when will this chapel be finished?" "When I can, Holy Father," said the artist. At that the Pope, who had a staff in his hand, struck Michelangelo and exclaimed, "When I can—when I can! I'll make thee finish it, and quickly." But no sooner had Michelangelo returned to his house to prepare for the journey than the pontiff's chamberlain brought five hundred crowns to pacify him. The chamberlain excused the Pope, declaring that these outbursts must be considered marks of His Holiness' favor. Michelangelo knew the Pope and was, after all, much attached to him. He laughed at what had happened, the more readily because things of this kind always turned out to his profit, and he saw that the Pope was anxious to keep him as a friend.

• • •

I do not propose to describe this work [the *Last Judgment*],[12] which has so often been reproduced. It will be enough to say that the purpose of the master was to render the human form in the absolute perfection of proportion and the greatest variety of attitude and to express the passions with force and truth. With this in mind he gave little attention to coloring or to minutiae. . . .

---

[12]This is on the end wall of the Sistine Chapel behind the altar and was painted after the ceiling was completed.

When it was three quarters done, Pope Paul went to see it. Messer Biagio de Cesena, the master of ceremonies, when asked to give his opinion, said that he thought it very improper to have so many nude forms, shameless in their nakedness, in that sacred place. He added that such pictures were suited to a bath or a wineshop. Messer Biagio had no sooner left than our artist drew his portrait from memory, with a serpent wound around him surrounded by devils in hell. Nor could Messer Biagio persuade the Pope to have the portrait removed.[13]

Michelangelo fell from the scaffolding and hurt his leg, but would not allow a surgeon to come near him. Messer Baccio Rontini, his great friend and admirer, went to his house and knocked. Getting no answer he finally forced his way in and found the master in a desperate state. Baccio never left his bedside until the leg was cured.

When he was well, Michelangelo completed the painting. This great work may be described in the words of Dante, "Dead are the dead, the living seem to live." Michelangelo surpassed himself. The seated figure of Our Lord, terrible in his anger, turns toward the condemned, thundering anathema. Our Lady cowers in her mantle at the sight of that destruction. In a word, we have here the true Last Judgment, the real Condemnation, the effectual Resurrection. Those who thought they knew art are overcome by this work. They gaze upon the evidence of power in these contours and they tremble with fear as though some great spirit had possessed himself of the art of design. The more they examine this work, the more they are bewildered at the thought of a comparison of other paintings with this paragon. . . .

Meanwhile Michelangelo pressed on the work at Saint Peter's in an effort to bring it to such a state that no further changes could be made. About this time he was told that Paul IV wished to change the paintings in the chapel because some of the figures in the *Last Judgment* were shamefully nude. Michelangelo said, "Tell His Holiness that this is a mere trifle, and can easily be done. Let him mend the world; paintings are easily mended."

• • •

In Lent of this year, Leonardo [Buonarroti], Michelangelo's nephew, resolved to go to Rome. Perhaps he sensed that his kinsman was near the end of his life. Michelangelo was already suffering from a slow fever

---

[13]The Pope is said to have replied, "If the painter had put you in purgatory, I would have done my utmost, but since he has sent you to hell, it is useless for you to come to me, since from there, as you know, there is no redemption."

and he had his doctor, Messer Federigo Donato, write Leonardo to hasten his coming. But the malady increased, in spite of the care of those around him. Still in perfect self possession, the master at length made his will in three clauses. He left his soul to God, his body to the earth, and his goods to his nearest relatives. He recommended his attendants to think upon the sufferings of Christ, and departed to a better life on February 17, 1564. . . .

But now, to conclude, I will only add, that Michelangelo had an excellent constitution, a spare form, and strong nerves. He was not robust as a child, and as a man he suffered two serious attacks of illness, but he could endure much fatigue. In his latter years he wore stockings of dogskin for months together, and when he took them off the skin of the leg sometimes came with them. His face was round, the brow square and ample, with seven direct lines upon it. The temples projected much beyond the ears, which were somewhat large and stood a little off from the cheeks. His nose had been flattened by the blow of Torrigiano. His eyes were rather small, dark, with blue and yellowish points. The eyebrows had few hairs. The lips were thin and the lower slightly projected. The chin was well formed, and the beard and hair were black mingled with gray.

This master, as I said at the beginning, was certainly sent by God as an example of what an artist could be. I, who can thank God for unusual happiness, count it among the greatest of my blessings that I was born while Michelangelo still lived, was found worthy to have him for my master, and was accepted as his trusted friend. . . .

Michelangelo was followed to his tomb by all the artists and by his numerous friends. The Pope expressed his intention of commanding that a monument should be erected to his memory in Saint Peter's.

Michelangelo's nephew Leonardo did not arrive in Rome until it was all over, though he traveled post haste. When Duke Cosimo[14] heard of his death, he resolved that, since he had not been able to do the master honor in his lifetime, Michelangelo's body should be brought to Florence and his obsequies solemnized with all possible splendor. But Michelangelo's body had to be smuggled out of Rome in a sort of bale, such as merchants use, to prevent a tumult in the city.

A committee of four artists of the Academy of Painters and Sculptors of Florence was chosen to make all the arrangements. Agnolo Bronzino and Giorgio Vasari, painters, and the sculptors Benvenuto

[14]Cosimo de' Medici (1519-1574), Grand Duke of Tuscany (Florence and surrounding territory).

Cellini and Bartolommeo Ammanato formed the committee. First they decided to ask the duke if the funeral could be held in the church of San Lorenzo, where the greater part of Michelangelo's Florentine works were. Also, they requested that the distinguished Messer Benedetto Varchi pronounce the funeral oration. The duke most readily and graciously consented.

Leonardo Buonarroti directed the secret removal of his uncle's body from Rome and brought it to Florence, where it arrived on Saturday, March 11. The next day all the painters, sculptors, and architects assembled quietly, bearing only a pall of velvet rich with gold embroidery. This they placed over the coffin and the bier. At nightfall they gathered silently around the corpse. The oldest and most distinguished masters each took a torch, while the younger artists at the same moment raised the bier. Blessed was he who could get a shoulder under it! All desired the glory of having borne to earth the remains of the greatest man ever known to the arts.

25

Benvenuto Cellini

Autobiography

VASARI *wrote his* Lives of the
Artists *to praise the achievements of greater artists than he. He gives an impartial account of their careers. Benvenuto Cellini (1500–1571), on the other hand, writes a colorful account of his own life and deeds. It is a more vivid picture of the times than Vasari's and illustrates the daring, boastful, egoistic, individualistic aspects of the Renaissance.*

By his own account, Cellini was master of all arts and of all occasions. Early in life, in his native city of Florence, he was apprenticed, in the time-honored guild custom, to a goldsmith. After a series of troubles resulting from his too-vigorous participation in brawling, he went to Rome and established himself as an independent craftsman and artist, enjoying the patronage of rich merchants, nobles, and churchmen of high rank. There was no limit to Cellini's ambition nor, it seems, to his success. He enjoyed the favor of King Francis I, Pope Clement VII, and many of the famous and influential personages of his time. Forever asserting his individualism, having confidence in himself and his talent, and engaging in physical combat almost as often as in art, Cellini was one of the most memorable (though hardly most admirable) figures of the Renaissance.

His Autobiography, *in addition to revealing the self-assertive artist, gives a fascinating picture of the era and its personalities: the worldly papal court, which Cellini observes but does not judge; the rivalries of petty princes; the efforts of the nobles, merchants, and prelates to achieve splendor and dignity in their homes and palaces; and the importance of taste and connoisseurship in the life of the wealthy and cultured. How reliable these portrayals are can perhaps be judged by the comment of the English translator, J. A. Symonds, who observed that Cellini "was not deliberately untruthful." In the latter part of the*

*following selection, Cellini gives a dramatic account of the arduous molding and
casting of his statue of Perseus; considered Cellini's sculptural masterpiece, the
statue still stands today in Florence.*

———————

All men of whatsoever quality they be, who have done anything of
excellence, or which may properly resemble excellence, ought, if they
are persons of truth and honesty, to describe their life with their own
hand; but they ought not to attempt so fine an enterprise till they have
passed the age of forty. This duty occurs to my own mind, now that I
am travelling beyond the term of fifty-eight years, and am in Florence,
the city of my birth. Many untoward things can I remember, such as
happen to all who live upon our earth; and from those adversities I am
now more free than at any previous period of my career—nay, it seems
to me that I enjoy greater content of soul and health of body than ever I
did in bygone years. I can also bring to mind some pleasant goods and
some inestimable evils, which, when I turn my thoughts backward,
strike terror in me, and astonishment that I should have reached this age
of fifty-eight, wherein, thanks be to God, I am still travelling prosper-
ously forward.

• • •

Upon my arrival in Rome, I went to work in the shop of the
master-goldsmith Santi. He was dead; but a son of his carried on the
business. He did not work himself, but entrusted all his commissions to
a young man named Lucagnolo from Iesi, a country fellow, who while
yet a child had come into Santi's service. This man was short but well
proportioned, and was a more skilful craftsman than any one whom I
had met with up to that time; remarkable for facility and excellent in
design. He executed large plate only; that is to say, vases of the utmost
beauty, basins, and such pieces. Having put myself to work there, I
began to make some candelabra for the Bishop of Salamanca, a Spaniard. They were richly chased, so far as that sort of work admits. A
pupil of Raffaello da Urbino called Gian Francesco, and commonly
known as Il Fattore, was a painter of great ability; and being on terms of

AUTOBIOGRAPHY   Benvenuto Cellini, *The Life of Benvenuto Cellini*, trans. John Adding-
ton Symonds (New York: Brentano's, 1906), I, 71–72, 113–26; II, 253–69.

friendship with the Bishop, he introduced me to his favour, so that I obtained many commissions from that prelate, and earned considerable sums of money.

During that time I went to draw, sometimes in Michelangelo's chapel, and sometimes in the house of Agostino Chigi of Siena, which contained many incomparable paintings by the hand of that great master Raffaello. This I did on feast-days, because the house was then inhabited by Messer Gismondo, Agostino's brother. They plumed themselves exceedingly when they saw young men of my sort coming to study in their palaces. Gismondo's wife, noticing my frequent presence in that house—she was a lady as courteous as could be, and of surpassing beauty—came up to me one day, looked at my drawings, and asked me if I was a sculptor or a painter; to whom I said I was a goldsmith. She remarked that I drew too well for a goldsmith; and having made one of her waiting-maids bring a lily of the finest diamonds set in gold, she showed it to me, and bade me value it. I valued it at 800 crowns. Then she said that I had very nearly hit the mark, and asked me whether I felt capable of setting the stones really well. I said that I should much like to do so, and began before her eyes to make a little sketch for it, working all the better because of the pleasure I took in conversing with so lovely and agreeable a gentlewoman. When the sketch was finished, another Roman lady of great beauty joined us; she had been above, and now descending to the ground floor, asked Madonna Porzia what she was doing there. She answered with a smile: "I am amusing myself by watching this worthy young man at his drawing; he is as good as he is handsome." I had by this time acquired a trifle of assurance, mixed, however, with some honest bashfulness; so I blushed and said: "Such as I am, lady, I shall ever be most ready to serve you." The gentlewoman, also slightly blushing, said: "You know well that I want you to serve me"; and reaching me the lily, told me to take it away; and gave me besides twenty golden crowns which she had in her bag, and added: "Set me the jewel after the fashion you have sketched, and keep for me the old gold in which it is now set." On this the Roman lady observed: "If I were in that young man's body, I should go off without asking leave." Madonna Porzia replied that virtues rarely are at home with vices, and that if I did such a thing, I should strongly belie my good looks of an honest man. Then turning round, she took the Roman lady's hand, and with a pleasant smile said: "Farewell, Benvenuto." I stayed on a short while at the drawing I was making, which was a copy of a Jove by Raffaello. When I had finished it and left the house, I set myself to making a little model of wax, in order to show how the jewel would look when it was completed. This I took to Madonna Porzia, whom I found with the same Roman lady. Both of them were highly satisfied with my work, and treated me so kindly that, being somewhat emboldened, I promised the jewel should be twice as good as the model. Accordingly I set hand to it, and in twelve days I finished it in the form of a fleur-de-lys, as I have said above, ornamenting it with little masks, children, and animals, exquisitely enamelled, whereby the diamonds which formed the lily were more than doubled in effect.

While I was working at this piece, Lucagnolo, of whose ability I have before spoken, showed considerable discontent, telling me over and over again that I might acquire far more profit and honour by helping him to execute large plate, as I had done at first. I made him answer that, whenever I chose, I should always be capable of working at great silver pieces; but that things like that on which I was now engaged were not commissioned every day; and beside their bringing no less honour than large silver plate, there was also more profit to be made by them. He laughed me in the face, and said: "Wait and see, Benvenuto; for by the time that you have finished that work of yours, I will make haste to have finished this vase, which I took in hand when you did the jewel; and then experience shall teach you what profit I shall get from my vase, and what you will get from your ornament." I answered that I was very glad indeed to enter into such a competition with so good a craftsman as he was, because the end would show which of us was mistaken. Accordingly both the one and the other of us, with a scornful smile upon our lips, bent our heads in grim earnest to the work, which both were now desirous of accomplishing; so that after about ten days, each had finished his undertaking with great delicacy and artistic skill.

Lucagnolo's was a huge silver piece, used at the table of Pope Clement, into which he flung away bits of bone and the rind of divers fruits, while eating; an object of ostentation rather than necessity. The vase was adorned with two fine handles, together with many masks, both small and great, and masses of lovely foliage, in as exquisite a style of elegance as could be imagined; on seeing which I said it was the most beautiful vase that ever I set eyes on. Thinking he had convinced me, Lucagnolo replied: "Your work seems to me no less beautiful, but we shall soon perceive the difference between the two." So he took his vase and carried it to the Pope, who was very well pleased with it, and ordered at once that he should be paid at the ordinary rate of such large plate. Meanwhile I carried mine to Madonna Porzia, who looked at it with astonishment, and told me I had far surpassed my promise. Then she bade me ask for my reward whatever I liked; for it seemed to her my desert was so great that if I craved a castle she could hardly recompense me; but since that was not in her hands to bestow, she added laughing that I must beg what lay within her power. I answered that the greatest reward I could desire for my labour was to have satisfied her ladyship. Then, smiling in my turn, and bowing to her, I took my leave, saying I wanted no reward but that. She turned to the Roman lady and said: "You see that the qualities we discerned in him are companied by virtues, and not vices." They both expressed their admiration, and then Madonna Porzia continued: "Friend Benvenuto, have you never heard it said that when the poor give to the rich, the devil laughs?" I replied: "Quite true! and yet, in the midst of all his troubles, I should like this time to see him laugh"; and as I took my leave, she said that this time she had no will to bestow on him that favour.

When I came back to the shop, Lucagnolo had the money for his vase in a paper packet; and on my arrival he cried out: "Come and compare the price of your jewel with the price of my plate." I said that he must leave things as they were till the next day, because I hoped that even as my work in its kind was not less excellent than his, so I should be able to show him quite an equal price for it.

On the day following, Madonna Porzia sent a majordomo of hers to my shop, who called me out, and putting into my hands a paper packet full of money from his lady, told me that she did not choose the devil should have his whole laugh out: by which she hinted that the money sent me was not the entire payment merited by my industry, and other messages were added worthy of so courteous a lady. Lucagnolo, who was burning to compare his packet with mine, burst into the shop; then in the presence of twelve journeymen and some neighbours, eager to behold the result of this competition, he seized his packet, scornfully exclaiming "Ou ou!" three or four times, while he poured his money on the counter with a great noise. They were twenty-five crowns in giulios; and he fancied that mine would be four or five crowns *di moneta*.[1] I for my part, stunned and stifled by his cries, and by the looks and smiles of the bystanders, first peeped into my packet; then, after seeing that it contained nothing but gold, I retired to one end of the

[1]Silver coins. Cellini's money, being gold, was worth far more than Lucagnolo's silver coins.

counter, and, keeping my eyes lowered and making no noise at all, I lifted it with both hands suddenly above my head, and emptied it like a mill hopper. My coin was twice as much as his; which caused the onlookers, who had fixed their eyes on me with some derision, to turn round suddenly to him and say: "Lucagnolo, Benvenuto's pieces, being all of gold and twice as many as yours, make a far finer effect." I thought for certain that, what with jealousy and what with shame, Lucagnolo would have fallen dead upon the spot; and though he took the third part of my gain, since I was a journeyman (for such is the custom of the trade, two-thirds fall to the workman and one-third to the masters of the shop), yet inconsiderate envy had more power in him than avarice: it ought to have worked quite the other way, he being a peasant's son from Iesi. He cursed his art and those who taught it him, vowing that thenceforth he would never work at large plate, but give his whole attention to those whoreson gewgaws, since they were so well paid. Equally enraged on my side, I answered that every bird sang its own note; that he talked after the fashion of the hovels he came from; but that I dared swear that I should succeed with ease in making his lubberly lumber, while he would never be successful in my whoreson gewgaws. Thus I flung off in a passion, telling him that I would soon show him that I spoke truth. The bystanders openly declared against him, holding him for a lout, as indeed he was, and me for a man, as I had proved myself.

It happened at that time that one Giangiacomo of Cesena, a musician in the Pope's band, and a very excellent performer, sent word through Lorenzo, the trumpeter of Lucca, who is now in our Duke's service, to inquire whether I was inclined to help them at the Pope's Ferragosto,[2] playing soprano with my cornet in some motets of great beauty selected by them for that occasion. Although I had the greatest desire to finish the vase I had begun [for the Bishop of Salamanca], yet, since music has a wondrous charm of its own, and also because I wished to please my old father, I consented to join them. During eight days before the festival we practised two hours a day together; then on the first of August we went to the Belvedere, and while Pope Clement was at table, we played those carefully studied motets so well that his Holiness protested he had never heard music more sweetly executed or with better harmony of parts. He sent for Giangiacomo, and asked him where and how he had procured so excellent a cornet for soprano, and

[2]Holiday occurring on the first of August.

inquired particularly who I was. Giangiacomo told him my name in full. Whereupon the Pope said: "So, then, he is the son of Maestro Giovanni?" On being assured I was, the Pope expressed his wish to have me in his service with the other bandsmen. Giangiacomo replied: "Most blessed Father, I cannot pretend for certain that you will get him, for his profession, to which he devotes himself assiduously, is that of a goldsmith, and he works in it miraculously well, and earns by it far more than he could do by playing." To this the Pope added: "I am the better inclined to him now that I find him possessor of a talent more than I expected. See that he obtains the same salary as the rest of you; and tell him from me to join my service, and that I will find work enough by the day for him to do in his other trade." Then stretching out his hand, he gave him a hundred golden crowns of the Camera[3] in a handkerchief, and said: "Divide these so that he may take his share."

When Giangiacomo left the Pope, he came to us, and related in detail all that the Pope had said; and after dividing the money between the eight of us, and giving me my share, he said to me: "Now I am going to have you inscribed among our company." I replied: "Let the day pass; to-morrow I will give my answer." When I left them, I went meditating whether I ought to accept the invitation, inasmuch as I could not but suffer if I abandoned the noble studies of my art. The following night my father appeared to me in a dream, and begged me with tears of tenderest affection, for God's love and his, to enter upon this engagement. Methought I answered that nothing would induce me to do so. In an instant he assumed so horrible an aspect as to frighten me out of my wits, and cried: "If you do not, you will have a father's curse; but if you do, may you be ever blessed by me!" When I woke, I ran, for very fright, to have myself inscribed. Then I wrote to my old father, telling him the news, which so affected him with extreme joy that a sudden fit of illness took him, and well-nigh brought him to death's door. In his answer to my letter, he told me that he too had dreamed nearly the same as I had.

Knowing now that I had gratified my father's honest wish, I began to think that everything would prosper with me to a glorious and honourable end. Accordingly, I set myself with indefatigable industry to the completion of the vase I had begun for Salamanca. That prelate was a very extraordinary man, extremely rich, but difficult to please.

[3]Coins of the Camera, that is, the treasury.

He sent daily to learn what I was doing; and when his messenger did not find me at home, he broke into fury, saying that he would take the work out of my hands and give it to others to finish. This came of my slavery to that accursed music. Still I laboured diligently night and day, until, when I had brought my work to a point when it could be exhibited, I submitted it to the inspection of the Bishop. This so increased his desire to see it finished, that I was sorry I had shown it. At the end of three months I had it ready, with little animals and foliage and masks, as beautiful as one could hope to see. No sooner was it done than I sent it by the hand of my workman, Paulino, to show that able artist Lucagnolo, of whom I have spoken above. Paulino, with the grace and beauty which belonged to him, spoke as follows: "Messer Lucagnolo, Benvenuto bids me say that he has sent to show you his promises and your lumber, expecting in return to see from you his gew-gaws." This message given, Lucagnolo took up the vase, and carefully examined it; then he said to Paulino: "Fair boy, tell your master that he is a great and able artist, and that I beg him to be willing to have me for a friend, and not to engage in aught else." The mission of that virtuous and marvellous lad caused me the greatest joy; and then the vase was carried to Salamanca, who ordered it to be valued. Lucagnolo took part in the valuation, estimating and praising it far above my own opinion. Salamanca, lifting up the vase, cried like a true Spaniard: "I swear by God that I will take as long in paying him as he has lagged in making it." When I heard this, I was exceedingly put out, and fell to cursing all Spain and every one who wished well to it.

• • •

Having succeeded so well with the cast of the Medusa,[4] I had great hope of bringing my Perseus through; for I had laid the wax on, and felt confident that it would come out in bronze as perfectly as the Medusa. The waxen model produced so fine an effect, that when the Duke[5] saw it and was struck with its beauty—whether somebody had persuaded him it could not be carried out with the same finish in metal, or whether he thought so for himself—he came to visit me more frequently than usual, and on one occasion said: "Benvenuto, this figure cannot succeed in bronze; the laws of art do not admit of it." These words of his

---

[4]One of the Gorgons, creatures whose look turned men into stone. Perseus avoided this fate by looking at her reflection in a polished shield and was thus able to approach and kill her.

[5]Cosimo de' Medici, grand duke of Tuscany. He commissioned the statue of Perseus holding aloft the head of the Medusa to symbolize victory over tyranny.

Excellency stung me so sharply that I answered: "My lord, I know how very little confidence you have in me; and I believe the reason of this is that your most illustrious Excellency lends too ready an ear to my calumniators, or else indeed that you do not understand my art." He hardly let me close the sentence when he broke in: "I profess myself a connoisseur, and understand it very well indeed." I replied: "Yes, like a prince, not like an artist; for if your Excellency understood my trade as well as you imagine, you would trust me on the proofs I have already given. These are, first, the colossal bronze bust of your Excellency, which is now in Elba; secondly, the restoration of the Ganymede[6] in marble, which offered so many difficulties and cost me so much trouble, that I would rather have made the whole statue new from the beginning; thirdly, the Medusa, cast by me in bronze, here now before your Excellency's eyes, the execution of which was a greater triumph of strength and skill than any of my predecessors in this fiendish art have yet achieved. Look you, my lord! I constructed that furnace anew on principles quite different from those of other founders; in addition to many technical improvements and ingenious devices, I supplied it with two issues for the metal, because this difficult and twisted figure could not otherwise have come out perfect. It is only owing to my intelligent insight into means and appliances that the statue turned out as it did; a triumph judged impossible by all the practitioners of this art. I should like you furthermore to be aware, my lord, for certain, that the sole reason why I succeeded with all those great and arduous works in France under his most admirable Majesty King Francis, was the high courage which that good monarch put into my heart by the liberal allowances he made me, and the multitude of workpeople he left at my disposal. I could have as many as I asked for, and employed at times above forty, all chosen by myself. These were the causes of my having there produced so many masterpieces in so short a space of time. Now then, my lord, put trust in me; supply me with the aid I need, I am confident of being able to complete a work which will delight your soul. But if your Excellency goes on disheartening me, and does not advance me the assistance which is absolutely required, neither I nor any man alive upon this earth can hope to achieve the slightest thing of value."

It was as much as the Duke could do to stand by and listen to my pleadings. He kept turning first this way and then that; while I, in

---

[6]An antique statue of Ganymede, cup-bearer to Zeus, that had been given to the duke.

despair, poor wretched I, was calling up remembrance of the noble state I held in France, to the great sorrow of my soul. All at once he cried: "Come, tell me, Benvenuto, how is it possible that yonder splendid head of Medusa, so high up there in the grasp of Perseus, should ever come out perfect?" I replied upon the instant: "Look you now, my lord! If your Excellency possessed that knowledge of the craft which you affirm you have, you would not fear one moment for the splendid head you speak of. There is good reason, on the other hand, to feel uneasy about this right foot, so far below and at a distance from the rest." When he heard these words, the Duke turned, half in anger, to some gentlemen in waiting, and exclaimed: "I verily believe that this Benvenuto prides himself on contradicting everything one says." Then he faced round to me with a touch of mockery, upon which his attendants did the like, and began to speak as follows: "I will listen patiently to any argument you can possibly produce in explanation of your statement, which may convince me of its probability." I said in answer: "I will adduce so sound an argument that your Excellency shall perceive the full force of it." So I began: "You must know, my lord, that the nature of fire is to ascend, and therefore I promise you that Medusa's head will come out famously; but since it is not in the nature of fire to descend, and I must force it downwards six cubits by artificial means, I assure your Excellency upon this most convincing ground of proof that the foot cannot possibly come out. It will, however, be quite easy for me to restore it." "Why, then," said the Duke, "did you not devise it so that the foot should come out as well as you affirm the head will?" I answered: "I must have made a much larger furnace, with a conduit as thick as my leg; and so I might have forced the molten metal by its own weight to descend so far. Now, my pipe, which runs six cubits to the statue's foot, as I have said, is not thicker than two fingers. However, it was not worth the trouble and expense to make a larger; for I shall easily be able to mend what is lacking. But when my mould is more than half full, as I expect, from this middle point upwards, the fire ascending by its natural property, then the heads of Perseus and Medusa will come out admirably; you may be quite sure of it." After I had thus expounded these convincing arguments, together with many more of the same kind, which it would be tedious to set down here, the Duke shook his head and departed without further ceremony.

Abandoned thus to my own resources, I took new courage, and banished the sad thoughts which kept recurring to my mind, making me often weep bitter tears of repentance for having left France; for though I did so only to revisit Florence, my sweet birthplace, in order that I might charitably succour my six nieces, this good action, as I well perceived, had been the beginning of my great misfortune. Nevertheless, I felt convinced that when my Perseus was accomplished, all these trials would be turned to high felicity and glorious well-being.

Accordingly I strengthened my heart, and with all the forces of my body and my purse, employing what little money still remained to me, I set to work. First I provided myself with several loads of pinewood from the forests of Serristori, in the neighbourhood of Montelupo. While these were on their way, I clothed my Perseus with the clay which I had prepared many months beforehand, in order that it might be duly seasoned. After making its clay tunic (for that is the term used in this art) and properly arming it and fencing it with iron girders, I began to draw the wax out by means of a slow fire. This melted and issued through numerous air-vents I had made; for the more there are of these, the better will the mould fill. When I had finished drawing off the wax, I constructed a funnel-shaped furnace all round the model of my Perseus. It was built of bricks, so interlaced, the one above the other, that numerous apertures were left for the fire to exhale at. Then I began to lay on wood by degrees, and kept it burning two whole days and nights. At length, when all the wax was gone, and the mould was well baked, I set to work at digging the pit in which to sink it. This I performed with scrupulous regard to all the rules of art. When I had finished that part of my work, I raised the mould by windlasses and stout ropes to a perpendicular position, and suspending it with the greatest care one cubit above the level of the furnace, so that it hung exactly above the middle of the pit, I next lowered it gently down into the very bottom of the furnace, and had it firmly placed with every possible precaution for its safety. When this delicate operation was accomplished, I began to bank it up with the earth I had excavated; and, ever as the earth grew higher, I introduced its proper air-vents, which were little tubes of earthenware, such as folk use for drains and suchlike purposes. At length, I felt sure that it was admirably fixed, and that the filling-in of the pit and the placing of the air-vents had been properly performed. I also could see that my workpeople understood my method, which differed very considerably from that of all the other masters in the trade. Feeling confident, then, that I could rely upon them, I next turned to my furnace, which I had filled with numerous pigs of copper and other bronze stuff. The pieces were piled according to the laws of art, that is to say, so resting one upon the other that the flames could play freely through them, in order that the metal might heat and liquefy the sooner. At last I called out heartily to set the furnace going. The logs of pine were heaped in, and, what with the unctuous resin of the wood and the good draught I had given, my furnace worked so well that I was obliged to rush from side to side to keep it going. The labour was more than I could stand; yet I forced myself to strain every nerve and muscle. To increase my anxieties, the workshop took fire, and we were afraid lest the roof should fall upon our heads; while, from the garden, such a storm of wind and rain kept blowing in, that it perceptibly cooled the furnace.

Battling thus with all these untoward circumstances for several hours, and exerting myself beyond even the measure of my powerful constitution, I could at last bear up no longer, and a sudden fever, of the utmost possible intensity, attacked me. I felt absolutely obliged to go and fling myself upon my bed. Sorely against my will having to drag myself away from the spot, I turned to my assistants, about ten or more in all, what with master-founders, hand-workers, country-fellows, and my own special journeymen, among whom was Bernardino Man-nellini of Mugello, my apprentice through several years. To him in particular I spoke: "Look, my dear Bernardino, that you observe the rules which I have taught you; do your best with all despatch, for the metal will soon be fused. You cannot go wrong; these honest men will get the channels ready; you will easily be able to drive back the two plugs with this pair of iron crooks; and I am sure that my mould will fill miraculously. I feel more ill than I ever did in all my life, and verily believe that it will kill me before a few hours are over." Thus, with despair at heart, I left them, and betook myself to bed.

No sooner had I got to bed, than I ordered my serving-maids to carry food and wine for all the men into the workshop; at the same time I cried: "I shall not be alive to-morrow." They tried to encourage me, arguing that my illness would pass over, since it came from excessive fatigue. In this way I spent two hours battling with the fever, which steadily increased, and calling out continually: "I feel that I am dying." My housekeeper, who was named Mona Fiore da Castel del Rio, a very notable manager and no less warm-hearted, kept chiding me for my discouragement; but, on the other hand, she paid me every kind attention which was possible. However, the sight of my physical pain and moral dejection so affected her, that, in spite of that brave heart of hers, she could not refrain from shedding tears; and yet, so far as she was able, she took good care I should not see them. While I was thus terribly afflicted, I beheld the figure of a man enter my chamber, twisted in his body into the form of a capital S. He raised a lamentable, doleful voice, like one who announces their last hour to men condemned to die upon the scaffold, and spoke these words: "O Benvenuto! your statue is spoiled, and there is no hope whatever of saving it." No sooner had I heard the shriek of that wretch than I gave a howl which might have been heard from the sphere of flame. Jumping from my bed, I seized my clothes and began to dress. The maids, and my lad, and every one who came around to help me, got kicks or blows of the fist, while I kept crying out in lamentation: "Ah! traitors! enviers! This is an act of treason, done by malice prepense! But I swear by God that I will sift it to the bottom, and before I die will leave such witness to the world of what I can do as shall make a score of mortals marvel."

When I had got my clothes on, I strode with soul bent on mischief toward the workshop; there I beheld the men, whom I had left erewhile in such high spirits, standing stupefied and downcast. I began at once and spoke: "Up with you! Attend to me! Since you have not been able or willing to obey the directions I gave you, obey me now that I am with you to conduct my work in person. Let no one contradict me, for in cases like this we need the aid of hand and hearing, not of advice." When I had uttered these words, a certain Maestro Alessandro Lastricati broke silence and said: "Look you, Benvenuto, you are going to attempt an enterprise which the laws of art do not sanction, and which cannot succeed." I turned upon him with such fury and so full of mischief that he and all the rest of them exclaimed with one voice: "On then! Give orders! We will obey your least commands, so long as life is left in us." I believe they spoke thus feelingly because they thought I must fall shortly dead upon the ground. I went immediately to inspect the furnace, and found that the metal was all curdled; an accident which we express by "being caked." I told two of the hands to cross the road, and fetch from the house of the butcher Capretta a load of young oak-wood, which had lain dry for above a year; this wood had been previously offered me by Madame Ginevra, wife of the said Capretta. So soon as the first armfuls arrived, I began to fill the grate beneath the furnace. Now oak-wood of that kind heats more powerfully than any other sort of tree; and for this reason, where a slow fire is wanted, as in the case of gun-foundry, alder or pine is preferred. Accordingly, when the logs took fire, oh! how the cake began to stir beneath that awful heat, to glow and sparkle in a blaze! At the same time I kept stirring up the channels and sent men upon the roof to stop the conflagration, which had gathered force from the increased combustion in the furnace; also I caused boards, carpets, and other hangings to be set up against the garden, in order to protect us from the violence of the rain.

When I had thus provided against these several disasters, I roared out first to one man and then to another: "Bring this thing here! Take that thing there!" At this crisis, when the whole gang saw the cake was on the point of melting, they did my bidding, each fellow working with the strength of three. I then ordered half a pig of pewter to be brought, which weighed about sixty pounds, and flung it into the middle of the cake inside the furnace. By this means, and by piling on wood and stirring now with pokers and now with iron rods, the curdled mass rapidly began to liquefy. Then, knowing I had brought the dead to life again, against the firm opinion of those ignoramuses, I felt such vigour fill my veins, that all those pains of fever, all those fears of death, were quite forgotten.

All of a sudden an explosion took place, attended by a tremendous flash of flame, as though a thunderbolt had formed and been discharged amongst us. Unwonted and appalling terror astonied every one, and me more even than the rest. When the din was over and the dazzling light extinguished, we began to look each other in the face. Then I discovered that the cap of the furnace had blown up, and the bronze was bubbling over from its source beneath. So I had the mouths of my mould immediately opened, and at the same time drove in the two plugs which kept back the molten metal. But I noticed that it did not flow as rapidly as usual, the reason being probably that the fierce heat of the fire we kindled had consumed its base alloy. Accordingly I sent for all my pewter platters, porringers, and dishes, to the number of some two hundred pieces, and had a portion of them cast, one by one, into the channels, the rest into the furnace. This expedient succeeded, and every one could now perceive that my bronze was in most perfect liquefaction, and my mould was filling; whereupon they with all heartiness and happy cheer assisted and obeyed my bidding, while I, now here, now there, gave orders, helped with my own hands, and cried aloud: "O God! Thou that by Thy immeasurable power didst rise from the dead, and in Thy glory didst ascend to heaven!" . . . even thus in a moment my mould was filled; and seeing my work finished, I fell upon my knees, and with all my heart gave thanks to God.

After all was over, I turned to a plate of salad on a bench there, and ate with hearty appetite, and drank together with the whole crew. Afterwards I retired to bed, healthy and happy, for it was now two hours before morning, and slept as sweetly as though I had never felt a touch of illness. My good housekeeper, without my giving any orders, had prepared a fat capon for my repast. So that, when I rose, about the hour for breaking fast, she presented herself with a smiling countenance, and said: "Oh! is that the man who felt that he was dying? Upon my word, I think the blows and kicks you dealt us last night, when you were so enraged, and had that demon in your body, as it seemed, must have frightened away your mortal fever! The fever feared that it might catch it too, as we did!" All my poor household, relieved in like measure from anxiety and overwhelming labour, went at once to buy earthen vessels in order to replace the pewter I had cast away. Then we dined together joyously; nay, I cannot remember a day in my whole life when I dined with greater gladness or a better appetite.

After our meal I received visits from the several men who had assisted me. They exchanged congratulations, and thanked God for our success, saying they had learned and seen things done which other masters judged impossible. I too grew somewhat glorious; and deeming I had shown myself a man of talent, indulged in a boastful humour. So I thrust my hand into my purse, and paid them all to their full satisfaction.

That evil fellow, my mortal foe, Messer Pier Francesco Ricci, majordomo of the Duke, took great pains to find out how the affair had gone. In answer to his questions, the two men whom I suspected of having caked my metal for me, said I was no man, but of a certainty some powerful devil, since I had accomplished what no craft of the art could do; indeed they did not believe a mere ordinary fiend could work such miracles as I in other ways had shown. They exaggerated the whole affair so much, possibly in order to excuse their own part in it, that the majordomo wrote an account to the Duke, who was then in Pisa, far more marvellous and full of thrilling incidents than what they had narrated.

After I had let my statue cool for two whole days, I began to uncover it by slow degrees. The first thing I found was that the head of Medusa had come out most admirably, thanks to the air-vents; for, as I had told the Duke, it is the nature of fire to ascend. Upon advancing farther, I discovered that the other head, that, namely, of Perseus, had succeeded no less admirably; and this astonished me far more, because it is at a considerably lower level than that of the Medusa. Now the mouths of the mould were placed above the head of Perseus and behind his shoulders; and I found that all the bronze my furnace contained had been exhausted in the head of this figure. It was a miracle to observe that not one fragment remained in the orifice of the channel, and that nothing was wanting to the statue. In my great astonishment I seemed to see in this the hand of God arranging and controlling all.

I went on uncovering the statue with success, and ascertained that everything had come out in perfect order, until I reached the foot of the right leg on which the statue rests. There the heel itself was formed, and going farther, I found the foot apparently complete. This gave me great joy on the one side, but was half unwelcome to me on the other, merely because I had told the Duke that it could not come out. However, when I reached the end, it appeared that the toes and a little piece above them were unfinished, so that about half the foot was wanting. Although I knew that this would add a trifle to my labour, I was very well pleased, because I could now prove to the Duke how well I understood my business. It is true that far more of the foot than I expected had been perfectly formed; the reason of this was that, from causes I have recently described, the bronze was hotter than our rules of art prescribe; also that I had been obliged to supplement the alloy with my pewter cups and platters, which no one else, I think, had ever done before.

Having now ascertained how successfully my work had been accomplished, I lost no time in hurrying to Pisa, where I found the Duke. He gave me a most gracious reception, as did also the Duchess; and although the majordomo had informed them of the whole proceedings, their Excellencies deemed my performance far more stupendous and astonishing when they heard the tale from my own mouth. When I arrived at the foot of Perseus, and said it had not come out perfect, just as I previously warned his Excellency, I saw an expression of wonder pass over his face, while he related to the Duchess how I had predicted this beforehand. Observing the prince to be so well disposed towards me, I begged leave from the Duke to go to Rome. He granted it in most obliging terms, and bade me return as soon as possible to complete his Perseus; giving me letters of recommendation meanwhile to his ambassador, Averardo Serristori. We were then in the first years of Pope Giulio de Monti.

26
Montaigne

Essays: In Defense of
Raymond Sebond

MICHEL Eyquem, *Seigneur de
Montaigne (1533–1592), was another of the multi-talented individuals who
characterized the Renaissance. Having frequented the court of the French kings
and served as counselor in the Bordeaux parlement, he "retired" at age
thirty-eight to his castle of Montaigne and devoted most of the rest of his life to
study and writing. Except for two terms as mayor of Bordeaux (1581–1585),
Montaigne's chief occupation during the last years of his life was the composition
of his* Essays.

The Essays *reflect a discursive examination of what Montaigne had learned
from books, acquaintances, and his own experience. They reveal a cool,
rational intelligence, and show that he was always patient and humorously
observant. "Others fashion man"; he said, "I repeat him."*

*Not swayed by the new religious doctrines of his time, nor concerned with the
defense of the old, Montaigne remarked, "The ancientest evil, if it be known to
us, bears always lighter on us than a new one of which we know but little." Even
new scientific discoveries seemed to him only possible contributors to further
confusion. Nevertheless, Montaigne was sure that there were such qualities as
greatness and magnanimity, which he saw demonstrated occasionally by people
of his own time (more often by the common people than by the rulers) as well as
by the ancients. His essays deal with such diverse subjects as the education of
children and the true nature of Roman grandeur.*

*Montaigne's epicureanism links him with the life of contented reason that
was the goal of one of his favorite authors, Lucretius, whom he quotes extensively. The greatest influence of Montaigne's essays was upon intellectuals and
writers. In England the translation of his essays (by John Florio in 1603)
became standard reading for anyone with pretensions to wit and learning. The
following selection is from* In Defense of Raymond Sebond—*Sebond was a*

professor of medicine, philosophy, and theology at the University of Toulouse in the 1430s—a long essay in which Montaigne presents his own skeptical views on religious controversy and on human aspirations to power, virtue, and wisdom.

Consider if it is not by our hands that we shape religion, drawing as from wax so many contrary figures from a rule so straight and so firm. When has that been more evident than in France nowadays? Those who have seized it on the left hand, those who have seized it on the right, those who use black to portray it and those who use white, employ religion in such a similar way in their violent and ambitious enterprises, behave according to a pattern so identical in excess and injustice, that they render doubtful and hard to believe the contradictory opinions which they claim to hold concerning the thing on which depend the conduct and principle of our life. Can one see come out of the same school and the same doctrine ways of acting more uniform, more completely identical?

• • •

Let us confess the truth: were one to sift out of the army, even the average legitimate army, those who participate in it solely through the zeal of a religious devotion, and also those who are concerned only with the protection of the laws of their country or the service of the prince, one would not be able to form with them a complete company of soldiers. Whence comes it that there are so few who have maintained a uniform will and effort in our public disturbances and that we see them sometimes advance at a walk, sometimes gallop at top speed, and the same men sometimes harm our cause by their violence and harshness, sometimes by their lack of zeal, their softness, and their slowness, unless it be that they are moved by personal and casual considerations according to the varying nature of which they bestir themselves?

ESSAYS: IN DEFENSE OF RAYMOND SEBOND   From Montaigne, *In Defense of Raymond Sebond,* translated by A. H. Beattie. Copyright © 1959 by the Frederick Ungar Publishing Co. Reprinted by permission of The Ungar Publishing Company. [Pp. 7–10, 17–22, 34–35, 37–41, 60–65, 85–87.]

This I see clearly, that we readily give to religion only the services which flatter our passions. There is no hostility so fine as Christian hostility. Our zeal does marvels when it supports our inclination toward hatred, cruelty, ambition, avarice, slander, rebellion. On the contrary, toward kindness, gentleness, temperance, unless by a miracle some rare quirk of character drives it in that direction, it neither runs nor flies.

Our religion is made to root out vices; we use it to cover them, feed them, encourage them.

One must not offer God straw instead of grain (as the popular saying goes). If we believed in him, I do not say through faith, but with a simple belief, indeed (and I say it to our great confusion) if we believed in him and knew him as we might some other matter, as we might know one of our companions, we should love him above all other things for the infinite goodness and beauty which shine in him; at least he would occupy in our affection the same rank as wealth, pleasures, glory, and our friends.

The best of us does not fear to offend him as he fears offending his neighbor, his relative, his master. Is there a mind so simple that, having on the one side the object of one of our vicious pleasures, and on the other, equally clearly known and understood, the state of an immortal glory, it would give the latter in exchange for the former? And yet we often renounce that glory out of pure disdain: for what desire attracts us to blasphemy unless by chance the very desire to offend?

CONVICTIONS ARE WEAK
IF EXTERNAL EVENTS ALTER THEM

The philosopher Antisthenes,[1] as he was being initiated into the Orphic mysteries, was told by a priest that those who devoted themselves to that religion were destined to receive after their death eternal and perfect gifts. "Why, then, don't you die yourself?" he asked the priest. Diogenes, more abruptly according to his manner, and on a somewhat different subject, said to the priest who was exhorting him similarly to join his order so that he might attain the blessings of the

---

[1]Practically all of the names and quoted passages in Montaigne's essay are either from Greek and Roman writers and philosophers or from Scripture. Montaigne makes his references readily understandable by providing an adequate context or clarifying quotation, thus limiting the need for extensive footnotes here.

next world: "Don't you want me to believe that Agesilaus and Epaminondas, such great men, will be wretched, and that you, who are only a
fool, will be blessed because you are a priest?"

If we received with the same authority as a philosophical discourse
these great promises of eternal blessedness, we should no longer view
death with the horror in which we now hold it.

> No longer would the dying man lament
> His dissolution, but he would rejoice
> To leave the body as the snake is freed
> Of its worn skin, or as the stag grown old
> Lets fall at last its horns now overlong.
>
> [Lucretius III, 613]

I wish to be dissolved, we should say, and to be with Jesus Christ. The
force of Plato's teaching concerning the immortality of the soul encouraged indeed some of his disciples to seek death in order to enjoy more
promptly the hopes which he gave them.

All that is a very obvious sign that we receive our religion only in our
way, and by our hands, and not otherwise than other religions are
received. We happened to be in the region where it was observed; or we
esteem its antiquity or the authority of the men who have taught it; or
we fear the threats which it directs against unbelievers; or we are drawn
by its promises. Those considerations must be employed for our belief,
but as secondary supports: they are based on human ties. A different
region, other witnesses, similar promises and threats, might impress
upon us in the same way a contrary belief. We are Christians for the
same reason that we are either Perigordians[2] or Germans. . . .

Let us then consider for the moment man alone, without outside
help, armed only with his own weapons, and stripped of grace and
divine understanding, which are all his honor, his strength, and the
foundation of his being. Let us see what kind of figure he cuts in such a
fine array. Let him make me understand by the effort of his reason upon
what foundations he has built those great advantages which he thinks
he has over all other creatures. What has convinced him that this
admirable motion of the vault of heaven, the eternal light of those
torches revolving so proudly above his head, the awe-inspiring movements of that infinite sea, were established and have continued for so
many centuries for his convenience and in order to serve him? Is it
possible to imagine anything so ridiculous as that wretched and puny

---

[2]Natives of Perigord, a region of southwestern France.

creature, who is not even master of himself, exposed to offenses from all things, and who yet proclaims himself master and emperor of the universe, concerning which it is not within his power to know the slightest part, let alone govern? And this privilege that he attributes to himself of being alone in this great creation in having the capacity to recognize its beauty and understand its structure, in being able to give thanks to the architect and to note the balance of income and outlay of the world—who placed the seal upon this privilege accorded him? Let him show us the patent of this fine and great prerogative.

Was it granted in favor of the wise only? It concerns few people, then. Are the foolish and wicked worthy of such an extraordinary favor, and they who are the worst part of creation, should they be given a privileged position above all the rest?

Shall we believe on this score him who says: "For whom then shall we say that the world was made? Doubtless for animate beings who have the use of reason. These are gods and men, to whom surely nothing is superior." [Cicero, *De natura deorum* II, 53] It is impossible ever to ridicule sufficiently the impudence of thus associating gods and men.

But, puny creature that he is, what has man in himself worthy of such a privileged position? Considering the incorruptible life of the heavenly bodies, their beauty, their greatness, their movement continued according to so precise a rule:

> When we lift up our eyes to the celestial vaults
> Of this great universe, and toward the heaven set
> With shining stars, and when we call to mind the course
> Of moon and sun;
>
> > [Lucretius V, 1205]

considering, too, the domination and power which those bodies have not only over our lives and the conditions of our fortune,

> For he has made the deeds and lives of men
> Dependent on the stars,
>
> > [Manilius III, 58]

but over our very inclinations, our reasonings, our wills which they govern, drive and stir at the mercy of their influences, as our reason teaches us and reveals,

> For reason recognizes that those stars we see
> So distant from us, govern men by hidden laws;

> That movements of the universe entire are ruled
> By periodic causes, and the turns of fate
> Revealed by certain signs;
>
> [Manilius I, 60]

seeing that not a single man, not a king, escapes their influence, but that monarchies, empires, and this whole world here below move in accord with the slightest tremor of the celestial movements,

> How great are the effects the slightest motion brings:
> So mighty is that power which governs even kings!
>
> [Manilius I, 55 and IV, 93]

if our virtue, our vices, our competence and learning, and this very conclusion which we draw concerning the power of the stars, and this comparison of them with ourselves, if all that comes, as our reason judges, by their means and their favor,

> One, mad with love,
> Is doomed to cross the sea and Troy town overthrow;
> Another's fated to draw up a nation's laws;
> Here children slay their parents, and parents slay their sons;
> And armed against his brother, one fights in cruel affray.
> This war's not of our doing; fate wills these agitations,
> And makes them hurt themselves, slashing each other's limbs.
> And fate wills too that I should thus discourse of fate;
>
> [Manilius IV, 79 and 118]

if we owe to heaven's distribution this share of reason which we possess, how can it make us heaven's equal? How can its essence and its conditions be subject to our learning? Everything which we see in those bodies awes us. "What was the effort, what were the instruments, the levers, the machines, the workers who erected so vast an edifice?" [Cicero, *De natura deorum* I, 8] Why do we consider them without soul, and life, and reason? Have we recognized in them some heavy and unfeeling stupidity, we whose only relationship to them is one of obedience? Shall we say that we have seen in no other creature but man the employment of a reasoning soul? What then! Have we seen anything similar to the sun? Must we say that it does not exist because we have never seen anything like it? And that its movements do not exist because they are without parallel? If what we have not observed does not exist, our learning is wonderfully restricted: "How narrow are the limits of our mind!" [Cicero, *De natura deorum* I, 31] Is it not a dream of human vanity to make of the moon a celestial earth, to imagine on it mountains and valleys as Anaxagoras did, to set up there human habitations and abodes, and to establish there colonies for our convenience as Plato and Plutarch do, and of our earth to make a light-giving and luminous star? "Among other infirmities of human nature is this blindness of the mind which not only forces it to err, but which makes it love its errors." [Seneca, *De ira* II, 10] "The corruptible body weighs down the soul, and its earthly covering oppresses it even in the exercise of thought." [St. Augustine, *City of God* XII, 15, citing *Book of Wisdom*]

MAN'S SUPERIORITY OVER ANIMALS A DELUSION BASED ON PRIDE

Presumption is our natural and original malady. The most calamitous and fragile of all creatures is man, and at the same time the proudest. He sees and feels himself placed here in the mire and dung of the world, attached and fixed in the worst, most lifeless, and most corrupt part of the universe, on the meanest floor of the house and the farthest removed from the vault of heaven, with animals of the worst condition of the three; and he goes installing himself in his imagination above the circle of the moon and bringing the heavens beneath his feet. It is by the vanity of this same imagination that he makes himself God's equal, that he ascribes to himself divine attributes, that he winnows himself and separates himself from the mass of other creatures, determines the share allowed the animals, his colleagues and companions, and distributes to them such elements of faculties and powers as seem good to him. How does he know, by the effort of his intelligence, what inwardly and secretly moves animals? By what comparison of them with ourselves does he deduce the stupidity which he attributes to them?

When I play with my cat, who knows whether she is not making me her pastime more than I make her mine? Plato, in depicting the golden age under Saturn,[3] counts among the principal advantages of the man of those days the ability he had to communicate with the animals, for questioning them and learning from them, he knew the real qualities of each; in that way he acquired a quite perfect understanding and wisdom, and in consequence conducted his life far more happily than we can do. Do we need a better proof to judge human presumption

[3] In ancient mythology Saturn was the god of agriculture. His reign was called a golden age of peace, plenty, and contentment.

concerning animals? That great author gave it as his opinion that so far as the corporal form which nature gave them is concerned, she had regard, in the main, only for the prognostications which one was accustomed to draw from them in his day.

• • •

But, to return to my subject, we have as part of our lot inconstancy, irresolution, incertitude, mourning, superstition, concern about things to come (even after our life), ambition, avarice, jealousy, envy, appetites which are lawless, frenzied, and uncontrollable, war, falsehood, disloyalty, slander, and curiosity. Certainly we have paid strangely and dearly for that fine reason in which we glory, and that capacity to judge and know, if we have bought them at the price of this infinite number of passions to which we are a constant prey. That is, unless it still pleases us to insist, as Socrates does indeed, upon that notable prerogative over the other animals which we enjoy in that nature, whereas she has prescribed for them certain seasons and limits to sexual pleasure, has given us a free rein at all times and under all circumstances.

> "As wine is rarely good for invalids and is also most often harmful to them, so it is better not to give them any at all than to expose them to a manifest harm in the hope of a problematical advantage; so, perhaps, it would be better for mankind had nature refused us that activity of thought, that penetration, that industry which we call reason and which she has so liberally accorded us, since that activity is healthful to only a small number and fatal to all others."
>
> [Cicero, *De natura deorum* III, 27]

Of what profit can we consider that understanding of so many things to have been to Varro[4] and Aristotle? Did it free them from the annoyances of human life? Were they spared the accidents which beset a common porter? Did they draw from logic some consolation for the gout? Because they knew how that humor settles in the joints, did they suffer any less from it? Were they reconciled with death for knowing that some nations rejoice at it, and with cuckoldry for knowing that in some regions wives are held in common? On the contrary, having held the highest rank for knowledge, one among the Romans and the other among the Greeks, and in the age when learning flourished most, we have not, however, learned that they had any special excellence in their

---

[4]Roman linguist and writer (first century B.C.), famous for his extensive knowledge.

lives; indeed the Greek is rather hard put to it to clear his name of certain noteworthy stains.

Has it been found that pleasure and health are more keenly enjoyed by one who knows astrology and grammar . . . and that shame and poverty are less a burden?

> Illness and weakness you will doubtless thus escape,
> And will be spared both grief and cares; a longer life
> And better fate will then be granted you.
>   [Juvenal XIV, 156]

I have in my day seen a hundred artisans, a hundred peasants, wiser and happier than university rectors, and whom I should prefer to resemble. Scholarship, so I believe, has a place among the things necessary for life, like honor, nobility, dignity, or at most like beauty, wealth, and such other qualities which really contribute to it, but from afar, and somewhat more through imagination than by their essential value.

We need scarcely more services, rules, and laws of living, in our society, than cranes and ants do in theirs. And yet we see that they behave in a very well-ordered way without erudition. If man were wise, he would attribute to each thing its proper worth according as it was most useful and fitting for his life.

• • •

PRESUMPTION LEADS TO VAIN BOASTING ABOUT MAN'S STATE AND POWERS

There is general agreement among all the philosophers of all schools that the sovereign good consists in tranquility of soul and body. But where do we find it?

> In short, the sage sees none above him save great Jove;
> For he is handsome, honored, rich, and free—indeed,
> The very king of kings; but most of all he knows
> Good health—unless he be afflicted with a cold.
>   [Horace, *Epistles* I, i, 106]

It seems indeed that nature, to console us for our wretched and puny state, has bestowed on us only presumption. That is what Epictetus says—that man has nothing peculiarly his own except the use he makes of his opinions. We have received as our portion only wind and smoke. The gods possess health as part of their essence, says philosophy, and illness only in imagination; man, on the contrary, possesses his gifts only in fancy, and his woes are part of his essence. We have been right to insist upon the powers of our imagination, for all our blessings are only fanciful. Just hear the boastings of this poor and calamity-stricken animal. "There is nothing," says Cicero [*Tusculan Disputations* V, 36 and I, 26], "so pleasant as the pursuit of letters, those letters, I say, by means of which the infinity of things, the immense greatness of nature, the very skies of this world and the lands and seas are revealed to us; it is they which have taught us religion, moderation, greatness, and courage, and which have snatched our soul away from darkness to show it all things, the lofty and the low, the first and the last, and what lies in between; it is they which furnish us what is necessary to live well and happily, and guide us to spend our life without displeasure and harm." Does he not seem to be speaking of the condition of the eternal and almighty God?

And so far as practice is concerned, a thousand unimportant women led in their village a life more equable, more pleasant, and more consistent than was his.

> A god he was, indeed a very god, who found,
> O noble Memmius, that rule of life which now
> We call Philosophy, and by his wit and skill
> Gave life a firm foundation, quite secure from storms
> And such great darkness, and who brought it forth at last
> Into such great tranquility and such clear light.
>
> [Lucretius V, 8]

These are quite magnificent and beautiful words; but a very slight accident reduced the understanding of their author to a worse state than that of the meanest peasant, in spite of the teachings of that guiding god and that divine wisdom. Of similar impudence is this promise of the book of Democritus: "I am going to talk to you about all things" [Cicero, *Academica* II, 23]; and this stupid title which Aristotle bestows on us, calling us "mortal gods"; and the judgment of Chrysippus, that Dion was as virtuous as God. And my Seneca recognized, he says, that God had given him life, but that he himself was responsible for living well; this is in keeping with another dictum: "With reason do we pride ourselves upon our virtue, which would not be the case if we held it as a gift from God, and not through our own efforts." [Cicero, *De natura deorum* III, 36] This is also from Seneca: that the wise man has fortitude comparable to God's, but in the midst of human weakness; and for that reason he surpasses God. There is nothing so ordinary as to encounter remarks of such rashness. There is none of us who takes such offense at seeing himself exalted to the level of God as he does at seeing himself pushed back to the level of the other animals: so much more jealous are we of our own interest than of our creator's.

But we must trample down that foolish vanity, and sharply and boldly overthrow the ridiculous foundations on which these false opinions are built. So long as he thinks he has some freedom of action and some power in himself, man will never recognize what he owes to his master; he will always count his chickens before they are hatched, as they say; he must be stripped of all but his shirt.

Let us see a few noteworthy examples of the effect of this philosophy.

Posidonius, being afflicted with such a painful illness that it made him wring his hands and gnash his teeth, thought that he was defying pain by crying out to it: "It does you no good to rack me, if I do not admit that you are hurting me." He feels the same emotions as my servant, but he boasts because he at least holds his tongue according to the laws of his philosophic school. "It was not proper to be boastful in speech, but to yield in fact." [Cicero, *Tusculan Disputations* II, 13]

Arcesilaus was ill with the gout; Carneades, having come to visit him and going away deeply afflicted, Arcesilaus called him back and pointing first to his feet and then his chest: "What bothers me there," he said to him, "has not affected me here." He has somewhat better grace, for he recognizes that he is suffering and would like to be rid of his infirmity; but his heart, however, has not been overwhelmed and weakened by it. The other maintains his inflexibility, more verbal, in my opinion, than real. And Dionysius of Heraclea, afflicted with a great burning sensation in his eyes, was induced thereby to abandon these Stoic resolves.

IGNORANCE AIDS MORE THAN KNOWLEDGE IN ENDURING MISFORTUNES

But even though learning should achieve what they say, blunting and reducing the bitterness of the misfortunes which pursue us, what does it do that in a more direct and more obvious way ignorance doesn't do? The philosopher Pyrrho, undergoing at sea the hazard of a great storm, presented to those who were with him, as an example to imitate, only the security of a pig that was traveling with them and that looked out on the storm without fright. Philosophy, finding its precepts useless, refers us to the example of an athlete and a mule-driver, in whom one sees ordinarily much less fear of death, of pain, and of other troubles, and more steadfastness than learning ever furnished to anyone who wasn't born to it and prepared for it himself by natural habit. What brings it about that one makes an incision and cuts the tender members of a child more readily than ours, unless it is ignorance? And what about those of a horse? How many have been made ill by the mere force of imagination? We customarily see people bled, purged, and doctored in order to cure ills which they feel only in their minds. When we lack real ills, our learning lends us its own. This color and complexion indicate that you will have some catarrhal discharge; this hot season threatens you with a feverish disturbance; this break in the life line of your left hand warns you of some important illness about to come. And finally imagination turns destructively upon good health itself. That animation and vigor of youth cannot remain stable; we must remove some of their blood and strength lest they turn against you. Compare the life of a man subjected to such imaginations with that of a peasant letting himself go according to his natural inclination, measuring things only by the way he feels at the moment, without science, and without foreseeing woes to come, who has illness when it actually strikes him. In contrast, the other one often has the stone in his mind before he has it in his kidneys; as if it were not soon enough to suffer illness when it is at hand, he anticipates it in imagination, and hastens to meet it.

• • •

When we say that the infinite number of centuries, both past and future, are to God only an instant; that his goodness, wisdom, power are one with his essence, our words declare it, but our intelligence does not understand it. And yet our presumption wishes to sift the divine through our sieve. And from that are born all the fanciful ideas and errors which this world has seized upon, bringing to its balance and weighing therein something so remote from its measure. "It is a marvel how far the arrogance of the human heart goes, encouraged by the slightest success." [Pliny, II, 23]

May it please nature one day to open her bosom and to reveal to us as they are the means and operation of its movements, and to prepare our eyes for that revelation! O God! What errors, what misconceptions we should find in our poor science! I am mistaken if science has grasped a single thing correctly; and I shall leave here ignorant of everything except my ignorance.

THE TEACHINGS OF PHILOSOPHY
ARE MERE POETIC SPECULATIONS

Have I not read in Plato this divine remark, that nature is nothing but an enigmatic poem? As perhaps one might say a veiled and obscure painting, gleaming with an infinite variety of reflections to invite our conjectures. "All those things are enveloped and hidden in thick darkness, and there is nothing in the human mind sharp enough to penetrate to heaven and to probe into the depths of the earth." [Cicero, *Academica* II, 39]

And certainly philosophy is only a sophisticated poetry. Where do those ancient authors draw all their authorities if not from poets? And the first philosophers were poets themselves and treated philosophy in their art. Plato is only a poet writing in a loose, disconnected style. Timon calls him, as an insult, a great forger of miracles.

Just as women use ivory teeth to replace their own that are missing and, instead of the real complexion, make a false one of foreign matter; as they pad their thighs with cloth and felt, and their busts with cotton, obviously and to everyone's knowledge embellish themselves with a false and borrowed beauty, so too does science (and even our jurisprudence has, they say, legal fictions upon which it founds the truth of its justice).

Our science offers us as an explanation, and as underlying principles of the universe, things that she herself informs us were the product of human imagination. Those epicycles, eccentrics, and concentrics which astrology uses to explain the movement of its stars, it gives them to us as the best it has been able to invent on this subject. Similarly, moreover, philosophy presents to us not what is, or what it believes, but the most pleasant and imposing of its inventions. Plato, speaking of his discussion of the state of our body and that of beasts, declares: "That what we have said is true, we should affirm it if we had on that point the confirmation of an oracle; we can only declare that it has the greatest appearance of truth of what we could say.". . .

I am grateful to the woman of Miletus who, seeing the philosopher Thales occupy himself continually in contemplation of the celestial vault and always keep his eyes turned heavenward, placed something in his way to make him stumble, in order to warn him that it would be time to amuse his thought with things that were in the clouds when he had taken care of those which were at his feet. She surely gave him good advice in advising him to look to himself rather than to heaven. For, as Cicero has Democritus say,

> What lies before his feet, no man regards;
> His eyes explore the vaulted arch of heaven.
> [Cicero, *De divinatione* II, 13]

But our condition makes the knowledge of what we have within our hands as remote from us, and as far above the clouds, as knowledge of the stars. As Socrates says in Plato, to whoever dabbles in philosophy one can reproach what that woman reproached Thales with, that he sees nothing of what is before him. For every philosopher is ignorant of what his neighbor does, yes, and of what he does himself, and of what they both are, whether beasts or men.

OUR OWN BEING IS BEYOND OUR UNDERSTANDING

Those people who consider Sebond's arguments too weak, who are ignorant of nothing, who govern the universe, who know everything,

> What causes rule the sea; what regulates the seasons;
> If stars move at their own free will or by command;
> What veils in darkness the moon's orb, and what reveals it;
> What is the will and power in nature's complex plan
> Which joins in perfect harmony discordant things;
> [Horace, *Epistles* I, xii, 16]

have they not sometimes probed, amid their books, the difficulties which stand in the way of their knowing their own being? We see indeed that the finger moves and that the foot moves; that some parts move by themselves, without our leave, and that our will controls others; that a certain fear makes us flush, and a certain other turn pale; this notion affects our spleen only, and that one our brain; one makes us laugh, and another weep; a certain other chills us and paralyzes all our senses, and stops the movement of our limbs. At a certain sight, our stomach rises; at a certain other, some lower part. But how a spiritual impression produces such an effect in a massive and solid subject, and the nature of the linking and union of these admirable mechanisms, never has man known that. "All these things are impenetrable to human reason and hidden in the majesty of nature," says Pliny [*Natural History* II, 37]; and St. Augustine declares: "The manner in which the spirit is united with the body is completely marvelous, nor can it be understood by man; yet that union is man himself." [*City of God* XXXI, x] Such considerations, however, do not arouse men's doubts, for their opinions are received according to ancient beliefs, with authority and credit, as if they were religion and law. One accepts, as by rote, what is commonly held; one accepts this truth with all its structure and appendages of arguments and proofs, as a firm and solid whole which one no longer shakes, which one no longer judges. On the contrary, each vies with the others in plastering and fortifying this accepted belief with all that his reason can add—and the reason is an adaptable instrument, which can be made to serve any form. Thus the world is full of, and steeped in, inanities and falsehood.

• • •

Now out of the knowledge of this changeable nature of mine, I have by chance engendered within myself some constancy of opinions, and I have scarcely altered my early and natural ones. For, whatever plausibility there may be in new ideas, I do not change readily lest I have occasion to lose in so doing. And, since I am not capable of choosing, I take the choice of others and remain in the position where God placed me. Otherwise, I could not keep myself from rolling constantly. So, by God's grace, I have kept completely, without agitation and disturbance of my conscience, the old beliefs of our religion, in spite of all the sects and divisions which our century has produced. The writings of the ancients (I mean the good writings, substantial and solid) attract me and stir me almost as they wish; the one I am listening to seems to me always the strongest; I find that each in turn is right, even though they contradict one another. One must recognize that facility which great minds have to make whatever they wish seem plausible, and the fact that there is nothing so strange but they undertake to color it sufficiently to fool a simple nature such as mine; that shows obviously the weakness of their proof. The sky and the stars revolved for three thousand years; everyone had believed so until Cleanthes of Samos or, according to Theophrastus, Nicetas of Syracuse took it into his head to maintain that it was the earth which moved around the oblique circle of the Zodiac, spinning on its axis; and, in our day, Copernicus has so well established that doctrine that he uses it in a quite systematic way for all astronomical computations. What shall we draw from that, if not that we should not worry which of the two systems is true? And who knows that a third opinion, a thousand years from now, may not overthrow the two previous ones?

> So rolling time affects the status of all things:
> What once was held in high esteem, from honor falls;
> Now something new prevails, emerging out of scorn—
> Each day it's more desired, receives bouquets of praise,
> And among men it holds a place of highest honor.
>   [Lucretius V. 1275]

DISTRUST OF NEW DOCTRINES

Thus when we encounter some new doctrine, we have good reason to distrust it, and to consider that before it was produced its contrary was in vogue; and as that earlier doctrine was overthrown by this one, there can well be born in the future a third discovery which will similarly upset the second one. Before the principles which Aristotle introduced were generally accepted, other principles satisfied the human reason as his satisfy us now. What warrant do his have, what special privilege, that the course of our seeking ends with them, and that to them belongs for all time dominion over our belief? They are no more exempt from being ousted than were the ideas which preceded them. When a new argument is urged upon me, it is up to me to consider that, where I cannot find a satisfactory answer, someone else will; for to believe all the appearances which we cannot explain away is to be a great simpleton. Such willingness to believe would lead the common throng of men (and we are all of the common throng) to have beliefs which spin about like a weather-vane; for their soul, being soft and without resistance, would be forced to receive unceasingly new impressions one on top of the other, the latest always effacing the trace of the preceding one. He who feels weak must answer, as they do in the law courts, that he will seek advice on the matter, or rely upon those wiser men under whom he served his apprenticeship. How long has the art of medicine existed? They say that a newcomer, Paracelsus by name, is changing and overthrowing the whole order of ancient rules, and maintains that heretofore medicine has served only to kill men. I believe that he will easily verify that; but as for submitting my life to the test of his new experience, I think that would not be great wisdom.

One must not believe everyone, the saying goes, because everyone can say all manner of things.

27

Queen Elizabeth I of England

Address to the Troops AND
The Golden Speech

ELIZABETH I *(1533–1603) came to the throne in 1558 at a time of great social and cultural change. The nation-state was supplanting the feudal monarchy. Religious conflict divided Europe. The changes of the Renaissance that began in Italy were reaching England. England, with Elizabeth as guide and governor, came through this period more successfully than other countries of Europe in large measure because of her talents and strengths.*

Elizabeth learned her consummate skills as adroit political maneuverer and negotiator at an early age, mastering the art of survival in a turbulent and dangerous time and in hazardous circumstances. When she was a child, she lived under a cloud of rejection, since her mother, Anne Boleyn, the second wife of Henry VIII, had been executed for high treason. Later, she was the object of the envious suspicion of her older sister, Queen Mary, who had her imprisoned for a while in the Tower of London.

When she became queen, she was faced with the enmity of Spain and with many plots against her in her own country. She managed, however, to avoid becoming embroiled in major wars and to keep England free from religious civil warfare. At the same time, she maintained a strong, central government and furthered the growth of England as a nation-state.

Her shrewdness and intelligence enabled her to put to good use an excellent Renaissance education that gave her knowledge of history, acquaintance with theology and philosophy, appreciation of literature (Shakespeare's plays were sometimes performed at court), and skill in writing and speaking. She also acquired a mastery of Latin, Greek, French, and Italian. It has been said that she was excessively proud of her language skills and used them to surprise, charm, and impress foreign ambassadors.

She was an excellent public speaker, often talking informally, as in the first of the following speeches. On more formal occasions, like the second example, she may have had a draft prepared by one of her advisers. But she undoubtedly reviewed and revised it to make it her own in form as well as in content.

Much of her success as a ruler has been attributed to her ability to choose the right words at precisely the right time to inspire the patriotic loyalty of her subjects. An example is the first of the following speeches. She spoke before the London militia at Tilbury, east of London, mobilized against the threat of a Spanish invasion in 1588.

The second speech is known as the "Golden Speech," 1601. It was her last formal address to Parliament. She spoke to representatives of the House of Commons, who later reported to the rest of Parliament. In the speech she expresses her great love for her people and her deep concern for their welfare. The occasion of the speech was the House of Commons' refusal to discuss taxes to support the government until after the government dealt with the abuse of granting monopolies in commerce and manufacturing to powerful nobles. She promises to correct the abuse, and as usual ends by gaining the fervent loyalty of these representatives.

To the soldiers she said, "I have the heart of a king." To the members of the House of Commons she said, "I have reigned with your loves." Both statements were true, and both gained her such popularity and loyalty as have seldom been given to any ruler.

TO THE TROOPS AT TILBURY, 1588

My loving people: We have been persuaded by some that are careful of our safety to take heed how we commit ourselves to armed multitudes for fear of treachery. But I assure you I do not desire to live to distrust my faithful and loving people. Let tyrants fear! I have always so behaved myself that under God I have placed my chief strength and safeguard in the loyal hearts and good will of my subjects. And therefore I am come amongst you, as you see, at this time, not for my recreation and disport; but being resolved in the midst of the heat of the

ADDRESS TO THE TROOPS AND THE GOLDEN SPEECH   From *The Public Speaking of Queen Elizabeth* by George P. Rice, Jr. (New York: Columbia University Press, 1951). Copyright © 1979, Columbia University Press. By permission. Pp. 96–97, 106–109.

battle[1] to live or die amongst you all; to lay down for my God and for my Kingdom and for my people my honor and my blood even in the dust.

I know I have the body but of a weak and feeble woman; but I have the heart and stomach of a king, and of a king of England too, and think foul scorn that Parma[2] or Spain or any prince of Europe should dare to invade the borders of my realm; to which, rather than any dishonor should grow by me, I myself will take up arms; I myself will be your general, judge, and rewarder of every one of your virtues in the field.

I know already for your forwardness you have deserved rewards and crowns; and we do assure you on the word of a prince they shall be duly paid you.

In the meantime, my lieutenant-general[3] shall be in my stead, than whom never prince commanded a more noble or worthy subject; not doubting but by your obedience to my general, by your concord in the camp, and your valor in the field, we shall shortly have a famous victory over those enemies of my God, of my kingdom, and of my people.

THE "GOLDEN SPEECH" OF 1601

Mr. Speaker: We have heard your declaration and perceive your care of our state, by falling into the consideration of a grateful acknowledgment of such benefits as you have received; and that your coming is to present thanks unto us, which I accept with no less joy than your loves can have desire to offer such a present. I do assure you that there is no prince that loveth his subjects better, or whose love can countervail our love. There is no jewel, be it of never so rich a prize, which I prefer before this jewel, I mean your love, for I do more esteem it than any treasure or riches, for that we know how to prize. That love and thanks I count inestimable. And though God has raised me high, yet this I count the glory of my crown, that I have reigned with your loves. This

---

[1]The Queen is speaking metaphorically. She is referring to war in general and to her leadership of her people, not to a specific battle. She did not, of course, command troops in action.

[2]The Duke of Parma, commander of Spanish forces in The Netherlands, had been ordered by the King of Spain to concentrate his troops preparatory to invading England. The invasion never occurred, for the Spanish fleet, the "Invincible Armada," was destroyed before it could land any forces in England.

[3]The Earl of Leicester.

makes me that I do not so much rejoice that God hath made me to be a queen as to be a queen over so thankful a people. Therefore I have cause to wish nothing more than to content the subject, and that is a duty which I owe. Neither do I desire to live longer days than that I may see your prosperity, and that is my only desire. And as I am that person that still, yet under God, hath delivered you, so I trust, by the almighty power of God, that I still shall be His instrument to preserve you from envy, peril, dishonor, shame, tyranny, and oppression, partly by means of your intended helps, which we take very acceptably, because it manifests the largeness of your loves and loyalties unto your sovereign. Of myself I must say this: I never was any greedy, scraping grasper, nor a strait fast-holding prince, nor yet a waster; my heart was never set on worldly goods, but only for my subjects' good. What you do bestow on me I will not hoard up, but receive it to bestow on you again. Yea, mine own properties I count yours, to be expended for your good. Therefore render unto them, I beseech you, Mr. Speaker, such thanks as you imagine my heart yieldeth, but my tongue cannot express.

[During these words the assemblage had knelt. Because she had yet more to say and was conscious of their possible discomfort, Elizabeth invited the men to stand.]

Mr. Speaker, I would wish you and the rest to stand up, for I shall yet trouble you with longer speech.

Mr. Speaker, you give me thanks, but I doubt me I have more cause to thank you all than you me: and I charge you to thank them of the House of Commons from me, for had I not received a knowledge from you, I might have fallen into the lap of an error only for lack of true information. Since I was queen, yet never did I put my pen to any grant, but that upon pretext and semblance made unto me that it was both good and beneficial to the subjects in general, though a private profit to some of my ancient servants who had deserved well. But the contrary being found by experience, I am exceedingly beholding to such subjects as would move the same at first. And I am not so simple to suppose but that there be some of the Lower House whom these grievances never touched, and for them I think they speak out of zeal to their countries and not out of spleen or malevolent affection, as being parties grieved. And I take it exceeding grateful from them because it gives us to know that no respects or interests had moved them, other than the minds they bear to suffer no diminution of our honor and our subjects' love unto us. The zeal of which affection, tending to ease my people and knit their hearts unto me, I embrace with a princely care. Far above all earthly treasure I esteem my people's love, more than which I desire not to merit. That my grants should be grievous to my people and oppressions to be privileged under color of our patents, our kingly dignity shall not suffer it. Yea, when I heard it, I could give no rest to my thoughts until I had reformed it. Shall they think to escape unpunished that have thus oppressed you and have been respectless of their duty and regardless of our honor? No. Mr. Speaker, I assure you, were it more for conscience' sake than for any glory or increase of love that I desire these errors, troubles, vexations, and oppressions done by these varlets and lewd persons, not worthy the name of subjects, should not escape without condign punishment. But I perceive they dealt with me like physicians who, ministering a drug, make it more acceptable by giving it a good aromatical savour, or when they give pills, do gild them all over. I have ever used to set the last judgment day before mine eyes and so to rule as I shall be judged to answer before a higher Judge. To Whose judgment seat I do appeal that never thought was cherished in my heart that tended not to my people's good. And if my kingly bounty have been abused and my grants turned to the hurt of my people, contrary to my will and meaning, or if any in authority under me have neglected or perverted what I have committed to them, I hope God will not lay their culps [faults] and offences to my charge. And though there were danger in repealing our grants, yet what danger would not I rather incur for your own good, than I would suffer them still to continue? I know the title of a king is a glorious title, but assure yourself that the shining glory of princely authority hath not so dazzled the eyes of our understanding but that we well know and remember that we also are to yield an account of our actions before the Great Judge. To be a king and wear a crown is more glorious to them that see it than it is pleasure to them that bear it. For myself, I was never so much enticed with the glorious name of a king or royal authority of a queen as delighted that God hath made me this instrument to maintain His truth and glory, and to defend this kingdom, as I said, from peril, dishonor, tyranny, and oppression. There will never queen sit in my seat with more zeal to my country or care to my subjects, and that will sooner with willingness yield and venture her life for your good and safety than myself. And though you have had and may have many princes more mighty and wise sitting in this seat, yet you never had or shall have any that will be more careful and loving. Should I ascribe anything to myself and my sexly weakness, I were not worthy to live then, and of all most unworthy of the mercies I have had from God, Who hath ever yet given me a heart which never yet feared foreign or home enemies. I speak it to give God the praise as a testimony before you, and not to attribute anything unto myself. For I, O Lord, what am I, whom practices and perils past should not fear! *O what can I do that I should speak for any glory!* God forbid. This, Mr. Speaker, I pray you deliver unto the House, to whom heartily recommend me. And so I commit you all to your best fortunes and further counsels. And I pray you, Mr. Comptroller, Mr. Secretary, and you of my council, that before these gentlemen depart into their counties, you bring them all to kiss my hand.

28

William Shakespeare

Othello

*T*HE *second half of the sixteenth century was a period of intense cultural activity, especially in England, where Queen Elizabeth gave her name to the age. Indeed, in reference to art and literature the term* Elizabethan *has come to mean daring elaboration, colorful adornment, and a range of moods varying from exaltation to melancholy. The Elizabethans excelled in poetry, drama, and music, and the most highly valued of their literary works are those associated with William Shakespeare (1564–1616).*

What we know of Shakespeare's youth and upbringing indicates that he came from a middle-class family that lived in the town of Stratford-upon-Avon, where his father was prominent in the community and earned his living as a craftsman. Shakespeare's education was excellent for the time. Schooled in the classics and knowledgeable in history and in religious doctrine, he was attuned to both Renaissance and Reformation. He moved to London early in his literary career and soon enjoyed both artistic and financial success, the London theater having become in his day largely an independent commercial enterprise. Fairly well-to-do, he retired to Stratford about 1610 and lived there until his death.

Though his poems and sonnets have become a study in themselves, the reputation of Shakespeare rests primarily on his dramas, some two dozen of the thirty-eight plays attributed to him meriting the term masterpiece. *Including comedies, histories, and tragedies, these plays incorporated many of the medieval characteristics of the native dramatic tradition and added numerous classical themes and references. Working with well-known stories of his own and earlier eras, Shakespeare combined plots and characterizations to fashion new creations.*

Othello *(1603) is based on a plot borrowed from a collection of Italian short stories, a plot that Shakespeare enhances through character conflict and melodra-*

matic action. Othello is portrayed as an honorable man trapped by his own flawed character as well as by the deceit of Iago, literature's masterstudy of the malicious villain. Iago seems at first a Machiavellian schemer, but audiences and critics later find that his villainy has deeper roots than the creed of Machiavellian expediency. The play is one of Western literature's most shocking, fascinating, and moving studies of the interplay of good and evil in human motivations and actions.

Dramatis Personae

DUKE OF VENICE
BRABANTIO, *a Senator*
OTHER SENATORS
GRATIANO, *brother to Brabantio*
LODOVICO, *kinsman to Brabantio*
OTHELLO, *a noble Moor*
   in the service of
   the Venetian state
CASSIO, *his lieutenant*
IAGO, *his ancient*
MONTANO, *Othello's predecessor*
   in the government of Cyprus

RODERIGO, *a Venetian gentleman*
CLOWN, *servant to Othello*
DESDEMONA, *daughter to*
   Brabantio and wife to Othello
EMILIA, *wife to Iago*
BIANCA, *mistress to Cassio*
SAILOR, MESSENGER, HERALD,
   OFFICERS, GENTLEMEN,
   MUSICIANS, *and* ATTENDANTS

ACT I

SCENE I. *Venice. A street.*

[*Enter* RODERIGO *and* IAGO.]

RODERIGO.   Tush, never tell me. I take it much unkindly
   That thou, Iago, who hast had° my purse
   As if the strings were thine, shouldst know of this.   3

Act I, SCENE I: 2. *had:* used.

IAGO.   'Sblood,° but you will not hear me.
    If ever I did dream of such a matter,
    Abhor me.
RODERIGO.   Thou told'st me thou didst hold him in thy hate.
IAGO.   Despise me if I do not. Three great ones of the city,
    In personal suit° to make me his Lieutenant,
    Off-capped° to him. And, by the faith of man,   10
    I know my price, I am worth no worse a place.
    But he, as loving his own pride and purposes,
    Evades them, with a bombast circumstance°
    Horribly stuffed with epithets of war.°
    And, in conclusion,
    Nonsuits° my mediators, for, "Certes,"° says he,
    "I have already chose my officer."
    And what was he?
    Forsooth, a great arithmetician,°
    One Michael Cassio, a Florentine,   20
    A fellow almost damned in a fair wife,°
    That never set a squadron in the field,
    Nor the division of a battle° knows
    More than a spinster, unless the bookish theoric,°
    Wherein the toged° Consuls° can propose
    As masterly as he—mere prattle without practice
    Is all his soldiership. But he, sir, had the election.
    And I, of whom his eyes had seen the proof
    At Rhodes, at Cyprus, and on other grounds
    Christian and heathen must be beleed° and calmed   30
    By debitor and creditor. This countercaster,°
    He, in good time,° must his Lieutenant be,
    And I—God bless the mark!°—his Moorship's Ancient.°

---

4. *'Sblood:* by God's blood.   9. *In . . . suit:* making this request in person.   10. *Off-capped:* stood cap in hand.   13. *bombast circumstance:* bombastic phrases. Bombast is cotton padding used to stuff out a garment.   14. *stuffed . . . war:* padded out with military terms.   16. *Nonsuits:* rejects the petition of; *Certes:* assuredly.   19. *arithmetician:* Contemporary books on military tactics are full of elaborate diagrams and numerals to explain military formations. Cassio is a student of such books.   21. *almost . . . wife:* a much-disputed phrase. It is probably best understood as Iago's mockery of Cassio's genteel appearance and manners.   23. *division . . . battle:* organization of an army.   24. *bookish theoric:* student of war: not a practical soldier.   25. *toged:* wearing a toga; *Consuls:* councilors (see I.ii 43).   30. *beleed:* placed on the lee (or unfavorable) side.   31. *countercaster:* calculator (repeating the idea of arithmetician). Counters were used in making calculations.   32. *in . . . time:* a phrase expressing indignation.   33. *God . . . mark:* an exclamation of impatience; *Ancient:* ensign, a low-ranking officer.

RODERIGO.   By Heaven, I rather would have been his hangman.
IAGO.   Why, there's no remedy 'Tis the curse of service,
Preferment goes by letter and affection,
And not by old gradation,° where each second
Stood heir to the first. Now, sir, be judge yourself
Whether I in any just term am affined°
To love the Moor.
RODERIGO.   I would not follow him, then.   40
IAGO.   Oh, sir, content you,
I follow him to serve my turn upon him.
We cannot all be masters, nor all masters
Cannot be truly followed. You shall mark
Many a duteous and knee-crooking knave
That doting on his own obsequious bondage
Wears out his time, much like his master's ass,
For naught but provender, and when he's old, cashiered.°
Whip me such honest knaves. Others there are
Who, trimmed in forms and visages of duty,°   50
Keep yet their hearts attending on themselves,
And throwing but shows of service° on their lords
Do well thrive by them, and when they have lined their coats
Do themselves homage.° These fellows have some soul,
And such a one do I profess myself. For, sir,
It is as sure as you are Roderigo,
Were I the Moor, I would not be Iago.
In following him, I follow but myself.
Heaven is my judge, not I for love and duty,
But seeming so, for my peculiar° end.   60
For when my outward action doth demónstrate
The native act and figure of my heart°
In compliment extern,° 'tis not long after
But I will wear my heart upon my sleeve
For daws° to peck at. I am not what I am.°

36–37. *Preferment . . . gradation:* Promotion comes through private recommendation and favoritism and not by order of seniority.   39. *affined:* tied by affection.
48. *cashiered:* dismissed. The word at this time did not imply dishonorable discharge.
50. *trimmed . . . duty:* decking themselves out with the outward forms of loyal service.   52. *throwing . . . service:* serving merely in outward show.   54. *Do . . . homage:* serve themselves; *homage:* an outward act signifying obedience.   60. *peculiar:* particular, personal.   62. *native . . . heart:* natural actions and shape of my secret designs.
63. *extern:* outward.   65. *daws:* jackdaws; that is, fools; *I . . . am:* Iago's mockery of Jehovah' "I am that I am." Exodus 3:14.

RODERIGO.   What a full fortune° does the thick-lips owe°
  If he can carry't thus!°
IAGO.   Call up her father,
  Rouse him. Make after him, poison his delight,
  Proclaim him in the streets. Incense her kinsmen,
  And though he in a fertile climate dwell,   70
  Plague him with flies. Though that his joy be joy,
  Yet throw such changes of vexation on 't
  As it may lose some color.°
RODERIGO.   Here is her father's house, I'll call aloud.
IAGO.   Do, with like timorous° accent and dire yell
  As when, by night and negligence, the fire
  Is spied in populous cities.
RODERIGO.   What ho, Brabantio! Signior Brabantio, ho!
IAGO.   Awake! What ho, Brabantio! Thieves! Thieves! Thieves!
  Look to your house, your daughter and your bags!°   80
  Thieves! Thieves!

          [BRABANTIO *appears above, at a window.*]
BRABANTIO.   What is the reason of this terrible summons?
  What is the matter there?
RODERIGO.   Signior, is all your family within?
IAGO.   Are your doors locked?
BRABANTIO.   Why, wherefore ask you this?
IAGO.   'Zounds,° sir, you're robbed. For shame, put
    on your gown,°
  Your heart is burst, you have lost half your soul.
  Even now, now, very now, an old black ram
  Is tupping° your white ewe. Arise, arise,
  Awake the snorting° citizens with the bell,   90
  Or else the Devil° will make a grandsire of you.
  Arise, I say.
BRABANTIO.   What, have you lost your wits?
RODERIGO.   Most reverend signior, do you know my voice?
BRABANTIO.   Not I. What are you?
RODERIGO.   My name is Roderigo.

---

66. *full fortune:* overflowing good luck; *owe:* own.   67. *carry't thus:* that is, bring off this marriage.   72–73. *throw . . . color:* cause him some annoyance by way of variety to tarnish his joy.   75. *timorous:* terrifying.   80. *bags:* moneybags.   86. *'Zounds:* by God's wounds; *gown:* dressing gown.   89. *tupping:* covering.   90. *snorting:* snoring. 91. *Devil:* The Devil in old pictures and woodcuts was represented as black.

BRABANTIO.   The worser welcome.
  I have charged thee not to haunt about my doors.
  In honest plainness thou hast heard me say
  My daughter is not for thee, and now, in madness,
  Being full of supper and distempering draughts,°
  Upon malicious bravery° dost thou come   100
  To start° my quiet.
RODERIGO.   Sir, sir, sir——
BRABANTIO.   But thou must needs be sure
  My spirit and my place have in them power
  To make this bitter to thee.
RODERIGO.   Patience, good sir.
BRABANTIO.   What tell'st thou me of robbing? This is Venice,
  My house is not a grange.°
RODERIGO.   Most grave Brabantio,
  In simple and pure soul I come to you.
IAGO.   'Zounds, sir, you are one of those that will not serve
  God if the Devil bid you. Because we come to do you
  service and you think we are ruffians, you'll have your   110
  daughter covered with a Barbary° horse, you'll have
  your nephews° neigh to you, you'll have coursers for
  cousins,° and jennets° for germans.°
BRABANTIO.   What profane wretch art thou?
IAGO.   I am one, sir, that comes to tell you your daughter
  and the Moor are now making the beast with two
  backs.
BRABANTIO.   Thou art a villain.
IAGO.   You are—a Senator.
BRABANTIO.   This thou shalt answer. I know thee, Roderigo.
RODERIGO.   Sir, I will answer anything. But I beseech you   120
  If't be your pleasure and most wise consent,
  As partly I find it is, that your fair daughter,
  At this odd-even° and dull° watch o' the night,
  Transported with no worse nor better guard
  But with a knave of common hire, a gondolier,
  To the gross clasps of a lascivious Moor—

---

99. *distempering draughts:* intoxicating drinks.   100. *bravery:* defiance.   101. *start:* startle.   106. *grange:* lonely farm.   111. *Barbary:* Moorish.   112. *nephews:* grandsons.
113. *cousins:* near relations; *jennets:* Moorish ponies; *germans:* kinsmen.   123. *odd-even:* about midnight; *dull:* heavy, sleepy.

If this be known to you, and your allowance,°
We then have done you bold and saucy wrongs.
But if you know not this, my manners tell me
We have your wrong rebuke. Do not believe   130
That from the sense of all civility°
I thus would play and trifle with your reverence.
Your daughter, if you have not given her leave,
I say again, hath made a gross revolt,°
Tying her duty, beauty, wit, and fortunes
In an extravagant° and wheeling° stranger
Of here and everywhere. Straight satisfy yourself.
If she be in her chamber or your house,
Let loose on me the justice of the state
For thus deluding you.

BRABANTIO.   Strike on the tinder,° ho!   140
Give me a taper!° Call up all my people!
This accident is not unlike my dream.
Belief of it oppresses me already.
Light, I say! Light!

                                                    [*Exit above.*]

IAGO.   Farewell, for I must leave you.
It seems not meet, nor wholesome to my place,°
To be produced—as if I stay I shall—
Against the Moor. For I do know the state,
However this may gall° him with some check,°
Cannot with safety cast° him. For he's embarked
With such loud reason to the Cyprus wars,   150
Which even now stand in act,° that, for their souls,
Another of his fathom° they have none
To lead their business. In which regard,
Though I do hate him as I do Hell pains,
Yet for necessity of present life

127. *your allowance:* by your permission.   131. *from . . . civility:* disregarding all sense
of decent behavior.   134. *gross revolt:* indecent rebellion.   136. *extravagant:* vagabond;
wheeling: wandering.   140. *tinder:* the primitive method of making fire, used before
the invention of matches. A spark, made by striking flint on steel, fell on the tinder,
some inflammable substance such as charred linen, which was blown into flame.
141. *taper:* candle.   145. *place:* that is, as Othello's officer.   148. *gall:* make sore; *check:*
rebuke.   149. *cast:* dismiss from service.   151. *stand in act:* are on the point of beginning.   152. *fathom:* depth.

I must show out a flag° and sign of love,
Which is indeed but sign. That you shall surely find him,
Lead to the Sagittary° the raisèd search,
And there will I be with him. So farewell.

[*Exit.*]

[*Enter, below,* BRABANTIO, *in his nightgown,
and* SERVANTS *with torches.*]

BRABANTIO.   It is too true an evil. Gone she is,   160
And what's to come of my despisèd time°
Is naught but bitterness. Now, Roderigo,
Where didst thou see her? Oh, unhappy girl!
With the Moor, say'st thou? Who would be a father!
How didst thou know 'twas she? Oh, she deceives me
Past thought! What said she to you? Get more tapers.
Raise all my kindred. Are they married, think you?
RODERIGO.   Truly, I think they are.
BRABANTIO.   Oh Heaven! How got she out? Oh, treason
of the blood!°
Fathers, from hence trust not your daughters' minds   170
By what you see them act. Are there not charms°
By which the property° of youth and maidhood
May be abused?° Have you not read, Roderigo,
Of some such thing?
RODERIGO.   Yes, sir, I have indeed.
BRABANTIO.   Call up my brother. Oh, would you had had her!
Some one way, some another. Do you know
Where we may apprehend her and the Moor?
RODERIGO.   I think I can discover him, if you please
To get good guard and go along with me.
BRABANTIO.   Pray you, lead on. At every house I'll call,   180
I may command° at most. Get weapons, ho!
And raise some special officers of night.
On, good Roderigo, I'll deserve your pains.°

[*Exeunt.*]

---

156. *flag:* a sign of welcome.   158. *Sagittary:* presumably some building in Venice, not
identified, used as a meeting place for the Council.   161. *what's . . . time:* the rest of
my wretched life.   169. *treason . . . blood:* treachery of my own child.   171. *charms:*
magic spells.   172. *property:* nature.   173. *abused:* deceived.   181. *command:* find sup-
porters.   183. *deserve . . . pains:* reward your labor.

SCENE II. *Another street.*

[*Enter* OTHELLO, IAGO, *and* ATTENDANTS, *with torches.*]

IAGO.   Though in the trade of war I have slain men,
Yet do I hold it very stuff° o' the conscience
To do no contrivèd° murder. I lack iniquity
Sometimes to do me service. Nine or ten times
I had thought to have yerked° him here under the ribs.

OTHELLO.   'Tis better as it is.

IAGO.   Nay, but he prated
And spoke such scurvy and provoking terms
Against your honor
That, with the little godliness I have,
I did full hard forbear him.° But I pray you, sir,
Are you fast° married? Be assured of this,
That the Magnifico° is much beloved,
And hath in his effect° a voice potential
As double as° the Duke's. He will divorce you,
Or put upon you what restraint and grievance
The law, with all his might to enforce it on,
Will give him cable.°

OTHELLO.   Let him do his spite.
My services which I have done the signiory°
Shall outtongue his complaints. 'Tis yet to know°—
Which, when I know that boasting is an honor,
I shall promulgate°—I fetch my life and being°
From men of royal siege,° and my demerits°
May speak unbonneted° to as proud a fortune
As this that I have reached. For know, Iago,
But that I love the gentle Desdemona,
I would not my unhousèd° free condition

SCENE II: 2. *stuff:* material, nature. 3. *contrived:* deliberately planned. 5. *yerked:* jabbed. 10. *full . . . him:* had a hard job to keep my hands off him. 11. *fast:* securely. 12. *Magnifico:* the title of the chief men of Venice. 13. *in . . . effect:* what he can do. 13–14. *potential . . . as:* twice as powerful as. 17. *cable:* rope. 18. *signiory:* the state of Venice. 19. *'Tis . . . know:* it has still to be made known. 21. *promulgate:* proclaim; *fetch . . . being:* am descended. 22. *royal siege:* throne; *demerits:* deserts. 23. *unbonneted:* A disputed phrase. Usually it means "without a cap": that is, in sign that the wearer is standing before a superior. But Othello means that his merits are such that he need show deference to no man. 26. *unhoused:* unmarried.

Put into circumscription and confine°
For the sea's worth. But look! What lights come yond?

IAGO.   Those are the raisèd father and his friends.
You were best go in.

OTHELLO.   Not I, I must be found.   30
My parts,° my title, and my perfect° soul
Shall manifest me rightly. Is it they?

IAGO.   By Janus,° I think no.

> [*Enter* CASSIO, *and certain* OFFICERS *with torches.*]

OTHELLO.   The servants of the Duke, and my Lieutenant.
The goodness of the night upon you, friends!
What is the news?

CASSIO.   The Duke does greet you, General,
And he requires your haste-posthaste° appearance,
Even on the instant.

OTHELLO.   What is the matter, think you?

CASSIO.   Something from Cyprus, as I may divine.
It is a business of some heat. The galleys°   40
Have sent a dozen sequent° messengers
This very night at one another's heels,
And many of the consuls, raised and met,
Are at the Duke's already. You have been hotly called for
When, being not at your lodging to be found,
The Senate hath sent about three several° quests
To search you out.

OTHELLO.   'Tis well I am found by you.
I will but spend a word here in the house
And go with you.

                                        [*Exit.*]

CASSIO.   Ancient, what makes he here?

IAGO.   Faith, he tonight hath boarded a land carrack.°   50
If it prove lawful prize, he's made forever.

---

27. *confine:* confinement.   31. *parts:* abilities; *perfect:* ready.   33. *Janus:* the two-faced God of Romans, an appropriate deity for Iago.   37. *haste-posthaste:* with the quickest possible speed. When it was necessary to urge the postboy to greater speed than usual, the letter or dispatch was inscribed "haste, posthaste."   40. *galleys:* Venetian ships manned and rowed by slaves and prisoners; the fastest of craft.   41. *sequent:* following one after another.   46. *several:* separate.   50. *carrack:* the largest type of Spanish merchant ship.

CASSIO.   I do not understand.
IAGO.   He's married.
CASSIO.   To who?

[*Re-enter* OTHELLO]

IAGO.   Marry,° to——Come, Captain, will you go?
OTHELLO.   Have with you.
CASSIO.   Here comes another troop to seek for you.
IAGO.   It is Brabantio. General, be advised,°   55
He comes to bad intent.

[*Enter* BRABANTIO, RODERIGO, *and* OFFICERS
with torches and weapons.]

OTHELLO.   Holloa! Stand there!
RODERIGO.   Signior, it is the Moor.
BRABANTIO.   Down with him, thief!

[*They draw on both sides.*]

IAGO.   You, Roderigo! Come, sir, I am for you.
OTHELLO.   Keep up° your bright swords, for the dew
will rust them.
Good signior, you shall more command with years   60
Than with your weapons.
BRABANTIO.   O thou foul thief, where hast thou
stowed my daughter?
Damned as thou art, thou has enchanted her.
For I'll refer me to all things of sense°
If she in chains of magic were not bound,
Whether a maid so tender, fair, and happy,
So opposite to marriage that she shunned
The wealthy curlèd darlings of our nation,
Would ever have, to incur a general mock,
Run from her guardage° to the sooty bosom   70
Of such a thing as thou, to fear, not to delight.
Judge me the world if 'tis not gross in sense°
That thou hast practiced on her with foul charms,
Abused her delicate youth with drugs or minerals
That weaken motion.° I'll have 't disputed on,°

---

53. *Marry:* Mary, by the Virgin—with a pun.   55. *advised:* careful.   59. *Keep up:*
sheathe.   64. *refer . . . sense:* that is, by every rational consideration.   70. *guardage:*
guardianship.   72. *gross in sense:* that is, plain to the perception.   75. *motion:* sense;
disputed on: argued in the courts of law.

'Tis probable, and palpable° to thinking.
I therefore apprehend and do attach° thee
For an abuser of the world, a practicer
Of arts inhibited and out of warrant.°
Lay hold upon him. If he do resist,   80
Subdue him at his peril.

OTHELLO.   Hold your hands,
Both you of my inclining and the rest.
Were it my cue to fight, I should have known it
Without a prompter. Where will you that I go
To answer this your charge?

BRABANTIO.   To prison, till fit time
Of law and course of direct session°
Call thee to answer.

OTHELLO.   What if I do obey?
How may the Duke be therewith satisfied,
Whose messengers are here about my side
Upon some present° business of the state   90
To bring me to him?

1ST OFFICER.   'Tis true, most worthy signior.
The Duke's in Council, and your noble self
I am sure is sent for.

BRABANTIO.   How! The Duke in Council!
In this time of the night! Bring him away.
Mine's not an idle° cause. The Duke himself,
Or any of my brothers of the state,
Cannot but feel this wrong as 'twere their own.
For if such actions may have passage free,°
Bondslaves and pagans shall our statesmen be.

                                              [*Exeunt.*]

SCENE III. *A council chamber.*

[*The* DUKE *and* SENATORS *sitting at a table,* OFFICERS *attending.*]

DUKE.   There is no composition° in these news°
That gives them credit.

---

76. *palpable:* clear. 77. *attach:* arrest. 79. *arts . . . warrant:* forbidden and illegal acts;
that is, magic and witchcraft. 86. *course . . . session:* trial in the ordinary courts, where
witches and other criminals are tried—and not by special commission as a great man.
90. *present:* immediate. 95. *idle:* trivial. 98. *have . . . free:* be freely allowed.
SCENE III: 1. *composition:* agreement; *news:* reports.

1ST SENATOR.   Indeed they are disproportioned.
    My letters say a hundred and seven galleys.
DUKE.   And mine, a hundred and forty.
2ND SENATOR.   And mine, two hundred.
    But though they jump not on a just account°—
    As in these cases, where the aim reports,°
    'Tis oft with difference—yet do they all confirm
    A Turkish fleet, and bearing up° to Cyprus.
DUKE.   Nay, it is possible enough to judgment.
    I do not so secure me in the error,°   10
    But the main article° I do approve
    In fearful° sense.
SAILOR [*within*]   What ho! What ho! What ho!
1ST OFFICER.   A messenger from the galleys.

                [*Enter* SAILOR.]

DUKE.   Now, what's the
    business?
SAILOR.   The Turkish preparation makes for Rhodes.
    So was I bid report here to the state
    By Signior Angelo.
DUKE.   How say you by this change?
1ST SENATOR.   This cannot be,
    By no assay of reason.° 'Tis a pageant°
    To keep us in false gaze.° When we consider
    The importancy of Cyprus to the Turk,   20
    And let ourselves again but understand
    That as it more concerns the Turk than Rhodes,
    So may he with more facile question bear° it,
    For that it stands not in such warlike brace°
    But altogether lacks the abilities
    That Rhodes is dressed° in—if we make thought of this,
    We must not think the Turk is so unskillful
    To leave that latest which concerns him first,

---

5. *jump . . . account:* do not agree with an exact estimate.   6. *aim reports:* that is, intelligence reports of an enemy's intention often differ in details.   8. *bearing up:* making course for.   10. *I . . . error:* I do not consider myself free from danger, because the reports may not all be accurate.   11. *main article:* general purport.   12. *fearful:* to be feared.   18. *assay of reason:* reasonable test; *pageant:* show.   19. *false gaze:* looking the wrong way.   23. *with . . . bear:* take it more easily.   24. *brace:* state of defense. 26. *dressed:* prepared.

Neglecting an attempt of ease and gain
To wake and wage° a danger profitless.   30
DUKE.   Nay, in all confidence, he's not for Rhodes.
1ST OFFICER.   Here is more news.

[*Enter a* MESSENGER.]

MESSENGER.   The Ottomites,° Reverend and Gracious,
Steering with due course toward the isle of Rhodes,
Have there injointed° them with an after-fleet.°
1ST. SENATOR.   Aye, so I thought. How many, as you guess?
MESSENGER.   Of thirty sail. And now they do restem°
Their backward course, bearing with frank appearance°
Their purposes toward Cyprus. Signior Montano,
Your trusty and most valiant servitor,   40
With his free duty recommends you thus,°
And prays you to believe him.
DUKE.   'Tis certain then for Cyprus.
Marcus Luccicos, is not he in town?
1ST SENATOR.   He's now in Florence.
DUKE.   Write from us to him. post-posthaste dispatch.
1ST SENATOR.   Here comes Brabantio and the valiant Moor.

[*Enter* BRABANTIO, OTHELLO, IAGO, RODERIGO, *and* OFFICERS.]

DUKE.   Valiant Othello, we must straight employ you
Against the general enemy Ottoman.
[*To* BRABANTIO] I did not see you. Welcome, gentle signior.
We lacked your counsel and your help tonight.   51
BRABANTIO.   So did I yours. Good your Grace, pardon me.
Neither my place nor aught I heard of business
Hath raised me from my bed, nor doth the general care
Take hold on me. For my particular° grief
Is of so floodgate° and o'erbearing nature
That it engluts° and swallows other sorrows,
And it is still itself.
DUKE.   Why, what's the matter?
BRABANTIO.   My daughter! Oh, my daughter!
ALL.   Dead?

---

30. *wage:* risk.   33. *Ottomites:* Turks.   35. *injointed:* joined; *after-fleet:* following, second fleet.   37. *restem:* steer again.   38. *frank appearance:* no attempt at concealment.
41. *With . . . thus:* with all due respect thus advises.   55. *particular:* personal.   56. *flood-
gate:* that is, like water rushing through an opened sluice.   57. *engluts:* swallows.

BRABANTIO.   Aye, to me.
    She is abused, stol'n from me and corrupted   60
    By spells and medicines bought of mountebanks.°
    For nature so preposterously to err,
    Being not deficient, blind, or lame of sense,
    Sans° witchcraft could not.
DUKE.   Whoe'er he be that in this foul proceeding
    Hath thus beguiled your daughter of herself°
    And you of her, the bloody book of law
    You shall yourself read in the bitter letter
    After your own sense—yea, though our proper° son
    Stood in your action.
BRABANTIO.   Humbly I thank your Grace.   70
    Here is the man, this Moor, whom now, it seems,
    Your special mandate for the state of affairs
    Hath hither brought.
ALL.   We are very sorry for 't.
DUKE [*to* OTHELLO].   What in your own part can you say to this?
BRABANTIO.   Nothing but this is so.
OTHELLO.   Most potent, grave, and reverend signiors,
    My very noble and approved° good masters,
    That I have ta'en away this old man's daughter,
    It is most true—true, I have married her.
    The very head and front° of my offending   80
    Hath this extent, no more. Rude° am I in my speech,
    And little blest with soft phrase of peace.
    For since these arms of mine had seven years' pith°
    Till now some nine moons wasted, they have used
    Their dearest° action in the tented field.
    And little of this great world can I speak,
    More than pertains to feats of broil and battle,
    And therefore little shall I grace my cause
    In speaking for myself. Yet, by your gracious patience,
    I will a round unvarnished tale° deliver   90
    Of my whole course of love—what drugs, what charms,

61. *mountebanks:* quack doctors, who dealt in poisons and love potions. 64. *Sans:* without. 66. *beguiled . . . herself:* cheated your daughter of herself; that is, caused her to be "beside herself." 69. *proper:* own. 77. *approved:* tested; that is, found good masters by experience. 80. *front:* forehead. 81. *Rude:* rough, uncultured. 83. *pith:* marrow. 85. *dearest:* most important. 90. *round . . . tale:* direct, unadorned account.

What conjuration and what mighty magic—
For such proceeding I am charged withal—
I won his daughter.

BRABANTIO.   A maiden never bold,
Of spirit so still and quiet that her motion
Blushed at herself,° and she—in spite of nature,
Of years, of country, credit,° everything—
To fall in love with what she feared to look on!
It is a judgment maimed and most imperfect
That will confess° perfection so could err   100
Against all rules of nature, and must be driven
To find out practices° of cunning Hell
Why this should be. I therefore vouch° again
That with some mixture° powerful o'er the blood,°
Or with some dram conjured° to this effect,
He wrought upon her.

DUKE.   To vouch this is no proof
Without more certain and more overt° test
Than these thin habits° and poor likelihoods°
Of modern seeming° do prefer° against him.

1ST SENATOR.   But Othello, speak.   110
Did you by indirect and forcèd° courses
Subdue and poison this young maid's affections?
Or came it by request, and such fair question
As soul to soul affordeth?

OTHELLO.   I do beseech you
Send for the lady to the Sagittary,
And let her speak of me before her father.
If you do find me foul in her report,
The trust, the office I do hold of you,
Not only take away, but let your sentence
Even fall upon my life.

DUKE.   Fetch Desdemona hither.   120

OTHELLO.   Ancient, conduct them, you best know the place.

                          [*Exeunt* IAGO *and* ATTENDANTS.]

95–96. *Of . . . herself:* she was so shy that she blushed at the slightest cause; *motion:* outward behavior. 97. *credit:* reputation. 100. *will confess:* would believe. 102. *practices:* plots. 103. *vouch:* declare. 104. *mixtures:* drugs; *blood:* passions. 105. *conjured:* mixed with spells. 107. *overt:* open. 108. *thin habits:* slight evidence; lit., thin clothes; *poor likelihoods:* unconvincing charges. 109. *modern seeming:* slight suspicions; *prefer:* make a charge against. 111. *forcèd:* unnatural.

And till she comes, as truly to Heaven
I do confess the vices of my blood,
So justly to your grave ears I'll present
How I did thrive in this fair lady's love
And she in mine.
DUKE.   Say it, Othello.
OTHELLO.   Her father loved me, oft invited me,
Still° questioned me the story of my life
From year to year, the battles, sieges, fortunes,
That I have passed.   130
I ran it through, even from my boyish days
To the very moment that he bade me tell it.
Wherein I spake of most disastrous chances,°
Of moving accidents° by flood and field,
Of hairbreadth 'scapes i' the imminent deadly breach,°
Of being taken by the insolent foe
And sold to slavery, of my redemption thence,
And portance° in my travels' history.
Wherein of antres° vast and deserts idle,°
Rough quarries, rocks, and hills whose heads touch heaven,
It was my hint° to speak—such was the process.°   141
And of the cannibals that each other eat,
The anthropophagi,° and men whose heads
Do grow beneath their shoulders. This to hear
Would Desdemona seriously incline.
But still the house affairs would draw her thence.
Which ever as she could with haste dispatch,
She'd come again, and with a greedy ear
Devour up my discourse. Which I observing,
Took once a pliant° hour and found good means   150
To draw from her a prayer of earnest heart
That I would all my pilgrimage dilate,°
Whereof by parcels° she had something heard,
But not intentively.° I did consent,
And often did beguile her of° her tears

---

128. *Still:* always, continually. 133. *chances:* accidents. 134. *accidents:* occurrences.
135. *breach:* assault on a city. 138. *portance:* bearing. 139. *antres:* caves; *idle:* worthless. 141. *hint:* occasion; *process:* proceeding, order. 143. *anthropophagi:* cannibals.
150. *pliant:* suitable. 152. *dilate:* relate at length. 153. *parcels:* portions. 154. *inten-*
tively: intently. 155. *beguile . . . of:* draw from her.

When I did speak of some distressful stroke
That my youth suffered. My story being done,
She gave me for my pains a world of sighs.
She swore, in faith, 'twas strange, 'twas passing strange,
'Twas pitiful, 'twas wondrous pitiful.   160
She wished she had not heard it, yet she wished
That Heaven had made her° such a man. She thanked me,
And bade me, if I had a friend that loved her,
I should but teach him how to tell my story
And that would woo her. Upon this hint I spake.
She loved me for the dangers I had passed,
And I loved her that she did pity them.
This only is the witchcraft I have used.
Here comes the lady, let her witness it.

      [*Enter* DESDEMONA, IAGO, *and* ATTENDANTS.]

DUKE.   I think this tale would win my daughter too.   170
  Good Brabantio,
  Take up this mangled matter at the best.°
  Men do their broken weapons rather use
  Than their bare hands.
BRABANTIO.   I pray you hear her speak.
  If she confess that she was half the wooer,
  Destruction on my head if my bad blame
  Light on the man! Come hither, gentle mistress.
  Do you perceive in all this noble company
  Where most you owe obedience?
DESDEMONA.   My noble Father,   180
  I do perceive here a divided duty.
  To you I am bound for life and education,
  My life and education both do learn° me
  How to respect you, you are the lord of duty,°
  I am hitherto your daughter. But here's my husband,
  And so much duty as my mother showed
  To you, preferring you before her father
  So much I challenge that I may profess
  Due to the Moor my lord.

---

162. *her:* for her. 172. *Take . . . best:* make the best settlement you can of this confused business. 183. *learn:* teach. 184. *lord of duty:* the man to whom I owe duty.

BRABANTIO.   God be with you! I have done.
   Please it your Grace, on to the state affairs.   190
   I had rather adopt a child than get° it.
   Come hither, Moor.
   I here do give thee that with all my heart
   Which, but thou hast already, with all my heart
   I would keep from thee. For your sake, jewel,
   I am glad at soul I have no other child,
   For thy escape would teach me tyranny,
   To hang clogs on them. I have done, my lord.
DUKE.   Let me speak like yourself, and lay a sentence°
   Which, as a grise° or step, may help these lovers   200
   Into your favor.
   When remedies are past, the griefs are ended
   By seeing the worst, which late on hopes depended.°
   To mourn a mischief that is past and gone
   Is the next way to draw new mischief on.
   What cannot be preserved when fortune takes,
   Patience her injury a mockery makes.°
   The robbed that smiles steals something from the thief.
   He robs himself that spends a bootless° grief.
BRABANTIO.   So° let the Turk of Cyprus us beguile,   210
   We lose it not so long as we can smile.
   He bears the sentence well that nothing bears
   But the free comfort which from thence he hears.
   But he bears both the sentence and the sorrow
   That, to pay grief, must of poor patience borrow.
   These sentences, to sugar or to gall,
   Being strong on both sides, are equivocal.
   But words are words. I never yet did hear
   That the bruised heart was piercèd through the ear.
   I humbly beseech you, proceed to the affairs of state.   220

---

191. *get:* beget. 199. *sentence:* proverbial saying. 200. *grise:* degree, step.
202–03. *When . . . depended:* our anxieties end when the feared event happens.
207. *Patience . . . makes:* that is, when we are not unduly disturbed by our misfortunes, we mock Fortune. 209. *bootless:* vain. 210–19. *So . . . ear:* Brabantio retaliates sarcastically with a few "sentences" of his own: Let the Turk take Cyprus; it is no loss if we smile at it. It is easy enough to produce sententious consolation, it costs nothing; but the man who has to endure both consolation and the sorrow itself must needs be patient. These sentences work both ways; mere words hurt no one.

DUKE.   The Turk with a most mighty preparation makes for
Cyprus. Othello, the fortitude of the place is best known
to you, and though we have there a substitute° of most
allowed° sufficiency,° yet opinion, a sovereign mistress
of effects, throws a more safer voice on you.° You must
therefore be content to slubber° the gloss of your new
fortunes with this more stubborn and boisterous expedi-
tion.

OTHELLO.   The tyrant custom, most grave Senators,
Hath made the flinty and steel couch of war   230
My thrice-driven° bed of down. I do agnize°
A natural and prompt alacrity
I find in hardness,° and do undertake
These present wars against the Ottomites.
Most humbly therefore bending to your state,
I crave fit disposition for my wife,
Due reference of place° and exhibition,°
With such accommodation and besort°
As levels with her breeding.°

DUKE.   If you please,
Be 't at her father's.

BRABANTIO.   I'll not have it so.   240

OTHELLO. Nor I.

DESDEMONA.   Nor I. I would not there reside
To put my father in impatient thoughts
By being in his eye. Most gracious Duke,
To my unfolding° lend your prosperous° ear,
And let me find a charter° in your voice
To assist my simpleness.

DUKE.   What would you, Desdemona?

DESDEMONA.   That I did love the Moor to live with him,
My downright violence and storm of fortunes

---

223. *substitute:* deputy commander.   224. *allowed:* admitted; *sufficiency:* efficency.
224–25. *yet . . . you:* yet public opinion, which controls our actions, is such that we
regard you as a safer choice.   226. *slubber:* tarnish.   231. *thrice driven:* three times refined; *agnize:* confess.   233. *hardness:* hardship.   237. *Due . . . place:* that is, that she
shall be treated as becomes my wife; *exhibition:* allowance.   238. *besort:* attendants.
239. *levels . . . breeding:* as suits her birth.   244. *unfolding:* plan; literally, revealing;
prosperous: favorable.   245. *charter:* privilege.

May trumpet to the world. My heart's subdued   250
Even to the very quality of my lord.°
I saw Othello's visage in his mind,
And to his honors and his valiant parts
Did I my soul and fortunes consecrate.
So that, dear lords, if I be left behind,
A moth of peace,° and he go to the war,
The rites for which I love him are bereft me,
And I a heavy interim° shall support
By his dear absence. Let me go with him.
OTHELLO.   Let her have your voices.   260
   Vouch° with me, Heaven, I therefore beg it not
   To please the palate of my appetite,
   Nor to comply with heat—the young affects
   In me defunct°—and proper satisfaction,
   But to be free and bounteous° to her mind.°
   And Heaven defend° your good souls, that you think
   I will your serious and great business scant
   For she is with me. No, when light-winged toys°
   Of feathered Cupid seel° with wanton dullness
   My speculative and officed instruments,°   270
   That my disports° corrupt and taint my business,
   Let housewives make a skillet° of my helm,
   And all indign° and base adversities
   Make head against° my estimation!°
DUKE.   Be it as you shall privately determine,
   Either for her stay or going. The affair cries haste,
   And speed must answer 't. You must hence tonight.
DESDEMONA.   Tonight, my lord?
DUKE.   This night.
OTHELLO.   With all my heart.

248–51. *That . . . lord:* my love for the Moor is publicly shown by the way in which I
have violently taken my fortunes in my hands; my heart has become a soldier like my
husband; *quality:* profession.   256. *moth of peace:* a useless creature living in luxury.
258. *interim:* interval.   261. *Vouch:* certify.   263–64. *young . . . defunct:* in me the passion of youth is dead.   265. *bounteous:* generous; *to . . . mind:* Othello repeats Desdemona's claim that this is a marriage of minds.   266. *defend:* forbid.   268. *toys:* trifles.
269. *seel:* close up; a technical term from falconry.   270. *speculative . . . instruments:*
powers of sight and action; that is, my efficiency as your general.   271. *disports:*
amusements.   272. *skillet:* saucepan.   273. *indign:* unworthy.   274. *Make . . . against:*
overcome; *estimation:* reputation.

DUKE.   At nine i' the morning here we'll meet again.
    Othello, leave some officer behind,   280
    And he shall our commission° bring to you,
    With such things else of quality and respect
    As doth import you.°
OTHELLO.   So please your Grace, my Ancient,
    A man he is of honesty and trust.
    To his conveyance I assign my wife,
    With what else needful your good grace shall think
    To be sent after me.
DUKE.   Let it be so.
    Good night to everyone. [*To* BRABANTIO] And, noble signior,
    If virtue no delighted beauty lack,
    Your son-in-law is far more fair than black.°   290
1ST SENATOR.   Adieu, brave Moor. Use Desdemona well.
BRABANTIO.   Look to her, Moor, if thou hast eyes to see.
    She has deceived her father, and may thee.°

                 [*Exeunt* DUKE, SENATORS, OFFICERS, *etc.*]

OTHELLO.   My life upon her faith! Honest Iago,
    My Desdemona must I leave to thee.
    I prithee, let thy wife attend on her,
    And bring them after in the best advantage.°
    Come, Desdemona, I have but an hour
    Of love, of worldly matters and direction,
    To spend with thee. We must obey the time.   300

                 [*Exeunt* OTHELLO *and* DESDEMONA.]

RODERIGO.   Iago!
IAGO.   What say'st thou, noble heart?
RODERIGO.   What will I do, thinkest thou?
IAGO.   Why, go to bed and sleep.
RODERIGO.   I will incontinently° drown myself.
IAGO.   If thou dost, I shall never love thee after.
    Why, thou silly gentleman!

---

281. *commission:* formal document of appointment.   282–83. *With . . . you:* with other matters that concern your position and honor.   289–90. *If . . . black:* if worthiness is a beautiful thing in itself, your son-in-law, though black, has beauty.   293–95. *Look . . . thee:* Iago in the background takes note of these words, and later reminds Othello of them with deadly effect (see III.iii.206).   297. *in . . . advantage:* at the best opportunity.   305. *incontinently:* immediately.

RODERIGO.   It is silliness to live when to live is torment, and
then have we a prescription to die when death is our
physician.   310
IAGO.   Oh, villainous! I have looked upon the world for four
times seven years, and since I could distinguish betwixt a
benefit and an injury I never found man that knew how
to love himself. Ere I would say I would drown myself
for the love of a guinea hen, I would change my humanity with a baboon.
RODERIGO.   What should I do? I confess it is my shame to be
so fond,° but it is not in my virtue° to amend it.
IAGO.   Virtue! A fig! 'Tis in ourselves that we are thus or
thus. Our bodies are gardens, to the which our wills° are   320
gardeners. So that if we will plant nettles or sow lettuce,
set hyssop and weed up thyme, supply it with one gen-
der° of herbs or distract it with many, either to have it
sterile with idleness or manured with industry—why,
the power and corrigible° authority of this lies in our
wills. If the balance of our lives had not one scale of
reason to poise° another of sensuality, the blood and
baseness of our natures would conduct us to most pre-
posterous conclusions. But we have reason to cool our
raging motions, our carnal stings,° our unbitted° lusts,   330
whereof I take this that you call love to be a sect or
scion.°
RODERIGO.   It cannot be.
IAGO.   It is merely a lust of the blood and a permission of the
will. Come, be a man. Drown thyself! Drown cats and
blind puppies. I have professed me thy friend, and I
confess me knit to thy deserving with cables of per-
durable° toughness. I could never better stead° thee than
now. Put money in thy purse, follow thou the wars,
defeat thy favor with an usurped beard°—I say put   340
money in thy purse. It cannot be that Desdemona should
long continue her love to the Moor—put money in thy

318. *fond:* foolishly in love; *virtue:* manhood.   320. *wills:* desires.   323. *gender:* kind.
325. *corrigible:* correcting, directing.   327. *poise:* weigh.   330. *carnal stings:* fleshly desires; *unbitted:* uncontrolled.   332. *sect or scion:* Both words mean a slip taken from a
tree and planted to produce a new growth.   338. *predurable:* very hard; *stead:* help.
340. *defeat . . . beard:* disguise your face by growing a beard.

purse—nor he his to her. It was a violent commencement, and thou shalt see an answerable sequestration°—
put but money in thy purse. These Moors are changeable
in their wills.—Fill thy purse with money. The food that
to him now is as luscious as locusts° shall be to him
shortly as bitter as coloquintida.° She must change for
youth. When she is sated with his body, she will find the
error of her choice. She must have change, she must—   350
therefore put money in thy purse. If thou wilt needs
damn thyself, do it a more delicate way than drowning.
Make all the money thou canst.° If sanctimony and a frail
vow betwixt an erring° barbarian and a supersubtle Venetian be not too hard for my wits and all the tribe of
Hell, thou shalt enjoy her—therefore make money. A
pox of drowning thyself! It is clean out of the way. Seek
thou rather to be hanged in compassing° thy joy than to
be drowned and go without her.

RODERIGO.   Wilt thou be fast to my hopes if I depend on the   360
issue?

IAGO.   Thou art sure of me. Go, make money. I have told
thee often, and I retell thee again and again, I hate the
Moor. My cause is hearted,° thine hath no less reason.
Let us be conjunctive° in our revenge against him. If
thou canst cuckold° him, thou dost thyself a pleasure, me
a sport. There are many events in the womb of time,
which will be delivered. Traverse,° go, provide thy
money. We will have more of this tomorrow. Adieu.

RODERIGO.   Where shall we meet i' the morning?   370
IAGO.   At my lodging.
RODERIGO.   I'll be with thee betimes.°
IAGO.   Go to, farewell. Do you hear, Roderigo?
RODERIGO.   What say you?
IAGO.   No more of drowning, do you hear?
RODERIGO.   I am changed. I'll go sell all my land.

                                                    [*Exit.*]

---

344. *answerable sequestration:* corresponding separation; that is, reaction. 347. *locusts:* It
is not known what fruit was called a locust. 348. *coloquintida:* known as "bitter apple," a form of gherkin from which a purge was made. 353. *Make . . . canst:* turn all
you can into ready cash. 354. *erring:* vagabond. 358. *compassing:* achieving.
364. *hearted:* heartfelt. 365. *conjunctive:* united. 366. *cuckold:* make him a cuckold.
368. *Traverse:* quickstep. 372. *betimes:* in good time, early.

IAGO.   Thus do I ever make my fool my purse,
For I mine own gained knowledge should profane
If I would time expend with such a snipe
But for my sport and profit. I hate the Moor,   380
And it is thought abroad that 'twixt my sheets
He has done my office. I know not if 't be true,
But I for mere suspicion in that kind
Will do as if for surety. He holds me well,
The better shall my purpose work on him.
Cassio's a proper° man. Let me see now,
To get his place, and to plume up° my will
In double knavery——How, how?—Let's see.—
After some time, to abuse Othello's ear
That he is too familiar with his wife.   390
He hath a person and a smooth dispose
To be suspected,° framed to make women false.
The Moor is of a free and open nature
That thinks men honest that but seem to be so,
And will as tenderly be led by the nose   395
As asses are.
I have't. It is engendered.° Hell and night
Must bring this monstrous birth to the world's light.

                                                        [*Exit.*]

ACT II

SCENE I. *A seaport in Cyprus. An open place near the wharf.*

[*Enter* MONTANO *and two* GENTLEMEN.]

MONTANO.   What from the cape can you discern at sea?
1ST GENTLEMAN.   Nothing at all. It is a high-wrought flood.°
I cannot 'twixt the heaven and the main°
Descry a sail.
MONTANO.   Methinks the wind hath spoke aloud at land,
A fuller blast ne'er shook our battlements.

---

386. *proper:* handsome.   387. *plume up:* glorify.   391–92. *He . . . suspected:* an easy
way with him that is naturally suspected.   397. *engendered:* conceived.
Act II, SCENE I: 2. *high-wrought flood:* heavy sea.   3. *main:* sea.

If it hath ruffianed° so upon the sea,
What ribs of oak, when mountains melt on them,
Can hold the mortise?° What shall we hear of this?
2ND GENTLEMAN.   A segregation° of the Turkish fleet.   10
For do but stand upon the foaming shore,
The chidden billow seems to pelt the clouds,
The wind-shaked surge, with high and monstrous mane,
Seems to cast water on the burning Bear,°
And quench the guards of the ever-fixèd Pole.°
I never did like molestation° view
On the enchafèd° flood.
MONTANO.   If that the Turkish fleet
Be not ensheltered and embayed,° they are drowned.
It is impossible to bear it out.
                  [*Enter a* THIRD GENTLEMAN]
3RD GENTLEMAN.   News, lads! Our wars are done.   20
The desperate tempest hath so banged the Turks
That their designment halts.° A noble ship of Venice
Hath seen a grievous wreck and sufferance°
On most part of their fleet.
MONTANO.   How! Is this true?
3RD GENTLEMAN.   The ship is here put in,
A Veronesa. Michael Cassio,
Lieutenant to the warlike Moor Othello,
Is come on shore, the Moor himself at sea,
And is in full commission° here for Cyprus.
MONTANO.   I am glad on 't. 'Tis a worthy governor.   30
3RD GENTLEMAN.   But this same Cassio, though he
      speak of comfort
Touching the Turkish loss, yet he looks sadly
And prays the Moor be safe, for they were parted
With foul and violent tempest.
MONTANO.   Pray Heavens he be,
For I have served him, and the man commands
Like a full° soldier. Let's to the seaside, ho!

7. *ruffianed:* played the ruffian.   9. *hold . . . mortise:* remain fast joined.   10. *segregation:* separation.   14. *Bear:* the Great Bear.   15. *guards . . . Pole:* stars in the "tail" of the Little Bear constellation.   16. *molestation:* disturbance.   17. *enchafed:* angry.   18. *embayed:* anchored in some bay.   22. *designment halts:* plan is made lame.   23. *sufferance:* damage.   29. *in . . . commission:* with full powers (see I.iii.280–81).   36. *full:* perfect.

As well to see the vessel that's come in
As to throw out our eyes for brave Othello,
Even till we make the main and the aerial blue
An indistinct regard.°

3RD GENTLEMAN.   Come, let's do so.   40
For every minute is expectancy
Of more arrivance.°

[*Enter* CASSIO.]

CASSIO.   Thanks, you the valiant of this warlike isle
That so approve the Moor! Oh, let the heavens
Give him defense against the elements,
For I have lost him on a dangerous sea.

MONTANO.   Is he well shipped?°

CASSIO.   His bark is stoutly timbered, and his pilot
Of very expert and approved allowance.°
Therefore my hopes, not surfeited° to death,   50
Stand in bold cure.° [*A cry within:* "A sail, a sail, a sail!"]

[*Enter a* FOURTH GENTLEMAN.]

CASSIO.   What noise?

4TH GENTLEMAN.   The town is empty. On the brow o' the sea
Stand ranks of people, and they cry "A sail!"

CASSIO.   My hopes do shape° him for the governor.

[*Guns heard.*]

4TH GENTLEMAN.   They do discharge their shot of courtesy.
Our friends, at least.

CASSIO.   I pray you, sir, go forth,
And give us truth who 'tis that is arrived.

2ND GENTLEMAN.   I shall.

[*Exit.*]

MONTANO.   But, good Lieutenant, is your General wived?   60

CASSIO.   Most fortunately. He hath achieved° a maid
That paragons° description and wild fame,
One that excels the quirks of blazoning pens

39–40. *Even . . . regard:* until we can no longer distinguish between sea and sky.
41–42. *For . . . arrivance:* every minute more arrivals are expected. 47. *well shipped:* in
a good ship. 49. *approved allowance:* proved skill. 50. *surfeited:* sickened. 51. *Stand
. . . cure:* have every hope of cure. 55. *shape:* imagine. 61. *achieved:* won. 62. *paragons:*
surpasses.

And in the essential vesture of creation
Does tire the ingener.°

      ⌈*Re-enter* SECOND GENTLEMAN.⌉

                How now! Who has put in?

2ND GENTLEMAN. 'Tis one Iago, Ancient to the General.
CASSIO. He has had most favorable and happy speed.
    Tempests themselves, high seas, and howling winds,
    The guttered° rocks, and congregated sands,   70
    Traitors ensteeped° to clog the guiltless keel,
    As having sense of beauty, do omit
    Their mortal natures,° letting go safely by
    The divine Desdemona.
MONTANO.   What is she?
CASSIO. She that I spake of, our great Captain's captain,
    Left in the conduct° of the bold Iago,
    Whose footing° anticipates our thoughts
    A sennight's° speed. Great Jove, Othello guard,
    And swell his sail with thine own powerful breath,
    That he may bless this bay with his tall ship,   80
    Make love's quick pants in Desdemona's arms,
    Give renewed fire to our extincted° spirits,
    And bring all Cyprus comfort.

  ⌈*Enter* DESDEMONA, EMILIA, IAGO, RODERIGO, *and* ATTENDANTS.⌉

                  Oh, behold,
    The riches of the ship is come on shore!
    Ye men of Cyprus, let her have your knees.
    Hail to thee, lady! And the grace of Heaven,
    Before, behind thee, and on every hand,
    Enwheel° thee round!
DESDEMONA.   I thank you, valiant Cassio.
    What tidings can you tell me of my lord?
CASSIO. He is not yet arrived, nor know I aught   90
    But that he's well and will be shortly here.

63–65. *One . . . ingener:* one that is too good for the fancy phrases (*quirks*) of painting
pens (i.e., poets) and in her absolute perfection wearies the artist (i.e., the painter).
Cassio is full of gallant phrases and behavior, in contrast to Iago's bluntness; *ingener:*
inventor. 70. *guttered:* worn into channels. 71. *ensteeped:* submerged. 72–73. *omit
. . . natures:* forbear their deadly nature. 76. *conduct:* escort. 77. *footing:* arrival.
78. *sennight:* week. 82. *extincted:* extinguished. 88. *Enwheel:* encompass.

DESDEMONA.   Oh, but I fear——How lost you company?

CASSIO.   The great contention of the sea and skies
Parted our fellowship.°—But, hark! A sail.

[*A cry within:* "A sail, a sail!" *Guns heard.*]

2ND GENTLEMAN.   They give their greeting to the citadel.
This is likewise is a friend.

CASSIO.   See for the news.

[*Exit* GENTLEMAN.]

Good Ancient, you are welcome. [*To* EMILIA.]
                          Welcome, mistress.
Let it not gall your patience, good Iago,
That I extend my manners.° 'Tis my breeding°
That gives me this bold show of courtesy.° [*Kissing her.*]   100

IAGO.   Sir, would she give you so much of her lips
As of her tongue she oft bestows on me,
You'd have enough.

DESDEMONA.   Alas, she has no speech.

IAGO.   In faith, too much,
I find it still° when I have list° to sleep.
Marry, before your ladyship, I grant,
She puts her tongue a little in her heart
And chides with thinking.

EMILIA.   You have little cause to say so.

IAGO.   Come on, come on. You are pictures° out of doors,   110
Bells° in your parlors, wildcats in your kitchens,
Saints in your injuries,° devils being offended,
Players in your housewifery, and housewives in your beds.

DESDEMONA.   Oh, fie upon thee, slanderer!

IAGO.   Nay, it is true, or else I am a Turk.°
You rise to play, and go to bed to work.

EMILIA.   You shall not write my praise.

IAGO.   No, let me not.

DESDEMONA.   What wouldst thou write of me if thou
shouldst praise me?

---

94. *fellowship:* company. 99. *extend my manners:* that is, salute your wife; *breeding:*
bringing-up. 100. *bold . . . courtesy:* that is, of saluting your wife with a kiss—a piece
of presumptuous behavior which indicates that Cassio regards himself as Iago's social
superior. 105. *still:* continuously; *list:* desire. 110. *pictures:* that is, painted and
dumb. 111. *Bells:* i.e., ever clacking. 112. *Saints . . . injuries:* saints when you hurt
anyone else. 115. *Turk:* heathen.

IAGO.   O gentle lady, do not put me to 't,
   For I am nothing if not critical.°   120
DESDEMONA.   Come on, assay.°—There's one gone to the harbor?
IAGO.   Aye, madam.
DESDEMONA.   I am not merry, but I do beguile
   The thing I am by seeming otherwise.
   Come, how wouldst thou praise me?
IAGO.   I am about it, but indeed my invention
   Comes from my pate as birdlime does from frieze°—
   It plucks out brains and all. But my Muse labors,
   And thus she is delivered.
   If she be fair and wise, fairness and wit,   130
   The one's for use, the other useth it.
DESDEMONA.   Well praised! How if she be black and witty?
IAGO.   If she be black, and thereto have a wit,
   She'll find a white° that shall her blackness fit.
DESDEMONA.   Worse and worse.
EMILIA.   How if fair and foolish?
IAGO.   She never yet was foolish that was fair,
   For even her folly helped her to an heir.
DESDEMONA.   These are old fond paradoxes° to make fools
   laugh i' the alehouse. What miserable praise hast thou for   140
   her that's foul and foolish?
IAGO.   There's none so foul, and foolish thereunto,
   But does foul pranks which fair and wise ones do.
DESDEMONA.   Oh, heavy ignorance! Thou praisest the worst
   best. But what praise couldst thou bestow on a deserv-
   ing woman indeed, one that in the authority of her
   merit did justly put on the vouch of very malice itself?°
IAGO.   She that was ever fair and never proud,
   Had tongue at will° and yet was never loud,
   Never lacked gold and yet went never gay,   150
   Fled from her wish and yet said "Now I may,"
   She that, being angered, her revenge being nigh,
   Bade her wrong stay and her displeasures fly,

---

120. *critical:* bitter. 121. *assay:* try. 126–27. *my . . . frieze:* my literary effort (*inven-tion*) is as hard to pull out of my head as frieze (cloth with a nap) stuck to birdlime.
134. *white:* with a pun on *wight* (l. 158). man, person. 139. *fond paradoxes:* foolish
remarks, contrary to general opinion. 146–47. *one . . . itself:* one so deserving that
even malice would declare her good. 149. *tongue . . . will:* a ready flow of words.

She that in wisdom never was so frail
To change the cod's head for the salmon's tail,°
She that could think and ne'er disclose her mind,
See suitors following and not look behind,
She was a wight, if ever such wight were——

DESDEMONA.   To do what?

IAGO.   To suckle fools and chronicle small beer.°   160

DESDEMONA.   Oh, most lame and impotent conclusion! Do
not learn of him, Emilia, though he be thy husband.
How say you, Cassio? Is he not a most profane and
liberal° counselor?

CASSIO.   He speaks home,° madam. You may relish° him
more in the soldier than in the scholar.

IAGO [aside].   He° takes her by the palm. Aye, well said,
whisper. With as little a web as this will I ensnare as
great a fly as Cassio. Aye, smile upon her, do, I will
gyve° thee in thine own courtship. You say true, 'tis so   170
indeed. If such tricks as these strip you out of your Lieu-
tenantry, it had been better you had not kissed your three
fingers° so oft, which now again you are most apt to
play the sir° in. Very good, well kissed! An excellent
courtesy! 'Tis so indeed. Yet again your fingers to your
lips? Would they were clyster pipes° for your sake!
[Trumpets within.] The Moor! I know his trumpet.

CASSIO.   'Tis truly so.

DESDEMONA.   Let's meet him and receive him.

CASSIO.   Lo where he comes!   180

[Enter OTHELLO and ATTENDANTS.]

OTHELLO.   O my fair warrior!°

DESDEMONA.   My dear Othello!

OTHELLO.   It gives me wonder great as my content
To see you here before me. O my soul's joy!
If after every tempest come such calms,

---

155. *To . . . tail:* to prefer the tail end of a good thing to the head of a poor thing.
160. *chronicle . . . beer:* write a whole history about trifles (*small beer:* thin drink).
164. *liberal:* gross.   165. *home:* to the point; *relish:* appreciate.   167–76. *He . . . sake:*
As so often, Shakespeare without using elaborate stage directions exactly indicates the
action in the dialogue.   170. *gyve:* fetter.   172–73. *kissed . . . fingers:* a gesture of gallantry.   174. *play . . . sir:* act the fine gentleman.   176. *clyster pipes:* an enema
syringe.   181. *warrior:* because she is a soldier's wife (see I.iii.250).

May the winds blow till they have wakened death!
And let the laboring bark climb hills of seas
Olympus-high,° and duck again as low
As Hell's from Heaven! If it were now to die,
'Twere now to be most happy, for I fear
My soul hath her content so absolute   190
That not another comfort like to this
Succeeds in unknown fate.
DESDEMONA.   The Heavens forbid
But that our loves and comforts should increase,
Even as our days do grow!
OTHELLO.   Amen to that, sweet powers!
I cannot speak enough of this content.
It stops me here,° it is too much of joy.
And this, and this, the greatest discords be [*kissing her*]
That e'er our hearts shall make!
IAGO [*aside*].   Oh, you are well tuned now.
But I'll set down the pegs° that make this music,   200
As honest as I am.
OTHELLO.   Come, let us to the castle.
News, friends. Our wars are done, the Turks are drowned.
How does my old acquaintance of this isle?
Honey, you shall be well desired in Cyprus,
I have found great love amongst them. O my sweet,
I prattle out of fashion,° and I dote
In mine own comforts. I prithee, good Iago,
Go to the bay and disembark my coffers.°
Bring thou the master° to the citadel.
He is a good one, and his worthiness   210
Does challenge° much respect. Come, Desdemona,
Once more well met at Cyprus.

                    [*Exeunt all but* IAGO *and* RODERIGO.]

IAGO.   Do thou meet me presently° at the harbor. Come
hither. If thou beest valiant—as they say base men being
in love have then a nobility in their natures more than is

187. *Olympus-high:* high as Olympus, the highest mountain in Greece.   196. *here:* that is, in
the heart.   200. *set . . . pegs:* that is, make you sing a in a different key. A stringed instrument was tuned by the pegs.   206. *prattle . . . fashion:* talk idly.   208. *coffers:* trunks.
209. *master:* captain of the ship.   211. *challenge:* claim.   213. *presently:* immediately.

native to them—list me. The Lieutenant tonight watches
on the court of guard.° First, I must tell thee this. Desdemona is directly in love with him.

RODERIGO.   With him! Why, 'tis not possible.

IAGO.   Lay thy finger thus,° and let thy soul be instructed.   220
Mark me with what violence she first loved the Moor,
but for° bragging and telling her fantastical lies. And will
she love him still for prating? Let not thy discreet heart
think it. Her eye must be fed, and what delight shall she
have to look on the Devil?° When the blood is made dull
with the act of sport, there should be, again to inflame it
and to give satiety a fresh appetite, loveliness in favor,°
sympathy in years, manners, and beauties, all which the
Moor is defective in. Now, for want of these required
conveniences, her delicate tenderness will find itself   230
abused, begin to heave the gorge,° disrelish and abhor
the Moor. Very nature will instruct her in it and compel
her to some second choice. Now, sir, this granted—as it
is a most pregnant and unforced position°—who stands
so eminently in the degree of this fortune as Cassio does?
A knave very voluble, no further conscionable° than in
putting on the mere form of civil and humane seeming°
for the better compassing of his salt° and most hidden
loose affection? Why, none, why, none. A slipper° and
subtle knave, a finder-out of occasions, that has an eye   240
can stamp and counterfeit advantages,° though true advantage never present itself. A devilish knave! Besides,
the knave is handsome, young, and hath all those requi-
sites in him that folly and green° minds look after. A
pestilent complete knave, and the woman hath found
him already.

RODERIGO.   I cannot believe that in her. She's full of most
blest condition.°

216–17. *watches . . . guard:* is on duty with the guard. The court of guard meant both the
guard itself and the guardroom.   220. *finger thus:* that is, on the lips.   222. *but for:* only
for.   225. *Devil:* See I.i.91,n.   227. *favor:* face.   231. *heave . . . gorge:*retch; *gorge:*
throat.   234. *pregnant . . . position:* very significant and probable argument.   236. *no
. . . conscionable:* who has no more conscience.   237. *humane seeming:* courteous appearance.   238. *salt:* lecherous.   239. *slipper:* slippery.   241. *stamp . . . advantages:* forge false
opportunities.   244. *green:* inexperienced, foolish.   248. *condition:* disposition.

IAGO. Blest fig's-end!° The wine she drinks is made of
grapes. If she had been blest, she would never have   250
loved the Moor. Blest pudding! Didst thou not see her
paddle° with the palm of his hand? Didst not mark that?
RODERIGO. Yes, that I did, but that was but courtesy.
IAGO. Lechery, by this hand, an index° and obscure prologue to the history of lust and foul thoughts. They met
so near with their lips that their breaths embraced
together. Villainous thoughts, Roderigo! When these
mutualities° so marshal the way, hard at hand comes the
master and main exercise, the incorporate° conclusion.
Pish! But, sir, be you ruled by me. I have brought you   260
from Venice. Watch you tonight. For the command, I'll
lay 't upon you. Cassio knows you not. I'll not be far
from you. Do you find some occasion to anger Cassio,
either by speaking too loud, or tainting° his discipline, or
from what other course you please which the time shall
more favorably minister.°
RODERIGO. Well.
IAGO. Sir, he is rash and very sudden in choler,° and haply°
may strike at you. Provoke him, that he may, for even
out of that will I cause these of Cyprus to mutiny, whose   270
qualification° shall come into no true taste again but by
the displanting° of Cassio. So shall you have a shorter
journey to your desires by the means I shall then have to
prefer° them, and the impediment most profitably removed without the which there were no expectation of
our prosperity.
RODERIGO. I will do this, if I can bring it to any opportunity.
IAGO. I warrant thee. Meet me by and by at the citadel. I
must fetch his necessaries ashore. Farewell.   280
RODERIGO. Adieu.

[*Exit.*]

---

249. *Blest fig's-end:* blest nonsense, a phrase used as a substitute in contempt for a
phrase just used, as is also *blest pudding* (l. 251). 252. *paddle:* play. 254. *index:* table
of contents. 258. *mutualities:* mutual exchanges. 259. *incorporate:* bodily.
264. *tainting:* disparaging. 266. *minister:* provide. 268. *choler:* anger; *haply:* perhaps.
271. *qualification:* appeasement. 272. *displanting:* removal. 274. *prefer:* promote.

IAGO.   That Cassio loves her, I do well believe it.
That she loves him, 'tis apt and of great credit.°
The Moor, howbeit that I endure him not,
Is of a constant, loving, noble nature,
And I dare think he'll prove to Desdemona
A most dear husband. Now, I do love her too,
Not out of absolute lust, though peradventure
I stand accountant for as great a sin,
But partly led to diet° my revenge   290
For that I do suspect the lusty Moor
Hath leaped into my seat. The thought whereof
Doth like a poisonous mineral° gnaw my inwards.
And nothing can or shall content my soul
Till I am evened with him, wife for wife.
Or failing so, yet that I put the Moor
At least into a jealousy so strong
That judgment° cannot cure. Which thing to do,
If this poor trash of Venice, whom I trash°
For his quick hunting, stand the putting-on,°   300
I'll have our Michael Cassio on the hip,
Abuse him to the Moor in the rank garb°—
For I fear Cassio with my nightcap too—
Make the Moor thank me, love me, and reward me
For making him egregiously° an ass
And practicing upon° his peace and quiet
Even to madness. 'Tis here, but yet confused.
Knavery's plain face is never seen till used.

[Exit.]

SCENE II. A street.

[Enter a HERALD with a proclamation, PEOPLE following.]

HERALD.   It is Othello's pleasure, our noble and valiant General, that upon certain tidings now arrived, importing
the mere perdition° of the Turkish fleet, every man put

---

283. *apt . . . credit:* likely and very credible.   290. *diet:* feed.   293. *poisonous mineral:*
corrosive poison (see I.ii.74).   298. *judgment:* reason.   299. *trash . . . trash:* rubbish . . .
discard.   300. *putting-on:* encouraging.   302. *rank garb:* gross manner; that is, by
accusing him of being Desdemona's lover.   305. *egregiously:* notably.   306. *practicing
upon:* plotting against.
SCENE II. 3. *mere perdition:* absolute destruction.

himself into triumph°—some to dance, some to make
bonfires, each man to what sport and revels his addic-
tion° leads him, For, besides these beneficial news, it is
the celebration of his nuptial. So much was his pleasure
should be proclaimed. All offices° are open, and there is
full liberty of feasting from this present hour of five till
the bell have told eleven. Heaven bless the isle of Cyprus   10
and our noble General Othello!

                                         [Exeunt.]

SCENE III. *A hall in the castle.*

[Enter OTHELLO, DESDEMONA, CASSIO, *and* ATTENDANTS.]

OTHELLO.   Good Michael, look you to the guard tonight.
    Let's teach ourselves that honorable stop,
    Not to outsport discretion.°
CASSIO.   Iago hath direction what to do,
    But notwithstanding with my personal eye
    Will I look to 't.
OTHELLO.   Iago is most honest.
    Michael, good night. Tomorrow with your earliest°
    Let me have speech with you. Come, my dear love,
    The purchase made, the fruits are to ensue—
    That profit's yet to come 'tween me and you.   10
    Good night.

           [Exeunt OTHELLO, DESDEMONA, *and* ATTENDANTS.]
                    [Enter IAGO.]

CASSIO.   Welcome, Iago. We must to the watch.
IAGO.   Not this hour, Lieutenant, 'tis not yet ten o' the
    clock. Our General cast° us thus early for the love of his
    Desdemona, who let us not therefore blame. He hath not
    yet made wanton the night with her, and she is sport for
    Jove.
CASSIO.   She's a most exquisite lady.

3–4. *put . . . triumph:* celebrate. 6. *addiction:* inclination. 8. *offices:* the kitchen and
buttery—that is, free food and drink for all.
SCENE III: 3. *outsport discretion:* let the fun go too far. 7. *with . . . earliest:* very early.
14. *cast:* dismissed.

IAGO.   And, I'll warrant her, full of game.

CASSIO.   Indeed she's a most fresh and delicate creature.   20

IAGO.   What an eye she has! Methinks it sounds
   a parley to provocation.°

CASSIO.   An inviting eye, and yet methinks right modest.

IAGO.   And when she speaks, is it not an alarum° to love?

CASSIO.   She is indeed perfection.

IAGO.   Well, happiness to their sheets! Come, Lieutenant, I
   have a stoup° of wine, and here without are a brace of
   Cyprus gallants that would fain° have a measure to the
   health of black Othello.

CASSIO.   Not tonight, good Iago. I have very poor and un-   30
   happy brains for drinking. I could well wish courtesy
   would invent some other custom of entertainment.

IAGO.   Oh, they are our friends. But one cup—I'll drink for
   you.

CASSIO.   I have drunk but one cup tonight, and that was
   craftily qualified° too, and behold what innovation° it
   makes here. I am unfortunate in the infirmity, and dare
   not task° my weakness with any more.

IAGO.   What, man! 'Tis a night of revels. The gallants desire
   it.   40

CASSIO.   Where are they?

IAGO.   Here at the door. I pray you call them in.

CASSIO.   I'll do 't, but it dislikes° me.   [Exit.]

IAGO.   If I can fasten but one cup upon him,
   With that which he hath drunk tonight already
   He'll be as full of quarrel and offense
   As my young mistress' dog. Now my sick fool Roderigo,
   Whom love hath turned almost the wrong side out,
   To Desdemona hath tonight caroused°
   Potations pottle-deep,° and he's to watch.   50
   Three lads of Cyprus, noble swelling° spirits
   That hold their honors in a wary distance,°

21–22. *sounds . . . provocation:* invites to a love talk.   24. *alarum:* call to arms.
27. *stoup:* large drinking vessel.   28. *fain:* gladly.   36. *craftily qualified:* cunningly
mixed; *innovation:* revolution, disturbance.   38. *task:* burden.   43. *dislikes:* dis-
pleases.   49. *caroused:* drunk healths.   50. *pottle-deep:* "Bottoms up"; a pottle held two
quarts.   51. *swelling:* bursting with pride.   52. *hold . . . distance:* "have a chip on their
shoulders."

The very elements° of this warlike isle,
Have I tonight flustered with flowing cups,
And they watch too. Now, 'mongst this flock of drunkards,
Am I to put our Cassio in some action
That may offend the isle. But here they come.
If consequences do but approve my dream,°
My boat sails freely, both with wind and stream.

[*Re-enter* CASSIO, *with him* MONTANO
and GENTLEMEN, SERVANTS *following with wine.*]

CASSIO.   'Fore God, they have given me a rouse° already.   60
MONTANO.   Good faith, a little one—not past a pint, as I am
   a soldier.
IAGO.   Some wine, ho! [*Sings*]
       "And let me the cannikin° clink, clink,
         And let me the cannikin clink.
           A soldier's a man,
           A life's but a span.°
        Why, then let a soldier drink."
   Some wine, boys!
CASSIO.   'Fore God, an excellent song.   70
IAGO.   I learned it in England, where indeed they are most
   potent in potting.° Your Dane, your German, and your
   swag-bellied° Hollander—Drink, ho!—are nothing to
   your English.
CASSIO.   Is your Englishman so expert in his drinking?
IAGO.   Why, he drinks you with facility your Dane dead
   drunk, he sweats not° to overthrow your Almain,° he
   gives your Hollander a vomit° ere the next pottle can be
   filled.
CASSIO.   To the health of our General!   80
MONTANO.   I am for it, Lieutenant, and I'll do you justice.
IAGO.   O sweet England! [*Sings*]
       "King Stephen was a worthy peer,

---

53. *very elements:* typical specimens.   58. *If . . . dream:* if what follows proves my
dream true.   60. *rouse:.* a deep drink.   64. *cannikin:* large drinking pot.   67. *span:*
literally, the measure between the thumb and little finger of the outstretched hand;
about 9 inches.   72. *potent in potting:* desperate drinkers.   73. *swag-bellied:* with loose
bellies.   77. *sweats not:* has no need to labor excessively; *Almain:* German.   78. *gives
. . . vomit:* drinks as much as will make a Dutchman throw up.

His breeches cost him but a crown.
He held them sixpence all too dear,°
    With that he called the tailor lown.°
"He was a wight of high renown,
    And thou art but of low degree.
'Tis pride that pulls the country down.
    Then take thine auld cloak about thee."   90
Some wine, ho!

CASSIO.   Why, this is a more exquisite song than the other.

IAGO.   Will you hear 't again?

CASSIO.   No, for I hold him to be unworthy of his place that does those things. Well, God's above all, and there be souls must be saved and there be souls must not be saved.

IAGO.   It's true, good Lieutenant.

CASSIO.   For mine own part—no offense to the General, nor any man of quality°—I hope to be saved.   100

IAGO.   And so do I too, Lieutenant.

CASSIO.   Aye, but, by your leave, not before me. The Lieutenant is to be saved before the Ancient. Let's have no more of this, let's to our affairs. God forgive us our sins! Gentlemen, let's look to our business. Do not think, gentlemen, I am drunk. This is my Ancient, this is my right hand and this is my left. I am not drunk now, I can stand well enough and speak well enough.

ALL.   Excellent well.

CASSIO.   Why, very well, then, you must not think then that   110
I am drunk.

                                          [*Exit.*]

MONTANO.   To the platform,° masters. Come, let's set the watch.°

IAGO.   You see this fellow that is gone before.
He is a soldier fit to stand by Caesar
And give direction. And do but see his vice.
'Tis to his virtue a just equinox,°
The one as long as the other. 'Tis pity of him.

---

85. *sixpence . . . dear:* too dear by sixpence.   86. *lown:* lout.   100. *quality:* rank.
112. *platform:* the level place on the ramparts where the cannon were mounted;
set . . . watch: mount guard.   117. *just equinox:* exact equal.

I fear the trust Othello puts him in
On some odd time° of his infirmity   120
Will shake this island.

MONTANO.   But is he often thus?

IAGO.   'Tis evermore the prologue to his sleep.
He'll watch the horologe a double set,°
If drink rock not his cradle.

MONTANO.   It were well
The General were put in mind of it.
Perhaps he sees it not, or his good nature
Prizes the virtue that appears in Cassio
And looks not on his evils. Is not this true?

                    [*Enter* RODERIGO.]

IAGO [*aside to him*].   How now, Roderigo! I pray you, after
the Lieutenant. Go.   130

                    [*Exit* RODERIGO.]

MONTANO.   And 'tis great pity that the noble Moor
Should hazard such a place as his own second
With one of an ingraft° infirmity.
It were an honest action to say
So to the Moor.

IAGO.   Not I, for this fair island.
I do love Cassio well, and would do much
To cure him of this evil—But, hark! What noise?

                    [*A cry within:* "Help! help!"]
                    [*Re-enter* CASSIO, *driving in* RODERIGO.]

CASSIO.   'Zounds! You rogue! You rascal!

MONTANO.   What's the matter, Lieutenant?

CASSIO.   A knave teach my my duty!
But I'll beat the knave into a wicker bottle.°   140

RODERIGO.   Beat me!

CASSIO.   Dost thou prate, rogue? [*Striking* RODERIGO.]

MONTANO.   Nay, good Lieutenant, [*staying him*]
I pray you, sir, hold your hand.

---

120. *some . . . time:* some time or other.   123. *watch . . . set:* stay awake the clock
twice around.   133. *ingraft:* engrafted, firmly fixed.   140. *But . . . bottle:* one of those
bad-tempered threatening phrases which have no very exact meaning, like "I'll knock
him into a cocked hat." *wicker bottle:* large bottle covered with wicker, demijohn

CASSIO.   Let me go, sir,
Or I'll knock you o'er the mazzard.°
MONTANO.   Come, come, you're drunk.
CASSIO.   Drunk!   [*They fight.*]
IAGO [*aside to* RODERIGO].   Away, I say. Go out and cry a mutiny.°
                                                          [*Exit* RODERIGO.]
Nay, good Lieutenant! God's will, gentlemen!
Help, ho!—Lieutenant—sir—Montano—sir—
Help, masters!—Here's a goodly watch indeed!
                        [*A bell rings.*]
Who's that that rings the bell?—Diablo,° ho!   150
The town will rise. God's will Lieutenant, hold—
You will be shamed forever.
                    [*Re-enter* OTHELLO *and* ATTENDANTS.]
OTHELLO.   What is the matter here?
MONTANO.   'Zounds, I bleed still, I am hurt to the death. [*Faints.*]
OTHELLO.   Hold, for your lives!
IAGO.   Hold, ho! Lieutenant—sir—Montano—gentlemen—
Have you forgot all sense of place and duty?
Hold! The General speaks to you. Hold, hold, for shame!
OTHELLO.   Why, how now, ho! From whence ariseth this?
Are we turned Turks, and to ourselves do that
Which Heaven hath forbid the Ottomites?   160
For Christian shame, put by this barbarous brawl.
He that stirs next to carve for his own rage°
Holds his soul light, he dies upon his motion.°
Silence that dreadful bell. It frights the isle
From her propriety.° What is the matter, masters?
Honest Iago, that look'st dead with grieving,
Speak, who began this? On thy love, I charge thee.
IAGO.   I do not know. Friends all but now, even now,
In quarter and in terms like bride and groom
Devesting° them for bed. And then, but now,   170
As if some planet had unwitted men,°

---

144. *mazzard:* head, a slang word.   146. *cry . . . mutiny:* cry that a mutiny has broken
out; i.e., raise a riot.   150. *Diablo:* the Devil.   162. *carve . . . rage:* to satisfy his hunger
for rage.   163. *upon . . . motion:* at his first movement.   165. *propriety:* natural behavior.   170. *Devesting:* taking off their clothes.   171. *planet . . . men:* as if some evil
star had made men mad.

Swords out, and tilting° one at other's breast
In opposition bloody. I cannot speak
Any beginning to this peevish odds,°
And would in action glorious I had lost
Those legs that brought me to a part of it!
OTHELLO.　How comes it, Michael, you are thus forgot?°
CASSIO.　I pray you, pardon me, I cannot speak.
OTHELLO.　Worthy Montano, you were wont be civil.°
　　The gravity and stillness° of your youth　　　　　　　　180
　　The world hath noted, and your name is great
　　In mouths of wisest censure.° What's the matter
　　That you unlace° your reputation thus,
　　And spend yor rich opinion° for the name
　　Of a night brawler? Give me answer to it.
MONTANO.　Worthy Othello, I am hurt to danger.
　　Your officer, Iago, can inform you—
　　While I spare speech, which something now offends me—
　　Of all that I do know. Nor know I aught
　　By me that's said or done amiss this night,　　　　　　190
　　Unless self-charity° be sometimes a vice,
　　And to defend ourselves it be a sin
　　When violence assails us.
OTHELLO.　　　　　　　　　　Now, by Heaven,
　　My blood begins my safer guides to rule,
　　And passion, having my best judgment collied,°
　　Assays to lead the way. If I once stir,
　　Or do but lift this arm, the best of you
　　Shall sink in my rebuke. Give me to know
　　How this foul rout° began, who set it on,
　　And he that is approved° in this offense,　　　　　　　200
　　Though he had twinned with me, both at a birth,
　　Shall lose me. What! In a town of war,
　　Yet wild, the people's hearts brimful of fear,
　　To manage° private and domestic quarrel,
　　In night, and on the court and guard of safety!
　　'Tis monstrous. Iago, who began 't?

---

172. *tilting:* thrusting.　174. *peevish odds:* silly disagreement.　177. *are . . . forgot:* have
so forgotten yourself.　179. *civil:* well behaved.　180. *stillness:* staid behavior.
182. *censure:* judgment.　183. *unlace:* undo.　184. *spend . . . opinion:* lose your good
reputation.　191. *self-charity:* love for oneself.　195. *collied:* darkened.　199. *rout:* riot,
uproar.　200. *approved:* proved guilty.　204. *manage:* be concerned with.

MONTANO.   If partially affined, or leagued in office
    Thou dost deliver° more or less than truth,
    Thou art no soldier.
IAGO.   Touch me not so near.
    I had rather have this tongue cut from my mouth   210
    Than it should do offense to Michael Cassio.
    Yet I persuade myself to speak the truth
    Shall nothing wrong him. Thus it is, General.
    Montano and myself being in speech,
    There comes a fellow crying out for help,
    And Cassio following him with determined sword
    To execute upon him. Sir, this gentleman
    Steps in to Cassio and entreats his pause.°
    Myself the crying fellow did pursue,
    Lest by his clamor—as it so fell out—   220
    The town might fall in fright. He, swift of foot,
    Outran my purpose, and I returned the rather
    For that I heard the clink and fall of swords,
    And Cassio high in oath, which till tonight
    I ne'er might say before. When I came back—
    For this was brief—I found them close together,
    At blow and thrust, even as again they were
    When you yourself did part them.
    More of this matter cannot I report.
    But men are men, the best sometimes forget.   230
    Though Cassio did some little wrong to him,
    As men in rage strike those that wish them best,
    Yet surely Cassio, I believe, received
    From him that fled some strange indignity,
    Which patience could not pass.
OTHELLO.   I know, Iago,
    Thy honesty and love doth mince this matter,
    Making it light to Cassio. Cassio, I love thee,
    But never more be officer of mine.

          [*Re-enter* DESDEMONA, *attended.*]

    Look, if my gentle love be not raised up!
    I'll make thee an example.

207–08. *If . . . deliver:* if, because you are influenced by partiality or because he
is your fellow officer, you report; *affined:* bound.   218. *entreats . . . pause:* begs him
to stop.

DESDEMONA.   What's the matter?   240
OTHELLO.   All's well now, sweeting.° Come away to bed.

           ⌈*To* MONTANO, *who is led off*⌉

Sir, for your hurts, myself will be your surgeon.
Lead him off.
Iago, look with care about the town,
And silence those whom this vile brawl distracted.
Come, Desdemona. 'Tis the soldier's life
To have their balmy slumbers waked with strife.

            [*Exeunt all but* IAGO *and* CASSIO.]

IAGO.   What, are you hurt, Lieutenant?
CASSIO.   Aye, past all surgery.
IAGO.   Marry, Heaven forbid!   250
CASSIO.   Reputation, reputation, reputation! Oh, I have lost
     my reputation! I have lost the immortal part of myself,
     and what remains is bestial. My reputation, Iago, my
     reputation!
IAGO.   As I am an honest man, I thought you had received
     some bodily wound. There is more sense in that than in
     reputation. Reputation is an idle and most false imposi-
     tion,° oft got without merit and lost without deserving.
     You have lost no reputation at all unless you repute
     yourself such a loser. What, man! There are ways to re-   260
     cover the General again. You are but now cast in his
     mood,° a punishment more in policy° than in malice—
     even so as one would beat his offenseless dog to affright
     an imperious lion.° Sue to him again and he's yours.
CASSIO.   I will rather sue to be despised than to deceive so
     good a commander with so slight, so drunken, and so
     indiscreet an officer, Drunk? And speak parrot?° And
     squabble? Swagger? Swear? And discourse fustian° with
     one's own shadow? O thou invisible spirit of wine, if
     thou hast no name to be known by, let us call thee devil!   270
IAGO.   What was he that you followed with your sword?
     What had he done to you?

---

241. *sweeting:* sweetheart. 258. *imposition:* a quality laid on a man by others.
261–62. *cast . . . mood:* dismissed because he is in a bad mood. 262. *in policy:* that is,
because he must appear to be angry before the Cypriots. 263–64. *even . . . lion:* a
proverb meaning that when the lion sees the dog beaten, he will know what is coming
to him. 267. *speak parrot:* babble. 268. *fustian:* nonsense; literally, cheap cloth.

CASSIO.   I know not.

IAGO.   Is't possible?

CASSIO.   I remember a mass of things, but nothing distinctly—a quarrel, but nothing wherefore. Oh God, that men should put an enemy in their mouths to steal away their brains! That we should, with joy, pleasance,° revel, and applause, transform ourselves into beasts!

IAGO.   Why, but you are now well enough. How came you thus recovered?   280

CASSIO.   It hath pleased the devil drunkenness to give place to the devil wrath. One unperfectness shows me another, to make me frankly despise myself.

IAGO.   Come, you are too severe a moraler.° As the time, the place, and the condition of this country stands, I could heartily wish this had not befallen. But since it is as it is, mend it for your own good.

CASSIO.   I will ask him for my place again, he shall tell me I am a drunkard! Had I as many mouths as Hydra,° such   290
an answer would stop them all. To be now a sensible man, by and by a fool, and presently a beast! Oh, strange! Every inordinate° cup is unblest, and the ingredient is a devil.

IAGO.   Come, come, good wine is a full familiar creature, if it be well used. Exclaim no more against it. And, good Lieutenant, I think you think I love you.

CASSIO.   I have well approved it, sir. I drunk!

IAGO.   You or any man living may be drunk at some time, man. I'll tell you what you shall do. Our General's wife   300
is now the General. I may say so in this respect, for that he hath devoted and given up himself to the contemplation, mark, and denotement° of her parts and graces. Confess yourself freely to her, importune her help to put you in your place again. She is of so free, so kind, so apt,° so blessed a disposition, she holds it a vice in her goodness not to do more than she is requested. This broken joint between you and her husband entreat her to splinter° and, my fortunes against any lay° worth nam-

278. *pleasance:* a gay time.   285. *moraler:* moralizer.   290. *Hydra:* a hundred-headed beast slain by Hercules.   293. *inordinate:* excessive.   303. *denotement:* careful observation.   306. *apt:* ready.   309. *splinter:* put in splints; *lay:* bet.

ing, this crack of your love shall grow stronger than it   310
was before.

CASSIO.   You advise me well.

IAGO.   I protest, in the sincerity of love and honest kindness.

CASSIO.   I think it freely, and betimes in the morning I will
beseech the virtuous Desdemona to undertake for me. I
am desperate of my fortunes if they check me here.°

IAGO.   You are in the right. Good night, Lieutenant, I must
to the watch.

CASSIO.   Good night, honest Iago.

[*Exit.*]

IAGO.   And what's he then that says I play the villain?   320
When this advice is free I give and honest,
Probal° to thinking, and indeed the course
To win the Moor again? For 'tis most easy
The inclining Desdemona to subdue
In any honest suit. She's framed° as fruitful
As the free elements.° And then for her
To win the Moor, were 't to renounce his baptism,
All seals and symbols of redeemèd sin,
His soul is so enfettered to her love
That she may make, unmake, do what she list,   330
Even as her appetite shall play the god
With his weak function.° How am I then a villain
To counsel Cassio to this parallel course,
Directly to his good? Divinity of Hell!
When devils will the blackest sins put on,
They do suggest° at first with heavenly shows,
As I do now. For whiles this honest fool
Plies° Desdemona to repair his fortunes,
And she for him pleads strongly to the Moor,
I'll pour this pestilence into his ear,   340
That she repeals° him for her body's lust.
And by how much she strives to do him good,
She shall undo her credit with the Moor.
So will I turn her virtue into pitch,

315–16. *I . . . here:* I despair of my future if my career is stopped short here.   322. *Probal:*
probable.   325. *framed:* made.   326. *free elements:* that is, the air.   332. *function:* intelligence.   336. *suggest:* seduce.   338. *Plies:* vigorously urges.   341. *repeals:* calls back.

And out of her own goodness make the net
That shall enmesh them all.

[*Enter* RODERIGO.]

How now, Roderigo!

RODERIGO.   I do follow here in the chase, not like a hound
that hunts but one that fills up the cry.° My money is almost spent, I have been tonight exceedingly well cud-
geled, and I think the issue will be I shall have so much   350
experience for my pains and so, with no money at all
and a little more wit, return again to Venice.

IAGO.   How poor are they that have not patience!
What wound did ever heal but by degrees?
Thou know'st we work by wit and not by witchcraft,
And wit depends on dilatory Time.°
Does't not go well? Cassio hath beaten thee,
And thou by that small hurt hast cashiered Cassio.
Though other things grow fair against the sun,
Yet fruits that blossom first will first be ripe.°   360
Content thyself awhile. By the mass, 'tis morning.
Pleasure and action make the hours seem short.
Retire thee, go where thou art billeted.
Away, I say. Thou shalt know more hereafter.
Nay, get thee gone.

[*Exit* RODERIGO.]

Two things are to be done:
My wife must move for° Cassio to her mistress,
I'll set her on,
Myself the while to draw the Moor apart
And bring him jump° when he may Cassio find
Soliciting his wife. Aye, that's the way.   370
Dull not device° by coldness and delay.

[*Exit.*]

---

348. *one . . . cry:* that is, one of the pack chosen merely for its bark.   356. *And . . .*
Time: and cleverness must wait for Time, who is in no hurry.   360. *Though . . . ripe:*
Though the fruit ripens in the sun, yet the first fruit to ripen will come from the
earliest blossoms; that is, our first plan—to get Cassio cashiered—has succeeded, the
rest will soon follow.   366. *move for:* petition for.   369. *jump:* at the moment, just.
371. *Dull . . . device:* do not spoil the plan.

ACT III

SCENE I. *Before the castle.*

[*Enter* CASSIO *and some* MUSICIANS.]

CASSIO. Masters, play here, I will content your pains°—
Something that's brief, and bid "Good morrow, General."°

[*Music.*]

[*Enter* CLOWN.]

CLOWN. Why, masters, have your instruments been in Naples,° that they speak i' the nose thus?

1ST MUSICIAN. How, sir, how?

CLOWN. Are these, I pray you, wind instruments?

1ST MUSICIAN. Aye, marry are they, sir.

CLOWN. Oh, thereby hangs a tail.

1ST MUSICIAN. Whereby hangs a tale, sir?

CLOWN. Marry, sir, by many a wind instrument that I   10
know. But, masters, here's money for you. And the
General so likes your music that he desires you, for
love's sake, to make no more noise with it.

1ST MUSICIAN. Well, sir, we will not.

CLOWN. If you have any music that may not be heard, to 't
again. But, as they say, to hear music the General does
not greatly care.

1ST MUSICIAN. We have none such, sir.

CLOWN. Then put up your pipes in your bag, for I'll away.
Go, vanish into air, away!   20

[*Exeunt* MUSICIANS.]

CASSIO. Dost thou hear, my honest friend?

CLOWN. No, I hear not your honest friend, I hear you.

CASSIO. Prithee keep up thy quillets.° There's a poor piece of
gold for thee. If the gentlewoman that attends the Gen-

Act III, SCENE I: 1. *content . . . pains:* reward your labor. 2. *bid . . . General:* It was a
common custom to play or sing a song beneath the bedroom window of a distinguished guest or of a newly wedded couple on the morning after their wedding night.
3. *in Naples:* a reference to the Neapolitan (i.e., venereal) disease. 23. *keep . . . quillets:* Put away your wisecracks.

eral's wife be stirring, tell her there's one Cassio entreats
her a little favor of speech. Wilt thou do this?

CLOWN.   She is stirring, sir. If she will stir hither, I shall
seem to notify unto her.

CASSIO.   Do, good my friend.

[*Exit* CLOWN.]

[*Enter* IAGO.]
In happy time,° Iago.

IAGO.   You have not been abed, then?   30

CASSIO.   Why, no, the day had broke
Before we parted. I have made bold, Iago,
To send in to your wife. My suit to her
Is that she will to virtuous Desdemona
Procure me some access.

IAGO.   I'll send her to you presently,
And I'll devise a mean to draw the Moor
Out of the way, that your convérse and business
May be more free.

CASSIO.   I humbly thank you for 't.

[*Exit* IAGO.]

I never knew
A Florentine more kind° and honest.   40

[*Enter* EMILIA.]

EMILIA.   Good morrow, good Lieutenant. I am sorry
For your displeasure,° but all will sure be well.
The General and his wife are talking of it,
And she speaks for you stoutly. The Moor replies
That he you hurt is of great fame in Cyprus
And great affinity,° and that in wholesome wisdom
He might not but° refuse you. But he protests he loves you,
And needs no other suitor but his likings°
To take the safest occasion by the front
To bring you in° again.

---

29. *In . . . time:* that is, I am glad to see you.   40. *Florentine . . . kind:* Iago is a Venetian. Cassio means: even one of my own people could not have been kinder.   42. *your
displeasure:* that is, that Othello is displeased with you.   46. *affinity:* kindred.
47. *might . . . but:* that is, he must.   48. *likings:* affections.   49–50. *safest . . . in:* to
take the first opportunity to restore you to your position; *front:* forehead; that is, to
take time by the forelock.

CASSIO.   Yet I beseech you,   50
　　If you think fit, or that it may be done,
　　Give me advantage of some brief discourse
　　With Desdemona alone.
EMILIA.   Pray you, come in.
　　I will bestow you where you shall have time
　　To speak your bosom freely.°
CASSIO.   I am much bound to you.

[*Exeunt.*]

SCENE II. *A room in the castle.*

[*Enter* OTHELLO, IAGO, *and* GENTLEMEN.]

OTHELLO.   These letters give, Iago, to the pilot,
　　And by him do my duties° to the Senate.
　　That done, I will be walking on the works.°
　　Repair there to me.
IAGO.   Well, my good lord, I'll do't.
OTHELLO.   This fortification, gentlemen, shall we see 't?
GENTLEMEN.   We'll wait upon your lordship.

[*Exeunt.*]

SCENE III. *The garden of the castle.*

[*Enter* DESDEMONA, CASSIO, *and* EMILIA.]

DESDEMONA.   Be thou assured, good Cassio, I will do
　　All my abilities in thy behalf.
EMILIA.   Good madam, do. I warrant it grieves my husband
　　As if the case were his.
DESDEMONA.   Oh, that's an honest fellow. Do not doubt, Cassio,
　　But I will have my lord and you again
　　As friendly as you were.
CASSIO.   Bounteous madam,
　　Whatever shall become of Michael Cassio,
　　He's never anything but your true servant.

55. *speak . . . freely:* declare what is on your mind.
SCENE II: 2. *do . . . duties:* express my loyalty. 3. *works:* fortifications.

DESDEMONA.   I know't. I thank you. You do love my lord.   10
    You have known him long, and be you well assured
    He shall in strangeness stand no farther off
    Than in a politic distance.°
CASSIO.   Aye, but, lady,
    That policy may either last so long,
    Or feed upon such nice and waterish diet,°
    Or breed itself so out of circumstance,°
    That, I being absent and my place supplied,°
    My General will forget my love and service.
DESDEMONA.   Do not doubt° that. Before Emilia here
    I give thee warrant of thy place.° Assure thee,   20
    If I do vow a friendship, I'll perform it
    To the last article. My lord shall never rest.
    I'll watch him tame° and talk him out of patience,
    His bed shall seem a school, his board a shrift.°
    I'll intermingle every thing he does
    With Cassio's suit. Therefore be merry, Cassio,
    For thy solicitor shall rather die
    Than give thy cause away.

              [*Enter* OTHELLO *and* IAGO, *at a distance.*]

EMILIA.   Madam, here comes my lord.
CASSIO.   Madam, I'll take my leave.   30
DESDEMONA.   Nay, stay and hear me speak.
CASSIO.   Madam, not now. I am very ill at ease,
    Unfit for my own purposes.°
DESDEMONA.   Well, do your discretion.

                    [*Exit* CASSIO.]

IAGO.   Ha! I like not that.
OTHELLO.   What dost thou say?
IAGO.   Nothing, my lord. Or if—I know not what.
OTHELLO.   Was that not Cassio parted from my wife?

SCENE III: *12–13. He . . . distance:* that is, his apparent coldness to you shall only be so much as his official position demands for reasons of policy. *15. nice . . . diet:* have such weak encouragement. *16. breed . . . circumstance:* become so used to the situation. *17. supplied:* filled by another. *19. doubt:* fear. *20. give . . . place:* guarantee that you will be restored to your position. *23. watch . . . tame:* as wild hawks are made tame by keeping them from sleep. *24. shrift:* place of confession and absolution. *33. Unfit . . . purposes:* in no condition to plead my own cause.

IAGO.   Cassio, my lord! No, sure, I cannot think it,
That he would steal away so guilty-like,
Seeing you coming.
OTHELLO.   I do believe 'twas he.   40
DESDEMONA.   How now, my lord!
I have been talking with a suitor here,
A man that languishes in your displeasure.
OTHELLO.   Who is't you mean?
DESDEMONA.   Why, your Lieutenant, Cassio. Good my lord,
If I have any grace or power to move you,
His present reconciliation take.°
For if he be not one that truly loves you,
That errs in ignorance and not in cunning,°
I have no judgment in an honest face.   50
I prithee call him back.
OTHELLO.   Went he hence now?
DESDEMONA.   Aye, sooth, so humbled
That he hath left part of his grief with me,
To suffer with him. Good love, call him back.
OTHELLO.   Not now, sweet Desdemona, some other time.
DESDEMONA.   But shall't be shortly?
OTHELLO.   The sooner, sweet, for you.
DESDEMONA.   Shall't be tonight at supper?
OTHELLO.   No, not tonight.
DESDEMONA.   Tomorrow dinner then?
OTHELLO.   I shall not dine at home.
I meet the captains at the citadel.
DESDEMONA.   Why, then tomorrow night or Tuesday morn.   60
On Tuesday noon, or night, on Wednesday morn.
I prithee name the time, but let it not
Exceed three days. In faith, he's penitent,
And yet his trespass, in our common reason°—
Save that, they say, the wars must make examples
Out of their best—is not almost° a fault
To incur a private check.° When shall he come?
Tell me, Othello. I wonder in my soul

---

47. *His . . . take:* accept his immediate apology and forgive him.   49. *in cunning:*
knowingly.   64. *common reason:* common sense.   66. *not almost:* hardly.   67. *check:*
rebuke.

What you would ask me that I should deny,
Or stand so mammering° on. What! Michael Cassio,   70
That came a-wooing with you, and so many a time
When I have spoke of you dispraisingly
Hath ta'en your part—to have so much to do
To bring him in! Trust me, I could do much——
OTHELLO.   Prithee, no more. Let him come when he will.
I will deny thee nothing.
DESDEMONA.   Why, this is not a boon.°
'Tis as I should entreat you wear your gloves,
Or feed on nourishing dishes, or keep you warm,
Or sue to you to do a peculiar° profit
To your own person. Nay, when I have a suit   80
Wherein I mean to touch your love indeed,
It shall be full of poise° and difficult weight,°
And fearful to be granted.°
OTHELLO.   I will deny thee nothing.
Whereon I do beseech thee grant me this,
To leave me but a little to myself.
DESDEMONA.   Shall I deny you? No. Farewell, my lord.
OTHELLO.   Farewell, my Desdemona. I'll come to thee straight.
DESDEMONA.   Emilia, come. Be as your fancies teach you.°
Whate'er you be, I am obedient.

[*Exeunt* DESDEMONA *and* EMILIA.]

OTHELLO.   Excellent wretch! Perdition catch my soul   90
But I do love thee! And when I love thee not,
Chaos° is come again.
IAGO.   My noble lord——
OTHELLO.   What dost thou say, Iago?
IAGO.   Did Michael Cassio, when you wooed my lady,
Know of your love?
OTHELLO.   He did, from first to last. Why dost thou ask?
IAGO.   But for a satisfaction of my thought,
No further harm.
OTHELLO.   Why of thy thought, Iago?

70. *mammering:* hesitating.   76. *boon:* great favor.   79. *peculiar:* particular.   82. *poise:* weight in the scales; *difficult weight:* hard to estimate.   83. *fearful . . . granted:* only granted with sense of fear.   88. *Be . . . you:* please yourself.   92. *Chaos:* the utter confusion that existed before order was established in the universe.

IAGO.   I did not think that he had been acquainted with her.

OTHELLO.   Oh, yes, and went between us very oft.   100

IAGO.   Indeed!

OTHELLO.   Indeed! Aye, indeed. Discern'st thou aught in that?
　　　Is he not honest?

IAGO.   Honest, my lord!

OTHELLO.   Honest! Aye, honest.

IAGO.   My lord, for aught I know.

OTHELLO.   What dost thou think?

IAGO.   Think, my lord!

OTHELLO.   Think, my lord! By Heaven, he echoes me
　　　As if there were some monster in this thought
　　　Too hideous to be shown. Thou dost mean something.
　　　I heard thee say even now thou likedst not that
　　　When Cassio left my wife. What didst not like?   110
　　　And when I told thee he was of my counsel
　　　In my whole course of wooing, thou criedst "Indeed!"
　　　And didst contract and purse thy brow together
　　　As if thou then hadst shut up in thy brain
　　　Some horrible conceit.° If thou dost love me,
　　　Show me thy thought.

IAGO.   My lord, you know I love you.

OTHELLO.   I think thou dost,
　　　And for° I know thou'rt full of love and honesty
　　　And weigh'st thy words before thou givest them breath,
　　　Therefore these stops of thine fright me the more.   120
　　　For such things in a false disloyal knave
　　　Are tricks of custom, but in a man that's just
　　　They're close delations,° working from the heart,
　　　That passion cannot rule.

IAGO.   For Michael Cassio,
　　　I dare be sworn I think that he is honest.

OTHELLO.   I think so too.

IAGO.   Men should be what they seem,
　　　Or those that be not, would they might seem none!°

OTHELLO.   Certain, men should be what they seem.

IAGO.   Why, then I think Cassio's an honest man.

---

115. *conceit:* conception, notion. 118. *for:* since. 123. *close delations:* concealed accusations. 127. *seem none:* that is, not seem to be honest men.

OTHELLO.   Nay, yet there's more in this.   130
  I prithee speak to me as to thy thinkings,
  As thou dost ruminate and give thy worst of thoughts
  The worst of words.
IAGO.   Good my lord, pardon me.
  Though I am bound to every act of duty,
  I am not bound to that all slaves are free to.
  Utter my thoughts? Why, say they are vile and false,
  As where's that palace whereinto foul things
  Sometimes intrude not? Who has a breast so pure
  But some uncleanly apprehensions
  Keep leets and law days, and in session sit   140
  With meditations lawful?°
OTHELLO.   Thou dost conspire against thy friend, Iago.
  If thou but think'st him wronged and makest his ear
  A stranger to thy thoughts.
IAGO.   I do beseech you—
  Though I perchance am vicious in my guess,
  As, I confess, it is my nature's plague
  To spy into abuses, and oft my jealousy°
  Shapes faults that are not—that your wisdom yet,
  From one that so imperfectly conceits,°
  Would take no notice, nor build yourself a trouble   150
  Out of his scattering° and unsure observance.°
  It were not for your quiet nor your good,
  Nor for my manhood, honesty, or wisdom,
  To let you know my thoughts.
OTHELLO.   What dost thou mean?
IAGO.   Good name in man and woman, dear my lord,
  Is the immediate° jewel of their souls.
  Who steals my purse steals trash—'tis something, nothing,
  'Twas mine, 'tis his, and has been slave to thousands—
  But he that filches from me my good name

138–41. *Who . . . lawful:* whose heart is so pure but that some foul suggestion will sit
on the bench alongside lawful thoughts; that is, foul thoughts will rise even on the
most respectable occasions; *leet:* court held by the lord of the manor; *law days:* days
when courts sit; *session:* sitting of the court.   147. *jealously:* suspicion.   149. *conceits:*
conceives, imagines.   151. *scattering:* scattered, casual; *observance:* observation.
156. *immediate:* most valuable.

Robs me of that which not enriches him   160
And makes me poor indeed.
OTHELLO.   By Heaven, I'll know thy thoughts.
IAGO.   You cannot if my heart were in your hand,
Nor shall not whilst 'tis in my custody.
OTHELLO.   Ha!
IAGO.   Oh, beware, my lord, of jealousy.
It is the green-eyed monster which doth mock°
The meat° it feeds on. That cuckold lives in bliss
Who, certain of his fate, loves not his wronger.°
But, oh, what damnèd minutes tells he o'er
Who dotes, yet doubts, suspects, yet strongly loves!   170
OTHELLO.   Oh, misery!
IAGO.   Poor and content is rich, and rich enough,
But riches fineless° is as poor as winter
To him that ever fears he shall be poor.
Good Heaven, the souls of all my tribe defend
From jealousy!
OTHELLO.   Why, why is this?
Think'st thou I'd make a life of jealousy,
To follow still the changes of the moon
With fresh suspicions? No, to be once in doubt
Is once to be resolved.° Exchange me for a goat   180
When I shall turn the business of my soul
To such exsufflicate and blown surmises,
Matching thy inference.° 'Tis not to make me jealous
To say my wife is fair, feeds well, loves company,
Is free of speech, sings, plays, and dances well.
Where virtue is, these are more virtuous.
Nor from mine own weak merits will I draw
The smallest fear or doubt of her revolt,°
For she had eyes, and chose me. No, Iago,
I'll see before I doubt, when I doubt, prove,   190

166. *doth mock:* makes a mockery of.   167. *meat:* i.e., victim.   167–68. *That . . . wrong-er:* that is, the cuckold who hates his wife and knows her falseness is not tormented by suspicious jealousy.   173. *fineless:* limitless.   179–80. *to . . . resolved:* whenever I find myself in doubt, I at once seek out the truth.   181–83. *When . . . inference:* when I shall allow that which concerns me most dearly to be influenced by such trifling suggestions as yours; *exsufflicate:* blown up, like a bubble.   188. *revolt:* faithlessness.

And on the proof, there is no more but this—
Away at once with love or jealousy!
IAGO.   I am glad of it, for now I shall have reason
To show the love and duty that I bear you
With franker spirit. Therefore, as I am bound,
Receive it from me. I speak not yet of proof.
Look to your wife. Observe her well with Cassio.
Wear your eye thus, not jealous nor secure.°
I would not have your free and noble nature
Out of self-bounty° be abused, look to 't.   200
I know our country disposition well.
In Venice° they do let Heaven see the pranks
They dare not show their husbands. Their best conscience
Is not to leav't undone, but keep't unknown.
OTHELLO.   Dost thou say so?
IAGO.   She did deceive her father,° marrying you,
And when she seemed to shake and fear your looks,
She loved them most.
OTHELLO.   And so she did.
IAGO.   Why, go to, then.
She that so young could give out such a seeming
To seel° her father's eyes up close as oak——   210
He thought 'twas witchcraft—but I am much to blame.
I humbly do beseech you of your pardon
For too much loving you.
OTHELLO.   I am bound to thee forever.
IAGO.   I see this hath a little dashed your spirits.
OTHELLO.   Not a jot, not a jot.
IAGO.   I' faith, I fear it has.
I hope you will consider what is spoke
Comes from my love, but I do see you're moved.
I am to pray you not to strain my speech
To grosser issues° nor to larger reach°
Than to suspicion.   220

198. *secure:* overconfident.   200. *self-bounty:* natural goodness.   202. *In Venice:*
Venice was notorious for its loose women; the Venetian courtesans were among
the sights of Europe and were much commented upon by travelers.   206. *She . . .
father:* Iago deliberately echoes Brabantio's parting words (see I.iii.292–93).   210. *seel:*
blind (see I.iii.269,n.).   219. *grosser issues:* worse conclusions; *larger reach:* that is,
more widely.

OTHELLO.   I will not.
IAGO.   Should you do so, my lord,
    My speech should fall into such vile success°
    As my thoughts aim not at. Cassio's my worthy friend.—
    My lord, I see you're moved.
OTHELLO.   No, not much moved.
    I do not think but Desdemona's honest.°
IAGO.   Long live she so! And long live you to think so!
OTHELLO.   And yet, how nature erring from itself——
IAGO.   Aye, there's the point. As—to be bold with you—
    Not to affect° many proposed matches°
    Of her own clime, complexion, and degree,   230
    Whereto we see in all things nature tends°——
    Foh! One may smell in such a will most rank,°
    Foul disproportion, thoughts unnatural.
    But pardon me. I do not in position
    Distinctly speak of her, though I may fear
    Her will, recoiling to her better judgment,
    May fall to match° you with her country forms,°
    And happily° repent.
OTHELLO.   Farewell, farewell.
    If more thou dost perceive, let me know more.
    Set on thy wife to observe. Leave me, Iago.   240
IAGO [*going*].   My lord, I take my leave.
OTHELLO.   Why did I marry? This honest creature doubtless
    Sees and knows more, much more, than he unfolds.
IAGO [*returning*].   My lord, I would I might entreat your honor
    To scan this thing no further. Leave it to time.
    Though it be fit that Cassio have his place,
    For sure he fills it up with great ability,
    Yet if you please to hold him off awhile,
    You shall by that perceive him and his means.
    Note if your lady strain his entertainment°   250

222. *success:* result.   225. *honest:* When applied to Desdemona, "honest" means
"chaste," but applied to Iago it has the modern meaning of "open and sincere."
229. *affect:* be inclined to; *proposed matches:* offers of marriage.   231. *in . . . tends:* that
is, a woman naturally marries a man of her own country, color, and rank.   232. *will
. . . rank:* desire most lustful.   237. *match:* compare; *country forms:* the appearance of
her countrymen; that is, white men.   238. *happily:* haply, by chance.   250. *strain . . .
entertainment:* urge you to receive him.

With any strong or vehement importunity—
Much will be seen in that. In the meantime,
Let me be thought too busy in my fears—
As worthy cause I have to fear I am—
And hold her free, I do beseech your Honor.
OTHELLO.   Fear not my government.°
IAGO.   I once more take my leave.

[*Exit.*]

OTHELLO.   This fellow's of exceeding honesty,
And knows all qualities,° with a learned spirit,
Of human dealings.° If I do prove her haggard,
Though that her jesses were my dear heartstrings,   260
I'd whistle her off and let her down the wind
To prey at fortune.° Haply, for I am black
And have not those soft parts of conversation
That chamberers° have, or for I am declined
Into the vale of years—yet that's not much—
She's gone, I am abused, and my relief
Must be to loathe her. Oh, curse of marriage,
That we can call these delicate creatures ours,
And not their appetites! I had rather be a toad
And live upon the vapor of a dungeon   270
Than keep a corner in the thing I love
For others' uses. Yet, 'tis the plague of great ones,
Prerogatived° are they less than the base.
'Tis destiny unshunnable, like death.
Even then this forkèd plague° is fated to us
When we do quicken.° Desdemona comes.

[*Re-enter* DESDEMONA *and* EMILIA.]

If she be false, oh, then Heaven mocks itself!
I'll not believe 't.
DESDEMONA.   How now, my dear Othello!

---

256. *government:* self-control.   258. *qualities:* different kinds.   258–59. *with . . . deal-ings:* with wide experience of human nature.   259–62. *If . . . fortune:* . . . If I find that she is wild, I'll whistle her off the game and let her go where she will, for she's not worth keeping . . . *haggard:* a wild hawk; *jesses:* the straps attached to a hawk's legs.   264. *chamberers:* playboys.   273. *Prerogatived:* privileged.   275. *forkèd plague:* that is, to be cuckold.   276. *quicken:* stir in our mother's womb.

Your dinner, and the generous° islanders
By you invited, do attend your presence.   280
OTHELLO.   I am to blame.
DESDEMONA.   Why do you speak so faintly?
    Are you not well?
OTHELLO.   I have a pain upon my forehead here.
DESDEMONA.   Faith, that's with watching,° 'twill away again.
    Let me but bind it hard, within this hour
    It will be well.
OTHELLO.   Your napkin° is too little.

    [*He puts the handkerchief from him, and she drops it.*]

    Let it alone. Come, I'll go in with you.
DESDEMONA.   I am very sorry that you are not well.

                        [*Exeunt* OTHELLO *and* DESDEMONA.]

EMILIA.   I am glad I have found this napkin.
    This was her first remembrance from the Moor.   290
    My wayward° husband hath a hundred times
    Wooed me to steal it, but she so loves the token,
    For he conjured° her she should ever keep it,
    That she reserves it evermore about her
    To kiss and talk to. I'll have the work ta'en out,°
    And give 't Iago. What he will do with it
    Heaven knows, not I.
    I nothing but to please his fantasy.°

                        [*Re-enter* IAGO.]

IAGO.   How now! What do you here alone?
EMILIA.   Do not you chide, I have a thing for you.   300
IAGO.   A thing for me? It is a common thing——
EMILIA.   Ha!
IAGO.   To have a foolish wife.
EMILIA.   Oh, is that all? What will you give me now
    For that same handkerchief?
IAGO.   What handkerchief?

---

279. *generous:* noble, of gentle blood. 284. *watching:* lack of sleep. 286. *napkin:*
handkerchief. 291. *wayward:* unaccountable. 293. *conjured:* begged with an oath.
295. *work . . . out:* pattern copied. 298. *fantasy:* whim.

EMILIA.   What handkerchief?
Why, that the Moor first gave to Desdemona,
That which so often you did bid me steal.
IAGO.   Hast stol'n it from her?
EMILIA.   No, faith, she let it drop by negligence,   310
And, to the advantage,° I being here took 't up.
Look, here it is.
IAGO.   A good wench. Give it me.
EMILIA.   What will you do with 't, that you have been so earnest
To have me filch it?
IAGO [*snatching it*].   Why, what's that to you?
EMILIA.   If 't be not for some purpose of import,
Give 't me again. Poor lady, she'll run mad
When she shall lack it.
IAGO.   Be not acknown on 't,° I have use for it.
Go, leave me.

                                        [*Exit* EMILIA.]

I will in Cassio's lodging lose this napkin,   320
And let him find it. Trifles light as air
Are to the jealous confirmations strong
As proofs of Holy Writ. This may do something.
The Moor already changes with my poison.
Dangerous conceits are in their natures poisons,
Which at the first are scarce found to distaste,°
But with a little° act upon the blood
Burn like the mines of sulphur. I did say so.°
Look where he comes!

                [*Re-enter* OTHELLO.]
                            Not poppy,° nor mandragora,°
Nor all the drowsy syrups of the world   330
Shall ever medicine thee to that sweet sleep
Which thou owedst° yesterday.
OTHELLO.   Ha! Ha! False to me?
IAGO.   Why, how now, General! No more of that.

---

311. *to . . . advantage:* thereby giving me the opportunity.   318. *Be . . . on 't:* know
nothing about it.   326. *distaste:* taste unpleasantly.   327. *with a little:* in a little while.
328. *I . . . so:* As Iago says this, Othello enters from the back of the stage, with all the
signs of his agitation outwardly visible.   329. *poppy:* opium; *mandragora:* called also
mandrake, a root used as a drug to bring sleep.   332. *owedst:* owned, possessed.

OTHELLO.   Avaunt!° Be gone! Thou hast set me on the rack.°
      I swear 'tis better to be much abused
      Than but to know 't a little.
IAGO.   How now, my lord!
OTHELLO.   What sense had I of her stol'n hours of lust?
      I saw 't not, thought it not, it harmed not me.
      I slept the next night well, was free and merry.
      I found not Cassio's kisses on her lips.   340
      He that is robbed, not wanting° what is stol'n,
      Let him not know 't and he's not robbed at all.
IAGO.   I am sorry to hear this.
OTHELLO.   I had been happy if the general camp,
      Pioners° and all, had tasted her sweet body,
      So I had nothing known. Oh, now forever
      Farewell the tranquil mind! Farewell content!
      Farewell the plumèd° troop and the big wars
      That make ambition virtue! Oh, farewell,
      Farewell the neighing steed and the shrill trump,   350
      The spirit-stirring drum, the ear-piercing fife,
      The royal banner and all quality,°
      Pride, pomp, and circumstance of glorious war!
      And, O you mortal engines,° whose rude throats
      The immortal Jove's dread clamors counterfeit,°
      Farewell! Othello's occupation gone!
IAGO.   Is 't possible, my lord?
OTHELLO.   Villain, be sure thou prove my love a whore,
      Be sure of it, give me the ocular proof.
      Or by the worth of man's eternal soul,   360
      Thou hadst been better have been born a dog
      Than answer my waked wrath!
IAGO.   Is 't come to this?
OTHELLO.   Make me to see 't, or at the least so prove it
      That the probation° bear no hinge nor loop
      To hang a doubt on, or woe upon thy life!
IAGO.   My noble lord——

334. *Avaunt:* be off! *on . . . rack:* that is, in torment.   341. *wanting:* missing.
345. *Pioners:* pioneers, the lowest type of soldier.   348. *plumèd:* wearing plumes in the
helmet.   352. *quality:* military rank.   354. *mortal engines:* deadly cannon.
355. *conterfeit:* imitate.   364. *probation:* proof.

OTHELLO.   If thou dost slander her and torture me,
    Never pray more, abandon all remorse.°
    On horror's head horrors accumulate,
    Do deeds to make Heaven weep, all earth amazed,   370
    For nothing canst thou to damnation add
    Greater than that.
IAGO.   Oh, grace! Oh, Heaven defend me!
    Are you a man? Have you a soul or sense?
    God be wi' you, take mine office. O wretched fool,
    That livest to make thine honesty a vice!
    O monstrous world! Take note, take note, O world,
    To be direct and honest is not safe.
    I thank you for this profit,° and from hence
    I'll love no friend, sith° love breeds such offense.
OTHELLO.   Nay, stay. Thou shouldst be honest.   380
IAGO.   I should be wise, for honesty's a fool.
    And loses that it works for.
OTHELLO.   By the world,
    I think my wife be honest, and think she is not.
    I think that thou art just, and think thou art not.
    I'll have some proof. Her name, that was as fresh
    As Dian's° visage, is now begrimed and black
    As mine own face. If there be cords, or knives,
    Poison, or fire, or suffocating streams,
    I'll not endure it. Would I were satisfied!
IAGO.   I see, sir, you are eaten up with passion.   390
    I do repent me that I put it to you.
    You would be satisfied?
OTHELLO.   Would! Nay, I will.
IAGO.   And may, but, how? How satisfied, my lord?
    Would you, the supervisor,° grossly gape on?
    Behold her topped?
OTHELLO.   Death and damnation! Oh!
IAGO.   It were a tedious difficulty, I think,
    To bring them to that prospect.° Damn them then,
    If ever mortal eyes do see them bolster°
    More than their own! What then? How then?

---

368. *remorse:* pity.   378. *profit:* profitable lesson.   379. *sith:* since.   386. *Dian:* Diana, goddess of chastity.   394. *supervisor:* looker-on.   397. *prospect:* sight.   398. *bolster:* sleep together.

What shall I say? Where's satisfaction?   400
It is impossible you should see this,
Were they as prime° as goats, as hot as monkeys,
As salt° as wolves in pride,° and fools as gross
As ignorance made drunk. But yet I say
If imputation° and strong circumstances,
Which lead directly to the door of truth,
Will give you satisfaction, you may have 't.
OTHELLO.   Give me a living° reason she's disloyal.
IAGO.   I do not like the office.
But sith I am entered in this cause so far,   410
Pricked° to 't by foolish honesty and love,
I will go on. I lay with Cassio lately,
And being troubled with a raging tooth,
I could not sleep.
There are a kind of men so loose of soul
That in their sleeps will mutter their affairs.
One of this kind is Cassio.
In sleep I heard him say "Sweet Desdemona,
Let us be wary, let us hide our loves."
And then, sir, would he gripe° and wring my hand,   420
Cry, "O sweet creature!" and then kiss me hard,
As if he plucked up kisses by the roots
That grew upon my lips. Then laid his leg
Over my thigh, and sighed and kissed, and then
Cried "Cursed fate that gave thee to the Moor!"
OTHELLO.   Oh, monstrous! Monstrous!
IAGO.   Nay, this was
    but his dream.
OTHELLO.   But this denoted a foregone conclusion.
    'Tis a shrewd doubt,° though it be but a dream.
IAGO.   And this may help to thicken other proofs
    That do demónstrate thinly.
OTHELLO.   I'll tear her all to pieces.   430
IAGO.   Nay, but be wise. Yet we see nothing done.
    She may be honest yet. Tell me but this:

---

402. *prime:* lustful.   403. *salt:* eager; *in pride:* in heat.   405. *imputation:* probability.
408. *living:* tangible.   411. *Pricked:* spurred on.   420 *gripe:* grip.   428. *shrewd doubt:*
bitter suspicion.

Have you not sometimes seen a handkerchief
Spotted with strawberries° in your wife's hand?
OTHELLO.   I gave her such a one, 'twas my first gift.
IAGO.   I know not that. But such a handkerchief—
    I am sure it was your wife's—did I today
    See Cassio wipe his beard with.
OTHELLO.   If it be that——
IAGO.   If it be that, or any that was hers,
    It speaks against her with the other proofs.   440
OTHELLO.   Oh, that the slave had forty thousand lives!
    One is too poor, too weak, for my revenge.
    Now do I see 'tis true. Look here, Iago,
    All my fond love thus do I blow to Heaven—
    'Tis gone.
    Arise, black Vengeance, from thy hollow cell!
    Yield up, O Love, thy crown and hearted° throne
    To tyrannous hate! Swell, bosom, with thy fraught,°
    For 'tis of aspics'° tongues!
IAGO.   Yet be content.
OTHELLO.   Oh, blood, blood, blood!
IAGO.   Patience, I say. Your mind perhaps may change.
OTHELLO.   Never, Iago. Like to the Pontic Sea,
    Whose icy current and compulsive course
    Ne'er feels retiring ebb but keeps due on
    To the Propontic and the Hellespont;°
    Even so my bloody thoughts, with violent pace,
    Shall ne'er look back, ne'er ebb to humble love,
    Till that capable° and wide revenge
    Swallow them up. Now, by yond marble Heaven,
    In the due reverence of a sacred vow [*kneels*]   460
    I here engage° my words.
IAGO.   Do not rise yet. [*Kneels.*]
    Witness, you ever burning lights above,
    You elements that clip° us round about,

---

434. *with strawberries:* with a pattern of strawberries.   447. *hearted:* in my heart.
448. *fraught:* freight, load.   449. *aspic:* asp, a small poisonous snake.   452–55. *Like
. . . Hellespont:* In Pliny's *Natural History*, translated by Philemon Holland in 1601, it
was noted that "the sea Pontus (Black Sea) evermore floweth and runneth out into
Propontis (Sea of Marmora) but the sea never returneth back again within Pontus."
Hellespont: The Dardenelles.   458. *capable:* comprehensive, complete.   461. *engage:*
pledge.   463. *elements . . . clip:* skies that embrace, surround.

Witness that here Iago doth give up
The execution of his wit, hands, heart,
To wronged Othello's service! Let him command,
And to obey shall be in me remorse,°
What bloody business ever.

[*They rise.*]

OTHELLO.   I greet thy love,
  Not with vain thanks, but with acceptance bounteous,
  And will upon the instant put thee to 't.°   470
  Within these three days let me hear thee say
  That Cassio's not alive.
IAGO. My friend is dead. 'Tis done at your request.
  But let her live.
OTHELLO. Damn her, lewd minx! Oh, damn her!
  Come, go with me apart. I will withdraw,
  To furnish me with some swift means of death
  For the fair devil. Now art thou my Lieutenant.
IAGO. I am your own forever.

[*Exeunt.*]

SCENE IV. *Before the castle.*

[*Enter* DESDEMONA, EMILIA, *and* CLOWN.]

DESDEMONA. Do you know, sirrah, where Lieutenant Cassio
  lies?
CLOWN. I dare not say he lies anywhere.
DESDEMONA. Why, man?
CLOWN. He's a soldier, and for one to say a soldier lies is
  stabbing.
DESDEMONA. Go to. Where lodges he?
CLOWN. To tell you where he lodges is to tell you where I
  lie.
DESDEMONA. Can anything be made of this?   10
CLOWN. I know not where he lodges, and for me to devise a
  lodging, and say he lies here or he lies there, were to lie
  in mine own throat.

---

467. *remorse:* solemn obligation. 470. *put . . . to 't:* put you to the proof.

DESDEMONA.   Can you inquire him out and be edified by
     report?°
CLOWN.   I will catechize the world for him; that is, make
     questions and by them answer.
DESDEMONA.   Seek him, bid him come hither. Tell him I
     have moved my lord on his behalf and hope all will be
     well.   20
CLOWN.   To do this is within the compass of man's wit, and
     therefore I will attempt the doing it.

                                                                           [*Exit.*]

DESDEMONA.   Where should I lose that handkerchief, Emilia?
EMILIA.   I know not madam.
DESDEMONA.   Believe me, I had rather have lost my purse
     Full of crusados.° And, but my noble Moor
     Is true of mind and made of no such baseness
     As jealous creatures are, it were enough
     To put him to ill thinking.
EMILIA.   Is he not jealous?
DESDEMONA.   Who, he? I think the sun where he was born   30
     Drew all such humors° from him.
EMILIA.   Look where he comes.
DESDEMONA.   I will not leave him now till Cassio
     Be called to him.
                         [*Enter* OTHELLO.]
               How is 't with you, my lord?
OTHELLO.   Well, my good lady. [*Aside.*] Oh, hardness to dissemble!
     How do you, Desdemona?
DESDEMONA.   Well, my good lord.
OTHELLO.   Give me your hand. This hand is moist,° my lady.
DESDEMONA.   It yet has felt no age nor known no sorrow.
OTHELLO.   This argues fruitfulness and liberal heart.
     Hot, hot, and moist—this hand of yours requires
     A sequester° from liberty, fasting and prayer,   40
     Much castigation, exercise devout.

SCENE IV: 15. *edified by report:* enlighted by the information. Desdemona speaks with
mock pomposity.   ˙26. *crusados:* small gold Portugeuse coins.   31. *humors:* moods;
literally, dampnesses.   36. *moist:* a hot moist palm was believed to show desire.
40. *sequester:* separation.

For here's a young and sweating devil here,
That commonly rebels. 'Tis a good hand,
A frank one.
DESDEMONA.   You may indeed say so,
For 'twas that hand that gave away my heart.
OTHELLO.   A liberal° hand. The hearts of old gave hands,
But our new heraldry is hands, not hearts.°
DESDEMONA.   I cannot speak of this. Come now, your promise.
OTHELLO.   What promise, chuck?°
DESDEMONA.   I have sent to bid Cassio come speak with you.   50
OTHELLO.   I have a salt and sorry rheum° offends me.
Lend me thy handkerchief.
DESDEMONA.   Here, my lord.
OTHELLO.   That which I gave you.
DESDEMONA.   I have it not about me.
OTHELLO. Not?
DESDEMONA.   No indeed, my lord.
OTHELLO.   That's a fault. That handkerchief
Did an Egyptian° to my mother give.
She was a charmer, and could almost read   60
The thoughts of people. She told her while she kept it
'Twould make her amiable and subdue my father
Entirely to her love, but if she lost it
Or made a gift of it, my father's eye
Should hold her loathed and his spirits should hunt
After new fancies. She dying gave it me,
And bid me, when my fate would have me wive,
To give it her. I did so. And take heed on 't,
Make it a darling like your precious eye.
To lose 't or give 't away were such perdition   70
As nothing else could match.
DESDEMONA.   Is 't possible?
OTHELLO.   'Tis true. There's magic in the web of it.
A sibyl° that had numbered in the world

---

46. *liberal:* overgenerous. 46–47. *The . . . hearts:* Once love and deeds went together, but now it is all deeds (i.e., faithlessness) and no love. . . . 49. *chuck:* a term of affection, but not the kind of word with which a person of Othello's dignity would normally address his wife. He is beginning to treat her with contemptuous familiarity (see IV.ii.24). 51. *rheum:* common cold. 59. *Egyptian:* gypsy. 73. *sibyl:* prophetess.

The sun to course two hundred compasses
In her prophetic fury° sewed the work.
The worms were hallowed that did breed the silk,
And it was dyed in mummy° which the skillful
Conserved° of maidens' hearts.
DESDEMONA.   Indeed! Is 't true?
OTHELLO.   Most veritable, therefore look to 't well.
DESDEMONA.   Then would to God that I had never seen 't.   80
OTHELLO.   Ha! Wherefore?
DESDEMONA.   Why do you speak so startlingly and rash?
OTHELLO.   Is 't lost? Is 't gone? Speak, is it out o' the way?
DESDEMONA.   Heaven bless us!
OTHELLO.   Say you?
DESDEMONA.   It is not lost, but what an if it were?
OTHELLO.   How!
DESDEMONA.   I say it is not lost.
OTHELLO.   Fetch 't, let me see it.
DESDEMONA.   Why, so I can, sir, but I will not now.   90
    This is a trick to put me from my suit.
    Pray you let Cassio be received again.
OTHELLO.   Fetch me the handkerchief. My mind misgives.
DESDEMONA.   Come, come,
    You'll never meet a more sufficient man.
OTHELLO.   The handkerchief!
DESDEMONA.   I pray talk me of Cassio.
OTHELLO.   The handkerchief!
DESDEMONA.   A man that all his time
    Hath founded his good fortunes on your love,
    Shared dangers with you——
OTHELLO.   The handkerchief!   100
DESDEMONA.   In sooth, you are to blame.
OTHELLO.   Away!

                                                    [*Exit.*]

EMILIA.   Is not this man jealous?
DESDEMONA.   I ne'er saw this before.
    Sure there's some wonder in this handkerchief.
    I am most unhappy in the loss of it.

―――――――

75. *fury:* inspiration.   77. *mummy:* a concoction made from Egyptian mummies.
78. *Conserved:* prepared.

EMILIA.   'Tis not a year or two shows us a man.°
　　They are all but stomach and we all but food.
　　They eat us hungerly, and when they are full
　　They belch us. Look you, Cassio and my husband.   110

　　　　　　　　[*Enter* CASSIO *and* IAGO.]

IAGO.   There is no other way, 'tis she must do 't.
　　And, lo, the happiness!° Go and impórtune her.
DESDEMONA.   How now, good Cassio! What's the news with you?
CASSIO.   Madam, my former suit. I do beseech you
　　That by your virtuous means I may again
　　Exist, and be a member of his love
　　Whom I with all the office of my heart
　　Entirely honor. I would not be delayed.
　　If my offense be of such mortal kind
　　That nor my service past nor present sorrows   120
　　Nor purposed merit in futurity°
　　Can ransom me into his love again,
　　But to know so must be my benefit.
　　So shall I clothe me in a forced content
　　And shut myself up in some other course
　　To Fortune's alms.°
DESDEMONA.　　　　　　　Alas, thrice-gentle Cassio!
　　My advocation° is not now in tune.
　　My lord is not my lord, nor should I know him
　　Were he in favor as in humor altered.°
　　So help me every spirit sanctified,   130
　　As I have spoken for you all my best
　　And stood within the blank° of his displeasure
　　For my free speech! You must awhile be patient.
　　What I can do I will, and more I will
　　Than for myself I dare. Let that suffice you.
IAGO.   Is my lord angry?

---

107. *'Tis . . . man:* It does not take a couple of years for us to discover the nature of a man; that is, he soon shows his real nature.   112. *And . . . happiness:* What good luck, here she is.   121. *Nor . . . futurity:* nor my good resolutions for the future.   123–26. *But . . . alms:* If I know that Othello will not restore me to my position, it will have this benefit: I shall force myself to be contented and try my luck elsewhere; *Fortune's alms:* what Fortune may give me.   127. *advocation:* advocacy, pleading.   129. *favor . . . altered:* as changed in face as in mood.   132. *blank:* aim. The blank is the bull's-eye of a target.

EMILIA.   He went hence but now,
  And certainly in strange unquietness.
IAGO.   Can he be angry? I have seen the cannon
  When it hath blown his ranks into the air,
  And, like the Devil, from his very arm   140
  Puffed his own brother, and can he be angry?
  Something of moment then. I will go meet him.
  There's matter in 't indeed if he be angry.
DESDEMONA.   I prithee do so.

                                                  [*Exit* IAGO.]

                          Something sure of state,
  Either from Venice, or some unhatched practice
  Made demonstrable° here in Cyprus to him,
  Hath puddled° his clear spirit. And in such cases
  Men's natures wrangle with inferior things,
  Though great ones are their object.° 'Tis even so,
  For let our finger ache and it indues°   150
  Our other healthful members even to that sense
  Of pain. Nay, we must think men are not gods,
  Nor of them look for such observancy
  As fits the bridal.° Beshrew me° much, Emilia,
  I was, unhandsome warrior° as I am,
  Arraigning his unkindness with my soul,
  But now I find I had suborned the witness,°
  And he's indicted falsely.
EMILIA.   Pray Heaven it be state matters, as you think,
  And no conception nor no jealous toy°   160
  Concerning you.
DESDEMONA.   Alas the day, I never gave him cause!
EMILIA.   But jealous souls will not be answered so.
  They are not ever jealous for the cause,
  But jealous for they are jealous. 'Tis a monster
  Begot upon itself, born on itself.

145–46. *unhatched . . . demonstrable:* some plot, not yet matured, which has been revealed.   147. *puddled:* muddied, stirred up.   147–49. *in . . . object:* When men are disturbed by great matters, they show their temper in small things.   150. *indues:* endows,
pervades.   154. *bridal:* honeymoon; *Beshrew me:* plague on me.   155. *unhandsome war-*
rior: clumsy soldier. Desdemona continually thinks of herself as Othello's companion
in arms (see I.iii.248ff.).   157. *suborned . . . witness:* corrupted the evidence; that is, it is
my fault, not his.   160. *jealous toy:* silly suspicion.

DESDEMONA.   Heaven keep that monster from Othello's mind!
EMILIA.   Lady, amen.
DESDEMONA.   I will go seek him. Cassio, walk hereabout,
  If I do find him fit, I'll move your suit,   170
  And seek to effect it to my uttermost.
CASSIO.   I humbly thank your ladyship.

                                [Exeunt DESDEMONA *and* EMILIA.]
                           [Enter BIANCA.]

BIANCA.   Save you, friend Cassio!
CASSIO.   What make you from° home?
  How is it with you, my most fair Bianca?
  I' faith, sweet love, I was coming to your house.
BIANCA.   And I was going to your lodging, Cassio.
  What, keep a week away? Seven days and nights?
  Eightscore eight hours? And lovers' absent hours,
  More tedious than the dial eightscore times?°
  Oh, weary reckoning!
CASSIO.   Pardon me, Bianca.   180
  I have this while with leaden thoughts been pressed,
  But I shall in a more continuate time°
  Strike off this score of absence. Sweet Bianca

        [giving her DESDEMONA'S *handkerchief]*,
  Take me this work out.°
BIANCA.   O Cassio, whence came this?
  This is some token from a newer friend.
  To the felt absence now I feel a cause.
  Is 't come to this? Well, well.
CASSIO.   Go to, woman!
  Throw your vile guesses in the Devil's teeth,
  From whence you have them. You are jealous now
  That this is from some mistress, some remembrance.   190
  No, by my faith, Bianca.
BIANCA.   Why, whose is it?
CASSIO.   I know not, sweet. I found it in my chamber.
  I like the work well. Ere it be demanded—

---

173. *make . . . from:* are you doing away from.   178–79. *And . . . times:* When one's
lover is absent for a week, does it not seem far longer than a hundred and sixty clock
hours?   182. *continuate time:* that is, when my time is not continually being inter-
rupted.   184. *Take . . . out:* copy this pattern.

As like enough it will—I'd have it copied.
Take it, and do 't, and leave me for this time.
BIANCA.   Leave you! Wherefore?
CASSIO.   I do attend here on the General,
  And think it no addition,° nor my wish,
  To have him see me womaned.°
BIANCA.   Why, I pray you?
CASSIO.   Not that I love you not.
BIANCA.   But that you do not love me.
  I pray you bring me on the way a little,   201
  And say if I shall see you soon at night.
CASSIO.   'Tis but a little way that I can bring you,
  For I attend here. But I'll see you soon.
BIANCA.   'Tis very good, I must be circumstanced.°

                                                    [*Exeunt.*]

ACT IV

SCENE I. *Cyprus. Before the castle.*

[*Enter* OTHELLO *and* IAGO.]

IAGO.   Will you think so?
OTHELLO.   Think so, Iago!
IAGO.   What,
  To kiss in private?
OTHELLO.   An unauthorized kiss.
IAGO.   Or to be naked with her friend in bed
  An hour or more, not meaning any harm?
OTHELLO.   Naked in bed, Iago, and not mean harm!
  It is hypocrisy against the Devil.°
  They that mean virtuously and yet do so,
  The Devil their virtue tempts and they tempt Heaven.°
IAGO.   So° they do nothing, 'tis a venial° slip.
  But if I give my wife a handkerchief——   10

---

198. *addition:* honor. 199. *womaned:* with a girl. 205. *circumstanced:* put off.
Act IV, SCENE I: 6. *hypocrisy . . . Devil:* "double-crossing the Devil"; that is, they are
behaving in a most suspicious way. 7–8. *They . . . Heaven:* that is, those who go to
bed together and mean no harm are asking the Devil to tempt them, and they make
God suspect their innocence. 9. *So:* so long as; *venial:* pardonable.

OTHELLO.   What then?

IAGO.   Why, then, 'tis hers my lord, and being hers,
She may, I think bestow 't on any man.

OTHELLO.   She is protectress of her honor too.
May she give that?

IAGO.   Her honor is an essence that's not seen.
They have it very oft that have it not.°
But for the handkerchief——

OTHELLO.   By Heaven, I would most gladly have forgot it.
Thou said'st—oh, it comes o'er my memory,   20
As doth the raven o'er the infected house,°
Boding° to all—he had my handkerchief.

IAGO.   Aye, what of that?

OTHELLO.   That's not so good now.

IAGO.   What,
If I had said I had seen him do you wrong?
Or heard him say—as knaves be such abroad,
Who having, by their own importunate suit,
Or voluntary dotage° of some mistress,
Convincèd or supplied° them, cannot choose
But they must blab——

OTHELLO.   Hath he said anything?

IAGO.   He hath, my lord, but be you well assured,   30
No more than he'll unswear.

OTHELLO.   What hath he said?

IAGO.   Faith, that he did——I know not what he did.

OTHELLO.   What? What?

IAGO.   Lie——

OTHELLO.   With her?

IAGO.   With her, on her, what you will.

OTHELLO.   Lie° with her! Lie on her!—We say lie on her
when they belie her.—Lie with her! 'Zounds, that's fulsome!° Handkerchief—confessions—handkerchief!—To
confess, and be hanged for his labor. First to be hanged,
and then to confess. I tremble at it. Nature would not in-

---

17. *They . . . not:* that is, many are honored who have no honor.   21. *As . . . house:*
that is, as a bird of prey waits for its victim to die.   22. *Boding:* foretelling evil.
27. *dotage:* infatuation.   28. *Convincèd or supplied:* overcome or satisfied their desires.
35–43. *Lie . . . devil:* Othello breaks into incoherent muttering before he falls down in
a fit.   37. *fulsome:* disgusting.

vest herself in such shadowing passion without some in-   40
struction.° It is not words that shake me thus. Pish! Noses,
ears, and lips. Is 't possible?—Confess?—Handkerchief?
—Oh, devil!   [*Falls in a trance.*]
IAGO.   Work on,
My medicine, work! Thus credulous fools are caught,
And many worthy and chaste dames even thus,
All guiltless, meet reproach. What ho! My lord!
My lord, I say! Othello!

[*Enter* CASSIO.]

How now, Cassio!
CASSIO.   What's the matter?
IAGO.   My lord is fall'n into an epilepsy.   50
This is his second fit, he had one yesterday.
CASSIO.   Rub him about the temples.
IAGO.   No, forbear,
The lethargy° must have his quiet course.
If not, he foams at mouth and by and by
Breaks out to savage madness. Look, he stirs.
Do you withdraw yourself a little while,
He will recover straight. When he is gone,
I would on great occasion speak with you.

[*Exit* CASSIO.]

How is it, General? Have you not hurt your head?°
OTHELLO.   Dost thou mock me?
IAGO.   I mock you! No, by Heaven.   60
Would you would bear your fortune like a man!
OTHELLO.   A hornèd man's a monster and a beast.
IAGO.   There's many a beast, then, in a populous city,
And many a civil° monster.
OTHELLO.   Did he confess it?
IAGO.   Good sir, be a man.
Think every bearded fellow that's but yoked°
May draw with you.° There's millions now alive

39–41. *Nature . . . instruction:* Nature would not fill me with such overwhelming emotion unless there was some cause.   53. *lethargy:* epileptic fit.   59. *Have . . . head:* With
brutal cynicism Iago asks whether Othello is suffering from cuckold's headache.
64. *civil:* sober, well-behaved citizen.   66. *yoked:* married.   67. *draw . . . you:* literally,
be your yoke fellow, share your fate.

That nightly lie in those unproper beds
Which they dare swear peculiar.° Your case is better.
Oh, 'tis the spite of Hell, the Fiend's archmock,   70
To lip° a wanton in a secure couch°
And to suppose her chaste! No, let me know,
And knowing what I am, I know what she shall be.
OTHELLO.   Oh, thou art wise, 'tis certain.
IAGO.   Stand you awhile apart,
Confine yourself but in a patient list.°
Whilst you were here o'erwhelmèd with your grief—
A passion most unsuiting such a man—
Cassio came hither. I shifted him away,
And laid good 'scuse upon your ecstasy,°
Bade him anon return and here speak with me,   80
The which he promisèd. Do but encave° yourself,
And mark the fleers,° the gibes, and notable scorns,
That dwell in every region of his face.
For I will make him tell the tale anew,
Where, how, how oft, how long ago, and when
He hath and is again to cope° your wife.
I say but mark his gesture. Marry, patience,
Or I shall say you are all in all in spleen,°
And nothing of a man.
OTHELLO.   Dost thou hear, Iago?
I will be found most cunning in my patience,   90
But—dost thou hear?—most bloody.
IAGO.   That's not amiss,
But yet keep time in all. Will you withdraw?

                                        [OTHELLO *retires.*]

Now will I question Cassio of Bianca,
A housewife° that by selling her desires
Buys herself bread and clothes. It is a creature
That dotes on Cassio, as 'tis the strumpet's plague
To beguile many and be beguiled by one.

68–69. *That . . . peculiar:* that lie nightly in beds which they believe are their own but which others have shared.   71. *lip:* kiss; *secure couch:* literally, a carefree bed; that is, a bed which has been used by the wife's lover, but secretly.   75. *patient list:* confines of patience.   79. *ecstasy:* fit.   81. *encave:* hide.   82. *fleers:* scornful grins.   86. *cope:* encounter.   88. *spleen:* hot tempered.   94. *housewife:* hussy.

He, when he hears of her, cannot refrain
From the excess of laughter. Here he comes.

[*Re-enter* CASSIO.]

As he shall smile, Othello shall go mad,   100
And his unbookish° jealousy must construe°
Poor Cassio's smiles, gestures, and light behavior
Quite in the wrong. How do you now, Lieutenant?

CASSIO.   The worser that you give me the addition°
Whose want even kills me.

IAGO.   Ply° Desdemona well, and you are sure on 't.
Now, if this suit lay in Bianca's power,
How quickly should you speed!

CASSIO.   Alas, poor caitiff!°

OTHELLO.   Look how he laughs already!

IAGO.   I never knew a woman love man so.   110

CASSIO.   Alas, poor rogue! I think, i' faith, she loves me.

OTHELLO.   Now he denies it faintly and laughs it out.

IAGO.   Do you hear, Cassio?

OTHELLO.   Now he impórtunes him
To tell it o'er. Go to. Well said, well said.

IAGO.   She gives it out that you shall marry her.
Do you intend it?

CASSIO.   Ha, ha, ha!

OTHELLO.   Do you triumph, Roman?° Do you triumph?

CASSIO.   I marry her! What, a customer!° I prithee bear some   120
charity to my wit. Do not think it so unwholesome. Ha,
ha, ha!

OTHELLO.   So, so, so, so. They laugh that win.°

IAGO.   Faith, the cry goes that you shall marry her.

CASSIO.   Prithee say true.

IAGO.   I am a very villain else.

OTHELLO.   Have you scored° me? Well.

CASSIO.   This is the monkey's own giving out. She is persuaded I will marry her out of her own love and flattery,
not out of my promise.   130

---

101. *unbookish:* unlearned, simple; *construe:* interpret.   104. *addition:* title (Lieutenant)
which he has lost.   106. *Ply:* urge.   108. *caitiff:* wretch.   119. *triumph, Roman:* The
word "triumph" suggests "Roman" because the Romans celebrated their victories
with triumphs, elaborate shows, and processions.   120. *customer:* harlot.   123. *They
. . . win:* a proverbial saying.   127. *scored:* marked, as with a blow from a whip.

OTHELLO.   Iago beckons me, now he begins the story.

CASSIO.   She was here even now. She haunts me in every
place. I was the other day talking on the sea bank with
certain Venetians, and thither comes the bauble,° and, by
this hand, she falls thus about my neck——

OTHELLO.   Crying "O dear Cassio!" as it were. His gesture
imports it.

CASSIO.   So hangs and lolls and weeps upon me, so hales°
and pulls me. Ha, ha, ha!

OTHELLO.   Now he tells how she plucked him to my cham-   140
ber. Oh, I see that nose of yours, but not that dog I shall
throw it to.

CASSIO.   Well, I must leave her company.

IAGO.   Before me!° Look where she comes.

CASSIO.   'Tis such another fitchew!° Marry, a perfumed one.

[*Enter* BIANCA]

What do you mean by this haunting of me?

BIANCA.   Let the Devil and his dam° haunt you! What did
you mean by that same handkerchief you gave me even
now? I was a fine fool to take it. I must take out the
work? A likely piece of work, that you should find it in   150
your chamber and not know who left it there! This is
some minx's token, and I must take out the work?
There, give it your hobbyhorse.° Wheresoever you had
it, I'll take out no work on 't.

CASSIO.   How now, my sweet Bianca! How now! How now!

OTHELLO.   By Heaven, that should be my handkerchief!

BIANCA.   An° you'll come to supper tonight, you may. An
you will not, come when you are next prepared for.

[*Exit.*]

IAGO.   After her, after her.

CASSIO.   Faith, I must, she'll rail i' the street else.   160

IAGO.   Will you sup there?

CASSIO.   Faith, I intend so.

IAGO.   Well, I may chance to see you, for I would very fain°
speak with you.

---

134. *bauble:* toy, plaything.   138. *hales:* hauls, drags.   144. *Before me:* by my soul, a
mild oath.   145. *fitchew:* polecat, a creature most demonstrative in the mating season.
147. *dam:* mother.   153. *hobbyhorse:* harlot.   157. *An:* if.   163. *fain:* gladly.

CASSIO.   Prithee, come, will you?

IAGO.   Go to. Say no more.

[*Exit* CASSIO.]

OTHELLO [*advancing*].   How shall I murder him, Iago?

IAGO.   Did you perceive how he laughed at his vice?

OTHELLO.   Oh, Iago!

IAGO.   And did you see the handkerchief?   170

OTHELLO.   Was that mine?

IAGO.   Yours, by this hand. And to see how he prizes the foolish woman your wife! She gave it him, and he hath given it his whore.

OTHELLO.   I would have him nine years a-killing. A fine woman! A fair woman! A sweet woman!

IAGO.   Nay, you must forget that.

OTHELLO.   Aye, let her rot, and perish, and be damned to-night, for she shall not live. No, my heart is turned to stone, I strike it and it hurts my hand. Oh, the world   180 hath not a sweeter creature. She might lie by an emperor's side, and command him tasks.

IAGO.   Nay, that's not your way.°

OTHELLO.   Hang her! I do but say what she is, so delicate with her needle, an admirable musician—oh, she will sing the savageness of out of a bear—of so high and plenteous wit and invention—

IAGO.   She's the worse for all this.

OTHELLO.   Oh, a thousand thousand times. And then, of so gentle a condition!°   190

IAGO.   Aye, too gentle.

OTHELLO.   Nay, that's certain. But yet the pity of it, Iago! O Iago, the pity of it, Iago!

IAGO.   If you are so fond° over her iniquity, give her patent° to offend, for if it touch not you, it comes near nobody.

OTHELLO.   I will chop her into messes.° Cuckold me!

IAGO.   Oh, 'tis foul in her.

OTHELLO.   With mine officer!

---

183. *Nay . . . way:* that is, don't get soft thoughts about her.   190. *condition:* nature.
194. *fond:* foolish; *patent:* a grant by the King of some special privilege.   196. *messes:* little pieces.

IAGO. That's fouler.

OTHELLO. Get me some poison, Iago, this night. I'll not ex-   200
postulate° with her, lest her body and beauty unprovide°
my mind again. This night, Iago.

IAGO. Do it not with poison, strangle her in her bed, even
the bed she hath contaminated.

OTHELLO. Good, good. The justice of it pleases. Very good.

IAGO. And for Cassio let me be his undertaker.° You shall
hear more by midnight.

OTHELLO. Excellent good. [*A trumpet within.*] What trumpet
is that same?

IAGO. Something from Venice, sure. 'Tis Lodovico   210
Come from the Duke. And see, your wife is with him.

[*Enter* LODOVICO, DESDEMONA, *and* ATTENDANTS.]

LODOVICO. God save the worthy General!

OTHELLO.   With all my heart, sir.

LODOVICO. The Duke and Senators of Venice greet you.

                                  [*Gives him a letter.*]

OTHELLO. I kiss the instrument° of their pleasures.

                           [*Opens the letter, and reads.*]

DESDEMONA. And what's the news, good Cousin Lodovico?

IAGO. I am very glad to see you, signior.
Welcome to Cyprus.

LODOVICO. I thank you. How does Lieutenant Cassio?

IAGO. Lives, sir.

DESDEMONA. Cousin, there's fall'n between him and my lord
An unkind breach, but you shall make all well.   221

OTHELLO. Are you sure of that?

DESDEMONA. My lord?

OTHELLO [*reads*]. "This fail you not to do, as you will——"

LODOVICO. He did not call, he's busy in the paper.
Is there division 'twixt my lord and Cassio?

DESDEMONA. A most unhappy one. I would do much
To atone° them, for the love I bear to Cassio.

---

201. *expostulate:* argue; *unprovide:* weaken.   206. *be . . . undertaker:* undertake to manage his business. In Shakespeare's plays the word does *not* mean "mortician."   214. *instrument:* that is, the official letter which he has just received.   228. *atone:* reconcile.

OTHELLO.   Fire and brimstone!

DESDEMONA.   My lord?

OTHELLO.   Are you wise?°

DESDEMONA.   What, is he angry?

LODOVICO.   Maybe the letter moved him,   230
    For, as I think, they do command him home,
    Deputing Cassio in his government.°

DESDEMONA.   By my troth,° I am glad on 't.

OTHELLO.   Indeed!

DESDEMONA.   My lord?

OTHELLO.   I am glad to see you mad.

DESDEMONA.   Why, sweet Othello?

OTHELLO.   Devil! [*Striking her.*]

DESDEMONA.   I have not deserved this.

LODOVICO.   My lord, this would not be believed in Venice
    Though I should swear I saw 't. 'Tis very much.°
    Make her amends, she weeps.

OTHELLO.   O devil, devil!
    If that the earth could teem with a woman's tears,   240
    Each drop she falls would prove a crocodile.°
    Out of my sight!

DESDEMONA.   I will not stay to offend you. [*Going.*]

LODOVICO.   Truly, an obedient lady.
    I do beseech your lordship, call her back.

OTHELLO.   Mistress!

DESDEMONA.   My lord?

OTHELLO.   What would you with her, sir?

LODOVICO.   Who, I, my lord?

OTHELLO.   Aye, you did wish that I would make her turn.
    Sir, she can turn and turn, and yet go on
    And turn again. And she can weep, sir, weep.   250
    And she's obedient, as you say, obedient,
    Very obedient. Proceed you in your tears.

---

229. *Are . . . wise:* that is, in saying you bear love to Cassio.   232. *in . . . government:* in his place as governor.   233. *troth:* truth.   238. *'Tis . . . much:* this is too much. 240–41. *If . . . crocodile:* If the earth could breed from woman's tears, each tear that she lets fall would become a crocodile. It was believed that the crocodile would cry and sob to attract the sympathetic passerby, who was then snapped up.

Concerning this, sir—oh, well-painted passion!°—
I am commanded home. Get you away.
I'll send for you anon. Sir, I obey the mandate,
And will return to Venice. Hence, avaunt!

[*Exit* DESDEMONA.]

Cassio shall have my place. And, sir, tonight,
I do entreat that we may sup together.
You are welcome, sir, to Cyprus. Goats and monkeys!

[*Exit.*]

LODOVICO.   Is this the noble Moor whom our full Senate   260
    Call all-in-all sufficient? This the nature
    Whom passion could not shake? Whose solid virtue
    The shot of accident nor dart of chance
    Could neither graze nor pierce?
IAGO.   He is much changed.
LODOVICO.   Are his wits safe? Is he not light of brain?
IAGO.   He's that he is. I may not breathe my censure°
    What he might be. If what he might he is not,
    I would to Heaven he were!°
LODOVICO.   What, strike his wife!
IAGO.   Faith, that was not so well, yet would I knew
    That stroke would prove the worst!
LODOVICO.   Is it his use?°   270
    Or did the letters work upon his blood,
    And new-create this fault?
IAGO.   Alas, alas!
    It is not honesty in me to speak
    What I have seen and known. You shall observe him,
    And his own courses° will denote him so
    That I may save my speech. Do but go after,
    And mark how he continues.
LODOVICO.   I am sorry that I am deceived in him.

[*Exeunt.*]

---

253. *well-painted passion:* cleverly imitated emotion; passion is any violent emotion.
266. *censure:* opinion, judgment.   268. *I . . . were:* I wish he were the man he ought to
be. Once more Iago hints that he is holding back some unpleasant fact.   270. *Is . . .
use:* Does he always behave like this?   275. *courses:* ways, behavior.

SCENE II. *A room in the castle.*

[*Enter* OTHELLO *and* EMILIA.]

OTHELLO. You have seen nothing, then?

EMILIA. Nor ever heard, nor ever did suspect.

OTHELLO. Yes, you have seen Cassio and she together.

EMILIA. But then I saw no harm, and then I heard
Each syllable that breath made up between them.

OTHELLO. What, did they never whisper?

EMILIA. Never, my lord.

OTHELLO. Nor send you out o' the way?

EMILIA. Never.

OTHELLO. To fetch her fan, her gloves, her mask, nor nothing?

EMILIA. Never, my lord. 10

OTHELLO. That's strange.

EMILIA. I durst, my lord, to wager she is honest,
Lay down my soul at stake.° If you think other,
Remove your thought, it doth abuse your bosom.
If any wretch have put this in your head,
Let Heaven requite it with the serpent's curse!°
For if she be not honest, chaste, and true,
There's no man happy, the purest of their wives
Is foul as slander.

OTHELLO. Bid her come hither. Go.

[*Exit* EMILIA.]

She says enough. Yet she's a simple bawd° 20
That cannot say as much. This is a subtle whore,
A closet° lock and key of villainous secrets.
And yet she'll kneel and pray, I have seen her do't.

[*Enter* DESDEMONA *with* EMILIA.]

DESDEMONA. My lord, what is your will?

OTHELLO. Pray, chuck,° come hither.

DESDEMONA. What is your pleasure?

OTHELLO. Let me see your eyes.
Look in my face.

DESDEMONA. What horrible fancy's this?

SCENE II: 13. *at stake:* as the stake, the bet. 16. *serpent's curse:* that is, the curse laid on the serpent in the Garden of Eden. 20. *bawd:* keeper of a brothel. 22. *closet:* box in which secret papers are kept. 24. *chuck.* See III.iv.49,n.

OTHELLO [*to* EMILIA].　　Some of your function,° mistress.
　　Leave procreants alone and shut the door,
　　Cough, or cry hem, if anybody come.
　　Your mystery,° your mystery. Nay, dispatch.°　　　　　30
　　　　　　　　　　　　　　　　　　　　[*Exit* EMILIA.]
DESDEMONA.　　Upon my knees, what doth your speech import?
　　I understand a fury in your words,
　　But not the words.
OTHELLO.　　Why, what art thou?
DESDEMONA.　　Your wife, my lord, your true and loyal wife.
OTHELLO.　　Come swear it, damn thyself,
　　Lest, being like one of Heaven,° the devils themselves
　　Should fear to seize thee. Therefore be double-damned.
　　Swear thou art honest.
DESDEMONA.　　　　　　　　Heaven doth truly know it.
OTHELLO.　　Heaven truly knows that thou art false as Hell.　　40
DESDEMONA.　　To whom, my lord? With whom? How am I false?
OTHELLO.　　O Desdemona! Away! Away! Away!
DESDEMONA.　　Alas the heavy day! Why do you weep?
　　Am I the motive of these tears, my lord?
　　If haply you my father do suspect
　　An instrument of this your calling-back,
　　Lay not your blame on me. If you have lost him,
　　Why, I have lost him too.
OTHELLO.　　　　　　　　　Had it pleased Heaven
　　To try me with affliction, had they rained
　　All kinds of sores and shames on my bare head,　　　　50
　　Steeped me in poverty to the very lips,
　　Given to captivity me and my utmost hopes,
　　I should have found in some place of my soul
　　A drop of patience. But, alas, to make me
　　A fixèd figure for the time of scorn
　　To point his slow unmoving finger at!°
　　Yet could I bear that too, well, very well.

---

27. *Some . . . function:* Get about your business; that is, prostitution. Othello pretends
that Emilia is keeper of a brothel and Desdemona one of the women.　30. *mystery:*
profession; *dispatch:* be quick.　37. *being . . . Heaven:* because you look like an angel.
55–56. *A . . . at:* a difficult image, much discussed. . . . Probably it means "a perpetual mark for scorn to point at with motionless finger." *time of scorn:* (perhaps) scorn
for all time.

But there where I have garnered up my heart,°
Where either I must live or bear no life,
The fountain from the which my current runs   60
Or else dries up—to be discarded thence!
Or keep it as a cistern for foul toads
To knot and gender° in! Turn thy complexion there,
Patience, thou young and rose-lipped cherubin—
Aye, there, look grim as Hell!

DESDEMONA.   I hope my noble lord esteems me honest.

OTHELLO.   Oh, aye, as summer flies are in the shambles,°
That quicken even with blowing.° O thou weed,
Who art so lovely fair and smell'st so sweet
That the sense aches at thee, would thou hadst ne'er been born!

DESDEMONA.   Alas, what ignorant sin have I committed?   71

OTHELLO.   Was this fair paper,° this most goodly book,
Made to write "whore" upon? What committed!
Committed! O thou public commoner!°
I should make very forges of my cheeks°
That would to cinders burn up modesty
Did I but speak thy deeds. What committed!
Heaven stops the nose at it, and the moon winks.
The bawdy wind, that kisses all it meets,
Is hushed within the hollow mine° of earth   80
And will not hear it. What committed!
Impudent strumpet!

DESDEMONA.   By Heaven, you do me wrong.

OTHELLO.   Are not you a strumpet?

DESDEMONA.   No, as I am a Christian
If to preserve this vessel for my lord
From any other foul unlawful touch
Be not to be a strumpet, I am none.

OTHELLO.   What, not a whore?

DESDEMONA.   No, as I shall be saved.

OTHELLO.   Is't possible?

DESDEMONA.   Oh, Heaven forgive us!

---

58. *garnered . . . heart:* stored the harvest of my love. 63. *gender:* mate. 67. *shambles:*
slaughterhouse. 68. *quicken . . . blowing:* come to life as soon as the eggs are laid.
72. *fair paper:* that is, her white body. 74. *public commoner:* one who offers herself to
all comers. 75. *I . . . cheeks:* that is, my cheeks would be as hot as a forge if I told the
truth. 80. *hollow mine:* that is, the cave where the winds were supposed to be kept.

OTHELLO.   I cry you mercy, then.
   I took you for that cunning whore of Venice   90
   That married with Othello. [*Raising his voice.*] You, mistress,
   That have the office opposite to Saint Peter,°
   And keep the gate of Hell!
                [*Re-enter* EMILIA.]
               You, you, aye, you!
   We have done our course, there's money for your pains.
   I pray you turn the key, and keep our counsel.°
                                 [*Exit.*]

EMILIA.   Alas, what does this gentleman conceive?°
   How do you, madam? How do you, my good lady?
DESDEMONA.   Faith, half-asleep.
EMILIA.   Good madam, what's the matter with my lord?
DESDEMONA.   With who?   100
EMILIA.   Why, with my lord, madam.
DESDEMONA.   Who is thy lord?
EMILIA.   He that is yours, sweet lady.
DESDEMONA.   I have none. Do not talk to me, Emilia.
   I cannot weep, nor answer have I none
   But what should go by water.° Prithee tonight
   Lay on my bed my wedding sheets. Remember,
   And call thy husband hither.
EMILIA.   Here's a change indeed!
                                 [*Exit.*]

DESDEMONA.   'Tis meet I should be used so, very meet.
   How have I been behaved that he might stick
   The small'st opinion on my least misuse?°   110
           [*Re-enter* EMILIA *with* IAGO.]

IAGO.   What is your pleasure, madam? How is 't with you?
DESDEMONA.   I cannot tell. Those that do teach young babes
   Do it with gentle means and easy tasks.
   He might have chid me so, for, in good faith.
   I am a child to chiding.
IAGO.   What's the matter, lady?

92. *office . . . Peter:* St. Peter kept the keys to Heaven.   95. *counsel:* that is, secret.
96. *conceive:* imagine.   105. *should . . . water:* be expressed in tears.   109–110. *How
. . . misuse:* What have I done that he could find the smallest reason to find fault with
my least mistake?

EMILIA.   Alas, Iago, my lord hath so bewhored her,
    Thrown such despite and heavy terms upon her,
    As true hearts cannot bear.
DESDEMONA.   Am I that name, Iago?
IAGO.   What name, fair lady?
DESDEMONA.   Such as she says my lord did say I was.   120
EMILIA.   He called her whore. A beggar in his drink
    Could not have laid such terms upon his callet.°
IAGO.   Why did he so?
DESDEMONA.   I do not know. I am sure I am none such.
IAGO.   Do not weep, do not weep. Alas the day!
EMILIA.   Hath she forsook so many noble matches,
    Her father and her country and her friends,
    To be called whore? Would it not make one weep?
DESDEMONA.   It is my wretched fortune.
IAGO.   Beshrew him for 't!
    How comes this trick upon him?
DESDEMONA.   Nay, Heaven doth know.   130
EMILIA.   I will be hanged if some eternal villain,
    Some busy and insinuating rogue,
    Some cogging, cozening° slave, to get some office,
    Have not devised this slander. I'll be hanged else.
IAGO.   Fie, there is no such man, it is impossible.
DESDEMONA.   If any such there be, Heaven pardon him!
EMILIA.   A halter pardon him! And Hell gnaw his bones!
    Why should he call her whore? Who keeps her company?
    What place? What time? What form? What likelihood?
    The Moor's abused by some most villainous knave,   140
    Some base notorious knave, some scurvy fellow.
    O Heaven, that such companions° Thou'dst unfold,°
    And put in every honest hand a whip
    To lash the rascals naked through the world
    Even from the east to the west!
IAGO.   Speak withindoor.°
EMILIA.   Oh, fie upon them! Some such squire° he was
    That turned your wit the seamy side without,
    And made you to suspect me with the Moor.

---

122. *laid . . . callet:* used such words about his moll. 133. *cogging, cozening:* deceiving,
cheating. 142. *companions:* low creatures; *unfold:* bring to light. 145. *Speak withindoor:* Don't shout so loud that all the street will hear you. 146. *squire:* fine fellow.

IAGO. You are a fool. Go to.°
DESDEMONA.   O good Iago,
   What shall I do to win my lord again?   150
   Good friend, go to him, for, by this light of Heaven,
   I know not how I lost him. Here I kneel.
   If e'er my will did trespass 'gainst his love
   Either in discourse of thought or actual deed,
   Or that mine eyes, mine ears, or any sense
   Delighted them in any other form,
   Or that I do not yet, and ever did,
   And ever will, though he do shake me off
   To beggarly divorcement, love him dearly,
   Comfort forswear° me! Unkindness may do much,   160
   And this unkindness may defeat° my life,
   But never taint my love. I cannot say "whore,"
   It doth abhor me now I speak the word.
   To do the act that might the addition° earn
   Not the world's mass of vanity° could make me.
IAGO. I pray you be content, 'tis but his humor.
   The business of the state does him offense,
   And he does chide with you.
DESDEMONA.   If'twere no other——
IAGO. 'Tis but so, I warrant.   170
                    [*Trumpets within.*]
   Hark how these instruments summon to supper!
   The messengers of Venice stay the meat.°
   Go in, and weep not, all things shall be well.
                  [*Exeunt* DESDEMONA *and* EMILIA.]
                  [*Enter* RODERIGO.]
   How now, Roderigo!
RODERIGO. I do not find that thou dealest justly with me.
IAGO. What in the contrary?
RODERIGO. Every day thou daffest° me with some device,
   Iago, and rather, as it seems to me now, keepest from
   me all conveniency° than suppliest me with the least ad-
   vantage of hope. I will indeed no longer endure it, nor   180

149. *Go to:* an expression of derision. 160. *forswear:* repudiate. 161. *defeat:* destroy.
164. *addition:* title. 165. *vanity:* that is, riches. 172. *meat:* serving of supper.
177. *thou daffest:* you put me aside. 179. *conveniency:* opportunity.

am I yet persuaded to put up in peace what already I
have foolishly suffered.

IAGO.   Will you hear me, Roderigo?

RODERIGO.   Faith, I have heard too much, for your words
and performances are no kin together.

IAGO.   You charge me most unjustly.

RODERIGO.   With naught but truth. I have wasted myself out
of my means. The jewels you have had from me to
deliver to Desdemona would half have corrupted a votarist.° You have told me she hath received them, and re-   190
turned me expectations and comforts of sudden respect
and acquaintance, but I find none.

IAGO.   Well, go to, very well.

RODERIGO.   Very well! Go to! I cannot go to, man, nor 'tis
not very well. By this hand, I say 'tis very scurvy, and
begin to find myself fopped° in it.

IAGO.   Very well.

RODERIGO.   I tell you 'tis not very well. I will make myself
known to Desdemona. If she will return me my jewels, I
will give over my suit and repent my unlawful solicita-   200
tion. If not, assure yourself I will seek satisfaction of
you.

IAGO.   You have said now.°

RODERIGO.   Aye, and said nothing but what I protest intend-
ment of doing.

IAGO.   Why, now I see there's mettle° in thee, and even from
this instant do build on thee a better opinion than ever
before. Give me thy hand, Roderigo. Thou hast taken
against me a most just exception,° but yet I protest I
have dealt most directly in thy affair.   210

RODERIGO.   It hath not appeared.

IAGO.   I grant indeed it hath not appeared, and your suspicion is not without wit° and judgment. But, Roderigo, if
thou hast that in thee indeed which I have greater reason
to believe now than ever—I mean purpose, courage, and
valor—this night show it. If thou the next night following enjoy not Desdemona, take me from this world with
treachery and devise engines° for my life.

---

190. *votarist:* one who has taken a vow, here a nun.   196. *fopped:* fooled.   203. *You . . .
now:* or in modern slang, "Oh yeah."   206. *mettle:* metal, good stuff.   209. *just exception:* reasonable grievance.   213. *wit:* wisdom.   218. *engines:* instruments of torture.

RODERIGO.   Well, what is it? Is it within reason and compass?

IAGO.   Sir, there is especial commission come from Venice to   220
depute Cassio in Othello's place.

RODERIGO.   Is that true? Why, then Othello and Desdemona
return again to Venice.

IAGO.   Oh, no. He goes into Mauritania, and takes away
with him the fair Desdemona, unless his abode be
lingered here by some accident. Wherein none can be so
determinate° as the removing of Cassio.

RODERIGO.   How do you mean, "removing of" him?

IAGO.   Why, by making him uncapable° of Othello's place,
knocking out his brains.   230

RODERIGO.   And that you would have me to do?

IAGO.   Aye, if you dare do yourself a profit and a right. He
sups tonight with a harlotry,° and thither will I go to
him. He knows not yet of his honorable fortune. If you
will watch his going thence, which I will fashion to fall
out between twelve and one, you may take him at your
pleasure. I will be near to second your attempt, and he
shall fall between us. Come, stand not amazed at it, but
go along with me. I will show you such a necessity in his
death that you shall think yourself bound to put it on   240
him. It is now high suppertime, and the night grows to
waste. About it.

RODERIGO.   I will hear further reason for this.

IAGO.   And you shall be satisfied.

[*Exeunt.*]

SCENE III. *Another room in the castle.*

[*Enter* OTHELLO, LODOVICO, DESDEMONA,
EMILIA, *and* ATTENDANTS.]

LODOVICO.   I do beseech you, sir, trouble yourself no further.

OTHELLO.   Oh, pardon me, 'twill do me good to walk.

LODOVICO.   Madam, good night. I humbly thank your ladyship.

DESDEMONA.   Your Honor is most welcome.

OTHELLO.   Will you walk, sir?
Oh—Desdemona——

---

227. *determinate:* decisive.   229. *uncapable:* unable to take.   233. *harlotry:* harlot.

DESDEMONA.   My lord?

OTHELLO.   Get you to bed on the instant, I will
   be returned forthwith.
   Dismiss your attendant there. Look it be done.

DESDEMONA.   I will, my lord.

[*Exeunt* OTHELLO, LODOVICO, *and* ATTENDANTS.]

EMILIA.   How goes it now? He looks gentler than he did.   10

DESDEMONA.   He says he will return incontinent.°
   He hath commanded me to go to bed,
   And bade me to dismiss you.

EMILIA.   Dismiss me!

DESDEMONA.   It was his bidding, therefore, good Emilia,
   Give me my nightly wearing,° and adieu.
   We must not now displease him.

EMILIA.   I would you had never seen him!

DESDEMONA.   So would not I. My love doth so approve° him
   That even his stubbornness, his checks, his frowns—
   Prithee, unpin me—have grace and favor in them.   20

EMILIA.   I have laid those sheets you bade me on the bed.

DESDEMONA.   All's one. Good faith, how foolish are our minds!
   If I do die before thee, prithee shroud me
   In one of those same sheets.

EMILIA.   Come, come, you talk.

DESDEMONA.   My mother had a maid called Barbara.
   She was in love, and he she loved proved mad
   And did forsake her. She had a song of "willow"°—
   An old thing 'twas, but it expressed her fortune,
   And she died singing it. That song tonight
   Will not go from my mind. I have much to do   30
   But to go hang my head all at one side
   And sing it like poor Barbara. Prithee, dispatch.

EMILIA.   Shall I go fetch your nightgown?

DESDEMONA.   No, unpin me here.
   This Lodovico is a proper man.

EMILIA.   A very handsome man.

DESDEMONA.   He speaks well.

SCENE III: 11. *incontinent:* immediately.   15. *nightly wearing:* nightgown.   18. *approve:*
commend.   27. *willow:* the emblem of the forlorn lover.

EMILIA.   I know a lady in Venice would have walked bare-
   foot to Palestine for a touch of his nether° lip.
DESDEMONA [*singing*].
      "The poor soul sat sighing by a sycamore tree,
         Sing all a green willow.   40
      Her hand on her bosom, her head on her knee,
         Sing willow, willow, willow.
      The fresh streams ran by her, and murmered her moans,
         Sing willow, willow, willow.
      Her salt tears fell from her, and softened the stones—"
  Lay by these—[*singing*]
         "Sing willow, willow, willow."
  Prithee, hie thee, he'll come anon.°—[*singing*]
      "Sing all a green willow must be my garland.
         Let nobody blame him, his scorn I approve——"   50
  Nay, that's not next. Hark! Who is 't that knocks?
EMILIA.   It's the wind.
DESDEMONA [*singing*].
      "I called my love false love, but what said he then?
         Sing willow, willow, willow.
      If I court moe° women, you'll couch with moe men."
  So get thee gone, good night. Mine eyes do itch.
  Doth that bode weeping?
EMILIA.   'Tis neither here nor there.
DESDEMONA.   I have heard it said so. Oh, these men, these men!
  Dost thou in conscience think—tell me, Emilia—
  That there be women do abuse their husbands   60
  In such gross kind?
EMILIA.   There be some such, no question.
DESDEMONA.   Wouldst thou do such a deed for all the world?
EMILIA.   Why, would not you?
DESDEMONA.   No, by this heavenly light!
EMILIA.   Nor I neither by this heavenly light. I might do 't as
  well i' the dark.
DESDEMONA.   Wouldst thou do such a deed for all the world?
EMILIA.   The world's a huge thing. It is a great price
  For a small vice.
DESDEMONA.   In troth, I think thou wouldst not.

---

38. *nether:* lower. 48. *anon:* soon. 55. *moe:* more.

EMILIA.   In troth, I think I should, and undo 't when I had
    done. Marry, I would not do such a thing for a joint   70
    ring,° nor for measures of lawn,° nor for gowns, pet-
    ticoats, nor caps, nor any petty exhibition;° but for the
    whole world—why, who would not make her husband a
    cuckold to make him a monarch? I should venture Pur-
    gatory for 't.
DESDEMONA.   Beshrew me if I would do such a wrong
    For the whole world.
EMILIA.   Why, the wrong is but a wrong i' the world, and
    having the world for your labor, 'tis a wrong in your
    own world and you might quickly make it right.   80
DESDEMONA.   I do not think there is any such woman.
EMILIA.   Yes, a dozen, and as many to the vantage° as would
    Store° the world they played for.
    But I do think it is their husbands' faults
    If wives do fall. Say that they slack their duties
    And pour our treasures into foreign laps,
    Or else break out in peevish jealousies,
    Throwing restraint° upon us, or say they strike us,
    Or scant our former having in despite,°
    Why, we have galls,° and though we have some grace,   90
    Yet we have some revenge. Let husbands know
    Their wives have sense like them. They see and smell
    And have their palates both for sweet and sour,
    As husbands have. What is it that they do
    When they change us for others? Is it sport?
    I think it is. And doth affection breed it?
    I think it doth. Is't frailty that thus errs?
    It is so too. And have not we affections,
    Desires for sport, and frailty, as men have?
    Then let them use us well. Else let them know   100
    The ills we do, their ills instruct us so.
DESDEMONA.   Good night, good night. Heaven me such uses° send,
    Not to pick bad from bad, but my bad mend!

                                    [Exeunt.]

---

71. *joint ring:* ring made in two pieces, a lover's gift. *measures of lawn:* lengths of finest
lawn, or as a modern woman would say, "sheer nylon."   72. *petty exhibition:* small
allowance of money.   82. *as . . . vantage:* and more too; *vantage* is that added to the
exact weight to give generous measure.   83. *store:* stock, fill up.   88. *Throwing restraint:* putting restraints.   89. *scant . . . despite:* for spite cut down our allowance.
90. *galls:* bile, the cause of bitterness.   102. *uses:* practices.

ACT V

SCENE I. *Cyprus. A street.*

[*Enter* IAGO *and* RODERIGO]

IAGO.   Here, stand behind this bulk,° straight° will he come.
Wear thy good rapier bare, and put it home.
Quick, quick, fear nothing, I'll be at thy elbow.
It makes us, or it mars us. Think on that,
And fix most firm thy resolution.
RODERIGO.   Be near at hand, I may miscarry in 't.
IAGO.   Here, at thy hand. Be bold, and take thy stand.

[*Retires.*]

RODERIGO.   I have no great devotion to the deed,
And yet he hath given me satisfying reasons.
'Tis but a man gone. Forth, my sword. He dies.   10
IAGO.   I have rubbed this young quat° almost to the sense,°
And he grows angry. Now, whether he kill Cassio,
Or Cassio him, or each do kill the other,
Every way makes my gain. Live Roderigo,
He calls me to a restitution large°
Of gold and jewels that I bobbed° from him
As gifts to Desdemona.
It must not be. If Cassio do remain,
He hath a daily beauty in his life
That makes me ugly,° and besides, the Moor   20
May unfold° me to him. There stand I in much peril.
No, he must die. Be't so. I hear him coming.

[*Enter* CASSIO.]

RODERIGO.   I know his gait, 'tis he. Villain, thou diest!

[*Makes a pass at* CASSIO.]

CASSIO.   That thrust had been mine enemy indeed
But that my coat is better than thou know'st.°
I will make proof of thine.

[*Draws, and wounds* RODERIGO.]

Act V, SCENE I: 1. *bulk:* stall outside a shop; *straight:* straightway.   11. *quat:* pimple; *to
. . . sense:* To the quick, to the raw.   15. *large:* full.   16. *bobbed:* cheated.   19–20. *He
. . . ugly:* by comparison with him I am a poor thing. Iago is conscious of his lack
of social graces.   21. *unfold:* expose.   25. *coat . . . know'st:* that is, I wear mail under
my coat.

RODERIGO.   Oh, I am slain!

[IAGO *from behind wounds* CASSIO *in the leg, and exit.*]

CASSIO.   I am maimed for ever. Help, ho! Murder! Murder!

[*Falls.*]

[*Enter* OTHELLO.]

OTHELLO.   The voice of Cassio. Iago keeps his word.

RODERIGO.   Oh, villain that I am!

OTHELLO.   It is even so.

CASSIO.   Oh, help, ho! Light! A surgeon!   30

OTHELLO.   'Tis he. O brave Iago, honest and just,
That hast such noble sense of thy friend's wrong!
Thou teachest me. Minion,° your dear lies dead,
And your unblest fate hies.° Strumpet, I come!
Forth of my heart those charms, thine eyes, are blotted.
Thy bed lust-stained shall with lust's blood be spotted.

[*Exit.*]

[*Enter* LODOVICO *and* GRATIANO.]

CASSIO.   What ho! No watch?° No passage?° Murder! Murder!

GRATIANO.   'Tis some mischance, the cry is very direful.

CASSIO.   Oh, help!

LODOVICO.   Hark!   40

RODERIGO.   Oh, wretched villain!

LODOVICO.   Two or three groan. It is a heavy° night.
These may be counterfeits.° Let's think 't unsafe
To come in to the cry without more help.

RODERIGO.   Nobody come? Then shall I bleed to death.

LODOVICO.   Hark!

[*Re-enter* IAGO, *with a light.*]

GRATIANO.   Here's one comes in his shirt, with light and weapons.

IAGO.   Who's there? Whose noise is this that cries on° murder?

LODOVICO.   We do not know.

IAGO.   Did not you hear a cry?

CASSIO.   Here, here! For Heaven's sake, help me!

IAGO.   What's the matter?

GRATIANO.   This is Othello's Ancient, as I take it.   51

LODOVICO.   The same indeed, a very valiant fellow.

---

33. *Minion:* darling, in a bad sense.   34. *hies:* comes on quickly.   37. *watch:* citizen police force; *No passage:* "Is nobody passing by?"   42. *heavy:* thick.   43. *counterfeits:* fakes.   47. *cries on:* cries out.

IAGO.   What are you here that cry so grievously?

CASSIO.   Iago? Oh, I am spoiled, undone by villains!
Give me some help.

IAGO.   Oh me, Lieutenant! What villains have done this?

CASSIO.   I think that one of them is hereabout,
And cannot make away.

IAGO.   Oh, treacherous villains!
[*To* LODOVICO *and* GRATIANO] What are you there? Come in
and give some help.

RODERIGO.   Oh, help me here!   60

CASSIO.   That's one of them.

IAGO.   Oh, murderous slave! Oh, villain! [*Stabs* RODERIGO.]

RODERIGO.   Oh, damned Iago! Oh, inhuman dog!

IAGO.   Kill men i' the dark! Where be these bloody thieves?
How silent is this town! Ho! Murder! Murder!
What may you be? Are you of good or evil?

LODOVICO.   As you shall prove us, praise us.

IAGO.   Signior Lodovico?

LODOVICO.   He, sir.

IAGO.   I cry you mercy. Here's Cassio hurt by villains.   70

GRATIANO.   Cassio!

IAGO.   How is 't, brother?

CASSIO.   My leg is cut in two.

IAGO.   Marry, Heaven forbid!
Light, gentlemen. I'll bind it with my shirt.

[*Enter* BIANCA.]

BIANCA.   What is the matter, ho? Who is 't that cried?

IAGO.   Who is 't that cried!

BIANCA.   Oh, my dear Cassio! My sweet Cassio!
Oh, Cassio, Cassio, Cassio!

IAGO.   Oh, notable strumpet! Cassio, may you suspect
Who they should be that have thus mangled you?

CASSIO.   No.   80

GRATIANO.   I am sorry to find you thus. I have been to seek you.

IAGO.   Lend me a garter. So. Oh, for a chair,
To bear him easily hence!

BIANCA.   Alas, he faints! Oh, Cassio, Cassio, Cassio!

IAGO.   Gentlemen all, I do suspect this trash
To be party in this injury.
Patience awhile, good Cassio. Come, come,

Lend me a light. Know we this face or no?
Alas, my friend and my dear countryman
Roderigo? No—yes, sure. Oh Heaven! Roderigo.   90

GRATIANO.   What, of Venice?

IAGO.   Even he, sir. Did you know him?

GRATIANO.   Know him! Aye.

IAGO.   Signior Gratiano? I cry you gentle pardon.°
These bloody accidents must excuse my manners,
That so neglected you.

GRATIANO.   I am glad to see you.

IAGO.   How do you, Cassio? Oh, a chair, a chair!

GRATIANO.   Roderigo!

IAGO.   He, he, 'tis he.

> *[A chair is brought in.]*
Oh, that's well said, the chair.
Some good man bear him carefully from hence.
I'll fetch the General's surgeon. [*To* BIANCA] For you, mistress,
Save you your labor. He that lies slain here, Cassio,   101
Was my dear friend. What malice was between you?

CASSIO.   None in the world, nor do I know the man.

IAGO [*to* BIANCA].   What, look you pale? Oh, bear him out
o' the air.

> *[*CASSIO *and* RODERIGO *are borne off.]*
Stay you, good gentlemen. Look you pale, mistress?
Do you perceive the gastness° of her eye?
Nay, if you stare, we shall hear more anon.
Behold her well, I pray you look upon her.
Do you see, gentlemen? Nay, guiltiness will speak,
Though tongues were out of use.   110

> *[Enter* EMILIA.]
EMILIA.   'Las, what's the matter? What's the matter, husband?

IAGO.   Cassio hath here been set on in the dark
By Roderigo, and fellows that are 'scaped.
He's almost slain, and Roderigo dead.

EMILIA.   Alas, good gentlemen! Alas, good Cassio!

IAGO.   This is the fruit of whoring. Prithee, Emilia,
Go know of Cassio where he supped tonight.
What, do you shake at that?

---

93. *I . . . pardon:* I beg you kindly pardon me.   106. *gastness:* ghastly look.

BIANCA.   He supped at my house, but I therefore shake not.

IAGO.   Oh, did he so? I charge you, go with me.   120

EMILIA.   Fie, fie upon thee, strumpet!

BIANCA.   I am no strumpet, but of life as honest
    As you that thus abuse me.

EMILIA.   As I! Foh! Fie upon thee!

IAGO.   Kind gentlemen, let's go see poor Cassio dressed.°
    Come, mistress, you must tell 's another tale.
    Emilia, run you to the citadel,
    And tell my lord and lady what hath happed!
    Will you go on? I pray. [*Aside.*] This is the night
    That either makes me or fordoes° me quite.

                                     [*Exeunt.*]

SCENE II. *A bedchamber in the castle.*
DESDEMONA *in bed asleep, a light burning.*

[*Enter* OTHELLO.]

OTHELLO.   It is the cause,° it is the cause, my soul.
    Let me not name it to you, you chaste stars!
    It is the cause. Yet I'll not shed her blood,
    Nor scar that whiter skin of hers than snow
    And smooth as monumental alabaster.°
    Yet she must die, else she'll betray more men.
    Put out the light, and then put out the light.
    If I quench thee, thou flaming minister,°
    I can again thy former light restore,
    Should I repent me. But once put out thy light,   10
    Thou cunning'st° pattern of excelling nature,
    I know not where is that Promethean heat°
    That can thy light relume.° When I have plucked the rose,
    I cannot give it vital growth again,

---

124. *dressed:* that is, his wound dressed.   129. *fordoes:* ruins.
SCENE II: 1. *It . . . cause:* The meaning of the opening lines of this speech has been
much discussed. The *cause* is Desdemona's supposed faithlessness; Othello, at this moment, sees himself as embodied vengeance, the avenger of man betrayed by woman.
5. *monumental alabaster:* Alabaster is white translucent stone, much used for memorial
effigies on Elizabethan tombs.   8. *minister:* servant.   11. *cunning'st:* most skillfully
made.   12. *Promethean heat:* fire from Heaven. Prometheus stole fire from Heaven and
first gave it to man.   13. *relume:* relight.

It needs must wither. I'll smell it on the tree [*Kissing her*].
Ah, balmy breath, that dost almost persuade
Justice to break her sword! One more, one more.
Be thus when thou art dead, and I will kill thee,
And love thee after. One more, and this the last.
So sweet was ne'er so fatal. I must weep,   20
But they are cruel tears. This sorrow's heavenly,
It strikes where it doth love. She wakes.
DESDEMONA.   Who's there? Othello?
OTHELLO.   Aye, Desdemona.
DESDEMONA.   Will you come to bed, my lord?
OTHELLO.   Have you prayed tonight, Desdemona?
DESDEMONA.   Aye, my lord.
OTHELLO.   If you think yourself of any crime
    Unreconciled as yet to Heaven and grace,
    Solicit for it straight.
DESDEMONA.   Alas, my lord, what may you mean by that?   30
OTHELLO.   Well, do it, and be brief. I will walk by.
    I would not kill thy unprepared spirit.
    No, Heaven forfend! I would not kill thy soul.°
DESDEMONA.   Talk you of killing?
OTHELLO.   Aye, I do.
DESDEMONA.   Then Heaven have mercy on me!
OTHELLO.   Amen, with all my heart!
DESDEMONA.   If you say so, I hope you will not kill me.
OTHELLO.   Hum!
DESDEMONA.   And yet I fear you, for you are fatal° then   40
    When your eyes roll so. Why I should fear I know not,
    Since guiltiness I know not, but yet I feel I fear.
OTHELLO.   Think on thy sins.
DESDEMONA.   They are loves I bear to you.
OTHELLO.   Aye, and for that thou diest.
DESDEMONA.   That death's unnatural that kills for loving.
    Alas, why gnaw you so your nether lip?
    Some bloody passion shakes your very frame.
    These are portents,° but yet I hope, I hope,
    They do not point on me.
OTHELLO.   Peace, and be still!

27–33. *If . . . soul:* Othello will be a merciful murderer. *forfend:* forbid.   40. *fatal:*
deadly.   48. *portents:* signs fortelling disaster.

DESDEMONA.   I will so. What's the matter?   50
OTHELLO.   That handkerchief which I so loved and gave thee
Thou gavest to Cassio,
DESDEMONA.   No, by my life and soul!
Send for the man, and ask him.
OTHELLO.   Sweet soul, take heed,
Take heed of perjury, thou art on thy deathbed.
DESDEMONA.   Aye, but not yet to die.
OTHELLO.   Yes, presently.°
Therefore confess thee freely of thy sin,
For to deny each article with oath
Cannot remove nor choke the strong conception°
That I do groan withal. Thou art to die.
DESDEMONA.   The Lord have mercy on me!
OTHELLO.   I say amen.   60
DESDEMONA.   And have you mercy too! I never did
Offend you in my life, never loved Cassio
But with such general warranty° of Heaven
As I might love. I never gave him token.
OTHELLO.   By Heaven, I saw my handkerchief in 's hand.
O perjured woman! Thou dost stone° my heart,
And makest me call what I intend to do
A murder, which I thought a sacrifice.
I saw the handkerchief.
DESDEMONA.   He found it, then,
I never gave it him. Send for him hither.   70
Let him confess a truth.
OTHELLO.   He hath confessed.
DESDEMONA.   What, my lord?
OTHELLO.   That he hath used thee.
DESDEMONA.   How? Unlawfully?
OTHELLO.   Aye.
DESDEMONA.   He will not say so.
OTHELLO.   No, his mouth is stopped.
Honest Iago hath ta'en order for 't.
DESDEMONA.   Oh, my fear interprets! What, is he dead?
OTHELLO.   Had all his hairs been lives, my great revenge
Had stomach for them all.

---

55. *presently:* at once.   58. *conception:* thought.   63. *warranty:* permission.   66. *stone:*
turn to stone.

DESDEMONA.   Alas, he is betrayed, and I undone!   80
OTHELLO.   Out, strumpet! Weep'st thou for him to my face?
DESDEMONA.   Oh, banish me, my lord, but kill me not!
OTHELLO.   Down, strumpet!
DESDEMONA.   Kill me tomorrow, let me live tonight!
OTHELLO.   Nay, if you strive——
DESDEMONA.   But half an hour!
OTHELLO.   Being done, there is no pause.
DESDEMONA.   But while I say one prayer!
OTHELLO.   It is too late. [*He stifles her.*]
EMILIA [*within*].   My lord, my lord! What ho! My lord, my lord!
OTHELLO.   What noise is this? Not dead? Not yet quite dead?
   I that am cruel am yet merciful,   90
   I would not have thee linger in thy pain.
   So, so.
EMILIA [*within*].   What ho! My lord, my lord!
OTHELLO.   Who's there?
EMILIA [*within*].   Oh, good my lord, I would speak a word with you!
OTHELLO.   Yes, 'tis Emilia. By and by. She's dead.
   'Tis like she comes to speak of Cassio's death.
   The noise was here. Ha! No more moving?
   Still as the grave. Shall she come in? Were 't good?
   I think she stirs again. No. What's best to do?
   If she come in, she'll sure speak to my wife.   100
   My wife! My wife! What wife? I have no wife.
   Oh, insupportable! Oh, heavy hour!
   Methinks it should be now a huge eclipse
   Of sun and moon, and that the affrighted globe
   Should yawn at alteration.°
EMILIA [*within*].   I do beseech you
   That I may speak with you, O good my lord!
OTHELLO.   I had forgot thee. Oh, come in, Emilia.
   Soft, by and by. Let me the curtains° draw.
   Where art thou?   [*Unlocks the door.*]
                 [*Enter* EMILIA.]
            What's the matter with thee now?
EMILIA.   Oh, my good lord, yonder 's foul murders done!   110
OTHELLO.   What, now?

---

105. *yawn at alteration:* gape with wonder at some monstrous change.   108. *curtains:*
that is, of the bed.

EMILIA.   But now, my lord.

OTHELLO.   It is the very error° of the moon.
She comes more nearer earth than she was wont
And makes men mad.

EMILIA.   Cassio, my lord, hath killed a young Venetian
Called Roderigo.

OTHELLO.   Roderigo killed!
And Cassio killed!

EMILIA.   No, Cassio is not killed.

OTHELLO.   Not Cassio killed! Then murder's out of tune,
And sweet revenge grows harsh.   120

DESDEMONA.   Oh, falscly, falsely murdered!

EMILIA.   Alas, what cry is that?

OTHELLO.   That! What?

EMILIA.   Out and alas! That was my lady's voice.
Help! Help, ho! Help! O lady, speak again!
Sweet Desdemona! O sweet mistress, speak!

DESDEMONA.   A guiltless death I die.

EMILIA.   Oh, who hath done this deed?

DESDEMONA.   Nobody, I myself. Farewell.
Commend me to my kind lord. Oh, farewell!   [*Dies.*]

OTHELLO.   Why, how should she be murdered?   130

EMILIA.   Alas, who knows?

OTHELLO.   You heard her say herself it was not I.

EMILIA.   She said so. I must needs report the truth.

OTHELLO.   She's like a liar gone to burning Hell.
'Twas I that killed her.

EMILIA.   Oh, the more angel she,
And you the blacker devil!

OTHELLO.   She turned to folly,° and she was a whore.

EMILIA.   Thou dost belie her, and thou art a devil.

OTHELLO.   She was false as water.

EMILIA.   Thou art rash as fire to say
That she was false. Oh, she was heavenly true!   140

OTHELLO.   Cassio did top her, ask thy husband else.
Oh, I were damned beneath all depth in Hell
But that I did proceed upon just grounds
To this extremity. Thy husband knew it all.

EMILIA.   My husband!

---

113. *error:* wandering out of her proper course.   137. *folly:* lewdness.

OTHELLO.   Thy husband.

EMILIA.   That she was false to wedlock?

OTHELLO.   Aye, with Cassio. Nay, had she been true,
If Heaven would make me such another world
Of one entire and perfect chrysolite,°   150
I'd not have sold her for it.

EMILIA.   My husband!

OTHELLO.   Aye, 'twas he that told me first.
An honest man he is, and hates the slime
That sticks on filthy deeds.

EMILIA.   My husband!

OTHELLO.   What needs this iteration,° woman? I say thy husband.

EMILIA.   Oh, mistress, villainy hath made mocks with love!
My husband say that she was false!

OTHELLO.   He, woman.
I say thy husband. Dost understand the word?
My friend, thy husband, honest, honest Iago.

EMILIA.   If he say so, may his pernicious soul   160
Rot half a grain a day! He lies to the heart.
She was too fond of her most filthy bargain.

OTHELLO.   Ha!

EMILIA.   Do thy worst.
This deed of thine is no more worthy Heaven
Than thou wast worthy her.

OTHELLO.   Peace, you were best.

EMILIA.   Thou hast not half that power to do me harm
As I have to be hurt. O gull!° O dolt!°
As ignorant as dirt! Thou hast done a deed——
I care not for thy sword, I'll make thee known,   170
Though I lost twenty lives. Help! Help, ho! Help!
The Moor hath killed my mistress! Murder! Murder!

                [*Enter* MONTANO, GRATIANO, IAGO, *and others.*]

MONTANO.   What is the matter? How now, General!

EMILIA.   Oh, are you come, Iago? You have done well,
That men must lay their murders on your neck.

GRATIANO.   What is the matter?

EMILIA.   Disprove this villain, if thou be'st a man.
He says thou told'st him that his wife was false.

---

150. *chrysolite:* a semiprecious stone, usually green in color.   155. *iteration:* repetition.
168. *gull:* dupe; *dolt:* dull-witted ass.

I know thou didst not, thou'rt not such a villain.
Speak, for my heart is full. 180
IAGO. I told him what I thought, and told no more
Than what he found himself was apt° and true.
EMILIA. But did you ever tell him she was false?
IAGO. I did.
EMILIA. You told a lie, an odious, damnèd lie,
Upon my soul, a lie, a wicked lie!
She false with Cassio! Did you say with Cassio?
IAGO. With Cassio, mistress. Go to, charm your tongue.°
EMILIA. I will not charm my tongue, I am bound to speak.
My mistress here lies murdered in her bed. 190
ALL. Oh, Heavens forfend!
EMILIA. And your reports have set the murder on.
OTHELLO. Nay, stare not, masters. It is true indeed.
GRATIANO. 'Tis a strange truth.
MONTANO. Oh, monstrous act!
EMILIA. Villainy, villainy, villainy!
I think upon 't. I think I smell 't. Oh, villainy!
I thought so then.° I'll kill myself for grief.
Oh, villainy, villainy!
IAGO. What, are you mad? I charge you, get you home.
EMILIA. Good gentlemen, let me have leave to speak. 200
'Tis proper I obey him, but not now.
Perchance, Iago, I will ne'er go home.
OTHELLO. Oh! Oh! Oh! [*Falling on the bed.*]
EMILIA. Nay, lay thee down and roar,
For thou hast killed the sweetest innocent
That e'er did lift up eye.
OTHELLO [*rising*]. Oh, she was foul!
I scarce did know you, Uncle. There lies your niece,
Whose breath indeed these hands have newly stopped.
I know this act shows horrible and grim.
GRATIANO. Poor Desdemona! I am glad thy father's dead.
Thy match was mortal° to him, and pure grief 210
Shore his old thread in twain.° Did he live now,
This sight would make him do a desperate turn—

---

182. *apt:* likely. 188. *charm . . . tongue:* be silent. 197. *I . . . then:* that is, I suspected this earlier—as for example when Iago took the handkerchief (see III.iii.314).
210. *match . . . mortal:* that is, grief at this marriage killed him. 211. *Shore . . . twain:* cut his thread of life in two.

Yea, curse his better angel from his side,
And fall to reprobation.°
OTHELLO.   'Tis pitiful, but yet Iago knows
That she with Cassio hath the act of shame
A thousand times committed. Cassio confessed it.
And she did gratify his amorous works
With that recognizance° and pledge of love
Which I first gave her, I saw it in his hand.   220
It was a handkerchief, an antique token
My father gave my mother.
EMILIA.   Oh, heaven! Oh, heavenly powers!
IAGO.   'Zounds! Hold your peace.
EMILIA.   'Twill out, 'twill out. I peace!
No, I will speak as liberal as the north.°
Let Heaven and men and devils, let them all,
All, all, cry shame against me, yet I'll speak.
IAGO.   Be wise, and get you home.
EMILIA.   I will not.

> [IAGO *offers to stab* EMILIA.]

GRATIANO.   Fie!
Your sword upon a woman!
EMILIA.   O thou dull Moor! That handkerchief thou speak'st of
I found by fortune and did give my husband,   231
For often with solemn earnestness,
More than indeed belonged to such a trifle,
He begged of me to steal it.
IAGO.   Villainous whore!
EMILIA.   She give it Cassio! No, alas, I found it,
And I did give 't my husband.
IAGO.   Filth, thou liest!
EMILIA.   By Heaven, I do not, I do not, gentlemen.
Oh, murderous coxcomb!° What should such a fool
Do with so good a wife?
OTHELLO.   Are there no stones° in Heaven
But what serve for the thunder? Precious villain!   240

> [*He runs at* IAGO. IAGO, *from behind, stabs* EMILIA, *and exits.*]

---

214. *reprobation:* damnation; that is, by self-murder.   219. *recognizance:* badge, token.
225. *liberal . . . north:* as freely as the north wind, which is loud and bitter.
238. *coxcomb:* conceited fool.   239. *stones:* thunderbolts.

GRATIANO.   The woman falls. Sure, he hath killed his wife.

EMILIA.   Aye, aye. Oh, lay me by my mistress' side.

GRATIANO.   He's gone, but his wife's killed.

MONTANO.   'Tis a notorious villain. Take you this weapon,
Which I have here recovered from the Moor.
Come, guard the door without, let him not pass,
But kill him rather. I'll after that same villain,
For 'tis a damnèd slave.

[Exeunt all but OTHELLO *and* EMILIA.]

OTHELLO.   I am not valiant neither.
But every puny whipster° gets my sword.
But why should honor outlive honesty?   250
Let it go all.

EMILIA.   What did thy song bode, lady?
Hark, canst thou hear me? I will play the swan,
And die in music.° [*Singing*]
          "Willow, willow, willow."
Moor, she was chaste. She loved thee, cruel Moor,
So come my soul to bliss as I speak true.
So speaking as I think, I die, I die.

[Dies.]

OTHELLO.   I have another weapon in this chamber.
It is a sword of Spain,° the ice brook's temper.°—
Oh, here it is. Uncle, I must come forth.

GRATIANO [*within*].   If thou attempt it, it will cost thee dear.   260
Thou hast no weapon, and perforce must suffer.

OTHELLO.   Look in upon me then, and speak with me,
Or, naked° as I am, I will assault thee.

[Re-enter GRATIANO.]

GRATIANO.   What is the matter?

OTHELLO.   Behold, I have a weapon,
A better never did itself sustain
Upon a soldier's thigh. I have seen the day
That with this little arm and this good sword
I have made my way through more impediments

---

249. *whipster:* whippersnapper. 252–53. *play . . . music:* that is, I will sing at my
death. It was believed that swans sang once only, just before they died. 258. *sword of
Spain:* Spanish swords and rapiers, from Toledo or Bilbao, were famous; *ice . . . tem-*
per: hardened in ice-cold water. 263. *naked:* unarmed.

Than twenty times your stop. But, on, vain boast!
Who can control his fate? 'Tis not so now.   270
Be not afraid, though you do see me weaponed.
Here is my journey's end, here is my butt°
And very sea mark of my utmost sail.°
Do you go back dismayed? 'Tis a lost fear.
Man but a rush° against Othello's breast,
And he retires? Where should Othello go?
Now, how dost thou look now? O ill-starred wench!
Pale as thy smock! When we shall meet at compt,°
This look of thine will hurl my soul from Heaven
And fiends will snatch at it. Cold, cold, my girl!   280
Even like thy chastity. Oh, cursèd slave!
Whip me, ye devils,
From the possession of this heavenly sight!
Blow me about in winds! Roast me in sulphur!
Wash me in steep-down gulfs° of liquid fire!
O Desdemona! Desdemona! Dead!
Oh! Oh! Oh!

[*Enter* LODOVICO, MONTANO, CASSIO *carried in a chair,
and* OFFICERS *with* IAGO, *prisoner.*]

LODOVICO.   Where is this rash and most unfortunate man?
OTHELLO.   That's he that was Othello. Here I am.
LODOVICO.   Where is that viper? Bring the villain forth.   290
OTHELLO.   I look down toward his feet,° but that's a fable.
    If that thou be'st a devil,° I cannot kill thee.

                                        [*Wounds* IAGO.]

LODOVICO.   Wrench his sword from him.
IAGO.   I bleed, sir, but not killed.
OTHELLO.   I am not sorry neither. I'd have thee live,
    For, in my sense, 'tis happiness to die.
LODOVICO.   O thou Othello, that wert once so good,
    Fall'n in the practice° of a damnèd slave,
    What shall be said to thee?

---

272. *butt:* aim.   273. *And . . . sail:* the mark that I have reached the end of my voyage;
sea mark: a conspicuous object by which the mariner checks his course.   275. *Man . .*
rush: attack with only a reed.   278. *compt:* account; that is, the Day of Judgment.
285. *steep-down gulfs:* sheer whirlpools.   291. *toward . . . feet:* that is, to see if he has the
cloven hoof of a devil.   292. *If . . . devil:* if you are an evil spirit and no man.
297. *Fall'n . . . practice:* destroyed by the plotting.

OTHELLO.   Why, anything.
    An honorable murderer, if you will,
    For naught did I in hate, but all in honor   300
LODOVICO.   This wretch hath part confessed his villainy.
    Did you and he consent in Cassio's death?
OTHELLO.   Aye.
CASSIO.   Dear General, I never gave you cause.
OTHELLO.   I do believe it, and I ask your pardon.
    Will you, I pray, demand that demidevil
    Why he hath thus ensnared my soul and body?
IAGO.   Demand me nothing. What you know, you know.
    From this time forth I never will speak word.
LODOVICO.   What, not to pray?
GRATIANO.   Torments will ope your lips.   310
OTHELLO.   Well, thou dost best.
LODOVICO.   Sir, you shall understand what hath befall'n,
    Which, as I think, you know not. Here is a letter
    Found in the pocket of the slain Roderigo,
    And here another. The one of them imports
    The death of Cassio to be undertook
    By Roderigo.
OTHELLO.   Oh, villain!
CASSIO.   Most heathenish and most gross!
LODOVICO.   Now here's another discontented paper,
    Found in his pocket too. And this, it seems,   320
    Roderigo meant to have sent this damnèd villain
    But that, belike, Iago in the interim
    Came in and satisfied him.
OTHELLO.   Oh, the pernicious caitiff!
    How came you, Cassio, by that handkerchief
    That was my wife's?
CASSIO.   I found it in my chamber.
    And he himself confessed but even now
    That there he dropped it for a special purpose
    Which wrought to his desire.
OTHELLO.   O fool! Fool! Fool!
CASSIO.   There is besides in Roderigo's letter
    How he upbraids Iago, that he made him   330
    Brave° me upon the watch, whereon it came

---

331. *Brave:* dare, insult.

That I was cast.° And even but now he spake
After long seeming dead, Iago hurt him,
Iago set him on.
LODOVICO.   You must forsake this room, and go with us.
Your power and your command is taken off,
And Cassio rules in Cyprus. For this slave,
If there be any cunning cruelty
That can torment him much and hold him long,°
It shall be his. You shall close prisoner rest   340
Till that the nature of your fault be known
To the Venetian state. Come, bring away.
OTHELLO.   Soft you,° a word or two before you go.
I have done the state some service, and they know 't.
No more of that. I pray you, in your letters,
When you shall these unlucky deeds relate,
Speak of me as I am, nothing extenuate,
Nor set down aught in malice. Then must you speak
Of one that loved not wisely but too well,
Of one not easily jealous, but, being wrought,   350
Perplexed in the extreme, of one whose hand,
Like the base Indian, threw a pearl away
Richer than all his tribe—of one whose subdued eyes,
Albeit unusèd to the melting mood,
Drop tears as fast as the Arabian trees
Their medicinal gum. Set you down this,
And say besides that in Aleppo once,
Where a malignant and a turbaned Turk
Beat a Venetian and traduced° the state,
I took by the throat the circumcisèd dog   360
    And smote him, thus.   [*Stabs himself.*]
LODOVICO.   Oh, bloody period!
GRATIANO.   All that's spoke is marred.°
OTHELLO.   I kissed thee ere I killed thee. No way but this,
Killing myself, to die upon a kiss.

                                [*Falls on the bed, and dies.*]
CASSIO.   This did I fear, but thought he had no weapon.
For he was great of heart.

---

332. *cast:* dismissed.   339. *hold . . . long:* that is, in dying.   343. *Soft you:* pause
awhile.   359. *traduced:* insulted.   362. *marred:* spoiled.

LODOVICO [*to* IAGO].   O Spartan° dog,
     More fell° than anguish, hunger, or the sea!
     Look on the tragic loading° of this bed,
     This is thy work. The object poisons sight,
     Let it be hid.° Gratiano, keep the house,   370
     And seize upon the fortunes of the Moor,
     For they succeed on you. To you, Lord Governor,
     Remains the censure of this hellish villain,
     The time, the place, the torture.
     Oh, enforce it!
     Myself will straight aboard, and to the state
     This heavy act with heavy heart relate.

                                                            [*Exeunt.*]

366. *Spartan:* that is, hardhearted.   367. *fell:* cruel.   368. *loading:* burden—the
bodies of Desdemona and Othello.   370. *Let . . . hid:* At these words the curtains are
closed across the inner stage (or chamber, if this scene was acted aloft), concealing all
three bodies.

29

Miguel de Cervantes

Don Quixote

*M*IGUEL *de Cervantes (1547–1616) had been writing—with only moderate success—poems, plays, and romances for twenty-five years before beginning his masterpiece, Don Quixote, in 1598. His early career as a soldier had been a promising one, and he later held several posts in the service of the Spanish king. However, he suffered repeated misfortunes. Severely wounded in battle, he was a prisoner of war in Algiers for several years and, after returning to Spain and being appointed collector of taxes, was twice imprisoned for alleged shortages in his accounts.*

Despite such comparatively unpromising beginnings, Cervantes produced the masterpiece of Spanish literature, The Ingenious Gentleman Don Quixote. *Like the works of Shakespeare, it is characteristic of the late Renaissance. It describes the many characters and conflicts of the author's world and addresses the general public rather than a scholarly audience. Although obviously a satire on earlier knightly romances, it goes beyond mere mockery to deal with some basic dilemmas of human experience. Human life, Cervantes seems to be saying, without ideals and imagination is a rather unpleasant affair. On the other hand, it is perilous to retreat into a world of fanciful, imaginative being.*

Don Quixote *has always had a large readership and has been the inspiration for many literary, musical, and pictorial works. Many people are familiar with the French artist Daumier's picture of the melancholy knight wistfully ambling along on his raw-boned nag, accompanied by the fat and faithful Sancho Panza on his patient donkey.*

The following selection includes the opening scene of Cervantes' story. Don Quixote, an impoverished country gentleman who has lost his wits from too-long immersion in tales of chivalry, sets out, accompanied by his servant Sancho Panza as his squire. He seeks knightly adventures that will involve him in fighting against evil, aiding the oppressed and poor, and serving the beautiful ideal lady whom he has named Dulcinea del Toboso.

Next follows the Don's encounter with windmills that in his disordered imagination are menacing giants. His last combat (with the Knight of the White Moon) is also included, and the selection ends with a passage from the conclusion of the book. This describes the Don's final recognition of his madness and his resignation to old age and death. The reader laughs at the Ingenious Gentleman Don Quixote, of course, but with the realization of the truth of the saying, "Pity the man who has not had some of Don Quixote's ideas."

In a certain village in La Mancha,[1] the name of which I do not choose to remember, there lived not long ago one of those country gentlemen who adorn their halls with a rusty lance and shield and ride out on a skinny nag and with a starved greyhound to go hunting. Three-fourths of his income was hardly sufficient to afford a bowl of stew in which there was more beef than mutton for dinner, a plate of cold meat for supper, leftovers on Saturdays, lentils on Fridays, and a pigeon or some such thing on Sundays. The rest of his income went to buy a fine black suit with velvet breeches and slippers to wear on holy-days and a coat of broadcloth which he wore the rest of the week.

He had a female housekeeper about forty years old, a niece about half that age, a trusty young fellow fit for field and market, who could turn his hand to anything, either to saddle the horse or handle the pruning hook.

Our gentleman, who was close to fifty, had a tough constitution. He was extremely thin and hard-featured, an early riser and a lover of hunting. He is said to have gone by the name of Quijada, or Quesada[2] (writers who mention the subject disagree) though it is most likely that

---

[1] A region of central Spain. Cervantes probably had no particular village in mind.

[2] Quijada and Quiseda were distinguished family names in Spain.

DON QUIXOTE   Adapted from *The History and Adventures of the Renowned Don Quixote* by Miguel de Cervantes Saavedra, trans. Tobias Smollett, London, 1755, repr. 1986 (New York: Farrar, Strauss, Giroux), 27–32, 62–64, 799–801, 841–45.

he was called Quijadas (meaning "jaws," with which he was well-endowed). But this is of small importance to this story, in the course of which it will be satisfactory if we do not stray too far from the truth.

Be it known, therefore, that this honest gentleman spent his leisure hours, that is, most of his time throughout the year reading books of chivalry, which he did with such devotion and concentration that he not only forgot the pleasures of hunting but neglected the management of his estate. To such an extent did this interest preoccupy him that he sold many acres of good land to purchase books about knightly adventures, with which he furnished his library as much as he possibly could. But none of these books pleased him as much as those written by Feliciano de Sylva,[3] whom he admired as the pearl of all authors for the brilliancy of his prose and the beautiful complexity of his expressions. How he was enraptured when he read those amorous passages that so often occur in these works.

"The reason of the unreasonable usage of my reason has met with, so unreasons my reason that I have reason to complain of your beauty." How he did enjoy this and other flowery compositions such as, "The high heaven of your divinity, which with stars divinely fortifies your beauty and renders you meritorious of that merit which by your highness is merited!"

The poor gentleman lost his senses in poring over and attempting to discover the meaning of these and other such rhapsodies, which Aristotle himself would not be able to unravel were he to rise from the dead for that purpose only. . . .

So eager and entangled was our gentleman in this kind of story that he would often read from morning to night, and from night to morning again without interruption. At last the moisture of his brain dried up from this unceasing study and he lost his wits. All that he had read of quarrels, enchantments, battles, challenges, wounds, tortures of love and its pangs, and other unlikely happenings took over his entire mind. He believed all those romantic exploits so completely that in his opinion Holy Scripture itself was not more true. . . .

In short, when he had lost his understanding altogether, he began to believe the strangest idea that ever entered the brain of a madman. This was no other than the belief that it was necessary not only for his own honor, but also for the good of the public that he should become a

---

[3] *Author of the Chronicle of Don Florizel de Niquea*, 1551. The first of the quotations which follow is from this work, and the second is from Antonio de Torquemada's *Olivante de Laura*, 1564.

knight-errant, one who rides through the world seeking adventures. He would be like those heroes whose exploits he had read, righting wrongs and risking dangers so that he would become famous. The poor lunatic imagined himself as good as crowned King of Trebizond.[4] Intoxicated with these pleasant imaginings, he resolved to put his plan into action at once.

In the first place, he cleaned an old suit of armor which had belonged to some of his ancestors and which he found in his attic where it had lain for years covered with mold and rust. When he had cleaned and scoured it as well as he could, he discovered that the helmet was missing its visor or face guard. This unlucky defect he remedied by making a visor out of cardboard, which, when fastened in place, made the helmet look complete. Unfortunately, when he tested it to see if it was strong enough and struck it a good slashing blow with his sword, he destroyed his whole week's work. Not approving of the ease with which he had been able to cut it to pieces, he set to work again and faced the helmet with an iron plate. Satisfied that this looked good and strong, he did not test it but looked at it as a well-finished piece of armor. . . .

Having found a satisfactory name, Rosinante, for his horse,[5] he thought he would do as much for himself and after eight days' study, assumed the title Don Quixote[6]. . . and, like the heroes of the romances he admired so much, added to it the name of the place of his birth. So he became Don Quixote de la Mancha, which, in his opinion, revealed his lineage and honored his fortunate country.

Accordingly, his armor being polished, his helmet repaired, himself and his horse suitably named, he reflected that nothing was missing but a lady to inspire him with love. A knight-errant without a lady would be like a tree without leaves or fruit, or a body without a soul. . . .

How the heart of our worthy knight danced with joy when he found a lady worthy of his affection! This, they say, was a healthy, buxom country wench called Aldonza Lorenzo, who lived in the neighborhood and with whom he had been in love. By all accounts she never knew about this, nor did she have the least concern about the matter. But he looked upon her as qualified in every respect to be the queen of his affection. Putting his mind to work again, he looked for a name that would be somewhat like her own and at the same time be suitable for a

[4]A medieval kingdom on the Black Sea.
[5]Rosinante comes from "rosin," meaning "hack" or "nag."
[6]Quixote literally means "the piece of armor that protects the thigh."

princess or a noble lady. He decided to call her Dulcinea del Toboso because she lived in that place and because, in his opinion, it was romantic, musical, and expressive, like the names he had chosen for himself and his horse.

Having made these preparations, he could no longer resist the desire of putting his plan into action at once. He thought impatiently of the harm his delay would cause to the world where there were so many grievances to be redressed, wrongs to be righted, errors corrected, and abuses reformed. Therefore, without telling anybody or being seen by a living soul, one morning at dawn in the scorching month of July he put his armor on, mounted Rosinante, fastened on his ill-made helmet, braced his shield, seized his lance, and rode through the gate of his back yard and joyfully on into the fields, happy because of this easy and successful beginning of his adventures.

• • •

[Don Quixote and Sancho Panza, a local peasant whom Quixote has persuaded to become his squire, set out on the open road. The Don rides the raw-boned Rosinante; Sancho rides a fat little donkey. *Ed.*]

As Don Quixote and Sancho rode along, they came upon thirty or forty windmills on the plain, and no sooner had Don Quixote seen them than he said to his squire, "Chance has governed our affairs even better than we could wish or hope for. Look there, friend Sancho, and behold thirty or forty evil giants, with whom I intend to engage in battle and put every one of them to death so that we may begin to enrich ourselves with their wealth, for it is a good thing for both man and God to eliminate such a wicked race from the face of the earth."

"What giants do you mean?" asked Sancho Panza in amazement.

"Those you see yonder," replied his master, "with widely stretched arms, some of which are two leagues long."

"I wish your worship would see correctly," answered Sancho. "What you see yonder are not giants, but windmills, and what seem to you arms are their sails, which, when turned by the wind, make the millstones go round."

"It seems very plain," said the knight, "that you are only a novice in adventures. These I affirm to be giants, and if you are afraid, get out of the reach of danger and pray for me while I attack them in fierce and unequal combat."

So saying, he put spurs to his steed Rosinante without paying the least attention to the cries of his squire Sancho, who assured him again that what he was going to attack were no giants but innocent windmills. But Don Quixote was so carried away by his belief that they were giants that he neither heard Sancho's advice nor believed the evidence of his own eyes as he rode toward the mills.

He called aloud, "Don't run away, you vile and cowardly creatures, for it is only a single knight that attacks you."

At that instant, a breeze sprang up and began turning the great sails. Seeing this, Don Quixote shouted, "Though you wave more arms than the giant Briareus,[7] I'll make you pay for your insolence."

So saying, and remembering his lady Dulcinea whom he implored to aid him in this danger, he held his shield ready and, with his lance extended, spurred Rosinante to a full gallop. He attacked the nearest windmill, thrusting his lance into one of the sails which was whirling at such speed that the lance was splintered and both knight and steed were tossed aside and sent rolling on the ground.

Sancho Panza rode to Don Quixote's assistance as fast as his donkey could carry him. When he reached the knight, he found him unable to move. Bruised and hurt, both he and Rosinante lay stretched on the ground.

"Lord have mercy upon us!" cried the squire. "Didn't I tell your worship to be careful what you were doing? Didn't I warn you that they were only windmills? Nobody could mistake them for anything else except someone who has windmills in his own head!"

"Be quiet, friend Sancho," replied Don Quixote. "The affairs of war are, more than anything else, subject to changes. I believe, indeed I am certain, that the magician Freston[8] . . . has changed those giants into mills in order to rob me of the honor of conquering them, so great is his hatred of me. But in the end all his treacherous arts won't help him against the strength of my sword."

"God's will be done," said Sancho Panza, who helped him get up and mount Rosinante, who stood by with joints half dislocated.

While they talked about what had happened, they followed the road that leads to the pass of Lapice. It was such a busy road that, as Don Quixote observed, they would be sure to have many more adventures.

---

[7]In Greek mythology, a hundred-armed giant.

[8]A magician in one of the romances the Don has been reading.

As he jogged along, worried by the loss of his lance, he said to his squire, "I remember reading about a Spanish knight called Diego Perez de Vargos who, having broken his sword in battle, tore off a huge bough from an oak. He performed such wonders with it and killed so many Moors that he was called the Machuca, the 'Bruiser' or 'Pounder.' All his descendants from that day forward have gone by the names of Vargos and Machuca. I mention this because I will tear a bough as big as his from the first oak or ash I find. I intend to perform such exploits that you will think yourself extremely lucky that I think you worthy of seeing and giving testimony about these feats of mine."

"With God's help," said Sancho, "I believe that everything will happen as your worship says. But please, sir, sit a little bit straighter, for you seem to lean strongly to one side, which must be the result of the bruises you received in your fall."

"You are right," answered Don Quixote, "and if I do not complain of the pain it is because knights-errant are not permitted to complain of any wound they receive even though their bowels may be dropping out of their bodies."

"If that is the case, I have nothing more to say," replied Sancho. "But God knows I should be glad if your worship would complain when anything causes you pain. I know this, that for my part, the smallest thing that hurts me would make me complain—unless that law of not complaining reaches to squires as well as knights."

Don Quixote could not help smiling at the simplicity of his squire, to whom he gave permission to complain as much and as often as he pleased and whether he had reason or not. As yet, he had not read anything to the contrary in his books of knight-errantry.

Sancho then observed that it was dinner time. His master said that he himself had no need of food, but that Sancho might eat when he pleased. With this permission Sancho seated himself as well as he could on his donkey and, taking out the provisions with which he had stuffed his saddlebag, dropped behind his master a good way and kept his jaws working as he jogged along. He raised his wine bottle from time to time with so much satisfaction that the most prosperous tavern keeper in all Malaga[9] might have envied him.

While he traveled in this way, repeating his agreeable swigs from the bottle every so often, he . . . thought that going in quest of adventures was not hardship but a sport, no matter how dangerous.

[9]A city on the south coast of Spain noted for its fine wines.

They passed that night in a grove of trees, from one of which Don Quixote tore a withered branch to serve instead of a lance. He fitted to it the iron head he had taken from the broken lance. All night long he stayed awake thinking of his lady Dulcinea, for such was what he should be doing. He had read about those knights-errant who passed many sleepless nights in woods and deserts remembering their ladies, and he felt he ought to do so too.

This was not the case with Sancho Panza, however, whose belly was well filled, and not with flavored water. He made one nap of the whole night, and even then if his master had not called him would not have been wakened by the sunbeams that shone on his face or the happy singing of the many birds that greeted the new day.

• • •

[After many adventures, Don Quixote and Sancho Panza are befriended by a nobleman in whose home by the sea they are given refuge. In the meantime, the Don's friends have decided that the only way to rescue him from the endless humiliations and defeats resulting from his mad attempts at knightly adventure is to use his delusion against him. Therefore, one of his friends, disguising himself as the Knight of the White Moon, overcomes him in open combat and compels him to surrender and return home. Ed.]

One morning, Don Quixote was riding along the beach completely armed, for, as he often observed, arms were his ornaments and fighting his recreation, and he never cared to appear without them. As he trotted along, he saw coming toward him a knight armed from head to foot and with a full moon painted on his shield. This figure was no sooner within hearing than he called out to Don Quixote, "Renowned knight, never-applauded-enough Don Quixote de la Mancha, I am the Knight of the White Moon, whose unheard-of exploits may perhaps be known to you. I have come to challenge you and test the strength of your arm, to compel you to admit that my lady, whoever she is, is more beautiful by far than your Dulcinea del Toboso. If you fairly and fully confess this, you will avoid your own death and spare me the trouble of being your executioner. But if you dare to engage in single combat with me and are defeated, all I will demand of you is that you lay aside your arms, cease traveling in search of adventures, and return to your home to stay for a year without drawing your sword, but living in peace and tranquillity for the benefit of your estate and your soul.

"On the other hand, if it is my fate to be vanquished, my life will be at your disposal. You will win my horse and arms, and the fame of my achievements will be added to your fame. Consider which of these choices you prefer and answer me at once, for on this very day this affair must be concluded."

Don Quixote was astonished at the arrogance of the Knight of the White Moon and amazed at the reason for his challenge. After a pause to collect his thoughts, he replied in a solemn tone and with a severe countenance.

"Sir Knight of the White Moon," he said, "whose exploits are as yet unknown to me, I dare swear that you have never seen the illustrious Dulcinea, for if you had, I know you would not make such a rash demand. One glimpse of her would have shown you your error and that there never was or will be any beauty comparable to that which she possesses now. I therefore do not say you lie; but you are wholly mistaken.

"I accept your challenge and the conditions you propose. I will fight you before the day you have decided on is over. There is this exception, however. I will not take the fame of your exploits because I do not know how, when, or why they were achieved. I am satisfied with my own, such as they are.

"Choose your ground. I will then take my side of the field. And let St. Peter bless whatever God may give."

People who had seen the Knight of the White Moon talking with Don Quixote informed the viceroy[10] . . . who, when he saw that they were about to engage in combat, hastened to come between them and demand the cause of their fighting. The Knight of the White Moon answered that it was a question of whose lady was more beautiful, and he briefly repeated the conditions he had proposed to Don Quixote, which they had both accepted. . . .

The viceroy was a little perplexed and dubious about whether he ought to allow the battle to take place. As he could not believe it was anything but a joke, he went off to one side and said to them, "Valiant knights, seeing that there is no other remedy than yielding or dying, for Señor Don Quixote persists in denying what you of the White Moon affirm to be true, I leave you to your fate, and may God stand by the righteous."

The Knight of the White Moon thanked the viceroy for the permission just granted, and Don Quixote followed his example. Then Don Quixote prayed to heaven and to his Dulcinea, according to his usual

---

[10]The official governing the territory as representative of the king.

practice before engaging in combat. He turned around to take a little more ground. His opponent was doing the same.

Then, without any blare of trumpet or other signal, both combatants wheeled about and charged. The Knight of the White Moon, having the fleeter horse, met his adversary before the Don had run one-third of the way. He raised his lance at the last moment in order not to wound the Don, whom, however, he crashed against with such tremendous force that he brought Rosinante and the Don to the ground in a terrible and dangerous fall.

The victor immediately leaped from his horse and thrust his lance against the fallen Don's visor. "Knight," he said, "you are vanquished. You are a dead man unless you say you accept the terms of my challenge."

The battered and astounded Don Quixote, without raising the visor of his helmet, replied in a weak voice that seemed to come from the tomb, "Dulcinea del Toboso is the most beautiful woman in the world, and I am the most unfortunate knight on earth. It cannot be that weakness can alter the truth. So, use your weapon, knight, and take my life, as you have already deprived me of my honor."

"By no means," said the Knight of the White Moon. "Let the fame of the lady Dulcinea's beauty flourish in full perfection. All the satisfaction I ask is that the great Don Quixote retire to his own house and remain there for the space of one year or until such time as I decide, according to the articles agreed upon before we fought."

Don Antonio, the nobleman at whose home the Don had been staying, the viceroy, and a number of other people heard Don Quixote answer that since the victor had demanded nothing derogatory to Dulcinea, he would comply with the other demands like a true and honorable knight.

The Knight of the White Moon, hearing this declaration, turned his horse and, bowing courteously to the viceroy, returned to the city at half-gallop. He was followed by Don Antonio, whom the viceroy had sent to find out about this mysterious stranger. In the meantime, they raised Don Quixote up and, uncovering his face, found him pale as death, his forehead covered with a cold sweat. Rosinante lay motionless from the rough treatment he had received.

Sancho Panza was so overwhelmed with sorrow that he did not know what to do or say. This unlucky incident seemed to be a dream, and he looked on the whole scene as a matter of enchantment. Seeing his lord and master overcome and compelled to lay aside his arms for a year, he feared that his master's bones were dislocated and poor Rosinante seemed maimed forever.

Finally, the viceroy ordered his servants to bring a stretcher to carry the Don to the city. The viceroy went along, for he wanted very much to know who this Knight of the White Moon was who had left Don Quixote in such a cruel dilemma.

• • •

[In obedience to the command of the victorious Knight of the White Moon, Don Quixote, accompanied by Sancho Panza, sets out for home. On the way, they have several more adventures. Upon arriving at home, Don Quixote tells his friends of his defeat and his promise to abandon his chivalrous career. He soon falls ill and is taken to his room where his friends visit him and try to console him. *Ed.*]

As nothing human is eternal, but every earthly thing, especially mankind, is always declining from its origin to its decay, Don Quixote had no special privileged exemption from heaven different from the common fate. The end of his existence arrived when he least expected its approach. Either because of the melancholy resulting from his defeat or because of some special judgment of heaven, he was seized by a fever which kept him in bed for six days, during which time he was often visited by his friends, the curate, the bachelor, and the village barber.[11] His good squire Sancho Panza never left his bedside.

Supposing that his sickness was caused by his humiliating defeat . . . his friends tried to cheer him up by all possible means. All their consolations, however, could not dispel Don Quixote's melancholy, and his friends at last called a physician, who felt his pulse and gave a gloomy forecast. He told them that they ought to be concerned about the health of Don Quixote's soul, for that of his body was in serious danger. The knight heard this report with heroic composure, but that was not the case with his housekeeper, niece, and squire, who began to weep and wail as if they had already seen him die.

Don Quixote felt sleepy and asked to be left alone. He slept six hours at a stretch, so that the housekeeper and niece began to fear that he would never wake up. At last he did awaken and cried out, "Praise be the almighty God for the great benefits I have received from his bounty! His mercies are boundless and not limited by man's sinful errors!"

[11]The curate (village priest), Sampson Carrasco (the bachelor, who held a bachelor's degree from a small university), and the village barber were Don Quixote's close friends. The bachelor had masqueraded as the Knight of the White Moon.

The niece, who had listened closely to these exclamations, which made more sense than anything else he had uttered since the beginning of his illness, said, "Uncle, what do you mean? Has anything new happened? What mercies and what sinful errors are these that you mention?"

"Mercies," replied the knight, "which heaven has granted me in spite of my sinful errors. I now enjoy my judgment undisturbed and cleared of those dark shadows of ignorance that clouded my understanding from incessant reading of those detestable books of chivalry. I now understand the falsity and folly they contain, and nothing causes me so much concern as knowing that this understanding comes too late to give me time enough to read other books that would enlighten my soul. I feel myself at the point of death, and I don't want to die in such a way that I could be remembered as a madman. Though I have acted like one, I don't want to act like one in my last moments. Dear niece, call my worthy friends the curate, the bachelor Sampson Carrasco, and master Nicholas the barber, for I want to confess and make my will."

The three came in just then, and she did not have to send them messages. Don Quixote greeted them, saying, "Good gentlemen, congratulate me and rejoice with me upon my no longer being Don Quixote de la Mancha but plain Alonso Quixano, surnamed the Good, on account of his innocence and simplicity of life. I am now an enemy of that whole tribe of heroes of tales of knight-errantry. Now I am aware of my own madness, into which I fell because of reading them, and now I abominate and abhor them."

The three friends were afraid that he was seized by some new madness. Sampson asked, "Why do you talk this way . . . have you decided to become a hermit? Please, be sensible and forget all about those foolish stories."

"Those stories which I used to believe have indeed caused my misfortune," said the knight, "but with heaven's aid I will turn them to my advantage. Therefore, jesting aside, let me have the aid of a priest to hear my confession and a notary to write my will. In such circumstances a man must not trifle with his own soul. . . ."

His friends looked at each other in amazement and, though still doubtful, decided to comply with his wishes. They felt that this sudden and easy transition from madness to sanity was a certain signal of his approaching death. Moreover, he went on to talk so reasonably, expressing so many sensible and religious sentiments, that their doubts about his sanity were removed.

The curate sent the others away and heard the penitent's confession. The bachelor went to look for the lawyer, with whom he returned in a little while, accompanied by Sancho, who, having learned about his master's condition and finding the housekeeper and niece in tears, began to pucker up his face and open the floodgates of his eyes.

When the confession was over the curate came out saying, "The good Alonso Quixano is really dying and without doubt restored to his senses. . . ."

These words caused the two ladies and the faithful squire to burst again into tears, and their bosoms heaved with sobs. For it must be said that whether in the role of Alonso the Good or Don Quixote de la Mancha, the poor gentleman had always been kindly and agreeable, for which he was loved not only by his own family but also by all those who had the pleasure of his acquaintance.

The notary went with them into the room in which the Don lay ill and listened to him make his will. First he disposed of his soul in the necessary Christian forms and then proceeded to the legacies. Among these was one for his squire: "Whereas Sancho Panza, whom in my madness I made my squire, has in his hands a certain sum of money for my use . . . if there is any surplus left over after he has deducted the payment of what I owe him, which must be a mere trifle, it shall be his own, and much good may it do him, for the innocency of his heart and the fidelity of his service." Then, turning to the squire, he said, "Forgive me, friend, for having been the cause of your appearing before the world as mad as I and for making you share my crazy notions about the life and adventures of knights-errant."

"Dear master," cried Sancho, blubbering, "do not die. Take my advice and live for many more years. The greatest madness a man be guilty of in this life is to let himself die without being slain by anyone or destroyed by any other weapon than the hands of melancholy. Get up and let us go walking in the fields . . . who knows that behind some bush we may find Lady Dulcinea, disenchanted and pretty to look at.

"If you take your defeat so much to heart, put the blame on me. Say you were vanquished because of my carelessness in not tightening Rosinante's saddle girth. Besides, you must have read in your books of chivalry that it was common for one knight to unhorse another and for him who was beaten today to win tomorrow."

"Very true," said Sampson. "Honest Sancho is very well informed in these matters."

"Gentlemen," replied the knight, "let us proceed fairly and carefully, without looking for this year's birds in last year's nests. I was mad, but now am in my right mind I was Don Quixote de la Mancha, but now, as I have said, I am Alonso Quixano the Good. And I hope that by my true repentance I can regain the respect I used to have from you. . . ."

At last death came to Don Quixote after he had received all the sacraments and repeated his condemnation in the strongest possible terms of all books of chivalry. The notary observed that in all books of that kind that he had read, no one had died quietly in bed, as a good Christian, like Don Quixote.

Amidst the tears and lamentations of all present, Don Quixote gave up the ghost. In other words, he died.

30

Martin Luther

Address to the Christian Nobility of the German Nation

MARTIN Luther (1483–1546) re-
ceived training in law and theology at the University of Erfurt. His career
turned suddenly and dramatically toward religion, however, when he undertook
a life of strict asceticism as a monk of the Augustinian order. Luther was later
sent to assist at the new University of Wittenberg, where he lectured on the New
Testament. These theological studies led him to question certain doctrines of the
Church, and, on the matter of indulgences (an explosive issue at that time), he
challenged papal authority with his famous Ninety-Five Theses (1517).
Luther's criticism soon broadened to a general attack, stemming from his belief
that the papacy of his day, far from being a God-ordained institution, was
actually a creation of men interested in perpetuating their own power. Believing
that the civil authority had the right and obligation to correct erroneous religious
beliefs and practices, Luther appealed to the German ruling class to expel the
"foreign tyranny of the papacy," as he termed it. Under the protection of the
rulers of the north German principalities, whose motives were nationalistic and
economic as well as religious, Luther's brand of Protestantism flourished.

The Address to the Christian Nobility of the German Nation (1520)
shows Luther at the height of his energies. As the central work in his attack upon
the papacy, it contains (in addition to forthright denunciations of Catholic
theory and practice) such fundamental points of Lutheran doctrine as the
"priesthood of all believers" and the supreme authority of the Scriptures. Its
vigorous language, intensely nationalistic spirit, and fervent denunciations of
the papacy appealed to many people. In their opinion, the Address, signaling
the complete and irreparable break with Rome, was of vital importance to the
success of Lutheranism—the first major branch of Protestantism to develop
during the Reformation.

To His Most Serene and Mighty Imperial Majesty
and to the Christian Nobility
of the German Nation
DR. MARTINUS LUTHER

The grace and might of God be with you, Most Serene Majesty, most gracious, well-beloved gentlemen!

It is not out of mere arrogance and perversity that I, an individual poor man, have taken upon me to address your lordships. The distress and misery that oppress all the Christian estates, more especially in Germany, have led not only myself, but every one else, to cry aloud and to ask for help, and have now forced me too to cry out and to ask if God would give His Spirit to any one to reach a hand to His wretched people. Councils have often put forward some remedy, but it has adroitly been frustrated, and the evils have become worse, through the cunning of certain men. Their malice and wickedness I will now, by the help of God, expose, so that, being known, they may henceforth cease to be so obstructive and injurious. God has given us a young and noble sovereign,[1] and by this has roused great hopes in many hearts; now it is right that we too should do what we can, and make good use of time and grace.

The first thing that we must do is to consider the matter with great earnestness, and, whatever we attempt, not to trust in our own strength and wisdom alone, even if the power of all the world were ours; for God will not endure that a good work should be begun trusting to our own strength and wisdom. He destroys it; it is all useless, as we read in Psalm xxxiii., "There is no king saved by the multitude of a host; a mighty man is not delivered by much strength." And I fear it is for that reason that those beloved princes the Emperors Frederick, the First and the Second,[2] and many other German emperors were, in former times, so piteously spurned and oppressed by the popes, though they were feared by all the world. Perchance they trusted rather in their own

---

[1]Charles V, elected Holy Roman emperor in 1519.

[2]Emperors of the Holy Roman Empire, during the eleventh century and the twelfth century respectively. Frederick II, having been involved in a dispute with the Church, died under excommunication.

ADDRESS TO THE CHRISTIAN NOBILITY   Martin Luther, *Address to the Christian Nobility of the German Nation Respecting the Reformation of the Christian Estate*, in *Luther's Primary Works*, ed. Henry Wace and C. A. Buchheim (London: Hodder and Stoughton, 1896), 161–80.

strength than in God; therefore they could not but fall; and how would the sanguinary tyrant Julius II[3] have risen so high in our own days but that, I fear, France, Germany, and Venice trusted to themselves? The children of Benjamin slew forty-two thousand Israelites, for this reason: that these trusted to their own strength (Judges xx., etc.).

That such a thing may not happen to us and to our noble Emperor Charles, we must remember that in this matter we wrestle not against flesh and blood, but against the rulers of the darkness of this world (Eph. vi. 12), who may fill the world with war and bloodshed, but cannot themselves be overcome thereby. We must renounce all confidence in our natural strength, and take the matter in hand with humble trust in God; we must seek God's help with earnest prayer, and have nothing before our eyes but the misery and wretchedness of Christendom, irrespective of what punishment the wicked may deserve. If we do not act thus, we may begin the game with great pomp; but when we are well in it, the spirit of evil will make such confusion that the whole world will be immersed in blood, and yet nothing be done. Therefore let us act in the fear of God and prudently. The greater the might of the foe, the greater is the misfortune, if we do not act in the fear of God and with humility. If popes and Romanists have hitherto, with the devil's help, thrown kings into confusion, they may still do so, if we attempt things with our own strength and skill, without God's help.

THE THREE WALLS OF THE ROMANISTS

The Romanists[4] have, with great adroitness, drawn three walls round themselves, with which they have hitherto protected themselves, so that no one could reform them, whereby all Christendom has fallen terribly.

Firstly, if pressed by the temporal power, they have affirmed and maintained that the temporal power has no jurisdiction over them, but, on the contrary, that the spiritual power is above the temporal.

Secondly, if it were proposed to admonish them with the Scriptures, they objected that no one may interpret the Scriptures but the Pope.

Thirdly, if they are threatened with a council, they pretend that no one may call a council but the Pope.

---

[3]Pope from 1503 to 1513.
[4]Supporters of the Pope and advocates of papal supremacy.

Thus they have secretly stolen our three rods, so that they may be unpunished, and intrenched themselves behind these three walls, to act with all the wickedness and malice, which we now witness. And whenever they have been compelled to call a council, they have made it of no avail by binding the princes beforehand with an oath to leave them as they were, and to give moreover to the Pope full power over the procedure of the council, so that it is all one whether we have many councils or no councils, in addition to which they deceive us with false pretences and tricks. So grievously do they tremble for their skin before a true, free council; and thus they have overawed kings and princes, that these believe they would be offending God, if they were not to obey them in all such knavish, deceitful artifices.

Now may God help us, and give us one of those trumpets that overthrew the walls of Jericho, so that we may blow down these walls of straw and paper, and that we may set free our Christian rods for the chastisement of sin, and expose the craft and deceit of the devil, so that we may amend ourselves by punishment and again obtain God's favour.

THE FIRST WALL

That the Temporal Power Has No Jurisdiction over the Spirituality

Let us, in the first place, attack the first wall.

It has been devised that the Pope, bishops, priests, and monks are called the *spiritual estate*, princes, lords, artificers, and peasants are the *temporal estate*. This is an artful lie and hypocritical device, but let no one be made afraid by it, and that for this reason: that all Christians are truly of the spiritual estate, and there is no difference among them, save of office alone. As St. Paul says (1 Cor. xii.), we are all one body, though each member does its own work, to serve the others. This is because we have one baptism, one Gospel, one faith, and are all Christians alike; for baptism, Gospel, and faith, these alone make spiritual and Christian people.

As for the unction by a pope or a bishop, tonsure, ordination, consecration, and clothes differing from those of laymen—all this may make a hypocrite or an anointed puppet, but never a Christian or a spiritual man. Thus we are all consecrated as priests by baptism, as St. Peter says: "Ye are a royal priesthood, a holy nation" (1 Peter ii. 9); and in the book of Revelations: "and hast made us unto our God (by Thy blood) kings and priests" (Rev. v. 10). For, if we had not a higher consecration in us than pope or bishop can give, no priest could ever be made by the consecration of pope or bishop, nor could he say the mass, or preach, or absolve. Therefore the bishop's consecration is just as if in the name of the whole congregation he took one person out of the community, each member of which has equal power, and commanded him to exercise this power for the rest; in the same way as if ten brothers, co-heirs as king's sons, were to choose one from among them to rule over their inheritance, they would all of them still remain kings and have equal power, although one is ordered to govern.

And to put the matter even more plainly, if a little company of pious Christian laymen were taken prisoners and carried away to a desert, and had not among them a priest consecrated by a bishop, and were there to agree to elect one of them, born in wedlock or not, and were to order him to baptise, to celebrate the mass, to absolve, and to preach, this man would as truly be a priest, as if all the bishops and all the popes had consecrated him. That is why in cases of necessity every man can baptise and absolve, which would not be possible if we were not all priests. This great grace and virtue of baptism and of the Christian estate they have quite destroyed and made us forget by their ecclesiastical law. In this way the Christians used to choose their bishops and priests out of the community; these being afterwards confirmed by other bishops, without the pomp that now prevails. So was it that St. Augustine, Ambrose, Cyprian,[5] were bishops.

Since, then, the temporal power is baptised as we are, and has the same faith and Gospel, we must allow it to be priest and bishop, and account its office an office that is proper and useful to the Christian community. For whatever issues from baptism may boast that it has been consecrated priest, bishop, and pope, although it does not beseem every one to exercise these offices. For, since we are all priests alike, no man may put himself forward or take upon himself, without our consent and election, to do that which we have all alike power to do. For, if a thing is common to all, no man may take it to himself without the wish and command of the community. And if it should happen that a man were appointed to one of these offices and deposed for abuses, he would be just what he was before. Therefore a priest should be nothing in Christendom but a functionary; as long as he holds his office, he has precedence of others; if he is deprived of it, he is a peasant or a citizen like the rest. Therefore a priest is verily no longer a priest after deposi-

[5]Bishops of the early Church, all elected by laymen.

tion. But now they have invented *characteres indelebiles*,[6] and pretend that a priest after deprivation still differs from a simple layman. They even imagine that a priest can never be anything but a priest—that is, that he can never become a layman. All this is nothing but mere talk and ordinance of human invention.

It follows, then, that between laymen and priests, princes and bishops, or, as they call it, between spiritual and temporal persons, the only real difference is one of office and function, and not of estate; for they are all of the same spiritual estate, true priests, bishops, and popes, though their functions are not the same—just as among priests and monks every man has not the same functions. And this, as I said above, St. Paul says (Rom. xii.; 1 Cor. xii.), and St. Peter (1 Peter ii.): "We, being many, are one body in Christ, and severally members one of another." Christ's body is not double or twofold, one temporal, the other spiritual. He is one Head, and He has one body.

We see, then, that just as those that we call spiritual, or priests, bishops, or popes, do not differ from other Christians in any other or higher degree but in that they are to be concerned with the word of God and the sacraments—that being their work and office—in the same way the temporal authorities hold the sword and the rod in their hands to punish the wicked and to protect the good. A cobbler, a smith, a peasant, every man, has the office and function of his calling, and yet all alike are consecrated priests and bishops, and every man should by his office or function be useful and beneficial to the rest, so that various kinds of work may all be united for the furtherance of body and soul, just as the members of the body all serve one another.

Now see what a Christian doctrine is this: that the temporal authority is not above the clergy, and may not punish it. This is as if one were to say the hand may not help, though the eye is in grievous suffering. Is it not unnatural, not to say unchristian, that one member may not help another, or guard it against harm? Nay, the nobler the member, the more the rest are bound to help it. Therefore I say, Forasmuch as the temporal power has been ordained by God for the punishment of the bad and the protection of the good, therefore we must let it do its duty throughout the whole Christian body, without respect of persons, whether it strike popes, bishops, priests, monks, nuns, or whoever it may be. If it were sufficient reason for fettering the temporal power that it is inferior among the offices of Christianity to the offices of priest or

---

[6]Indelible marks—that is, spiritual characteristics conferred by ordination that cannot be destroyed or taken away.

confessor, or to the spiritual estate—if this were so, then we ought to restrain tailors, cobblers, masons, carpenters, cooks, cellarmen, peasants, and all secular workmen, from providing the Pope or bishops, priests and monks, with shoes, clothes, houses, or victuals, or from paying them tithes. But if these laymen are allowed to do their work without restraint, what do the Romanist scribes mean by their laws? They mean that they withdraw themselves from the operation of temporal Christian power, simply in order that they may be free to do evil, and thus fulfill what St. Peter said: "There shall be false teachers among you, . . . and in covetousness shall they with feigned words make merchandise of you" (2 Peter ii. 1, etc.).

Therefore the temporal Christian power must exercise its office without let or hindrance, without considering whom it may strike, whether pope, or bishop, or priest: whoever is guilty, let him suffer for it.

Whatever the ecclesiastical law has said in opposition to this is merely the invention of Romanist arrogance. For this is what St. Paul says to all Christians: "Let every soul" (I presume including the popes) "be subject unto the higher powers; for they bear not the sword in vain: they serve the Lord therewith, for vengeance on evildoers and for praise to them that do well" (Rom. xiii. 1–4). Also St. Peter: "Submit yourselves to every ordinance of man for the Lord's sake, . . . for so is the will of God" (1 Peter ii. 13, 15). He has also foretold that men would come who should despise government (2 Peter ii), as has come to pass through ecclesiastical law.

Now, I imagine, the first paper wall is overthrown, inasmuch as the temporal power has become a member of the Christian body; although its work relates to the body, yet does it belong to the spiritual estate. Therefore it must do its duty without let or hindrance upon all members of the whole body, to punish or urge, as guilt may deserve, or need may require, without respect of pope, bishops, or priests, let them threaten or excommunicate as they will. That is why a guilty priest is deprived of his priesthood before being given over to the secular arm; whereas this would not be right, if the secular sword had not authority over him already by Divine ordinance.

It is, indeed, past bearing that the spiritual law should esteem so highly the liberty, life, and property of the clergy, as if laymen were not as good spiritual Christians, or not equally members of the Church. Why should your body, life, goods, and honour be free, and not mine, seeing that we are equal as Christians, and have received alike baptism, faith, spirit, and all things? If a priest is killed, the country is laid under an interdict: why not also if a peasant is killed? Whence comes this great difference among equal Christians? Simply from human laws and inventions.

It can have been no good spirit, either, that devised these evasions and made sin to go unpunished. For if, as Christ and the Apostles bid us, it is our duty to oppose the evil one and all his works and words, and to drive him away as well as may be, how then should we remain quiet and be silent when the Pope and his followers are guilty of devilish works and words? Are we for the sake of men to allow the commandments and the truth of God to be defeated, which at our baptism we vowed to support with body and soul? Truly we should have to answer for all souls that would thus be abandoned and led astray.

Therefore it must have been the arch-devil himself who said, as we read in the ecclesiastical law, If the Pope were so perniciously wicked, as to be dragging souls in crowds to the devil, yet he could not be deposed. This is the accursed and devilish foundation on which they build at Rome, and think that the whole world is to be allowed to go to the devil rather than they should be opposed in their knavery. If a man were to escape punishment simply because he is above the rest, then no Christian might punish another, since Christ has commanded each of us to esteem himself the lowest and the humblest (Matt. xviii. 4; Luke ix. 48).

Where there is sin, there remains no avoiding the punishment, as St. Gregory[7] says, We are all equal, but guilt makes one subject to another. Now let us see how they deal with Christendom. They arrogate to themselves immunities without any warrant from the Scriptures, out of their own wickedness, whereas God and the Apostles made them subject to the secular sword; so that we must fear that it is the work of antichrist,[8] or a sign of his near approach.

THE SECOND WALL

That No One May Interpret the Scriptures But the Pope

The second wall is even more tottering and weak: that they alone pretend to be considered masters of the Scriptures; although they learn nothing of them all their life. They assume authority, and juggle before us with impudent words, saying that the Pope cannot err in matters of

---

[7]Gregory the Great, pope from 590 to 604.

[8]The incarnation of all that is hostile to Christ and His kingdom.

faith, whether he be evil or good, albeit they cannot prove it by a single letter. That is why the canon law contains so many heretical and unchristian, nay unnatural, laws; but of these we need not speak now. For whereas they imagine the Holy Ghost never leaves them, however unlearned and wicked they may be, they grow bold enough to decree whatever they like. But were this true, where were the need and use of the Holy Scriptures? Let us burn them, and content ourselves with the unlearned gentlemen at Rome, in whom the Holy Ghost dwells, who, however, can dwell in pious souls only. If I had not read it, I could never have believed that the devil should have put forth such follies at Rome and find a following.

But not to fight them with our own words, we will quote the Scriptures. St. Paul says, "If anything be revealed to another that sitteth by, let the first hold his peace" (1 Cor. xiv. 30). What would be the use of this commandment, if we were to believe him alone that teaches or has the highest seat? Christ Himself says, "And they shall be all taught of God" (St. John vi. 45). Thus it may come to pass that the Pope and his followers are wicked and not true Christians, and not being taught by God, have no true understanding, whereas a common man may have true understanding. Why should we then not follow him? Has not the Pope often erred? Who could help Christianity, in case the Pope errs, if we do not rather believe another who has the Scriptures for him?

Therefore it is a wickedly devised fable—and they cannot quote a single letter to confirm it—that it is for the Pope alone to interpret the Scriptures or to confirm the interpretation of them. They have assumed the authority of their own selves. And though they say that this authority was given to St. Peter when the keys were given to him, it is plain enough that the keys were not given to St. Peter alone, but to the whole community. Besides, the keys were not ordained for doctrine or authority, but for sin, to bind or loose; and what they claim besides this from the keys is mere invention. But what Christ said to St. Peter: "I have prayed for thee that thy faith fail not" (St. Luke xxii. 32), cannot relate to the Pope, inasmuch as the greater part of the Popes have been without faith, as they are themselves forced to acknowledge; nor did Christ pray for Peter alone, but for all the Apostles and all Christians, as He says, "Neither pray I for these alone, but for them also which shall believe on Me through their word" (St. John xvii.). Is not this plain enough?

Only consider the matter. They must needs acknowledge that there are pious Christians among us that have the truth faith, spirit, understanding, word, and mind of Christ: why then should we reject their word and understanding, and follow a Pope who has neither understanding nor spirit? Surely this were to deny our whole faith and the Christian Church. Moreover, if the article of our faith is right, "I believe in the holy Christian Church," the Pope cannot alone be right; else we must say, "I believe in the Pope of Rome," and reduce the Christian Church to one man, which is a devilish and damnable heresy. Besides that, we are all priests, as I have said, and have all one faith, one Gospel, one Sacrament; how then should we not have the power of discerning and judging what is right or wrong in matters of faith? What becomes of St. Paul's words, "But he that is spiritual judgeth all things, yet he himself is judged of no man" (1 Cor. ii. 15), and also, "we having the same spirit of faith"? (2 Cor. iv. 13). Why then should we not perceive as well as an unbelieving Pope what agrees or disagrees with our faith?

By these and many other texts we should gain courage and freedom, and should not let the spirit of liberty (as St. Paul has it) be frightened away by the inventions of the Popes; we should boldly judge what they do and what they leave undone according to our own believing understanding of the Scriptures, and force them to follow the better understanding, and not their own. Did not Abraham in old days have to obey his Sarah, who was in stricter bondage to him than we are to any one on earth? Thus, too, Balaam's ass was wiser than the prophet.[9] If God spoke by an ass against a prophet, why should He not speak by a pious man against the Pope? Besides, St. Paul withstood St. Peter as being in error (Gal. ii.). Therefore it behooves every Christian to aid the faith by understanding and defending it and by condemning all errors.

THE THIRD WALL

That No One May Call a Council But the Pope

The third wall falls of itself, as soon as the first two have fallen; for if the Pope acts contrary to the Scriptures, we are bound to stand by the Scriptures, to punish and to constrain him, according to Christ's commandment, "Moreover, if thy brother shall tresspass against thee, go and tell him his fault between thee and him alone; if he shall hear thee,

---

[9] A reference to the biblical story of Balaam (Numbers 22: 21–35). Balaam's ass, miraculously given the ability to speak, saved his master's life.

thou hast gained thy brother. But if he will not hear thee, then take with thee one or two more, that in the mouth of two or three witnesses every word may be established. And if he shall neglect to hear them, tell it unto the Church; but if he neglect to hear the Church, let him be unto thee as a heathen man and a publican" (Matt. xviii. 15–17). Here each member is commanded to take care for the other; much more then should we do this, if it is a ruling member of the community that does evil, which by its evil-doing causes great harm and offence to the others. If then I am to accuse him before the Church, I must collect the Church together. Moreover, they can show nothing in the Scriptures giving the Pope sole power to call and confirm councils; they have nothing but their own laws; but these hold good only so long as they are not injurious to Christianity and the laws of God. Therefore, if the Pope deserves punishment, these laws cease to bind us, since Christendom would suffer, if he were not punished by a council. Thus we read (Acts xv.) that the council of the Apostles was not called by St. Peter, but by all the Apostles and the elders. But if the right to call it had lain with St. Peter alone, it would not have been a Christian council, but a heretical *conciliabulum*.[10] Moreover, the most celebrated council of all— that of Nicaea—was neither called nor confirmed by the Bishop of Rome, but by the Emperor Constantine; and after him many other emperors have done the same, and yet the councils called by them were accounted most Christian. But if the Pope alone had the power, they must all have been heretical. Moreover, if I consider the councils that the Pope has called, I do not find that they produced any notable results.

Therefore when need requires, and the Pope is a cause of offence to Christendom, in these cases whoever can best do so, as a faithful member of the whole body, must do what he can to procure a true free council. This no one can do so well as the temporal authorities, especially since they are fellow-Christians, fellow-priests, sharing one spirit and one power in all things, and since they should exercise the office that they have received from God without hindrance, whenever it is necessary and useful that it should be exercised. Would it not be most unnatural, if a fire were to break out in a city, and every one were to keep still and let it burn on and on, whatever might be burnt, simply because they had not the mayor's authority, or because the fire perchance broke out at the mayor's house? Is not every citizen bound in this case to rouse and call in the rest? How much more should this be done in

---

[10]A mere gathering of people, whereas a *concilium* would be a proper council.

the spiritual city of Christ, if a fire of offence breaks out, either at the Pope's government or wherever it may! The like happens if an enemy attacks a town. The first to rouse up the rest earns glory and thanks. Why then should not he earn glory that descries the coming of our enemies from hell and rouses and summons all Christians?

But as for their boasts of their authority, that no one must oppose it, this is idle talk. No one in Christendom has any authority to do harm, or to forbid others to prevent harm being done. There is no authority in the Church but for reformation. Therefore if the Pope wished to use his power to prevent the calling of a free council, so as to prevent the reformation of the Church, we must not respect him or his power; and if he should begin to excommunicate and fulminate, we must despise this as the doings of a madman, and, trusting in God, excommunicate and repel him as best we may. For this his usurped power is nothing; he does not possess it, and he is at once overthrown by a text from the Scriptures. For St. Paul says to the Corinthians "that God has given us authority for edification, and not for destruction" (2 Cor. x. 8). Who will set this text as nought? It is the power of the devil and of antichrist that prevents what would serve for the reformation of Christendom. Therefore we must not follow it, but oppose it with our body, our goods, and all that we have. And even if a miracle were to happen in favour of the Pope against the temporal power, or if some were to be stricken by a plague, as they sometimes boast has happened, all this is to be held as having been done by the devil in order to injure our faith in God, as was foretold by Christ: "There shall arise false Christs and false prophets, and shall show great signs and wonders, insomuch that, if it were possible, they shall deceive the very elect" (Matt. xxiv. 23); and St. Paul tells the Thessalonians that the coming of antichrist shall be "after the working of Satan with all power and signs and lying wonders" (2 Thess. ii. 9).

Therefore let us hold fast to this: that Christian power can do nothing against Christ, as St. Paul says, "For we can do nothing against Christ, but for Christ" (2 Cor. xiii. 8). But, if it does anything against Christ, it is the power of antichrist and the devil, even if it rained and hailed wonders and plagues. Wonders and plagues prove nothing, especially in these latter evil days, of which false wonders are foretold in all the Scriptures. Therefore we must hold fast to the words of God and with an assured faith; then the devil will soon cease his wonders.

And now I hope the false, lying spectre will be laid with which the Romanists have long terrified and stupefied our consciences. And it will be seen that, like all the rest of us, they are subject to the temporal sword; that they have no authority to interpret the Scriptures by force without skill; and that they have no power to prevent a council, or to pledge it in accordance with their pleasure, or to bind it beforehand, and deprive it of its freedom; and that if they do this, they are verily of the fellowship of antichrist and the devil, and have nothing of Christ but the name.

OF THE MATTERS TO BE CONSIDERED IN THE COUNCILS

Let us now consider the matters which should be treated in the councils, and with which Popes, cardinals, bishops, and all learned men should occupy themselves day and night, if they love Christ and His Church. But if they do not do so, the people at large and the temporal powers must do so, without considering the thunders of their excommunications. For an unjust excommunication is better than ten just absolutions, and an unjust absolution is worse than ten just excommunications. Therefore let us rouse ourselves, fellow-Germans, and fear God more than man, that we be not answerable for all the poor souls that are so miserably lost through the wicked, devilish government of the Romanists, and that the dominion of the devil should not grow day by day, if indeed this hellish government can grow any worse, which, for my part, I can neither conceive nor believe.

It is a distressing and terrible thing to see that the head of Christendom, who boasts of being the vicar of Christ and the successor of St. Peter, lives in a worldly pomp that no king or emperor can equal, so that in him that calls himself most holy and most spiritual there is more worldliness than in the world itself. He wears a triple crown, whereas the mightiest kings only wear one crown. If this resembles the poverty of Christ and St. Peter, it is a new sort of resemblance. They prate of its being heretical to object to this; nay, they will not even hear how unchristian and ungodly it is. But I think that if he should have to pray to God with tears, he would have to lay down his crowns; for God will not endure any arrogance. His office should be nothing else than to weep and pray constantly for Christendom and to be an example of all humility.

However this may be, this pomp is a stumbling-block, and the Pope, for the very salvation of his soul, ought to put it off, for St. Paul says, "Abstain from all appearance of evil" (1 Thess. v. 21), and again,

"Provide things honest in the sight of all men" (2 Cor. viii. 21). A simple mitre would be enough for the Pope: wisdom and sanctity should raise him above the rest; the crown of pride he should leave to antichrist, as his predecessors did some hundreds of years ago. They say, He is the ruler of the world. This is false; for Christ, whose vicegerent and vicar he claims to be, said to Pilate, "My kingdom is not of this world" (John xviii. 36). But no vicegerent can have a wider dominion than his Lord, nor is he a vicegerent of Christ in His glory, but of Christ crucified, as St. Paul says, "For I determined not to know anything among you save Jesus Christ, and Him crucified" (2 Cor. ii. 2), and "Let this mind be in you, which was also in Christ Jesus, who made Himself of no reputation, and took upon Himself the form of a servant" (Phil. ii. 5, 7). Again, "We preach Christ crucified" (1 Cor. i.). Now they make the Pope a vicegerent of Christ exalted in heaven, and some have let the devil rule them so thoroughly that they have maintained that the Pope is above the angels in heaven and has power over them, which is precisely the true work of the true antichrist.

What is the use in Christendom of the people called "cardinals"? I will tell you. In Italy and Germany there are many rich convents, endowments, fiefs, and benefices, and as the best way of getting these into the hands of Rome, they created cardinals, and gave them the sees, convents, and prelacies, and thus destroyed the service of God. That is why Italy is almost a desert now: the convents are destroyed, the sees consumed, the revenues of the prelacies and of all the churches drawn to Rome; towns are decayed, the country and the people ruined, because there is no more any worship of God or preaching; why? Because the cardinals must have all the wealth. No Turk could have thus desolated Italy and overthrown the worship of God.

Now that Italy is sucked dry, they come to Germany and begin very quietly; but if we look on quietly Germany will soon be brought into the same state as Italy. We have a few cardinals already. What the Romanists mean thereby the drunken Germans are not to see until they have lost everything—bishoprics, convents, benefices, fiefs, even to their last farthing. Antichrist must take the riches of the earth, as it is written (Dan. xi. 8, 39, 43). They begin by taking off the cream of the bishoprics, convents, and fiefs; and as they do not dare to destroy everything as they have done in Italy, they employ such holy cunning to join together ten or twenty prelacies, and take such a portion of each annually that the total amounts to a considerable sum. The priory of Würzburg gives one thousand guilders; those of Bamberg, Mayence,

Treves, and others also contribute. In this way they collect one thousand or ten thousand guilders, in order that a cardinal may live at Rome in a state like that of a wealthy monarch.

After we have gained this, we will create thirty or forty cardinals on one day, and give one St. Michael's Mount, near Bamberg, and likewise the see of Würzburg, to which belong some rich benefices, until the churches and the cities are desolated; and then we shall say, We are the vicars of Christ, the shepherds of Christ's flocks; those mad, drunken Germans must submit to it. I advise, however, that there be made fewer cardinals, or that the Pope should have to support them out of his own purse. It would be amply sufficient if there were twelve, and if each of them had an annual income of one thousand guilders.

What has brought us Germans to such a pass that we have to suffer this robbery and this destruction of our property by the Pope? If the kingdom of France has resisted it, why do we Germans suffer ourselves to be fooled and deceived? It would be more endurable if they did nothing but rob us of our property; but they destroy the Church and deprive Christ's flock of their good shepherds, and overthrow the service and word of God. Even if there were no cardinals at all, the Church would not perish, for they do nothing for the good of Christendom; all they do is to traffic in and quarrel about prelacies and bishoprics, which any robber could do as well.

If we took away ninety-nine parts of the Pope's Court and only left one hundredth, it would still be large enough to answer questions on matters of belief. Now there is such a swarm of vermin at Rome, all called papal, that Babylon itself never saw the like. There are more than three thousand papal secretaries alone; but who shall count the other office-bearers, since there are so many offices that we can scarcely count them, and all waiting for German benefices, as wolves wait for a flock of sheep? I think Germany now pays more to the Pope than it formerly paid the emperors; nay, some think more than three hundred thousand guilders are sent from Germany to Rome every year, for nothing whatever; and in return we are scoffed at and put to shame. Do we still wonder why princes, noblemen, cities, foundations, convents, and people grow poor? We should rather wonder that we have anything left to eat.

Now that we have got well into our game, let us pause a while and show that the Germans are not such fools as not to perceive or understand this Romish trickery. I do not here complain that God's commandments and Christian justice are despised at Rome; for the state of things in Christendom, especially at Rome, is too bad for us to complain of such high matters. Nor do I even complain that no account is taken of natural or secular justice and reason. The mischief lies still deeper. I complain that they do not observe their own fabricated canon law, though this is in itself rather mere tyranny, avarice, and worldly pomp, than a law. This we shall now show.

Long ago the emperors and princes of Germany allowed the Pope to claim the *annates* from all German benefices; that is, half of the first year's income from every benefice. The object of this concession was that the Pope should collect a fund with all this money to fight against the Turks and infidels, and to protect Christendom, so that the nobility should not have to bear the burden of the struggle alone, and that the priests should also contribute. The popes have made such use of this good simple piety of the Germans that they have taken this money for more than one hundred years, and have now made of it a regular tax and duty; and not only have they accumulated nothing, but they have funded out of it many posts and offices at Rome, which are paid by it yearly, as out of a ground-rent.

Whenever there is any pretence of fighting the Turks, they send out some commission for collecting money, and often send out indulgences under the same pretext of fighting the Turks. They think we Germans will always remain such great inveterate fools that we will go on giving money to satisfy their unspeakable greed, though we see plainly that neither *annates*, nor absolution money, nor any other—not one farthing—goes against the Turks, but all goes into the bottomless sack. They lie and deceive, form and make covenants with us, of which they do not mean to keep one jot. And all this is done in the holy name of Christ and St. Peter.

This being so, the German nation, the bishops and princes, should remember that they are Christians, and should defend the people, who are committed to their government and protection in temporal and spiritual affairs, from these ravenous wolves in sheep's clothing, that profess to be shepherds and rulers; and since the *annates* are so shamefully abused, and the covenants concerning them not carried out, they should not suffer their lands and people to be so piteously and unrighteously flayed and ruined; but by an imperial or a national law they should either retain the *annates* in the country, or abolish them altogether. For since they do not keep to the covenants, they have no right to the *annates*; therefore bishops and princes are bound to punish this thievery and robbery, or prevent it, as justice demands. And herein should they assist and strengthen the Pope, who is perchance too weak to prevent this scandal by himself, or, if he wishes to protect or support it, restrain and oppose him as a wolf and tyrant; for he has no authority to do evil or to protect evil-doers. Even if it were proposed to collect any such treasure for use against the Turks, we should be wise in future, and remember that the German nation is more fitted to take charge of it than the Pope, seeing that the German nation by itself is able to provide men enough, if the money is forthcoming. This matter of the *annates* is like many other Romish pretexts.

Moreover, the year has been divided among the Pope and the ruling bishops and foundations in such wise that the Pope has taken every other month—six in all—to give away the benefices that fall in his month; in this way almost all the benefices are drawn into the hands of Rome, and especially the best livings and dignities. And those that once fall into the hands of Rome never come out again, even if they never again fall vacant in the Pope's month. In this way the foundations come very short of their rights, and it is a downright robbery, the object of which is not to give up anything again. Therefore it is now high time to abolish the Pope's months and to take back again all that has thereby fallen into the hands of Rome. For all the princes and nobles should insist that the stolen property shall be returned, the thieves punished, and that those who abuse their powers shall be deprived of them. If the Pope can make a law on the day after his election by which he takes our benefices and livings to which he has no right, the Emperor Charles should so much the more have a right to issue a law for all Germany on the day after his coronation that in future no livings and benefices are to fall to Rome by virtue of the Pope's month, but that those that have so fallen are to be freed and taken from the Romish robbers. This right he possesses authoritatively by virtue of his temporal sword.

31

John Calvin

The Institutes of the Christian Religion

JOHN Calvin (1509–1564), born and educated in France, was trained both as a cleric and as a lawyer. He was also skilled in classical studies, especially the Greek of the New Testament. Until 1532, indeed, Calvin seems to have been more concerned with classical scholarship than with theology, but about that time he experienced a religious conversion that led him to reject the Catholic doctrine of justification by faith and works. Rather than try to reconcile his own beliefs with the professions of faith required by a position in the Church, Calvin publicly announced his beliefs, resigned his minor clerical offices, and became a leader of the French religious reformers. Under threat of persecution, he sought refuge in Basel, Switzerland. There he wrote and published The Institutes of the Christian Religion in 1536, in Latin, with a French translation appearing in 1540.

On a journey shortly after publication of the Institutes, Calvin stopped in Geneva, where many religious exiles had sought refuge, and was persuaded by the Protestant leaders of that city to remain. He became the leading minister of the community and, because of his influence in the pulpit, a powerful force in local politics as well. Calvin's opinion was sought on all matters that came before the city council: questions of law, maintenance of order, trade and manufacture, as well as matters of religious doctrine and church organization. Calvin's influence soon became international, whereas Luther's tended to remain concentrated only on matters concerning Germany.

The Institutes is one of the major works of Christian theology, and its logical presentation of Protestant doctrine—based on a belief in the infallibility of the Bible—was of primary importance in the Reformation. The following selection includes Calvin's discussion of the authority of the Scriptures, Christian liberty, predestination, and the sacraments of the Church. As understood by *many of his followers, Calvin's doctrines had a tendency toward perfectionism and demanded rigorous control over private and social behavior.*

Before I proceed any further, it is proper to introduce some remarks on the authority of the Scripture, not only to prepare the mind to regard it with due reverence, but also to remove every doubt. For, when it is admitted to be a declaration of the word of God, no man can be so deplorably presumptuous, unless he be also destitute of common sense and of the common feelings of men, as to dare to derogate from the credit due to the speaker. But since we are not favoured with daily oracles from heaven, and since it is only in the Scriptures that the Lord hath been pleased to preserve his truth in perpetual remembrance, it obtains the same complete credit and authority with believers, when they are satisfied of its divine origin, as if they heard the very words pronounced by God himself. The subject, indeed, merits a diffuse discussion, and a most accurate examination. But the reader will pardon me, if I attend rather to what the design of this work admits, than to what the extensive nature of the present subject requires. But there has very generally prevailed a most pernicious error, that the Scriptures have only so much weight as is conceded to them by the suffrages of the Church; as though the eternal and inviolable truth of God depended on the arbitrary will of men. For thus, with great contempt of the Holy Spirit, they inquire, Who can assure us that God is the author of them? Who can with certainty affirm, that they have been preserved safe and uncorrupted to the present age? Who can persuade us that this book ought to be received with reverence, and that expunged from the sacred number, unless all these things were regulated by the decisions of the Church? It depends, therefore, (say they) on the determination of the Church, to decide both what reverence is due to the Scripture, and what books are to be comprised in its canon. Thus sacrilegious men, while they wish to introduce an unlimited tyranny, under the name of the Church, are totally unconcerned with what absurdities they embarrass themselves and others, provided they can extort from the ignorant this

THE INSTITUTES OF THE CHRISTIAN RELIGION   From *The Institutes of the Christian Religion* by John Calvin, tr. John Allen. Published 1936, The Presbyterian Board of Christian Education. By permission. [I, 85–87, 314–16, II, 77–82, 170–74, 280–81, 730–31.]

one admission, that the Church can do every thing. But, if this be true, what will be the condition of those wretched consciences, which are seeking a solid assurance of eternal life, if all the promises extant concerning it rest only on the judgment of men? Will the reception of such an answer cause their fluctuations to subside, and their terrors to vanish? Again, how will the impious ridicule our faith, and all men call it in question, if it be understood to possess only a precarious authority depending on the favour of men!

But such cavillers are completely refuted even by one word of the Apostle. He testifies that the Church is "built upon the foundation of the apostles and prophets." If the doctrine of the prophets and apostles be the foundation of the Church, it must have been certain, antecedently to the existence of the Church. Nor is there any foundation for this cavil, that though the Church derive its origin from the Scriptures, yet it remains doubtful what writings are to be ascribed to the prophets and apostles, unless it be determined by the Church. For if the Christian Church has been from the beginning founded on the writings of the prophets and the preaching of the apostles, wherever that doctrine is found, the approbation of it has certainly preceded the formation of the Church; since without it the Church itself had never existed. It is a very false notion, therefore, that the power of judging of the Scripture belongs to the Church, so as to make the certainty of it dependent on the Church's will. Wherefore, when the Church receives it, and seals it with her suffrage, she does not authenticate a thing otherwise dubious or controvertible; but, knowing it to be the truth of her God, performs a duty of piety, by treating it with immediate veneration. But, with regard to the question, How shall we be persuaded of its Divine original, unless we have recourse to the decree of the Church? this is just as if any one should inquire, How shall we learn to distinguish light from darkness, white from black, sweet from bitter? For the Scripture exhibits as clear evidence of its truth, as white and black things do of their colour, or sweet and bitter things of their taste.

• • •

I shall be content with citing a single passage, which, however, will resemble a very lucid mirror, in which we may behold at full length the image of our nature. For the Apostle,[1] when he wishes to demolish the arrogance of mankind, does it by these testimonies: "There is none

---

[1]St. Paul.

righteous, no, not one; there is none that understandeth, there is none that seeketh after God. They are all gone out of the way, they are together become unprofitable; there is none that doeth good, no, not one. Their throat is an open sepulchre; with their tongues they have used deceit; the poison of asps is under their lips; whose mouth is full of cursing and bitterness; their feet are swift to shed blood; destruction and misery are in their ways; there is no fear of God before their eyes." In this terrible manner he inveighs, not against particular individuals, but against all the posterity of Adam. He does not declaim against the depraved manners of one or another age, but accuses the perpetual corruption of our nature. For his design in that passage is not simply to rebuke men, in order that they may repent, but rather to teach us that all men are overwhelmed with an inevitable calamity, from which they can never emerge unless they are extricated by the mercy of God. As this could not be proved unless it were evinced by the ruin and destruction of our nature, he has adduced these testimonies, which demonstrate our nature to be totally ruined. Let this, then, be admitted, that men are such as they are here described, not only by corrupt habits, but also by a depravity of nature; for otherwise the reasoning of the Apostle could not be supported, "that there is no salvation for man but from the mercy of God; since in himself he is in a ruined and desperate condition." Here I shall not attempt to establish the application of the testimonies, to preclude the appearance of their being improperly introduced. I shall treat them just as if they had been originally uttered by Paul, and not quoted from the Prophets. He divests man first of righteousness, that is, integrity and purity, and then of understanding. Defect of understanding is proved by apostasy from God, the seeking of whom is the first step in the path of wisdom; but this loss must necessarily befall those who have revolted from God. He adds, that all have gone out of the way, and are become altogether corrupt, that there is not one that does good. Then he subjoins the flagitious crimes, with which they, who are once abandoned to iniquity, contaminate all the members of their bodies. Lastly, he declares them to be destitute of the fear of God, the rule by which all our steps ought to be directed. If these are the hereditary characters of mankind, in vain do we seek in our nature for any thing that is good. I grant, indeed, that all these crimes are not exhibited in every individual; yet it cannot be denied that this monster lurks in the hearts of all. For as the body, which already contains within itself the cause and matter of a disease, although it has yet no sensation of pain, cannot be said to enjoy good health, neither can the soul be esteemed healthy, while it is full of such moral maladies; although this similitude will not correspond in every particular; for in the body, however diseased, there remains the vigour of life; but the soul, immersed in this gulf of iniquity, is not only the subject of vices, but totally destitute of every thing that is good.

A question, nearly the same as we have already answered, here presents itself to us again. For in all ages there have been some persons, who, from the mere dictates of nature, have devoted their whole lives to the pursuit of virtue. And though many errors might perhaps be discovered in their conduct, yet by their pursuit of virtue they afforded a proof, that there was some degree of purity in their nature. The value attached to virtues of such a description before God, we shall more fully discuss when we come to treat of the merits of works; yet it must be stated also in this place, so far as is necessary for the elucidation of the present subject. These examples, then, seem to teach us that we should not consider human nature to be totally corrupted; since, from its instinctive bias, some men have not only been eminent for noble actions, but have uniformly conducted themselves in a most virtuous manner through the whole course of their lives. But here we ought to remember, that amidst this corruption of nature there is some room for Divine grace, not to purify it, but internally to restrain its operations. For should the Lord permit the minds of all men to give up the reins to every lawless passion, there certainly would not be an individual in the world, whose actions would not evince all the crimes, for which Paul condemns human nature in general, to be most truly applicable to him. For can you except yourself from the number of those whose feet are swift to shed blood, whose hands are polluted with rapine and murder, whose throats are like open sepulchres, whose tongues are deceitful, whose lips are envenomed, whose works are useless, iniquitous, corrupt, and deadly, whose souls are estranged from God, the inmost recesses of whose hearts are full of pravity, whose eyes are insidiously employed, whose minds are elated with insolence—in a word, all whose powers are prepared for the commission of atrocious and innumerable crimes? If every soul be subject to all these monstrous vices, as the Apostle fearlessly pronounces, we clearly see what would be the consequence, if the Lord should suffer the human passions to go all the lengths to which they are inclined. There is no furious beast, that would be agitated with such ungovernable rage; there is no river, though ever so rapid and violent, that would overflow its boundaries with such impetuosity. In his elect, the Lord heals these maladies by a method which we shall hereafter describe. In others, he restrains them, only to prevent their ebullitions so far as he sees to be necessary for the preservation of the universe. Hence some by shame, and some by fear of the laws, are prevented from running into many kinds of pollutions, though they cannot in any great degree dissemble their impurity; others, because they think that a virtuous course of life is advantageous, entertain some languid desires after it, others go further, and display more than common excellence, that by their majesty they may confine the vulgar to their duty. Thus God by his providence restrains the perverseness of our nature from breaking out into external acts, but does not purify it within.

• • •

Christian liberty, according to my judgment, consists of three parts. The first part is, that the consciences of believers, when seeking an assurance of their justification before God, should raise themselves above the law, and forget all the righteousness of the law. For since the law, as we have elsewhere demonstrated, leaves no man righteous, either we must be excluded from all hope of justification, or it is necessary for us to be delivered from it, and that so completely as not to have any dependence on works. For he who imagines, that in order to obtain righteousness he must produce any works, however small, can fix no limit or boundary, but renders himself a debtor to the whole law. Avoiding, therefore, all mention of the law, and dismissing all thought of our own works, in reference to justification, we must embrace the Divine mercy alone, and turning our eyes from ourselves, fix them solely on Christ. For the question is, not how we can be righteous, but how, though unrighteous and unworthy, we can be considered as righteous. And the conscience that desires to attain any certainty respecting this, must give no admission to the law. Nor will this authorize any one to conclude, that the law is of no use to believers, whom it still continues to instruct and exhort, and stimulate to duty, although it has no place in their consciences before the tribunal of God. For these two things, being very different, require to be properly and carefully distinguished by us. The whole life of Christians ought to be an exercise of piety, since they are called to sanctification. It is the office of the law to remind them of their duty, and thereby to excite them to the pursuit of holiness and integrity. But when their consciences are solicitous how God may be propitiated, what answer they shall make, and on what they shall rest their confidence, if called to his tribunal, there must then be no consideration of the requisitions of the law, but Christ alone must be proposed for righteousness, who exceeds all the perfection of the law.

• • •

The second part of Christian liberty, which is dependent on the first, is, that their consciences do not observe the law, as being under any legal obligation; but that, being liberated from the yoke of the law, they yield a voluntary obedience to the will of God. For being possessed with perpetual terrors, as long as they remain under the dominion of the law, they will never engage with alacrity and promptitude in the service of God, unless they have previously received this liberty. We shall more easily and clearly discover the design of these things from an example. The precept of the law is, "Thou shalt love the Lord thy God with all thine heart, and with all thy soul, and with all thy might." That this command may be fulfilled, our soul must be previously divested of every other perception and thought, our heart must be freed from all desires, and our might must be collected and contracted to this one point. Those who, compared with others, have made a very considerable progress in the way of the Lord, are yet at an immense distance from this perfection. For though they love God with their soul, and with sincere affection of heart, yet they have still much of their heart and soul occupied by carnal desires, which retard their progress towards God. They do indeed press forward with strong exertions, but the flesh partly debilitates their strength, and partly attracts it to itself. What can they do in this case, when they perceive that they are so far from observing the law? They wish, they aspire, they endeavour, but they do nothing with the perfection that is required. If they advert to the law, they see that every work they attempt or meditate is accursed. Nor is there the least reason for any person to deceive himself, by concluding that an action is not necessarily altogether evil, because it is imperfect, and that therefore the good part of it is accepted by God. For the law, requiring perfect love, condemns all imperfection, unless its rigour be mitigated. Let him consider his work, therefore, which he wished to be thought partly good, and he will find that very work to be a transgression of the law, because it is imperfect.

See how all our works, if estimated according to the rigour of the law, are subject to its curse. How, then, could unhappy souls apply themselves with alacrity to any work for which they could expect to receive nothing but a curse? On the contrary, if they are liberated from the severe exaction of the law, or rather from the whole of its rigour, and hear God calling them with paternal gentleness, then with cheerfulness and prompt alacrity they will answer to his call and follow his guidance. In short, they who are bound by the yoke of the law, are like slaves who have certain daily tasks appointed by their masters. They think they have done nothing, and presume not to enter into the presence of their masters without having finished the work prescribed to them. But children, who are treated by their parents in a more liberal manner, hesitate not to present to them their imperfect, and in some respects faulty works, in confidence that their obedience and promptitude of mind will be accepted by them, though they have not performed all that they wished. Such children ought we to be, feeling a certain confidence that our services, however small, rude, and imperfect, will be approved by our most indulgent Father. This he also confirms to us by the Prophet:[2] "I will spare them," saith he, "as a man spareth his own son that serveth him;" where it is evident, from the mention of *service*, that the word *spare* is used to denote indulgence, or an overlooking of faults. And we have great need of this confidence, without which all our endeavors will be vain; for God considers us as serving him in none of our works, but such as are truly done by us to his honour. But how can this be done amidst those terrors, where it is a matter of doubt whether our works offend God or honour him?

This is the reason why the author[3] of the Epistle to the Hebrews refers to faith, and estimates only by faith, all the good works which are recorded of the holy patriarchs. On this liberty there is a remarkable passage in the Epistle to the Romans, where Paul reasons that sin ought not to have dominion over us, because we are not under the law, but under grace. For after he had exhorted believers, "Let not sin, therefore, reign in your mortal body; neither yield ye your members as instruments of unrighteousness; but yield yourselves unto God, as those that are alive from the dead, and your members as instruments of righteousness unto God,"—they might, on the contrary, object that they yet carried about with them the flesh full of inordinate desires, and that sin dwelt in them; but he adds the consolation furnished by their

---

[2]Malachi 3:17 (in the Old Testament).
[3]St. Paul.

liberty from the law; as though he had said, Although you do not yet experience sin to be destroyed, and righteousness living in you in perfection, yet you have no cause for terror and dejection of mind, as if God were perpetually offended on account of your remaining sin; because by grace you are emancipated from the law, that your works may not be judged according to that rule. But those, who infer that we may commit sin because we are not under the law, may be assured that they have no concern with this liberty, the end of which is to animate us to virtue.

The third part of Christian liberty teaches us, that we are bound by no obligation before God respecting external things, which in themselves are indifferent; but that we may indifferently sometimes use, and at other times omit them. And the knowledge of this liberty also is very necessary for us; for without it we shall have no tranquility of conscience, nor will there be any end of superstitions. Many in the present age think it a folly to raise any dispute concerning the free use of meats, of days, and of habits, and similar subjects, considering these things as frivolous and nugatory; but they are of greater importance than is generally believed. For when the conscience has once fallen into the snare, it enters a long and inextricable labyrinth, from which it is afterwards difficult to escape; if a man begin to doubt the lawfulness of using flax in sheets, shirts, handkerchiefs, napkins, and table cloths, neither will he be certain respecting hemp, and at last he will doubt of the lawfulness of using tow; for he will consider with himself whether he cannot eat without table cloths or napkins, whether he cannot do without handkerchiefs. If any one imagine delicate food to be unlawful, he will ere long have no tranquility before God in eating brown bread and common viands, while he remembers that he might support his body with meat of a quality still inferior. If he hesitate respecting good wine, he will afterwards be unable with any peace of conscience to drink the most vapid; and at last he will not presume even to touch purer and sweeter water than others. In short, he will come to think it criminal to step over a twig that lies across his path. For this is the commencement of no trivial controversy; but the dispute is whether the use of certain things be agreeable to God, whose will ought to guide all our resolutions and all our actions. The necessary consequence is, that some are hurried by despair into a vortex of confusion, from which they see no way of escape; and some, despising God, and casting off all fear of him, make a way of ruin for themselves. For all, who are involved in such doubts, which way soever they turn their views, behold something offensive to their consciences presenting itself on every side.

• • •

The covenant of life[4] not being equally preached to all, and among those to whom it is preached not always finding the same reception, this diversity discovers the wonderful depth of the Divine judgment. Nor is it to be doubted that this variety also follows, subject to the decision of God's eternal election. If it be evidently the result of the Divine will, that salvation is freely offered to some, and others are prevented from attaining it,—this immediately gives rise to important and difficult questions, which are incapable of any other explication, than by the establishment of pious minds in what ought to be received concerning election and predestination—a question, in the opinion of many, full of perplexity; for they consider nothing more unreasonable, than that, of the common mass of mankind, some should be predestinated to salvation, and others to destruction. But how unreasonably they perplex themselves will afterwards appear from the sequel of our discourse. Besides, the very obscurity which excites such dread, not only displays the utility of this doctrine, but shows it to be productive of the most delightful benefit. We shall never be clearly convinced as we ought to be, that our salvation flows from the fountain of God's free mercy, till we are acquainted with his eternal election, which illustrates the grace of God by this comparison, that he adopts not all promiscuously to the hope of salvation, but gives to some what he refuses to others. Ignorance of this principle evidently detracts from the Divine glory, and diminishes real humility. But according to Paul, what is so necessary to be known, never can be known, unless God, without any regard to works, chooses those whom he has decreed. "At this present time also, there is a remnant according to the election of grace. And if by grace, then it is no more of works; otherwise, grace is no more grace. But if it be of works, then it is no more grace; otherwise, work is no more work." If we need to be recalled to the origin of election, to prove that we obtain salvation from no other source than the mere goodness of God, they who desire to extinguish this principle, do all they can to obscure what ought to be magnificently and loudly celebrated, and to pluck up humility by the roots. In ascribing the salvation

[4]Promises made by God to man concerning eternal life.

of the remnant of the people to the election of grace, Paul clearly testifies, that it is then only known that God saves whom he will of his mere good pleasure, and does not dispense a reward to which there can be no claim.

They who shut the gates to prevent any one from presuming to approach and taste this doctrine, do no less injury to man than to God; for nothing else will be sufficient to produce in us suitable humility, or to impress us with a due sense of our great obligations to God. Nor is there any other basis for solid confidence, even according to the authority of Christ, who, to deliver us from all fear, and render us invincible amidst so many dangers, snares, and deadly conflicts, promises to preserve in safety all whom the Father has committed to his care. Whence we infer, that they who know not themselves to be God's peculiar people will be tortured with continual anxiety; and therefore, that the interest of all believers, as well as their own, is very badly consulted by those who, blind to the three advantages we have remarked, would wholly remove the foundation of our salvation. And hence the Church rises to our view, which otherwise, as Bernard[5] justly observes, could neither be discovered nor recognized among creatures, being in two respects wonderfully concealed in the bosom of a blessed predestination, and in the mass of a miserable damnation. But before I enter on the subject itself, I must address some preliminary observations to two sorts of persons. The discussion of predestination—a subject of itself rather intricate—is made very perplexed, and therefore dangerous, by human curiosity, which no barriers can restrain from wandering into forbidden labyrinths, and soaring beyond its sphere, as if determined to leave none of the Divine secrets unscrutinized or unexplored. As we see multitudes every where guilty of this arrogance and presumption, and among them some who are not censurable in other respects, it is proper to admonish them of the bounds of their duty on this subject. First, then, let them remember that when they inquire into predestination, they penetrate the innermost recesses of Divine wisdom, where the careless and confident intruder will obtain no satisfaction to his curiosity, but will enter a labyrinth from which he will find no way to depart. For it is unreasonable that man should scrutinize with impunity those things which the Lord has determined to be hidden in himself; and investigate, even from eternity, that sublimity of wisdom which God would have us to adore and not

[5]St. Bernard, twelfth-century churchman and reformer.

comprehend, to promote our admiration of his glory. The secrets of his will which he determined to reveal to us, he discovers in his word; and these are all that he foresaw would concern us or conduce to our advantage.

"We are come into the way of faith," says Augustine; "let us constantly pursue it. It conducts into the king's palace, in which are hidden all the treasures of wisdom and knowledge. For the Lord Christ himself envied not his great and most select disciples when he said, 'I have many things to say unto you, but ye cannot bear them now.' We must walk, we must improve, we must grow, that our hearts may be able to understand those things of which we are at present incapable. If the last day finds us improving, we shall then learn what we never could learn in the present state." If we only consider that the word of the Lord is the only way to lead us to an investigation of all that ought to be believed concerning him, and the only light to enlighten us to behold all that ought to be seen of him, this consideration will easily restrain and preserve us from all presumption. For we shall know that when we have exceeded the limits of the word, we shall get into a devious and darksome course, in which errors, slips, and falls will often be inevitable. Let us, then, in the first place, bear in mind, that to desire any other knowledge of predestination than what is unfolded in the word of God, indicates as great folly, as a wish to walk through unpassable roads, or to see in the dark. Nor let us be ashamed to be ignorant of some things relative to a subject in which there is a kind of learned ignorance. Rather let us abstain with cheerfulness from the pursuit of that knowledge, the affectation of which is foolish, dangerous, and even fatal. But if we are stimulated by the wantonness of intellect, we must oppose it with a reflection calculated to repress it, that as "it is not good to eat much honey, so for men to search their own glory, is not glory." For there is sufficient to deter us from that presumption, which can only precipitate us into ruin.

Others, desirous of remedying this evil, will have all mention of predestination to be as it were buried; they teach men to avoid every question concerning it as they would a precipice. Though their moderation is to be commended, in judging that mysteries ought to be handled with such great sobriety, yet, as they descend too low, they have little influence on the mind of man, which refuses to submit to unreasonable restraints. To observe, therefore, the legitimate boundary on this side also, we must recur to the word of the Lord, which affords a certain rule for the understanding. For the Scripture is the school of the

Holy Spirit, in which, as nothing necessary and useful to be known is omitted, so nothing is taught which it is not beneficial to know. Whatever, therefore, is declared in the Scripture concerning predestination, we must be cautious not to withhold from believers, lest we appear either to defraud them of the favour of their God, or to reprove and censure the Holy Spirit for publishing what it would be useful by any means to suppress. Let us, I say, permit the Christian man to open his heart and his ears to all the discourses addressed to him by God, only with this moderation, that as soon as the Lord closes his sacred mouth, he shall also desist from further inquiry. This will be the best barrier of sobriety, if in learning we not only follow the leadings of God, but as soon as he ceases to teach, we give up our desire of learning. Nor is the danger they dread, sufficient to divert our attention from the oracles of God. It is a celebrated observation of Solomon, that "it is the glory of God to conceal a thing." But, as both piety and common sense suggest that this is not to be understood generally of every thing, we must seek for the proper distinction, lest we content ourselves with brutish ignorance under the pretext of modesty and sobriety. Now, this distinction is clearly expressed in a few words by Moses. "The secret things," he says, "belong unto the Lord our God; but those things which are revealed belong unto us, and to our children for ever, that we may do all the words of this law." For we see how he enforces on the people attention to the doctrine of the law only by the celestial decree, because it pleased God to promulgate it; and restrains the same people within those limits with this single reason, that it is not lawful for mortals to intrude into the secrets of God.

• • •

From what has been said, I conceive it must now be evident what judgment we ought to form respecting the Church, which is visible to our eyes, and falls under our knowledge. For we have remarked that the word *Church* is used in the sacred Scriptures in two senses. Sometimes, when they mention the Church, they intend that which is really such in the sight of God, into which none are received but those who by adoption and grace are the children of God, and by the sanctification of the Spirit are the true members of Christ. And then it comprehends not only the saints at any one time resident on earth, but all the elect who have lived from the beginning of the world. But the word *Church* is frequently used in the Scriptures to designate the whole multitude, dispersed all over the world, who profess to worship one God and Jesus

Christ, who are initiated into his faith by baptism, who testify their unity in true doctrine and charity by a participation of the sacred supper, who consent to the word of the Lord, and preserve the ministry which Christ has instituted for the purpose of preaching it. In this Church are included many hypocrites, who have nothing of Christ but the name and appearance; many persons ambitious, avaricious, envious, slanderous, and dissolute in their lives, who are tolerated for a time, either because they cannot be convicted by a legitimate process, or because discipline is not always maintained with sufficient vigour. As it is necessary, therefore, to believe that Church, which is invisible to us, and known to God alone, so this Church, which is visible to men, we are commanded to honour, and to maintain communion with it.

As far, therefore, as was important for us to know it, the Lord has described it by certain marks and characters. It is the peculiar prerogative of God himself to "know them that are his," as we have already stated from Paul. And to guard against human presumption ever going to such an extreme, the experience of every day teaches us how very far his secret judgments transcend all our apprehensions. For those who seemed the most abandoned, and were generally considered past all hope, are recalled by his goodness into the right way; while some, who seemed to stand better than others, fall into perdition. "According to the secret predestination of God," therefore as Augustine observes, "there are many sheep without the pale of the Church, and many wolves within." For he knows and seals those who know not either him or themselves. Of those who externally bear his seal, his eyes alone can discern who are unfeignedly holy, and will persevere to the end; which is the completion of salvation. On the other hand, as he saw it to be in some measure requisite that we should know who ought to be considered as his children, he has in this respect accommodated himself to our capacity. And as it was not necessary that on this point we should have an assurance of faith, he has substituted in its place a judgment of charity, according to which we ought to acknowledge as members of the Church all those who by a confession of faith, an exemplary life, and a participation of the sacraments, profess the same God and Christ with ourselves. But the knowledge of the body itself being more necessary to our salvation, he has distinguished it by more clear and certain characters.

Hence the visible Church rises conspicuous to our view. For wherever we find the word of God purely preached and heard, and the sacraments administered according to the institution of Christ, there, it is not to be doubted, is a Church of God; for his promise can never deceive—"where two or three are gathered together in my name, there am I in the midst of them."

• • •

The readers may now see, collected into a brief summary, almost every thing that I have thought important to be known respecting these two sacraments; the use of which has been enjoined on the Christian Church from the commencement of the New Testament until the end of time; that is to say, baptism, to be a kind of entrance into the Church, and an initiatory profession of faith; and the Lord's supper, to be a continual nourishment, with which Christ spiritually feeds his family of believers. Wherefore, as there is but "one God, one Christ, one faith," one Church, the body of Christ, so there is only "one baptism" and that is never repeated; but the supper is frequently distributed, that those who have once been admitted into the Church, may understand that they are continually nourished by Christ. Beside these two, as no other sacrament has been instituted by God, so no other ought to be acknowledged by the Church of believers. For that it is not left to the will of man to institute new sacraments, will be easily understood if we remember what has already been very plainly stated—that sacraments are appointed by God for the purpose of instructing us respecting some promise of his, and assuring us of his good-will towards us; and if we also consider, that no one has been the counsellor of God, capable of affording us any certainty respecting his will, or furnishing us any assurance of his disposition towards us, what he chooses to give or to deny us. Hence it follows, that no one can institute a sign to be a testimony respecting any determination or promise of his; he alone can furnish us a testimony respecting himself by giving a sign. I will express myself in terms more concise, and perhaps more homely, but more explicit—that there can be no sacrament unaccompanied with a promise of salvation. All mankind, collected in one assembly, can promise us nothing respecting our salvation. Therefore they can never institute or establish a sacrament.

Let the Christian Church, therefore, be content with these two, and not only neither admit nor acknowledge any other at present, but neither desire nor expect any other to the end of the world.

32

St. Ignatius of Loyola

The Spiritual Exercises

S T. *Ignatius of Loyola (1491–1556)*
was a soldier until age thirty, when, recovering from a severe wound, he
experienced a spiritual turmoil that resulted in his abandoning the profession of
arms and turning to the Church. His military training is evident, however, in
the fact that he called himself the knight of Christ and that his followers used
military discipline and terminology.

On his return from a pilgrimage to Jerusalem, Loyola undertook studies at
Barcelona; later, while at the University of Paris, he gathered together a small
group of fellow students who bound themselves by vows of poverty, chastity,
and obedience, and offered their services to the pope for whatever missions he
might choose. Meanwhile, the group continued to teach, offer spiritual counsel,
and tend the sick and needy. Ordained a priest in 1537, Loyola persisted in his
efforts on behalf of the association, which he named (in military terms) the
Company of Jesus; later it became known as the Society of Jesus. He gained
formal recognition of the order from the pope in 1540. The Jesuits, "the shock
troops of the papacy," as they have been called, were instrumental in checking
the further spread of Protestantism in the sixteenth century. The Jesuits' reliance
on rigorous education as a way of preventing the growth of heresy encouraged a
more systematic and widespread education for the clergy and laity than the
Church had hitherto provided.

After 1540 Loyola was principally concerned with drawing up the Constitutions *(in which he prescribed the duties of his followers in their missionary*
and educational work on behalf of the papacy) and The Spiritual Exercises,
which he completed in 1548. The latter work reflects the spirit of Catholic
Christianity and embodies the aims of the sixteenth-century Catholic Reforma-
tion. It reaffirms religious discipline for both the clergy and the laity and
reasserts the role of the Church as the guardian of spiritual welfare. The

Exercises *are so arranged that the reader is provided with a regular pattern of devotion and spiritual instruction. The following selection illustrates this pattern and includes guides for the individual seeking to attain harmony of thought and action with the Church.*

ANNOTATIONS

The first annotation is that the term Spiritual Exercises means any method of examining one's own conscience—of meditating, contemplating, praying mentally and vocally, and, finally, of performing any other spiritual operation that will be described hereafter. Just as walking, traveling, and running are bodily exercises, preparing the soul to remove ill-ordered affections, and after their removal seeking and finding the will of God with respect to the ordering of one's own life and the salvation of one's soul, are Spiritual Exercises.

The second annotation is that he who gives another the order and method of meditating or contemplating should set forth faithfully the facts of the meditation or contemplation, going briefly through the chief points only and adding merely a very brief exposition, so that he who is about to meditate, having first understood the foundation of the historical truth, may afterwards go over the ground and reason by himself. The effect of this will be that when he finds anything which may furnish more elucidation or understanding (whether this be effected by his own reasoning or by divine illumination of the mind), he will experience a more delightful taste and more abundant fruit than if the matter itself had been set forth in greater detail by another. It is not the abundance of the knowledge, but the inner feeling which satisfies the soul.

The third annotation is that, whereas in all of the following Spiritual Exercises we use acts of the intellect when we reason, but of the will when we are affected, we must notice that . . . while we converse vocally or mentally with the Lord God or His Saints a greater reverence is required of us than when we use the intellect to attain understanding.

The fourth annotation is that the following Exercises are divided into four weeks: in the first week the consideration may be of sins; in the second, concerning the life of our Lord Jesus Christ up to His entrance

THE SPIRITUAL EXERCISES   *The Spiritual Exercises of St. Ignatius of Loyola*, trans. Charles Seager (London: Dolman, 1847), 1–4, 15–17, 25–26, 173–85. (This is an adaptation.)

into Jerusalem on Palm Sunday; in the third, concerning His Passion; in the fourth, concerning His Resurrection and Ascension. Then the three methods of prayer are added. Yet these weeks are not to be understood as if each should contain seven or eight days. It happens that some are slower, others more ready in attaining what they seek (for instance, in the first week contrition, grief, and tears for their sins), and that some are more or less agitated and tried by various spirits. It is, therefore, sometimes expedient that any week should be cut down or extended according to the nature of the subject matter. The Exercises customarily take up the space of thirty days or thereabouts.

The fifth annotation is that he who receives the Exercises is wonderfully assisted if, coming to them with a liberal mind, he offers his whole desire and will to his Creator, so that he may serve Him according to His will.

The sixth is that he who gives the Exercises, if he perceives that the one who receives them undergoes no spiritual commotions of the mind, such as sadness, nor any agitations of different spirits, ought carefully to inquire whether he performs the Exercises themselves at the prescribed times and in what way.

• • •

The seventh annotation is that he who has the care of the exercising of another, if he sees him affected by desolation or temptation, ought to take care not to show himself hard or austere, but rather mild and gentle. He should strengthen his mind to act vigorously in the future and, having laid open to him the wiles of our enemy, prepare him for the consolation to follow.

• • •

CERTAIN SPIRITUAL EXERCISES BY WHICH A MAN MAY BE ABLE TO CONQUER HIMSELF AND, WITH DECISIONS FREE FROM HARMFUL DESIRES, PLAN HIS LIFE

In the first place, in order that exercises of this kind benefit him who gives and him who receives, it must be presupposed that every pious Christian prefers to put a good interpretation on another's opinion or proposition than to condemn it. But if he can in no way defend it, let him inquire the speaker's meaning and, if he thinks erroneously, correct him kindly. If this does not suffice, all suitable means should be tried to render his meaning sound and safe from error.

Man was created that he might praise and reverence the Lord his God, and, serving Him, at length be saved. But the other things which are placed on the earth were created for man's sake, that they might assist him in pursuing the end of his creation; whence it follows that they are to be used or abstained from in proportion as they profit or hinder him in pursuing that end.

· · ·

DAILY AND PARTICULAR EXAMINATION

The first time of examining is morning when a man ought, as soon as he rises from sleep, to decide to guard against some particular sin or fault which he desires to overcome.

The second is the afternoon in which he must ask of God the grace to be able to remember how often he has fallen into that particular sin or fault and to beware of it in the future. Then let him perform the first reexamination, asking account of his soul concerning the sin or fault already spoken of and, running through the parts of the day from the hour in which he rose down to the present, see how many times he has committed it.

· · ·

The third time will be the evening in which, after the hour of supper, another review will have to be made by running through in like manner the several hours which have elapsed from the former examination to the present and in the same way remembering and enumerating the times he has been in fault.

· · ·

A METHOD OF GENERAL EXAMINATION IN FIVE POINTS

The first point is to thank the Lord our God for the benefits we have received.

The second, to entreat grace for the knowledge and expulsion of our sins.

The third, to ask account of our soul concerning the sins committed during the present day, searching through the several hours from the time when we rose. Thoughts should come first, then words and deeds, in the same order laid down in the particular examination.

The fourth, to ask pardon concerning our faults.

The fifth, to propose amendment with the grace of God—and after all the above to say the Lord's Prayer.

THE USE OF GENERAL CONFESSION AND OF COMMUNION

From a general confession voluntarily made many advantages are gained, especially these three:

The first: although he who confesses at least once every year is not obliged to make a general confession, yet the person who does so gains much more merit on account of the greater sorrow he experiences for his sins and for the wickedness of his past life.

The second: having seen by means of the Spiritual Exercises much more clearly than before the nature and wickedness of sin, he will gain greater advantage and merit.

The third: it is reasonable to expect that he who has thus rightly confessed and is thus rightly disposed will be much better prepared for the reception of the Eucharist, which aids in the highest degree both the expulsion of sin and the preservation and increase of grace received.

This general confession will be best placed after the exercises of the first week.

SOME RULES TO BE OBSERVED IN ORDER THAT WE MAY THINK WITH THE ORTHODOX CHURCH

The first: removing all judgment of one's own, one must always keep one's mind prepared and ready to obey the true Spouse of Christ, our Holy Mother, which is the Orthodox, Catholic, and Hierarchical Church.

The second: it is proper to commend confession of sins to the priest and the receiving of the Eucharist at least once a year. It is more commendable to receive the same Sacrament every eighth day or at least once in each month.

• • •

The third: one should commend to Christ's faithful people the frequent and devout hearing of the holy rite or sacrifice of the Mass; also the saying of the Church hymns, the psalms, and long prayers, either within the Churches or outside; also to approve the hours marked out for the Divine Office, for prayers of whatever kind, and for the Canonical Hours.

The fourth: to praise vows . . . of chastity, poverty, and perpetual obedience, and other works of perfection and supererogation. Here it must be noted in passing that . . . a vow relates to those things which lead more closely to the perfection of Christian life. Concerning other things which lead away from perfection, for example . . . matrimony, a vow is never never to be made.

· · ·

The sixth: to praise relics, the veneration and invocation of Saints, also the stations and pious pilgrimages, indulgences, jubilees, the candles lighted in the Churches, and other such aids to our piety and devotion.

The seventh: to praise abstinence and fasts, such as Lent, Ember Days, Vigils, Fridays, Saturdays, and others undertaken for the sake of devotion; also voluntary afflictions of one's self, which we call penances, not merely internal, but external.

The eighth: to praise the construction of Churches and their adornment; also images . . . to be venerated . . . for the sake of what they represent.

The ninth: to uphold all the precepts of the Church and not impugn them in any manner; but, on the contrary, to defend them promptly, with reasons drawn from all sources against those who do impugn them.

The tenth: we ought to be more ready to approve and praise the statutes, recommendations, and the lives of our superiors than to reprove them; because, although sometimes they may not be worthy of praise, to speak against them either in public preaching or in speaking before the common people would cause murmuring and scandals rather than good. Consequently, the people would be angry with their superiors, either spiritual or temporal. Therefore, as it is mischievous to speak ill to the people concerning superiors who are absent, so it may be useful to speak concerning their evil lives to those persons who can remedy them.

The eleventh: to put the highest value on sacred teaching, both the positive and the Scholastic, as they are commonly called. For as it was the object of the ancient holy Doctors, Jerome, Augustine, Gregory,[1] and the like, to stir up men's minds to embrace the love and worship of God, so it is characteristic of Blessed Thomas, Bonaventure, the Master of the Sentences,[2] and other more modern Divines, to lay down and define more exactly the things necessary for salvation, and, according to what was fitting for their own times and for posterity, helpful in the confutation of heresies. Moreover, the Doctors of this kind, being later in date, are not merely endowed with the understanding of the Sacred Scripture, and assisted by the writings of the old authors, but also with the influx of the Divine Light, and use, happily for the help of our salvation, the decisions of Councils, the decrees, and various constitutions of Holy Church.

The twelfth: we must avoid the comparison of men still living on the earth, however worthy of praise, with the Saints, saying this man is more learned than St. Augustine, that man is another St. Francis, he is equal to St. Paul in holiness, or in some virtue he is not inferior, and so on.

The thirteenth: finally, so as to be altogether of the same mind and in conformity with the Church herself, if she shall have defined anything to be black which to our eyes appears to be white, we ought in like manner to pronounce it to be black. For we must undoubtingly believe that the Spirit of our Lord Jesus Christ, and the Spirit of the Orthodox Church, His Spouse, by which Spirit we are governed and directed to salvation, is the same; and that the God who of old delivered the precepts of the Decalogue is the same who now instructs and governs the Hierarchical Church.

The fourteenth: it must also be borne in mind that although it be most true that no one is saved except he who is predestinated, we must speak with circumspection concerning this matter lest, perchance stretching too far the grace of predestination of God, we should seem to wish to shut out the force of free will and the merits of good works, or on the other hand, attributing to the latter more than belongs to them. . . . .

The fifteenth: for the like reason we should not speak on the subject of predestination frequently, and if it occur occasionally, we ought so to

---

[1]Jerome, Augustine, and Gregory were writers and teachers of the early Church.

[2]The Blessed Thomas (St. Thomas Aquinas), St. Bonaventure, and the Master of the Sentences (Peter Lombard) were twelfth- and thirteenth-century churchmen and teachers.

temper what we say as to give the people no occasion of erroneously saying: If my salvation or damnation is already determined regardless of whether I do ill or well, it cannot happen differently. It happens, consequently, that many neglect good works and other helps of salvation.

The sixteenth: it also happens not infrequently that from immoderate preaching and praise of faith without distinction or explanation being added, the people . . . become indifferent to good works which precede faith or follow it.

• • •

The seventeenth: nor must we push to such a point the preaching and inculcating of the grace of God that there may creep into the minds of the hearers the deadly error of denying the faculty of our free will. Concerning grace itself, therefore, it is allowable, indeed, to speak fully, God inspiring us, but no more than redounds to His more abundant glory, lest in our dangerous times both the use of free will and efficacy of good works be taken away.

The eighteenth: although it is in the highest degree praiseworthy and useful to serve God from pure love, yet the fear of the Divine Majesty is greatly to be commended. And not that fear only which we call filial, which is the most pious and holy, but also the other which is called servile, as being . . . very often necessary . . . because it helps much towards rising from mortal sin. After a person has emerged from this, he easily arrives at the filial fear which is altogether acceptable and agreeable to our Lord God because it is inseparably joined with Divine love.